COOK'S

ILLUSTRATED

~ 1998 ~

Published by

Boston Common Press Limited Partnership

17 Station Street

Brookline MA 02445

ISBN: 0-936184-32-9

ISSN: 1068-2821

To get home delivery of future issues of *Cook's Illustrated*
magazine, call 800-526-8442. To order any of the book titles
from the *Cook's Illustrated Library*, call 800-611-0759,
or write to the address above.

$29.95

COOK'S ILLUSTRATED INDEX

Key: FC/BC= Front Cover/ Back Cover   QT= Quick Tips   MO= Mail-Order Sources   NR= Notes from Readers

Key: FC/BC= *Front Cover/ Back Cover*   QT= *Quick Tips*   MO= *Mail-Order Sources*   NR= *Notes from Readers*

Key: FC/BC= Front Cover/ Back Cover   QT= Quick Tips   MO= Mail-Order Sources   NR= Notes from Readers

Key: FC/BC= Front Cover/ Back Cover   QT= Quick Tips   MO= Mail-Order Sources   NR= Notes from Readers

Key: FC/BC= Front Cover/ Back Cover   QT= Quick Tips   MO= Mail-Order Sources   NR= Notes from Readers

Key: FC/BC= Front Cover/ Back Cover   QT= Quick Tips   MO= Mail-Order Sources   NR= Notes from Readers

⋛ N ⋜

Key: FC/BC= Front Cover/ Back Cover   QT= Quick Tips   MO= Mail-Order Sources   NR= Notes from Readers

Key: FC/BC= Front Cover/ Back Cover   QT= Quick Tips   MO= Mail-Order Sources   NR= Notes from Readers

∋ Q ∈

∋ R ∈

⋛ S ⋚

Key: FC/BC= Front Cover/ Back Cover   QT= Quick Tips   MO= Mail-Order Sources   NR= Notes from Readers

∍ Y ∊

∍ Z ∊

NUMBER THIRTY

JANUARY & FEBRUARY 1998

COOKS
ILLUSTRATED

Best Spaghetti & Meatballs
Rich Meatballs with a Soft, Creamy Interior

The New Carrot Cake
Here's a Light, Delicate Version of the 1970's Classic

Beef Broth Tasting
Are Canned Supermarket Broths Any Good?

The Truth About Microwave Ovens
42 Kitchen Tests Reveal What Really Works

Fluffy Scrambled Eggs
High Heat Is the Secret

Jewish Rye Bread
Rating Dutch Ovens
Bakery-Style Bran Muffins
Noodles & Greens
Tasting California Zinfandels

$4.00 U.S./$4.95 CANADA

CONTENTS

January & February 1998

COOK'S
ILLUSTRATED

PUBLISHER AND EDITOR
Christopher Kimball

EXECUTIVE EDITOR
Pam Anderson

SENIOR EDITOR
John Willoughby

SENIOR WRITER
Jack Bishop

ASSOCIATE EDITOR
Adam Ried

CONTRIBUTING EDITORS
Mark Bittman
Stephanie Lyness

TEST KITCHEN DIRECTOR
Eva Katz

TEST COOK
Dawn Yanagihara

ASSISTANT EDITOR
Maryellen Driscoll

TEST KITCHEN INTERN
Marnie DuBois

ART DIRECTOR
Amy Klee

CORPORATE MANAGING EDITOR
Barbara Bourassa

EDITORIAL PROD. MANAGER
Sheila Datz

COPY EDITOR
Amy Finch

MARKETING DIRECTOR
Adrienne Kimball

CIRCULATION DIRECTOR
David Mack

FULFILLMENT MANAGER
Larisa Greiner

CIRCULATION MANAGER
Darcy Beach

MARKETING ASSISTANT
Connie Forbes

CIRCULATION ASSISTANT
Steven Browall

VICE PRESIDENT
PRODUCTION AND TECHNOLOGY
James McCormack

SYSTEMS ADMINISTRATOR
James Burke

DESKTOP PUBLISHING MANAGER
Kevin Moeller

PRODUCTION ARTIST
Robert Parsons

PRODUCTION ASSISTANT
Daniel Frey

CONTROLLER
Lisa A. Carullo

SENIOR ACCOUNTANT
Mandy Shito

STAFF ACCOUNTANT
William Baggs

OFFICE MANAGER
Livia McRee

SPECIAL PROJECTS
Fern Berman

WINTER SQUASHES The simplest way to cook most small- to medium-sized winter squash is to halve them and bake, cut side down on a baking sheet, in a 350 degree oven until tender. Cooked squash is easier than raw to seed and to separate from the skin.

The weight of a winter squash is a good indication of the texture of the flesh. A Butternut squash, for instance, is heavier than a like-sized Acorn squash because its flesh has a lower moisture content and is denser. This means the Butternut, when cooked, will be notably smooth and creamy compared to the Acorn. It also means that the Butternut will be harder and more difficult to cut.

COVER PAINTING: BRENT WATKINSON, BACK COVER ILLUSTRATION: JOHN BURGOYNE

HERE AT THE COUNTRY FAIR

Late every August, our family drives over to the Washington County Fair, where the kids flock to the bumper cars, the flying school bus, the spinning tea cups, and the haunted double-wide trailer. They spend their carefully hoarded change on games one never wins, trying to throw ping-pong balls into the narrow mouths of goldfish bowls, softballs into old milk cans, or land a dime in the middle of a small painted galloping horse, its body drawn in such a manner that it looks a bit bigger than it is.

But for me, the fair has always been a tale of two eras—a melancholy mix of low-key agricultural exhibits and the harsh commerce of the midway. I walk through the quiet farm exhibits and see booths tended by the Farm Credit Bureau, Boujmatic Dairy Equipment, and farm machinery from New Holland, Kubota, and John Deere. The sheds of show cows include Guernsey, Ayshire, Jersey, and Holstein, with names like Becca, Winnie, Orea, Brittany, Moxy, Athena, Prudence, 7-Up, Petula, and Spot. Teenage girls tend to them carefully in the night, forking away the fresh manure and straw, using electric razors to trim unsightly whiskers that might lose them points during the judging. Next door in the old farm machinery museum, one can find scrapers for butchering hogs, all manner of metal fence tighteners, sheep pokes, egg candlers, old containers of Smith's Compound for Horses and Smith's Laxative Colic Drops, saw setters, steel neck gates for horses, bush cutters, corn shellers, hay pulleys, manual cow dehorners, flox breakers, double hole corn shellers, a Babcock Milk Tester, and milk aerators.

As the sun starts to ebb and twilight seeps over the fairgrounds, the lights of the midway grow brighter and the clang of the bells and incessant repetition of the barkers takes over. My two-year-old son rides the small green train and my oldest daughter begs to go one more time on the ride that snaps her thin body around, contorts her face with centrifugal force and breathless fright, transported like Vermont farmers at a rodeo to another world. Her dreams are of lights, and noise, and blinding speed, of exhilaration at the end of a painted metal arm that slings her back and forth, up and down. My dreams are quieter these days; they're of the clicking of a horse-drawn mower, the clacking back and forth of the scythe bar, the hollow echoes of a workhorse's huge shod feet on the thick wooden floorboards of the stable. She is still looking for change, for a way out of childhood into a world she glimpses dimly at best; her mother and father stopping for a kiss by the kitchen sink, or perhaps the scent and pace of a friend's home, offer a different view of the universe.

Christopher Kimball

As the country fair changes every year, I wonder what will become of the silence, the stillness of life in the country, of making our own fun without paying someone else to provide it for us. I will miss those gallon jars of silage more than I can say, when they are no longer put on display at the fair but stored in a museum with the rope stretchers and milk testers.

But for our family in a small valley in the Green Mountains of Vermont, the past is still the present. I listen to the piercing, thin wailing of the coyotes late at night, as they come down out of the hollow toward the chicken coop just across the road. It is a wild cry, bearing as much resemblance to the bark of a dog as the real Wild West does to the rodeo at the fair. For now, the wild things still come out in the dark of night, two bears hoot at each other across the ridges behind our house, the red-tailed hawks circle in the late August afternoon, their keening a constant companion and reminder that there are things beyond the range of human understanding. As I walk with my nine-year-old daughter toward home one evening, through a field littered with fallen birch and poplar, she looks up at the circling hawk and senses the connection saying, "I wish it would drop us a feather." Although still a child, she wants to reach out and touch the wildness, to carry the feather with her through life so when the hawk is gone, and the silage jars are on museum shelves, and the wilderness has retreated to just a memory, she can remember those days at the close of the twentieth century when she walked with her dad through the darkening hollow, when she looked up and saw a ghost in the sky and wanted to reach out and touch it. When my turn comes and I, too, am a ghost in the twilight, I hope to leave her a feather, memories of sudden storms, tall corn, and quiet moments, of walking hand-in-hand back home after a long summer day. It is our solemn responsibility to do this for our children, for those who will live in a world after the last old-time Vermont farmer is dead and gone, committed back to the soil that will no longer raise crops or graze cows. I think it is the earth itself we will miss most, the gravelly hardscrabble or the rich loam of the river valleys. I often dream of those old farmers at rest through the long winters and dry summers, whispering to us from their stony graves, their wordless song carried by the murmur of a brook or the rustle of leaves before a storm. I dream of their calling us until we are reborn with the call of the wild, and the pastures once again feel the roots of young buckwheat, pushing down into the earth, seeking moisture and inspiration.

Boiling Point and Altitude

What was your altitude when you tested the instant-read thermometers in the July/August 1997 issue? My understanding is that each 500 foot increase in altitude from sea level causes a drop of about 1 degree in the boiling point. The boiling point at sea level is 212 degrees, but at 5000 feet, where I live, water boils at 202 degrees. This would affect one of your tests for accuracy.

W.R. FRANZ
ALBUQUERQUE, NM

➤ Your understanding that the boiling point drops about 1 degree for every 500 foot gain in altitude is correct, and several of our food science sources confirmed it. The reason is that atmospheric pressure, or the weight of air pressing against any surface, decreases at higher altitudes simply because there is less air. When water boils, liquid molecules transform into gas (steam) and escape from the surface of the water. To do so, though, they push against the air molecules pressing down on the water's surface. Less air means less pressure at the water's surface, so less energy (temperature) is required for the molecules to escape. Hence, a lower boiling point. In fact, even the high or low pressure of a specific weather system can affect the boiling point slightly.

The Brookline Town Hall, about three relatively flat blocks from our office where we conducted the testing, is 40 feet above sea level. So we are confident of the 212 degree boiling point in our test kitchen. We conducted the thermometer accuracy tests several times in the same morning, and while none of us recalls the weather on that day, the fact that more than half the thermometers did register 212 degrees in boiling water indicates the reliability of that test and our findings.

Nonetheless, you made a good catch. Readers who are unsure of their altitude above sea level would be better off testing thermometer accuracy in an ice and water slurry, which should register 32 degrees regardless of atmospheric pressure.

Easy Pan Cleanup

If I have a skillet or other pan with cooking residue caked onto the bottom after the food has been removed, I heat up the pan and deglaze it with water. Most of the residue will be released, and clean-up will be a relative breeze.

JIM HARB
KNOXVILLE, TN

➤ A simple variation of this method is standard operating procedure in our test kitchen. Rather than heating the dirty pan while empty, we fill it with water first, and set the full pan over high heat until the water boils. As the temperature of the water increases, the gunk inside the pan loosens and we can scrape it free with a wooden spoon. Be careful of sloshing the water too much while scraping, and while transferring the hot, water-filled pan to the sink, so that you don't burn yourself.

Pesto Process

You were definitely onto something with the pesto recipe you ran in summer '96 (*see* "Pesto at Its Best," July/August 1996). Blanching the garlic and bruising the basil improved the flavor, but the texture of the pesto was all wrong for me. In a cooking class I took in Italy a couple of years ago, the instructor said that if we had to use a food processor—she thought a mortar and pestle was better—we should first grind the nuts with a little oil until they were totally broken down, then add the garlic and break that down, too, and then process in the basil and salt. While the basil was whirring around, we added the rest of the oil and the cheese through the tube until it was all taken up and the pesto was really smooth and homogenous. I've used this method ever since. Try it and see if you can tell a difference.

ROSIE HUNTINGTON
HOPE, ME

➤ We pitted a batch of pesto made according to our July/August 1996 recipe against a second batch made with our ingredients but your procedure. In a side-by-side test, the difference was noticeable indeed. Your technique produced an impressively smooth sauce, almost mayonnaise-like in texture. This stands to reason because all the ingredients that could contribute to a coarse texture, including the cheese, are ground much more extensively.

We did note, however, that achieving this texture required extra effort. Constant stops to scrape down the sides of the workbowl were necessary to puree a mere one-quarter cup of nuts into a smooth paste in either a full size or a mini food processor. Incorporating the garlic into the paste required more stops, though we found that adding another tablespoon or two of the oil along with the garlic helped the process. In all, we stopped to scrape a total of seven times, as opposed to three with the original method. If you don't mind the repeated stops, you will be rewarded by an incomparably smooth-textured pesto.

Safe Temperature for Pork

Many pork recipes these days, including some in *Cook's Illustrated*, call for cooking the meat to a much lower internal temperature than we used to twenty or thirty years ago. I've tried it once or twice and agree that the meat stays more tender and juicy at lower temperatures, but I'm leery about safety. Are these lower temperatures really safe?

REMI NAYEM
BROOKLYN, NY

➤ In keeping with your comment, Pam Anderson, in her article "Holiday Pork Roast" in the November/December 1997 issue, found that not overdoing the internal temperature was one key to a well-roasted rack. For years the standard internal temperature for pork was 180 degrees—an appropriate temperature for pre-WWII pork, but hardly right for today's young, lean, "other white meat." The National Pork Producers Council currently promotes 160 degrees as the new standard, but in her testing, Anderson found loins roasted to this temperature were still too dry. Instead, she settled on an internal temperature of 145 degrees, which increases an extra three or four degrees during the post-cooking resting period, at which point the roast has just lost the last of its pink color and is still very juicy.

Is it safe to cook pork to this temperature? In a word, yes. Given the controlled grain-based diet of pigs these days, trichinosis is virtually non-existent. According to David Meisinger, assistant vice president of pork quality for the National Pork Producers Council, the few reported incidents are a result of privately raised pigs and rustic production conditions. Even so, trichinosis is killed at 140 degrees.

Because the inside of the roast is bacteria-free (unless it has been punctured accidentally with a knife), only the cut surfaces of the roast might potentially be contaminated. As long as the outside of the roast reaches 140 degrees within four hours, the meat is safe.

Reviving Wilted Greens

My grandmother taught me to revive wilted parsley or lettuce by soaking the leaves in cold water for a few minutes. Provided the greens aren't too far gone, the trick works well, but neither she nor I can say why. Can you enlighten us?

FRANK JACE
OWOSSO, MI

➤ You're right about this trick. Ten minutes in an ice water bath gave new life to a bunch of wilted, sad-looking parsley in our test kitchen. As explained by food scientists Shirley Corriher, in *CookWise* (Morrow, 1997) and Harold McGee, in

On Food and Cooking (Collier, 1984), the cells that make up fresh, healthy plants are turgid, or stuffed so full of water that the cell walls bulge to accommodate it. The pressure exerted on one another by the filled cells results in firm, erect plant tissue, which we read as crisp when we bite or cut into it.

If the water concentration outside the cells drops, which it will when the plant is exposed to air, water exits the cells through semi-permeable membranes. For plants still rooted in the ground, this is no problem because the roots replenish lost water in the tissues. In harvested plants, though, the water exodus leaves tissue wilted and limp. But permeability is a two-way street. When water concentration outside the plant cells increases, as it obviously will when you submerge the plant in water, the membranes allow water back into the cells, restoring turgor, and with it, texture.

Alternative Pie Weights

Vis-à-vis Eva Katz's article about prebaking pie shells in the September/October '97 issue, I've discovered a great technique for blind baking pastry. I bought a 30-inch stainless steel choke dog collar to drape over the dough in place of the traditional pie weights or dry beans. The collar won't spill or scatter and it's easy to store in a drawer or on a hook.

LISA KUHN
OAKLAND, CA

➤ We too have accidentally scattered pie weights across the test kitchen floor by knocking over the storage jar. So we eagerly tested your dog collar method and found that it not only eliminated that risk, it browned the pastry as deeply and evenly as the loose weights because, like the weights, the metal conducts heat well. Since the metal touches the tin foil lining rather than the pastry itself, you can use either the collar or an equal length of light chain purchased from a hardware store.

Flavoring a Frozen Roast

If I'm defrosting a roast that I eventually want to flavor with garlic, I rub a fresh garlic clove over the meat while it is still frozen. The rough surface of the meat grates the garlic and helps it cling.

JUDY POLY
SAN JOSE, CA

➤ We tried your method and found that it does help impart a nice, very subtle, garlic essence to the meat when it is cooked. This process is similar to flavoring bruschetta with garlic, as described on our September/October 1996 issue (see "Bruschetta: Italian Garlic Bread," page 8). The jagged edges of the toasted bread, or the frozen meat in this case, rips tiny bits of garlic from the clove as it is rubbed over the surface. If you prefer a stronger garlic taste, try studding the meat with slivered garlic, or rubbing the outside prior to cooking with a spice paste that includes garlic.

Skillet Pizza Reheating

Years ago, I learned the best way to avoid a soggy crust when reheating pizza - use a skillet. Place the slices, cheese side down, in a preheated skillet for one minute to start the cheese melting. Don't go for any longer, though, because the cheese could burn. Flip the slices over and heat the crust thoroughly, about 3 minutes.

PAT ALEXANDER
CHICAGO, IL

➤ Your method proved especially successful in our well-seasoned cast iron skillet. In fact, since the pizza probably rode around for a while en route to the test kitchen, the reheated pizza came out crisper than when it was delivered "fresh."

Troubleshooting Rugelach

➤ In our September/October 1997 story "Homemade Rugelach," there was an unfortunate discrepancy between the text, which said there was an egg yolk in the dough, and the recipe, which did not include the yolk. The recipe was correct; there is no egg yolk. We apologize for the mistake.

Several readers thought the missing yolk might be responsible for their difficulty in handling this unusually sticky dough. Not so, since there should be no yolk, but the inquiries led us back to the test kitchen to troubleshoot. We've come up with three tips which should make handling the dough easier.

First, be certain not to overprocess the fats and dry ingredients in the food processor. The dough really will resemble small, uneven curds when it is just coming together, at which point a few quick kneads will make it cohesive. Processing beyond the curd stage will soften the butter and cream cheese too much, resulting in super-sticky, unwieldy dough. Second, try an extra 30 minute refrigeration period after dividing and shaping the dough log into four equal disks and before rolling each disk into the 8½-inch circles. Cold dough will be stiffer and easier to handle. Also, be certain that all portions of the dough with which you are not working at the moment stay refrigerated. Last, try flouring lightly the bottom sheet of plastic wrap on which the dough will be rolled, and, if need be, the surface of the dough on which the top sheet of plastic will be laid. Most of the extra flour will not incorporate into the dough, and it should make the removal of the plastic wrap from the rolled circle easier.

Errata

➤ In the Master Recipe in the article "A Simple Chocolate Truffle" on page 25 of our November/December 1997 issue, the list of possible flavoring liqueurs and liquors inadvertently included four that the author, Nick Malgieri, finds inappropriate: Frangelico, Amaretto, Kahlua, and port. In addition, Mr. Malgieri advises that he does not recommend adding sugar when processing the nuts for the Chocolate Nut Truffles on the same page.

WHAT IS IT?

We've had this kitchen tool—at least I think it's a kitchen tool—for many years. It appears to be some kind of press, with a bowl that measures 2-by 2¼-inches, at the end of a handle that is about 6 inches long. One side of the bowl has ¾-inch metal teeth, with several notches protruding from each tooth, while the other side has ¼-inch teeth, with small indentations to accept the notches. The teeth on each side do not appear to meet when the bowl is closed. It seems to be made of very light metal. Other than the word "Japan" in tiny letters on one handle, there are no identifying marks or numbers.

VIC BASTIEN
TULSA, OK

➤ As much a tool for the bar as for the kitchen, you have a manual ice crusher, designed to crack one cube of ice at a time. We found a German-made aluminum version. Like yours, ours has a bowl with two sides, one deep with short, indented teeth, and the other shallow, with larger, extended teeth. The two sides, each with a 6-inch metal handle, are attached by a hinge so that they can open and close onto each other. The side of the bowl with the ¼-inch, grooved teeth is deep enough to cradle a single cube, which is broken apart by lowering the top, shallow portion of the bowl, with it's ¾-inch notched teeth, down onto it.

Crushing ice one cube at a time is a slow way to go, which is fine when making drinks for one or two people. For large quantities of ice to serve a crowd, we'd stick to the old stress-relieving method of placing the cubes in a heavy-duty freezer bag, wrapping that in a brown paper grocery bag, and whacking away on the ground outside with a heavy cast iron pan or a mallet. Or, even easier, buy a bag of crushed ice at a convenience store.

Quick Tips

Roasting Chile Peppers

JoEllen Osteen of Smyrna, Georgia, finds that it is tedious and inefficient to hold small chile peppers over a flame with tongs to roast them, so she devised this method to roast a few chiles. Place the chiles on a wire cooling rack and lay the rack flat on top of the burner. You can easily shake the rack, and therefore turn the chiles, by grasping at the outer edge with an oven mitt or tongs.

Shaping Meat Balls

Our test kitchen found that the best and easiest way to shape the meatballs in the story on page 8 was to use a one and one-half inch cookie scooper.

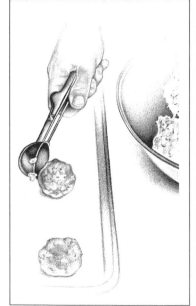

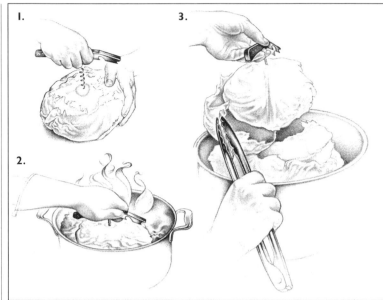

Blanching Cabbage Leaves

Need blanched cabbage leaves for a recipe? Cindy Chudy of Pleasant Hill, California, has developed a method that is easier than cutting out the core and separating the leaves prior to their water bath.

1. After trimming the core of the cabbage by about one inch, she screws a corkscrew into the core.

2. The corkscrew acts as a handle by which you can grasp (using a pot holder) the head of cabbage and lower it into a pot of boiling water for a few seconds at a time.

3. When the outer leaves are softened, pull the head out of the water and trim off the blanched leaves with a pair of tongs. Repeat the process as many times as necessary to get the number of blanched leaves you need.

Freezing Cake in Slices

After eating only one or two slices from a cake, Kate Bech Gardner of Lansdowne, Pennsylvania, often freezes the rest. To avoid defrosting the whole cake when she wants just a few pieces, she first wraps a sheet of wax paper around the point and against the sides of each slice, then reassembles the cake and freezes. This way, you can remove as many slices as you like without defrosting the whole thing.

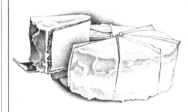

Kitchen String Dispenser

If you do not have a drawer beneath your work surface in which to keep a ball of kitchen string as we recommend in How to Tie Meat (see page 16), you may like the solution that Christina Walker-Green of Churchill, Pennsylvania, found to keep the ball of string from falling off the counter and unraveling in a mess.

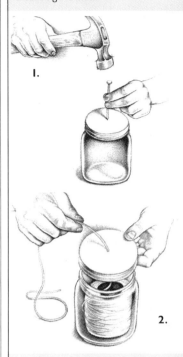

1. Using a hammer and nail or an ice pick, punch a hole through the center of the tin lid of a glass storage jar.

2. Place the ball of string inside the container and thread the end through the hole in the lid.

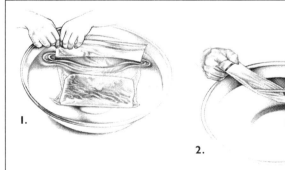

Vacuum-Packing Foods

One way to remove air from a zipper-lock bag of food before freezing is to suck it out through a straw. Rokshana Thanadar of Suffolk, Virginia, found that she never seems to have a straw within reach, so she uses the following method in her kitchen sink.

1. Fill the sink or a large bowl with water and submerge the food-filled bag almost to the top, taking care not to spill water into the bag.

2. The pressure from the water forces the air in the bag up around the food and out of the bag. When the bag has collapsed around the food, seal it immediately, dry it off, and it's ready to go in the freezer.

Cleaning Up Vegetable Scraps

It is a bad idea to leave vegetable, fruit, and meat trimmings sitting in the garbage pail for too long, as they will begin to break down and smell. To solve this problem, Daphna Caperonis of New York, New York, wraps the handles of a plastic grocery bag around the corners of a drawer beneath her work surface and closes the drawer. The bag stays open so that scraps can be swept right in. When she is finished, she simply ties the handles together and disposes of the whole package.

Foaming Milk for Cappuccino

If you love foamed milk in your cafe latte or cappuccino but don't feel like firing up (or cleaning up) the espresso machine, Sheri Reed of Atlanta, Georgia, has the answer. All you really need is a good quality whisk with a thick handle.

1. Heat a mug or a large measuring cup filled halfway with skim milk in a microwave until small bubbles have formed around the edges, one to two minutes. Place the bulb of the whisk into the mug or measuring cup, grasp the handle between your outstretched palms, and rub your hands back and forth rapidly to rotate the whisk briskly.

2. When the foam reaches the top of the mug, spoon foam out and repeat.

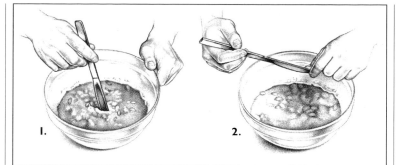

Making Sure Leftovers are Hot

Maryetta Bitzer of Stroudsburg, Pennsylvania, has devised this method to make sure that leftover casseroles, baked pasta dishes, stews, chilis, and so forth are thoroughly reheated before serving.

1. Insert a small paring or table knife into the food and hold it there for 30 seconds.

2. Remove the knife and feel the flat sides with your fingers. If it is hot, so is the food. If not, continue heating.

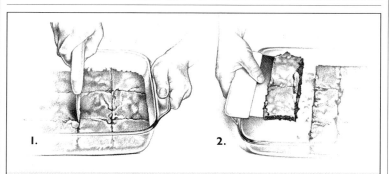

New Use for a Bench Knife

Bench knives are used primarily by bakers to divide masses of unbaked dough or to scrape flour and dried dough off their work surfaces. Virginia Graham of Lake San Marcos, California, finds that this tool, which is wider than most spatulas, is very useful for cutting and neatly serving bar cookies and lasagne.

1. Press down firmly to cut a section, moving down the same line from one end of the pan to the other.

2. When all the pieces are cut and the first one removed, slide the wide blade under the next piece and lift it neatly up and out.

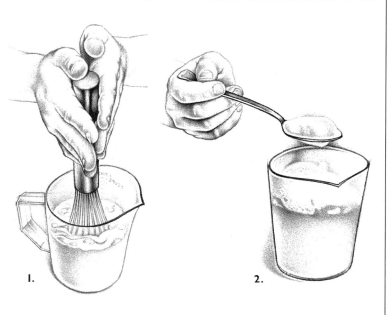

Ridding Egg Whites of Yolk

When separating eggs, Joan Grace of Bath, Maine, finds that a Q-Tip is ideal for blotting up small specks of egg yolk that accidentally get in the whites.

Making the Strainer Fit

Sally McQuail of Downington, Pennsylvania, makes big batches of stock which have to be strained through her small strainer into a bowl large enough to accommodate all the liquid. To suspend the strainer over the bowl, she lays a skewer across the bowl and rests the strainer handle on it.

Send Us Your Tip

The editors of Cook's Illustrated would like to thank all of our readers who have sent us their quick tips. We have enjoyed reading every one of them and have learned a lot. Keep them coming. We will provide a one-year complimentary subscription for each quick tip that we print. Send a description of your special technique to Cook's Illustrated, P.O. Box 569, Brookline, MA 02147-0569. Please write "Attention: Quick Tips" on the envelope and include your name, address, and daytime phone number. Unfortunately, we can only acknowledge receipt of tips that will be printed in the magazine. In case the same tip is received from two readers, the one postmarked first will be selected. Also, be sure to let us know what particular cooking problems you would like us to investigate in upcoming issues.

The Best Black Beans

For the most full-flavored beans, avoid pre-soaking, cook in liquid flavored
with a ham hock, then add a sofrito and the bright taste of acids.

⋺ BY STEPHANIE LYNESS ⋲

Although I've always considered myself something of a bean lover, I've never lived, traveled, or cooked in a country where beans are a daily staple. Friends who've vacationed in Central and Latin America, though, rave about rice and beans, a dish they never tired of eating, even while consuming it three times a day. So I set out with great enthusiasm to unearth this new world of flavors. I was looking for beans that were more than a side dish; I wanted mine to be flavorful enough to serve as a main course with rice and accompanied by a simple salad or, at most, another vegetable.

Looking for Perfect Texture

I started my research by cooking several basic bean recipes culled from Central and Latin American and Caribbean cookbooks. By the end of the day, I'd narrowed my research to black beans: despite the wonderfully creamy texture of kidney beans, I preferred the more pronounced flavor of the black.

While I focused on flavor, I also paid close attention to texture. The perfect bean was tender without being mushy, with enough tooth for a satisfying chew. In pursuit of this perfect texture, I discovered that it was important to cook the beans in enough water; too little water and the beans on the top cooked more slowly than the beans underneath and the whole pot took forever to cook. (Twelve cups is sufficient water to cook 1 pound of beans.) I further tested beans that had been soaked overnight against a batch of unsoaked, as well as against a batch softened by a "quick-soak" method in which the beans were brought to a boil, simmered 2 minutes, then covered to let stand 1 hour off the heat. The quick-soak method caused a large percentage of the beans to burst during cooking. This reduced the chew I was after, so I nixed that method. Contrary to my expectation, overnight soaking only decreased the cooking time by about half an hour and didn't improve the texture. Because I'm rarely organized enough to soak the night before, I no longer soak.

Next, to test the theory that salting toughens the skin of beans and lengthens the cooking time, I tested beans salted at the end of cooking against those salted three-quarters of the way through, as well as against beans salted at the beginning. In a blind tasting, I couldn't tell any difference be-

The key to unsplit beans is cooking them over very low heat. If simmered hard, they burst.

tween the skins but only those beans salted from the beginning had enough salt for my taste, so I salt them then.

In Pursuit of Flavor: Sofritos and Acids

Now that I had discovered how to cook beans with the texture I wanted, it was time to discover the best way to build more layers of flavor onto this base without drowning the earthy flavor of the beans.

In search of my answer, I travelled to Miami, New York, and Connecticut, gathering techniques from a number of cooks whose culinary roots lay in Cuba, the home of black beans and rice.

In the Connecticut kitchen of Olga Rigsby, a Cuban emigré, I learned the basics of adding flavor to my simple beans. To satisfy my desire for a vegetarian version, Olga agreed to cook two examples, one with pork and one without.

Olga started by cooking both pots of beans in salted water on the lowest possible heat. She basically cooked the beans the same way that I had, but added a ham hock and a green bell pepper, a vegetable I hadn't experimented with that's used a lot in Cuban cuisine.

Once the beans were cooked, Olga stirred up a mixture that she called a sofrito, a crucial element in many Cuban dishes. She sautéed chopped onion, garlic, and green bell pepper in

olive oil until soft. Then she added some of the cooked black beans with their liquid, along with dried oregano, vinegar, salt, and lots of cumin. She threw this whole mixture into the blender and pureed it. She then stirred it back into the beans, thus thickening the sauce, and cooked everything another thirty minutes to marry the flavors.

When Olga was finished, her Cuban-style beans had the complexity of flavor I was after. The beans still retained their distinctive taste, but the sofrito offered an additional layer of fresh flavor. The bell pepper in the cooking water added yet another dimension of sweetness to the beans and a bite at the end. The sofrito and the mashed beans thickened the sauce well. And I was sold on the pork. Olga had been right—it added richness and body to the beans. Finally, pureeing some of the beans with the sofrito made the bean liquid thick enough to sauce rice, a texture that I found preferable to the watery bean liquid served in several other versions I had sampled.

Sure that I was on the right track, I returned to my own kitchen to play with the new techniques and flavorings.

Having determined that meat gave me a necessary depth of flavor, I tested the beans with a ham hock, bacon, ham, and pork loin. I liked all four and each gave the beans a slightly different flavor; ham hock gave a smooth background taste, while bacon and ham were saltier and more in the foreground. Pork loin was the most subtle of the pork choices.

Wondering if pureeing was really necessary, I tested a pureed sofrito against one in which the beans were simply mashed into the whole sofrito and the liquid reduced, a method I had learned from Nieves Feal, a Cuban restaurateur in Miami. I decided on the latter technique. Pureeing intensified the flavor of the vegetables enough to almost overwhelm the beans, and the pureed onion gave me a gray color and a slightly grainy texture that I didn't like. I could thicken the sauce

Getting the Most for Your Bean

Having found a technique for cooking black beans that delivered the flavor I was looking for, I began to wonder what was actually going on in the cooking. How does flavor get into the bean? So I called food scientist Shirley Corriher to get the scientific explanation.

I found out that there are at least two processes going on in the development of flavor in the bean. First, according to Corriher, the bean itself develops flavor as it cooks. She explained that beans are full of starch granules made up of layers of tightly packed starch molecules, arranged something like the layers of an onion. As the bean soaks or cooks, the liquid seeps into the bean through the tiny white area on its side, the hilium, where the bean was originally connected to the plant. (The rest of the seed coat is impermeable.) As the liquid leaks in, slowly at first and then more quickly, it gets in between the layers of starch and the granules begin to swell. Eventually, the granules swell to the point of cracking and the

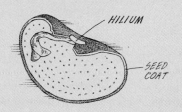

HILIUM

SEED COAT

starch rushes into the bean in a process called gelatinization. This process not only alters the texture of the beans, but it improves their flavor. So, in cooking terms, a well-cooked bean has more flavor than one that's not adequately cooked.

I went back to the kitchen to test this myself, tasting beans cooked in plain water every ten minutes after the first hour of cooking until the beans burst. I found that the beans changed over time from a starchy, acrid taste with a chalky texture, to a less acrid, rounder flavor with a velvety texture. Once the beans burst, they actually lost flavor as if it were being washed away by the water.

Second, I asked Corriher to explain how flavor outside the bean is infused into it. She explained that when you cook beans with vegetables and herbs, the water-soluble flavor compounds in those ingredients dissolve and flavor the water, and then enter and swell the bean, thus flavoring it. Good enough. But, I wondered, would it then be necessary to introduce the flavorings at the outset? Would beans that were brought to a boil with plain water using the quick-soak method, and then cooked with aromatics, be less flavorful than a batch of beans that were cooked with aromatics from the beginning? I tested this and found the answer to be yes. Corriher confirmed my results: Once the starch molecule has totally swollen, it ceases to take in water; therefore flavorings must be added at the beginning.   —Stephanie Lyness

adequately with the mashed beans and reduction.

I ran several experiments with flavorings: I tested to see whether sugar was necessary and found that I didn't like the additional sweetness. I also tested to find out whether I preferred the cumin simmered in with the beans, or in the sofrito. The flavor of the spice got lost when simmered with the beans; I decided to save the cumin for the sofrito. Inspired by the red pepper I'd noticed in Feal's restaurant, I made a sofrito with red pepper and found that it tasted particularly good in beans flavored with bacon.

While dining at Patria restaurant in New York, I found that acids can play a key role in flavoring black beans. So I tested red wine vinegar against balsamic and cider vinegars as well as lime and lemon juices. I found all of the acids to be delicious with the exception of cider vinegar, which I found harsh. I also discovered that sherry is particularly delicious with ham.

BLACK BEANS WITH HAM HOCKS, CILANTRO, AND LIME
SERVES 6

Serve with Fluffy White Rice (*Cook's Illustrated*, May/June 1996). Garnish the dish with a spoonful of sour cream, minced red onion, and a dash or two of hot red pepper sauce.

Beans
1	pound black beans, picked over and rinsed
12	cups water
1	smoked ham hock (about 2/3 pound), rinsed
1	green bell pepper, stemmed, seeded, and quartered
1	medium onion, minced
6	medium garlic cloves, minced
2	bay leaves
1 1/2	teaspoons table salt or 1 tablespoon kosher salt

Sofrito
2	tablespoons olive oil
1	medium onion, minced
1	small green bell pepper, stemmed, seeded, and minced
8	medium garlic cloves, minced
2	teaspoons dried oregano
3/4	teaspoon table salt or 1 1/2 teaspoons kosher salt, or to taste
1 1/2	teaspoons ground cumin
1	tablespoon juice from one medium lime
1/2	cup chopped fresh cilantro leaves
	Ground black pepper

1. *For the beans:* Bring all bean ingredients to

TECHNIQUE | THICKENING THE SAUCE

Add 1 cup of the cooked beans and 2 cups of the bean cooking liquid to the sofrito and mash the beans with a potato masher or a fork. The mashed beans will thicken the sauce.

boil over medium-high heat in heavy soup kettle or Dutch oven, skimming surface as scum rises. Reduce heat to low and simmer, partially covered, adding more water if cooking liquid reduces to level of beans, until tender but not splitting (taste several, as they cook unevenly), about 2 hours. Remove ham hock from beans. When cool enough to handle, remove ham from bone, discard bone and skin, and cut meat into bite-size pieces; set aside.

2. *For the sofrito:* Meanwhile, heat oil in large skillet over medium heat; add ingredients from onion through salt; sauté until vegetables soften, 8 to 10 minutes. Add cumin; sauté until fragrant, about 1 minute longer.

3. *To finish dish:* Scoop 1 cup beans and 2 cups cooking liquid into pan with sofrito; mash beans with potato masher or fork until smooth. Simmer over medium heat until liquid is reduced and thickened, about 6 minutes. Return sofrito mixture to bean pot; simmer until beans are creamy and liquid thickens to sauce consistency, 15 to 20 minutes. Add lime juice; simmer 1 minute longer. Stir in cilantro, adjust seasoning with pepper and salt if necessary, and serve hot over fluffy white rice.

BLACK BEANS WITH HAM HOCKS AND DRY SHERRY

Follow recipe for Black Beans with Ham Hocks (above), adding 1 teaspoon ground coriander to sofrito along with cumin, substituting 1 tablespoon dry sherry for lime juice, and omitting cilantro.

BLACK BEANS WITH BACON, BALSAMIC VINEGAR, AND SWEET PEPPER

Fry 1/2 pound bacon, cut into 1/2-inch strips, in medium skillet over medium heat until crisp and brown, about 5 minutes. Transfer with slotted spoon to paper towel–lined plate. Follow recipe for Black Beans with Ham Hocks (above), substituting bacon fat for olive oil and 1 medium red bell pepper for the green pepper in sofrito. Add cooked bacon to beans with sofrito, and substitute 2 teaspoons balsamic vinegar for lime juice.

Spaghetti and (Great) Meatballs

Buttermilk-soaked bread is the key to meatballs with a soft, creamy interior and pleasantly rich, tangy flavor.

⇒ BY JACK BISHOP ⇐

Like most Italian-Americans, I have fond memories of my grandmother's Sunday dinner. As a main course, she served two kinds of sausage, braciole (rolled flank steak stuffed with cheeses, herbs, and garlic), and meatballs, all simmered in tomato sauce and all designed to be eaten over spaghetti. It was delicious and decadent.

Although my grandmother is a fabulous cook, her meatballs were never the best part of the meal. (My siblings and I fought over the braciole or spicy sausage.) However, it's the meatball part of this traditional Italian-American feast that most other Americans are familiar with as part of the now-classic spaghetti and meatballs.

For this story, I wanted to make great meatballs (something the kids in my family would fight over) and try to streamline the recipe in the process. My grandmother would spend the better part of the weekend cooking Sunday dinner. I wanted to develop a spaghetti and meatball recipe that could be on the table in less-than an hour— a breeze for weekend cooking and doable on weeknights when pressed for time.

Right Texture, Right Binder

The problem with most meatballs is that they are too dense and heavy. Serving meatballs over thin, long noodles is already a bit awkward. If the meatballs are compact, overcooked little hamburgers, the dish can be so leaden that Alka-Seltzer is the only dessert that makes sense.

Many cooks think of meatballs as hamburgers with seasonings (cheese, herbs, garlic, etc.) and a round shape. This is partly true. However, unlike hamburgers, which are best cooked rare or medium-rare, meatballs are cooked through until well-done. At this point, ground beef and seasonings will form dry, tough hockey pucks. Meatballs require additional ingredients to keep them moist and lighten their texture. My testing first focused on ingredients that would give meatballs a moister, softer consistency.

I started out with a simple recipe (ground beef plus a little cheese, parsley, salt, and pepper) and tested the various binders—eggs, dried bread crumbs, fresh bread crumbs, ground crackers, and bread soaked in milk—that were common in the recipes uncovered during my research.

I started with a whole egg and decided that it was a welcome addition. Meatballs made without

Because the crust is cut off the before the bread is used, any good quality bread will work well in these meatballs.

egg were heavier and drier.

Next I added dried supermarket bread crumbs (the choice of my grandmother and most meatball recipe writers) to one batch and crustless bread soaked in milk (the second most popular bread binder) to another. The differences were quite clear. The crumbs soaked up any available moisture and compounded the problems caused by cooking meatballs to the well-done stage. Adding bread crumbs might be a way to extend the meat—an idea with appeal in less prosperous times—but hardly necessary in an age where the meat for this recipe cost $2. In comparison, the meatballs made with the soaked bread were moister, creamier, richer, and even more pâté-like in consistency. Clearly, milk was an important part of the equation.

There were a few problems with my first test using torn bread and milk. I soaked the crustless bread and then squeezed it dry as directed in many recipes but was still having trouble getting the bread to meld seamlessly into the meatball mixture. I saw a recipe where the crustless, torn bread cubes were cooked with milk into a paste. Although this method worked fine, I found myself waiting around for the mixture to cool before adding it to the meat.

The idea of mashing the bread and milk into a

paste was good; I just wondered if I could do it without cooking. After several attempts, I devised the following scheme. I starting by tearing the bread into small cubes. I placed the bread in a small bowl, drizzled the milk over it, and then started mashing with a fork. I continued to mash every few minutes as the bread absorbed the liquid and eventually formed a smooth, thick paste. (In the meantime, I prepared the other ingredients for the meatballs.) By the time the bread was ready, so were the rest of the ingredients and I just added the entire bread-milk mixture to the bowl with the meat and seasonings.

Besides solving the problem of bread chunks being recognizable in my meatballs, this method has an added benefit. With more milk, the meatballs were even creamier and moister than versions made with bread that had been soaked and squeezed. Of course, there is limit to how much milk that can be added before the meatball mixture is to hard to handle. But ½ cup milk added per pound of ground beef was clearly the winner in this first round of testing.

My colleague Pam Anderson found that yogurt adds a delicious flavor to meat loaf (see "Memorable Meat Loaf," September/ October 1996). Yogurt is too thick to properly soften bread by my method so I tried thinning it with some milk. Meatballs made with thinned yogurt were even richer, creamier, and more flavorful than those made with plain milk. I also tried buttermilk and the results were equally delicious, and there was no need to thin the liquid before adding it to the bread.

With the dairy and bread part of the binder decided, I went back to the issue of the egg one more time and tried the yolk only. As I suspected, the fats and emulsifiers in the yolk added moistness and richness to the meatballs. The white was only making the mixture sticky and harder to handle, so I eliminated it.

Meats and Seasonings

I next experimented with various meats. Until this point, I had been using all ground chuck. I tried leaner ground round but, as expected, the meatballs were dry. Ground veal was too bland and not worth adding, in my opinion. A little ground pork gives meatballs another flavor dimension. After several tests, I settled on a ratio of three parts chuck to one part pork as my ideal, although you can use all chuck if you prefer.

Freshly grated Parmesan cheese was clearly needed for flavor, as was a little fresh parsley. I tried basil in the meatballs but felt that its delicate flavor was better showcased in the tomato sauce. Raw garlic improved the flavor of the meatballs but raw onions were problematic because they tended to shrink during cooking and caused little pockets to form in the meatballs. I tried cooking the onions first, which was an improvement, but in the end the meatballs were delicious without them and I wanted to avoid precooking ingredients if possible, so I recommend just leaving them out.

With my ingredients in order, I then tested three cooking techniques—roasting, broiling, and traditional pan-frying. I had high hopes for roasting. I knew it would be cleaner and make my house less smelly. After twenty-five minutes at 450 degrees the meatballs emerged from the oven nicely browned. But one bite revealed the problem with this method—the meatballs were dry and crumbly. Broiling proved messier than pan-frying and also dried out the meatballs. Pan-frying was my method of choice.

When pan-frying, it is important to wait until the oil is quite hot before adding the meatballs. Once in the pan, turn the meatballs several times to brown all sides. Meatballs should have a dark brown crust so they don't become too soggy when placed in the tomato sauce. In order to pan-fry the meatballs in a single batch, choose a 10- or 11-inch sauté pan with straight sides.

I wondered if I could save clean-up time and add flavor by building the tomato sauce in the same pan used to fry the meatballs. I emptied the vegetable oil, leaving behind the browned bits on the bottom of the pan. I then added a little fresh olive oil and started my tomato sauce. Not only did this method prove convenient, but it gave depth to my quick-cooking sauce.

Meatballs need a thick, smooth sauce—the kind produced by canned crushed tomatoes. I added a little garlic and basil to the tomatoes, but otherwise kept the flavorings simple so that the focus would remain on the meatballs. Once the tomato sauce thickens, the browned meatballs are added and simmered just until heated through.

By this time the pasta should be almost cooked (the meatballs can sit in the tomato sauce for a few minutes without getting soggy, but not for a few hours, as is common in most restaurants), and dinner is ready to go. While I think that a pound of pasta usually feeds four, this dish is so hearty that it may yield six servings, especially when feeding several kids.

CLASSIC SPAGHETTI AND MEATBALLS
SERVES 4 TO 6

This streamlined recipe can be on the table in under an hour. See the illustrations below for helpful tips. In our testing of canned crushed tomatoes (see March/April 1997), we found that Progresso and Muir Glen were the best choices because of their fresh tomato flavor. Redpack and Contadina also showed well in that tasting, but should be considered backup choices.

Meatballs

- 2 slices white sandwich bread (crusts discarded), torn into small cubes
- 1/2 cup buttermilk or 6 tablespoons plain yogurt thinned with 2 tablespoons sweet milk
- 3/4 pound ground chuck mixed with 1/4 pound ground pork or 1 pound ground chuck
- 1/4 cup freshly grated Parmesan cheese
- 2 tablespoons minced fresh parsley leaves
- 1 large egg yolk
- 1 small garlic clove, minced (1 teaspoon)
- 3/4 teaspoon salt
  Ground black pepper
  Vegetable oil for pan-frying (about 1 1/4 cups)

Simple Tomato Sauce

- 2 tablespoons extra-virgin olive oil
- 1 teaspoon minced garlic
- 1 can (28 ounces) crushed tomatoes
- 1 tablespoon minced fresh basil leaves
  Salt and ground black pepper

- 1 pound spaghetti
  Freshly grated Parmesan cheese

1. *For the meatballs:* combine bread and buttermilk in small bowl, mashing occasionally with fork, until smooth paste forms, about 10 minutes.

2. Mix all meatball ingredients, including bread mixture and pepper to taste in medium bowl. Lightly form 3 tablespoons of mixture into 1½-inch round meatballs; repeat with remaining mixture to form approximately 14 meatballs. (Compacting them can make the meatballs dense and hard. Can be placed on large plate, covered loosely with plastic wrap, and refrigerated for several hours.)

3. Bring 4 quarts of water to boil in large pot for cooking pasta.

4. Meanwhile, heat ¼-inch vegetable oil over medium-high heat in 10- or 11 inch sauté pan. When edge of meatball dipped in oil sizzles, add meatballs in single layer. Fry, turning several times, until nicely browned on all sides, about 10 minutes, regulating heat as needed to keep oil sizzling but not smoking. Transfer browned meatballs to paper towel–lined plate; set aside. Repeat, if necessary, with remaining meatballs.

5. *For the sauce,* discard oil in pan, leaving behind any browned bits. Add olive oil along with garlic; sauté, scraping up any browned bits, just until garlic is golden, about 30 seconds. Add tomatoes, bring to boil, and simmer gently until sauce thickens, about 10 minutes. Stir in basil; add salt and pepper to taste. Add meatballs and simmer, turning them occasionally, until heated through, about 5 minutes. Keep warm over low flame.

6. Meanwhile, add 1 tablespoon salt and pasta to boiling water. Cook until al dente, drain, and return to pot. Ladle several large spoonfuls of tomato sauce (without meatballs) over spaghetti and toss until noodles are well coated. Divide pasta among individual bowls and top each with a little more tomato sauce and 2 to 3 meatballs. Serve immediately with grated cheese passed separately.

TECHNIQUE | MAKING MEATBALLS

1. Mash the bread cubes and buttermilk together with a fork. Let stand, mashing occasionally, until a smooth paste forms, about 10 minutes.

2. Once all the ingredients for the meatballs are in the bowl, mix with a fork to roughly combine. At this point, use your hands to make sure that the flavorings are evenly distributed throughout the mixture.

3. Meatballs must be browned well on all sides. This may involve standing meatballs on their sides near the end of the cooking process. If necessary, lean them up against each other to get the final sides browned.

The Microwave Chronicles

Can a microwave oven actually cook food or is it just an expensive tool for reheating coffee? Well, some of each.

≥ BY CHRISTOPHER KIMBALL WITH DAWN YANAGIHARA ≤

The fact that microwave ovens are mostly used for defrosting, reheating leftovers, and cooking hot dogs is no secret. As with the Internet, wild claims of ubiquitous application are long gone, replaced in this case by the deflated expectations of millions of home cooks who have abandoned attempts at microwave osso buco but are quite content to heat up cold coffee or defrost bacon. But, as if the microwave were a highly-touted and overpriced weapons system that failed in battle, the publicity mavens keep up a stream of counter-intelligence while the troops know the truth: this dog won't hunt.

In recent years, however, a few books have appeared that promote the microwave as a cooking tool much like a food processor or standing mixer. According to these books, it can soften butter, melt chocolate, toast breadcrumbs, and peel tomatoes, as well as perform a few simple culinary chores such as cooking grains, rice, and beans; poaching fruit; preparing corn on the cob; baking apples; and steaming broccoli and cauliflower. These techniques share a common theme: They purport to be ideally suited to the cooking method used by a microwave, which uses the vibration of water molecules to generate heat.

We were intrigued enough by a few successes to draw up a list of techniques most likely to succeed. What follows is a blow-by-blow account of our microwave adventures. In our evaluations, we used a few simple guidelines: Is the microwave oven truly better than other (stovetop or conventional oven) methods? Does it do a better job? Is it truly faster? (Shaving mere seconds off a recipe is not important.) Is it more convenient?

As we tested, we became aware that a microwave reduces the window of time during which a particular food is properly cooked, thus increasing the likelihood of overcooking. The walnuts we tested, for example, were underdone at six minutes yet burned at seven minutes, an unacceptable margin of error. This problem is compounded by the fact that different models and different wattages perform differently.

There were also issues of convenience. Because most microwave ovens are small in comparison to conventional models, the food must be removed from the oven to stir it, taste it, or add to it. Different quantities of food can also dramatically change cooking times—just try baking three potatoes at a time instead of one, or doubling your favorite oatmeal recipe. And don't even attempt to defrost poultry or other odd-shaped frozen foods. Because a whole chicken is an odd amalgam of bones, skin, meat, and air, the ends of the drumsticks are fully cooked when the ice in the body cavity just starts to thaw.

Many of the most frequently recommended microwave techniques turned out to be duds. When we tried roasting butternut squash, for example, we ended up with squash that was unevenly cooked, with a wet texture and a gray, unappealing appearance. Similarly, apples steamed rather than baked in the microwave, and bacon emerged from the nuke dry and unevenly cooked. Bulgur took just as long to cook in the microwave as on the stove, and ended up firm and chewy rather than tender and fluffy like the stovetop version. Even steamed broccoli, reputed to be one of the microwave's fortes, was not suc-

cessful. The microwave-steamed broccoli had a duller color than the stovetop version, with a rubbery texture and a rather listless flavor.

Our testing did reveal, however, sixteen different techniques and simple recipes that we do recommend. To check on standardization of recipes, we conducted all tests with two different machines, the first a Sharp R4H17 with 1,000 watts and 1.2 cubic feet of space, the second a General Electric JE740GW, with only 700 watts of output and .7 cubic feet.

16 Methods That Really Work

These winners are divided into two categories: basic cooking techniques and simple, building-block recipes. Note that cooking times are usually given in ranges, as different wattage and size ovens cook at different rates. The lower times are for 1,000-watt ovens and the longer times are for 700-watt models, unless otherwise indicated.

11 Basic Techniques

➤ *Melting Chocolate:* Melting choclate is the all-time best use for a microwave. It's fast and easy. Note that the chocolate will hold its shape even when melted so be sure to stir the chocolate to gauge its texture. Because fats such as butter, cream, or shortening heat more quickly than chocolate, add them during the first stirring rather than at the beginning. Increase microwave time for larger quantities of chocolate.

Microwave four 1-ounce squares or 4 ounces chopped chocolate at 50% power in a 2-cup Pyrex measuring cup to partially melt, about 1½ minutes. Stir with a wooden spoon; continue to mi-

Defrosting Ground Meat For best results, break the frozen meat into chunks. Cover loosely with plastic wrap.

Softening Brown Sugar A piece of bread provides moisture to the sugar.

Proofing Dough This simple technique cuts rising time by as much as 20 minutes.

crowave at 50% power until fully melted, about 1 minute longer.

➤ *Softening Butter:* The outside of the stick will melt a bit, making this not ideal for creaming, but for all other uses, the microwave is a winner. Don't forget to remove foil wrapping.

Place 1 stick refrigerated butter in the microwave oven; microwave at 30% power until softened, about 1 minute.

➤ *Defrosting Butter:* The outside of the butter starts to melt at the point the interior is malleable, but in a pinch this method is worth it, as frozen butter takes one-and-one-half hours to soften.

Place 2 sticks frozen butter in microwave oven; microwave at 50% power for 2 minutes. Turn butter over and continue to microwave at 50% power 1 minute longer.

➤ *Melting Butter:* The big benefit of using the microwave is that the butter separates cleanly, making it easy to clarify. If melting only four tablespoons butter, reduce microwave time to one-and-one-half minutes.

Place 1 stick butter, cut into 8 pieces, in a 2-cup Pyrex measuring cup; cover loosely with plastic wrap. Microwave at 50% power until melted, 2 to 2½ minutes.

➤ *Defrosting Ground Meat:* Oven wattage makes a big difference here, so check the meat as you go along. Both of our ovens did a good job, however, and the microwave is well-suited to this task.

Place 1 pound ground meat in a glass pie dish; cover loosely with plastic wrap and microwave at 30% power until partially defrosted, about 3 minutes. Break meat into 8 to 10 pieces and arrange them doughnut-style around the dish. Cover and continue to microwave at 30% power until almost defrosted, 3 to 4 minutes longer. Let stand until fully defrosted, about 5 minutes longer.

➤ *Defrosting Bacon:* Defrosting is a bit uneven but not a problem, because the bacon does not start to cook before the strips can be pulled apart.

Wrap frozen bacon in plastic wrap; microwave at 30% power, turning bacon halfway through cooking time, until defrosted, 2½ to 3 minutes.

➤ *Softening Brown Sugar:* This is a quick and easy way to bring back rock-hard brown sugar.

Place 1 cup sugar on a glass pie plate, cover with a small piece of wax paper, and then top with a slice of bread to provide a bit of moisture. Cover with plastic wrap. Microwave at 100% power until softened, about 30 seconds.

➤ *Warming Eggs:* Waiting for eggs to come to room temperature is like waiting for water to boil. The microwave, on the other hand, can take an egg from 45 degrees to 70 degrees in just 10 seconds! For each additional egg, add 5 seconds.

Place cold egg in a ramekin or small bowl; microwave at 30% power for 10 seconds.

➤ *Warming Syrup:* This is fast, easy, and the syrup can be heated right in the serving pitcher. Microwave ½ cup syrup in a 1-cup Pyrex measuring cup or small microwave-safe pitcher at 100% power until warm, about 30 seconds.

➤ *Warming Up Rice:* The microwave wins out here because the rice can be reheated in the serving dish, and larger quantities are easier to handle than on the stovetop. In addition, reheating rice is particularly tricky on the stovetop because stirring tends to make the rice sticky.

Sprinkle one cup cooked rice with 2 teaspoons water; cover with vented plastic wrap. Microwave at 100% power until rice is soft and hot, about 1½ minutes; let stand for 2 minutes.

➤ *Proofing Bread:* Another good use of the microwave, this technique cut rising time by 20 minutes for sweet yeast bread and American-style yeast bread doughs. Although we do not usually recommend using a microwave for boiling water, here the boiled water creates a warm, moist environment which promotes quick rising.

Microwave 2 cups water to boil at 100% power in a 1-quart Pyrex measuring cup. Alongside the water, place bowl of dough, covered with plastic wrap. Close microwave door; let stand until dough doubles in size.

5 Simple Recipes

STEAMED SALMON FILLETS
SERVES 2

Although we prefer a cooking method that lends more flavor to fish, if you like your fish steamed, this is an excellent method.

2   8-ounce salmon steaks

Place salmon steaks in a glass pie dish and cover with vented plastic wrap. Cook at 100% power for about 3½ minutes. Let stand for 2 minutes.

STEAMED LITTLENECK CLAMS
MAKES 8 TO 15 CLAMS

Although the opening clams sound like minor explosions, they emerge tender, flavorful, and with plenty of wonderful juices.

8-15   littlenecks

Place 8 to 15 littlenecks, hinge side out, around a microwave-safe pie dish, cover with vented plastic wrap, and microwave at 100% power until clams open, 1½ to 2 minutes for 8 clams, up to 3½ minutes for 15 clams.

POLENTA
MAKES 3½ CUPS

Unlike the stovetop method, microwave polenta does not require constant stirring. After testing different grinds of cornmeal, we found the medium-grind varieties, sold as polenta, are best.

1   cup medium-grind cornmeal
3½   cups water
1   teaspoon salt

In a 2-quart Pyrex measuring cup, covered with plastic wrap, microwave cornmeal, water, and salt at 100% power for 6 minutes. Uncover and stir thoroughly, then continue to microwave at 100% power until polenta is creamy and fully cooked, 5 to 6 minutes longer.

STEAMERS
MAKES 1 DOZEN

Arrange one dozen steamers, hinge side out, on a microwave-safe pie dish, cover with vented plastic wrap. Microwave at 100% power for 1 minute. Rearrange steamers to promote even cooking, cover, and microwave at 100% power until clams open, about 1 minute longer.

CORN ON THE COB
MAKES 2 TO 4 EARS

Nuked corn is just as good as boiled corn, and much faster too.

2-4   unhusked and unsilked ears corn

Rinse 2 to 4 unhusked, unsilked ears under cold water; microwave at 100% power, 4 to 6 minutes for 2 ears, 8 to 9 minutes for 4 ears. Let stand in microwave for 3 minutes longer.

How To Make Flavorful Beef Soup

Contrary to modern kitchen wisdom, it takes a lot of browned beef and a few small bones to make good soup broth.

⇒ BY PAM ANDERSON WITH MELISSA HAMILTON ⇐

I began cooking seriously in the '70s, the height of mainstream fascination with French cooking. One of my early attempts was making classic beef stock for French onion soup. I followed the instructions to the letter, a process that involved three types of beef bones, some aromatic vegetables, and hours and hours of roasting and simmering. But after taking a few sips from an oversized spoon, I realized my beef stock tasted like bone-enhanced vegetable liquid.

I blamed myself for the failed attempt, and swore I'd get it right at some point. In the meantime, I opted for chicken stock whenever I had a choice, and used canned beef broth when I absolutely had to. Every few winters I'd attempt a pot of beef stock, but I was never overjoyed with the results. The broth I was looking for would taste like beef—almost as intense as pot roast jus or beef stew broth—flavorful enough to need only a few vegetables and a handful of noodles or barley for support. I didn't want this broth to demand a trip to the butcher, nor did I want to spend all day making it.

Strong On Body, Weak On Flavor

We began our testing by making a traditional stock using four pounds of beef bones fortified with a generous two pounds of beef, as well as celery, carrot, onion, tomato, and fresh thyme, all covered with four quarts of water. Our plan was to taste the stock after four, six, eight, twelve, and sixteen

For broth this rich, use beef shanks or a combination of beef chuck and small marrow bones.

hours of simmering. Despite my unsuccessful history with beef stock, I was rooting for it; I wanted to report that the classic was a "must" when the best was required.

At hours four, six, and even eight our stock was weak and tasted mostly of vegetables. And while the texture of the twelve- and sixteen-hour stocks was richly gelatinous, the flavors of vegetables and bones still predominated. Not willing to give up on this method quite yet, we found a recipe that instructed us to roast then simmer beef bones, onions, and tomatoes—no celery and carrots—for twelve hours. During the last three hours of cooking, three pounds of beef were added to the pot. This, we thought, could be our ideal—a stock with great body from the bones, minimal vegetable flavor, and generous hunks of beef to enhance the rich, reduced stock. Once again, however, the stock was beautifully textured, but with very little flavor; the vegetal taste was gone, but there was no real, deep beef flavor in its place. Time to move on.

The Search Is On

Knowing now that it was going to take more meat than bones to get great flavor, we started our next set of tests by making broths with different cuts of meat, including chuck, shank, round, arm-blade, oxtail, and shortribs. We browned two pounds of meat and one pound of small marrow bones (or three pounds bone-in cuts like shank, shortribs, and oxtails), and an onion. We covered the browned ingredients and let them "sweat" for twenty minutes. We added only a quart of water to each pot and simmered them until the meat in each pot was done.

With so little added water, these broths were more braise-like than broth-like. But because more traditional methods yielded bland broths, we decided to start with the flavor we were looking for and add water from there.

After a 1½-hour simmer, our broths were done, most tasting unmistakably beefy. Upon a blind tasting of each, we both agreed that the shank broth was our favorite, followed by the marrow bone-enhanced brisket and chuck. Not only was the broth rich, beefy, and full of body, the shank meat was soft and gelatinous, perfect for shredding and adding to a pot of soup. Because it appeared that our broth was going to require a generous amount of meat, brisket's high price ($3.99 per pound compared to $1.99 for both the shanks and chuck) knocked it out of the running.

Though not yet perfect, this broth was on its way to fulfilling our requirements. First, it didn't require a trip to the butcher. It could be made from common supermarket cuts like shank, chuck, and marrow bones. Second, it didn't take all day. This broth was done in about two and one-half hours and was full-flavored as soon as the meat was tender. Unlike traditional stocks, which require a roasting pan, stock pot, oven, and burner, this was a one-pot, stovetop-only affair. Finally, this broth didn't require a cornucopia of vegetables to make it taste good. To us, the more vegetables, the weaker the beef flavor. At this point, our recipe called for one lone onion.

What we sacrificed in vegetables, however, we were apparently going to have to compensate for in meat. Our two pounds of meat was yielding only one quart of broth. But now that we had a flavor we liked, we decided to see if we could achieve an equally beefy broth with less meat.

In order to stretch the meat a bit further, we increased the amount of meat and bones by fifty per cent, but doubled the amount of water. Unfortunately, the extra water diluted the meat

If using shanks for your broth, cut the meat away from the bone in the largest possible pieces. Both meat and bones contribute flavor to the final product.

flavor, and though better than many broths we had tried, we missed the strong beef flavor of our original formula. To intensify flavor, we tried adding a pound of ground beef to the three pounds of meat, thinking we would throw away the spent meat during straining. But ground beef only fattened up the broth, and its distinctive hamburger flavor muddied the waters. Also, fried ground beef does not brown well, and this burger-enhanced broth confirmed that browning not only deepened the color, but beefed up the flavor as well.

We went back to the original proportions, doubling both the meat and bones as well as the water. Not surprisingly, the broth was deeply colored, richly flavored, and full-bodied. We were finally convinced that a good beef broth requires a generous portion of meat. Though our broth required more meat than was necessary for the soup, the leftover beef was delicious, good for sandwiches and cold salads.

At this point our richly flavored broth needed enlivening. Some broth recipes accomplished this with a splash of vinegar, others with tomato. Although we liked tomatoes in many of the soups we developed, they didn't do much for our broth. And although vinegar was an improvement, red wine made the broth even better. We ultimately fortified our broth with a modest one-half cup of red wine, adding it to the kettle after browning the meat.

We had followed our method for making chicken broth without giving it much thought—browning then sweating a generous portion of meat and bones, adding water just to cover, and simmering for a relatively short time. We knew the ratio of meat to water was right, but we questioned whether sweating the meat for twenty minutes before adding the water was really a necessary step. Side-by-side tests proved that sweating the meat did result in a richer-flavored broth. Moreover, the sweated meat and bones did not release foamy scum, thus eliminating the need to skim.

After much testing, we came to the inescapable conclusion: If you want to make beef soup right, you just can't skimp on the meat.

RICH BEEF BROTH FOR SOUP
MAKES SCANT 2 QUARTS

2 tablespoons vegetable oil
6 pounds of shank, meat cut from bone in large chunks, or 4 pounds chuck and 2 pounds of small marrow bones
1 large onion, halved
½ cup dry red wine
½ teaspoon salt

1. Heat 1 tablepoon oil in a large soup kettle or Dutch oven over medium-high heat; brown meat, bones, and onion halves on all sides in batches, making sure not to overcrowd the pan, and adding the additional teaspoon and a half of oil to the pan if necessary. Remove and set aside. Add red wine to the empty kettle; cook until reduced to a syrup, 1 to 2 minutes. Return browned bones, meat, and onion to kettle. Reduce heat to low, then cover and sweat meat and onions until they have released about ¾ cup dark, very intensely flavored liquid, about 20 minutes. Increase heat to medium-high, add 2 quarts water and salt; bring to a simmer, reduce heat to very low, partially cover, and barely simmer until meat is tender, 1½ to 2 hours.
2. Strain broth, discard bones and onions, and set meat aside, reserving half of the meat for another use. (At this point broth and meat can be cooled to room temperature and covered and refrigerated up to 5 days.) Let broth stand until fat rises to the top; skim and discard fat. When the unreserved meat is cool enough to handle, shred into bite-size pieces. Continue with one of the following soup recipes.

BEEF NOODLE SOUP
SERVES 6

1 tablespoon vegetable oil
1 medium onion, cut into medium dice
2 medium carrots, cut into medium dice
1 celery stalk, cut into medium dice
½ teaspoon dried thyme or 1½ teaspoons minced fresh thyme leaves
½ cup canned tomatoes, cut into medium dice
1 recipe Rich Beef Broth, strained and skimmed of fat and 2 cups meat shredded into bite-sized pieces
2 cups egg noodles for soup
¼ cup minced fresh parsley leaves
   Salt and ground black pepper

Heat oil over medium-high heat in a soup kettle or Dutch oven. Add onion, carrots, and celery; sauté until softened, about 5 minutes. Add thyme and tomatoes, then beef broth and meat; bring to simmer. Reduce heat to low; simmer until vegetables are no longer crunchy and flavors have blended, about 15 minutes. Add noodles; simmer until fully cooked, about 5 minutes longer. Stir in parsley, adjust seasonings, including salt and pepper to taste, and serve.

BEEF BARLEY SOUP WITH MUSHROOMS AND THYME
SERVES 6

2 tablespoons vegetable oil
1 medium onion, cut into medium dice
2 medium carrots, cut into medium dice
12 ounces domestic or wild mushrooms, stems removed, wiped clean, and sliced thin
½ teaspoon dried thyme or 1½ teaspoons minced fresh thyme leaves
½ cup canned tomatoes, cut into medium dice
1 recipe Rich Beef Broth, strained and skimmed of fat and 2 cups meat shredded into bite-sized pieces
½ cup pearl barley
¼ cup minced fresh parsley leaves
   Salt and ground black pepper

Heat oil over medium-high heat in a soup kettle or Dutch oven. Add onion and carrots; sauté until almost soft, 3 to 4 minutes. Add mushrooms; sauté until softened and liquid almost evaporates, 4 to 5 minutes longer. Add thyme and tomatoes, then beef broth, meat, and barley; bring to simmer. Reduce heat to low; simmer until barley is just tender, 45 to 50 minutes. Stir in parsley, adjust seasonings, including salt and pepper to taste, and serve.

SCIENCE | SO MUCH BEEF, SO LITTLE BROTH

Before I actually began testing, I would not have believed how much meat was required to make a rich, beefy-flavored broth. Why, I questioned, did a good beef soup require six pounds of beef and bones when a mere three-pound chicken could beautifully flavor the same size pot of soup?

Though I had always thought of beef as the heartier-flavored meat, I began to understand chicken's strength when making broths for this story. In one of my time-saving beef broth experiments, I used the four pounds of beef called for in the recipe, but substituted two pounds of quicker-cooking hacked-up chicken bones for the beef bones. The result was surpising. Even with twice as much meaty beef than chicken bones, the chicken flavor predominated. With the help of my colleagues, I venture a few speculations.

Despite what it might seem, says food scientist and cookbook author Shirley Corriher, the flavor compounds in chicken are very strong, possibly stronger than those of beef. She points to mild-flavored boiled beef to prove her point. It's the browning or searing that contributes much of the robust beefy flavor to a good steak or stew. Skin and bones may be another reason why less chicken is required to flavor a broth. Chicken skin, predominantly fat, tastes like the animal. Beef fat, on the other hand, tastes "rich," but not beefy, as evidenced by french fries cooked in beef tallow. In addition, chicken bones, filled with rich, dark marrow, also contribute flavor. Beef bones, on the other hand, offer incredible body to stocks and broths, but their flavor is predominately and unmistakably that of bone, not of beef.

Finally, according to the USDA, chicken contains more water than beef—61% in chuck compared to 77% in drumsticks and 73% to 74% for wings and backs. This means that, when simmered, chicken is releasing 11% to 16% more liquid—and flavor—into the pot.
　　　　　　　　　　　　　　　　　　　　　　　　　　　　　　　　　　　—Pam Anderson

The Best Way to Cook Bacon

For perfectly crisp, evenly cooked bacon with no hassle,
use the oven instead of the frying pan.

⋑ BY DOUGLAS BELLOW ⋐

For me, bacon is one of those enduring guilty addictions; I love those little salty, smoky strips of hog fat no matter how bad they may be for my health.

So I was very interested when I recently noticed while eating a B.L.T. that the directions on the back of a bacon package suggest microwaving (a method that I had previously rejected out of hand) or skillet cooking (the traditional method), but omit a technique for oven cooking. Having worked around restaurant kitchens, I knew that oven roasting bacon is the method most preferred by chefs who have to cook a lot of it. I decided to compare these three techniques in my own kitchen and try to find the best method—an excellent excuse to eat a lot of the stuff.

After a bit of testing, I came up with some interesting results. For most tests I used three pieces of bacon as a single serving. For each cooking technique, I varied temperature, timing, and material, cooking both a typical store-bought bacon and a thick-cut mail-order bacon. The finished strips were compared in terms of flavor, texture, and appearance, while the techniques were compared for consistency, safety, and ease.

While the microwave would seem to have the apparent advantage of ease—stick the pieces in and forget about them—it turned out that this was not the case. My microwave produced such a narrow window of doneness that extreme care had to be taken, leaving very little margin for error. Strips were still raw at one minute and thirty seconds; at two minutes they were medium-well-done in most spots, but still uneven; but by two minutes and thirty seconds the strips were hard and flat and definitely overcooked.

In addition, the finished product didn't warrant the investment of time it would take to figure out the perfect number of seconds. The texture of microwave bacon is not crisp, the color is pink/gray even when well-done, and I really felt that the taste was blander—less bright, smoky, and sweet—than that afforded by the other methods.

The skillet made for a significantly better finished product than the microwave. The bacon flavors were much more pronounced than in the nuked version, the finished color of the meat was a more appealing brick-red, and the meat had a pleasing crispness. There were, however, a number of drawbacks to pan cooking. In addition to the functional problems of grease splatter and the

number of eleven-inch strips you can fit into a twelve-inch round shape, there were problems of consistency and convenience. Because all of the heat comes from below the meat, the strips brown on one side before the other. Moreover, even when using a cast iron pan, as I did, heat is not distributed perfectly evenly across the bottom of the pan. This means that to get consistent strips of bacon you have to turn them over and rotate them in the pan. In addition, when more strips are added to an already-hot pan, they tend to wrinkle up, making for raw or burned spots in the finished product.

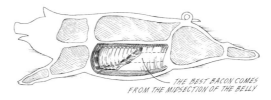

THE BEST BACON COMES
FROM THE MIDSECTION OF THE BELLY

Thick-cut strips only accentuated these problems. They wrinkled less than the thin brand, but tended to curl lengthwise, with the center lifting up off of the cooking surface and the edges browning too quickly. The best results in a pan came when I lowered the heat from medium to medium-low—just hot enough to sizzle. The right temperature allowed the strips to render their grease more slowly, with a lot less curling and spitting out of the pan. Of course, this added to cooking time somewhat, and it did not alleviate the need for vigilance. I even tried pouring off two-thirds of the grease halfway through cooking, but it did nothing to speed the cooking time or to improve the crispness of the finished strips.

Oven-frying seemed to combine the advantages of both of these techniques while eliminating most of the problems. I tried three strips in a preheated 400-degree oven on a 9"x12" cookie sheet with a raised lip to contain the grease. Bacon was medium-well-done after nine to ten minutes and crispy after eleven to twelve minutes. The texture was more like a seared piece of meat than a cracker, the color was that nice brick-red, and all of the flavors were just as bright and obvious as pan-cooked. Oven-frying also provided a greater margin of timing error than either of the other methods, and surprisingly, it was just about as easy as microwaving, with only the added steps of pre-heating and draining. Finally, the oven-roasted

strips of bacon were more consistently cooked throughout, showing no raw spots, and requiring no turning or flipping during cooking. Because the heat hits the strip from all sides, there is no particular impetus for curling in one direction, and curly areas cook as quickly as flat ones.

Lastly, I tried twelve pieces—a pretty full tray—in a preheated oven. This was also quite successful. The pieces were very consistent, the only difference being between those in the back and those in the front of the oven; this inconsistency was corrected by one rotation of the tray during cooking. That was about the limit of the contact with the hot grease. Thick-cut bacon also did well in the oven.

So, when is it worth it to use the oven, as opposed to the pan? Clearly, the added cooking time is a drawback. However, when cooking more than a few strips of bacon, that issue becomes irrelevant—you can add more strips to the oven without significantly increasing cooking time. For crisp, evenly cooked bacon that you have to pay virtually no attention to during cooking, the oven is definitely the way to go.

OVEN-FRIED BACON
SERVES 4- 6

Use a large, rimmed baking sheet, such as a jelly-roll pan, that is shallow enough to promote browning, yet tall enough (at least ¾ inch in height) to contain the rendered bacon fat. To save time, you can add the bacon to the oven before it reaches 400 degrees, but exact cooking time will vary from oven to oven. If cooking more than one tray of bacon, exchange their oven positions once about halfway through the cooking process.

12 slices bacon, thin- or thick-cut

Adjust oven rack to middle position and heat oven to 400 degrees. Arrange bacon slices in a large jelly-roll pan or other shallow baking pan. Roast until fat begins to render, 5 to 6 minutes; rotate pan front-to-back. Continue roasting until crisp and brown, 5 to 6 minutes longer for thin-sliced bacon, 8 to 10 minutes for thick-cut. Transfer with tongs to paper towel–lined plate, drain, and serve.

Douglas Bellow lives, cooks, and writes in Cambridge, Massachusetts.

Fluffy Scrambled Eggs

For soft, pillowy eggs, you need a slow hand, a heavy nonstick pan,
and (despite much advice to the contrary) high heat.

⋺ BY ELAINE CORN ⋞

Scrambled eggs should be a dreamy mound of big, softly wobbling curds, yellow as a legal pad, glistening, a hair breadth away from undercooking. When cut, the eggs should be cooked enough to hold their shape but soft enough to eat with a spoon—a cross between a custard gone right and wrong. If you can't deliver on the texture and consistency, you can kiss the taste good-bye.

My first advice is to stop muscling the raw eggs into a tight froth. Overbeating can cause premature coagulation of the eggs' protein—even without heat! So it makes eggs tough before they hit the pan. For a smooth yellow color and no streaks of white, I whip eggs in a medium-sized bowl with a fork and stop while the bubbles are large. For ten or twelve eggs, I've found a balloon whisk does the trick just fine.

Before beating, the eggs get a few important additions—salt, pepper, and milk rather than water. Compared side by side, scrambled eggs made with water are less flavorful, don't fluff as nicely, form wrinkled curds, and aren't as soft as those made with milk. With its traces of sugar, proteins, and fats, milk has a wonderful pillowy effect and helps create large curds—the bigger you can get the curds, the more steam you'll trap inside, for puff all the way to the table.

I've tried lots of pans and have discovered that a nonstick surface is best for scrambled eggs. Make that a nonstick coating in a pan that's thicker than a U.S. dime. Cheap, thin pans overheat and are difficult to control on high heat. Thicker pans may take longer to heat up, but they hold heat evenly without hot spots. Eggs need this special consideration.

Pan size is important, too. When I used a ten-inch skillet for two eggs, the batter spread out so thinly that while I was busy moving one area of the eggs, another area overcooked. The more the eggs are contained, the bigger the curds. A eight-inch skillet kept the two-egg batter at a depth of about one quarter inch, and curds came out nice and plump.

When you add butter to a pan that's been sitting on a burner three minutes, five minutes—who knows?—the butter burns. So I always put the butter into the cold pan and heat both at the same time over high heat. The progress of the butter's melting is a good indicator of the readiness of the pan. I wait for the butter to foam,

A key to fluffy scrambled eggs is recognizing the exact moment at which the eggs must leave the pan.

then wait a few seconds for the foam to subside but not disappear. I know that the pan is hot, but not so hot that it will burn the butter.

I've tried cooking scrambled eggs over medium heat for a longer time, but that proved irritating. The eggs got tough, dried out, and over-coagulated, like a badly made meringue that "weeps." A hot pan will begin to cook eggs instantaneously, for the quickest coagulation. My tradeoff for using high heat is absolute vigilance in making sure the eggs are off the heat before serious damage is done; plus, I keep the eggs in constant, steady motion.

The movement of utensils upon the cooking batter is as deliberate as an exercise in tai chi. Call it body language, posture, or the approach—physical address goes a long way. Stirring the eggs in the pan with a fork or spoon is inadequate. To compensate for what these utensils fail to do per stroke, I stirred too much and knotted the curds. But when I switched to a wooden spatula or an upside-down pancake turner, the flat edge snowplowed a two- to three-inch swath of eggs across the pan in one pass. The idea is to slowly push, lift, and fold. Two eggs should cook into big curds in about thirty seconds.

When are the eggs done? The idea behind big voluptuous curds is to trap steam. I ask myself, "If I pull the eggs off the heat now, then the eggs will cook how much by the time I take a bite?" It is up to me to anticipate. The larger the curds,

the more steam is pocketed inside, and the more the eggs will continue to cook once off the heat. I like scrambled eggs soft and juicy, so they look positively undone when I make that final fold and push them out of the pan. But if you get the eggs off the heat when they're still juicy, you'll always get lush scrambled eggs with big curds that melt in your mouth.

FLUFFY SCRAMBLED EGGS
SERVES 4

These eggs cook very quickly, so it's important to be ready to eat before you start to cook them.

8	large eggs
½	teaspoon salt and several grinds of ground black pepper
½	cup milk
1	tablespoon butter

1. Crack eggs into a medium bowl. Add salt, pepper, and milk. Whip with a fork until streaks are gone and color is pure yellow; stop beating while the bubbles are still large.

2. Meanwhile, put butter in a 10-inch nonstick skillet, then set the pan over high heat. When the butter foams, swirl it around and up the sides of the pan. Before foam completely subsides, pour in beaten eggs. With a wooden spatula or a nonstick-safe egg turner, push eggs from one side of the pan to the other, slowly but deliberately, lifting and folding eggs as they form into curds, until eggs are nicely clumped into a single mound, but remain shiny and wet, 1½ to 2 minutes. Serve immediately.

For two eggs, season with ⅛ teaspoon salt, 1 grind of pepper, and 2 tablespoons milk. Heat only 1½ teaspoons butter, use a 8-inch skillet. Cooking time is only 30 to 45 seconds.

For four eggs, season with ¼ teaspoon salt, 2 grinds of pepper, and ¼ cup milk. Heat ¾ tablespoon butter and use a 10-inch skillet. Cooking time is about 1 minute.

For one dozen eggs, season with ¾ teaspoon salt, 6 grinds of pepper, and ¾ cup milk. Heat 1½ tablespoons butter and use a 12-inch skillet. Cooking time is 2½ to 3 minutes.

Elaine Corn is the author of *365 Ways to Cook Eggs* (HarperCollins, NY 1996).

How to Tie Meat

Many cuts of meat, such as leg of lamb, are unevenly shaped by nature. As a result, they cook more evenly if molded and then tied into shape. Stuffed, butterflied cuts also need tying to hold their shape. In the process of testing and retesting to determine the best ways to tie various cuts of meat, we found a few less obvious perks: Tying makes a piece of meat easier to handle, helps to hold in juices, and lends to better presentation.

By Maryellen Driscoll

THE TWINE

When tying meat, place the butcher's twine on the handle of a meat pounder or put in a drawer to prevent contaminating the entire spool.

LEARNING THE ROPES

To practice tying the knot, use a roll of paper towel.

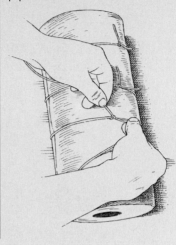

TYING A BASIC KNOT

There's no such thing as a standard butcher's knot, but this one is simpler than most, allows you to adjust tension, and holds snug.

1. Draw the end of the string, known as the bitter, away from you so that it passes under the meat, then draw it back over the top.

2. Cross the bitter under the left side of the bottom strand. With your left hand, pinch the point where the strings intersect. Cross the bitter up and over the right side of the top strand, leaving a large keyhole opening.

3. Pull the bitter under and through the keyhole. Tug the bitter down, closing the knot.

4. Pull the strings away from each other to tighten the knot. Secure with a final basic knot, making sure it is snug but not too tight or the meat fibers will tear and the juices will spill. Trim knot ends with scissors.

5. Space the ties evenly, about three fingers apart.

Illustration: John Burgoyne

1.

2.

3.

4.

5.

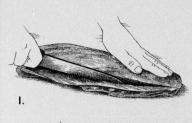

1.

2.

3.

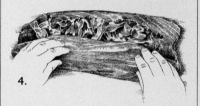

4.

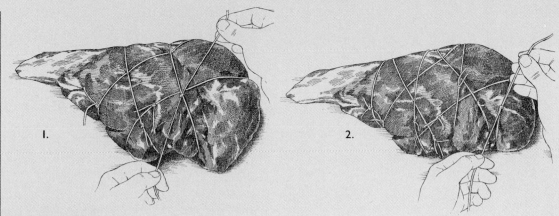

1.
2.

LEG OF LAMB

Tying is imperative to hold together the multiple small muscles on a semi-boned leg of lamb. (Have your butcher remove as much fat and silver skin from this cut as possible.)

1. Tie twice diagonally, once around the upper part of the leg and again at the opposite angle.

2. Tie four times around the width to secure.

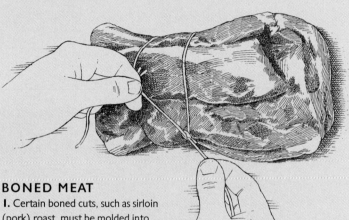

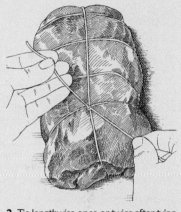

BONED MEAT

1. Certain boned cuts, such as sirloin (pork) roast, must be molded into shape before tying.

2. Tie lengthwise once or twice after tying widthwise in order to hold its shape.

BUTTERFLIED MEATS

Butterflied and stuffed meats need tying. We like this butterflying method for beef tenderloin used in "Chez Panisse Cooking" (Random House, 1988), because it adds 25 percent more length to the meat roll than if it were simply butterflied across the center width.

1. Positioning your knife about ¾" from the edge, make a lengthwise cut two-thirds of the way down. Fold back the cut edge.

2. Slice horizontally until you are about ¾" from the other edge. Fold the flap open like a book.

3. Slice the flap horizontally until you are about ¾" from the other edge. Fold the flap open like a book.

4. After spreading filling on the opened meat, roll and tie, following steps 1—5 opposite page.

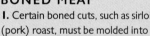

1.
2.

RIB EYE STEAKS

1. At Savenor's specialty foods in Boston, owner and butcher Ronald Savenor likes to remove the thick vein of fat and gristle in rib eye steaks.

2. He then ties each steak around its width to hold it together. This tying method also works well for beef tenderloin medallions.

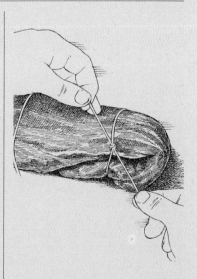

TENDERLOIN

1. Curl and tie the tapered tip of a tenderloin. Tie the tip so that it cooks at the same rate as the rest of the cut.

Noodles with Winter Greens

By cooking noodles and winter greens together, then adding the sauce, you can save considerable time and still end up with full-flavored weeknight fare.

⇒ BY EVA KATZ ⇐

The sharp, peppery flavor of winter greens is a perfect match for the mild wheaty tones and silken texture of noodles. I wanted to find a way to make weeknight dishes by combining these two with savory sauces. Blanching turned out to be the optimal method for cooking these greens, maintaining their vibrant green color but taming their bitterness. When I started testing, I had three pots going—one for the greens, one for the noodles, and one for the sauce. After a few experiments, I found that it worked best to cook the greens right along with the noodles. This technique cut one pot and two steps out of the whole production. I didn't have to worry about removing the greens from the boiling water or about running them under cold water to stop them from cooking, because once the noodles and greens are done they are simply drained together and added to the sauce.

If you're using fresh noodles, the greens need to be put in the water before the noodles. With dried noodles or pasta, adding the greens after the noodles is the way to go.

BROCCOLI RABE AND ORECCHIETTE WITH WHITE BEAN-ANCHOVY SAUCE
SERVES 4

 3 tablespoons olive oil
 4 anchovy fillets, minced
 4 medium garlic cloves, minced
 1 can (15-ounces) white beans, drained and rinsed
 ⅔ cup chicken stock or low-sodium canned chicken broth
   Salt and ground black pepper
 1 pound orecchiette, penne, or other short, tubular pasta
 1½ pounds broccoli rabe, washed well, trimmed, and cut into 1½-inch pieces
   Freshly grated pecorino Romano cheese

1. Heat oil, anchovy, and garlic in medium skillet over medium-low heat, stirring until anchovy dissolves, 1–2 minutes. Add beans and stock; simmer to thicken, 4 to 5 minutes. Off heat, season with salt and pepper to taste, and cover.

2. Meanwhile, add 1 tablespoon salt and pasta to 5 quarts boiling water; cook until pasta just begins to soften, about 5 to 6 minutes. Add greens; cook until greens are wilted fully and pasta is al dente, 3 to 4 minutes longer. Reserve ⅓ cup pasta water; drain pasta and greens and return to pot. Add sauce and reserved water and cook over medium-low heat, stirring to meld flavors, about 1 minute. Adjust seasoning, and serve immediately, passing grated cheese separately.

MUSTARD GREENS AND UDON NOODLES WITH SHIITAKE-GINGER SAUCE
SERVES 4

Find fresh Japanese udon noodles in the produce section of large supermarkets. If they are not available, substitute dried or frozen udon or dried fettuccini and follow cooking instructions for Broccoli Rabe and Orecchiette with White Bean-Anchovy Sauce, because dried noodles take longer to cook than fresh.

 1½ cups chicken stock or low sodium canned chicken broth
 ¼ cup rice wine vinegar
 ¼ cup mirin (Japanese rice wine)
 2 medium garlic cloves, crushed with flat side of a chef's knife blade
 ½ pound shiitake mushrooms, or a combination of white button and shiitake mushrooms, wiped clean and sliced thin
 1 1-inch chunk fresh gingerroot, halved and smashed with flat side of a chef's knife blade
 ½ teaspoon Asian chili paste
 2 tablespoons soy sauce
 1 teaspoon Asian sesame oil
   Salt and ground black pepper
 1½ pounds mustard greens (1 large bunch), washed well, leaves trimmed from ribs and cut into 2-inch pieces
 1 package (14-ounces) fresh udon noodles

1. Simmer chicken stock through sesame oil in a large saucepan or large skillet over high heat until liquid thickens and reduces by half, 8 to 10 minutes. Off heat, remove garlic and ginger; season with salt and pepper to taste, and cover.

2. Meanwhile, add 1 tablespoon salt and greens to 5 quarts boiling water; cook until greens are almost tender, 4 to 5 minutes. Add noodles; cook until greens and noodles are tender, about 2 minutes longer. Reserve ⅓ cup noodle water; drain noodles and greens and return to pot. Add sauce and reserved water and cook over medium-low heat, stirring to meld flavors, about 1 minute. Adjust seasoning and serve immediately.

BOK CHOY AND CHINESE EGG NOODLES WITH SPICY BEEF SAUCE
SERVES 4

Dried linguine can be substituted if fresh Chinese egg noodles are not available, but follow cooking instructions for Broccoli Rabe and Orecchiette with White Bean-Anchovy Sauce, because dried noodles take longer to cook than fresh.

 1½ tablespoons vegetable oil
 2 3-inch cinnamon sticks, broken in half
 2 whole cloves
 1 teaspoon anise seed
 4 medium garlic cloves, slivered
 1 1-inch chunk fresh gingerroot, cut into fine julienne
 1 cup chicken stock or low sodium canned chicken broth
 1½ teaspoons Asian chili paste
 ½ pound beef sirloin or rib eye steak, halved crosswise, each half sliced thin across the grain
   Salt and ground black pepper
 1½ pounds bok choy, washed well, bottom 2 inches of base discarded, remainder cut crosswise into ¾-inch pieces
 1 package (12 ounces) fresh Chinese egg noodles

1. Heat oil in a large sauté pan over medium-high heat until shimmering but not smoking. Add cinnamon sticks, cloves, and anise seed, stirring until cinnamon sticks unfurl and cloves pop, about 1 minute. Add garlic and ginger, cook until they begin to soften, about 2 minutes longer. Add chicken stock and chili paste, reduce heat to medium-low; simmer until liquid reduces by half, about 4 minutes. Remove cinnamon sticks and cloves; add beef and simmer until meat is gray around edges and still slightly pink in center, about 1 minute longer. Off heat, season with salt and ground black pepper to taste, and cover.

2. Continue with step 2 in Mustard Greens and Udon Noodles with Shiitake-Ginger Sauce, substituting bok choy for mustard greens and egg noodles for udon.

Jewish Rye Bread

For a chewy, tangy, deli-style rye bread that won't go soggy or limp when piled with a stack of pastrami, use bran-free rye flour and the overnight sponge method.

≥ BY EVA KATZ WITH DAWN YANAGIHARA ≤

Jewish rye, a.k.a. New York rye, is one of my favorite breads. I love its tang and chew. Unfortunately, it's difficult to find good Jewish rye these days. The mass-produced varieties in supermarkets (and even the rye bread in my local Jewish bakery in Boston) are too refined, fluffy, and soft, with only a hint of rye flavor. The rye bread I hanker for should be slightly moist and chewy but not too dense. It should have a tight, uneven crumb, a hard, thin, almost brittle crust, and a tangy rye flavor. Perhaps most importantly, the bread shouldn't become soggy or limp when stacked with a pile of pastrami.

I discovered myriad of rye bread recipes during my research. Not just the Jewish varieties, but Old-World recipes containing buttermilk, sour cream, mashed potatoes, molasses, ginger, and even sauerkraut! Intriguing as these were, I stuck to the basics: rye and white flours, water, a sweetener, salt, fat, and caraway seeds.

The Key Variables

I identified three variables that I thought would affect the texture and flavor of the bread: the method of leavening, the type of rye flour, and the ratio of rye to white flour.

I focused first on two basic methods for leavening the dough, both of which are practical for home cooks. The "sponge" starter method involves first mixing a small amount of flour, water, and yeast, then leaving this starter to ferment for a defined period of time. More flour and water are then added to make the dough. In the second method, flour and water are mixed and the yeast is added directly to make the dough.

Using a variety of cookbook rye bread recipes, I did side-by-side testing of the sponge and direct methods. I found the sponge method clearly preferable. Because the slow rise allows time for the creation of fermentation byproducts that add flavor, this method produced a bread with strong, tangy flavor and a chewy, pleasantly uneven texture. I also liked the way the bread made using the sponge method maintained its moistness during storage. The bread made with the direct method had a tighter web of holes and a more even crumb.

I also tested different sponge fermentation times, including thirty minutes, two-and-a-half hours, and overnight. As I increased the fermentation time, the rise and proof were faster, the

Rye flakes give our bread a deeper rye flavor and more chew, but are not essential.

bread baked higher, the crumb was more uneven, the bread was chewier, and the flavor was stronger. The sponge fermentation time can, therefore, be varied to taste, two and one half hours being the minimum. I personally prefer an overnight sponge fermentation, and I find that the initial intense and slightly sour rye flavor improves with cooling and storage. However, I was looking for more chew and a sharper tang than even my longest fermentation time could give. In search of this, I turned to the choice and ratio of different flours.

Flour Power

I suspected that different rye flours might affect the texture and flavor of the rye bread. However, many rye bread recipes don't even specify the type of rye flour to use. Up to this point all of my testing had been done using a whole grain rye flour. I now proceeded to round up all the rest of the nationally available rye flours to test—white

rye, medium rye, whole grain, and pumpernickel. The breads they produced were dramatically different. I preferred the breads made with King Arthur light rye and Pillsbury medium rye, both of which had an earthy, tangy flavor with a slight springiness. (See "Rye Awry," page 21.)

Following the successes with these two flours, I moved on to test different ratios of rye to white flour. Rye flour alone does not contain gluten-forming proteins to make the bread rise enough, so some protein-rich wheat flour must be used, as well. When water is mixed with wheat flour, the proteins glutenin and gliadin bind to each other and to the water molecules to form gluten. Kneading shapes the protein/gluten into elastic sheets that trap and hold air and the gases produced by the yeast, the combination of which allows the bread to rise.

My test recipe had three cups of rye flour and four and a half cups of all-purpose unbleached white flour. As I reduced the rye flour (increasing

Bakery-Style Bran Muffins

Full-flavored, moist muffins require a mix of whole wheat and all-purpose flour, wheat bran, buttermilk, and a dash of sour cream.

≥ BY LISA YOCKELSON ≤

There are two basic types of bran muffins popular among those of us who love to bake them—"refrigerator" muffins and muffins based on a classic batter. The batter for the refrigerator muffins, which contains bran cereal, is simply mixed together then stored in the refrigerator until you are ready to bake. The second type is made by combining ingredients either by the "creamed" method (just like putting together a butter cake batter) or by using the "two-bowl" method (mixing dry ingredients with a whisked liquid mixture).

When I baked and compared batches of both muffin varieties, it was immediately obvious that the classic muffins, made with wheat bran, far exceeded the refrigerator type in taste, texture, and appearance. Compared to the wheat bran variety, the cereal-based bran muffins had a muddy look, a somewhat rubbery texture, and an oddly chewy quality. The bran flavor was dull and muted, and they lacked that all-around depth I expected from a bran muffin. By contrast, the classic bran muffins tasted deeply of bran and had a better (although far from perfect) texture.

Next I compared muffins made by the creaming and the two-bowl method. Just as Pam Anderson did in her earlier exploration of muffins (see "Big, Beautiful Muffins," January/February, 1997), I found that creaming the butter and sugar together and then alternately stirring in wet and dry ingredients created a fuller, more tender muffin.

With the mixing method decided, I moved on to the ingredients. A standard muffin batter is composed of flour, sugar, leavening, eggs, flavorings, milk, and fat. The batter's volume is built on a higher proportion of flour relative to fat and liquid. But when you reduce a portion of the flour to accommodate the bran, you disrupt the balance of liquid and dry ingredients, because wheat bran isn't actually absorbed into the batter the way flour is. This means that you need to rework the proportion of liquid and dry ingredients.

To understand this dynamic, it is important to know a bit about bran. Bran, the exterior covering of wheat kernels, is milled into flakes. These flakes, known as wheat bran, are high in insoluble fiber. As a result, they are actually suspended in the batter, making a denser muffin. The bran flakes also tend to dry out and "break up" the batter, in much the same way that chocolate chips or nuts break up the batter in cookies.

When I started baking the muffins, I used a whopping two cups of bran. You could probably imagine the result: Dry, crumbly muffins that tasted (and acted) just like sawdust. After much fine-tuning, I found that I could achieve a fuller, more tempered flavor and a pleasing texture by replacing a little of the all-purpose flour with whole wheat flour. This allowed me to cut the bran down to one-and-one-half cups without losing the flavor I wanted.

After many tests with individual ingredients, I concluded that bran muffins are best made by juggling a proper amount of wheat bran with all-purpose and whole wheat flour; adding buttermilk and sour cream for smoothness and moisture; using butter as the fat for creaming; and brightening the batter with vanilla extract, spices, and molasses if needed.

Finally, I noticed that bran muffins tend to overbake in a flash. A tray of muffins are baked through when they retract ever so slightly from the sides of the cups and the tops spring back very gently. Don't look for an active spring. The muffins will still be baked through even though a wooden pick withdraws from the centers with a few moist crumbs clinging to it.

THE BEST BRAN MUFFINS
MAKES 12 SMALL MUFFINS OR 6 JUMBO MUFFINS

Wheat bran is available at health foods stores or in boxes, labeled Quaker Unprocessed Bran, in supermarkets.

1¼	cups bleached all-purpose flour
¼	cup whole wheat flour
1¼	teaspoons baking powder
½	teaspoon baking soda
¾	teaspoon salt
1¼	teaspoons ground cinnamon
¾	teaspoon ground allspice
½	teaspoon freshly grated nutmeg
7	tablespoons unsalted butter, softened
½	cup plus 2 tablespoons dark brown sugar
2	large eggs
2½	teaspoons vanilla extract
3	tablespoons unsulphured molasses
¼	cup sour cream
1	cup plus 3 tablespoons buttermilk
1½	cups wheat bran
1	cup raisins

The ideal bran muffin is moist and lightly sweetened with substantial bran flavor.

1. Adjust oven rack to lower middle position and heat oven to 375 degrees. Mix flour through nutmeg in medium bowl; set aside.

2. Beat butter in large bowl of electric mixer or with handheld mixer at medium speed until light and fluffy, 1 to 2 minutes. Add brown sugar, increase speed to medium-high, and beat until combined and fluffy, about 1 minute longer. Add eggs one at a time, beating thoroughly before adding the next. Beat in vanilla, molasses, and sour cream until thoroughly combined and creamy, about 1 minute longer. Reduce speed to low; beat in buttermilk and half the flour mixture until combined, about 1 minute. Beat in remaining flour mixture until incorporated and slightly curdled looking, about 1 minute longer, scraping sides of bowl as necessary. Stir in bran and raisins.

3. Spray a twelve mold muffin tin (each mold measuring ½ cup) or a six mold muffin tin (each mold measuring one cup) with cooking spray or coat lightly with butter; divide batter evenly among molds using spoon or ice cream scoop. Bake until a toothpick inserted into center withdraws cleanly or with a few moist particles adhering to it, about 25 minutes. Set on wire rack to cool slightly, about 5 minutes. Remove muffins from tin and serve warm.

Lisa Yockelson is the author of *Layer Cakes and Sheet Cakes* (HarperCollins, 1996).

Tasting Beef Broth

After sampling a dozen commercial beef broths, our tasters were left asking, "Where's the beef?"

≽ BY MARYELLEN DRISCOLL ≼

Beef broth is a traditional European and American staple, a key ingredient in many classic sauces as well as the basis for popular beef soups. Over the past years, however, sales of beef broth have lagged. While more folks buy beef broth from a can than beef bouillon, chicken bouillon sales top both, according to consumer trend reports by ACNielsen. The most recent statistics for annual sales show that more than four times as many cans of chicken broth are sold than cans of beef broth.

When we tasted commercial beef broths, it became obvious why this situation has developed: Most beef broths simply do not deliver full-bodied, beefy flavor. There might be subtle beef suggestions, but after tasting nearly all of the selected broths—bouillon-based, canned, gourmet, organic, and classic homemade—there remained one nagging question: "Where's the beef?"

Well, as it stands, U.S. regulations for beef broth do not require much beef. A commercial beef broth need contain only one part protein to one hundred and thirty-five parts of moisture, according to the United States Department of Agriculture's standards. That translates to less than about an ounce of meat (or about one-quarter of a hamburger) to one gallon of water. And, says meat scientist William Mikel, Ph.D., of the University of Kentucky, "Most commercial products are very close to that limit, strictly because of economics." Generally, according to Mikel, manufactured beef broth derives its flavor from bare beef bones and a boost of various additives. A glance at the label on the side of any canned broth or boxed bouillon cubes will confirm this.

We wanted to talk to the manufacturers of beef broths to verify our impressions of the way they make their products, but calls to broth giants Hormel Foods and Campbell Soup Company were dead ends. Both declined to answer questions as to how their commercial beef broths are made. But beef bones plus additives would certainly explain why of the thirteen broths we tasted, only one—our homemade recipe made with six pounds of meat (see page 13)—carried a full-bodied, beefy flavor. Nearly all the other broths were thin and flavorless with the exception of "off" or artificial flavors.

What seems to distinguish most supermarket broths from homemade, gourmet, or natural foods store broths is a riddling of flavor additives. Monosodium glutamate can be found in nearly all supermarket beef broths (see "The Plus Side of MSG," right). Disodium guanylate and disodium isonate, which are both yeast-based, hydrolyzed soy protein, are also typically added to commercial broths. Yeast extracts also find their way into most of these broths. All FDA-approved, these additives are intended to "enhance" flavor. As one FDA spokesperson explained, "You've got something that's kind of 'blah,' so to give it a little more taste they add these things."

Salt—and lots of it—also adds to the flavor of these broths. Most beef broth products contain about thirty-five percent of the daily allowance for sodium per serving. Salt is also added to help extract the needed protein from the bones, according to food scientist Mikel.

Surprisingly, making a homemade stock from beef bones in the old-fashioned way did not turn out to be the answer, nor did going organic. Tasters found the broth with the least beef flavor (or none at all, according to most of our tasters) to be one made in our test kitchen from a classic French cookbook stock recipe. (Unlike broth, a stock is typically made of bones only, but is also typically used as a soup base.) And the more expensive gourmet and organic commercial broths, such as those made by Williams-Sonoma and Walnut Acres, not only failed to deliver beef flavor but also proved among the least palatable of the pack.

As the runner-up in overall liking to our own beef broth recipe, tasters chose a jarred beef base, Superior Touch "Better Than Bouillon," but with an unflattering score of 4.6 on a 0 to 10 scale. Herb Ox Beef Bouillon Cubes tagged not too far behind. While these are the "top finishers," we would not recommend that you use them in a recipe where the flavor of beef broth predominates, such as in a beef soup. They would be forgivable if used as background in a sauce or gravy, if necessary. Depending on the recipe, a good alternative might be a flavorful chicken broth (see "Taking Stock of Chicken Broth," Jan./Feb. 1994). But if you truly seek beef flavor, bypass the broth aisle in your supermarket and head straight to the meat department to make a broth at home. And be sure to freeze extra in small batches for those critical instances when you might find yourself reaching for a can.

The Plus Side of MSG

Because so many commercial broths use monosodium glutamate (MSG) as a flavor enhancer, we decided to find out just how this product affects flavor. To provide the most dramatic illustration, we cooked up a batch of the most tasteless liquid in our tasting—a classic French stock. We then tasted it plain and with one-half teaspoon of MSG per quart.

The difference was more distinct than we had expected. The plain stock was characterized by excessive vegetable and sweet flavors while beef flavors were indiscernable. By contrast, the stock with MSG had, as one taster described, "higher flavor notes" that included beefy and more savory flavors and a subdued sweetness. In fact, it tasted nothing like the lowest-rated broths.

Just how that half-teaspoon of MSG can make such a difference, however, is something scientists cannot fully explain, says Food Science Professor F. Jack Francis of the University of Massachusetts at Amherst. MSG, like many other flavor enhancers, does not actually change the flavor of the substance to which it is added. Instead, it is believed to enhance the response of a person's taste buds, especially to meats and proteins, says Francis. Exactly how this happens scientists have yet to learn. Some describe it as not just a taste enhancer but a stimulator of a fifth taste perception in addition to sweet, sour, salty, and bitter.

While MSG might be popular with many commercial broth makers, it has not been popular with the American public. In the 1980's, people began to associate it with "Chinese restaurant syndrome," which includes headaches, digestive upset, and chest pains. Even though numerous studies have failed to turn up an association between such symptoms and MSG, the reputation has stuck. It has been speculated that a bacteria quick to grow on cooked rice left at room temperature and able to cause food poisoning has been the real cause of troubles for those Chinese restaurant goers.

Nowadays most Chinese restaurants will tout "No MSG" on their menus. Yet many people do not realize that it's still lurking in their hot and sour soup as well as many other non-Chinese dishes. That's because MSG is the salt form of glutamate, a naturally-occurring substance found in such foods as peanut butter, rice, flour, and mushrooms.   —Maryellen Driscoll

TASTING BEEF BROTH

For our tasting, we identified a dozen widely available beef broths sold in supermarkets, whole foods stores, and gourmet stores. They included bouillon and bases as well as canned and jarred broths. We also included two homemade beef broths, one made from our own recipe (see page 13), the other from a traditional French recipe. Our tasting was attended by three chefs from the New England Soup Factory in Brookline, Massachusetts, as well as 15 staff members of our editorial and circulation departments. Broths are listed in accordance with tasters' ranking. Their company or distributor's name and location are listed in parentheses. Prices indicate actual retail cost.

HIGHLY RECOMMENDED

Our Homemade Recipe (SEE PAGE 13)

➤ Makes 2 quarts for $9 to $12.
Our beef soup recipe, found on page 13 and shown at left, uses our homemade beef broth recipe. It's worth the extra money to get this kind of flavor. This was the only sample to offer the distinct beefiness that tasters demanded. As one wrote, "The clear winner of the group, head and shoulders above the other samples." This broth took tops in all the desirables—roasted, beefy flavor and aroma, not too salty, and ample body.

RECOMMENDED IN A PINCH

Superior Touch "Better Than Bouillon" Beef Base (SUPERIOR QUALITY FOODS, ONTARIO, CA)

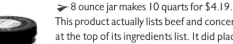

➤ 8 ounce jar makes 10 quarts for $4.19.
This product actually lists beef and concentrated beef stock at the top of its ingredients list. It did place second in the tasting, with more beef flavor than any of the other commercial brands. But it did not come near the winning broth in terms of beefy flavor or overall liking. "Nothing seems overly assertive"—except, perhaps, the salt, about which many tasters complained.

NOT RECOMMENDED

Herb Ox Beef Bouillon Cubes (HORMEL FOODS, AUSTIN, MN)

➤ 25 cubes makes about 6 quarts for $2.09.
While this was the best bouillon, tasters knew that it was a bouillon-based broth. Some of the comments included: "slightly beef flavored salt cube," "tastes like it was produced in a lab, not a kitchen," and "watery, almost no beef flavor—a cow walked near the stock pot?" This broth lacked balance and depth of flavor.

Health Valley Beef Flavored Broth (HEALTH VALLEY COMPANY, INC., IRWINDALE, CA)

➤ 14 1/4 ounce can for $1.29.
Tasters found this fat-free broth carried little flavor but were somewhat forgiving because what flavor it did have was not offensive. It scored the highest among all of the canned broths. While there's a low-salt version to this line, this one contained only 7 percent of the daily value of sodium per serving versus the average 35 percent of many other products.

Campbell's Beef Broth (CAMPBELL SOUP COMPANY, CAMDEN, NJ)

➤ 10 1/2 ounce can for $.99.
The distinguishing characteristics of this canned broth were its dark coffee-like appearance and extreme saltiness. Its acidic (and salty) flavor was repeatedly described by tasters as soy sauce with the addition of beef base.

Wyler's Bouillon Granules (BORDEN, INC., COLUMBUS, OH)

➤ 2 1/4 ounce jar makes 4 1/2 quarts for $1.69.
One taster targeted this as more of a vegetable broth and another considered it more like a chicken broth. In sum: "beef is elusive." It also scored low in terms of body.

Knorr Beef Bouillon (CPC SPECIALTY PRODUCTS, INC., INDIANAPOLIS, IN)

➤ 12 cubes make 6 quarts for $1.39.
"Where's the beef?" asked one taster. Perhaps somewhere lingering behind the salt? Broth made from these bouillon cubes was one of the most salty and greasy products tasted. Tasters also complained of "commercial" and "industrial" flavors. Other comments included "wouldn't use it for a sauce nor soup" and "lacks a heartiness I'd expect."

Bovril Concentrated Beef Flavored Liquid Bouillon (CPC SPECIALTY PRODUCTS, INC., INDIANAPOLIS, IN)

➤ 4.2 ounce jar makes 6 quarts for $1.39.
Tasters liked the look of the broth made from this rich-colored liquid bouillon but as one taster said, "Looks better than it is." Like too many of the other products, tasters rejected this product for its "blah flavor."

Swanson's Beef Broth (CAMPBELL SOUP COMPANY, CAMDEN, NJ)

➤ 14 1/2 ounce can for $.79.
Off flavors in this major-brand beef broth were a big turn-off for tasters. "Tastes extremely fake," wrote one taster. The consensus was that this broth was too greasy as well.

College Inn (NABISCO, INC., EAST HANOVER, NJ)

➤ 13 3/4 ounce can for $.79
"Off" flavors pervaded this canned broth also. Some described it as burnt plastic and others metallic. "Horrific" was a repeated descriptor. It did not perform well in any of the categories.

Williams-Sonoma Beef Cooking Stock (WILLIAMS-SONOMA, SAN FRANCISCO, CA)

➤ Makes 2 cups for $4.50.
So little stock for so many dollars and all for what one taster described as "the black hole of beef stock." The flavor complaints echoed: no beef, sour, metallic, and burnt. A slight roasted flavor was barely detectable next to strong tomato accents and off flavors.

Walnut Acres Beef Broth (PENNS CREEK, PA)

➤ 15 1/2 ounce can for $2.99.
This organic broth took everyone by surprise. As one taster said, "I thought it could not get any worse." Floating grease globules merited this the most greasy of all. Beef flavors went undetected.

Classic French Beef Stock Recipe, makes 3 to 4 quarts for $12.50.
Do not even waste your money making a homemade stock from a batch of bones. This traditional recipe rendered nothing more than flavorless, discolored water or "dishwater," as one taster commented. Made from 4 pounds of beef bones, herbs, vegetables, and water.

Rating Large Dutch Ovens

To our surprise, we found that shape and color of interior finish are more important than weight—and we don't like nonstick.

⇒ BY ADAM RIED WITH EVA KATZ AND DAWN YANAGIHARA ⇐

Most cooks own a large, cheap pot for cooking pasta or blanching vegetables. As long as they'll bring water to a boil, the subtler performance characteristics of these pots are unimportant. For braises, stews, soups, and sauces, however—often dependent on moist-heat cooking procedures that begin with browning—these pots will not do. Enter the Dutch oven, a large, lidded pot or kettle designed specifically for these tasks.

As with most cookware products, Dutch oven choices are dizzying and prices vary widely. We wanted to test the same spectrum of brands, materials, finishes, and prices that most cooks would encounter while shopping. So we chose twelve pots, each of which satisfied our two primary criteria: large capacity (we agreed that six to eight quarts was the most useful size) and open stock availability (models sold only as part of larger cookware sets were not considered). In some cases, due usually to our capacity requirement, the pot we tested was not called a Dutch oven, but rather a casserole, sauce pot, or stock pot. If a manufacturer offered several cookware lines that each included a Dutch oven, we asked company representatives which line was the most widely distributed or best-selling and went with that.

As we cooked, the shape of the pots became increasingly important to us. We prefer pots that are wider and shallower because they are easier to see into, reach into, and they offer more bottom surface to accommodate larger batches of meat for browning. This reduces the number of batches required to brown a given quantity of meat, and with it, the chances of burning the flavorful pan drippings.

Though we did include a number of tall, deep pots in our full battery of tests, we eventually realized that comparing them to wide, shallow pots in the type of cooking we were testing was like comparing apples to oranges. To avoid unfair comparisons, we figured all of the pots' ratios of bottom surface area to height by dividing the diameter measurement by the height measurement, and decided to eliminate from further consideration the four pots with diameter-to-height ratios that

were less than 2-to-1, including candidates from WearEver, Chantal, Farberware, and Revere.

We had also planned to test the T-Fal Armaral Sovereign Dutch Oven along with the others, until a T-Fal representative confirmed that it was not oven-worthy. Because many of the braised or pot roast recipes for which most home cooks use these pots require oven cooking, we considered the T-Fal's shortcoming to be a fatal flaw and knocked it out of the running.

Our final lineup included pots in stainless steel from All-Clad, Tramontina, and Cuisinart; in enameled cast iron from Le Creuset; in cast iron from Lodge; in cast aluminum from Berndes; and in anodized aluminum from Calphalon and Circulon. The Berndes and Circulon both had non-stick interior finishes.

Running the Tests

We first ran two tests to observe the pots' browning performance. In doing so, we looked at heat conduction, evenness of heat distribution, and response time, as well as the effects of bottom surface area and interior finish.

First, we cooked a pot roast by browning it on the stovetop over medium-high heat and then finishing it in the oven. All-Clad and Le Creuset excelled at browning because the pots did not overheat, so they did not burn either the meat itself or the pan drippings. In addition, both of these pans had light-colored interior finishes that made it easy to judge the caramelization of the pan drippings at a glance. Tramontina and Cuisinart also benefited from stainless steel interiors, though both pots ran a bit too hot during browning, slightly burning

both meat and drippings. Pots with dark interior finishes, including both non-sticks, the dark gray anodized aluminum Calphalon, and the cast iron Lodge, masked the color of the drippings, making it difficult to determine whether they were burning. Once the Lodge heated up, which took longer than any other pot, its browning ability was on par with All-Clad and Le Creuset.

In a second round of testing, we cooked the beef soup recipe (*see* page 13) in each pot. This involved browning six pounds of beef shanks in three batches over medium-high heat on the stovetop. Because the drippings remained in the pot through all three batches, this was a more extreme test of the pots' ability to brown without burning.

Again, All-Clad and Le Creuset ran away with top honors, browning thoroughly, evenly, and with minimal threat of burning. Both Tramontina and Cuisinart did a better job browning the shanks than the roast, largely because the smaller shanks exuded more liquid during cooking. The Lodge cast iron also browned the shanks very well, but despite our attempts to caramelize the drippings in each pot to the same point, soups made in the dark-finished Lodge and Calphalon tasted slightly bitter, indicating that the drippings had overcaramelized or burned. The Berndes and Circulon represented the other side of that phenomenon, both producing soups that tasted thin and light, indicating under development of the drippings. In both cases, a light-colored interior would have made it easier to judge the degree of caramelization.

Dark interior finishes were not the only problem with the non-stick pots. In contrast to our

---

ILLUSTRATION: JOHN BURGOYNE

TERMINOLOGY | BUT WHAT IS A DUTCH OVEN?

A "Dutch" oven is nothing more than a wide, deep pot, usually with a wire handle. It was originally manufactured with "ears" on the side (small, round tabs used to pick up the pot) and a top that had a lip around the edge. The latter design element was important because a Dutch oven was heated through coals placed both underneath and on top of the pot. The lip kept the coals on the lid from falling off. One could bake biscuits, cobblers, stews, beans, just about anything with this method. Some cooks also used it for baking bread and pies; others used it to steam steaks and roasts or cook rice, hominy, and oatmeal. It was, in the full sense of the word, an oven. It was also a key feature of chuck wagons; photographs from the latter half of the 19th century show four or five huge Dutch ovens in use around a campfire, each one cooking a different dish.

And the name? The best explanation that I have read is that, for some time, the best cast iron came from Holland and the pots were therefore referred to as Dutch ovens. —Christopher Kimball

COALS

RATINGS OF DUTCH OVENS

Eight Dutch ovens, each with a capacity of six to eight quarts and available from their manufacturers in open stock, were tested and evaluated according to the following criteria. All stovetop cooking tests were performed over 10,000 BTU gas burners on the KitchenAid home ranges in our test kitchen. The Testers' Comments augment the information on the chart with observations about unusual or noteworthy aspects of the pots and their performance.

PRICE: Prices listed at Boston-area retail outlets, in mail-order catalogs, or Manufacturer's Suggested Retail Promotional price. Because cookware is often heavily discounted, you may see different prices for the same item in your local stores.

MATERIALS: The materials for each pot (in some cases the exterior and interior are different), as well as the lid, are listed. Stainless steel pots are made with a core of conductive metal such as aluminum. If this layer goes all the way up through the sides of the pot, the note reads "complete aluminum core." If the conductive metal layer does not extend up the sides, the note reads "aluminum sandwich bottom."

CAPACITY AND MEASUREMENTS: The measurements listed are the diameter, measured across the top of the pan from inside edge to inside edge and height, measured from inside of the bottom surface to the top inside edge of the pan wall. Pans with a wider diameter were preferred.

WEIGHT: Measured with the lid on.

BROWNING: In the pot roast test, pots that produced a dark brown, even crust on the meat in two to four minutes were preferred. Pots that produced an uneven crust that was too light or dark in some spots, and took longer than four minutes, were downgraded slightly. Pots that smoked or burned the drippings were downgraded severely. In the beef soup test, pots that browned thoroughly and evenly, at a medium pace, were preferred. Pots that smoked or burned the pan drippings during any of the batches were downgraded.

SAUTÉ SPEED: Pans that produced soft, pale gold onions with no burned edges in ten to twelve minutes were considered medium speed and were preferred. Pans that took a little longer were considered slow and were downgraded slightly, and fast pans that burned the onions were downgraded seriously.

SIMMER: A slow, steady simmer, with bubbles barely visible, that produced evenly cooked, fluffy rice with minimal sticking was rated good. If the simmer was faster, with more bubbles noticeable, and the rice cooked unevenly or stuck a little bit, but did not burn, we rated the pot fair. If the simmer was very fast and looked as though it might approach a boil, with many bubbles visible, and the rice burned or stuck to the bottom, we rated the pot poor.

BOILING WATER: In part one, pots that brought the water to a boil in twenty to twenty-four minutes were rated good; those that took between twenty-five and twenty-nine minutes were rated fair; and those that required thirty minutes or more were rated poor. In part two, pots in which six or more cups of water remained would have been rated good; pots in which five to six cups remained were rated fair; and pots in which four to five cups remained were rated poor.

Brand	Price	Materials	Capacity	Weight	Browning	Sauté Speed	Simmer	Boiling	Testers' Comments
BEST DUTCH OVEN **All-Clad** Stainless Stockpot, Model 5508	$187	Stainless exterior and interior with complete aluminum core; stainless steel lid	8 QUARTS 10 3/8" X 5 1/4"	5 LBS., 8 1/2 OZ.	★★★ POT ROAST / ★★★ BEEF BROTH	MEDIUM	★★★	★★★ PART I / ★★ PART II	Comfortable heft and great heat distribution. In browning, this pot seemed to need higher heat than the manufacturer's recommended medium.
BEST BUY **Lodge** Dutch Oven, Size 10	$45	Cast-iron pot and lid	7 QUARTS 11 1/2" X 4 3/4"	6 LBS., 15 1/2 OZ.	★★★ POT ROAST / ★★★ BEEF BROTH	MEDIUM-SLOW	★★	★★ PART I / ★★ PART II	Though it has distinct advantages, its colossal weight will make it difficult for some to use on an everyday basis. Other problems include demanding maintenance in that it must be seasoned regularly.
Le Creuset Round French Oven, Model 2501280901	$170	Enameled cast-iron pot and lid	7 QUARTS 11" X 3 3/4"	12 LBS., 7 OZ.	★★★ POT ROAST / ★★★ BEEF BROTH	MEDIUM	★★★	★★ PART I / ★ PART II	This handsome pot was clearly the beauty of the group, but heavy to lift and slow to heat up. Once it's hot, it simmers and browns well.
Tramontina Sterling II Dutch Oven/Casserole, Model 6503/28	$70	Stainless steel pot with aluminum sandwich bottom; stainless steel lid	7 QUARTS 11" X 4 1/4"	5 LBS., 15 OZ.	★★ POT ROAST / ★★★ BEEF BROTH	MEDIUM-FAST	★★	★ PART I / ★ PART II	Very light lid that jumps around noticeably when water is boiled vigorously, yet sticks to the pan via amazing suction when ingredients are sweated without liquid. Browning, simmering, and sautéing all run fast.
Cuisinart Stainless Steel Everyday Collection Saucepot, Model 944-26	$102	Stainless steel pot with copper sandwich bottom; stainless steel lid	7 QUARTS 10 1/8" X 4 7/8"	4 LBS., 12 OZ.	★ POT ROAST / ★★ BEEF BROTH	VERY FAST	★★	★★★ PART I / ★★ PART II	A relative lightweight that is prone to scorching in key browning, simmering, and sautéing tests.
Calphalon Deep Casserole with Domed Cover, Model GC8788-1/2HC	$194	Anodized aluminum pot and lid	8 1/2 QUARTS 12" X 4 1/2"	7 LBS., 7 1/2 OZ	★★ POT ROAST / ★ BEEF BROTH	MEDIUM	★★	★★★ PART I / ★ PART II	The dark gray interior finish made it difficult to see, and therefore judge, whether drippings were caramelizing or burning. Beware the handles, which get scorching hot even on the stovetop, and the lid, on which condenses a lake's worth of steam that splashes over you and the stovetop.
Circulon Covered Dutch Oven	$139	Anodized aluminum pot; grooved nonstick-coated interior; domed stainless steel lid	8 1/2 QUARTS 12" X 4 1/2"	7 LBS., 7 1/2 OZ.	★★ POT ROAST / ★ BEEF BROTH	MEDIUM	★★	★★★ PART I / ★ PART II	A great shape with which to work, but lackluster performance in key areas. The dark interior finish makes it very difficult to judge pan drippings.
Berndes TraditionCast Casserole/Dutch Oven, Model 74030	$135	Nonstick coated cast aluminum; Pyrex lid	7 1/4 QUARTS 11" X 4 1/4"	5 LB., 15 OZ.	★★ POT ROAST / ★ BEEF BROTH	MEDIUM-SLOW	★	★★ PART I / ★ PART II	Looks are deceiving with this pot. It appears as though it would be heavy, so mentally you prepare for a real heave. But you end up almost throwing the pot across the room because it's actually quite light.

preference for nonstick interiors in two quart saucepans (*see* "Choosing the Right Saucepan," May/June 1997), we actually do want some sticking in our Dutch ovens. The sticking, caramelization, and deglazing of drippings in the pan is a key technique for building flavor in moist heat cooking methods. Non-stick finishes retard this process in the name of easy cleaning, but what you gain in cleaning ease you sacrifice in flavor. All-Clad and Le Creuset impressed us precisely because they picked up excellent drippings and allowed them to caramelize without burning over the course of continued cooking.

Any Dutch oven will see some sautéing action during the course of normal use, so we sautéed one and one-half cups of minced onion in three tablespoons of butter over medium heat to determine sauté speed and to test even, scorch-free cooking ability. All-Clad, Le Creuset, and Calphalon all sautéed at a steady, medium pace that was ideal. Lodge, Berndes, and Circulon were slightly slow, but generally even. Tramontina was a little faster than ideal, but easily monitored. Don't turn your back on the Cuisinart, though—it sautéed much too fast, quickly burning the onions.

Another important test was to cook a double batch of long-grain white rice over the lowest possible heat. Though most cooks make rice in a large saucepan, this test illustrated each pot's slow simmering characteristics, as well as the presence of any obvious hot spots. All Clad and Le Creuset maintained the slowest, most even simmers of the group, producing rice that was fluffy and evenly cooked. A little rice stuck to the bottom of the All-Clad and a lot more stuck to the stainless steel interior of the Tramontina and Cuisinart, which otherwise simmered well. The Calphalon and the Lodge also simmered reasonably well and saw some sticking. The non-stick Berndes and Circulon both simmered too fast, but, needless to say, sticking was not an issue.

Though our two boiling water tests carried less weight in the ratings than browning, simmering, and sautéing, we ran them because some cooks may not have a second large pot, and might therefore use their Dutch oven to boil water for pasta or veggies. First, we clocked the time each pot required to bring five quarts of water to a rolling boil over medium-high heat, which we thought to be a good indication of heat conductivity speed. All-Clad and Cuisinart were best, at about twenty minutes. The rest of the pack fell way behind, taking anywhere from twenty-six minutes for the Calphalon to thirty-three minutes for the Tramontina. Our second boiling water test evaluated the fit of the lid, which bears on the pots' liquid reduction characteristics, and therefore the flavor of any sauce made from that liquid. This time, we boiled two quarts of water vigorously for half an hour and then measured the remaining quantity. The tighter the lid fit, the more water re-

The Dutch Ovens We Tested

BEST DUTCH OVEN
All-Clad Stainless Stockpot, Model 5508
Pricey, but distributes heat evenly, browns perfectly, and boils fast.

BEST BUY
Lodge Dutch Oven, Size 10
Weighs a ton but browns like a pro.

Le Creuset Round French Oven, Model 2501280901
Very attractive, browns well, but heats up slowly.

Tramontina Sterling II Dutch Oven/Casserole Model 6503/28
Burned drippings a bit, very slow to boil.

Cuisinart Stainless Steel Everyday Collection Saucepot Model 944-26
Lightweight pan is prone to scorching.

Calphalon Deep Casserole with Domed Cover Model GC8788-1/2HC
Dark interior is problematic, handles get scorching hot.

Circulon Covered Dutch Oven
Great shape but lackluster performance.

Berndes TraditionCast Casserole/Dutch Oven, Model 74030
Very light pan excelled in no areas.

mained. None of the pots managed to retain six or more cups of water. All-Clad, Cuisinart, Circulon, and Lodge all kept between five and six cups, beating Le Creuset, Tramontina, Calphalon, and Berndes, which kept five cups or less.

Recommendations

The All-Clad, which can approach $200, is hardly a bargain, but it is the top-notch performer of the group. It browns, simmers, and sautés reliably; it can handle high heat; its shape and finish are right; and its medium weight makes it easy to handle. If you can spare the cash, it will be money well-spent. The Le Creuset matched All-Clad's performance in the key areas, but it is very heavy to lift and took a little longer to heat up, so it fell to second place. At one-quarter the price of the top two finishers, the Lodge cast iron is also worthy of consideration. Price and great browning are the Lodge's pros; dark interior finish and colossal weight are its cons. In addition, you must remember to season the Lodge regularly.

Tasting California Zinfandels

Unlike their predecessors from the 1970's, today's California zins are lush, fruity, and well-made. All this and inexpensive, to boot. BY MARK BITTMAN

When I started writing about wine nearly 20 years ago, California zinfandels—or zins, as they are affectionately called—were the latest rage. In those days, winemakers spent their time figuring out how to get maximum alcohol, maximum extraction, and maximum concentration out of the grape—in other words, how to make the strongest wine possible. The resulting wines were "interesting," but so tannic they sucked the teeth out of your mouth, and so high in alcohol that a couple of glasses sent you reeling.

Needless to say, those zinfandels never caught on with the public at large. But the thousands of acres of zinfandel grapes were put to good use when market-conscious wineries used them to produce "blush" wines, the smash hit of the late '80s. These somewhat sweet, varietally indistinct wines were inoffensive at best, but convinced a whole generation of wine drinkers that "zinfandel" was synonymous with "pink."

In the past few years, the tables have turned again and red zinfandel, real zinfandel, is back—and better than ever. Dozens of wineries are now producing fruity, lush wines from what may be North America's finest indigenous grape.

In fact, when we began to assemble our list of reasonably priced zinfandels of good reputation for our tasting, we were startled to find that more than one hundred qualified. In order to pare the list down to a manageable level for the panel of tasters, we selected fifteen wines based on current reputation (Rosenblum and Ravenswood, for example), length of time making zinfandel (Ridge and Mt. Veeder), stature in the industry at large (Mondavi, Fetzer, and Beaulieu Vineyards), and our guess at those we thought would represent good value (Cline and Napa Ridge).

Generally, the results were about what we'd anticipated; almost all of the wines were enjoyable. Indeed, with the exception of the two wines that fell into our Not Recommended category, I'd happily drink any of them with most grilled foods, pasta-and-tomato dishes (they're an excellent alternative to generally pricier Chianti), and roasted meats—including turkey. As a class, the wines have luscious, ripe-tasting fruit, and are tannic enough to stand up to most anything. They're wonderful with cheese but their forward, fairly uncomplicated fruit makes them pleasant to drink by the glass, with no food at all.

I believe that two generalizations can be drawn from this tasting. One, zinfandel has finally become a quality, food-friendly wine—most zinfandels can be bought with confidence that they will complement a wide variety of foods. And two, quality appears to be less dependent on price than it is with many other grapes. In many of our tastings, one or two inexpensive wines make their way into the top half of the rankings; here, wines under $15 are in the majority, and those under $10 make a great showing.

THE JUDGES' RESULTS | CALIFORNIA ZINFANDELS

The wines in our tasting—held at Mt. Carmel Wine and Spirits, in Hamden, Connecticut—were judged by a panel made up of both wine professionals and amateur wine lovers. The wines were all purchased in the Northeast; prices will vary considerably throughout the country. All the wines are from California.

Within each category, wines are listed based on the number of points scored. In this tasting, the "Highly Recommended" wines had almost exclusively positive comments and "Recommended" wines had a majority of positive comments. Those labeled "Recommended with Reservations" had mixed comments—some positive, some negative, with no clear majority.

HIGHLY RECOMMENDED

1994 Burgess, $14 "Big, Barolo-like wine," "complex with lots of fruit and good balance." You can't say much more than that, except that at $14 it's a bargain.

NV Marietta Old Vine Cuvee Red, Lot #20, $10. An interesting blend of grapes dominated by zinfandel. We included it to see how a zin-dependent blend would do, and were pleased with the results. "Ripe, rich, and full," with "intense nose," "lovely fruit and good finish."

1995 Cline California, $8. Our tasting panel seems to love the Cline style—everyone ranked this wine somewhere. It seemed to be the typical zinfandel: "Berry-like fruit and lush finish." A little strong in the alcohol department for some, but note the price.

RECOMMENDED

1994 Rosenblum Old Vines, $15 "Lush fruit, more Bordeaux-like, with good balance," with a "powerfully fine nose of cedar." "Beautiful nose, but not as interesting on the palate," was a typical comment of those with reservations.

1995 Ridge Paso Robles, $23. A typical wine from the granddaddy of good zin makers. "Chocolate nose" in this "well-rounded, chewy, well-made wine."

1994 Napa Ridge Central Coast, $9. "A complex, mushroomy wine that just tastes good." "Spicy and lively," but a "bit hot."

1994 Mondavi, $19. There was more controversy about this wine than any other in this category: "Nice, open, berry-like nose followed by delicious, fruity flavors—will be even better in three years," wrote one. "Nondescript nose, and the taste follows," wrote another. But the majority gave it a "yea."

1995 Beuhler Vineyards Estate Bottled, $27. A good example of a wine with almost completely positive comments—"Meaty and yummy," "open and complex," "delicious, with good structure"—that did not translate into votes.

1995 Ravenswood Vintners Blend, $11. This wine has become the default choice of many diners when confronted with an unenticing restaurant wine list; "Simple but decent," "good fruit and balance," "lovely hit of fruit." Strong, almost harsh finish cost it points.

1995 Frog's Leap, Napa, $18. "Really quite yummy" wine with "Asian spice in the nose," that was found to be "short, with no complexity" by some.

1995 Beaulieu Vineyards Napa Valley, $15. "Luscious on the nose, with sweet fruit," would make you a believer. Some tasters found it "short" and "burnt."

RECOMMENDED WITH RESERVATIONS

1994 Renwood Amador County Old Vines, $15. "Port-like" and "over-ripe" comments led to relatively low score, mitigated by "big," with "sweetness and texture."

1994 Mt. Veeder, $27. "Intense, with minty nose and fruit on the palate," said one taster. But the majority found this "too tame," with "just old fruit."

Tour Guides to Liguria

Choose a genial, breezy tour guide of Italy's western province or a dour, but compelling, intellectual. BY CHRISTOPHER KIMBALL

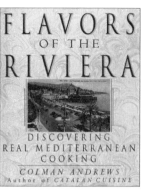

Cookbooks about Italy are so popular that they can now focus on small regions of the country. These two books, for example, are concerned with the cuisine of Liguria, a province in the northwest of Italy. Although often referred to by foreigners as the Italian Riviera, this region also extends inland. (Colman Andrews also extends the reach of his book into France as far as Nice.) Fortunately for readers, the cooking of this region is a frugal, full-flavored cuisine that even a Burger King addict would find compelling. Not only does it include the usual suspects—pine nuts, anchovies, polenta, walnuts, basil, potatoes, sardines, and chickpeas—it also enchants with more unusual fare such as fried mine-strone, goat with white beans, and marjoram noodle soup. The spirit of this cuisine is perhaps caught best by a friend of Andrews', a restauranteur from Portofino who described the perfect pasta dish. "You catch some sardines, then you grill them right on deck. Then you put oil, capers, and garlic in a pan—that's all—and throw in the sardines. Put that on some pasta and you simply don't need anything else. It's the best."

Because the food and the region are both so compelling—a rustic black hole that is rapidly sucking American culinary trends into its vortex— the first question for an armchair gourmet is obvious: Which tour guide do I prefer? Fred Plotkin is a breezy, genial sort, pointing out statues of lions, antique market signs, and ancient communal ovens. He'll look after you like a cheery uncle, stopping the minivan to offer particularly good photo opportunities of quaint alleyways and mar-

REVIEWS

Recipes from Paradise
By Fred Plotkin
(Little Brown, $24.95)

Flavors of the Riviera
By Colman Andrews
(Bantam, $24.95)

kets filled with fresh sardines, great clumps of basil, and Swiss chard. He also has a good command of local history and is not shy with his adjectives or his translations of the earthy vernacular. This guy is likable.

At the other end of the spectrum is Andrews, a rather dour intellectual who describes, in somewhat academic terms, his experiences at the carnival in Nice. Nestled just above a rather romantic post-card view of the event, Andrews wraps up his small aside with the following words: "I found it all rather forced, and not very much fun, and decided not to stay." Spoken, I would guess, like a true Ligurian.

But don't jump onto Plotkin's tour bus just yet. Andrews grows on you; his depth of culinary knowledge is impressive and his no-nonsense tone a refreshing change of pace from the happy, sun-drenched prose of Plotkin. Although I yearn to grab Colman by the shoulders, shake him, and ask, "Aren't you having fun yet?", it's hard not to cotton to someone who really knows what he is talking about. But he's quite a sight, having dinner up in the mountains of Piedmont, the grassy hills extending almost to the sea, seated at a wooden table in front of a wood-burning oven, drinking homemade wine, feasting on flat-bread, wild boar prosciutto, a radicchio sprout salad with raw onion, slow-roasted lamb, and home-made ricotta—and his most compelling memory is the taste of the pecorino. Damn the view!

Andrews has also developed his recipe head-notes to an academic art. Like a great culinary fisherman, he trolls original documents, gets on the phone, ventures out to homes and restaurants, all in an effort to sniff out some reasonable approximation of the truth, however obscure. And his double-barreled research and deadpan delivery frequently bears fruit. He reveals, in the same erudite monotone he uses throughout the book, that the inhabitants of different Ligurian towns have been awarded nicknames over the years, according to what is perceived to be their favorite foodstuff. Fava eaters, gourdies, snailies, panissies, honeys, oil dousers, bean eaters, and then he ends with the punchline, the caga-bléa, the chard shitters.

As for the food, well, this is a hard call. These are full-fledged cookbooks for which no claims of authenticity have been made by the authors. (In fact, Andrews pronounces that his recipes cannot be considered authentic because, for example, true Genovese ravioli must contain spinal marrow and heifer's udder.) As a result, the recipe cannot be viewed as a mere exercise in academia, but must deliver in an American kitchen. Judged solely on the recipes, I find both books problematic. We tested twenty-three recipes, nine of them in my home kitchen. I found that they tended to be laborious and sometimes lackluster in flavor. In addition, the cooking times were frequently off and we often felt left at sea by the authors. When you bake ricotta cheese for fifteen minutes, for instance, should it come out of the oven firm and dry, firm and moist, or still wet and sloppy?

Purely on the basis of recipe testing, Andrews wins the contest. I found five out of nine of his recipes worth making again, while Plotkin scored on only two out of twelve. Overcooked fish, seven cups of fritter batter for just two apples, grossly inaccurate cooking times, unnecessarily arduous preparation, and a curious lack of seasoning (although many authentic Italian dishes are quite modest in this regard) were among the problems.

But in defense of both authors, I had difficulty putting these books down. Neither is promoting an ersatz, tourist's version of Ligurian cuisine. This alone is very compelling amidst the current love-fest for all things Italian. Of course, in search of authenticity one must engage in labors of love: seeking out fresh sardines, removing the spines from thirty basil leaves to make pesto, or stirring constantly for fifty minutes. But such labors should have been more precisely tested and presented; the authors should have evidenced a more serious interest in the American home cook. Instead, Plotkin and Andrews, both confirmed intellectuals, invite us on a grand tour of Liguria, one that is steeped in culinary lore, interesting historical notes, and a glimpse of culinary paradise. On this level they succeed admirably. But when the trip was over, I felt like a weary tourist, the trip just a fading memory. I wanted to bring a bit of Liguria back to my own kitchen, but was left instead with souvenirs, recipes that required serious interpretation.

Briefly noted: Congratulations to Shirley Corriher, our science adviser, on the publication of her book *CookWise* (Morrow, 1997).

Most of the ingredients and materials necessary for the recipes in this issue are available at your local supermarket, gourmet store, or kitchen supply shop. The following are mail-order sources for particular items. Prices listed below were current at press time and do not include shipping or handling unless otherwise indicated. We suggest that you contact companies directly to confirm up-to-date prices and availability.

Dutch Ovens

In our Dutch oven tests on page 27 the All-Clad and Le Creuset ran neck and neck. They excelled at browning, sautéing and simmering, as well as handling high heat. The stainless steel All-Clad outranked enameled cast iron Le Creuset, however, because of the latter's cumbersome weight (more than twelve pounds) and slower heating rate. **A Cook's Wares (211 37th Street, Beaver Falls, PA 15010-2103; 800-915-9788)** sells the eight-quart All-Clad Stainless Stockpot, Model 5508, for $186.30. The Le Creuset Round French Oven can also be purchased for $170 from **A Cook's Wares**. It is sold in blue, white, flame, black, green, and red.

Rye Flour

While we tested a number of different rye flours, we were only able to get the Jewish deli-style bread we were looking for from Pillsbury Medium Rye Flour and King Arthur Flour's White Rye Flour (see page 19). Both are milled only from the endosperm of the rye berry. Without any bran to cut the gluten strands of the dough and weigh down the bread, we found these flours gave us a light, holey, springy bread with a good chew. Many major supermarkets nationwide carry Pillsbury Medium Rye Flour. King Arthur White Rye Flour can be purchased by mail order through their **Baker's Catalogue (P.O. Box 876, Norwich, VT 05055-0876; 800-827-6836)**. A two-pound bag costs $1.95 and a five-pound bag costs $4.50.

Greater Zester

Our executive editor and our test kitchen director are both hooked on the Greater Zester. Eight-and-one-half inches long, one-inch wide, and three-eigths of an inch deep, the Greater Zester resembles a thin, metal ruler with tiny, square-edged teeth that run across its width at a close-cropped diagonal. Woodworkers might recognize this tool as a rasp blade for carving wood. We particularly like this tool in the kitchen because, unlike any other grater we have tried, it can grate dried cheese into fluffy, fine wisps. It also grates ginger into a near paste versus the scattered strands you get from the fine teeth of a regular box grater. Easy to handle and longer than a box grater, so that less sweeps are required, the Greater Zester is also useful for zesting citrus rinds or grating chocolate for garnish. Order by mail for $13.50 from **Cooking by the Book, Inc. (13 Worth Street, New York, NY 10013; 212-966-9799)**. To care for this stainless steel tool, wash by hand with soap and water.

Bench Knife

A Quick Tip on page 5 suggests using a bench knife to score and lift bar cookies and lasagne. A bench knife also quickly remedies the frustration of peeling dough scraps off your work surface or dividing up a sticky ball of dough. **New York Cake and Baking Distributor (56 West 22nd Street, New York, NY 10010; 800-942-2539)** sells a six-inch-wide bench knife with a dishwasher-safe polypropylene handle for $6.99. If you typically work with particularly sticky doughs you can also buy a nonstick bench knife with a wooden handle for $14.70 from the **King Arthur Baker's Catalogue (P.O. Box 876, Norwich, VT 05055-0876; 800-827-6836)**. Both knives have blunt stainless steel blades that are safe to use on most countertops.

Bread Lamé

While the markings on a loaf of bread are best known for indicating the kind of bread it is (diagonal slashes for baguettes, for example), they're also necessary to help the bread dough expand evenly and to prevent the crust from bursting while baking. We preferred to use a bread lamé to score across our rye bread because a knife often pulls or tears the dough and scissors often are not sharp enough. A lamé resembles a rubber spatula but has a double-edged stainless steel razor held at the bottom of the plastic handle. **A Cook's Wares (211 37th Street, Beaver Falls, Pennsylvania 15010-2103; 800-915-9788)** sells a lamé that has a four-inch blade and a separate acrylic sheath for $4.80.

Instant-Read Thermometer Update

While **Owen Instruments Thermapen 5** topped our instant-read thermometer ratings in our July/August 1997 issue, we did miss the automatic shutoff feature that the Cooper Digital Test Thermometer offered. Since the story's publication, the Thermapen has been updated with an automatic shutoff feature so that the battery will not wear out if you forget to turn it off. Instead of an "on/off" switch, the new model turns on when you unfold the probe from its case. If the probe is accidentally left extended, the automatic shutoff feature will turn the thermometer off after five minutes. You can order the updated thermometer for $59 by contacting **ThermoWorks, Inc. (P.O. Box 605, American Fork, Utah 84003; 801-756-7705)**.

Thick-Handled Whisks

In a Quick Tip on page 5, a whisk is rubbed rapidly between two hands to make foam out of hot milk for cappuccino. To do this you need a thick-handled whisk with enough surface area to roll between your palms. We also like thick-handled whisks for their overall ease of grip. **New York Cake and Baking Distributor (56 West 22nd Street, New York, NY 10010; 800-942-2539)** sells a variety of thick-handled whisks at bargain prices. For this Quick Tip we used a twelve-inch French or sauce whisk. The stiff wires of this pear-shaped whisk are useful for mixing, emulsifying, or aerating sauces. **New York Cake** sells this stainless steel whisk with a thick metal handle for $6.50. It also carries French whisks with thick metal handles in ten-, fourteen-, and sixteen-inch sizes. French whisks with thick wooden handles are sold in the same sizes, except sixteen inches.

Statement of Ownership, Management, and Circulation (United States Postal Service). Publication Title: Cook's Illustrated. Filing Date: 10/1/97. Issue Frequency: Bi-Monthly. Number of Issues Published Annually: 6. Annual Subscription Price: $24.95. Complete Mailing Address of Known Office of Publication: Boston Common Press, 17 Station Street, Brookline, MA 02146. Telephone: 617 232-1000. Publisher: Christopher Kimball, Boston Common Press, 17 Station St., Brookline, MA 02146. Editor: Same as Publisher. Managing Editor: Keith Powers, Boston Common Press, 17 Station St., Brookline, MA 02146. Owner: Boston Common Press Limited Partnership, 500 Boylston St., #1880, Boston, MA (Christopher Kimball).

RECIPE INDEX

Black Beans with Bacon, Balsamic Vinegar, and Sweet Pepper
PAGE 7

Classic Spaghetti and Meatballs **PAGE 9**

Bok Choy and Chinese Egg Noodles with Spicy Beef Sauce **PAGE 18**

Oven-Fried Bacon, Fluffy Scrambled Eggs and Bran Muffins
PAGES 14, 15 & 24

Beef Barley Soup with Mushrooms and Thyme and Deli-Style Rye Bread
PAGES 13 & 20

Carrot Cake with Cream Cheese Frosting **PAGE 23**

PHOTOGRAPHY: CARL TREMBLAY

DELICATA

RED TURBAN

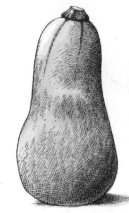

BUTTERNUT

ACORN

PUMPKIN

BUTTERCUP

RED KURI

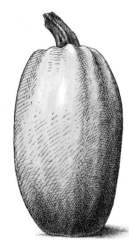

SPAGHETTI

SWEET
DUMPLING

CARNIVAL

BLUE HUBBARD

WINTER SQUASHES

NUMBER THIRTY-ONE

MARCH & APRIL 1998

COOK'S
ILLUSTRATED

Secrets of Homemade Chili
Fresh Roasted Chiles Yield
Rich, Deep Flavors

Cheap Baking Sheet Wins Testing
Spend $5 not $25

Easy Flourless Chocolate Cake
Three Ingredients, Rich Texture,
and True Chocolate Flavor

Chicken and Rice
Improving an American Classic

How to Oven-Poach Whole Salmon

Better Banana Bread
Grilled Cheese Perfected
Rating Inexpensive Chardonnays
Simple Clam Chowder
Best Peanut Butter Cookie

$4.00 U.S./$4.95 CANADA

CONTENTS
March & April 1998

COOK'S ILLUSTRATED

PUBLISHER AND EDITOR
Christopher Kimball

EXECUTIVE EDITOR
Pam Anderson

SENIOR EDITOR
John Willoughby

SENIOR WRITER
Jack Bishop

ASSOCIATE EDITORS
Adam Ried
Maryellen Driscoll

CONTRIBUTING EDITORS
Mark Bittman
Stephanie Lyness

TEST KITCHEN DIRECTOR
Susan Logozzo

TEST COOK
Anne Yamanaka

EDITORIAL INTERN
Jessica Drench

ART DIRECTOR
Amy Klee

CORPORATE MANAGING EDITOR
Barbara Bourassa

EDITORIAL PRODUCTION
MANAGER
Sheila Datz

COPY EDITOR
Amy Finch

MARKETING DIRECTOR
Adrienne Kimball

CIRCULATION DIRECTOR
David Mack

FULFILLMENT MANAGER
Larisa Greiner

CIRCULATION MANAGER
Darcy Beach

MARKETING ASSISTANT
Connie Forbes

CIRCULATION ASSISTANT
Steven Browall

VICE PRESIDENT
PRODUCTION AND TECHNOLOGY
James McCormack

SYSTEMS ADMINISTRATOR
James Burke

DESKTOP PUBLISHING MANAGER
Kevin Moeller

PRODUCTION ARTIST
Robert Parsons

PRODUCTION ASSISTANT
Daniel Frey

CONTROLLER
Lisa A. Carullo

SENIOR ACCOUNTANT
Mandy Shito

STAFF ACCOUNTANT
William Baggs

OFFICE MANAGER
Livia McRee

SPECIAL PROJECTS
Fern Berman

DRIED CHILES Dried chiles are both more intense and more varied in flavor than fresh chiles. This means that a specific dried chile will often perform best in a particular setting. Earthy, sweet, relatively mild ancho chiles, for example, are the workhorse of the genre, with a wide range of uses in cooked dishes. On the other hand, chipotles, which are dried, smoked jalapeños, have a more distinctive flavor, and therefore tend to be used more sparingly. Chiles are also somewhat fickle. A given type of chile, for instance, may be considerably hotter or milder depending on the time of year it was picked, the location of the individual plant, or even the location of the individual pepper on the same plant. The best policy is to try the whole range of dried chiles and let experience be your guide.

COVER PAINTING: BRENT WATKINSON, BACK COVER ILLUSTRATION: JOHN BURGOYNE

COUNTRY ROADS

Our town has but three main roads: One is the main road up to Beartown, another veers off to the west, through the notch (a narrow mountain pass) and down into the valley where we have our farm, and the third goes pretty much east, up over a four-wheel drive track, down into the next village. Most roads are named after old town families such as Wilcox or Woodcock, and they wind through hollows or around hills and mountains that ring with a small-town accent— Swearing Hill and Minister Hill, which face each other across the valley, or Red, Moffitt, and Bear Mountains, which rise to just over 3,000 feet. Our town is also blessed with many small streams, most of which feed into the Green River, including Terry Brook, Chunks Creek, and Baldwin Brook over on the west side, and Pruddy Brook, Hopper Brook, and Tidd Brook in the main part of town. I used to live near Tidd Brook as a child, catching small crawfish and trout under the barn-red wooden bridge. The sound of the cars rattling on the timbers, one at a time, echoed off the side hills of our small hollow, but today they are just a memory now that the bridge has been replaced by a quieter culvert. Back then, there weren't many cars on our roads and they moved slowly: old Charlie Bentley Sr. hunched over the steering wheel of a black 1950 Ford, or Fred Woodcock Sr. driving down to the row of mailboxes, anxious for his social security check. As each car moved across the bridge, every board had time to move up and down, the hollow thumping always in the same key but playing a song with different notes. In bed at the end of a summer day as the light was just fading to twilight, I would stare out my window at the side hill of thistle and wait for the sound of a crossing, for a sign of movement in the still, hot air, a promise of a chance visit to break the silence of the house.

Travelling along that road over the years, I have seen many things. There is the Skidmore place, just a few feet back from the main road into town, which offers a clear view of 55-gallon drums, a pickup with a smashed windshield, pools of rusted chain, and piles of worn tires strewn about as if some great wind funnel had sucked out the contents of the sagging garage and thrown them helter-skelter. For many years, one could also see Russell Baines, a metalworker who would park his blue station wagon by the side of the road, eat potato chips, read a romance novel, and go to sleep. He had moved in with Charlie Bentley, a local farmer. To get some privacy he'd start up the car every afternoon and go in search of a new place to park. Pretty soon, the whole town got used to the sight of Russell, head angled out the window, his large ears and thick black-frame glasses visible from the road, taking his nap, alone at last, peaceful in his car.

But it is the dirt road that passes by our farm that I love the most. During the long days of summer, we put the dishes in the sink to soak after dinner and take a walk down the road in the twilight. During the day, as I bush hog over a wet corner of the meadow I can smell sweet fern, the hot scent of wild sage, the occasional whiff of spearmint, feel the blast of heat from the tractor, see the birds swooping down over the mowed grass, an ocean of yellow and orange Indian paintbrushes against waves of large bright purple clover, overstuffed bumblebees as big as a thumb, and hear the rhythm of the engine and the mower, the hum of pistons, gears, axles, and whirring blades. But now, in the still of the

Christopher Kimball

evening, I walk down our road and witness hundreds of fireflies sparking over a field of sunflowers, a goat perched half-way up a small tree by a neighbor's barn, a sky that is tinged with pink clouds that turn into a broad swath of vermilion and magenta as the broad strokes are painted just above our small valley, a handsome bowl of trees and pasture and houses that is open to the universe yet hidden quietly in the mountain valley. I crouch next to one of our hives, listening to the buzzing of 40,000 bees, the wooden frames alive with newly minted workers, happy, I suppose, to be at the end of another day. I can hear our voices clear and soft drifting up over the valley on a slight breeze that stirs up out of the west. We walk slowly back home along the lazy "S" of the dusty road to our farmhouse, the last swath of sun lighting up the top of the ridges with deep ochres and golds. The children run ahead, thinking of great bowls of homemade vanilla ice cream with stewed rhubarb. They carry a small railroad lantern that swings back and forth as they race ahead down our dirt driveway by the old apple trees that need pruning and the young cornfield. The faint breath of wind washes in and out of us, an ebb and flow that is always just out of focus, like trying to follow the path of a lightning bug across a meadow. The light flashes on and off in bursts, but its dark path can only be inferred, never actually seen. On these evenings, I watch our three children, standing quietly by the side of a meadow, enchanted by a glimpse of the unknown in a thousand blinking lights moving across a field blanketed by twilight.

ABOUT COOK'S ILLUSTRATED

The Magazine Cook's Illustrated is published every other month (6 issues per year) and accepts no advertising. A one-year subscription is $24.95, two years is $45, and three years is $65. Add $6 postage per year for Canadian subscriptions and $12 per year for all other foreign countries. To order subscriptions call 800-526-8442. Gift subscriptions are available for $24.95 each.

Magazine-Related Items Cook's Illustrated is available in an annual hardbound, which includes an index, for $24.95 each plus shipping and handling. Discounts are available if more than one year is ordered at a time. Back issues are available for $5 each. The Cook's Illustrated 1998 calendar, featuring 12 of the magazine's covers reproduced in full color, is available for $12.95. Cook's also offers a 5-year index (1993-1997) of the magazine for $12.95. To order any of these products, call 800-611-0759.

Books Cook's Illustrated publishes a series of single topic books, available for $14.95 each. Current titles include: How To Make A Pie, How To Make An American Layer Cake, How To Stir Fry, How To Make Ice Cream, How To Make Pizza, How To Make Holiday Desserts, and How To Make Pasta Sauces. The Cook's Bible, written by Christopher Kimball and published by Little Brown, is available for $24.95. To order any of these books, call 800-611-0759.

Reader Submissions Cook's accepts reader submissions for both Quick Tips and Notes From Readers. We will provide a one-year complimentary subscription for each Quick Tip that we print. Send a description of your technique, along with your name, address, and daytime telephone number, to Quick Tips, Cook's Illustrated, P.O. Box 569, Brookline, MA 02147. Questions, suggestions, or other submissions for Notes From Readers should be sent to the same address.

Subscription Inquiries All queries about subscriptions or change of address notices should be addressed to Cook's Illustrated, P.O. Box 7446, Red Oak, IA 51591-0446.

Website Address Selected articles and recipes from Cook's Illustrated's, as well as subscription information, is now available online. You can access the Cook's website at: www.cooksillustrated.com.

All Bagels, All the Time

➤ Response to our September/October 1997 story "Better than Store-Bought Bagels" was brisk. Jeanne Meierhofer of Willmar, Minnesota, Mark Judman of Freehold, New Jersey, and Bruce Backman of Boston, Massachusetts, all inquired about adding vital wheat gluten powder to either bread flour or all-purpose flour to substitute for the high-gluten flour in the recipe. We experimented with both, adding one teaspoon of gluten and two teaspoons of water, as directed on the package, to each cup of flour in the recipe. The dough made from the bread flour mixture was very stiff, as was the Master Recipe dough, and the bagels were reasonably firm, chewy, and well-browned, but not as much as the Master Recipe. Dr. Debi Rogers, a cereal chemist at the American Institute of Baking, attributed the low performance of vital wheat gluten to its manufacturing process. Specifically, some of the proteins in the gluten unwind from their natural coiled state as they are extracted from wheat. Denaturing partially deactivates those proteins. On the whole, flour to which partially deactivated proteins have been added will not be as effective as flour with 100 percent of its protein intact and active. Rogers also said that added gluten will never distribute as uniformly throughout the volume of flour in the recipe as the gluten within the flour itself. In sum, bread flour with gluten added might do in a pinch, but it is no match for the true high-gluten flour in this recipe.

Several other bagel questions came in. Meierhofer also asked if the dough could be retarded in the refrigerator before it is shaped into rounds. The answer is yes, though the chilled dough will be even more difficult to work with than it is at room temperature. Also, Geri Davis of Prescott, Arizona, suggested intensifying the onion flavor in our onion bagels by adding one tablespoon of dried onion flakes, rehydrated in a bit of water and drained, to the dough along with the yeast and water. We tried it and liked the flavor boost, though it seemed less traditional than the onion topping alone.

Anise and Fennel

In your January/February 1998 issue, there was a recipe for Bok Choy and Chinese Egg Noodles with Spicy Beef Sauce that called for anise seed. I didn't have any anise on hand, so I substituted fennel seed, and the dish tasted fine. But this started me thinking…aren't anise and fennel the same thing?

SHERRY MEEK
MINNEAPOLIS, MN

➤ Fennel and anise share a characteristic licorice flavor and scent, but they are, in fact, two different herbs. Anise is used in the form of seeds, which resemble cumin seeds in their yellowish-brown color and ⅛-inch length, and it is often associated with aperitifs, liqueurs, desserts, sweet cookies, and breads. With fennel, on the other hand, all parts of the plant are used, as well as the yellowish-green, ¼-inch-long seeds. Fennel is generally associated with Mediterranean-style sausage, salami, pork and fish dishes, and tomato sauces.

In her book *Savoring Spices and Herbs* (Morrow, 1996), Julie Sahni attributed their similar flavor to the fact that they contain the same essential oil, called anethol, which imparts the flavor. We tasted the two side-by-side and noted, as did Sahni, that the anise was sweeter and had a somewhat stronger licorice flavor than the fennel.

Substituting anise and fennel back and forth in a tomato sauce, for example, would be fine, though the results will vary slightly according to which is used. However, spice expert Pamela Penzey, purchasing agent for the mail-order spice retailer Penzey's, Ltd., felt that substituting them in baking or sausage-making would be a mistake because of their different sweetness levels.

Pan Measurements

Many recipes from *Cook's* and other sources call for skillets of a specific size. I am confused about how to measure a skillet. Do you measure across the rim or the bottom surface?

JANE DORROWITZ
RICHMOND, VA

➤ Our contacts in the cookware manufacturing and retailing industries confirmed that measurements always refer to the top diameter of the pan, from outside rim to outside rim. Given that different manufacturers' pans vary in the angle of the sidewall flare and thickness of the metal, Hugh Rushing, executive vice president of the Cookware Manufacturers Association, added that industry standards allow a tolerance of plus or minus ¼ inch. Thus, a 10-inch pan could actually have a diameter anywhere between 9¾ and 10¼ inches.

Cast Iron Care

We use our cast iron often, from the Dutch oven to the griddle, but find that the edges build up crud that won't come off, even with heavy scrubbing. My grandmother's trick in this instance was to put the skillet (or Dutch oven or griddle) into the coals in the fireplace and let it all burn off. Some areas may need a day-long fire, but it's impossible to overdo it. Once it has been rinsed, dried, and re-seasoned, even my grandmother's original skillet comes out like new.

GINA WALKER FOX
RHINEBECK, NY

➤ Several readers have contacted us with their techniques for cleaning and seasoning cast iron, including Sandy Glass of Gunnison, Colorado, who also puts hers in a fire once every couple of years. This winter our editor, Christopher Kimball, tested that method by putting a cast iron skillet, the exterior of which was coated with a rough, pebbly residue built up over several years, into the hot coals left after a roaring fire. When the fire died down and the pan had cooled enough to retrieve, its surfaces were completely stripped down to the metal, and ready to re-season. The late chef and cookbook author Pierre Franey had an alternative but equally effective method for those without access to a live fire. He achieved the same result with a cast iron skillet into which sugar syrup had been badly burnt by running it through the self-cleaning cycle of an oven. The 500-degree temperature of the cleaning cycle handily incinerated the sugar and all other residue.

Reader Nancy Kohl of Lynn, Massachusetts, wrote to suggest deep frying in cast iron cookware helps keep it well seasoned, noting that "Years of occasional deep frying have left my skillets smooth, black, and shiny—and almost completely nonstick." Our executive editor, Pam Anderson, who also fries foods such as chicken, meatballs, and tortilla chips in her cast iron cookware, attested to this method. In fact, deep frying in cast iron is a classic win-win situation. As we found in our March/April 1997 article "The Best Buttermilk Doughnuts," cast iron is the best possible choice for deep frying due to its excellent heat retention. By the same token, the cast iron benefits from the hot oil bath of deep frying because its pores open to let the fat penetrate, and the fat polymerizes on the metal to create a stick-resistant coating (see "How to Season a Cast Iron Pan," May/June 1997).

Christopher Kimball goes the extra mile of re-seasoning his cast iron after every use. Each time he cleans a skillet, he dries it over high heat on the stovetop until he can hold his hand a couple of inches above the surface for just four or five seconds. This takes up to five minutes for a twelve-inch skillet. Off the heat, he re-seasons by wiping about one tablespoon of oil into the pan with a wad of paper towels, and leaves the pan to cool.

Panfrying Steaks

I believe that the best steaks are not the product of direct smoke and fire, but instead come out of that honorable piece of kitchen equipment, the old iron frying pan. So I read with interest Stephanie Lyness' article "The Secrets of Panfrying Steaks" (May/June 1997), and I have a secret that I'd like to add. Instead of lubricating the pan with oil, try using a small piece of fat cut off the steak. It will add to the steak's flavor.

ROD KEYS
WATERFORD, MI

➤ Your method fared well in a side-by-side tasting of oil- and fat-panfried steaks we held in our test kitchen. Though the difference between the two was subtle, all comers unanimously voted for the steak fried in its own fat, calling it slightly "richer" and "beefier" than the steak fried in oil.

The one precaution we offer is to leave the pan empty for eight minutes of the recommended ten-minute preheating time, then add the fat to heat for the last two minutes. When we added the fat at the beginning of the preheating period, it had started to burn by the time the pan was hot enough to use.

Knife Sharpening Steels

After receiving a set of Wusthof cutlery as a gift, I eagerly re-read the *Cook's Illustrated* March/April 1997 article "Do Electric Knife Sharpeners Really Work?" The author, however, did not include a sharpening steel, which was part of my Wusthof set, in the comparison. Can you explain the role of a sharpening steel?

BRYON HERBEL
DURHAM, NC

➤ Sharpening steels perform a different function from electric knife sharpeners, which is why they were not included in the test. In the days when knives were commonly made of soft carbon steel, a sharpening steel did just what its name implied. Because harder stainless steel and high-carbon stainless steel knives have replaced their rust-prone predecessors, the term sharpening steel has become something of a misnomer. Steels are very important, however, to maintain a knife's edge.

As Shane Levens of Stoddard's, a Boston store that has specialized in cutlery since 1800 explained, a knife's newly sharpened edge might appear impeccably smooth, but a peek through a microscope would reveal hair-like metal teeth. With every slice or chop these teeth go askew, like the bristles of a mashed brush. Running a blade down a steel realigns, or "trues" the teeth and straightens the blunted edge that results from using the knife. You can use a steel as often or as seldom as you wish, said Levens, but the less you use it, the sooner the blade will lose its edge. No matter how frequently you steel your knives, the blades will eventually lose their fine edges and become dull.

At this point, you'll need to grind metal away from the blade to sharpen the edge. In general, there are three ways to accomplish this: with a sharpening stone, a belt grinder (the technique used by many professional knife sharpeners), or an electric knife sharpener.

Somewhere between the steel and the stone is another option called the diamond steel. Made of hollow steel, the diamond steel's surface is covered with a very fine industrial-grade diamond dust that trims metal in addition to truing the teeth. This prolongs the time period between needed sharpenings, said Levens. *See* Sources and Resources, page 32, for steel, stone, and diamond steel availability.

Sharpening Serrated Blades

Do serrated bread knives need to be sharpened? If so, what is the proper technique?

LINDA SEBESTA
ROCHESTER, MN

➤ In general, serrated edges suffer less wear and tear than smooth-edged knives. The points of a serrated blade do the initial tearing of the food, which is often hard, crusty bread. The finer edges within the scallop-shaped serrations follow the points through the food, doing less work and enduring less friction. Therefore, the scallops degrade slower. This means that the need for honing and sharpening is much less critical than it is with straight-edged blades.

There are, however, several sharpeners for serrated blades available on the market. We bought two to test on four heavily used, never-sharpened serrated knives in our test kitchen. In general, we were not impressed. The Chef's Choice Diamond Hone Knife Sharpener Model 430, designed to be ambidextrous, was easy to use, but we noticed very little difference in the knives' cutting ability before and after sharpening. Another model, the DMT Diafold Diamond Serrated Knife Sharpener, looked like a mini steel, came with next-to-no instructions and was very tricky to use for right-handed testers. The difficulty arose because, as is often the case with serrated blades, all four of our test knives had the serrations ground into only one side of the blade. Each tester had to use his or her right hand to grasp the knife so that it could be held, as instructed, with the sharp edge facing away from you and the serrations facing up and exposed to the sharpener. This meant holding the sharpener rather unnaturally for right-handers in the left hand, making it difficult to control and use precisely. Stoddard's' Shane Levens warned that this arrangement increases the risk of breaking a tooth off the blade as you sharpen, which, in fact, we did.

So, if you really think the edge on your bread knife needs a lift, we recommend taking it to a professional knife sharpener.

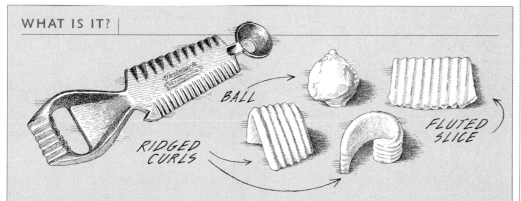

WHAT IS IT?

BALL

RIDGED CURLS

FLUTED SLICE

Every Christmas, we have a Secret Santa party at our office in which everyone receives a present from an office-mate whose identity remains a secret. Knowing that I love to cook, my Santa assembled a lovely gift basket of kitchen gadgets that included this item, but I don't know what it is. Will you find out for me?

GINNY ALTGEDD
FORT LAUDERDALE, FL

➤ Your present is a multifunction butter garnish cutter. When warmed in hot water, the cast aluminum cutter slices attractive pats of butter from a large, semifirm block. Each side of this tool, which is about six inches long, is cast with a different pattern. A little scoop on one end makes small balls of butter or melon. At the opposite end is a plane with a crimped lip that, when pulled across the butter block, shapes ridged curls. On either side of a central shaft are large and small grooved edges, used to make large and small fluted slices. We found the curler to be the most effective function, because the edges of the baller and the other two sides were too dull to make a nice, sharp definition.

The "multifunction" designation arises because there's a notch on the curler end to open bottles, and a conical point protruding from the baller end for piercing cans. Cutters can be ordered for $6.95, plus shipping costs, from Kitchen Kaboodle (3219 N.W. Guam, Portland, Oregon, 97210-1697; 800-366-0161). Ask for item number 22275 when ordering.

Quick Tips

Crumbling Hard-Boiled Eggs Extra Fine

Pat Welch of Marblehead, MA, could never chop hard boiled eggs as fine as she liked for garnishes. Then she learned that she could press the egg through a sieve for extra fine, even, crumbled egg. This works especially well for our recipe for Steamed Cauliflower with Bread Crumbs, Capers, and Chopped Egg on page 7.

Wrap and Foil Box Organizer

The boxes containing plastic sandwich bags, rolls of tin foil, plastic wrap, and the like can use up a lot of drawer space. Dolores Driscoll, of Topsfield, MA, solves this problem by storing the boxes upright in the slots of a cardboard six-pack beer bottle or soda container in a cabinet under the counter.

Quick-Drying Biscotti

Traditionally, biscotti dough is baked in a log and then cut into slices to be baked a second time—and flipped halfway through the baking time—to dry both sides of each slice. Marcia Stewart of Burnaby, British Columbia, has streamlined the method by laying the slices on a wire cooling rack set on a cookie sheet, then placing them in the oven. The rack elevates the slices, allowing air to circulate all the way around them, drying both sides at once.

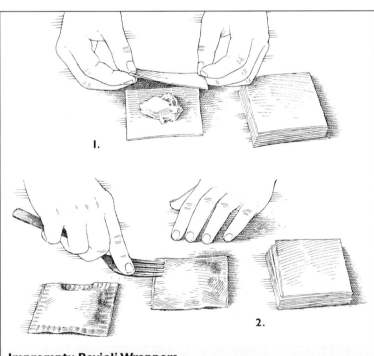

1.

2.

Impromptu Ravioli Wrappers

Jane Faraco of Solebury, PA, has found that store-bought wonton wrappers make a great substitute for homemade pasta when making ravioli.
1. Lay one wrapper on a work surface; place homemade filling on top.
2. Brush edges of dough with water and cover with another wrapper. Use the tines of a fork to seal edges of ravioli.

Preserving Over-ripe Bananas for Banana Bread

Rather than throwing over-ripe bananas away, Mary Logozzo of Meriden, CT, saves hers for banana bread by placing them in the freezer. Simply put the bananas in a plastic bag, seal, and freeze. When you're ready to use, just thaw until softened.

Protecting Nonstick Pans

In response to our previous tip about placing plastic coffee can lids between nonstick pans in a stack to protect their finishes, Joan Schulte of Edgerton, WI, pointed out that not everyone will have those lids available. Instead, she uses double sheets of paper towels, which everyone should have, between her pans.

Freezing Meat For Easy Slicing

When making recipes such as the Bok Choy and Chinese Egg Noodles with Spicy Beef Sauce in the January/February issue of *Cook's*, Associate Editor Adam Ried partially freezes the meat to make it easy to slice very thinly. For the thin steaks used in this particular recipe, two hours in the freezer usually does the trick.

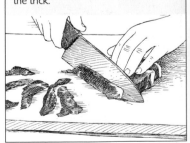

Send Us Your Tip We will provide a complimentary one-year subscription for each tip we print. See page 1 for information.

Shaping Lace Cookies Perfectly

Exact timing is crucial to successfully lift lace cookies off the pan and shape them before they harden and become brittle. Arlene Lentz of Santa Ana, CA, has a method that makes it easy to lift and manipulate the cookies while still hot. In addition, this method eliminates the need to move the hot cookies off the cookie sheet with a spatula, a process that often results in torn or bunched-up cookies.

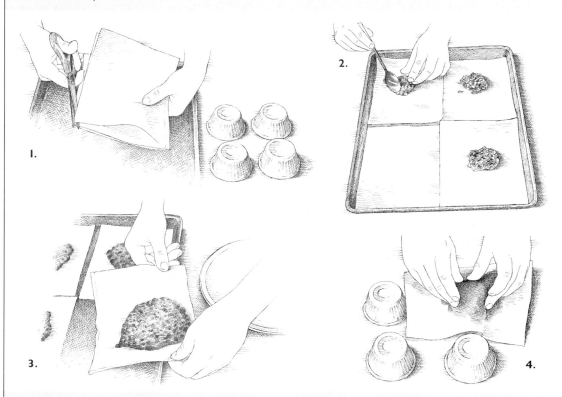

1. First, line up four upside-down ramekins or small bowls. Next, cut a sheet of parchment paper to fit the baking pan, and cut that sheet into four equal pieces.

2. Drop one tablespoon of batter onto the center of each piece of parchment and bake.

3. When the cookies come out of the oven, lift one of the parchment squares off the sheet and onto a plate to cool, leaving the other three on the hot pan to keep them warm and pliable.

4. When the cookie has cooled to the right consistency for molding, 30 to 60 seconds, pick up the parchment square, turn the cookie over, and lay it on the bottom of the bowl and shape it. Lift the parchment from the cookie. Cool the cookie completely, and then lift it off the bowl or ramekin.

Removing Tart Pan Rings

To free a baked tart from the ring of its pan, follow this tip from Roger Fillion of Chevy Chase, MD. Set a wide, stout can, such as a 28-ounce tomato can, on a flat surface and set the cooled tart and pan on the top of the can. Hold the pan ring and gently pull it downward—the can will support the pan base with the tart as you remove the ring.

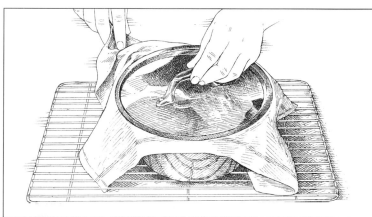

Preventing Soggy Mashed Potatoes

Having made our recipe for long-grain white rice, in which excess moisture is absorbed by a dishtowel placed between the pan and the lid, Sophie Green of Cambridge, MA, applied the same concept to a pot of mashed potatoes that was finished ahead of other dishes for the same meal. The towel absorbs the excess moisture created by the steam, preventing it from condensing on the pot lid and dripping down into the potatoes.

Ridding Artichokes of Their Thorns

Jon Candy of Loomis, CA, removes the thorns at the tips of artichoke leaves by holding the artichoke upside down (by the stem) and passing it quickly through the flame of a gas burner. The sharp points of the thorns will burn off almost instantly.

Quick, Long Cake Tester

When testing an especially deep or thick cake, such as a Bundt cake, for doneness, a toothpick will probably not be long enough. In its place, James Jengo of Rolling Hills Estates, CA, uses a strand of uncooked spaghetti.

Egg Slicer Redux

Linda Sebesta of Rochester, MN, recently suggested another good use of the common, everyday egg slicer. She uses the slicer to make perfect slices of strawberries (for shortcake), kiwi (as shown), or banana.

Two Ways with Cauliflower

Steaming brings out the fresh, sweet flavors, while browning
and braising intensify the nutty taste.

≥ BY EVA KATZ ≤

One of my most vivid childhood culinary memories is soggy, overcooked cauliflower flooded with congealing neon-yellow cheese. At that time, I was definitely only interested in the gooey cheese, and the cauliflower always got left on my plate. Until I started cooking for this article, my opinion of cauliflower had not really changed that much over the years. But after several days in the kitchen, I was pleased to discover that when properly cooked and imaginatively flavored, cauliflower can be nutty, slightly sweet, and absolutely delicious.

I spent those first few days trying to develop a quick stove-top method for cooking this sometimes overcooked vegetable. During my first round at the stove, I made two important observations. First, I noticed that cauliflower is very porous. This can work to cauliflower's advantage or disadvantage, depending on what the cauliflower absorbs during cooking. I identified two basic cooking methods that went hand-in-hand with this observation. In the first method the cauliflower is fully cooked (boiled, steamed, or microwaved), then flavored. In this scenario, keeping the water out is key. In the second method the cauliflower is flavored as it cooks, which means that you want to get liquid in. My new goal was to test the variables for both methods and devise two master recipes with plenty of creative variations.

Two Excellent Techniques

I first worked on perfecting the "cook first, flavor later" technique. In this method, the cauliflower is fully cooked by boiling, steaming, or microwaving, then tossed with a light vinaigrette or sautéed briefly in butter or oil with simple flavorings.

I began by comparing boiling, steaming, and microwaving. The boiled cauliflower tasted watery; regardless of how long I boiled it, from underdone to overcooked, the first flavor to reach my taste buds was the cooking water. The microwaved cauli-

Don't rely on the old test of slipping a knife into cooked cauliflower to test doneness; you have to actually sample a piece of the vegetable.

flower (cooked on full power for six minutes and left to stand for three minutes) had a sweet, nutty flavor, but some of the florets were perfectly cooked while others were seriously undercooked. Steaming the cauliflower for seven to eight minutes, on the other hand, produced evenly cooked florets with a clean, bright, sweet flavor.

To verify my strong impression that steamed cauliflower was less watery than the boiled version, I compared the raw and cooked weights of cauliflower cooked by each method. With steaming, there was no weight increase. With boiling, the cauliflower gained approximately ten percent of its original weight.

Next I moved to the "flavor while cooking" approach. The basic technique was braising, which involves cooking with a small amount of liquid in a covered container. I hoped that the cooking liquid—my foe in the previous method—would now become my friend. But I was curious as to how this was best done. Should the cauliflower simply be braised with no previous cooking? Or should it be sautéed first, then finished by braising? Or what about partially cooking via the steaming method and then braising?

After testing these three methods I immediately realized the benefits of sautéing the cauliflower first, then adding some flavorings and liquids and braising the vegetable until tender. Braising the dense vegetable with no pre-cooking simply took too long. Not only did I have to stand over the stove to make sure that it did not overcook, this method also created some of the same problems of liquid absorption that I had found when boiling. When I partially cooked the cauliflower by steaming it and then braised it, the taste was lackluster and flat. Sautéing it for seven minutes on medium high heat and then braising it, however, intensified the cauliflower's naturally mild flavors. Not only did the cauliflower absorb the flavors from the braising liquid, but the browned cauliflower also tasted wonderfully smoky and earthy.

Cauliflower Tips

Cooking cauliflower too long can release unpleasant sulfur-containing compounds in the vegetable that break down when exposed to heat. To avoid this problem, I found it best to cut the cauliflower into one-inch pieces which cook quite quickly. With the brown-and-braise method, I also liked how the cut surface of the florets lay flat in my sauté pan. Those cut surfaces browned beautifully and the sweetness of those florets was pronounced.

I also discovered that just because a tip of a knife slipped in and out the stem of the cauliflower easily did not necessarily mean the cauliflower was done. The best way to test for doneness is quite simply to sample a piece.

MASTER RECIPE FOR STEAMED
CAULIFLOWER
SERVES 4

The best complement to the fresh, delicate flavor of steamed cauliflower are mild seasonings, including dill, basil, nuts, and citrus, or simple flavor combinations such as those below.

1   **medium head cauliflower, trimmed, cored,
    florets cut according to illustrations 1
    through 4, page 7 (about 6 cups)**

Fit large saucepan with steamer basket; fill with enough water to reach just below the bottom of basket. Bring water to boil over high heat; add florets to basket. Reduce heat to medium; cover and steam until cauliflower is tender but still offers some resistance to the tooth when sampled, 7 to 8 minutes. Remove cauliflower from basket and serve or finish with one of the next two recipes.

STEAMED CAULIFLOWER WITH
DILL-WALNUT VINAIGRETTE
SERVES 4

- 1 teaspoon Dijon mustard
- 1 tablespoon red wine vinegar
- 1 tablespoon juice from one small lemon
- 1/2 medium shallot or scallion, minced
- 2 tablespoons minced fresh dill
- 2 tablespoons olive oil
  Salt and ground black pepper
- 1/2 cup toasted walnuts, chopped medium (about 1/3 cup)
- 1 recipe Steamed Cauliflower (*see* above)

Whisk first six ingredients (mustard through oil) in small bowl, plus salt and pepper to taste. Toss dressing immediately with walnuts and warm cauliflower; adjust seasonings and serve.

STEAMED CAULIFLOWER WITH BREAD
CRUMBS, CAPERS, AND CHOPPED EGG
SERVES 4

- 2 tablespoons butter
- 3 tablespoons dry bread crumbs
- 1 recipe Steamed Cauliflower (*see* above)
- 1 1/2 tablespoons juice from one small lemon
- 2 tablespoons minced fresh parsley leaves
- 2 tablespoons capers
- 1 hard boiled egg, pressed through a sieve to crumble very fine
  Salt and ground black pepper

Heat butter in large skillet over medium heat until foaming, about 1 1/2 minutes. Add bread crumbs; cook, stirring occasionally, until lightly browned, about 5 minutes. Add cauliflower; cook to heat through, about 1 minute. Add lemon juice, parsley, capers, and egg; toss lightly to distribute. Season to taste with salt and ground black pepper; serve immediately.

BROWNED AND BRAISED CAULIFLOWER
WITH GARLIC, GINGER, AND SOY
SERVES 4

The stronger flavor of browned cauliflower stands up well to bolder, more complex flavor combinations, such as the Asian flavorings.

- 1 1/2 tablespoons canola oil
- 1 medium head cauliflower, trimmed, cored, and florets cut according to illustrations 1 through 4, below
- 1 teaspoon Asian sesame oil
- 2 medium garlic cloves, minced
- 2 tablespoons minced fresh gingerroot
- 2 tablespoons soy sauce
- 1 tablespoon dry sherry
- 2 tablespoons rice vinegar
- 2 medium scallions, white and green parts, minced
  Ground black pepper

1. Heat large skillet over medium-high heat until pan is very hot, 3 to 4 minutes. Add canola oil, swirling pan to coat evenly. Add florets; sauté, stirring occasionally, until they begin to brown, 6 to 7 minutes.

2. Make a well in center of pan; add sesame oil, garlic, and ginger. Mash and stir garlic-ginger mixture in center of pan with rubber spatula until fragrant, about 1 minute. Stir to combine garlic-ginger mixture with cauliflower; sauté 30 seconds more. Reduce heat to low and add soy, sherry, vinegar, and 1/4 cup water. Cover and cook until florets are fully tender but still offer some resistance to the tooth when sampled, 4 to 5 minutes. Add scallions and toss lightly to distribute.

Season to taste with ground black pepper; serve immediately.

BROWNED AND BRAISED CAULIFLOWER
WITH INDIAN SPICES
SERVES 4

This is adapted from the recipe for Ful Gobi in Elizabeth Rozin's book *The Flavor Principle* (Hawthorne Books, 1973).

- 1 1/2 tablespoons canola oil
- 1 medium head cauliflower, trimmed, cored, and florets cut according to illustrations 1 through 4, below
- 1/2 medium onion, sliced thin
- 1 teaspoon ground cumin
- 1 teaspoon ground coriander
- 1 teaspoon ground turmeric
- 1/4 teaspoon hot red pepper flakes
- 1 tablespoon juice from one small lime
- 1/4 cup plain yogurt
- 1/4 cup chopped fresh cilantro leaves
- 1/2 cup frozen green peas, thawed (optional)
  Salt and ground black pepper

1. Heat large skillet over medium-high heat until pan is very hot, 3 to 4 minutes. Add canola oil, swirling pan to coat evenly. Add florets; sauté, stirring occasionally, until they just begin to soften, 2 to 3 minutes. Add onions; continue sautéing until florets begin to brown and onions soften, about 4 minutes longer.

2. Stir in cumin, coriander, turmeric, and pepper flakes; sauté until spices begin to toast and are fragrant, 1 to 2 minutes. Reduce heat to low and add lime juice, yogurt, and 1/4 cup water. Cover and cook until flavors meld, about 4 minutes. Add cilantro and peas (if using), toss to distribute, cover and sauté until florets are fully tender but still offer some resistance to the tooth when sampled, about 2 minutes more. Season to taste with salt and black pepper; serve immediately.

STEP-BY-STEP | CUTTING CAULIFLOWER INTO FLORETS

1. First, pull off all the outer leaves from the cauliflower and trim off the stem near the base of the head.

2. Next, turn the cauliflower upside down so the stem is facing up. Using a sharp knife, cut around the core to remove it.

3. Separate the individual florets from the inner stem using the tip of a chef's knife.

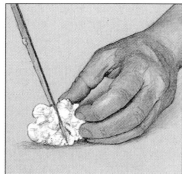

4. Cut the florets in half or quarters if necessary so that individual pieces are about one inch long.

Making Great Chili

The secret is using large cubes of beef chuck and a mixture of fresh and oven-roasted chiles.

⇒ BY ADAM RIED ⇐

In many parts of America, chili-making is a highly contentious matter. Cooks with prized personal recipes debate and tinker with every aspect of this seemingly simple dish, so the path to developing your own formula can be twisty. In fact, before arriving at the recipe in this piece, I made almost sixty pots of chili, consulted expert home and professional cooks, hit the road for Texas (where I sampled not just chili, but my first tastes of rattlesnake and wild boar), and journeyed into the thriving grassroots culture of devoted chiliheads and their competition cook-offs.

The work began with extensive recipe research and testing of recipes of different styles. Defined in the broadest possible sense, chili con carne consists of meat, dried red chiles, and liquid, more often than not seasoned with garlic, cumin, and oregano. But, of course, it's not that easy. My research turned up numerous distinct styles of chili, the most prevalent of which were from Texas, New Mexico, the Midwest, and Cincinnati.

Countless variations exist within each style, but generally speaking, Texas chili depends on either pureed or powdered ancho chile, uses beef, excludes tomato, onion, and beans, and features a high proportion of meat to chiles. New Mexican chili relies on different local varieties of dried New Mexico chiles, uses pork, and tends toward a relatively high proportion of chiles to meat. New Mexico is also known for chile verde, a meat and vegetable stew seasoned heavily with roasted fresh New Mexico chiles. Midwestern chili is based on ground beef, includes beans, lots of tomato, onion, and bell pepper, and is seasoned relatively mildly with chili powder. Last, Cincinnati chili includes sweet spices such as cinnamon, nutmeg, and allspice, and is served, heavily garnished, over noodles.

I felt strongly about narrowing my focus, and it was the Texas style that hit closest to home for me. My tasters and I agreed that the flavor combination of ancho chile and beef was satisfying and familiar, and that this would be the starting point for the testing of chile, meat, liquid, and spice that lay ahead. In my view, there was no reason for beans to be part of the chili; like most Texans, I prefer mine on the side. The chili I envisioned would be hearty, heavy on the meat, with a clear, multidimensional chile flavor, spici-

Our chili is beanless but a side dish of pinto or kidney beans is a good accompaniment.

ness without overwhelming heat, and a creamy consistency somewhere between soup and stew. The flavors would be balanced so that no single spice or seasoning stood out or competed with the chile. I was shooting for a chili with a vibrant, but not loud, character.

Chiles, the Central Question

Toward the beginning of my chili inquiry, I spent a weekend judging the International Chili Society's 1997 Massachusetts and Connecticut state chili cook-offs. Despite their rowdy joie de vivre, these die-hard chiliheads were seasoned, determined competitors, all vying for a chance to cook for a $25,000 prize in the world championship cookoff in Reno, Nevada. Not only did I sample more than fifty chilis in two days, I also

learned that some of the competitors blended up to nine types of chile, sometimes including commercial chili powders pre-blended with salt, garlic, cumin, and oregano, for their brews.

Because chiles are the heart of chili con carne, I had to learn about the different types. A nine-chile mixture, however, was far beyond my needs. I skipped over the more esoteric varieties and studied only those mentioned repeatedly in my research. What's more, I wanted to settle on no more than two of the most widely available for my recipe, so any home cook could easily make it. After considerable testing and tasting (*see* "Choosing the Chiles," page 9), I settled on a combination of ancho and New Mexico for the dried chiles, with a few jalapeños added for their fresh flavor and bite.

There was little question in my mind that toasting the dried chiles before preparing them would enhance their flavor, and it did. Chilis made with toasted chiles tasted noticeably fuller and warmer than those made with chiles left untoasted. The two main toasting methods were oven and skillet, and after trying both, I went with the oven simply because it required less attention and effort than skillet toasting. The chiles will puff in the oven, become fragrant, and dry out sufficiently after five to six minutes. One caveat, though: Overtoasted chiles can take on a distinctly bitter flavor, so don't let them go too long.

With the chiles chosen and toasted, the next big question was the best way to prepare them. The two options here were to either rehydrate the chiles in liquid and process them into a puree, or to grind them into a powder. It didn't take long for me to decide that I was a fan of the grinding method. It was easier, faster, and much less messy than making the puree, which all of my tasters and I felt produced a chili that was simply too rich, more like a Mexican enchilada sauce than a bowl of chili.

This felt like the right time to determine the best ratio of chile to meat. Many of the research recipes suggested that one tablespoon of ground chile per pound of meat was sufficient, but all of my tasters and I found these chilis to be bland and watery. Three tablespoons per pound of meat, on the other hand, produced chili with too much punch and richness. Two tablespoons per pound was the way to go.

In neither the interviews with chili cooks nor the research recipes was there much agreement about when the chili powder should be added to the chili. This is when I decided to borrow a technique from Stephanie Lyness, who discovered when making curries (see "Curry Demystified," January/February 1997) that sautéing the spices, including the chiles, was key to the success of that dish. Sautéing the chiles along with the onions deepened and developed the chile flavor. The only problem I encountered with this technique was the tendency of the chiles to scorch before adding the liquid to the pot. The solution to this problem came from Jay McCarthy, chef and owner of Jay's Mesteña in San Antonio. As I raced with Jay to a seven-course cactus dinner that he was hosting at the San Antonio Botanical Gardens, he mentioned off-handedly his trick of blending the chili powder with tequila. Though I wasn't sure that tequila had a place in my recipe, I did reason that blending the chili powder with water to make a paste might protect it from scorching in the pot, and it did.

Building Block Basics

Traveling around Texas, a state where chili is serious business (to wit, the highway billboard just north of San Antonio advertising an annual chili cook-off called the "Chilimpiad"), I found that while beasts from rattlesnake to buffalo find their way into the chili pot, the most typical choice is beef. Pork also appeared in some regional chilis, so I tried both. I distinctly preferred the beef. Pork was too mild and sweet for me, whereas the beef was rich and robust. Nothing was gained by blending the two, either.

Though my research recipes cited plenty of different beef cuts as the best for chili, I went with the findings of fellow *Cook's* editors Pam Anderson and Chris Kimball in their articles "Simple, Satisfying Beef Stew" (January/February 1996) and "How to Roast a Cheap Cut of Beef" (September/October 1996) and stuck with chuck.

There were still, however, aspects of the meat question yet to settle. Should the chuck be standard hamburger grind, coarser chili grind, hand-cut into tiny cubes, or a combination? The chili made from small cubes of beef was far more appealing than those made from either type of ground beef; they both had a grainy, extruded texture. Most of my research recipes specified that the meat should be, in the words of Maine food writers John and Matt Lewis Thorne, "... cut into the smallest pieces you have patience for." But I increased the size of the cubes from one-quarter to one inch after a visit to the Texas Chili Parlor in Austin, where they use a combination of ground beef and large, one-inch chunks. I still didn't care for the ground beef, but the larger chunks were great, substantial, and satisfying to chew. In addition, cutting a chuck roast into larger chunks was much, much faster and easier than breaking it down into a fussy, quarter-inch dice.

Next I set out to determine the best type, or types, of liquid for chili. The main contenders were water, chicken stock, beef stock, beer, black coffee, and red wine. I tried each one on its own, as well as in any combination I felt made sense. The surprise result was that I liked plain water best because it allowed the flavor of the chiles to come through in full force. Both stocks, whether on their own, combined in equal parts with each other, or with water, muddied the chile flavors. All of the other liquids, either alone, or mixed with an equal part of chicken stock or water, competed with the chile flavor. Though I was alone among my tasters in this opinion, I liked

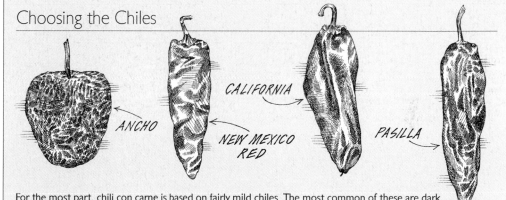

Choosing the Chiles

ANCHO

CALIFORNIA

NEW MEXICO RED

PASILLA

For the most part, chili con carne is based on fairly mild chiles. The most common of these are dark, mahogany red, wrinkly-skinned **ancho chiles,** which have a deep, sweet, raisiny flavor; **New Mexico Reds,** which have a smooth, shiny, brick-red skin and a crisp, slightly acidic, weedy, earthy flavor; **California chiles,** which are very similar to New Mexico in appearance but have a slightly milder flavor; and long, shiny, smooth, dark brown pasilla chiles. **Pasillas,** which are a little hotter than the other three varieties, have grapey, herby flavor notes, and, depending on the region of the country, are often packaged and sold as either ancho or mulato chiles.

My tasters and I sampled each of these types, as well as a selection of pre-blended commercial powders, alone and in various combinations in batches of chili. Though the individual chiles tasted much purer and fresher than any of the pre-mixed powders, they nonetheless seemed one-dimensional on their own. When all was said and done, the two-chile combination we favored was equal parts ancho, for its earthy, fruity sweetness and the stunning deep red color it imparted to the chili, and New Mexico, for its lighter flavor and crisp acidity.

Chile heat was another factor to consider. Hotter dried chiles that appear regularly in chili include guajillo, de Arbol, pequin, japonais, and cayenne. Though I did not want to develop a fiery, overly hot chili, I did want a subtle bite to give the dish some oomph. My counselor on the topic of heat and its application in chili was Cambridge cook Larry Flynt, a southwestern transplant to Massachusetts. "Initially," said Larry as we made our first batch of chili together, "I'll go conservative and undershoot the heat. Then, tasting as I go, I'll build layers of flavor and heat by using different types of chiles." Aside from using dark dried chiles for earthy sweetness and lighter dried chiles for brightness, Larry was a big believer in using some fresh chiles to add heat and a slight vegetal flavor. I followed his lead on this, mincing three jalapeño chiles and adding them to the pot with the garlic, and found that it added not just heat, but freshness and vitality to my chili. Because chili with three jalapeños was good, I tried a batch with five, and that was even better. I also tested roasting the jalapeños before adding them to the chili, but found that they lost some of the herby, green, vegetal flavor tones that they provided when raw. —A.R.

the combination of water and red wine. Another taster commented that it was like Boeuf Bourginon a la chili, but I thought it sweetened the chili in an interesting and complex way. Yuppie though it sounds, you may want to give it a try some time.

Another basic factor to determine was the right amount and type of garlic. Tasters agreed that three cloves was too little and eight was too much, so I settled on five cloves for my recipe. I was shocked to find that many of the research recipes called for powdered garlic rather than fresh, and even stranger, many of the competition chili cooks whom I interviewed also relied on it. Out of obligation, I tested the powdered garlic versus the fresh. Suffice it to say that I'll stick with fresh garlic in my chili.

Though common in modern recipes, Texas chili lore leaves tomatoes and onions out of the original formula. These two ingredients may break with tradition, but to my palate, chili wouldn't be chili without them. The acidity of tomato and the sweetness of onion, both in small amounts, add interest and dimension to chili. The batches I tested without them were decidedly dull. I tested various amounts and types of tomato products and determined that more than one cup of tomato pushed the flavor of the chili toward that of spaghetti sauce. Products with a smooth consistency, such as canned crushed or plain tomato sauce helped create the smooth sauce I wanted in my dish.

I also tested the onion, and like the garlic before it, found that I favored a moderate amount, one cup, of fresh onion to larger amounts or dehydrated onion.

Over a dinner based on wild game at his Austin restaurant, Hudson's on the Bend, executive chef and owner Jeff Blank inspired another flavor refinement. Among Jeff's other "secret" chili ingredients, his recipe called for bacon. I checked out the bacon idea when I got back to the test kitchen and found that it does, indeed, provide a subtly sweet, smoky essence to the chili that is most welcome.

An astonishing array of oddball flavorings showed up in my research. Some ingredients are added to give chilis various ethnic bents, including rum, pineapple juice, raisins, and coriander for Jamaican chili; a curry spice blend for Ethiopian chili; or orange zest and fennel for Mediterranean chili. But other ingredients appear, individually and somewhat arbitrarily, in familiar American chili recipes. The list included, but was in no way limited to, sweeteners such as honey, maple syrup, brown sugar, and Coke; herbs and spices such as woodruff, caraway, and

anise; and flavorings such as Sauternes, soy sauce, anchovy, mustard, chocolate, ginger, and peanut butter. Even Velveeta reared its head in a recipe. Curiosity got the best of me in this arena, so I tried chilis with Coke, which imparted a sourish, off taste; brown sugar, which cut the heat of the chiles too much; and cilantro, which added freshness and complemented the other flavors. I also tested a chili made with a one-ounce square of unsweetened baking chocolate, which I actually liked because it gave the chili a somewhat rounder, deeper flavor. Another surprise winner in this category was peanut butter. This was suggested by Texas chef Matt Martinez, Jr., because it, like the chocolate, ties chili to an early Mexican influence, mole sauce, which is made of nuts and seeds, among other things. A mere two teaspoons of peanut butter gave the chili a subtle, pleasant earthiness and notably creamy texture. I consider both unsweetened chocolate and peanut butter good additions, but not mandatory.

The Unexpected Importance of Thickening

Through most of my testing, I kept wondering why so many chili recipes called for a thickener to "tighten" the sauce at the end. So far, I had found that evaporation was producing a perfectly acceptable texture. Then I absentmindedly added an extra two cups of water to one of my test batches. Two hours later the meat was tender and flavorful, but still floating in a sea of chili liquid, so for the first time in the testing, I thickened the sauce with cornstarch, and the results were fantastic. The thicker consistency was smoother, softer, and more appealing than any before it.

A few more thickening tests, including flour, roux, cornstarch, and masa harina (a flour ground from lime-treated corn), helped refine my approach. Dredging the meat in flour before

browning and adding a roux along with the liquid were both effective, but made it more difficult to tailor the consistency of the finished product because both were introduced early in the cooking process. Roux added at the end of the cooking left a faint taste of raw flour. I did prefer thickening at the end of cooking, though, because I could control the consistency by adding thickener gradually until it was at the right stage. I like chili thick enough to coat the back of a wooden spoon, like the custard base of homemade ice cream.

My first choice for thickening was masa harina,

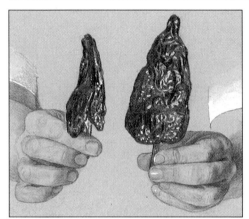

1. Dried chile pods toasted in a 350-degree oven for about 6 minutes become fragrant and puffed (right).

2. When cool enough to handle, remove stems and seeds from the pods, rip them into pieces, and process until powdery, 30 to 45 seconds.

added at the end of cooking. Masa both thickened and imparted a slightly sweet, earthy corn flavor to the chili. If masa harina is not available in your grocery store and you'd rather not mail-order it, use a cornstarch and water slurry. It brings no flavor to the chili, but it is predictable, easy to use, and gives the gravy a silky consistency and attractive sheen.

One last note. Time and time again, my tasters observed that chili, like many stews, always improved after an overnight rest because the flavors blended and mellowed. So if you have the chance, cook yours a day ahead. The result will be worth the wait.

CHILI CON CARNE
SERVES 6

To ensure the best chile flavor, I recommend toasting whole dried chiles and grinding them in a mini-chopper or spice-dedicated coffee grinder, all of which takes only ten (very well-spent) minutes. Select dried chiles that are moist and pliant, like dried fruit. Count on trimming one-half to a full pound of waste from your chuck roast, so start with a four-pound roast to end up with three to three-and-a-half pounds of beef cubes. For hotter chili, boost the heat with a pinch of cayenne, a dash of hot pepper sauce, or crumbled pequin chiles near the end of cooking. Serve the chili with any of the following side dishes: warm pinto or kidney beans, corn bread or chips, corn tortillas or tamales, rice, biscuits, or just plain crackers, and top with any of the following garnishes: chopped fresh cilantro leaves, minced white onion, diced avocado, shredded cheddar or jack cheese, or sour cream.

    3   tablespoons ancho chili powder or 3 medium
        pods (about ½ ounce), toasted and ground
        (*see* illustrations 1 and 2, page 10)
    3   tablespoons New Mexico chili powder or
        3 medium pods (about ¾ ounce), toasted and
        ground (*see* illustrations 1 and 2, page 10)
    2   tablespoons cumin seeds, toasted in a dry skillet
        over medium heat until fragrant, about
        4 minutes, and ground
    2   teaspoons dried oregano, preferably Mexican
    ½   cup water
    1   4-pound beef chuck roast, trimmed of excess fat
        and cut into 1-inch cubes
    2   teaspoons salt, plus extra for seasoning
    8   ounces bacon (7 or 8 slices), cut into
        ¼-inch pieces
    1   medium onion, minced (about 1 cup)
    5   medium garlic cloves, minced
  4-5   small jalapeño chile peppers, cored, seeded,
        and minced
    1   cup canned crushed tomatoes or plain
        tomato sauce
    2   tablespoons juice from 1 medium lime
    5   tablespoons masa harina or 3 tablespoons
        cornstarch
        Ground black pepper

1. Mix chili powders, cumin, and oregano in small bowl and stir in ½ cup water to form thick paste; set aside. Toss beef cubes with salt; set aside.

2. Fry bacon in large, heavy soup kettle or Dutch oven over medium-low heat until fat renders and bacon crisps, about 10 minutes. Remove bacon with slotted spoon to paper towel-lined plate; pour all but 2 teaspoons fat from pot into small bowl; set aside. Increase heat to medium-high; sauté meat in four batches until well-browned on all sides, about 5 minutes per batch, adding additional 2 teaspoons bacon fat to pot as necessary. Reduce heat to medium, add 3 tablespoons bacon fat to now-empty pan. Add onion; sauté until softened, 5 to 6 minutes. Add garlic and jalapeño; sauté until fragrant, about 1 minute. Add chili paste; sauté until fragrant, 2 to 3 minutes. Add reserved bacon and browned beef, crushed tomatoes or tomato sauce, lime juice, and 7 cups water; bring to simmer. Continue to cook at a steady simmer until meat is tender and juices are dark, rich, and starting to thicken, about 2 hours.

3. Mix masa harina with ⅔ cup water (or cornstarch with 3 tablespoons water) in a small bowl to form smooth paste. Increase heat to medium; stir in paste and simmer until thickened, 5 to 10 minutes. Adjust seasoning generously with salt and ground black pepper. Serve immediately, or preferably, cool slightly, cover, and refrigerate overnight or for up to 5 days. Reheat before serving.

SMOKY CHIPOTLE CHILI CON CARNE
SERVES 6

Grill-smoking the meat, a technique from food writers John and Matt Lewis Thorne, authors of the *Serious Pig* (North Point Press, 1996), in combination with chipotle chiles give this chili a distinct but not overwhelming, smoky flavor. Make sure you start with a chuck roast that is at least three inches thick. The grilling is meant to flavor the meat by searing the surface and smoking it lightly, not to cook it.

1. *To prepare meat:* Puree 4 medium garlic cloves with two teaspoons salt. Rub intact chuck roast with puree, and sprinkle evenly with 2 to 3 tablespoons New Mexico chili powder; cover and set aside. Meanwhile, build hot fire. When you can hold your hand 5 inches above grill surface for no more than 3 seconds, spread hot coals to area about the size of roast. Open bottom grill vents, scatter one cup soaked mesquite or hickory wood chips over hot coals, and set grill rack in place. Grill roast over hot coals, opening lid vents three-quarters of the way and covering so that vents are opposite bottom vents to draw smoke through and around roast. Sear meat until all sides are dark and richly colored, about 12 minutes per side. Remove roast to bowl; when cool to the touch, trim and cut into 1-inch cubes, reserving juices.

2. *For the chili:* Follow recipe for chili con carne, omitting the browning of the beef cubes and substituting 5 minced canned chipotle peppers in adobo sauce for jalapeños.

How Come You Don't Think It's Hot?

One enduring mystery among those partial to spicy food is why people have such varying tolerances for the heat of chile peppers. As it turns out, there are several reasons why your dinner companion may find a bowl of chili only mildly spicy while the same dish causes you to frantically summon a waiter for a glass of milk to cool the heat before you expire.

Your dining partner may be experiencing "temporary desensitization." This phenomenon, discovered by Barry Green of the Monell Chemical Senses Institute in Philadelphia, occurs when you eat something spicy hot, then lay off for a few minutes. "As long as you keep eating chiles, their effect keeps building," Green explained in a telephone interview. "But take a break—even as little as two to five minutes, depending on the individual—and when you go back to them, you are desensitized." In other words, a dish with the same amount of chiles will not seem as hot the second time around.

The most likely explanation, however, is that people who find chiles intensely, punishingly hot simply have more taste buds. According to Linda Bartoshuk, a psychophysicist at the Yale School of Medicine, humans can be neatly divided into three distinct categories when it comes to tasting ability: unfortunate "nontasters," pedestrian "medium tasters," and the aristocrats of the taste bud world, "supertasters" (*see* artist's representation, below).

This taste detection pecking order appears to correspond directly to the number of taste buds a person possesses, a genetically pre-determined trait which may vary by a factor of one hundred. Indeed, so radical is the difference among these three types that Bartoshuk speaks of them as inhabiting different "taste worlds."

Bartoshuk and her colleagues discovered the extent of this phenomenon a few years ago when they carried out experiments using a blue dye that turns the entire mouth blue except for the taste papillae (structures housing taste buds and other sensory receptors). After painting the front part of subjects' tongues with the dye, they were rather stunned at the differences they saw.

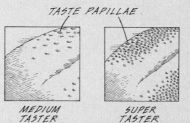

TASTE PAPILLAE

MEDIUM TASTER

SUPER TASTER

"We discovered, to our amazement, that a young male nontaster had eleven taste buds per square centimeter, while our best supertaster, a woman of the same age, had 1,100 taste buds in that same area," Bartoshuk recalls.

Further experiments confirmed that the ability to taste intensely was in direct proportion to the number of taste buds. Bartoshuk also found a rather startling sex difference. Women fell into all three categories of tasters, but in each category they are higher than men in numbers of taste buds, with about half being medium tasters, and over one-third being supertasters. In men, about 60 percent are medium tasters, and only 15 percent are supertasters.

So what does this have to do with how hot you find chiles? Well, it turns out that every taste bud in the mouth has a pain receptor literally wrapped around it. Along with extra taste buds comes an extra ability to feel pain. As a result, observed Bartashuk, "Super-tasters may have the capacity to experience 50 percent more pain from capsaicin, the chemical that gives chiles their heat."

–John Willoughby

Foolproof Chicken and Rice

Here is how to solve the twin problems of unevenly cooked chicken and heavy, greasy rice.

⇒ BY CHRISTOPHER KIMBALL WITH EVA KATZ ⇐

By reducing the liquid and stirring the rice during cooking, we managed to get fluffy, nongreasy rice.

Although there is no specific American tradition for a dish called "chicken and rice," its appeal is obvious: It's a one-dish supper, it's easy, and it's eminently variable. Yet, after having made a dozen attempts at perfecting this recipe, we found two major problems: The white meat tends to dry out before the dark meat is cooked, and the rice is often heavy and greasy.

First, we tackled the problem of overcooked breast meat. It turned out that the solution was rather simple. By adding the breast meat to the dish fifteen minutes after the thighs and legs, both cooked perfectly. Of course, one could make this dish with just dark or light meat but, like most cooks, I am more likely to have a whole chicken on hand than just thighs or breasts. In addition, my family of five has different taste preferences encompassing both kinds of meat.

The texture of the rice, however, was a more vexing issue. Our first thought was to reduce the amount of olive oil in which the chicken and onion are sautéed from two tablespoons to one. But this simply was not enough fat to get the job done, and the resulting rice was only fractionally less greasy. We thought that perhaps the chicken

skin was the culprit, but after making this dish with skinless chicken pieces, we were surprised to find that the rice was still heavy and the chicken, as we suspected, was tough and chewy without the skin to protect it during initial sautéing.

We then thought that perhaps reducing the amount of liquid would produce less-sodden rice. For one-and-one-half cups of long-grain white rice, we were using an equal amount of chicken stock plus two cups of water. We tried reducing the stock to a mere one-half cup; the rice was indeed less sodden, but the layer of rice on top was undercooked and dried out. Fortunately, this problem, too, was rather easily solved. We found that stirring the dish once when adding the breast meat, so that the rice on top was stirred into the bottom, produced more even cooking.

Next we made four different batches using different liquids: chicken stock (heavy rice); water (bland and flat tasting); a combination of wine and water (the acidity of the wine cuts through the fat, producing clean, clear flavors); and a combination of water, chopped canned tomatoes, and tomato liquid (the acid in the tomatoes punches up and enriches flavor). Learning from these tests, we tried a combination of white wine,

water, chopped canned tomatoes, and tomato liquid, with excellent results.

Finally, we tested different varieties of rice to see which held up best to this sort of cooking. A basic long-grain white rice was fine, with good flavor and decent texture; a medium-grain rice was creamy, with a risotto-like texture and excellent flavor (I found this version too heavy for my taste but others on the tasting panel overlooked the dense texture for the improved flavor); basmati rice was nutty, with separate, light grains (this was by far the lightest version but the basmati rice seemed somewhat out of place in such a pedestrian dish although well suited to the Indian Spice variation); and converted rice, which was absolutely tasteless although virtually indestructable (the tasting panel agreed that because converted rice is tasteless it is also worthless). So, while medium-grain and basmati rices have good results, we preferred basic long-grain white rice for this all-purpose dish.

MASTER RECIPE FOR CHICKEN AND RICE WITH TOMATOES, WHITE WINE, AND PARSLEY
SERVES 4

Though we rarely suggest stirring rice while it cooks, in this dish it is necessary, or the top layer might dry out or be undercooked. If you prefer, substitute two pounds of breast meat or boneless thighs for the pieces of a whole chicken.

1	chicken (3 to 4 pounds) rinsed, patted dry, and cut into 8 pieces, wings reserved for another use
	Salt and ground black pepper
2	tablespoons olive oil
1	medium onion, chopped fine
3	cloves garlic, minced very fine
1 1/2	cups long-grain white rice
1	can (14 1/2-ounces) diced tomatoes, drained (about 1 cup) and 1/2 cup liquid reserved
1/2	cup white wine
1	teaspoon salt
1/3	cup chopped fresh parsley leaves

1. Sprinkle chicken pieces liberally on both sides with salt and ground black pepper. Heat oil until shimmering in large, heavy, non-reactive Dutch oven over high heat. Add chicken pieces skin side down; cook, without moving them, until well browned, about 6 minutes. Turn chicken pieces over with tongs and cook, again without

moving them, until well browned on second side, about 6 minutes longer. Remove from pot and set aside.

2. Pour all but 2 tablespoons fat from pot; return to burner. Reduce heat to medium; add onion and sauté, stirring frequently, until softened, about 3 to 4 minutes. Add garlic and sauté until fragrant, approximately 1 minute longer.

Stir in rice and cook, stirring frequently, until coated and glistening, about 1 minute longer. Add tomatoes with reserved liquid, wine, salt, and 2 cups water, scraping browned bits off pot bottom with wooden spoon. Return chicken thighs and legs to pot; bring to boil. Reduce heat to low, cover, and simmer gently for 15 minutes. Add chicken breast pieces and stir ingredients

gently until rice is thoroughly mixed; replace cover and simmer until both rice and chicken are tender, 10 to 15 minutes longer. Stir in parsley, cover pot, and allow dish to rest for 5 minutes; serve immediately.

CHICKEN AND RICE WITH SAFFRON, PEAS, AND PAPRIKA
SERVES 4

Brown chicken as directed in recipe for Chicken and Rice with Tomatoes, White Wine, and Parsley. In step 2, along with onion, sauté 1 medium green bell pepper, cored, seeded, and cut into medium dice. Along with garlic, add 4 teaspoons paprika and ¼ teaspoon saffron and sauté until fragrant, about 1 minute. Continue with Master Recipe, stirring 1 cup thawed frozen peas into pot along with parlsey.

CHICKEN AND RICE WITH CHILE, CILANTRO, AND LIME
SERVES 4

Brown chicken as directed in recipe for Chicken and Rice with Tomatoes, White Wine and Parsley. In step 2, along with onion, sauté 2 jalapeño chiles, cored, seeded, and minced. Along with garlic, add 2 teaspoons each ground cumin and coriander, and 1 teaspoon chili powder and sauté until fragrant, about 1 minute. Continue with Master Recipe, substituting ¼ cup chopped fresh cilantro leaves and 3 tablespoons juice from one lime for parsley.

CHICKEN AND RICE WITH INDIAN SPICES
SERVES 4

Brown chicken as directed in recipe for Chicken and Rice with Tomatoes, White Wine, and Parsley. At the beginning of step 2, sauté one 3-inch piece cinnamon stick, stirring with wooden spoon, until it unfurls, about 15 seconds, before adding onion and 2 medium green bell peppers, cored, seeded, and cut into medium dice; sauté until onion and peppers are just soft, 5 to 6 minutes. Along with garlic, add 1 teaspoon each ground turmeric, coriander, and cumin. Continue with Master Recipe, omitting parsley.

CHICKEN AND RICE WITH ANCHOVIES, OLIVES, AND LEMON
SERVES 4

Brown chicken as directed in recipe for Chicken and Rice with Tomatoes, White Wine and Parsley. In step 2, along with onion, sauté 5 minced anchovy fillets. Continue with master recipe, adding 1 teaspoon minced lemon zest and 1 tablespoon juice from one small lemon and ½ cup imported black olives, pitted and halved, along with parsley.

STEP-BY-STEP | CUTTING A WHOLE CHICKEN

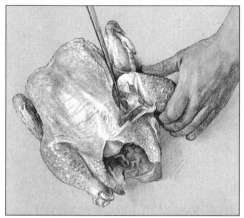

1. With a sharp chef's knife, cut through the skin around the leg where it attaches to the breast.

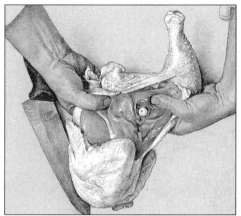

2. Using both hands, pop each leg out of its socket

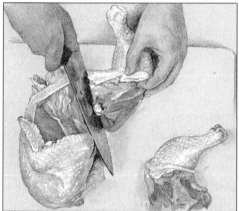

3. Use your chef's knife to cut through the flesh and skin to detach each leg from the body.

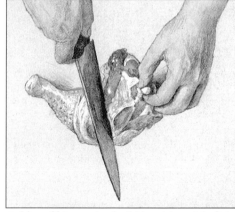

4. A line of fat separates the thigh and drumstick. Cut through the joint at this point.

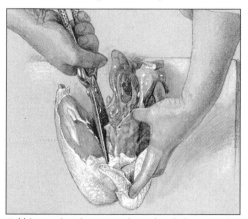

5. Using poultry sheers, cut down the ribs between the back and the breast to totally separate the back and wings from the breast.

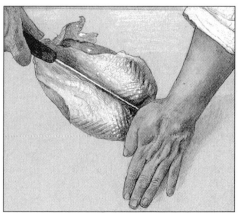

6. Place a chef's knife directly on the breast bone, then apply pressure to cut through the bone and separate the breasts.

Oven-Poaching Salmon

This simple method of poaching a whole salmon requires only aluminum foil and an oven.

⋛ BY MARK BITTMAN ⋛

I thought that poaching a whole salmon of, say, five or six pounds was a fairly straightforward task until I tried to get it right. As is so often the case, my first question was about money and space: Was I really ready to spend $80 for a fish poacher I might use once or twice a year? And, if I was, where was I going to put it on the remaining 363 days?

I decided to tackle the project without the aid of a poacher, figuring maybe something would happen that would convince me that the new hardware was unnecessary. Sure enough, it did.

Until now, I had cheated when I poached salmon: I simply cut the head and tail off the fish, or even cut it into a couple of large sections—whatever I deemed it necessary to get the fish to fit in my largest roasting pot. I'd fill the pot with water and seasonings, add the fish, bring it to a boil, cover, and turn off the heat. About thirty minutes later, the fish was done.

I liked this method, which I considered reliable enough to include in my book *Fish: The Complete Guide to Buying and Cooking* (Macmillian, 1994), but it only works if your style of entertaining is similar to my own: you don't really care how things look, only how they taste. A real poached salmon, of course, ought to be a lovely whole fish, which you can decorate with cucumber slices and dill, and which you can proudly display to all comers. Whacking the fish up into two or three pieces doesn't quite cut it. How, then, to fit a whole fish in a pot that's clearly too small? The answer was simple enough: Make the fish fit the pot. If you fill a stockpot with water and seasonings and gently bend a whole salmon to fit inside, the fish obediently remains along the pot's sides, cooks evenly, tastes delicious, and remains nicely intact. But the problem of presentation remains: The curved fish looks pretty, but it's nearly impossible to get at the meat on the inside of the curve, even after removing that from the outside.

Try as I might, I couldn't figure out a way to poach a whole salmon without a fish poacher, unless I altered its shape. So I did what I should have done in the first place: borrowed a fish poacher. And the results were good, especially when the fish was poached in a mildly acidic mixture containing aromatic vegetables (*see* "Poaching Salmon Steaks," page 15).

But I still wanted to figure out a way to moist-cook a whole fish without a poacher. It was then that I decided to get rid of the water altogether and steam the salmon in its own moisture. No one cares, I reasoned, how I get the poached salmon on the plate—just make it look and taste like a poached salmon and no one will ever know that it wasn't really poached.

I piled three long sheets of heavy-duty aluminum foil on the counter, plopped the fish down in the middle of them, seasoned it, and wrapped it up. I baked the fish on a baking sheet at 300 degrees, poking my trusty instant-read thermometer right through the foil into the thickest part of the fish every twenty minutes or so. And although my first couple of tries were near-disastrous failures—it seemed to take the fish about two hours go to from 33 degrees to 110 degrees, and then about two minutes to go from 110 degrees to 140 degrees—I felt that I was finally on the right track.

My first two salmons cooked at low oven heat had three problems: They were overcooked, resulting in a chalky, throat-clogging texture; the skin stuck to the foil; and the flavor was a little bland.

In an attempt to gain more control over the cooking process, I lowered the oven temperature to 250 degrees. This meant relatively long cooking times—still around two hours—but who cared? It was largely unattended anyway, once the timing was down. Still, I had problems with overcooking; the internal temperature of the fish, like that of most baked food, continued

to rise after I removed it from the oven. And, like most roasts of odd shape—think of leg of lamb—the thinner parts became overcooked before the thicker parts were done. I could compensate for the overcooking by removing the fish from the oven before it was done (that was easy enough) but what to do about the undercooking?

I gained more control by cooking the foil package directly on the oven rack; this kept the bottom from cooking more rapidly than the top. But in the end, all I could really do was undercook the thickest part slightly in hopes of keeping the slender tail end palatable. And, indeed, that was a fine solution; because fully cooked salmon is somewhat chalky, many people like it when it's slightly translucent, anyway. Serve from the thick body of the fish and, if there are any leftovers, they'll be from the overcooked tail (use them to make salmon croquettes).

Solving the skin-sticking was easy. I just sprayed the aluminum foil with virtually tasteless vegetable oil in an aerosol can. (I tried butter, but even that little amount hardened when the fish was chilled and gave it a dull, greasy look I didn't care for.)

All I needed to do to spark the fish's flavor was to give it a dose of vinegar and lemon juice. At that point, it was so close to "real" poached salmon that I returned the fish poacher, never to borrow it again.

OVEN "POACHED" WHOLE SALMON
SERVES 10 TO 12

Because the fish should lay flat as it cooks, measure your oven diagonally and make sure to buy a fish that will fit. If you do not have a thermometer to determine the internal temperature, gently insert the tip of a paring knife through the foil and into the fish. The flesh will separate easily and appear just barely translucent for medium-rare, or very light opaque pink for medium.

- 1 whole salmon (5 to 8 pounds) gutted, scaled, washed well, and fins trimmed away with kitchen shears
- 3 tablespoons cider, rice, or white-wine vinegar
- 1 tablespoon plus ½ teaspoon salt
- 2 lemons, one sliced and the other squeezed to yield 3 tablespoons juice

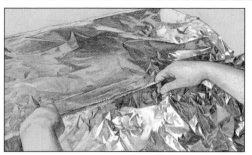

1. Cut three pieces of heavy-duty foil about a foot longer than the fish. Lay one piece down and the other two on top so they meet in the center; fold over to seal.

2. Center the fish on top of the foil, then wrap the fish with the foil, making a seam with the top edges of the top sheets and folding downward.

3. Roll up the ends. Do not close the foil too tightly.

1. Adjust oven rack to middle position and heat oven to 250 degrees. Using a pastry brush, generously brush fish with vinegar and sprinkle with 1 tablespoon salt, on both sides and in cavity; arrange lemon slices in cavity.

2. Following illustration 1 through 3, above, wrap fish in heavy-duty foil.

3. Transfer wrapped fish to oven rack and bake until an instant-read thermometer inserted through foil into thickest part of fish registers 125 to 130 degrees, between 1½ and 2½ hours, depending on weight of fish. Transfer fish to rimmed baking sheet, remove foil, and pour off liquid. At this point, fish can be covered loosely with plastic wrap and cooled to room temperature or refrigerated overnight.

4. Following illustrations 1 through 3 in "Preparing to Serve Oven-Poached Salmon," page 17, skin, bone, and prepare salmon for serving. Season bottom fillet with half the lemon juice and half the remaining salt. Replace both sections of top fillet to reassemble now-boneless fish. Season top fillet with remaining lemon juice and salt. Wipe platter edges, garnish fish and platter as desired, and serve, passing sauce separately.

HORSERADISH SAUCE
MAKES ABOUT 2 CUPS

The cream in this sauce is meant to be thickened only, not fully whipped.

- 1 cup heavy cream, chilled
- 1 2-inch piece fresh horseradish root, grated, or 2 tablespoons prepared horseradish, or to taste
  Salt and ground black pepper
- 2 teaspoons fresh lemon juice
- ¼ cup minced fresh chives

Beat cream in deep bowl with handheld mixer at medium speed until thick but not yet able to hold soft peaks, about 1½ minutes. Whisk in remaining ingredients until just combined. (Can be covered and refrigerated up to 2 hours; whisk briefly just before serving).

Poaching Salmon Steaks

Because salmon steaks and fillets do not pose the same problems of fitting into the pan as whole salmon does, it seemed that classic poaching was a good method for these cuts. So I set out to perfect the method for poaching salmon steaks and fillets. This involved finding the best poaching liquid and the easiest method.

I began by testing the poaching liquid. Referred to as court-bouillon, this mixture typically consists of water, an acid (vinegar, wine, or lemon), aromatics (carrots, onions, and celery), and herbs and spices.

First I needed to determine which acid, if any, should be included. To keep things simple, I left out the aromatics, herbs, and spices during this test. I simply poached fish in plain salted water as well as water spiked with three different acids, including cider vinegar, wine, or lemon juice. The plain salted water produced a fish that paradoxically tasted both overly rich and flat at the same time. By contrast, the cider vinegar produced a clean flavor that was bright and fresh. Acid, it seems, provides a nice counterpoint to the richness of the salmon and heightens the overall flavor. The bright, clean flavors were less pronounced with wine or lemon.

Having settled on vinegar, I put the aromatics, herbs, and spices back into the equation. I tried various flavor combinations using carrots, onions, celery, parsley, bay leaf, thyme, and peppercorns. Carrots and onions lend a lovely complementary sweetness, but celery overpowered some of the other flavors, so I eventually chose to leave it out. The herbs and peppercorns gave the fish a subtle flavor boost, while salt proved essential to heightening the flavor of the fish and making it taste of the sea.

To conclude the poaching liquid testing, I wanted to see how long the poaching liquid needed to be simmered before cooking the fish. I found 15 to 20 minutes adequate time for the vinegar to mellow and the vegetables to soften and infuse their flavor into the liquid. Any less and the liquid can taste harsh and unseasoned.

Up to this point, I was cooking the fish at a gentle sub-simmer with essentially no bubbling of the poaching liquid. I tested this technique against two other methods: boiling the poaching liquid with the fish in it, and bringing the liquid to a boil, adding the fish, then turning off the heat. Not surprisingly, the boiled version tasted watery, as if the flavors of the fish had been boiled away. The fish also cooked unevenly, with a 30-degree difference between the center and outside of the fish. Turning off the heat after submerging the fish was not that much better. It took longer to cook (16 minutes versus 10) and the cooking was also uneven. Based on this testing, my original method of poaching the fish in sub-simmer for about 10 minutes proved ideal.

CLASSIC POACHED SALMON STEAKS
SERVES 4

Though not essential, a few whole peppercorns, a bay leaf, and several sprigs of fresh parsley or thyme added to the poaching liquid will subtly flavor the fish steaks. The most accurate way to check the temperature of the medallions is to remove one from the simmering liquid before inserting the thermometer.

- 2 quarts cold water
- 1 cup cider or white wine vinegar
- 1 tablespoon salt
- ½ medium onion, chopped coarse (about ½ cup)
- 1 medium carrot, chopped coarse (about ½ cup)
- 4 salmon steaks (about 1-inch thick), boned and formed into medallions, following illustrations 1 through 6 on page 16

1. Bring all ingredients except salmon to boil in large soup kettle or Dutch oven; reduce heat to medium-low and simmer until flavors blend, about 20 minutes.

2. Reduce heat to lowest setting and place salmon medallions into liquid in pot. Simmer until fish is very light opaque pink, yet still barely translucent at center, and an instant-read thermometer inserted halfway through flesh registers 125 to 130 degrees.

3. Remove medallions to plate with slotted spoon or spatula and remove strings. Serve warm, or at room temperature, passing sauce, at left, separately. —Eva Katz

How to Cook & Serve Salmon

Rich, delicate salmon is probably the most popular eating fish in America. After extensive kitchen testing, we found that the best way to cook a whole salmon is to wrap it in tin foil and roast it in the oven (*see* recipe page 14). To combine ease of eating and attractive presentation, we like to bone the fish and reassemble it before serving. With salmon steaks, we prefer the more traditional approach of poaching in liquid (*see* recipe page 15). By following these step-by-step instructions, you will easily be able to prepare and cook your salmon by either method. By Eva Katz

PREPARING TO COOK SALMON STEAKS

1. Insert the tip of a chef's knife alongside the large central bone. While pressing the knife tip against the bone to avoid cutting off any extra meat, cut along the center to remove the one side of the steak.

2. Cut down the other side of the center bone to separate the other side.

3. Cut off the white, fatty belly flap on the narrow tip of each steak.

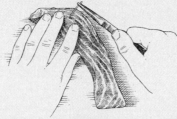

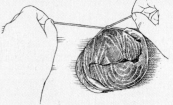

4. Gently rub the broad surface and sides of the steak with your fingers to locate any pin bones. Remove with needlenose pliers.

5. Place the two halves together, flesh sides facing and ends going in the opposite direction.

6. Move ends counterclockwise to form a medallion and secure with kitchen twine.

PREPARING TO COOK WHOLE SALMON

1. Trimming the salmon fins with kitchen scissors makes serving the fish easier. Cut the fins from both sides of the fish, then from its belly. Turn the fish over and cut the fins from along the back of the fish.

2. Generously sprinkle the fish with salt and brush with vinegar over both sides and inside the cavity.

3. Place the lemon slices inside the cavity.

4. Cut three pieces of foil, each about 12 inches longer than the fish. Following steps 1 through 3 on page 15, wrap the fish securely in the foil. Roll up the ends to seal, but do not close the foil too tight.

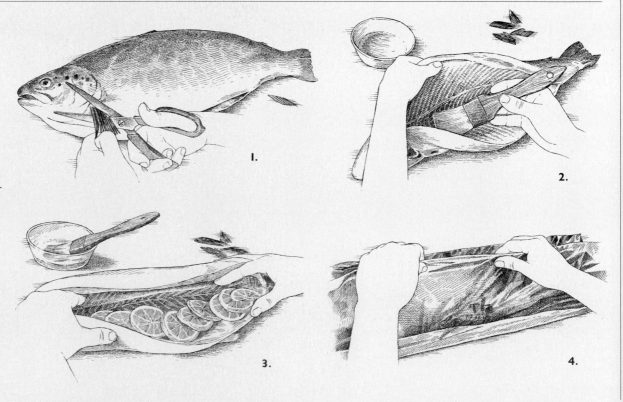

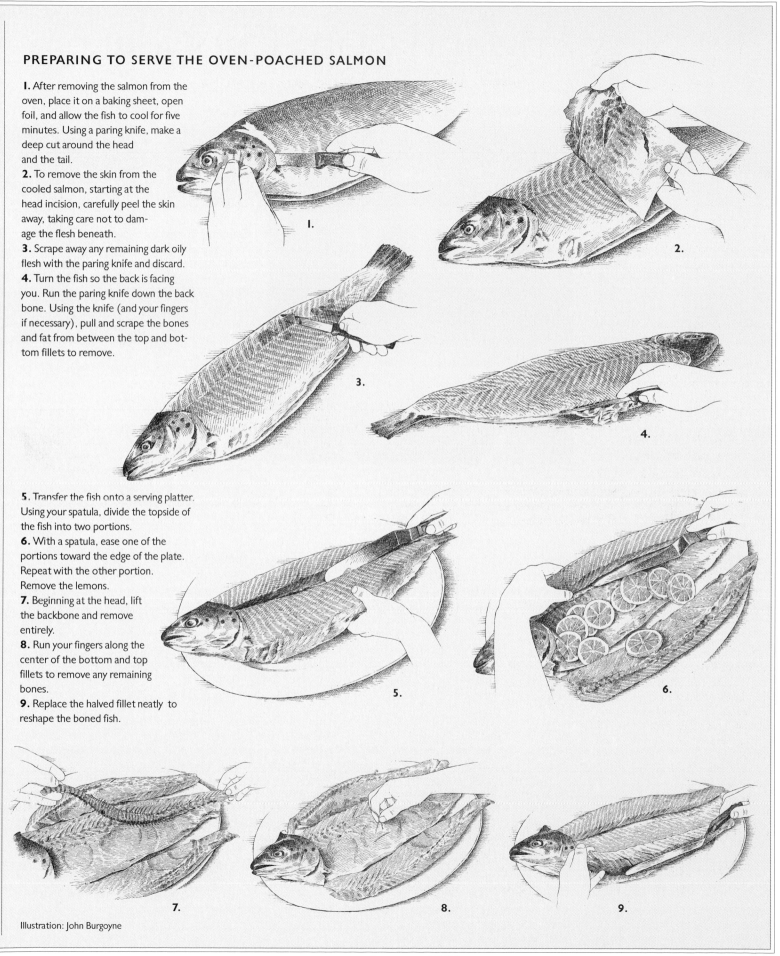

PREPARING TO SERVE THE OVEN-POACHED SALMON

1. After removing the salmon from the oven, place it on a baking sheet, open foil, and allow the fish to cool for five minutes. Using a paring knife, make a deep cut around the head and the tail.

2. To remove the skin from the cooled salmon, starting at the head incision, carefully peel the skin away, taking care not to damage the flesh beneath.

3. Scrape away any remaining dark oily flesh with the paring knife and discard.

4. Turn the fish so the back is facing you. Run the paring knife down the back bone. Using the knife (and your fingers if necessary), pull and scrape the bones and fat from between the top and bottom fillets to remove.

5. Transfer the fish onto a serving platter. Using your spatula, divide the topside of the fish into two portions.

6. With a spatula, ease one of the portions toward the edge of the plate. Repeat with the other portion. Remove the lemons.

7. Beginning at the head, lift the backbone and remove entirely.

8. Run your fingers along the center of the bottom and top fillets to remove any remaining bones.

9. Replace the halved fillet neatly to reshape the boned fish.

1.

2.

3.

4.

5.

6.

7.

8.

9.

Illustration: John Burgoyne

New England Clam Chowder

Here is an easy clam chowder that won't separate, is economical,
and has a rich, full-bodied taste and texture.

≥ BY PAM ANDERSON WITH KAREN TACK ≤

I love homemade clam chowder almost as much as I love good chicken soup, but I must confess I eat canned chowder more often than I prepare it from scratch. Because clam chowder is quicker to cook than chicken soup, I had to wonder why I would settle for eating it from a can.

Actually, the reasons came quickly to mind. For me, clams require a trip to the fish market. Although my local grocery store usually does carry small, pricey bags of littleneck clams, I once calculated that using them for a pot of chowder would cost me almost $30. Clams must also be processed fairly quickly or they'll spoil; a chicken can be frozen until ready to use.

Further, many chowder recipes demand that clams be purged of sand by soaking them in salt water with cornmeal or baking powder—yet another time-consuming step. Once made, chowder is more fragile than most other soups, and unless it is stabilized in some way, it curdles if brought to a boil.

Our goals for this soup, then, were multiple but quite clear. We wanted to develop a delicious, traditional chowder that was economical, stable, and almost as simple as opening a can.

Clam Digging
Before testing chowder recipes, we explored our clam options. Chowders are typically made with hard-shell clams, so we purchased (from smallest to largest) cockles, littlenecks, cherrystones, and chowder clams, often called quahogs. We were unable to get topnecks at the time of testing, but they are another hard-shell variety that falls between littlenecks and cherrystones.

Although they made delicious chowders, we eliminated littlenecks and cockles, both of which were just too expensive to toss into a chowder pot. Chowders made with the cheapest clams, however, weren't really satisfactory, either. The quahogs we purchased for testing were large (four to five inches in diameter), tough, and strong flavored. Their oversized bellies (and the contents therein) gave the chowder an overbearing mineral taste, detracting from its smooth, rich flavor.

Among hard-shell clams, we chose topnecks or cherrystones for their combination of flavor and affordability.

Though only a little more expensive, cherrystones offered good value and flavor. The chowder made from these slightly smaller clams was distinctly clam-flavored, without an inky aftertaste. Because there are no industry sizing standards for each clam variety (see "But How Many Clams Do I Need?", below), you may find some small quahogs labeled as cherrystones or large cherrystones labeled as quahogs. Regardless of designation, clams much over three inches in diameter will deliver a distinctly metallic, inky-flavored chowder.

Shucked, Baked, or Steamed
Steaming clams open is far easier than shucking them. Five minutes over simmering water, and the clams open as naturally as a budding flower. As long as they were pulled from the pot as soon as they opened, and as long as they weren't cooked too long in the finished chowder, they did not toughen up. In addition to steaming, we tried baking them open. Compared to steaming, baking takes longer and is more awkward. We also preferred steaming because of the wonderful broth that results when clam juices combine with the steaming liquid.

The extra step of purging or filtering hard-shell clams is unnecessary. All of the hard-shells we tested were relatively clean, and what little sediment there was sank to the bottom of the steaming liquid. Getting rid of the grit was as simple as leaving the last few tablespoons of broth in the pan when pouring it from the pot. If you find your clam broth is gritty, strain it through a coffee filter.

The Right Texture
After making several pots of chowder, we agreed with cookbook author Phillip Schulz (*As American as Apple Pie*, Simon and Schuster, 1990), who said chowders should be "slurpable, yet not watery. Thick, but not stew-like." Older recipes call for thickening the chowder with

But How Many Clams Do I Need?

Judging by most recipes, there is no consistent, accurate, or easily used method of designating the amount of clams needed for a given chowder. Some recipes call for a certain quantity of shucked clams, giving the cook no idea how many whole clams to buy. Other recipes call for X number of "hard-shell clams," apparently not taking into account the size differences between a quahog and a littleneck.

Likewise, there are no industry sizing standards for each clam variety. Clam size and name vary from source to source, so that one company's cherrystone clam might be another company's quahog. Simply calling for X number of cherrystones or quahogs was not a consistent measurement either.

We wondered if calling for X pounds of clams, regardless of size, would yield similar quantities of meat and liquid. Working with 1½-pound quantities, we shucked quahogs, cherrystones, and littlenecks. Although the number of clams per pound varied greatly (two of our quahogs equaled 1½ pounds, while it took 2 dozen littlenecks to equal the same weight), they consistently yielded a scant ½ cup of clams and ⅔ cup of clam juice.

Even though clams are usually sold by the piece at the fish market, we find it more accurate and consistent to give a weight rather than a number. Even most fish markets have a scale. So regardless of clam size, you'll need about seven pounds to make the clam chowder recipe that follows.   —P.A.

crumbled biscuits; breadcrumbs and crackers are modern stand-ins.

Standard breadcrumb-thickened chowders failed to impress. We wanted a smooth, creamy soup base for the potatoes, onions, and clams, but no matter how long the chowder was simmered, breadcrumbs or crackers never completely dissolved into the cooking liquid. Heavy cream alone, by contrast, did not give the chowder enough body, and we discovered fairly quickly that flour was necessary, not only as a thickener but as a stabilizer, because unthickened chowders separate and curdle. Of the two flour methods, we opted to thicken at the beginning of cooking rather than at the end. Because our final recipe was finished with cream, we felt the chowder didn't need the extra butter that would be required for the flour paste.

Because chowders call for potatoes, some cooks suggest that starchy baking potatoes, which tend to break down when boiled, can double as a thickener. But the potatoes did not break down sufficiently, and instead simply became soft and mushy. Waxy red boiling potatoes are best for chowders.

We now had two final questions to answer about our chowder. First, should it include salt pork or bacon, and if the latter, did the bacon need to be blanched? We ended up using such small amounts of this flavoring in the final recipe that either worked fine. Bacon is more readily available and, once bought, easier to use up. Blanching the bacon makes it taste more like salt pork, but we rather liked the subtle smokiness of the chowder made with unblanched bacon.

Finally, should the chowder be enriched with milk or cream? So much milk was required to make it look and taste creamy that the chowder started to lose its clam flavor and became more like mild bisque or the clam equivalent of oyster stew. Making the chowder with almost all clam broth (five cups of the cooking liquid from the steaming clams), then finishing the stew with a cup of cream gave us what we were looking for—a rich, creamy chowder that tasted distinctly of clams.

MASTER RECIPE FOR NEW ENGLAND CLAM CHOWDER
SERVES 6 (ABOUT 2 QUARTS)

During spring and summer, shellfish spawn, leaving them weak, perishable, and off-flavored. Although clams recover from their spawning phase more quickly than mussels and oysters, they should be avoided from late spring through midsummer.

- 7 pounds medium-size hard-shell clams, such as littleneck, topneck, or small cherrystone, washed and scrubbed clean

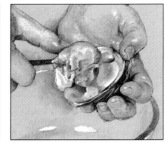

1. Steam clams until just open, at right, rather than completely open, as shown at left.

2. Open clams with a paring knife, holding over a bowl to catch juices.

3. Sever the muscle under the clam and remove it from the shell.

- 4 slices thick-cut bacon (about 4 ounces), cut into ¼-inch pieces
- 1 large Spanish onion, diced medium (about 2 cups)
- 2 tablespoons flour
- 3 medium boiling potatoes (about 1½ pounds), scrubbed and diced medium
- 1 large bay leaf
- 1 teaspoon fresh thyme leaves or ¼ teaspoon dried thyme
- 1 cup heavy cream
- 2 tablespoons minced fresh parsley leaves
  Salt and ground black or white pepper

1. Bring clams and 3 cups water to boil in large, covered soup kettle. Following illustration 1, above, steam until clams just open, 3 to 5 minutes. Transfer clams to large bowl; cool slightly. Following illustrations 2 and 3, remove clams from shells, reserving meat in bowl and discarding shells. Mince clams; set aside. Pour clam broth into 2-quart Pyrex measuring cup, holding back last few tablespoons broth in case of sediment; set clam broth aside. (Should have about 5 cups.) Rinse and dry kettle; return to burner.

2. Fry bacon in kettle over medium-low heat until fat renders and bacon crisps, 5 to 7 minutes. Add onion to bacon; sauté until softened, about 5 minutes. Add flour; stir until lightly colored, about 1 minute. Gradually whisk in reserved clam juice. Add potatoes, bay leaf, and thyme; simmer until potatoes are tender, about 10 minutes. Add clams, cream, parsley, and salt (if necessary) and ground pepper to taste; bring to simmer. Remove from heat and serve.

QUICK PANTRY CLAM CHOWDER
SERVES 6 (ABOUT 2 QUARTS)

Follow recipe for New England Clam Chowder, substituting for the fresh clams 4 cans (6.5 ounces each) minced clams, juice drained and reserved, along with 1 cup water and 2 bottles (8 ounces each) clam juice in medium bowl, and clam meat reserved in small bowl. Add reserved clam meat and juice at same points when fresh clam meat and juice would be added.

The Best Canned Clams

From late summer through winter, when clams are plentiful, you'll probably want to make fresh clam chowder. But if you're short on time or find clams scarce and expensive, we've found that the right canned clams and bottled clam juice deliver a chowder that's at least three notches above canned soup in quality. Are all canned clams the same? Taste-testing four varieties of minced canned clams (Doxsee, Progresso, Gorton's, and Cento) and three canned whole baby clams (3 Diamonds, Cento, and Chicken of the Sea), we discovered dramatic differences. Our findings are listed below; in the end, we preferred Doxsee minced clams teamed with Doxsee brand clam juice.

Minced Canned Clams
- Doxsee (No MSG) Minced Clams Best of the lot. Not too tough, not artificially tender.
- Progresso Recipe Ready, Gourmet Quality Minced Clams Apparently large, tough clams, are passed through a mechanical tenderizer, as the final product looks chewed up. Some taste chewy.
- Gorton's Chopped Clams Because clams are chopped, not minced, pieces are uneven, with larger pieces mixed in with minced. Bland tasting.
- Cento Minced Clams Gritty. The majority of meat looks like tough hinge muscle that's been artificially tenderized, and there are very few strips.

Small Whole Clams
- Chicken of the Sea Brand Baby Clams Our favorite of the baby clam variety. With their soft texture, they don't feel overly cooked. They also look natural and taste the most clam-like of the three.
- 3 Diamonds Whole Small Clams Very strong flavor. Bellies are very green and give the clams a bait-like flavor. A small crab was found in the can.
- Cento Whole Shelled Baby Clams Quite light in color. Very washed-out looking and tasting.
- Chopped fresh frozen clams (available at most grocery store fish counters and seafood markets) These clams were typically as chewy as rubber bands and gritty.

The Ultimate Flourless Chocolate Cake

Just three ingredients—whipped whole eggs, a good quality semisweet chocolate, and butter—will yield dense, rich texture and true chocolate flavor.

⇒ BY ALICE MEDRICH ⇐

To my knowledge, flourless chocolate cake is the only dessert that is named for a missing ingredient. Besides this, the word "cake" stretches the point in describing this very popular dessert; although some recipes replace flour or crumbs with ground nuts, the quintessence of the genre contains only chocolate, butter, and eggs—nothing that could conceivably be called a dry ingredient. The result is more confection than cake, like a dense baked mousse or chocolate cheesecake, with butter replacing cheese. This is a hardcore dessert!

As I reviewed recipes for this article, I saw enough variations to wonder just how I would survive the testing and the tasting. Ingredients were few—chocolate, butter, and eggs, sometimes sugar, and sometimes liquid such as water, coffee, or liqueur—but proportions as well as mixing and baking methods differed considerably.

I selected and baked six recipes that represented the array of choices. The results were staggering in their variety. One resembled a flourless fudge brownie, one was more like an ultra-dense, creamy custard, and one was a pouffy, fallen soufflé-like affair. Some were ultra bittersweet, others quite sweet. All, however, had the richness and intensity of a confection.

Although the desserts were almost all very enticing, I was quickly able to define my personal criteria for the ultimate flourless chocolate cake. I wanted something dense, moist, and ultra chocolate, but with some textural finesse. I wanted a mouth feel and texture somewhere between a substantial marquise au chocolat—that dense, buttery, and just slightly aerated chocolate mousse with a characteristic dry but creamy texture—and a heavy New York-style cheesecake, which requires the mouth to work for just a second before the stuff melts and dissolves with sublime flavor. I wanted the flavor and character of good eating-quality chocolate to reign supreme, with no unnecessary sweetness and not even the slightest grain of sugar on my palate. In short, I wanted an intense bittersweet "adult" dessert, not a piece of fudge or a brownie or a thick chocolate pudding—and certainly nothing fluffy.

To decorate this confection-like dessert, simply use a sieve to sprinkle the top with powdered sugar or cocoa.

Some recipes used unsweetened chocolate instead of semisweet or bittersweet chocolate, but I eliminated this notion after tasting just one cake made with unsweetened chocolate. Neither flavor nor texture were smooth or silky enough for this type of dessert, and there was a slight chalky sensation on the palate. This made perfect sense to me. Unsweetened chocolate is coarse and needs high heat to blend perfectly with the sugar required to sweeten it. It is most successful in desserts with a cakey or fudgy texture, when perfect smoothness is unnecessary. Hot fudge sauce made with unsweetened chocolate is smooth because it is cooked to a temperature high enough to melt the sugar and change the physical properties of the chocolate. But our flourless chocolate cake is more like chocolate mousse, chocolate

truffles, or ganache—ingredients are few, cooked very gently, and the results must be perfectly smooth. Made to be nibbled, semisweet and bittersweet chocolates are incomparably smooth, refined so that chocolate and sugar are intimately married and every particle is smaller than the human palate can detect.

The next decision had to do with the baking temperature and whether or not a water bath was indicated. The original recipe for this now-popular dessert was flawed by hard, crumbly edges—surely due to baking for a short time at a high temperature without a water bath. I tried a similar recipe baked at a high temperature for a short time but in a water bath. It was creamier by far but I could taste raw egg, which did not suit my palate and raised safety questions. I guessed that, like cheesecake, this dessert required a longer baking time at a lower temperature in a water bath to allow the interior to reach a safe temperature without overcooking the edges. I found that 325 degrees in a water bath produced a successful sample.

The trick in baking this cake, however, was knowing when to stop. Just like cheesecake, our flourless chocolate cake must be taken from the oven when the center still jiggles and looks quite underdone, as it continues to cook after it comes out of the oven.

At first I used a thermometer to make sure that the center of the cake had reached the safe temperature of 160 degrees. But this cake was clearly overbaked—the texture was dryish and chalky. Knowing that a temperature of at least 140 degrees held for five minutes also killed salmonella bacteria, I let the cake reach 140 degrees and then left it in the oven for five more minutes. It was over-baked as well. After trying four, three, and two extra minutes in the oven, I finally realized that I could remove the cake at 140 degrees and it would stay at or even above 140 degrees for at least five minutes (thus killing off salmonella) as the heat from the edges of the cake penetrated the center. The results were perfect.

Before determining the perfect quantities of butter and eggs for a pound of chocolate, I decided to test textures. I was pretty sure that my ultimate cake would need some form of aeration from beaten eggs to achieve the texture that I was looking for. I created a half-size test recipe for a six-inch pan and tested it three times. Each time I warmed the chocolate and butter together before adding eggs, but I handled the eggs differently in each sample. In the first test, I whisked the eggs over gentle heat to warm them (as for a genoise), and then beat them until about triple in volume and the consistency of soft whipped cream. I then folded the whipped eggs into the warm chocolate and butter in three parts. In the second test, I separated the eggs and whisked the yolks into the warm chocolate and butter and then beat the whites to a meringue before folding them in. In the third test, I simply whisked the eggs, one by one, into the warm chocolate and butter, as though making a custard.

The sample made with eggs simply whisked into the melted chocolate and butter was dense and smooth like a very rich custard or creme brulée. My definition of the ultimate flourless chocolate cake ruled this version out. The cake with beaten whole eggs differed from the one with yolks and meringue more than I expected. Surprisingly, the difference in flavor was greater than the difference in texture. Whole beaten eggs produced a dessert with nicely blended flavors, while the cake with separated eggs tasted as though the ingredients were not completely integrated. Along the way, I realized that I could eliminate the step of warming the eggs before beating them, since cold eggs produce a denser foam with smaller bubbles, which in turn gave the cake a more velvety texture.

THE ULTIMATE FLOURLESS CHOCOLATE CAKE
SERVES 12 TO 16

Even though the cake may not look done, pull it from the oven when an instant-read thermometer registers 140 degrees. (Make sure not to let tip of thermometer hit the bottom of the pan.) It will continue to firm up as it cools. If you use a 9-inch springform pan instead of the preferred 8-inch, reduce the baking time to 18 to 20 minutes.

8   large eggs, cold
I   pound bittersweet or semisweet chocolate (see "Which Chocolate Makes the Best Cake," right), coarsely chopped
1/2   pound (2 sticks) unsalted butter, cut into 1/2-inch chunks
1/4   cup strong coffee or liqueur (optional) Confectioners' sugar or cocoa powder for decoration

1. Adjust oven rack to lower middle position and heat oven to 325 degrees. Line bottom of 8-inch springform pan with parchment and grease pan sides. Cover pan underneath and along sides with sheet of heavy-duty foil and set in large roasting pan. Bring kettle of water to boil.

2. Beat eggs with hand-held mixer at high speed until volume doubles to approximately 1 quart, about 5 minutes. Alternately, beat in bowl of electric mixer fitted with wire whip attachment at medium speed (speed 6 on a KitchenAid) to achieve same result, about 5 minutes.

3. Meanwhile, melt chocolate and butter (adding coffee or liqueur, if using) in large heatproof bowl set over pan of almost simmering water, until smooth and very warm (about 115 degrees on an instant-read thermometer), stirring once or twice. (For the microwave, melt chocolate and butter together at 50 percent power until smooth and warm, 4 to 6 minutes, stirring once or twice.) Fold 1/3 of egg foam into chocolate mixture using large rubber spatula until only a few streaks of egg are visible; fold in half of remaining foam, then last of remaining foam, until mixture is totally homogenous.

4. Scrape batter into prepared springform pan and smooth surface with rubber spatula. Set roasting pan on oven rack and pour enough boiling water to come about halfway up side of springform pan. Bake until cake has risen slightly, edges are just beginning to set, a thin glazed crust (like a brownie) has formed on surface, and an instant read thermometer inserted halfway through center of cake registers 140 degrees, 22 to 25 minutes. Remove cake pan from water bath and set on wire rack; cool to room temperature. Cover and refrigerate overnight to mellow (can be covered and refrigerated for up to 4 days).

5. About 30 minutes before serving, remove springform pan sides, invert cake on sheet of

Which Chocolate Makes the Best Cake?

The labels on semisweet chocolate all have the same list of ingredients: sugar, chocolate liquor, cocoa butter, lecithin (a natural emulsifier), and vanilla. But the quality of the cocoa bean, the roasting levels, amounts of cocoa butter and sugar, and the conching or amalgamation of all the ingredients determines the ultimate taste and texture of the chocolate. Because there is such a high percentage of chocolate in this cake recipe, we decided to conduct additional tests to determine how different brands affected the outcome. For our tests, we chose Van Leer, Callebaut, and Ghiradelli, three specialty brands that tested well in *Cook's* chocolate tasting (November/December 1994), as well as two supermarket brands, Baker's and Nestle's.

Five cakes, each using one of the chosen brands, were baked according to the recipe. For these tests, I omitted the coffee liqueur so we could concentrate on the pure chocolate flavor. The baked cakes were judged for their taste and texture. We were specifically looking for depth of chocolate flavor, mouth feel, creaminess, underlying flavors, sweetness, and density.

Because of the subtleties in chocolate, it was not surprising to me that our tests revealed different preferences and opinions when the complex taste of chocolate in these cakes was evaluated.

Overall, the cake made with Ghiradelli chocolate received the most positive comments, such as "creamy taste, true chocolate flavor, and velvety texture." Callebaut was also highly praised for its "rich chocolate taste, aroma, and silky texture." Tasters liked the creamy texture of the cake made with Van Leer, but what one tester found to be "a balanced and intriguing taste," another found to be bland. Nestle's and Baker's appealed to some for the "mousse-like" texture they imparted and also for the "coffee and fruitiness" in their taste. A higher level of sweetness was also mentioned by everyone when tasting the cakes made with these chocolates.

None of the brands tested were ruled out for use as an ingredient in this recipe, but clearly there were differences in the textures and, especially, the tastes. Individual preferences, and perhaps availability, will dictate which brand you choose. If a deep, rich, chocolate taste is important, you'll probably reach for a specialty brand. If you prefer sweetness and light, a supermarket brand will suit your needs.

—Susan Logozzo

waxed paper, peel off parchment pan liner, and turn cake right side up on serving platter. Sieve light sprinkling of Confectioners' sugar or unsweetened cocoa powder over cake to decorate, if desired.

Alice Medrich is the author of *Chocolate and the Art of Low-Fat Desserts* (Warner Books, 1994).

The Best Peanut Butter Cookie

The key to a peanutty cookie that is crisp on the edges and chewy in the center?
Chunky commercial peanut butter and an extra hit of roasted, salted peanuts.

⇒ BY VICTORIA ABBOTT RICCARDI ⇐

When I was growing up, my mother used to make divine, chewy peanut butter cookies that tasted almost like candy. They were thin, smooth, and firm, with tremendous peanut flavor.

Over the years, however, my taste in peanut butter cookies has changed. Instead of being satisfied with this peanutty confection, I have been on a quest for a peanut butter cookie that is crisp around the edges, chewy in the center, slightly puffed, and that tastes buttery, sweet, and strongly of peanuts. This ideal cookie would combine the nutty flavor of my childhood cookie with the texture and appearance of a different recipe—a recipe I decided to develop because I could not find what I wanted at any bakery.

Searching for Texture and Flavor

I began by testing some fifteen different recipes to come up with a prototype. Overall, I noticed that these cookies fell into one of two camps: The cookies were either sweet and chewy with a mild peanut flavor because they contained significant amounts of sugar and butter and not much egg, or they were sandy and crumbly with a strong peanut flavor because they contained lots of peanut butter and not a lot of flour. The trick would be to come up with a recipe that combined the best of both worlds.

I selected as my working master one of the nuttiest-tasting, sweet and chewy recipes, because I figured it would be easier to pump up the peanut flavor in a chewy cookie rather than add chewiness to a sandy, peanutty cookie.

My first experiments focused on types and amounts of fats. I began by replacing the butter with peanut oil to add more peanut flavor. I quickly learned that oil is what makes a cookie sandy, while shortening adds crispness and chew. Curious to see if butter, margarine, or Crisco made a difference in texture or taste, I tested all three. Indeed, there were differences. Butter accentuated the cookie's peanut flavor, while margarine and Crisco lessened it. Butter also increased crispness. From now on, I would use butter.

I also noticed that peanut butter types mimicked the results I found with the fats. Early in my testing, I discovered that natural peanut butters, which have a layer of oil on top, made the cookie more grainy (like the peanut oil had), while com-

After testing scores of recipes, we finally got real peanut flavor and a non-sandy texture.

mercial brands, which contain partially hydrogenated vegetable oils, helped the cookie rise and achieve a crispier edge and chewier center (like the butter had). It was clear, at this point, that butter was necessary for flavor and crispness and commercial peanut butter was crucial for lightness and lack of sandiness. But how much of each ingredient would I need?

My working recipe contained equal amounts of peanut butter and butter. In an attempt to increase the cookie's peanut flavor, I increased the amount of peanut butter while proportionally decreasing the amount of butter. I did not taste a significant difference between the two recipes. Therefore, I continued adding peanut butter to the dough until I had eventually replaced the butter completely. The result was a cookie that had a strong peanut flavor, but a shortbread-like texture. I returned to an equal ratio of peanut butter to butter.

At this point I was getting close, but I still needed to find a way to make the cookie taste more peanutty and "less like a sugar cookie," said friends and family, who had become my critics.

With "sugar cookie" ringing in my ears, I decided to reduce the amount of sugar in my working master to bring out the cookie's peanut flavor. My working master called for equal

amounts of white granulated and light brown sugar, so I tried reducing the amounts of both. The result? I created a slightly more peanutty cookie, but I lost my chewy texture. Sugar clearly plays a significant role when it comes to chewiness.

Keeping this new discovery in mind, I made several attempts at using liquid sweeteners. I substituted a small amount of dark corn syrup for the light brown sugar, but the cookies spread and flattened when baked and took on a decidedly corn syrup tang. Next I tried sweetened condensed milk. The result was not bad, but the cookie had become candy-like. Molasses proved no better. From now on, I would stick with dry sweeteners.

About this time I decided that instead of cutting back on sugar to accentuate the richness of the peanut butter, I would try using different types of sugars. Using granulated brown sugar in place of granulated white sugar produced a dry dough and a brittle cookie with only modest peanut flavor. Dark brown sugar alone yielded an overly sweet cookie that had a very sugary center—almost like a praline. It was evident that the white sugar, in combination with the butter, peanut butter, and eggs, was an essential ingredient for producing a cookie that had crisp edges and a chewy center. Combining granulated white and dark brown sugar, my final sweetness experiment, enhanced chewiness and also added a certain richness that helped bring out the flavor of the nuts.

Oddly enough, in my testing I found that the amount of flour in the dough made a difference in peanut taste. Too little flour made the cookie taste greasy. As I increased the flour, the cookie's peanut taste intensified. Too much flour, however, and the cookie became too dry.

Some of the recipes I was looking at called for baking soda alone, while others called for a mixture of baking soda and baking powder. I found that baking soda was crucial for helping the cookie brown and, most importantly, for bringing out its peanut flavor. The baking powder added an important lift.

I had been baking the cookies at 350 degrees for 10 to 12 minutes and was very pleased with the results. Higher oven temperatures browned the cookies nicely, which contributed to their nutty flavor. But these high temperatures also caused the cookies to lose chewiness in the center. Lower oven temperatures lessened the browning and thus led to a less peanutty tasting cookie.

At this point, I felt I was coming down the home stretch. I was pleased with the texture of the peanut butter cookie I had developed thus far, based on equal amounts of butter and commercial peanut butter, the right number of eggs, equal amounts of white granulated and dark brown sugar, and the right oven temperature. And yet, I still wasn't satisfied with the cookie's flavor. It still needed a more powerful peanut punch.

To increase peanut flavor, I decided to add some toasted, ground, lightly salted peanuts to the dough. It helped considerably. The cookie had a much stronger peanut flavor, while still maintaining its crispy edges and chewy center. I then increased the salt and switched from sweet to lightly salted butter. These additional changes made a huge difference in flavor. The added peanuts and salt gave the cookie a strong roasted nut flavor, without sacrificing its wonderful texture. I was very pleased with the results, as were my critics. I had created my ideal peanut butter cookie.

BIG, SUPER-NUTTY PEANUT BUTTER COOKIES
MAKES APPROXIMATELY 3 DOZEN COOKIES

Bringing the butter, peanut butter, and eggs to room temperature makes it easier to blend the ingredients. Be sure to grind the peanuts, since whole, and even chopped peanuts tend to slip out of the dough. If using unsalted butter, increase salt to 1 teaspoon. Keep finished cookies refrigerated in airtight container. To restore just-baked chewiness, wrap a cookie in a sheet of paper towel and microwave for approximately 25 seconds. Cool before serving.

2½ cups all-purpose flour
½ teaspoon baking soda
½ teaspoon baking powder
½ teaspoon salt
½ pound butter (2 sticks), salted
1 cup firmly packed dark brown sugar
1 cup granulated sugar
1 cup extra-crunchy peanut butter, preferably Jif
2 large eggs
2 teaspoons vanilla extract
1 cup roasted salted peanuts, ground in food processor to resemble bread crumbs, about 14 pulses (about 1 cup, packed)

1. Adjust oven rack to low center position; heat oven to 350 degrees. Sift flour, baking soda, baking powder, and salt in medium bowl.
2. In bowl of electric mixer or by hand, beat butter until creamy. Add sugars; beat until fluffy, about 3 minutes with electric mixer, stopping to scrape down bowl as necessary. Beat in peanut butter until fully incorporated, then eggs, one at a time, then vanilla. Gently stir dry ingredients into peanut butter mixture. Add ground peanuts; stir gently until just incorporated.
3. Working with 2 tablespoons dough at a time (see illustration 1, below), roll into large balls, placing them 2 inches apart on a parchment-covered cookie sheet. Following illustration 2, below, press each dough ball with back of dinner fork dipped in cold water to make crisscross design. Bake until cookies are puffed and slightly brown along edges, but not top, 10 to 12 minutes (they will not look fully baked). Cool cookies on cookie sheet until set, about 4 minutes, then transfer to wire rack to cool completely. Cookies will keep, refrigerated in an airtight container, up to 7 days.

Victoria Abbott Riccardi is a food writer living in Boston.

A Barrel of Peanut Butters: Does Brand Matter?

Throughout my testing I used Skippy Super Chunk, not only for consistency, but also to pack as many peanuts as possible into the dough. However, once I had baked the ideal cookie, I tried making the recipe with several different national brands of peanut butter. For the sake of comparison, I made the cookies with chunky versions of Jif, Peter Pan, Reese's, and Skippy. To be honest, I was surprised with the final results, since my personal favorite eating peanut butter was not the winner. Peanut butters are listed in order of most to least favorite.

Brand	Ingredients	Comments
JIF	Roasted peanuts, sugar, molasses, partially hydrogenated vegetable oil (soybean), fully hydrogenated vegetable oils (rapeseed and soybean), mono- and diglycerides, salt	Dough quite thick with a slightly grainy texture. Cookies browned the best and had a rich, toasted peanut flavor. Only peanut butter without cottonseed oil. Perhaps molasses contributed to browning and richness.
PETER PAN	Roasted peanuts, sugar, partially hydrogenated vegetable oils (cottonseed and rapeseed), salt	Dough somewhat thick. Cookies had a good peanut flavor that was slightly more sugary than those made with Jif and Skippy. Only peanut butter without soybean oil.
REESE'S	Roasted peanuts, sugar, hydrogenated vegetable oil (rapeseed, cottonseed, and soybean), peanut oil, salt, molasses, monoglycerides	Dough neither too thick nor too thin. Cookies were the most crisp and light but were also the most sugary and least peanutty tasting. Only peanut butter with peanut oil, which perhaps contributed to lightness.
SKIPPY	Roasted peanuts, sugar, partially hydrogenated vegetable oils (rapeseed, cottonseed, and soybean), salt	Dough was the most thin. Cookies had a fairly good peanut taste, but a greasy, buttery flavor.

STEP-BY-STEP | SHAPING THE COOKIES

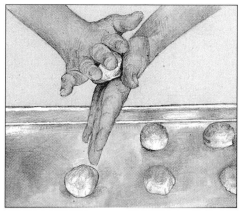

1. Measure two tablespoons of dough and with your hands roll into large ball.

2. For crisscross design, press each cookie twice with back of fork dipped in cold water.

Seeking "Real" Maple Syrup Flavor

Attracted by its dark, strong maple flavor, tasters pick a "lower grade" syrup as their favorite.

≥ BY MARYELLEN DRISCOLL ≤

At a friend's home in New Hampshire, I woke early one winter morning to find him whirring around the kitchen on roller blades. In between flipping pancakes, he would eye the mercury of a candy thermometer clipped to a pot of simmering sap, the March drippings of two front yard maples. A few more degrees and we would have syrup, with the most pure and alive maple flavor I can ever remember tasting.

In our blind taste test of maple syrups, we discovered that tasters wanted a similar maple syrup experience. They wanted a syrup that tasted like the "real thing." Reflecting consumer trends, our tasters leaned toward the darker maple syrups that pack more of a maple punch.

Making the Grade

While all "real" maple syrups are pure, their characteristics and price vary according to grade. In general, a syrup's grade is determined by the period during which it was made (the sugaring season lasts from February to early April).

Technically, the grades of maple syrup are measured by the amount of light that can pass through the syrup. Straight from the tree, maple sap is clear, consisting of about 98 percent water and 2 percent sugar. To make maple syrup, the water has to be boiled off to a concentration of 66 percent sugar. (This means boiling off about 39 gallons of water to get one gallon of syrup.)

Early in the season, maple syrups tend to be near-transparent because the sugar molecules in the boiled-down sap are able to reflect much light. As temperatures warm outside, wild yeasts in the sap begin feeding upon and breaking down the sugar. As a result light can be absorbed. So as the season progresses, the syrup darkens.

This breakdown of sugar also affects flavor. If maple sap is concentrated without boiling (e.g., by freeze drying), the syrup will taste sweet but otherwise have little flavor. The flavor we perceive as "maple" is actually the result of chemical reactions that occur when the sap is boiled, says Dr. Thomas Potter, a food and flavor chemist at the University of Massachusetts at Amherst's

Department of Food Science. One of the two primary flavor notes is derived from the compounds that form when sugar molecules break down. The process is similar to caramelizing. This may explain why the darker syrups produced later in the season have more of the caramel notes distinct to maple syrup, says Potter. The second flavor note is vanilla, which is produced from compounds in the sap that the tree uses to make wood.

While vanilla and caramel are essential maple flavor elements, the full flavor of maple is far more complex, says Potter. One producer's syrup can vary from a neighbor's because of differences in the soil, the tree chemistry, or the method of heating the sap.

The season's earliest sap flow produces Grade A light, or "Fancy" as it is called in Vermont. Honey gold and near-transparent, it has a pronounced sweetness and a delicate vanilla flavor. Grade A light can be the most expensive syrup and is not typically found in supermarkets. While it takes no more energy to produce than the other grades, its higher price was established more than 100 years ago, when "sugaring" was about just that—turning maple syrup into sugar. The lighter syrup made a finer sugar, so it sold at a higher cost, which simply never changed, says Sumner Williams, assistant director at the University of Vermont's Proctor Maple Research Center. Today Grade A light syrups are primarily used to make maple sugar candies.

The season's second syrup is Grade A medium amber. This has a warmer, caramel color with a medium-strength flavor. It is generally touted as the syrup for pancakes. Right on the heels of medium amber is Grade A dark amber, which is slightly deeper in color and has a more pronounced flavor.

After the ambers falls Grade B, the darkest and typically least expensive of the syrups on the market. It is traditionally considered cooking grade because of its strength of flavor. Only Vermont makes Grade B syrup for consumer table use. Other states make a similar syrup but only sell it in bulk to the food industry because it is deemed too strong and too dark. Some whole foods stores carry it in bulk.

Lastly, there is a Grade C, characterized by strong, almost molasses-like flavor. Sold only to the food industry, Grade C is used in table syrups.

Going for Gusto

Of the nine samples in the tasting, tasters de-

Best of the Imitators: Rating Table Syrups

Because pancake syrups far outsell real maple syrups, we decided to do an additional tasting of three top-selling national pancake syrups.

The high scorer was Aunt Jemima, which is made of high fructose corn syrup, with just four percent maple syrup.

We found Aunt Jemima's popularity a bit confusing considering tasters insisted upon strong maple flavor in the maple syrup tasting. Professor Sidney Mintz of Johns Hopkins University, however, was not surprised. It's the sugar appeal, explained the author of *Sweetness and Power* (Viking, 1985).

"[Sugar] is the equivalent in food as crack in drugs," said Mintz. And a product like Aunt Jemima "is sugar with its own distinctive signature." As for pure maple syrup, Mintz said its appeal is beyond that of sugar. "When they think maple, they want it to be intense." Thus,

the choice of Grade B in the maple syrup tasting.

The flavor of pancake syrups also carries with it keen memories of childhood indulgence. Most of us grew up on pancake syrup and many more children will continue to be raised on it primarily because it is affordable. Maple syrup can be two to eight times as expensive as table syrup. Last year, for every 34 pints of pancake syrup purchased at a U.S. supermarket, only one pint of real maple syrup was sold, according to ACNielson statistics.

Aunt Jemima Syrup (ILLINOIS)
➤ 24 fluid ounces sells for $3.59. Many tasters enjoyed the buttery flavor and thick, thick, thick texture, which one taster likened to "30-weight motor oil." While the mere four percent maple syrup content still gave this product a recognizable maple flavor, the fla-

vor of the high fructose corn syrup base was unmistakable.

Log Cabin Syrup (NEW YORK)
➤ 24 fluid ounces sells for $3.49. This dark, thick syrup looked good and carried the strongest aroma, but its evident corn syrup base rendered mixed reactions. Tasters were inclined to write "more maple, please." Extremely thick with a noted buttery flavor, Log Cabin contains two percent maple syrup.

Mrs. Butterworth's Original Syrup (ILLINOIS)
➤ 24 fluid ounces sells for $3.29. It's no surprise tasters found the maple flavor extremely weak—according to its ingredients label, there is none. Many also complained of excessive sweetness and "artificial" flavors. As one taster noted, "It has that gooey texture—definitely diner syrup."

TASTING MAPLE SYRUP

F or our tasting, we identified 10 widely available maple syrups sold in supermarkets, whole foods stores, gourmet stores, and major mail-order outlets. Our tasting was attended by 20 people from *Cook's* editorial staff and staff from our sister magazines, *Natural Health* and *Handcraft Illustrated*. Syrups were served with waffles, water, and orange slices. Tasters rated each syrup according to appearance, flavors, mouth feel, and overall appeal. Scores were based on a scale of 0 to 10. Syrups are listed in accordance with tasters' ranking. Their location of production is listed in parentheses. Prices indicate retail cost.

RECOMMENDED

Highland Sugarworks Grade B (VERMONT)

➤ 32 fluid ounces sells for $19.95.

This syrup, the color of dark rum, had the most assertive maple flavor and yet still carried a strong note of sweetness. Some tasters were tentative, but many were intrigued by its depth of color and flavor. Repeated comments included "great maple flavor" and "tastes real." One taster said, "This syrup has personality to it [and] the flavor still stands up on a waffle." The Guinness of syrups, this might have a bit too much oomph for pancake syrup diehards. Available by mail order from King Arthur Flour Baker's Catalogue (P.O. Box 876, Norwich, VT 05505-0876; 800-827-6836).

Spring Tree Grade A Dark Amber (CANADA)

➤ 8 fluid ounces sells for $3.99.

A close second as a favorite, tasters applauded this syrup for its "nutty, rich flavor." This syrup was the "most complete and engaging of them all," said one taster. Medium-bodied, this syrup's maple flavor was strong and complemented by a moderate sweetness. Available in whole foods stores and some supermarkets.

ACCEPTABLE

Howard's Grade A Dark Amber (CANADA)

➤ 8 fluid ounces sells for $2.79.

Tasters were attracted to the look of this dark, "handsome" syrup. Scores showed tasters were looking for a little more maple flavor but were appeased by its mild sweetness and medium body. A few tasters detected a slight smokiness in the maple flavor. Available in supermarkets.

Camp Grade A Dark Amber (CANADA)

➤ 12.5 fluid ounces sells for $3.79.

Tasters' comments on this caramel-colored maple syrup were devoid of superlatives. It was not "too" anything—it had medium body, medium sweetness, and medium strength of maple flavor. Safe but a bit of a snooze. Available in supermarkets.

NOT RECOMMENDED

President's Choice Grade A Medium Amber (CANADA)

➤ 12.7 fluid ounces sells for $4.59.

This syrup was "way too sweet" with one taster describing it as having an "artificial candy flavor." Tasters also were not impressed by the thin mouth feel.

Atwood's Grade A Medium Amber (NEW YORK)

➤ 16 ounces sells for $11.50.

"Very sugary taste," "too sugary, for most tasters" with a hint of butter and, as many tasters complained, not enough maple syrup flavor. Medium-bodied.

Maple Grove Farms Grade A Dark Amber (VERMONT AND CANADA)

➤ 8.5 fluid ounces sells for $2.79.

While this whole foods store brand scored unremarkably in terms of appearance, maple flavor, sweetness, and mouth feel, tasters were vocal about off flavors "like wood." Others described "pungent," "biting," and "sour" notes.

Palmer's Grade A Fancy (VERMONT)

➤ 18 ounces sells for $14.

This golden, honey colored syrup had the thinnest consistency of all syrups tasted, with the most delicate maple flavors. One taster wrote, "It grows on you. I didn't like it at first, but it gets better." Not enough tasters, however, experienced such a turnaround.

Sweet Life Grade A Dark Amber (CANADA)

➤ 8 fluid ounces sells for $2.59.

"Not a good smell" would aptly summarize tasters' initial response to this syrup. And this introduction proved ominous to the rest of their tasting experience. Many noted a "burnt" aroma and "off" flavors, as well as a "funky aftertaste."

---

cided that if they had the choice, they would reach for the Vermont "B" syrup in the tasting to drizzle on their pancakes. Most tasters were won over by the depth of flavor and the dark rum color of the syrup. Many wrote comments such as "tastes real." And unlike many of the syrups, which lost their distinction when poured on a waffle, this one's bold characteristics held up.

The close runner-up in our tasting was a Grade A dark amber by Spring Tree. Overall, tasters preferred the dark amber syrups to the medium ambers. According to Lynn Reynolds, whose Wisconsin family business, Reynolds Sugarbush Inc., is one of the country's largest and oldest maple syrup operations (established in 1630), the demand for dark amber has recently begun to exceed the demand for medium amber nationwide.

Likewise, the Grade A medium amber syrups in our tasting failed to spark tasters' interest, apparently because they were not bold enough. Not surprisingly, then, tasters flat-out rejected the one "Fancy" grade syrup we included in the tasting.

We purchased William-Sonoma's Grade A Medium Amber syrup, which sells for $16 in a one-quart ceramic jug, but excluded it from the chart because the syrup seemed spoiled. Another jug purchased separately also tasted fermented. Two experts said that ceramic, being porous, may have caused this syrup to spoil from exposure to oxygen.

None of our results indicated syrup made from one region or state is superior to another, and industry experts agreed that it is difficult, if not impossible, to determine by taste where a syrup is made. We also could not conclude that one grade of maple syrup is superior to another. Our winner was a Grade B, but it was the only Grade B in the tasting because it is not typically carried in mainstream shopping outlets. (We purchased ours through a mail-order food catalog.) We would suggest, then, that when purchasing a syrup, consider the strength of flavor and choose the best-ranking product in the above chart accordingly.

Cheap Cookie Sheet Tops Ratings

Save your money. An inexpensive model wins the testing in which surface color matters more than weight, material, or cost.

⇒ BY ADAM RIED WITH EVA KATZ ⇐

Baking scones for breakfast is part of my Sunday morning ritual. Unfortunately, so is listening to the clatter of my ancient cookie sheet warping in the oven heat. But this needn't be so. There are plenty of cookie sheet choices out there, and we set out to evaluate them in terms of materials, finishes, performance, and price, all with the aim of leading you to the best cookie sheet alternative, and me to quieter Sunday mornings.

To select the sheets, we shopped in local discount, department, cookware, and grocery stores. Our eleven sheets, each roughly 12-by-15 inches, covered all the variables— steel, aluminum, light and dark finishes, nonstick coated, heavy "professional" and standard gauges, insulated, and had a variety of sidewall designs. Prices ranged from $6.99 to $29.00, and brands included AirBake (by Mirro), Calphalon, Chicago Metallic, Ekco, Kaiser, Mirro, Nordic Ware, Revere, T-Fal, WearEver CushionAire (also by Mirro), and Wilton.

The sheets were subjected to three tests, all performed in the same oven in our test kitchen. In the first two tests, we baked vanilla icebox cookies and biscuits. Three factors were important: a rich golden, evenly browned bottom; uniform cooking despite their relative positions on the sheet; and even cooking all the way through the biscuits. The second test involved pecan lace cookies. The two most important aspects in this test were uniform, moderate caramelization without burning, and the spread of the cookie, which also dictated whether it became properly thin and gossamer or remained too thick.

Shiny Surfaces Succeed

The Kaiser, Mirro, Revere, AirBake, and Chicago Metallic sheets all browned evenly and well, be it biscuits or cookies. Also, the lace cookies that were baked on these sheets spread, as they should, into evenly thin, see-through, fairly round wafers. When we

The Baking Sheets We Tested

BEST BAKING SHEET

Kaiser Cookie Sheet
Extended rim on one side makes handling easy.

RECOMMENDED

Mirro Great Cooks II
Our favorite among the nonsticks.

Revere Professional Weight
Flat, rimless edge lets food slide on and off.

AirBake Insulated Bakeware
Good choice if you must use bottom rack.

Chicago Metallic Village Baker Commercial Weight
Relatively heavy with tall, straight sidewalls.

NOT RECOMMENDED

Ekco Baker's Secret Non-Stick
Popular supermarket choice warped.

WearEver CushionAire Nonstick Insulated Bakeware Cookie Sheet
No real advantage from insulation.

Nordic Ware Professional Hardcoat Nonstick Griddle/Baking Sheet
Heaviest sheet, performed poorly.

T-Fal Resistal Homebake Cookie Sheet
Gimmicky honeycomb-textured baking surface.

Wilton Enterprises Performance Pans Cookie Pan
Felt flimsier than others.

Calphalon Professional
Sturdy, but performed poorly.

reviewed our testing notes on these five sheets, we expected to see that they were similar in terms of weight, which is determined by the gauge, or thickness, of the metal, and/or the type of metal from which they were made. Not so. The top three sheets weighed two, three-quarters, and one-and-one-quarter pounds, respectively. Likewise, each was made of different materials, including tinned steel, aluminum, and stainless steel, respectively.

One clear pattern did emerge, however. Each of the winning sheets, with the exception of the Mirro, had a shiny silver baking surface without a nonstick coating. The rest of the pack, including the Mirro, were nonstick, with dark-colored baking surfaces ranging from light matte gray to black. The Mirro differed because its baking surface was, by far, the lightest in color of all the nonsticks, and its bottom surface was even lighter. The Ekco, incidentally, was also light gray like the Mirro, and showed reasonably good browning, but it was downgraded for warping in the oven. The Wilton also had a silver finish, but was marked down for denting, warping in the oven, and a flimsy feel.

As a group, the darker nonstick pans produced darker brown, often too dark, baked goods. This stands to reason because the darker color absorbs and retains more heat than the light, shiny surfaces, which deflect some heat.

It is true that the nonstick pans released their contents more readily than those without the coating, especially the sticky lace cookies, but the latter group performed far better than we anticipated in this department. With a modicum of extra pressure and finesse we removed the lace cookies, and certainly the biscuits and icebox cookies, from the conventional sheets without egregious incident. In light of their reliable and even browning characteristics, we were willing to put up with some minor sticking. Sticking, in fact, becomes a moot point when you bake on parchment paper, which saves cleaning effort and allows you to whisk a whole batch of cookies off the sheet in a single movement, and replace it with a raw batch just as easily. Our tests showed no difference in browning with and without parchment paper, so we see no reason not to use it.

All along, we had been curious about the much-touted insulated sheets, with two metal layers sandwiching an air layer meant to prevent burning. In fact, the dark-surfaced, nonstick insulated WearEver Cushion-Aire browned biscuits and cookies too much, like the other dark sheets. The light colored, insulated AirBake sheet, which was among our favorites, did effectively prevent burning by slowing the cooking. Biscuits and cookies took longer to bake, but browned slowly and uniformly in the extra time.

What's That Banging in the Oven?

So what causes some cookie sheets to warp with a resounding, metallic clang in a hot oven? According to Hugh Rushing, executive vice president of the Cookware Manufacturers Association, the primary culprit is stress.

Most cookie sheets start out as a flat sheet of metal that is then stretched into shape by a press. Stretching the metal thins it out, particularly where it bends up from the flat bottom to form the sidewall. The greater the sidewall's angle (as much as 90 degrees to the flat bottom), the more the metal is stretched, thinned, and thus stressed.

This "work-induced stress" results from increased molecular activity within the metal as it is bent. This stress causes the metal at those points to become brittle. When you later put the sheet into a hot oven, the heat increases molecular activity in the metal again and the sheet attempts to return to its original, perfectly flat, state. It cannot, of course, achieve this because the shape has been permanently altered. In the course of trying, however, the sheet may warp, giving off a loud "ping". Once out of the oven, the pan usually warps back in the other direction.

Aluminum is less likely than tinned steel to warp because it heats more evenly. Thicker sheets of metal are less likely to warp than thin ones because they have greater mass and aren't stretched as thin to begin with. Finally, a molded cookie sheet with straight sidewalls is more likely to warp than one with raked sidewalls.   —A.R.

RATING BAKING SHEETS

RATINGS
★★★
GOOD
★★
FAIR
★
POOR

We tested eleven baking sheets according to the following criteria. Performance differences among the sheets that did well were so minor that we would recommend any of them. Therefore, the sheets are listed in two categories—Recommended and Not Recommended. Our choice of best baking sheet was among the top three performers in all three of our tests, and it was the least expensive.
PRICE: Retail price paid in local stores.
MATERIAL/FINISH COLOR: Metal from which the sheet was made and color of baking surface.

BROWNING DEGREE: Sheets that browned biscuit and cookie bottoms to a rich golden shade were rated good. Browning that was moderately darker or lighter, or uneven, was rated fair. Very dark, burnt, or uneven bottoms were rated poor.
BROWNING EVENNESS: Assessed in two categories—the batch viewed in its entirety and the individual biscuit or cookie. Sheets that browned biscuits or cookies placed near the edges at the same rate as those near the center, and individual biscuits and cookies evenly from edge to center, were rated good. Sheets that produced moderate differences in either category were rated fair, and sheets that produced marked or extreme differences, such as burning, in either category were rated poor.

Brand	Price	Materials/Finish	Size	Browning Degree	Browning Evenness	Testers' Comments
BEST BAKING SHEET **Kaiser** Cookie Sheet	$6.99	Tinned Steel/Shiny Silver	14" X 16"	★★★	★★★	Great combination of qualities for very little money.
RECOMMENDED **Mirro** Great Cooks II	$9.39	Aluminum with nonstick	12" X 15½"	★★★	★★★	A good performer for the price, and nonstick to boot.
Revere Professional Weight	$16.99	Stainless Steel/Shiny Silver	12½" X 14½"	★★★	★★★	Lace cookies were a little thick, though within acceptable limits.
AirBake Insulated Bakeware	$16.99	Two sheets of aluminum with an air layer in between/Shiny Silver	14" X 16"	★★★	★★★	Baked biscuits and lace cookies a little bit slowly, but very evenly.
Chicago Metallic Village Baker Commercial Weight	$8.99	Tinned Steel/Shiny Silver	12" X 18"	★★★	★★★	Browned slowly, but a fine choice nonetheless.
NOT RECOMMENDED **Ekco** Baker's Secret Non-Stick	$8.99	Tinned Steel with nonstick coating/Light Gray	10¼" X 15¼"	★★★	★★	Ekco's downfall was warping in the oven, which caused the lace cookies to slide around on the pan and assume odd shapes.
WearEver CushionAire Nonstick Insulated Bakeware	$11.99	Two sheets of aluminum with an air layer in between/Nonstick finish in Medium Gray	14" X 16"	★★	★	Biscuits overcooked around the edges and lace cookies did not spread well.
Nordic Ware Professional Hardcoat Nonstick	$29.00	Heavy Cast Aluminum/Matte Black	13" X 19"	★	★★	Really heavy, and it both burned biscuits and cooked lace cookies unevenly.
T-Fal Resistal Homebake	$9.99	Aluminum with honeycomb textured nonstick coating/Matte Black	11" X 15"	★	★	Burning or uneven browning in all tests.
Wilton Enterprises Performance Pans Cookie Pan	$10.19	Aluminum with anodized finish/Matte Silver	12" X 18"	★	★	The only one to assume a dent during the course of testing, it also warped in the oven with both the icebox and the lace cookies, which therefore cooked unevenly.
Calphalon Professional	$22.99	Heavy Gauge Aluminum/Matte Black	14" X 17½"	★	★	The edges of both cookies and the biscuits browned too much, and too quickly, and the lace cookies spread poorly.

Inexpensive Chardonnays

Wines under $10 don't cut it here, but you don't need to spend much more than that to find good-tasting Chardonnays in a variety of styles. BY MARK BITTMAN

Chardonnay is one of the world's two great white-wine grapes (the other is Riesling), but there is no clear-cut standard for wine labeled "Chardonnay." In fact, I don't even know how many styles of Chardonnay there are anymore. A generation ago, when the vast majority of chardonnay grapes were grown in east-central France, there were at least three very distinct types: crisp, metallic Chablis, long considered the perfect seafood wine; buttery, almost fat stars of Burgundy, such as Montrachet; and the simple, reasonably priced wines of Mâcon.

That this is an oversimplification does not alter the fact that the globalization of Chardonnay has considerably increased the kinds on the market. Some are fruity, some bone-dry; some are aged in oak, some in stainless steel, some in concrete, some not at all; some are highly acidic which makes them great with food (but not for drinking alone), some so low in acid they taste flat, some so well balanced that they can be sipped at almost any time of day.

But the real difficulty lies in the fact that, outside of France, no region is associated with a single style. When wine lovers want a really special bottle of Chardonnay, they most often turn to the traditional wines of France, knowing that a good Chablis will give them one type of wine, a good Burgundy another.

These very good to great wines, however, almost always cost upwards of $30 per bottle. In the price range within which most of us shop most of the time, there are no hard and fast rules. Surprises abound, and sometimes the unpretentious wines at the low end of the scale finish higher in blind tastings than anything selling for three times as much—even though both might come from the same region. Because so many of the wines in this price range are made from grapes sold on the open market, the styles and quality of even "branded" wines may vary wildly from year to year.

Thus generalizations are difficult. In this tasting, we focused on the mid-tier Chardonnays that are most commonly found in wine shops, supermarkets, and restaurants. We excluded boxed and jug wines from the tasting (those are another story), as well as high-end wines, and even those in our price range (under $15) that are not widely available. The result was a tasting dominated by wines from California and France, with one entry each from Washington and Australia.

Despite its rather narrow focus, this tasting did not reveal much in the way of a pattern; the results were as scattered as the styles of wines themselves. Our first four finishers represented four different styles: an oaky, big wine that mimics Burgundy in a way that professionals find crude but amateurs clearly enjoy; a sharp, acidic wine with finesse; a complex but somewhat off-putting Burgundy; and a clean but somewhat sweet Californian. What these wines have in common is good craft, and it's safe to say that they each placed well in the tasting because the preferences of the dozen members of our panel cover as broad a spectrum as the wines themselves.

This means that you'd be well off to define your preferences before buying any of these wines. If a strong oak flavor is what you like, try the Kendall-Jackson; if you want Chablis-like wine, sample the Chateau Ste. Michelle. And so on. I feel safe in saying that all of the "recommended" wines are sound, but I am much less confident about those that are "recommended with reservations" because the reservations were many. As for those in the "not recommended" category, they may return as perfectly fine wines in the next vintage.

THE JUDGES' RESULTS | INEXPENSIVE CHARDONNAYS

The wines in our tasting—held at Mt. Carmel Wine and Spirits, in Hamden, Connecticut—were judged by a panel made up of both wine professionals and amateur wine lovers. The wines were all purchased in the Northeast; prices will vary considerably throughout the country.

Within each category, wines are listed based on the number of points scored. In this tasting, the "Recommended" wines had a majority of positive comments. Those labeled "Recommended with Reservations" had mixed comments—some positive, some negative, with no clear majority. "Not Recommended" wines garnered few, if any, positive comments.

RECOMMENDED

1996 Kendall-Jackson Vintners Reserve, CALIFORNIA $12. "Nice balance" with "buttery, oaky flavor" and "good acidity." The overwhelming choice of the amateurs, slightly disparaged by professionals for lack of sophistication.
1995 Chateau Ste. Michelle, COLUMBIA VALLEY, WASHINGTON. $12. "Has life," "balance," and "complexity." Chablis-like in spirit.
1996 Jadot, BURGUNDY, FRANCE. $12.50. "Little oak" but "very good" "fruit, acidity, and balance." "Gotta be French." Good hints of finer Burgundies.
1995 Beaulieu Vineyards, CARNEROS, CALIFORNIA. $13. "Nice nose" with "good balance" and a "touch of elegance." In my experience, one of the consistent California classics, a crisp wine with some oak.

RECOMMENDED WITH RESERVATIONS

1996 Latour, BURGUNDY, FRANCE. $10. "Clean, lovely wine; not big but good." "Overwhelming" acidity turned some off.
1995 Beringer, NAPA, CALIFORNIA. $15. "Oaky and a bit sweet," this "old-style California Chardonnay" may please some, but not all.
1995 Mondavi Coastal Chardonnay, CALIFORNIA. $10. "Not a strong wine," but "pleasant and good with food." Some found it "thin."
1995 Sebastiani, SONOMA, CALIFORNIA. $10. This wine confused almost everyone. Comments like "sweet but not fruity" and "rich but not classy" dominated.
1996 Macon-Lugny, LES CHARMES, FRANCE. $9. Once this was the inexpensive Chardonnay, full of character and life. Now it has "off-flavors" to go with its "real body" and "austere but good-tasting" fruit.
1996 Drouhin Laforet, BURGUNDY, FRANCE. $11. "Nicely balanced," "very clean but not impressive." Again, "high" acidity drove off some tasters.

NOT RECOMMENDED

1996 Rosemount Estate, SOUTH AUSTRALIA. $10.
1996 Fetzer Sundial, CALIFORNIA. $7.
1995 Glen Ellen Proprietors Reserve, CALIFORNIA. $6.
1995 Woodbridge, CALIFORNIA. $8.

The New Joy of Cooking

For better and for worse, this massive revision marks the decline of the enthusiastic amateur in American cooking. BY CHRISTOPHER KIMBALL

The new, revised edition of *Joy* (left) is certainly less whimsical than the original version (right).

In the original *Joy of Cooking*, author Irma Rombauer includes a quote from Goethe's *Faust*: "That which thy fathers have bequeathed to thee, earn it anew if thou wouldst possess it." These words, spoken at many German-American civic occasions from the late nineteenth century through World War I, were familiar to the German-descended Rombauer. She was the daughter of an immigrant, in a nation of immigrants, full of love for America and an intense enthusiasm that is carried only in the bosom of an amateur. Rombauer lived in a unique moment in our history, when one self-published cookbook could accurately reflect a broad melting pot of home cooks whose tastes and aspirations were remarkably homogenous. As I set out to test and review the new edition, the intriguing question was whether *Joy* could still reach out to millions, speaking a common language in an era of reverse gravity, when the mass of American culture no longer draws us toward the center.

The revised *Joy of Cooking* emerged from a multimillion dollar storm of controversy. The editor, Maria Guarnaschelli, is well known as a fierce, brilliant, mercurial intellect. Long before this book went to press, the media knives were being sharpened; this was one cookbook that everyone would love to hate. After all, a big New York publisher was spending a small fortune chain-sawing the seminal culinary work of twentieth century America. Here was the irrepressible Irma Rombauer, middle-class housewife from St. Louis, versus the greed and corruption of Gotham.

That's quite a story—but the machinations of

how a cookbook is written don't matter to most home cooks. We don't have to spend an evening with Guarnaschelli, we just have to cook out of her book—and I would argue that there is more of Guarnaschelli in this book than there is of Irma Rombauer, her daughter Marion Rombauer Becker, or her grandson Ethan Becker. So we turned to our test kitchen and prepared fifty dishes, sampled over three months.

Simply stated, the recipes work, and a whopping two-thirds are ones that we would make again. Many were straight-on, competent versions of American classics, and others were slightly more exotic, including vegetable stock, soy-braised chicken, biscotti, and a chocolate-glazed caramel tart. The clunkers included Ohio Lemon Pie, full of chewy, stringy, whole lemon slices; a few of the egg recipes; and oxtails smothered in onions. It should also be noted that the range of recipes is impressive. On the whole, a first-rate job and kudos to Guarnaschelli.

But the original *Joy* was no more just a cookbook than the New Testament is simply an historical account. Rombauer was a good writer with a clever and elegant turn of phrase. She refers to a cocktail party hostess as all "cheer and fluttering organdy" and says about making the most of a mishap during a party, "Capitalize on it, but not too heavily." Best of all, Rombauer knew her audience and spoke directly and honestly to each and every one of them. Her nonjudgmental air invited her readers in and made them comfortable.

The new *Joy* has the outlines right, but something is amiss. The prose is competent but impersonal, well-written but pedestrian. The way it echoes the words of the original author gives it a haunting quality, like an accomplished but unremarkable torch singer believing that he can successfully imitate every tonal nuance of Nat King Cole. Instead of Rombauer's wonderful turn of phrase regarding a mishap at a party, for example, the new *Joy* simply states that a minor castastrophe could be the making of your party.

And here lies the rub. For the new *Joy*, Guarnaschelli assembled the greatest team of

culinary experts in the history of cookbook publishing. In addition to the difficulties of writing a manuscript by committee, this changes the relationship with the reader. In fact, it is Rombauer's standing as an amateur that made her dialogue so compelling. Although she could put on airs, she was anti-elitist to the core, disdaining the heavy hand of the culinary expert. As Anne Mendelson comments in her biography *Stand Facing The Stove* (Henry Holt and Company, 1996), "She would never presume to lead American taste; the existing state of taste was fine with her." Rombauer's success was in reflecting her times. Instead of leading the masses to greener culinary pastures, she took them on a private lark, offering her companionship, her knowledge, her genteel enthusiasm. She invited others to see how she cooked; she didn't tell them how to cook.

By contrast, the new *Joy* seems unclear about both about its audience and its voice. While introducing us to Thai spices and Northern Italian cooking, for example, it also promotes an updated version of Golden Glow Gelatin Salad. One suspects that the gelatin salads were included for marketing purposes, that the publishers were afraid to throw out recipes that focus groups determined were dear to their constituents.

Of course, this is no reason not to purchase the new *Joy*. In fact, I highly recommend it. The recipes are vastly better than those in the previous edition, which was badly outdated. It is comprehensive, and given the limitations of updating a classic without losing its commercial imprimatur, it is a first-rate job. But when you hand over your $30, remember that even cookbooks should be part poetry. They are a reflection of not only the author but the times. Rombauer wasn't perfect, but she belonged to and reflected the tastes and aspirations of mid-century America. It is a warm, comforting image, one of imperfection and enthusiasm, one that can only be promoted by a true amateur. As we face the looking glass of the new *Joy*, we may be more accomplished and sophisticated cooks, but lacking, I think, the essence of the enterprise, the joy of cooking. Sadly, the latest edition tells us that we are a professionally packaged consensus of opinion, but hardly, in the words of Nat King Cole, unforgettable.

REVIEW

Joy of Cooking
Irma S. Rombauer,
Marion Rombauer
Becker, and
Ethan Becker
Charles Scribner & Sons, $30

Most of the ingredients and materials necessary for the recipes in this issue are available at your local supermarket, gourmet store, or kitchen supply shop. The following are mail-order sources for particular items. Prices listed below were current at press time and do not include shipping or handling unless otherwise indicated. We suggest that you contact companies directly to confirm up-to-date prices and availability.

Cookie Sheets
After baking batches and batches of cookies as well as dozens of biscuits in our test kitchen, Kaiser's tinned steel cookie sheet stood out as the number one cookie sheet for its ability to brown evenly without over- or undercooking baked goods (see page 28). And in addition to all that, it's affordable, costing only about $7. We also liked the design of this 14-by-16-inch cookie sheet because one short side has a raised lip for handling ease, while the other short side has an open edge to easily slide off finished baked goods. Both long sides have short angled rims to prevent foods from sliding off as the pans are placed in and pulled out of the oven. You can mail order the Kaiser cookie sheet for $6.99 from **Kitchen Etc. catalog services (Department TM, 32 Industrial Drive, Exeter, NH 03833; 800-232-4070).**

Ancho and New Mexico Chiles
A blend of dried ancho and New Mexico chiles was developed for our chili con carne recipe on page 10 because of their distinct yet complementary flavors as well as their widespread availability to home cooks. Ancho chiles, which in Spanish means "wide" chiles, are spade-shaped pods measuring about three to four inches long and approximately the same width at the top. New Mexico chiles taper to a blunt end and have narrower shoulders than the anchos, measuring about two inches wide and six inches long. More and more supermarkets are selling whole dried chiles, but if yours does not, you can order both the ancho and New Mexico chiles by mail from the **CMC Company (P.O. Box 322, Avalon, NJ 08202; 800-262-2780).** CMC sells six ounces of anchos for $6.00, and the same amount of New Mexico chiles for $5.50.

Chipotle en Adobo
Many chefs in America are hot on the flavor of the chipotle pepper, which is a dried, smoked jalapeño. Generally added to stews and sauces, chipotles are wrinkled, with yellowish brown skin and a smoky, sweet, almost chocolate flavor. As a takeoff from our master chili con carne recipe, we created a smoky chili con carne variation (see page 11) by searing the chuck roast on the grill and replacing fresh jalapeños with chipotles packed in an adobo sauce. The adobo sauce is a dark red, piquant vinegar and herb mixture. After opening a can of chipotles en adobo, store in a non-corrosive container and refrigerate. They should then keep for two or three weeks. **CMC Company (P.O. Box 322, Avalon, NJ 08202; 800-262-2780)** sells a seven-ounce can of chipotles en adobo sauce for $3.50.

Masa Harina
Masa harina is a finely ground corn flour used to make tortillas, tostadas, and tamales. It is made from dried corn kernels that have been cooked in limewater (water mixed with calcium oxide) and then ground into a powdery meal. The **CMC Company (P.O. Box 322, Avalon, NJ 08202; 800-262-2780)** sells a two-kilogram package of masa harina for $5.95. When stored well-wrapped in a dry place it should last about a year.

Mexican Oregano
Oregano, an herb whose name is derived from the Latin and Greek words meaning "joy of the mountains," has been used in cooking for more than 2,000 years. In that time, several varieties of the plant have been developed. Greek and Mexican oregano, two of the most widely used varieties, have distinctly different flavors and shouldn't be interchanged in recipes. Greek oregano, is sweet and strong, and is an essential ingredient in numerous Mediterranean dishes. Mexican oregano has a pungent, herbaceous taste and blends well with the spicy hot dishes of the region. Mexican oregano is also often paired with cilantro in salsas and guacamole. The **CMC Company (P.O. Box 322, Avalon, NJ 08202; 800-262-2780)** sells whole-leaf dried Mexican oregano at $2.85 for two ounces.

Springform Pans
A springform pan is round and shallow like a cake pan but has an expandable side with a clasp. The clasp forms a tight seal with the base for cooking but also snaps apart for easy removal. These pans are designed for delicate desserts such as cheesecakes, mousse cakes, and our flourless chocolate cake recipe (see page 23), as well as cakes with crumb crusts that are difficult to cleanly release from a pan. **Sur La Table (Catalog Division, 1765 Sixth Avenue South, Seattle, WA 98134-1608; 800-243-0852)** carries the hard-to-find eight-inch springform pan that we prefer for our flourless chocolate cake recipe. This stainless steel pan sells by mail order for $15.95. Sur La Table also sells the more popular nine-inch springform pan for $16.95. While our flourless chocolate cake recipe is designed for both pans, we prefer the look of the taller cake made in the eight-inch pan.

Semisweet Chocolates
The *Cook's* editorial staff tasted six flourless chocolate cakes, each made from different brands of semisweet chocolate. While preferences differed, there was agreement as to the taste and texture qualities of the cakes that each chocolate produced. Ghirardelli chocolate was applauded for its creamy, true chocolate flavor as well as its velvety texture. A four-ounce bar of Ghirardelli semisweet chocolate can be found in many supermarkets or ordered by mail for $1.99 from **Dairy Fresh Candies (57 Salem Street, Boston, MA 02113; 800-336-5536).** Dairy Fresh also sells blocks of Callebaut semisweet chocolate, which was characterized in the tasting as having a rich chocolate taste and silky texture, for $4.99 per pound. Van Leer, which gets its creamy texture from 39 percent cocoa butter, can be ordered in chunks for $5 per pound from **New York Cake and Baking Distributor (56 West 22nd Street, New York, NY 10010; 800-942-2539).** Nestle's and Baker's semisweet chocolates, which were noted for their "mousselike" texture and sweetness, can be found in supermarkets nationwide.

Diamond Steels
While traditional sharpening steels help maintain a knife's edge, the Ultimate Edge Diamond Sharpening Steel can bring back an edge and prolong the need for a thorough sharpening (see page 3). A diamond steel is made from an oval-shaped lightweight steel shaft with a 600-grit diamond mesh bond, which provides a hard surface to clean metal off a dulled knife and renew its edge. A 10-inch-long Ultimate Edge diamond steel will fit into most knife blocks and sells for $25 by mail order from both **Professional Cutlery Direct (170 Boston Post Road, Suite 135, Madison, CT 06443; 800-859-6994)** and **Stoddard's (50 Temple Place, Boston, MA 02111; 617-426-4187).** To hone a chef's knife with a diamond steel, hold the blade at a 20-degree angle away from the steel just as you would with a traditional sharpening steel.

Maple Syrup Six-Pack
Unsure of which grade of maple syrup you prefer? You can conduct your own mini taste test of the various grades of maple syrup to determine whether you prefer Fancy, Grade A medium or dark amber, or Grade B. **Vermont Only of Mile Square Farm, Inc.,** sells a six-pack of Vermont maple syrup containing one Fancy Grade sample, two Grade A medium amber samples, two Grade A dark amber samples, and one Grade B sample for $18.95. Each sample is packaged in a four-ounce tin. Order **by phone (888-868-6659)** or **through their web site (http://www.vtonly.com).**

RECIPE INDEX

Browned and Braised Cauliflower with Indian Spices
PAGE 7

Chile con Carne
PAGE 10

Oven "Poached" Whole Salmon
PAGE 14

Ultimate Flourless Chocolate Cake
PAGE 23

Grilled Fresh Mozzarella Sandwich with Olive Paste and Roasted Red
Peppers **PAGE 20**

Big, Super-Nutty Peanut Butter Cookies
PAGE 25

PHOTOGRAPHY: CARL TREMBLAY, STYLING: MYROSHA DZIUK

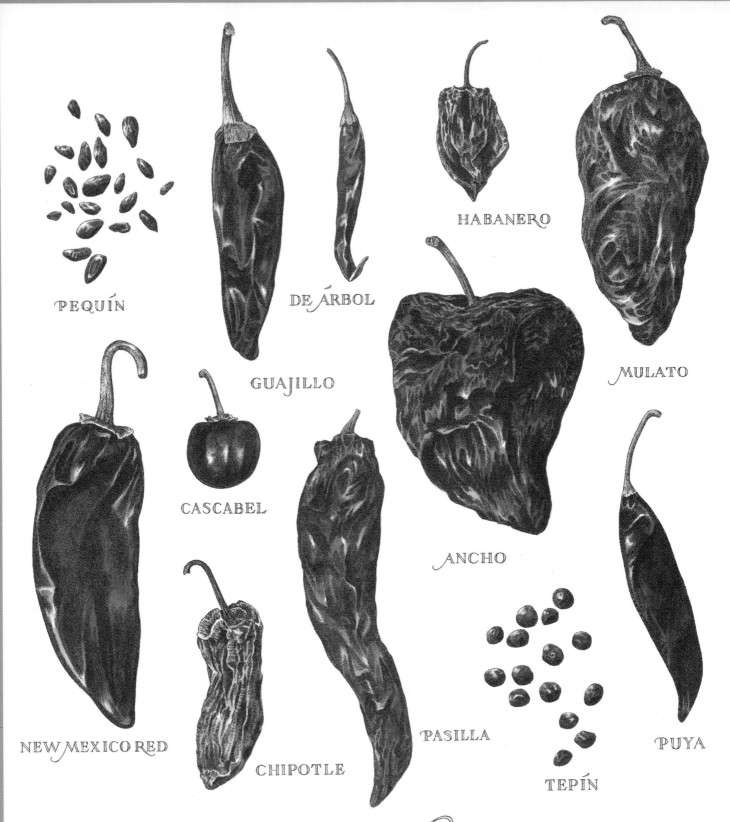

PEQUÍN

DE ÁRBOL

HABANERO

GUAJILLO

MULATO

CASCABEL

ANCHO

NEW MEXICO RED

CHIPOTLE

PASILLA

PUYA

TEPÍN

DRIED CHILES

COOK'S
ILLUSTRATED

Fresh Strawberry Pie
A Light, Fresh Pie
from Scratch

Rating Unsalted Butters
Should You Buy Expensive,
High-Fat Brands?

Grilling Tuna
No More Dry Fish Steaks

Testing Smokers
Electric Models Outperform Charcoal

Perfect Lemon Bars
Fresh, Lemony Filling and a
Crisp but Tender Crust

Southern Cornbread
Grilling Asparagus
Secrets of London Broil
How to Make Sangria
The Best Roast Potatoes
Grilled Lemon Chicken

$4.00 U.S./$4.95 CANADA

06 >

0 232816 4

62805

CONTENTS
May & June 1998

COOK'S ILLUSTRATED

PUBLISHER AND EDITOR
Christopher Kimball

EXECUTIVE EDITOR
Pam Anderson

SENIOR EDITOR
John Willoughby

SENIOR WRITER
Jack Bishop

ASSOCIATE EDITORS
Adam Ried
Maryellen Driscoll

TEST KITCHEN DIRECTOR
Susan Logozzo

TEST COOK
Anne Yamanaka

CONTRIBUTING EDITORS
Mark Bittman
Stephanie Lyness

EDITORIAL INTERN
Jessica Drench

ART DIRECTOR
Amy Klee

CORPORATE MANAGING EDITOR
Barbara Bourassa

EDITORIAL PROD. MANAGER
Sheila Datz

COPY EDITOR
Carol Parikh

MARKETING DIRECTOR
Adrienne Kimball

CIRCULATION DIRECTOR
David Mack

FULFILLMENT MANAGER
Larisa Greiner

CIRCULATION MANAGER
Darcy Beach

MARKETING ASSISTANT
Connie Forbes

PRODUCTS MANAGER
Steven Browall

VICE PRESIDENT
PRODUCTION AND TECHNOLOGY
James McCormack

SYSTEMS ADMINISTRATOR
James Burke

DESKTOP PUBLISHING MANAGER
Kevin Moeller

PRODUCTION ARTIST
Robert Parsons

PRODUCTION ASSISTANT
Daniel Frey

CONTROLLER
Lisa A. Carullo

SENIOR ACCOUNTANT
Mandy Shito

OFFICE MANAGER
Livia McRee

SPECIAL PROJECTS
Fern Berman

SALAD GREENS

SALAD GREENS In recent years, the variety of available greens has increased exponentially. For culinary purposes salad greens are best categorized in terms of their relative bitterness. Lowest on the bitterness scale are the lettuces, of which there are hundreds of varieties, including the green oak leaf and green romaine pictured here. Many other European-derived greens, including Belgian endive, mâche, and red beet leaf, are also relatively sweet, with only a slight edge of bitterness. Arugula, frisée, escarole, and radicchio, on the other hand, have a rather strong, peppery flavor. The newly popular Asian greens, such as mizuna, tatsoi, and red Asian mustard, are perhaps the bitterest of the greens, adding distinctive flavors to any dish.

COVER PAINTING: BRENT WATKINSON. BACK COVER ILLUSTRATION: JOHN BURGOYNE

THE COUNTRY STORE

Our local country store is a real working man's hangout, not a tourist destination. Like a bottomless wine jug out of some Greek myth, this store has everything. If you are in need of tools for painting, car repair, or rough carpentry, they have them. You can also find stacks of duct and masking tape, road flares, Tung-Sol auto lamps, and Goof Off paint remover. If you are sick, they have shelves packed with all the usual pharmaceuticals plus Dr. Seltzer's Hangover Helper and a box of ginseng tablets for energy. Hunters purchase their licenses here by the day, week, or year. If you need ammunition, that's no problem either; they stock everything from 22 shorts to 12-gauge shotgun shells for dove and quail (number 8 shot), rabbit and squirrel (number 6), and pheasant (number 4). You can also buy plenty of supplies for black powder rifles, including Pyrodex powder, .50-caliber lead-saboted boat-tail bullets, ramrods, nipple wrenches, cleaners, and patches, as well as standard rifle-cleaning equipment such as bore butter. Fishermen can find a broad assortment of Umpqua flies, including a Gray Yellow Hackle, an Elk Caddis, and a Trico Spinner. There is also plenty to chew on, from Skoal Long Cut to Red Man Tobacco, as well as Zig-Zag papers for rolling your own.

The proprietors, Doug and Nancy Schorn, have lots of merchandise to attract the kids as well. You can find Hacky Sack Footbags, Tippy Toes Finger Puppets, Jetfire Gliders, a jumbo bag of My Farm animals with 16 pieces, an Explorer H20 Rocket, a Woody Woodpecker Magic Draw, removable tattoos, Giant Outdoor Chalk, and a Bible Song Sing Along. For candy, there are bags of jelly beans, gumdrops, candy watches, and the original hard-chew Bazooka Joe bubble gum.

The real attraction, however, is the round table in the back, right next to the coffee shelf. This is the heart and soul of the town, especially early in the morning when the carpenters, electricians, and plumbers stop by for a cup of coffee and the opportunity to complain about the town selectmen, or the new town garage, or the seccession of our sovereign rights to the United Nations. A book entitled *Redneck Classics* lies open on the table, offering plenty of good advice. Former patrons have left a wall of hats behind, advertising everything from the Mall of America to Daytona Bike Week, Wilcox Lumber, Tri-State Mega Bucks, UPS, and Salem cigarettes. Although seemingly out of place, "Cat In The Hat" style headgear abounds as well, stuffed onto the head of a mannequin sporting hunting gear and propped onto the head of a buck, towering over its branched eight-point antlers. A postcard of the board of directors is posted right above the table: four donkeys staring out of a desert scene. You can also purchase copies of *Bass & Walleye Boats*, *X 4 Power*, *Vermont Deer Camp Recipes*, or *American Astrology*.

But what really makes a Vermont country store is the unexpected. You can still buy a small green can of Antiseptic Bag Balm for your cow, a one-dollar postcard from a grab bag, Larvex Cedarized Moth Balls, a candy apple kit, or bumper stickers that read, "My Kid Beat Up Your Honor Student" or "Just When You Think Life's a Bitch It Has Puppies." When the door opens, the old cow bell still rings with its deep, low clang. And as you walk in you can't help but see the sign that reads, "If We Don't Have It,

Christopher Kimball

You Don't Want It."

When I was a kid, a trip to the store meant a handful of Mallo Cups, dark chocolate rounds spiked with crispy coconut and filled with gooey marshmallow, or a box of Black Snake fire tablets, or a green plastic water pistol that would last about 24 hours, the trigger hanging loose from the fingerguard after just a few fill-ups. I usually stopped by after milking for an orange or grape soda, my T-shirt stuck with small spikes of hay. Although the Mallo Cups disappeared a few years back, the water pistols and snake tablets are still there, as are the balsa airplanes, smoke bombs, and cap pistols.

I sit out on the porch with a can of Dr. Pepper, watch the cheap American flag flutter occasionally in the hot breeze, listen to the clank of the cowbell, and wait for my children as they excitedly flit from one attraction to the next, trying to decide between candy lipstick and bubble gum tape or the small yellow plastic bank and the miniature finger puppets. I feel as if I have been sitting on this porch for 40 years now, winters and summers having come and gone, my kids first as newborns, now almost teenagers, soon to set off on their own journey, one that begins on the road that runs by this little store. They may go left or right, drive slow or push forward with great anticipation, but this old country road always comes back around. You find yourself, many years later, sitting on this narrow front porch, knowing that your grandchildren will someday take your place, listening to the dull clang of the same cowbell that greeted you so many years ago.

ABOUT COOK'S ILLUSTRATED

The Magazine *Cook's Illustrated* is published every other month (6 issues per year) and accepts no advertising. A one-year subscription is $24.95, two years is $45, and three years is $65. Add $6 postage per year for Canadian subscriptions and $12 per year for all other foreign countries. To order subscriptions call 800-526-8442. Gift subscriptions are available for $24.95 each.

Magazine-Related Items *Cook's Illustrated* is available in an annual hardbound edition, which includes an index, for $24.95 each plus shipping and handling. Discounts are available if more than one year is ordered at a time. Back issues are available for $5 each. The *Cook's Illustrated* 1998 calendar, featuring 12 of the magazine's covers reproduced in full color, is available for $12.95. *Cook's* also offers a 5-year index (1993-1997) of the magazine for $12.95. To order any of these products, call 800-611-0759.

Books *Cook's Illustrated* publishes a series of single-topic books, available for $14.95 each. Titles include: *How To Make A Pie, How To Make An American Layer Cake, How To Stir Fry, How*

To Make Ice Cream, How To Make Pizza, How To Make Holiday Desserts, How To Make Pasta Sauces, and *How To Grill.* The *Cook's Bible,* written by Christopher Kimball and published by Little Brown, is available for $24.95. To order any of these books, call 800 611 0759.

Reader Submissions *Cook's* accepts reader submissions for both Quick Tips and Notes From Readers. We will provide a one-year complimentary subscription for each Quick Tip that we print. Send a description of your technique, along with your name, address, and daytime telephone number, to Quick Tips, *Cook's Illustrated*, P.O. Box 569, Brookline, MA 02147. Questions, suggestions, or other submissions for Notes From Readers should be sent to the same address.

Subscription Inquiries All queries about subscriptions or change of address notices should be addressed to *Cook's Illustrated*, P.O. Box 7446, Red Oak, IA 51591-0446.

Website Address Selected articles and recipes from *Cook's Illustrated* and subscription information is available online. You can access the *Cook's* website at: www.cooksillustrated.com.

Make–Ahead Sauces

The recipes in Jack Bishop's September/October 1997 article "Quick Broccoli Side Dishes" were very appetizing. I must admit, though, however old-fashioned, that I prefer Hollandaise sauce on broccoli. I know that Hollandaise is best served right off the heat because reheating a cooled sauce can cause it to curdle, but I've heard that if you must make it ahead, Hollandaise can be held in a thermos for several hours without separating. Does this really work?

FLORENCE ROTHBAUM
PALM BEACH, FL

➤ Keeping finished sauce in a preheated thermos does work. Warm emulsion sauces such as Hollandaise are notoriously fragile when reheating, even in a bain-marie or double boiler, because the egg can easily overcook and curdle, or the butter can separate out in pools. The thermos method circumvents that risk and saves last-minute work.

Two easy tips can make a real difference, though. First, preheat the thermos for thirty seconds with hot water, taking care to dry it thoroughly after the water is emptied out. Second, use a small thermos that will be filled completely by the sauce. In our tests, Hollandaise remained in good condition for two and a half hours in a small thermos, cooling by only three degrees per hour. In a large thermos that was only partially full, however, the sauce dropped five degrees per hour, lasting in good condition for about one and a half hours. We also had success keeping a beurre blanc in the smaller thermos, so we'd use this method for any type of sauce we wanted to make ahead and keep warm for a couple of hours.

Salt Levels in Salted Butter

How much salt is in a quarter-pound stick of salted butter?

SUSAN LIBBEY
SANTA FE, NM

➤ Concurrent with our research for the rating story on unsalted butter on page 24 in this issue, we spoke to many food scientists and butter industry representatives about salted butter and found that there is no firm answer to your question. The exact amount of salt in butter varies from brand to brand, with a range of 1.25 to 1.75 percent by weight. Assuming an average of 1.5 percent, this works out to be about 1.7 grams of salt per ¼-pound stick, and 1.7 grams measured by volume equals around ⅓ teaspoon.

Our interest was roused, though, when someone on the Land O' Lakes hotline told us that it makes very little, if any, difference whether you use salted or unsalted butter in cooking. To see if this was true, we put a salted butter sample through the same paces as the unsalted butters in the testing story. We found the differences to be very subtle in preparations with strong flavors or many other ingredients, such as basic yellow cake or chocolate chip cookies. In preparations such as basic pie crust, beurre blanc, or buttercream, though, all of which depend heavily on butter for a fresh, delicate flavor, the differences between salted and unsalted were dramatic. Tasters called a beurre blanc made with salted butter "harsh," "off," and "stale," and the salted butter buttercream "overwhelming" and "horrible" in its saltiness.

In our view, substituting salted for unsalted butter in recipes poses two difficulties. First, it is not as easy to control the level of salt in the dish as it is when you add it yourself. Second, salted butter can be stored longer and sold later than unsalted, and therefore may be less fresh. The salt can mask off flavors in less-than-fresh butter that the heat of cooking will expose. So while it is possible to substitute salted butter for unsalted in some recipes, judge the type of dish very carefully and steer clear of those in which the butter is a primary flavoring.

Making Butter at Home

Recently, we wanted to see what would happen if you overwhipped cream, having heard that this was something to avoid. We put a pint of heavy whipping cream in our KitchenAid stand mixer and whipped it on high speed. After it passed the stage of nice whipped cream, it began to get grainy and taste buttery rather than creamy. We kept whipping. About four minutes later, the stuff started looking wet, then a milky liquid separated out and butter began to form around the beater. We drained the butter in a fine sieve over a bowl, and it tasted clean and lovely... even better than store-bought.

Besides finding one more cool thing to do with a stand mixer, this is a good thing to know if you ever do overwhip your cream...and it's a lot of fun watching the process.

JULIA GRAHAM AND NATHAN MESNIKOFF
BOULDER, CO

➤ We repeated your experiment in the test kitchen and our butter formed just as yours did. To finish the butter, though, we added two steps, rinsing and kneading, to the process. Both were suggested by Pennsylvania State University Professor of Food Science and former butter maker, Dr. Manfred Kroger.

After pouring the milky liquid, which is buttermilk, off the newly formed butter, we rinsed the granules in successive changes of very cold water until the water had lost its white tinge and was perfectly clear. Kroger explained that rinsing washes much of the milk solids, left behind from the cream, off the butter. This helps protect against spoilage, since the solids, which are protein, are the first components to spoil. This is why clarified butter, from which the milk solids are removed, keeps longer than regular butter.

Second, we kneaded the rinsed butter to change its texture from granular and separated, as it was right after forming in the mixer bowl, to smooth and waxy. We wrapped the butter in a doubled clean dishtowel and worked it by hand until it exuded very, very little liquid, about five minutes. At the same time, we kneaded a trace of salt into the butter to round out its flavor. When all was said and done, our two cups of cream yielded just under five ounces of butter.

For detailed information on the physical transformation of cream into butter, *see* "Cream vs. Butter" on page 24 in this issue.

Cobia

At the fish counter in my market, I recently noticed a fish I'd never seen before called cobia. It had white flesh and black skin, and the clerk told me to treat it like mahimahi. I checked all my cookbooks, my kitchen encyclopedia, and my dictionaries and could find no reference to cobia.

EVELYN CHASE
HOPKINTON, NH

➤ Mark Bittman, author of *Fish, the Complete Guide to Buying and Cooking* (Macmillan, 1994) and *Cook's* contributing editor and wine writer, reports that cobia is a fast-swimming fish found on both the East and Gulf coasts of the U.S. Also called sargentfish because its skin is very dark and striped, or crabeater, because it feeds on crustaceans among other things, cobia can grow as large as one hundred pounds. The flesh is meaty and fairly dense, with a texture similar to Mako shark or swordfish. On the rare occasions when cobia is available, you are most likely to see steaks or fillets.

According to Mark Godcharles, Fisheries Management Specialist at the National Marine Fisheries Service, both the federal government and the governments of coastal states from Texas to New York imposed stringent size and harvest restrictions on cobia fishing as early as 1983. With a harvest, or "bag," limit of no more than two fish per person per day, these restrictions preclude commercial cobia fishing. The restrictions were imposed in order to stabilize the population and sustain the resource.

We were not able to locate any cobia to sample ourselves, but Bittman suggests preparing it as you might Mako shark or swordfish.

Safer String Dispenser

In the January/February 1998 issue, you published a Quick Tip for making a kitchen string dispenser out of a jar (*see* January/February 1998, page 4). The illustration showed a nail being driven through a jar lid that was still affixed to the jar. I know from an experience I had as a child thirty years ago that if the blow is not perfect, the jar could easily shatter and cause injury. It is best to remove the lid before punching the hole. Otherwise, it is a great tip.

JERALD MADDOW
COLLINGSWOOD, NJ

➤ You make an excellent point, and we were lucky the jar did not break the couple of times we tried this tip in the test kitchen. It would be much safer to hammer the nail through a lid placed on the ground outside or in a garage (rather than on a countertop or cutting board which might be damaged by the nail point). We urge anyone who might try that tip to take the lid off the jar before poking the hole.

Putting the "Dutch" in Dutch Oven

Chris Kimball's sidebar "But What Is a Dutch Oven?" in the January/February 1998 equipment testing story "Rating Large Dutch Ovens" caught the interest of many readers, a couple of whom wrote to offer their own theories of how this type of pot got its name.

In a sidebar to the Dutch oven testing story in the January/February 1998 issue, you pass along the speculation that a Dutch oven is so named because the best cast iron came from Holland. That may be. I would like to share my speculation.

As an adjective, Dutch often means "false" or "imitation." My father sometimes called whiskey "Dutch courage," and when giving a friend stern advice, he would say he was acting as a "Dutch uncle." A "Dutch treat" is no treat at all—except for the pleasure of the other person's company. Similarly, a Dutch oven has many of the uses of an oven but is not an oven.

TIM DONAHUE
COLUMBIA, SC

I was interested in your explanation of how Dutch ovens were named. During the winter of 1988 we lived in Amsterdam, and I was amazed to discover that the kitchen in our flat was complete with everything but an oven! I mentioned this to our cleaning woman, who said that "it's rare to find a place around here that has an oven."

She went on to explain that most Dutch houses have only stovetops because traditionally people took their baking to be completed at the local bakery, or they simply purchased baked goods. Their means for cooking something that we would put in an oven was to use a large pot over low heat on the cooktop— hence the term "Dutch oven." This explanation made sense to me because almost every block of my shopping street in Amsterdam had a bakery, and I'd wondered why there were so many. This may well be folklore rather than fact, but I thought it added another dimension to your explanation of the term "Dutch oven."

VEDA BOTTOMLEY
VIENNA, VA

➤ Proving the origin of the term "Dutch oven" may be impossible. Adding one more theory to the ones advanced here by our readers and by Chris Kimball in his sidebar, two other sources we consulted claimed that the term derives from the popularity of this type of covered cooking pot among the Pennsylvania Dutch.

Microwave Meatloaf

I have also given up on the microwave for major cooking tasks and use it only for defrosting and melting and the like. I do, however, get good results with meatloaf. I start it in the microwave, at 70% power for seven minutes, and finish it in the oven.

NICKI PENDLETON WOOD
NASHVILLE, TN

➤ More of the readers who wrote to us regarding our assessment of the microwave's strengths and weaknesses (*see* "The Microwave Chronicles," January/February 1998) agreed with us than not. You were not the only reader, though, to suggest microwaved meatloaf. In fact, Benjamin Lobb of Bradenton, Florida, microwaves his meatloaf from start to finish.

Since we had never tried meatloaf in our testing for that article, we gave it a whirl. Following the recipe in our September/ October 1996 meatloaf article, we made three free-form loaves, cooking each until its internal temperature was 160 degrees. We cooked the first at full power for eighteen minutes in the microwave only, the second at 70% power in the microwave for seven minutes and then a 350 degree conventional oven for twenty minutes, and the third in the conventional oven only for just over sixty minutes. The texture and color differences among them were very minor. In fact, had the loaves not been sampled side-by-side, the differences would probably have been indistinguishable. That said, one taster considered the microwave-only loaf somewhat wetter at the center than the other two - not necessarily a positive trait. The loaf started in the microwave and finished in the oven was just as brown on top, and had as pleasing a texture as the oven-baked loaf, and saved thirty minutes of cooking time. This is a time-saver we'd recommend.

➤ Your son noticed that this item, called a rolling docker, looks more like an instrument of torture than the common baker's tool that it is. When rolled over unbaked puff pastry, the rolling docker, also called a pastry pricker, makes numerous uniform holes from which steam escapes in the oven. This controls the rise and creates compressed layers, so the resulting pastry is at once crisp, flaky, and flat, and well-suited to making Napoleons. The docker can also be used before baking to prick cracker or flatbread dough, or pie or tart pastry for free-form fruit tarts.

The barrel is usually about six-inches wide, with evenly spaced rows of slender plastic, carbon steel, or stainless steel spikes, all with sharply pointed ends like nails. The handle, usually wood but sometimes plastic, keeps the hand safely away from the spikes as they spin. A rolling docker might be handy when docking a huge quantity of pastry, but for home cooks who choose to dock (generally we do not, *see* "The Secrets of Prebaking Pie Shells," September/October 1997), the tines of a fork serve the purpose nicely.

Quick Tips

Dotting Baked Goods with Butter

Many recipes for pies and casseroles direct the cook to dot the surface with butter just before putting the dish into the oven. Sue Miller of Cleveland Heights, Ohio, has come up with a particularly neat and convenient method for this. She simply uses a vegetable peeler to shave the desired amount off a frozen stick of butter, letting it fall onto the food in fine curls.

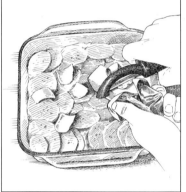

Air-Drying Wine Glasses Safely

With one wrong move or an inadvertent bump, a dish rack filled with drying dishes can wreak havoc on delicate wine glasses. To dry her glasses out of harm's way, Vicky Myint of Madison, Wisconsin, sets up two chopsticks (the square-sided kind are best) parallel to each other and about 1½ to 2 inches apart in a safe corner on the counter, then places the wet wineglasses on them to drain.

Freshening Stale Bread

It is not unusual for one half or one third of a loaf of bread to go uneaten at a meal. When you reach for the leftover the next day, you find that it has begun to go stale. George Locker of New York, New York, revives his stale bread by placing it inside a brown paper bag, sealing the bag, and moistening a portion of the outside of the bag with water. After placing it in a preheated 350-degree oven for about five minutes, the bread will emerge warm and soft.

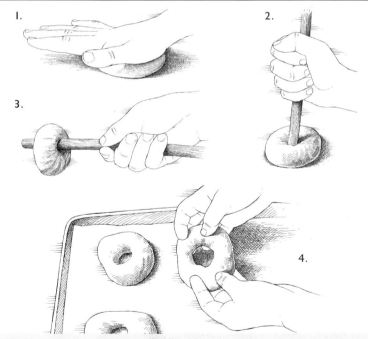

Shaping Dough Rings for Bagels

The bagel recipe we published in the September/October 1997 issue produces an exceptionally stiff, dry dough, which some cooks may have trouble shaping into rings. Instead of forming the dough ball into ropes and attaching the ends, Geri Davis of Prescott, Arizona, uses this method:

1. Slightly flatten the ball of dough with the palm of your hand.
2. Punch through the center of the ball with the handle of a wooden spoon.
3. Holding the spoon by the handle, spin gently to enlarge the dough ring to the desired size.
4. Stretch the hole with your fingers as you place the dough ring on a baking sheet.

Adding Flour in Food Processor Bread Recipes

Many food processor bread recipes call for adding flour in small increments. Lea Schwanhausser of DeLand, Florida, offers this tip for doing so without having to stand over the processor. Make a paper funnel using a doubled piece of parchment or wax paper and hold it in place in the feed tube. The flour will flow slowly, evenly, and steadily into the bowl.

Storing Bulk Parchment Paper

As with other nonperishables, parchment paper for baking is cheaper if bought in bulk. But storing the large quantity conveniently can be a problem. Nancy Hughes of Hanson, Massachusetts, has come up with this solution: Roll a quantity of parchment sheets into a tight roll and place it inside an empty gift-wrap tube, which can be easily stored in the pantry or kitchen. The sheets can be pulled out easily, one at a time.

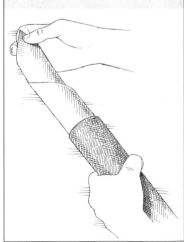

Hulling Strawberries Swiftly

Many cooks, including Robert Joseph of Somerville, Massachusetts, do not own a strawberry huller. He discovered, however, that a drinking straw pushed through the bottom up to the top cores and hulls whole strawberries quickly and easily.

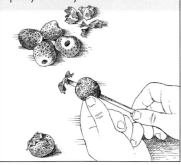

Moving Heavy Appliances

Since many food processors and standing mixers are heavy and don't slide easily, they can be very difficult for some people to move. Marcella Pascualy of Mercer Island, Washington, gets around this problem by placing her mixer on a towel or cloth place mat that can be pulled anywhere on the counter or tabletop with little effort.

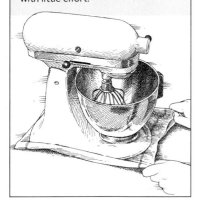

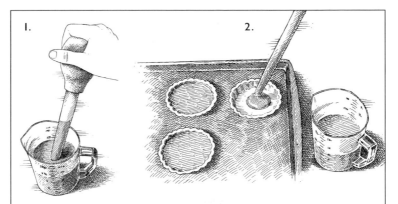

Filling Individual Tartlets Without Mess

Filling individual tartlet shells with a liquid custard or other filling can be both messy and tedious. To fill the shells with speed and precision, Karen Gernand of Redwood City, California, devised this technique.

1. Place the filling in a measuring cup, then fill a bulb baster from the cup.
2. Squirt out just the right amount of filling into the shell.

No-Mess Spraying of Nonstick Aerosols

Many cooks have encountered the oily film on their counter or workspace that results from using an aerosol nonstick cooking spray. To avoid this problem, Herbert Akers of Rockville, Maryland, suggests that you open the door to the dishwasher, lay the item to be greased right on the door, and spray away. Any excess or overspray will be cleaned off the door the next time you run the dishwasher.

Making Chipotles en Adobo Sauce Last

Because a little bit of chipotle chile goes a long way, it can be difficult to use up an entire can once it is opened. Rather than let the remaining chipotles go bad in the refrigerator, Kelsey Capps of Salem, Oregon, adapted our January/February 1996 Quick Tip for portioning tomato paste.

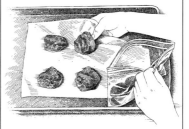

1. Spoon out the chipotles, each with a couple of teaspoons of adobo sauce, onto different areas of a cookie sheet lined with wax paper, then place in the freezer.
2. Once they are frozen, remove the chiles to a zipper-lock freezer bag, store in the freezer, and use as needed.

Skinning Chicken

Buying chickens whole and breaking them down into pieces yourself is less expensive than buying chicken parts. If you prefer your pieces skinless, Margaret Nordstrom of Shoreline, Washington, suggests that you simply grab the skin with a paper towel and pull. The paper towel provides the extra grip and simplifies the task considerably.

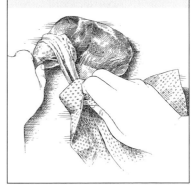

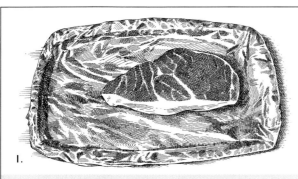

Be Healthful But Wash Fewer Platters

By now it is common knowledge that grilled meat, poultry, or fish should not be returned to the same platter that held it in its raw form. Instead of last-minute fumbling for a new platter, Tina Love of San Bernadino, California, has devised this method, which also leaves her with only one platter to clean.

1. Cover the platter with tinfoil before placing the raw food on it.
2. While the food is grilling, remove the foil so you can use the same platter when the food comes off the grill.

Grilled Lemon Chicken

The best way to get lemon flavor into chicken is not by marinating, not by basting, but with a quick, final dunk into a lemon-garlic-olive oil sauce.

⇒ BY PAM ANDERSON ⇐

If you like, add fresh herbs or toasted spices to the chicken marinade.

I've been watching my father grill for almost 40 years now. He's at least fifth generation Deep South—not the kind of man who would fire up his grill for some wimpy pizza, mahimahi, or basket of vegetables. For as long as I can remember, he's been grilling the same four things—steak, spareribs, barbecued pork butt, and finally, his signature dish, Lemon Chicken.

My father is a pretty confident griller, but that lemon chicken turned him into a nervous Nelly. Every time he made it he was obsessed with the same goal: to make sure that it absorbed as much lemon flavor as possible. After he'd arranged the chicken parts neatly over the the hot coals, he would brush each one with a mixture of lemon, oil, and garlic salt. He basted meticulously throughout the entire grilling process, carefully moving the chicken around and over to make sure each piece cooked evenly.

Dad almost dreaded taking that first bite for fear the lemon had not penetrated. Though we sometimes had to stretch the truth, Mom and I always assured him that it had. When the chicken was at its best, we marveled: "The lemon flavor's gone right into the bone!"

Because Dad felt his odds on whether the lemon would take or not were about fifty-fifty, he'd have me taste-test the chicken before he took it off the grill. About halfway through cooking, he'd start breaking off and feeding me the wings.

Even though I always told him they tasted lemony enough, he could read the truth in my eyes. (You can never trust a hungry 10-year-old who's been sitting still with her father for over an hour.) The grill lid would fly open, and he'd begin his basting again, hoping his fire would stay alive long enough to get a few more drops of lemon sauce onto the chicken.

Dipping the chicken in the leftover lemon basting sauce was always one of my favorite ways of ensuring good lemon flavor (salmonella was just a twinkle in the chicken's eye back then), but to Dad it meant failure. When he saw me sneak the leftover sauce to the table and slip a piece of my breast meat into the bowl, he'd start mentally kicking himself.

He tried a number of experiments over the years, but it wasn't until long after I'd left home that he called, his voice veering high with excitement. "I've finally discovered the secret to lemon chicken!" he exclaimed. It turned out that one day while frying fish, his oil cooled off and was absorbed by the fish. At this point, it suddenly occurred to him that over lower heat his cooked chicken might better absorb his lemon sauce. What was bad for the fish in oil, might be good for the chicken in lemon sauce.

This time, rather than baste the chicken from start to finish, he threw the salt and peppered chicken parts on the grill and cooked them until they were virtually done. At this point, he took the fire down really low and started brushing them. This, he said, consistently gave him the intense lemon flavor he was after. After 40 years, he had finally come up with a foolproof method.

He Was Right

I gave Dad's technique a try and realized he was onto something. I liked the fresh, perky lemon flavor of the chicken sauced at the end, but I couldn't really be sure that it was better than his

many lemon chicken experiments over the years. Which lemon chicken was best? Was it the one where the lemon mixture was applied before, during, or after cooking? So I grilled three chickens—one that was marinated in lemon juice, garlic, and oil for two hours, a second that was basted with the same mixture throughout grilling, and a third that was grilled by my father's method, rolling the cooked chicken around in the lemon mixture, returning it to the grill, and basting it for a few minutes longer. With each chicken, I used a two-level fire, with medium-hot coals under two-thirds of the grill grid and no coals at all under the remaining one-third. This allowed me to sear the chicken well over the coals but also to regulate its cooking, moving it to the no-coals area if it was cooking too quickly or if flare-ups occurred.

If you weren't comparing them with my father's newly discovered secret, you'd say the marinated and basted chickens were just fine. The chicken flavored at the end, however, stole the show. Not only did it have a fresher flavor, its juices had mingled with the lemon, garlic, and oil to make a wonderful sauce. The basted chicken, on the other hand, had lost much of its lemon juice to the fire, requiring more lemon mixture to complete the job, and even with more sauce, it turned out drier than the other two.

My Dad's technique became my favorite, especially after I made a few personal adjustments. First, I almost always brine poultry before cooking it, and brined lemon chicken was always preferred to unbrined in side-by-side tasting. Since brining made garlic salt out of the question, I tried using minced garlic, but because the chicken was on the grill for such a relatively short time after the marinade was applied, it tasted raw. I eventually found that mincing the garlic to almost a paste (a garlic press is helpful) and warming it in a small saucepan until it begins to sizzle improves the garlic flavor immensely.

Although my father would never consider doctoring up his chicken, I thought herbs like thyme, cilantro, rosemary, and oregano, and spices like cumin, coriander, and fennel might be nice additions. Herbs were easy. They could be stirred directly into the lemon mixture. But spices were questionable. Would they, like the garlic, taste raw with so little cooking time and over so low a heat? Once again, I made three batches of chicken—

one that was rubbed with crushed coriander seeds before cooking; a second that was brushed at the end with a marinade containing crushed coriander seeds; and a third that was brushed with a marinade containing toasted, then crushed coriander seeds. My tasters and I much preferred the last, where toasted seeds were crushed, stirred into the marinade, and applied at the end. The spices that cooked on the chicken the entire time were less flavorful and tended to char. And besides, toasted seeds, like toasted nuts, just taste better.

Since the lemon flavor was so much cleaner and brighter when the sauce was applied at the end of cooking, I thought other acids might work equally well. Lime, certainly, was good, but low-acid vinegar sauces, such as rice wine and balsamic vinegars, were less impressive primarily, I think, because there wasn't a fresh flavor to preserve.

Whether lemon chicken that's been brushed at the end of cooking is better because the lemon flavor actually permeates the meat, or because the flavors are brighter and fresher, or because there's an intensely flavored dipping sauce from the intermingled lemon, garlic, olive oil, and chicken juices, I don't know. What I do know is that after 40 years of guesswork, my father definitely got it right.

GRILLED LEMON CHICKEN
SERVES 6 TO 8

The 1½-hour brining time is highly recommended, but not essential; skip it if you're in a hurry. It's fine to use chicken parts, such as eight leg/thighs, separated or not, or eight breast/wings, separated at the joint connecting wing to breast. Grilling whole chickens is also an option, if you remove the backbones and butterfly each before brining. If flare-ups threaten to char the skin of the chicken, move the pieces temporarily to the cooler side of the grill. If you have it, 1 tablespoon minced fresh rosemary makes a nice addition to the lemon sauce.

- ¾ cup kosher or ½ cup table salt
- 2 whole chickens (about 3½ pounds each), cut into legs, thighs, breasts, and wings; backs reserved for another use
  Ground black pepper
- ¼ cup extra-virgin olive oil
- 4 large garlic cloves, minced and made into paste (*see* illustrations, above)
- I cup juice from 5 lemons
- I tablespoon minced fresh thyme leaves or 1½ teaspoons dried

1. Dissolve salt in 2 quarts water in large bowl or two 1-gallon zipper-lock plastic bags. Add chicken parts (seal zipper-lock bags, if using), and refrigerate until fully seasoned, about 1½ hours. Remove chicken from brine, rinse very well, dry thoroughly with paper towels, and sea-

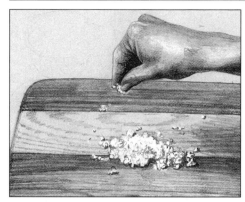

1. Once the garlic has been minced, sprinkle it lightly with salt.

2. Drag the flat side of a chef's knife over the garlic-salt mixture to form a paste.

son with pepper to taste.

2. Half an hour before cooking, ignite about 5 quarts hardwood charcoal or charcoal briquettes in a chimney and burn until completely covered with thin coating of light gray ash, 20 to 30 minutes. Dump out coals and, following illustration 1, below, spread coals over ⅔ of grill bottom, leaving ⅓ with no coals; position grill rack over coals and heat for 10 minutes. Coals should be medium-hot (you can hold your hand 5 inches above the grill surface for 4 seconds).

3. Heat olive oil and garlic in small saucepan over low heat until garlic starts to sizzle but not color, 1 to 2 minutes. Remove from heat; mix with lemon juice in large, shallow, nonreactive 13-by-9-inch baking dish or similar pan; set aside. (Dry herbs may be added at this point; fresh herbs should not be added until just before coating chicken.)

4. Place chicken skin side down on rack directly over hot coals; grill, pulling chicken over to empty side in case of flare-ups or if skin starts to char, and turning and moving pieces to ensure even cooking, until chicken is dark golden brown, 15 to 17 minutes for legs and wings and 18 to 20 minutes for thighs and breasts. When chicken pieces are well colored, place them in lemon sauce and roll to coat completely, following illustration 2, below. Return pieces to side of grill with no coals; heat until lemon sauce flavors meat, about 5 minutes longer, turning each piece and brushing with sauce once or twice more. Return chicken to pan and roll in lemon sauce once more; serve warm or at room temperature.

GRILLED LIME CHICKEN WITH JALAPEÑO AND CORIANDER
SERVES 6 TO 8

An equal amount of toasted and crushed cumin seeds may substituted for the coriander seeds.

Follow recipe for Grilled Lemon Chicken, adding 2 teaspoons minced fresh jalapeños along with garlic; substituting lime juice for lemon juice; substituting 2 tablespoons minced fresh cilantro for thyme; and adding 2 teaspoons toasted and crushed coriander seeds.

1. Once the coals are lit, create a two-level fire by moving the coals to one side of the grill bottom.

2. The final step is rolling the chicken in the sauce a second time.

How to Grill Tuna

Cook it well past rare, if you like—an hour's soak in extra-virgin olive oil takes the tough out of tuna.

⇒ BY STEPHANIE LYNESS ⇐

Grilled tuna has become such a familiar dish on the American home-cooking scene that it never occurred to me that it might also be a bear to cook. I had assumed that I could get a perfect tuna steak—beautifully seared on the outside, moist and tender on the inside—the same way I get a perfect beef or salmon steak: a quick sear over direct heat to brown and then, if the steak is really thick, a final few minutes over indirect heat to finish it. I also knew that tuna, lacking the fat of salmon, would be particularly susceptible to overcooking, so I would probably need to undercook it.

But a few days of testing proved tuna to be a tougher customer than I'd imagined. No matter what thickness I sliced it or how I cooked it—medium-rare to rare, direct or indirect heat—I was startled to find that steak after steak was almost inedible. Every one was tough and dry and tasted off-puttingly strong and fishy. Clearly more experimenting was in order.

Cooking Tests

I did all my testing on my 22½-inch kettle grill fired with hardwood charcoal. (Hardwood charcoal burns hotter than briquettes and gives a light, woody flavor that I like.) I worked with ¾- to 1-inch-thick steaks, the cut most available at supermarket fish counters.

First I tried grilling over direct heat, starting with an oiled and salted steak, for 3½ minutes on each side over a medium-hot fire. (I could hold my hand five inches above the grill for about four seconds.) The outside of the tuna was paler than I liked and the inside was overcooked. In successive tests I determined that a hotter fire (one over which I could hold my hand for only two to three seconds) seared better, particularly since the tuna needed to cook only 2½ minutes total for medium-rare, and 3 to 4 minutes for medium to well-done.

While the hotter fire was an improvement, the fish was still drier than I liked, particularly when it was cooked past medium-rare. So I experimented with indirect heat: I now tried searing the tuna 1½ minutes on each side over direct heat, and then pulled it to the side of the grill to finish cooking over indirect heat. The tuna came off the grill with the same texture but even less seared than before, so I gave up on the indirect heat approach.

I also tested different thicknesses over direct

Thin steaks cooked to medium are still tender if marinated in olive oil; thick steaks are best cooked rare or medium-rare.

heat and learned that if I wanted the tuna well seared and rare, it must be cut about 1½ inches thick; the standard supermarket steak, which is thinner, will be already cooked to at least medium-rare after the initial searing on both sides. But while I preferred the moistness of the thick, rare fish, I was concerned that some folks may not like to eat their tuna rare. In addition, I know that many consumers have difficulty locating thick steaks.

Marinating

Clearly, the problem wasn't going to be solved in the actual cooking. Something had to be done to the tuna before it hit the grill. My next inspiration was to test a marinade.

I'd recently eaten delicious tuna at Rivoli Restaurant in Berkeley, so I called chef Wendy Brucker to ask for her technique. She told me that she marinated her tuna for one hour in olive oil that had been infused with garlic, thyme, chili pepper, and lemon. This was strictly for flavor, she said—she didn't think that the oil moistened the tuna particularly. Back on the East Coast, I called Rick Moonen at Oceana Restaurant in Manhattan. He told me that he also marinates his tuna in herb-infused olive oil. Although he didn't know the science of it, he felt that the oil did moisten the tuna.

So I tried it. I marinated one 1½-inch-thick steak and one ½-inch-thick steak in Brucker's flavored oil for three hours, turning every now and then. Then I grilled the thick steak to rare, counting one minute apiece for the top and bottom, and 30 seconds more for each of the four remaining sides. I grilled the thin steak to medium, counting 2½ minutes total. The results were amazing. Both tunas were subtly flavored with olive oil and herbs, and their texture was moist and luscious. Perhaps most surprisingly, I liked the well-cooked tuna as well as the rare. Later tests showed that the thick steak, when cooked to rare or medium rare, needed only brushing with the oil-herb mixture; soaking it in the oil actually made it a bit too moist.

Finally I ran tests to determine whether the type of oil made a difference, and how long a soak was necessary. Comparing extra-virgin and pure olive oils with canola oil, I found that after one hour, only the extra-virgin oil had made a noticeable impact on the tuna. The pure olive oil seemed to catch up after another hour, but it didn't flavor the tuna appreciably until after three hours. The canola oil never affected the taste or the texture of the tuna.

Food scientist Shirley Corriher explained that an oil marinade tenderizes tuna in much the same way that marbling tenderizes beef. The oil coats the strands of protein, allowing a tuna steak to feel moist in the mouth even after most of the moisture has been cooked out of it. According to Corriher, the extra-virgin olive oil penetrated the fish more quickly than the other two oils because it was much richer in emulsifiers. Emulsifiers (mono- and di-glycerides) have a water-soluble molecule at one end and a fat-soluble molecule at the other; this double solubility increases their mobility and hence their ability to penetrate protein. Because the filtering process extracts emulsifiers, pure olive oil takes much longer than extra-virgin olive oil to coat the protein strands.

MASTER RECIPE FOR GRILLED TUNA
(³/₄-INCH STEAKS)
SERVES 4

It is difficult to avoid cooking tuna steaks thinner than ³/₄-inch to medium because the interior cooks almost as quickly as the surface. Piquant sauces and fresh salsas are natural partners for either thin or thick grilled tuna steaks (see "Five Easy Sauces for Fish," May/June 1994, page 13, and "Easy Summer Salsas," July/August 1996, page 21), or serve with the charmoula vinaigrette, below right.

- 4 tuna steaks (about ³/₄-inch thick and 8 ounces each)
- 3 tablespoons extra-virgin olive oil
  Salt and ground black pepper

1. Place tuna and oil in gallon-sized zipper-lock plastic bag; seal bag and refrigerate until fish has marinated fully, at least 1 and up to 24 hours.
2. Meanwhile, spread one large chimney's worth, about 5 quarts, hardwood charcoal or charcoal briquettes over ²/₃ of grill bottom. Refill chimney with charcoal, position on charcoal layer in grill, and ignite. Burn until charcoal in chimney is blazing, 5 to 8 minutes. Dump burning coals onto unlit charcoal, position grill rack over fire, and burn until all charcoal is completely covered with thin coating of light gray ash and fire is very hot (you can hold your hand 5 inches above grill surface for 1 to 2 seconds), 20 to 30 minutes more.
3. Remove tuna from bag; season both sides of each steak with salt and pepper. Grill over direct heat until well seared and grill marks appear, about 1½ minutes. Flip steaks over and grill on second side until fish is cooked to medium (opaque throughout, yet translucent at very center when checked with point of paring knife), 1 to 1½ minutes longer. Serve immediately.

GRILLED THICK TUNA STEAK VARIATION
(1 TO 1½ INCHES)

Whereas thinner tuna steaks cook to medium before you know it, thicker 1- to 1½-inch steaks can easily be cooked to rare or medium-rare. In addition, you need only to brush thick steaks with olive oil rather than to marinate them, because they are less likely to dry out during cooking.

Brush both sides of 4 tuna steaks (about 1 to 1½-inches thick and 8 ounces each) with olive oil. Follow Master Recipe for Grilled Tuna, omitting step 1. Grill steaks 2½ minutes on first side and 2½ to 3½ minutes on second side for rare (opaque near surfaces and still red and translucent at center when checked with point of paring knife) or 2½ to 3 minutes on first side and 3 to 4 minutes on second side for medium-rare (just opaque throughout, yet still pink at very center when checked with point of paring knife); serve immediately.

TUNA ANATOMY | THE BLOOD SPOT

Tuna is universally sold in the form of triangular-shaped, boneless steaks. These steaks are sliced from the four quarter sections, called loins, that are cut from the thick central spine when the fish is butchered. Each loin is a triangular quarter, wide at the head end and tapering towards the tail.

Sometimes when you buy a tuna steak, you'll see dark red coloration in the flesh. This is the bloodline, a piece of fibrous tissue heavily laden with blood vessels that runs from the gills to the tail on both sides of the spine. This specialized tissue makes possible the rapid bursts of speed that characterize tunas as they hunt for food: the bloodline fuels these bursts by dispersing oxygen quickly throughout the muscle. It tastes fishier and more bitter than the rest of the meat; I cut it off before cooking.
—S.L

LOIN

TUNA STEAK

BLOODLINE

GRILLED TUNA WITH WATERCRESS–PARSLEY SALAD AND CHARMOULA VINAIGRETTE
SERVES 4

Wendy Brucker of Rivoli Restaurant in Berkeley inspired this recipe.

- 1 recipe Grilled Tuna (³/₄- or 1½-inch thick; see recipe at left)
- 2½ tablespoons juice from 1 lemon
- 2 small cloves garlic, minced
- ½ teaspoon salt
- ½ teaspoon ground cumin
- ¼ teaspoon paprika
- ⅛ teaspoon cayenne
- 2 tablespoons chopped fresh cilantro leaves
- ½ cup extra-virgin olive oil
  Ground black pepper
- 1 bunch watercress, washed, dried well, and trimmed
- 1 cup flat Italian parsley leaves, washed and dried well

1. Follow Master Recipe or Grilled Thick Tuna Steak Variation.
2. For vinaigrette, whisk lemon juice, garlic, salt, cumin, paprika, cayenne, and cilantro in small bowl. Add oil in slow, steady stream, whisking constantly until smooth; season with pepper to taste.
3. Place watercress and parsley in medium bowl; drizzle with half the vinaigrette and toss to coat. Divide dressed greens among four serving plates; place a grilled tuna steak next to or on each bed of greens, drizzle with a portion of remaining vinaigrette, and serve immediately.

Good News—The Best Tuna Variety Is the Easiest to Get

To find out which of the five varieties of tuna available to consumers in the United States would make the tastiest grilled tuna, we held an informal blind taste test with the editorial staff of Cook's. The good news is that the fresh tuna most readily available, yellowfin, was the clear favorite. So if you're buying fresh tuna, you're probably buying the right one.

Yellowfin: The favorite of almost all tasters, who found it had the best combination of texture and flavor without tasting fishy or having a fatty mouth feel. In fact, previously frozen yellowfin, which tasters found had a slightly more fishy flavor, came in second, beating out fresh versions of other tuna varieties.

Bigeye: Although this is the variety most often used for sushi, it was only moderately popular with tasters. Several tasters did mention, however, that it had the most intense flavor of all the tunas. Probably the best choice for those who really love the taste of tuna.

Bluefin: We could not get fresh bluefin, and the previously frozen version was rated as "good but not outstanding" by most tasters.

Albacore: Most tasters found this fish dry and quite bland. Perhaps this is not surprising, since it is familiar to our taste buds as the only tuna that can legally be sold in cans as "white-meat tuna."

Skipjack: The least popular tuna in the tasting, skipjack was thought by almost all tasters to have too strong a flavor and too greasy a mouth feel.

Perfect Roast Potatoes

For a crisp, dense, velvety roast potato, take low-starch potatoes, cover for part of the cooking time, and flip them once.

⇒ BY ANNE YAMANAKA ⇐

My vision of the perfect roast potato is clear. It is crisp and deep golden brown on the outside, with moist, velvety, dense interior flesh. The potato's slightly bitter skin is intact, providing a contrast to the sweet, caramelized flavor that the flesh develops during the roasting process. It is rich, but never greasy, and it is accompanied by the heady taste of garlic and herbs.

Unfortunately, my attempts to roast potatoes in the past have left plenty to be desired. Sometimes the potatoes emerged a greasy mess, lacking texture or flavor; other times, they were dry and brittle, speckled with bitter remnants of burnt garlic. In frustration, I began to research recipes for roast potatoes.

I wanted to know how different types of potatoes would vary in texture, flavor, and color after roasting. I wondered what the best oven temperature would be for roasting potatoes, and for what length of time. Should potatoes be roasted raw, or should they be parcooked prior to roasting? I also needed to discover the best fat medium for both flavor and heat tolerance. Finally, wary of the unpleasant, bitter flavor produced by burnt garlic, I wanted to find the best way of infusing its flavor without scorching it.

Testing the Potatoes

My first task was to choose the best type of potato. As I soon found out, locating a specific variety of potato at most supermarkets can be quite confusing. Rather than being sold by varietal name (Yukon Gold, White Rose, Norgold Russet), many different varieties are offered under a generic name (All-Purpose, Baking, Red Creamer). After some research and a lot of confusion, I slowly began to make sense of how to choose potatoes at the supermarket. Instead of trying to locate specific varieties, I found it more helpful to group potatoes into three major categories, based on the ratio of solids (mostly starch) to water. The categories are high starch/low moisture potatoes, medium starch potatoes, and low starch/high moisture potatoes (*see* "But Which Potato Is Which?", next page).

I roasted potatoes from each of the three categories. The final products differed dramatically in texture, color, and flavor. The potatoes I liked least were the high starch/low moisture variety

For crisp new potatoes (as shown here), roast potatoes cut-side down, then turn them over during the last 5 to 10 minutes of roasting.

(I used Russet). They did not brown well, their dry, fluffy texture was more like baked than roast potatoes, and their flavor reminded me of raw potatoes. The medium starch all-purpose potatoes (I used Yukon Golds) produced a beautiful golden crust, but the interior flesh was still rather dry. The best roasting potatoes came from the low starch/high moisture category (I used Red Bliss). These potatoes emerged from the oven with a light, delicate crust and a moist, dense interior that had a more complex, nutty flavor than the others, with hints of bitterness and tang.

The primary reason for these differences, according to Dr. Alfred A. Bushway, professor of food science and human nutrition at the University of Maine, is that starch granules lose moisture when cooked in dry heat. As a result, high starch potatoes end up with a dry, fluffy texture when roasted. The low starch/high moisture varieties, on the other hand, retain moisture and, therefore, come out of the oven with the compact, dense texture that I like in roast potatoes.

Testing the Techniques

After choosing the Red Bliss potatoes, I began to

test oven temperatures. Temperatures had ranged from 350 degrees to 500 degrees in recipes that I had researched, so I decided to test my potatoes in oven temperatures ranging from 400 to 450 degrees in 25-degree increments. Baked at 400 degrees, the potatoes were golden brown outside and creamy on the inside, but the rather thick crust they developed made them a little dry. I tried roasting the potatoes at 450 degrees to see if this would cause quicker browning and, therefore, create a slightly thinner crust. After tasting the results, I concluded that this temperature was too high because the crust was very crisp, very dark, and bitter. At last, when I chose to roast the potato at 425 degrees, the result was an even colored, golden-brown potato with a thin, crisp crust and an interior that was soft and dense, although still slightly dry.

While researching, I came across some recipes that called for parboiling the potatoes before roasting them. Hoping that this approach would produce a texturally superior potato that retained more of its moisture after cooking, I tried boiling the potatoes for seven minutes prior to roasting. This produced a potato closer to my ideal, but required considerable attention due to the additional step. Steaming seemed like a possibility, but I knew that it, too, would complicate the roasting process.

Having established that parboiling really did reduce roasting time and thus allow these potatoes to retain more of their moisture, I now set out to find a simpler way of achieving this. Some recipes called for covering the potatoes for a portion of their roasting time, and I was especially drawn to this technique because it provided a way to steam the potatoes in their own moisture that required little extra effort on the cook's part. The results were fantastic! The crisp, deep golden-brown crust was perfectly balanced by a creamy, moist interior. This potato had a sweet and nutty caramelized flavor, with just a hint of tang from the skin. This simplest of methods had produced the very best potatoes.

Fats and Garlic

Now that I had a cooking method I was pleased with, I was ready to think about which fat I should use as the cooking medium, and how I should deal with the garlic. I decided to test butter, vegetable oil, and olive oil. I had come across other types of fat in my research, such as duck and bacon fat, but I did not want the hassle of rendering the fat, and I did want to test products that were likely to be in most pantries.

I started with butter and found that the milk solids burned before the potatoes were fully roasted, producing a potato with a bitter aftertaste. Both vegetable oil and olive oil yielded nicely browned potatoes with the texture that I was looking for, but I concluded that olive oil was the best choice. Not only does it have a higher smoking point than butter, which makes it better able to tolerate the high level of heat used to roast the potatoes, it also lends a pleasant fruity flavor to the finished product.

I was also concerned about how much fat was necessary. I began testing with two tablespoons of fat for two pounds of potatoes. Finding that the roast potatoes were a little dry, I added another tablespoon of fat. This yielded potatoes that had a rich mouthfeel but were not greasy.

The next step in the process was figuring out how to add garlic flavor to the potatoes. If I added minced garlic during the last five minutes of cooking, it burned almost instantly; coating the potatoes with garlic-infused oil failed to produce the strong garlic flavor that I was after; and roasting whole, unpeeled garlic cloves alongside the potatoes and squeezing the pulp out afterwards to add to the potatoes was too tedious. The best method turned out to be both very simple and very flavorful. You can just mash raw garlic into a paste, place it in a large stainless steel bowl, put the hot roast potatoes into the bowl, and toss. This method yields potatoes with a strong garlic flavor, but without the raw spiciness of uncooked garlic.

MASTER RECIPE FOR ROAST POTATOES
SERVES 4

To roast more than two pounds of potatoes at once, use a second pan rather than crowding the first. If your potatoes are small, like new potatoes, cut them in halves instead of wedges and turn them cut-side up during the final ten minutes of roasting.

2 pounds Red Bliss or other low-starch potatoes, scrubbed clean, dried, halved, and cut into ¾-inch wedges
3 tablespoons extra-virgin olive oil
   Salt and ground black pepper

1. Adjust oven rack to middle position and heat oven to 425 degrees. Toss potatoes and olive oil in medium bowl to coat; season generously with salt and pepper and toss again to blend.

2. Place potatoes flesh side down, in a single layer, on shallow roasting pan; cover tightly with aluminum foil and cook about 20 minutes. Remove foil; roast until side of potato touching pan is crusty golden brown, about 15 minutes more. Remove pan from oven and carefully turn potatoes over using metal spatula. (Press spatula against metal as it slides under potatoes to protect crusts.) Return pan to oven and roast until side of potato now touching pan is crusty golden brown and skins have raisin-like wrinkles, 5 to 10 minutes more. Remove from oven, transfer potatoes to serving dish (again, using metal spatula and extra care not to rip crusts), and serve warm.

ROAST POTATOES WITH GARLIC AND ROSEMARY
SERVES 4

Follow Master Recipe for Roast Potatoes. While potatoes roast, mince two medium garlic cloves; sprinkle with ⅛ teaspoon salt and mash with flat side of chef's knife blade until paste forms. Transfer garlic paste to large bowl; set aside. In last 3 minutes of roasting time, sprinkle 2 tablespoons chopped fresh rosemary evenly over potatoes. Immediately transfer potatoes to bowl with garlic; toss to distribute, and serve warm.

ROAST POTATOES WITH SPICY CARAMELIZED ONIONS
SERVES 4

Follow Master Recipe for Roast Potatoes. While potatoes roast, heat medium skillet over medium-high heat. Add 2 tablespoons olive oil and 1 medium yellow onion, sliced thin, and salt and ground black pepper to taste. Reduce heat to medium and cook, stirring occasionally, until onions are caramelized and deep golden brown, about 15 minutes. Stir in ¼ teaspoon cayenne and 1 teaspoon ground cumin; cook until fragrant, about 1 minute longer. Transfer to large bowl; add 1½ teaspoons lime juice, 2 tablespoons chopped fresh parsley leaves, and roast potatoes. Toss to distribute, and serve warm.

ROAST POTATOES WITH GARLIC, FETA, OLIVES, AND OREGANO
SERVES 4

Follow recipe for Roast Potatoes with Garlic and Rosemary, substituting 2 tablespoons chopped fresh oregano leaves for rosemary and adding ½ cup crumbled feta cheese, 12 pitted and chopped kalamata olives, and 1 tablespoon lemon juice along with garlic.

But Which Potato Is Which?

Potatoes are most frequently sold in supermarkets under generic names, such as "Baking Potato," that can include many different varieties. Below are some of the names under which potatoes with various starch levels are commonly sold.

High Starch/Low Moisture:
Baking Potato; Idaho; Russet; Russet Burbank; White Creamer

Medium Starch:
All-Purpose; Yukon Gold; Yellow Fin; Purple Peruvian

Low Starch/High Moisture:
Red Bliss; Red #1; Red Creamer; New Potato; White Rose; French Fingerlings; Red Pontiac

—A.Y.

STEP-BY-STEP | ROASTING POTATOES

1. Midway through cooking, remove the foil cover from the pan so the potatoes brown.

2. Flip the potatoes so both cut sides come into contact with the hot pan.

Asparagus Grilled or Broiled

Why grill or broil instead of steam or sauté? High heat develops the rich, subtle flavors of this complex vegetable.

≥ BY EVA KATZ ≤

I love grilled asparagus. As with meats, the flavor of this springtime vegetable is intensified by spending a few moments on the grill. Unlike the delicate taste and pristine appearance of steamed asparagus, the charred, rustic look and bold, robust flavors that result from grilling invite dressings with the aggressive flavorings that I prefer.

Despite my love for the smoky flavor of grilled asparagus, however, I'm not inclined to light the grill just for a vegetable side dish. But when I have the charcoal grill fired up for salmon or beef steaks, it seems only natural to throw on a few spears alongside.

Fortunately, broiling the asparagus in the oven produces similar results if you're careful not to let the asparagus overcook before it browns. I discovered that placing the pan about four inches from the heating element heats the pan enough so the tops and bottoms of the asparagus brown simultaneously. Grilling and broiling work best for thin to medium-thin asparagus spears, no more than 5/8-inch thick. Thicker spears will burn on the surface before they cook through.

All the recipes below can be prepared from start to finish in about fifteen minutes and will deliver beautifully browned and caramelized asparagus.

ASPARAGUS WITH PEANUT SAUCE
SERVES 4 AS A SIDE DISH

- 1   medium garlic clove, minced
- 1 1/2   teaspoons grated fresh ginger
- 1 1/2   teaspoons rice wine vinegar
- 1 1/2   teaspoons soy sauce
- 1   tablespoon Asian sesame oil
    Salt and ground black pepper
- 1 1/4   pounds asparagus spears, tough ends snapped off
- 1   tablespoon peanut butter
- 1   tablespoon minced fresh cilantro leaves
- 1   medium scallion, white and green parts, minced

1. Either light a medium fire in grill or preheat broiler. Whisk garlic, ginger, rice wine vinegar, soy sauce, and sesame oil, along with salt and pepper to taste, in medium bowl. Brush asparagus with about 1 tablespoon dressing to coat lightly.

2. Either grill asparagus, turning halfway through cooking time, until tender and streaked with light grill marks, 5 to 7 minutes, or line up spears in single layer on heavy jellyroll or rimmed baking sheet and broil, placing sheet about 4 inches from top heating element and shaking it once halfway through cooking to rotate spears, until tender and browned in some spots, 6 to 8 minutes.

3. Whisk peanut butter, cilantro, and 1 tablespoon water into remaining dressing; toss with asparagus. Transfer to serving platter, adjust seasoning with salt and pepper, sprinkle with minced scallion, and serve immediately.

ASPARAGUS AND PORTOBELLO MUSHROOMS WITH GOAT CHEESE
SERVES 4 AS A SIDE DISH

- 1   teaspoon fresh rosemary, minced
- 2   medium garlic cloves, minced
- 2   tablespoons juice from one lemon
- 1/4   cup extra-virgin olive oil
    Salt and ground black pepper
- 1 1/4   pounds asparagus spears, tough ends snapped off
- 2   large portobello mushroom caps
- 1   ounce goat cheese, crumbled

1. Either light a medium fire in grill or preheat broiler. Whisk rosemary, garlic, lemon juice, and oil, along with salt and pepper to taste, in medium bowl. Brush asparagus and mushrooms with about 2 tablespoons dressing to coat lightly.

2. Follow step 2 of recipe for Asparagus with Peanut Sauce. Along with asparagus, grill or broil mushroom caps, top side facing heat source, until tender and browned, 8 to 10 minutes.

3. Cool mushrooms slightly, then slice thin; toss with asparagus and remaining dressing. Transfer to serving platter, adjust seasoning with salt and pepper, sprinkle with goat cheese, and serve immediately.

ASPARAGUS AND COUNTRY BREAD WITH ANCHOVY DRESSING
SERVES 4 AS A SIDE DISH

- 3   anchovy fillets, rinsed and minced
- 2   medium garlic cloves, minced
- 2   tablespoons juice from one lemon
- 1/4   cup extra-virgin olive oil
    Salt and ground black pepper
- 1 1/4   pounds asparagus, tough ends snapped off
- 2   1/2-inch slices day-old, chewy country-style bread
- 1   small hunk (about 1 ounce) Parmesan cheese, shaved into strips with vegetable peeler

1. Either light a medium fire in grill or preheat broiler. Whisk anchovy, garlic, lemon juice, and oil, along with salt and pepper to taste, in medium bowl. Brush asparagus and bread with about 2 tablespoons dressing to coat lightly.

2. Follow step 2 of recipe for Asparagus with Peanut Sauce. Along with asparagus, grill or broil bread, turning once, until golden brown, about 3 minutes total on grill or 90 seconds total under broiler.

3. When bread is cool enough to handle, cut into 1/4-inch cubes; toss with asparagus and remaining dressing. Transfer to serving platter, adjust seasoning with salt and pepper, sprinkle with shaved Parmesan, and serve immediately.

ASPARAGUS AND HAM WITH MUSTARD–MINT VINAIGRETTE
SERVES 4 AS A SIDE DISH

- 2   medium scallions, white parts only, minced
- 2   tablespoons minced fresh mint leaves
- 1   teaspoon Dijon mustard
- 1 1/2   tablespoons juice from one lemon
- 3   tablespoons extra-virgin olive oil
    Salt and ground black pepper
- 1 1/4   pounds asparagus, tough ends snapped off
- 1   2-ounce piece deli or other ham, about 1/4-inch thick

1. Either light a medium fire in grill or preheat broiler. Whisk scallions, mint, mustard, lemon juice, and oil, along with salt and pepper to taste, in medium bowl. Brush asparagus and ham with about 2 tablespoons dressing to coat lightly.

2. Follow step 2 of recipe for Asparagus with Peanut Sauce. Along with asparagus, grill or broil ham, turning once, until spotty brown, about 3 minutes total on grill or 4 minutes total under broiler.

3. Cool ham slightly and cut into thin strips; toss with asparagus and remaining dressing. Transfer to serving platter, adjust seasoning with salt and pepper, and serve immediately.

Eva Katz, former Test Kitchen Director at Cook's Illustrated, now lives in Brisbane, Australia.

How To Make Sangria

The best sangria is based on cheap wine and uses oranges and lemons as the only fruit.

≥ BY ADAM RIED ≤

When I was a little kid, the hallmark of my parents' annual summer bash was their sangria. Pitcher after pitcher of this chilled Spanish wine-and-fruit punch flowed as friends talked, laughed, and let loose. This image has stayed with me into adulthood, and now that I'm the one throwing the parties, I'd like to bring sangria back with a recipe of my own.

Many people mistake sangria for an unruly collection of fruit awash in a sea of overly sweetened red wine. And forget the bottled, pre-made sangria sold in liquor stores, which is at once sugary, watery, and flavorless, with all the character and charm of Hi-C. Instead, I was after a robust, sweet-tart punch, with operative flavors of wine and citrus balanced against a simple, fruity background. I had no doubt that the choice of wine would be key. As if to keep my pride in check, however, testing proved that I was way off on this point.

I didn't discover this until the end. Working to find the right ingredient proportions for a standard 750 milliliter bottle of wine, my tasters and I started by testing the other building blocks of sangria—orange and lemon slices, juice, sugar, orange-flavored liqueur, and often a small amount of brandy.

After tinkering with various proportions of cut-up fruit, my tasters and I settled on a ratio of two oranges to one lemon. I tried limes, too, but found them too bitter. I did note that two sliced oranges and one sliced lemon in the pitcher made it difficult to pour the sangria, so I opted to squeeze the juice from one of the oranges. I wanted the fruit to act as a garnish, not an obstacle. I also tried peeling the fruit, on the theory that the zest and pith might be contributing some bitterness, but without them, the sangria tasted almost too winey, and a bit flat.

Last, I followed a cue from a recipe in John Willoughby and Chris Schlesinger's *Big Flavors of the Hot Sun* (Morrow, 1996) and tried mashing the fruit and the sugar together gently in the pitcher before adding the liquids. This improved the sangria by releasing some juice from the fruit and oils from the zest.

I wondered whether the type of sugar was important, since granulated, superfine, and a simple syrup of sugar dissolved in water had all appeared in recipes. The flavor difference turned out to be infinitesimal, as did any difference in texture, since each one dissolved completely, especially if the drink rested for a couple of hours before serving. What did matter was the amount of sugar—one-quarter cup gave the punch a pleasant, but not cloying, sweetness.

The orange liqueur that is part of all sangria recipes also gave some sweetness and fruitiness. I tried expensive brands such as Cointreau, Curaçao, and Grand Marnier, as well as the more pedestrian Triple Sec, which was the surprise winner for its bold, sweet flavor. One-quarter cup of Triple Sec was just right; using less, or none, made the sangria bland and one-dimensional.

The Wine

With the basic formula down, I turned to the choice of wine. Across the board, bartenders, wine merchants, and Spanish restaurateurs all advised me to keep it cheap. They argued that the addition of sugar and fruit would throw off the balance of the wine, anyhow, so why spend a lot on something carefully crafted and pricey? My testing so far had been done with a discount liquor store's house-label '96 Merlot, a medium-bodied wine which cost a whopping $4.49 a bottle. Other wines I had tried included Beaujolais-Villages, which tasters thought too fruity and light; Zinfandel, which tasted bright and acidic; jug Burgundy, which was somewhat richer and rounder; and Rioja, which tasters found a bit flat and dull. With Merlot out in front, I tried a more expensive bottle (1995 Clos du Bois, Sonoma County, $16.99), but only one taster out of five preferred the sangria made from it. My advice, then, is to use cheap wine whose character you know and can live with. Myself, I'll stick to the Merlot.

Many recipes I consulted moved well beyond the basic ingredients. Some had long lists of fruits, including apples, grapes, peaches, kiwis, cherries, and berries; others called for nonalcoholic filler ingredients, such as mineral or sparkling water, ginger ale, cold tea, lemonade, pineapple juice, or cranberry juice. One by one, my tasters and I sampled, and rejected, each of these. Consistently, we all preferred the straightforward flavor of citrus to the floating-fruit-salad approach, and everyone agreed that fillers, even in small amounts, diluted the wine and made it into a mere background flavor. Our reactions to more potent additions, including gin, sweet vermouth, port, and the traditional brandy, were similar. Even amounts as small as one tablespoon per batch gave the punch too much punch, moving it away from our ideal of a light, refreshing, quaffable summer drink.

Many recipes suggested preparing the sangria ahead of time and letting it rest in the refrigerator before serving. When all was said and done, I came to consider the resting time essential. After tasting an eight-hour-old sangria, a freshly made batch seemed harsh and edgy. That batch was a little better after one hour, and significantly better after two. In fact, a taste every hour up to eight revealed a better blended, more mellow flavor every time. My tasters and I tried the same batch again at hour number twelve, but found no significant improvement over the eight-hour taste. Rest assured, though, if you can't stand the anticipation, two hours of refrigeration serves the purpose adequately.

THE BEST SANGRIA
SERVES 4

The longer sangria sits before drinking, the more smooth and mellow it will taste. A full day is best, but if that's impossible, give it an absolute minimum of two hours to sit. Use large, heavy, juicy oranges and lemons for the best flavor. Doubling or tripling the recipe is fine, but you'll have to switch to a large punch bowl in place of the pitcher.

- 2   large juice oranges, washed; one orange sliced; remaining orange juiced
- 1   large lemon, washed and sliced
- ¼   cup sugar
- ¼   cup Triple Sec
- 1   750 milliliter bottle inexpensive, fruity, medium-bodied red wine, chilled (*see* above)

1. Add sliced orange and lemon and sugar to large pitcher; mash gently with wooden spoon until fruit releases some juice, but is not totally crushed, and sugar dissolves, about 1 minute. Stir in orange juice, Triple Sec, and wine; refrigerate for at least 2, and up to 8, hours.

2. Before serving, add 6 to 8 ice cubes and stir briskly to distribute settled fruit and pulp; serve immediately.

"Oven-Grilled" London Broil

For London broil that is both flavorful and inexpensive, choose the shoulder cut, sear it on the stove, then pop it into a blazing-hot oven.

⇒ BY MARK BITTMAN ⇐

First things first: London broil is a recipe, not a cut of meat. You take a thick steak, grill, broil, or pan-grill it, then slice it thin, on a bias across the grain. It's essentially a convenience food, a 20-minute protein blast that can form the backbone of any dinner and is complemented by almost any side dish.

The traditional cut for London broil is flank steak, a long, thin, boneless muscle that weighs a couple of pounds and comes from the flank section of the cow (*see* chart, next page). Since it has some marbling—a key to flavor in meat—and is not a super-tough cut, it's really the perfect choice. And, historically, it has been inexpensive. But these days, at around $7 a pound, flank

London broil must be sliced very thin against the grain.

steak is one of the more expensive cuts. At that price, most people will opt for porterhouse or rib-eye every time. Meatpackers and butchers know this, of course, which is how thick cuts of inexpensive round and shoulder steak have come to be labeled London broil, along with the required part-of-cow designation. You might see, for example, "top round steak for London broil." At as little as $1.79 a pound (and a ceiling of $3.99, at least where I live), these cheaper cuts seemed worth a try.

Before narrowing down the cuts, I decided to settle on a cooking technique. When the goal is simply a broiled steak, cooking shouldn't be much of a challenge. All you want, after all, is a crisp crust and a rare-to-medium-rare interior. (Because they are so lean, rareness is especially important for these cuts—once you cook the juices out, they are intolerably tough and dry.) Ideally, the dry crunch of the crust contrasts with the tender, juicy interior in every single slice. But my broiler doesn't really generate enough heat to brown the exterior of even a 1½–inch thick steak before the interior becomes overcooked. Grilling worked fine—and most steaks were perfectly done in four to eight minutes, turning only once—but I needed an alternative for indoor cooking.

Pan-grilling was the most obvious solution, but there was also an obvious problem: smoke. When I got a cast-iron skillet blazing hot and

threw the steak in there, it browned beautifully on both sides, and took about the same amount of time as grilling. But within a minute, the entire house—not just the kitchen—was filled with blue haze. (I knew enough to disconnect the smoke detectors, so at least I avoided that nuisance.)

Since high heat is necessary for this combination of good crust and rare interior, I decided to try the oven. Roasting couldn't possibly work; the oven wasn't going to produce the sudden "shock" that is so necessary for good searing. I thought about preheating my pan in the oven, but then I realized I could employ the same technique many restaurant chefs use—start the meat in a hot skillet on the stovetop, then transfer it to the hottest possible oven.

After some experimentation, I got this to work perfectly and, again, the total cooking time was less than 10 minutes. I set the oven rack at the lowest position and preheated the oven to 500 degrees. When it was ready, I preheated a skillet for a few minutes, then added the steak and immediately moved the skillet into the oven, using double potholders to protect my hand. After three or four minutes, I turned the steak and finished the cooking. The smoke problem was virtually eliminated, and I had a fairly crusty rare steak without having to light the grill. Eventually I made one further refinement to this technique: I used a pizza stone, and preheated my

oven for at least 30 minutes. The stone transferred more heat to the bottom of the skillet and produced a better crust, but I wouldn't consider it essential.

With all these techniques, timing varied according to the thickness of the steak. A one-inch-thick flank steak could be done in five minutes. A thicker shoulder or round steak—say, 1½ inches or more—might take eight minutes, or even a little longer. I learned to rely on my instant-read thermometer, and yanked the steak off the heat the second it read 120 degrees. When family members wanted the meat a little better done, I went to 125 degrees, still with good results.

Comparing the Cuts

Having settled on a cooking method, I began comparing the different cuts. To work as London broil, a cut must be made up of one muscle, because otherwise it simply falls apart when you slice it. There are only a few cuts of beef that meet this criterion. I eliminated one of them, the tri-tip cut, because it is too difficult for most consumers to find, and top sirloin along with the flank because it is too expensive. Eye of round has the wrong shape for steaks, while bottom round is almost always used for roasts.

That left me with two cuts—namely, the top round and the shoulder. When I began investigating them, I quickly made what turned out to be my most important discovery: Although supermarkets tend to market top round and shoulder the same way, the differences are enormous.

If you treat a 1 or 1½-inch thick cut of shoulder exactly like flank you'll get decent results, a chewy but fairly flavorful steak at a substantial savings. Not only is shoulder the least expensive steak you can buy, it also has a little bit of fat, which you want. If, however, you cook a thick cut of top round that way, you're going to be disappointed. Round is lean and tight-grained, with a liver-like flavor that's almost disgusting in quickly cooked muscle meat. Having experimented with top round alongside shoulder during the early stages of my work (and including it in my final tests), I would say that shoulder is the best inexpensive substitute for flank steak. A blind taste test by the *Cook's* editorial staff confirmed this. When they sampled London broil made from flank, shoulder, blade steak, and bottom and top round, they all preferred shoulder for its robust beef flavor and reasonably tender texture. While other cuts might have a slightly deeper flavor or better texture, none had the combination that shoulder offered.

Now that I had the right cut and had learned how to cook it, I thought I'd see what help I could give it. With a properly cooked shoulder steak, both flavor and texture were good, but the first could be stronger and the second had a somewhat flaccid quality I could do without. I tried marinades and spice rubs, but both simply added their flavors, creating a different critter from the plain, simple steak I wanted. There was another problem with these treatments: Instead of improving the texture of the steak, they detracted from the quality of its crust, which I had begun to consider essential. Even after I carefully dried the surface of the meat with paper towels, the wet marinades inhibited the formation of a good crust during the relatively short cooking times. And the dry rubs tended to burn or give the crust a completely foreign flavor.

I moved one step closer to my goal when I retreated into the past and began to serve the plain broiled steaks with a huge lump of compound butter. Its flavors complemented rather than overwhelmed the meat, but the taste of the butter still remained more distinctive than I wanted.

At that point my quest forked, and I pursued two roads at once. I began "aging" the meat in my refrigerator, both with salt and without. I knew the salt was a gamble because it would draw out moisture, which would leave the meat with even less juice and make cooking times more critical. But I hoped that salt would intensify the flavor, and I knew enzymatic action—the initial

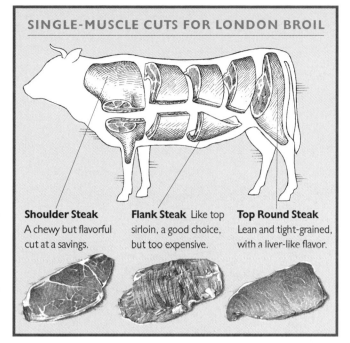

SINGLE-MUSCLE CUTS FOR LONDON BROIL

Shoulder Steak
A chewy but flavorful cut at a savings.

Flank Steak Like top sirloin, a good choice, but too expensive.

Top Round Steak Lean and tight-grained, with a liver-like flavor.

stages of spoilage, really—would tenderize the meat some. The aging worked, although much better with salt than without. The meat gained flavor and a certain firmness—it lost its flaccidity and became more like "real" steak. And the drier surface formed a better, crunchier crust than the untreated or wet-marinated steaks.

But there were considerable disadvantages to this process, not the least of which was that it required the kind of plan-ahead thinking that virtually destroyed the convenience of a simple steak. (If we all planned our dinners three days ahead—the amount of aging time I determined was best—we could abolish the frozen food aisle.) Furthermore, by drawing the liquids out of the meat, salting reduced the juiciness; I could see it on the plate and feel it in my mouth. And there was yet another problem with salting the meat. It became too salty for many people. Yet aging small pieces of meat like these without salting didn't do much at all. By the time the unsalted meat became tender and flavorful, it was so dried out that when I sliced it thin and left it raw, it resembled aged, air-dried beef like bresaola. To me, the results were clear. Salted meat was interesting, and different from "natural" meat, but not better. Its flavor was meatier, but only barely so, and its lack of juice was a real deterrent. Had the difference been more positive, I would say it was worth the effort, which is really more in the planning than in the execution. But I won't bother with this in the future.

When I was finished, I compared a well-cooked, untreated shoulder steak to a flank steak, the traditional cut for London broil. The flank steak had better texture and flavor, but the differences were not that great.

TECHNIQUE | OVEN GRILLING

To achieve the high heat necessary for a good crust, preheat a pizza stone on an oven rack set on the lowest rung.

And the fact that I can buy the shoulder steak more cheaply and in a thicker cut will make it my London broil of choice in summers to come.

"OVEN-GRILLED" LONDON BROIL
SERVES 4

Using a pizza stone in the oven helps super-heat the pan bottom, but this method works well without the stone, too.

1½-2 pounds boneless shoulder steak, about
  1½ inches thick, patted dry
Salt and ground black pepper

1. Adjust oven rack to lowest position; position pizza stone, if using, on rack and heat oven to 500 degrees at least 30 minutes.

2. Meanwhile, heat large, heavy, ovenproof skillet, preferably cast iron or stainless steel with an aluminum core, for at least 3 minutes over high heat. Generously sprinkle both sides of steak with salt and pepper; add to pan. As soon as steak smokes, about 5 seconds, carefully transfer pan to oven; cook 3½ to 4 minutes, then flip steak and cook until well seared and meat is medium-rare (125 degrees on an instant-read thermometer), 3½ to 4 minutes longer. Transfer steak to cutting board; let rest for 5 minutes. Following photograph on page 14, slice very thin, on bias against the grain; adjust seasoning with additional salt and pepper, and serve immediately with meat juices.

GRILLED LONDON BROIL
SERVES 4

1½-2 pounds boneless shoulder steak, about
  1½ inches thick, patted dry
Salt and ground black pepper

1. Spread one large chimney's worth, about 5 quarts, hardwood charcoal or charcoal briquettes over ⅔ of grill bottom. Refill chimney with charcoal, position on charcoal layer in grill, and ignite. Burn until charcoal in chimney is blazing, 5 to 8 minutes. Dump burning coals onto unlit charcoal, position grill rack over fire, and burn until all charcoal is completely covered with thin coating of light gray ash and fire is very hot (you can hold your hand 5 inches above grill surface for 2 seconds), 20 to 30 minutes more.

2. Generously sprinkle both sides of steak with salt and pepper. Grill over direct heat until well seared, about 3 minutes. Flip steak over and grill on second side until well seared and meat is medium-rare (125 degrees on an instant-read thermometer), about 3 minutes longer. Transfer to cutting board; let rest for 5 minutes. Following photograph on page 14, slice very thin, on bias against the grain; adjust seasoning with additional salt and pepper, and serve immediately.

Shaping Store-Bought Puff Pastry

Folding and turning the hundreds of layers of butter that give rise to puff pastry is a lot of work, and for the novice, the results can often be a disappointment. The accuracy of each turn of the dough is crucial, and the frequent chilling between turns is time-consuming. But there is a simple answer to this dilemma: store-bought puff pastry. Located in the frozen foods section of most supermarkets, it works well in a pinch for making shells for sweet and savory fillings. By Maryellen Driscoll

Illustration: John Burgoyne

PUFF PASTRY BASICS

As with the real thing, we found that the following precautions are necessary to avoid lopsided puff pastry (right) and ensure a successful rise (far right).

➤ To prepare: Thaw frozen pastry on the counter until pliable but still chilled (20 to 30 minutes). Unfold and place with creases opening onto a floured surface like a book set face down. Gently press the creases to make a smooth, even sheet.

➤ When using a cookie cutter: Dip the cutter periodically in flour so that it does not stick to the dough. Do not twist the cutter to cut. If the layers are pressed

together, the dough will not rise evenly.

➤ When using a knife: Make sure it is sharp, and do not drag it through the dough to cut. A pastry wheel or pizza cutter may also be used.

➤ Avoid dripping egg wash down the pastry's sides. This can seal the dough

to the pan and prevent the layers from rising.

➤ Avoid rolling over the dough edges with your rolling pin. It can press down the sides.

➤ Position your oven rack in the upper third of the oven to bake.

QUICK JAM TURNOVERS

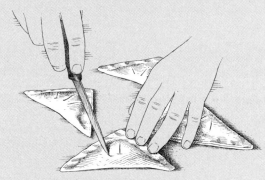

1. Roll the dough into a 12-inch square and cut into nine 4-inch squares. Brush egg wash (beaten whole eggs) along the perimeter of each square and fill with a tablespoon of jam before folding into a triangle.

2. After firmly pressing the edges, brush the tops with egg wash and make three ½-inch slashes. Sprinkle with sugar and transfer to a baking sheet. Bake at 400 degrees for 12 minutes. Place turnovers on a rack to cool.

PUFF PASTRY CUPS

These large puff pastry cups and the puff pastry diamonds (see page 17) are delicious with creamed chicken or seafood fillings, or fresh fruit topped with whipped cream. We recommend the smaller, bite-size cups for rich, sweet fillings, such as lemon curd or ganache, and for savory fillings such as egg salad, ratatouille, or finely diced sautéed mushrooms seasoned with garlic and herbs.

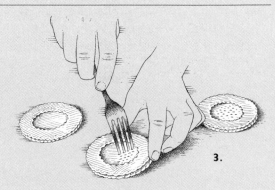

1.

1. Brush a 9-by-9-inch sheet of dough with egg wash and cut out eight circles with a 3-inch plain or scalloped cookie cutter (or a 2-inch cutter for smaller cups).

2. Center a 2-inch cutter in four of the circles to cut out rings (use a 1¼-inch cutter for smaller cups).

2.

3.

3. Place the rings onto the four remaining circles and press gently to seal. Thoroughly prick the center of the base with a fork. Bake at 400 degrees for 12 minutes or until golden brown. Place the cups on a rack to cool.

PUFF PASTRY FRUIT WRAPS

Use as a wrap for apples or pears. Since the pastry cooks quickly, the apples must be baked and the pears must be poached before wrapping.

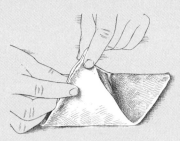
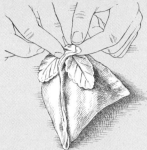

1. Cut a 9½-inch equilateral triangle and brush the perimeter with egg wash. (Join the side scraps to form another 9½-inch triangle.)

2. Center the prepared fruit upright (level the bottom if lopsided), and lift the corners of the dough. Press the edges together to encase the fruit.

3. Brush with egg wash and make slashes on each side. Decorate with leaf shapes. Bake on a parchment-lined baking sheet at 400 degrees for 15 minutes.

PUFF PASTRY DIAMONDS

See Puff Pastry Cups (page 16) for filling instructions.

1. Cut a 4-by-4-inch square. Brush with egg wash and fold into a triangle. Leave the tip of the triangle uncut. Starting ¾ inch in from each side of the tip, cut a ½-inch border down each side through the folded edge.

2. Unfold. Lay the square flat. Place each cut corner on the opposite corner to form the sides of the diamond. Brush raised border with the egg wash and prick the center square. Bake at 400 degrees for 12 minutes. Place on a rack to cool.

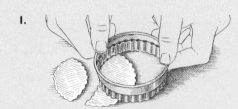

I.

DECORATIVE LEAVES

1. Cut oval-shaped leaves freehand with a sharp paring knife, or following illustration above, use a scalloped edge cookie cutter.

2. Without cutting through the dough, use a knife to press patterns into the leaves.

2.

CREAM HORNS

These are delicious filled with sweetened whipped cream or ice cream and sprinkled with powdered sugar.

1. Fold a 4-by-12-inch sheet of aluminum foil in half to make a 4-by-6-inch rectangle. Roll the foil around a baster (with its rubber bulb removed), holding firmly at the tip to form a small cone. Pinch the foil tip and lightly coat the foil with cooking spray.

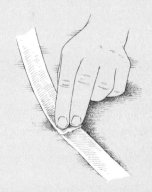

2. Cut two 9-by-1-inch strips of dough. Brush one end with egg wash and seal as above to form one long strip.

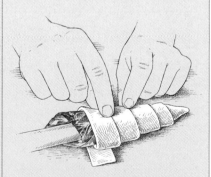

3. Starting at the tip, wrap the pastry strip around the foil cone. Brush the pastry with egg wash and remove the baster. Place the pastry-wrapped cone on a parchment-lined baking sheet. Bake at 400 degrees for 12 minutes, then remove the foil and continue baking for another 5 minutes. Place the horns on a rack to cool.

POT PIE TOPPING

Following our Simple Chicken Pot Pie recipe (May/June 1996), we developed this decorative topping for individual servings.

1. Invert an ovenproof bowl onto the pastry and cut a circle ½ inch larger than the bowl rim. Remove and fill the bowl with hot pie filling. Inside the pastry circle cut a second circle ¾ inch smaller.

2. Slash four steam vents in the inner circle and place on top of the hot filling.

3. Pinch pleats around the ring as illustrated.

4. Place the pleated ring around the pastry circle and brush with egg wash. Bake in a 400-degree oven until the pastry is golden brown and the filling is bubbly, 20 to 25 minutes.

New-Style Southern Cornbread

Cornmeal mush gives the bread a strong corn flavor and a moist, fine texture.

⇒ BY PAM ANDERSON WITH MELISSA HAMILTON ⇐

Although I've lived most of my adult life in the Midwest and the Northeast, I grew up in a small town on the Florida panhandle—and anybody who's been to the panhandle knows it's more Deep South than tropical paradise. Most often my family ate Southern-style, which meant there was hardly a noon or night meal without a couple of long-simmered, fatback-flavored vegetables, which we ate with a fork in the right hand and cornbread in the left. These, then, are my credentials: I know Southern cornbread.

Of course, having lived north of the Mason-Dixon Line for 20 years, I've sampled lots of Northern cornbread as well. Although the two ingredient lists may look similar, the cornbreads of the North and South are as different as Boston and Birmingham.

White, not yellow, is the cornmeal of choice for Southern-style cornbread. Unlike Northerners, Southerners use only trace amounts of flour, if any, and if sugar is included it is treated like salt, to be measured out in teaspoons, rather than by the cup. Buttermilk moistens, bacon drippings enrich, and a combination of baking powder and soda gives a lift. Classic Southern cornbread batter is poured into a scorching hot, greased cast-iron skillet, which causes it to develop a thin, shattery-crisp crust as the bread bakes. At its best, this bread is moist and tender, with the warm fragrance of the cornfield and the subtle flavor of the dairy in every bite. To my mind, it is the best possible accompaniment to soups, salads, chilis, and stews. So I set out to create a foolproof recipe for Southern-style cornbread.

Yellow's Not Mellow

I began by testing 11 different cornmeals in one simple Southern cornbread recipe. I tried as many nationally and regionally available brands as possible—Quaker, Indian Head, Martha White, and Arrowhead Mills—as well as brands from major mail-order houses—Walnut Acres, King Arthur, and Hoppin' John. While I was primarily interested in flavor differences between the two colors of meal, I also wondered whether the growing conditions (organic vs. nonorganic) and produc-

For an extra-crisp crust, heat your pan in the oven until it is very hot before adding the batter.

tion methods (stone ground vs. steel cut; whole grain vs. degerminated) would make much difference in the bread. (see "Understanding Cornmeal," page 19, for more information).

Before the cornmeal tests, I would have bet that color was a regional idiosyncrasy that had little to do with flavor. But tasting proved otherwise. Corn muffins made with yellow cornmeal consistently had a more potent corn flavor than those made with white meal. Less surprising, I found that breads made with stone ground, whole grain cornmeals were better textured and better flavored than those made with steel cut and degerminated grains. Whether organically grown corn results in superior cornmeal is debatable, but my two favorite meals—Walnut Acres and King Arthur—were yellow, whole grain, stone ground, and organic.

Although I didn't want these muffins to taste like dessert, I wondered whether a little sugar might enhance the corn flavor, much the way a little sugar in the cooking water can improve boiled corn. So I made three batches—one with no sugar, one with 2 teaspoons of sugar, and one with a heaping tablespoon. The higher-sugar bread was really too sweet for Southern cornbread, but 2 teaspoons of sugar seemed to enhance the natural sweetness of the corn without calling attention to itself.

Most Southern-style cornbread batters are made with just buttermilk, but I found recipes calling for the full range of acidic and sweet dairy products—buttermilk, sour cream, yogurt, milk, and cream—and made muffins with each of them. I still loved the pure, straightforward flavor of the buttermilk-based corn muffins, but those made with sour cream were not only more tasty, but also more shapely.

I was starting to become a little uneasy about where I was taking this bread. A couple of teaspoons of sugar might be overlooked; yellow cornmeal was a big blow; but my sour cream leanings felt like I was crossing the border.

A Rabbit Trail Pays Off

All my testing to this point had been done with a composite recipe under which most Southern cornbread recipes seemed to fall. There were two recipes, however, that didn't quite fit the mold—one very rich and one very lean—and now seemed like the right time to give them a try.

After rejecting the rich version as closer to spoonbread than cornbread, I went to the other extreme. In this simple version, boiling water is stirred into the cornmeal, then modest amounts of milk, egg, butter, salt, and baking powder are stirred into the resulting cornmeal mush and the whole thing is baked. So simple, so lean, so humble, so backwater, this recipe would have been easy to pass over. But given my options at this point, I decided to give it a quick test. Just one bite completely changed my direction. Unlike anything I had tasted so far, the crumb of this muffin was incredibly moist and fine and bursting with corn flavor, all with no flour and virtually no fat.

I was pleased, but since the foundation of this bread is cornmeal mush, the crumb was actually more mushy than moist. In addition, the baking powder, the only dry ingredient left, got stirred into the wet batter at the end. This just didn't feel right to me.

After a few unsuccessful attempts to make this cornbread less mushy, I started thinking that this great idea was a bust. As a last attempt, I decided to make mush out of only half the cornmeal and mix the remaining cornmeal with the leavener. To my relief, the bread made this way was much improved. Decreasing the mush even further—from a half to a third of the cornmeal—gave me exactly what I was looking for. I made the new, improved cornbread with buttermilk and mixed a bit of baking soda with the baking powder, and it tasted even better. Finally my recipe was starting to feel Southern again. Although I still preferred yellow cornmeal and a sprinkle of sugar, I had achieved a moist, tender, rather fine-crumbed bread without flour, and a nicely-shaped bread without the sour cream, thus avoiding two ingredients that would have interfered with the strong corn flavor I wanted.

With my new recipe in hand, I performed a few final tests. My recipe called for 1 tablespoon of butter, but many Southern cornbreads call for no more fat than is needed to grease the pan. I tried vegetable oil, peanut oil, shortening, butter, and bacon drippings, as well as a batch with no fat at all. To my delight, the cornbread with no added fat was as moist and delicious as the other breads. Butter and bacon drippings, however, were pleasant flavor additions.

Before these cornbread tests, I didn't think it was possible to bake cornbread in too hot an oven, but after tasting breads baked on the bottom rack of a 475 degree oven, I found that a dark brown crust makes bitter bread. I moved the rack up a notch and reduced the oven temperature to 450 degrees and was able to cook many loaves of bread and pans of muffins to golden brown perfection.

One final question: Do you need to heat up the skillet or muffin tin before adding the batter? The answer is no for non-Southerners. Although the bread will not be as crisp in an unheated pan, it will ultimately brown up with a longer baking time. The answer for Southerners like me is yes. More than the color

of the meal or the presence of sugar or flour, cornbread becomes Southern when the batter hits the hot fat in a cast-iron skillet.

MASTER RECIPE FOR SOUTHERN-STYLE CORNBREAD
MAKES ONE 8-INCH SKILLET OF BREAD

Unlike its sweet, cakey Northern counterpart, Southern cornbread is thin, crusty, and decidedly savory. Though some styles of Southern cornbread are dry and crumbly, I favor this dense, moist, tender version. Cornmeal mush of just the right texture (*see* illustrations 1 to 3, below) is essential to this bread. Though I prefer to make cornbread in a preheated cast-iron skillet, a 9-inch round cake pan or 9-inch square baking pan, greased lightly with butter and not preheated, will also produce acceptable results if you double the recipe and bake the bread for 25 minutes.

    4 teaspoons bacon drippings *or* I tablespoon
       melted butter and I teaspoon vegetable oil
    I cup yellow cornmeal, preferably stone ground
    2 teaspoons sugar
    ½ teaspoon salt
    I teaspoon baking powder
    ¼ teaspoon baking soda
    ⅓ cup rapidly boiling water
    ¾ cup buttermilk
    I large egg, beaten lightly

1. Adjust oven rack to lower middle position and heat oven to 450 degrees. Set 8-inch cast-iron skillet with bacon fat (or vegetable oil) in heating oven.

2. Measure ⅓ cup cornmeal into medium bowl. Mix remaining cornmeal, sugar, salt, baking powder, and baking soda in small bowl; set aside.

3. Pour boiling water all at once into the ⅓ cup cornmeal; stir to make a stiff mush. Whisk in buttermilk gradually, breaking up lumps until smooth, then whisk in egg. When oven is preheated and skillet very hot, stir dry ingredients

into mush mixture until just moistened. Carefully remove skillet from oven. Pour hot bacon fat (or melted butter) into batter and stir to incorporate, then quickly pour batter into heated skillet. Bake until golden brown, about 20 minutes. Remove from oven and instantly turn cornbread onto wire rack; cool for 5 minutes, then serve immediately.

SOUTHERN-STYLE CORN STICKS OR MUFFINS
MAKES 12 CORN STICKS OR 6 MUFFINS

Corn stick pans have anywhere from seven to 12 molds. If your pan has fewer than 12 molds, bake the sticks in two batches. If you wish, you can also follow these directions to make six muffins using a heavy-gauge 6-muffin mold tin (each mold measuring ½ cup). If making muffins, bake for 20 minutes.

Follow Master Recipe for Southern-style Cornbread, heating heavy-gauge corn stick pan instead of cast-iron skillet. Omit fat from batter. When oven is heated, remove pan from oven and generously brush molds with 4 teaspoons bacon drippings or 4 teaspoons vegetable oil. Continue with recipe, filling molds almost to rim with batter. Bake until golden brown, 18 to 20 minutes; turn corn sticks onto rack to cool. Wipe crumbs from molds, brush with more bacon fat or oil, and repeat baking process with remaining batter, if necessary.

SOUTHERN-STYLE CORNBREAD FOR NORTHERN TASTES
MAKES ONE 8-INCH SKILLET OF BREAD

The addition of extra sugar and cake flour moves this cornbread a small step away from its Southern roots. Though still very far removed from Northern-style cornbread, this version has a subtle sweetness and a very fine texture.

Follow Master Recipe for Southern-Style Cornbread, increasing sugar to 3 tablespoons and adding ¼ cup cake flour to dry ingredients.

TECHNIQUE | GETTING THE BATTER JUST RIGHT

I. If your mush looks like this, it is too firm; work in a tablespoon or two of hot water to loosen it before adding the wet ingredients.

2. If the water is not hot enough, the starch will not gelatinize, the batter will be too thin, and the mush will not form.

3. The mush should be like soft polenta: thick enough to give the batter body, but pliable enough to stir wet ingredients in easily.

The Best Lemon Bars

Most lemon bars are too sweet and have a thick, soggy crust. We developed a recipe that delivers a fresh, lemony filling paired with a thin, crisp crust.

⇒ BY SUSAN LOGOZZO ⇐

Lemon squares (or bars, as I like to refer to them, since it seems to give you permission to cut them into other than perfect squares) are a favorite classic American bar cookie. In this style of cookie, a bottom layer or "crust" is pressed into a pan, prebaked, then topped with a filling. The cookies are baked again, then cut into bars.

Lemon bars are easy to make—but that doesn't mean it's easy to get them just the way you want them. Whether from bakeries or home recipes, many versions are too sweet and lack true lemon flavor. The topping might be too gummy or too starchy; it might be skimpy relative to the amount of crust, or piled so high the bar doesn't hold its shape when cut. I have sampled crusts that are too thin, too dry, or too brittle; some lack flavor and others have so much fat they leave a greasy taste in your mouth.

With these variables in mind, I set out to develop a recipe for a lemon bar with a tender, melt-in-your-mouth crust that has a good balance of sweetness and richness. The lemon topping I was looking for needed to have a true, vibrant lemon taste, a light texture, and good mouthfeel. I also wanted to find just the right balance between filling and crust in terms of both texture and flavor. In addition, I wanted a good, clean cut when serving, without the crust crumbling or the topping falling over. Last but not least, since lemon bars are a casual treat to make without a lot of fuss, I wanted a recipe that was simple and straightforward.

The Crust

I knew that flour, butter, and sugar would be the main ingredients of the bottom layer. I also knew that since I wanted a cookie or shortbread texture rather than a pastry-type crust, I would need a fair amount of sugar. No liquid would be necessary because I wasn't trying to create the little pockets of steam that produce flakiness and layering in pastry.

My first challenges were to decide the proportion of flour to butter and the amount, as well as the type, of sugar. I decided, after several taste tests, that a crust made with ½ cup of butter per 1 cup of flour resulted in a crust that was too rich, a little greasy, and not quite sturdy enough to cut. Cutting back to ¼ cup, however, produced a crust that was hard and dry and crumbled when cut. An

One of the keys to great lemon bars is to achieve the right balance between the crust and the filling, so that neither dominates.

amount between these two—just over ⅓ cup of butter per cup of flour—proved to be just right.

Since sugar affects tenderness as well as sweetness, the amount and type of sugar needed to be determined along with the butter. Brown sugar proved too rich for my tasters' palates, while granulated sugar produced a crust that was a bit brittle and gritty. The best, most tender texture came from confectioners' sugar. To achieve the delicate crumb and melt-in-your-mouth quality of shortbread, I also added a bit of cornstarch to my formula.

Having decided on the basic ingredients, I began to investigate ways to combine and bake them. For most cookies and one type of pastry, the fat and sugar are creamed together in the first step. The alternative is to start by cutting the fat into the flour with your fingertips or a food processor, which is common in most pastry crusts. After testing both methods, I decided that because of the proportion of flour to butter and the absence of liquid, the second method was best suited for this crust. Cutting the butter into the flour created a crumbly mixture that could be pressed into the pan. To insure an evenly baked crust and prevent sogginess, I found it necessary to prebake the crust and discovered, through trial and error, that the standard temperature of 350 degrees worked best.

Once I had decided on a formula and the best techniques for making the bottom layer, all that remained was to discover the right proportion of crust to filling. The bottom layer must not only provide support for the topping but also balance the lemony taste. A crust that was about ¼-inch thick provided the right foundation for the amount of filling I wanted, which ended up being about ⅓ inch in depth.

The Lemon Layer

The usual method for making the lemon layer of these sweet bars is to mix eggs, sugar, lemon, and flour, pour it over the prebaked crust, and bake until set. But before trying this, I took a detour—I spread a precooked lemon filling over the prebaked crust and allowed it to set. This method worked only passably well because it required a filling that was made with butter and thickened with cornstarch, which turned out to be dull and a bit gummy.

Returning to the original method of baking, I proceeded to discover the amount of fresh lemon juice I would need for a clear, tart lemon flavor. I knew that 2 tablespoons of lemon juice, the minimum amount in the recipes I had researched, would not produce the zing that I was after, and initial tests proved this to be true. The flavor was bland and uninteresting. I kept adding more, and eventually ended up with 11 tablespoons of juice and 2 teaspoons of zest. Even tasters who initially thought that this was too lemony ended up liking it. The 11 tablespoons of juice also provided enough liquid for a topping that was attractively light.

However, I eventually decided that I wanted a topping that was just a little less intense, so I tried replacing some of the lemon juice with other liquids. Water thinned it out too much, and heavy cream not only adversely affected the lightness, but also cut the lemony taste. Adding a small amount of whole milk, though, seemed to balance the flavor with the texture. I also found that baking the topping at a slightly lower temperature than was used for the crust (325 degrees

1. Lay first sheet of paper lengthwise in pan. Dot the first sheet with butter and lay second sheet crosswise over it.

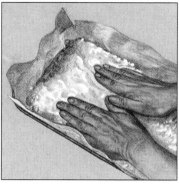

2. Use fingers to press a crust mixture into a ¼-inch layer over the bottom and about ½ inch up the sides of the pan.

3. After cooling the bars, grasp the edges of the lengthwise paper and lift the bars onto a cutting board.

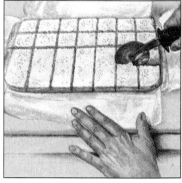

4. Peel the paper down and off the edges, then cut serving-size bars using a knife or pizza cutter.

rather than 350 degrees) helped produce the smooth texture I wanted, since eggs do not curdle when cooked at lower temperatures.

In my first round of tests, I thought it was unnecessary to thicken the filling with flour, which I wanted to avoid because I had detected its starchy taste in mixtures that had a high proportion of it. After more tests, though, I discovered two very good reasons to use it. First, some of the fillings baked without flour seemed to have a mealy texture after cooling, a result of the eggs being exposed to the oven heat during baking. Second, toppings made without flour became watery after sitting for only an hour or so. Adding just a small amount of flour solved both these problems without adding any starchy taste — buffering the eggs produced a smooth texture and effectively halted the "weeping."

To investigate thickening properties a bit more, I tried adding an extra egg yolk in one test and cornstarch in a few others. The additional yolk produced a bright yellow color, a heavier texture, and an unwanted eggy taste. Cornstarch also yielded surprisingly negative results. The cornstarch filling did not thicken well because cornstarch cannot withstand high heat for an extended amount of time. But what surprised me most was the taste. Not only could you detect the starch on your tongue, you could also find its strong, metallic flavor in the filling.

Now I had only one last problem to solve. During all my tests, the filling would inevitably shift and stick to the sides of the pan, which made it difficult to cut the bars along the edges. I solved this problem by lining the pan with paper, either parchment or waxed, the sides as well as the bottom. I cut two pieces to fit the pan, one for each direction, and held them in place with a small amount of butter. After baking, I lifted the uncut lemon bars from the pan by holding onto the edges of the paper. Because the paper could be cut or peeled away from the sides of the bars and there was no obstruction from the pan edges, I found it easy to cut them into even,

presentable pieces, using either a knife or a large pizza wheel. A sifting of powdered sugar, and I had my lemon bars.

PERFECT LEMON BARS
MAKES ABOUT TWO DOZEN 1½- TO 2-INCH SQUARES

The lemon filling must be added to a warm crust. The 30-minute chilling and 20-minute baking of the crust should allow plenty of time to prepare the filling. If not, make the filling first and stir to blend just before pouring it into the crust. Any leftover bars can be sealed in plastic wrap and refrigerated for up to two days.

The Crust
1¾	cups all-purpose flour
⅔	cup confectioners' sugar, plus extra to decorate finished bars
¼	cup cornstarch
¾	teaspoon salt
12	tablespoons unsalted butter (1½ sticks), at very cool room temperature, cut into 1-inch pieces, plus extra for greasing pan

Lemon Filling
4	large eggs, beaten lightly
1⅓	cups granulated sugar
3	tablespoons all-purpose flour
2	teaspoons finely grated zest from two large lemons
⅔	cup juice from 3 to 4 large lemons, strained
⅓	cup whole milk
⅛	teaspoon salt

1. *For the crust:* Adjust oven rack to middle position and heat oven to 350 degrees. Lightly butter a 13-by-9-inch baking dish and line with one sheet parchment or wax paper. Dot paper with butter, then lay second sheet crosswise over it (*see* illustration 1, above).

2. Pulse flour, confectioners' sugar, cornstarch, and salt in food processor workbowl fitted with steel blade. Add butter and process to blend, 8 to

10 seconds, then pulse until mixture is pale yellow and resembles coarse meal, about three 1-second bursts. (To do this by hand, mix flour, confectioners' sugar, cornstarch, and salt in medium bowl. Freeze butter and grate it on large holes of box grater into flour mixture. Toss butter pieces to coat. Rub pieces between your fingers for a minute, until flour turns pale yellow and coarse.) Sprinkle mixture into lined pan and, following illustration 2, press firmly with fingers into even, ¼-inch layer over entire pan bottom and about ½ inch up sides. Refrigerate for 30 minutes, then bake until golden brown, about 20 minutes.

3. *For the filling:* Meanwhile, whisk eggs, sugar, and flour in medium bowl, then stir in lemon juice, milk, and salt to blend well.

4. *To finish the bars:* Reduce oven temperature to 325 degrees. Stir filling mixture to reblend; pour into warm crust. Bake until filling feels firm when touched lightly, about 20 minutes. Transfer pan to wire rack; cool to near room temperature, at least 30 minutes. Following illustrations 3 and 4, above, transfer to cutting board, fold paper down, and cut into serving-size bars, wiping knife or pizza cutter clean between cuts, as necessary. Sieve confectioners' sugar over bars, if desired.

Lemon bars made with extra egg yolks and relatively little filling (1) were flat and edgy; our final recipe (2), has the tender but firm texture we liked best; bars made with extra filling and no starch (3) oozed when cut; those made with extra lemon but no milk (4) had an unpleasantly sticky texture.

Fresh Strawberry Pie

To preserve the pristine taste of fresh strawberries, thicken with a combination of cornstarch and pectin that's designed for lower sugar recipes.

⇒ BY TODD BUTCHER ⇐

Nothing says that summer and its promise of ripening abundance has arrived like a slice of fresh strawberry pie. And nothing could be simpler—fresh berries in a sweet glaze set on a flaky crust—a casual, delicious statement of the season.

I've had both commercially made and homemade strawberry pies, and I've never been completely satisfied with either. I like the smooth texture of a commercially produced strawberry pie. It's the phony flavor and color and the less-than-fresh berries that I have a problem with. I prefer the natural taste and top-notch berries in a homemade pie, but not the glaze, which is usually stiffly jelled and cloudy. I wanted to develop a strawberry pie with the best characteristics of both—fresh, juicy berries held together by a soft, sweet glaze. I also wanted it to be a pie that is easy to prepare, utilizes ingredients available at the local market, and emphasizes the rich flavor and color of fresh strawberries.

In researching the subject, I quickly discovered that there is no shortage of recipes for fresh strawberry pie and that they are remarkably similar in method: Prepare a glaze by boiling mashed berries, sugar, and thickener until the sugar is dissolved; stir in fresh berries; pour the mixture into a prebaked pie shell; and chill until set.

Thickening

I knew that thickening was the key element in getting the filling right, so I tried every thickener I could get my hands on, including old standbys like cornstarch and gelatin (see "Testing Pie Thickeners," page 23). None of them produced exactly the filling I was looking for, but cornstarch and arrowroot came closest. Although arrowroot had made a glaze with a slightly brighter color, I finally settled on cornstarch because the cornstarch glaze was more evenly textured.

Unfortunately, however, I also found that a glaze made with cornstarch alone would begin to leak liquid soon after being chilled. A pie that would go into the refrigerator with a good consistency would emerge several hours later loose and watery. This was a tendency shared by all the starches that I tested, except the modified ones.

For an explanation, I called Wulf Doerry, retired Director of Cereal Technology at the American Institute of Baking in Manhattan, Kansas. Doerry explained that the initial thickening of a starch

Place berry halves in concentric circles, flat side down and pointed ends toward center, starting at center and working toward the outer edge.

solution is not always an accurate indicator of the final product. When heated, the starch will bind up most of the water in the solution. As the mixture cools, however, it contracts, and some of the mixture is squeezed out in a process called syneresis. According to Doerry, commercial food producers avoid this by using modified food starches that have been chemically or physically altered to manipulate their thickening properties. But these modified starches are not readily available to the home cook. To make a pie viable using cornstarch as the thickener, I would need to address the problem of syneresis some other way.

In one of my earlier experiments I had combined cornstarch and a brand of pectin called Sure Jell for Lower Sugar Recipes. I knew that ordinary pectin relies on a very specific ratio of pectin, sugar, and acid to set properly. I also knew that my glaze recipe contained a lower proportion of sugar to fruit than what is recommended for ordinary pectin, so the pectin formulated for recipes with less sugar seemed like a better choice. I had rejected this filling because of its overly firm gel, but now I remembered that it had not become as watery as the other pies. I conducted some additional tests, gradually reducing the amount of pectin to soften the glaze. In a glaze prepared with

two cups of pureed strawberries, one cup of sugar, and three tablespoons of cornstarch, one tablespoon of pectin proved sufficient to inhibit the leakage without causing the glaze to set into a stiff gel. My fresh strawberry pie was close at hand. The glaze had the rich red color of fresh strawberries, and after chilling for several hours the pie had not become watery.

A food scientist at Kraft Foods speculated that the small amount of pectin I was adding to the glaze was delaying the syneresis by providing additional water-binding capacity and helping the starch to hold the water in place longer. He also explained that Sure Jell for Lower Sugar Recipes sets by combining with calcium ions, which is why it requires little or no sugar to perform properly and was more effective in my pie than ordinary pectin.

A Flaky Crust Is Best

With the glaze completed, I turned to the question of the crust. Initially, I had hoped to discover a way to prolong the life of the pie by preventing the crust from soaking up juices from the filling. However, I soon found that long before the pie crust became saturated and soggy, the berries themselves began to soften and lose their appeal. So I lost my interest in crust longevity—strawberry pie, like so many of summer's simple pleasures, is transitory and meant to be savored in the moment.

I tried pies using a vanilla wafer crumb crust, a graham cracker crumb crust, and the traditional flaky pie crust recipe featured in the September/October 1997 issue of *Cook's Illustrated*. For flavor and appearance, the traditional flaky pie crust won hands down. It provided a crisp, buttery counterpoint to the tart strawberries and smooth glaze, unlike the crumb crusts, which competed with rather than complemented the other flavors in the pie. The firmer pie shell also provided additional support to the slice.

So when strawberry season arrives this year, grab some fresh berries and celebrate summer. In no time at all, you can easily make a pie with a rich, thick strawberry glaze that can be prepared with ingredients that are probably already in your cupboard.

FRESH STRAWBERRY PIE
SERVES 8

For the glaze to be the right consistency, you must start with 1¼ cups of strawberry puree. Varying that amount will yield glaze that is either too thick or too thin. Likewise, be certain that the glaze mixture has cooled before adding the berries; if it is too hot, the berries might begin to cook and soften. Pectin for lower sugar recipes is important here because this pie does not have enough sugar for ordinary pectin to set properly. Serve the pie with softly whipped cream.

2　quarts fresh strawberries, washed and hulled; one quart halved (4 cups); remaining quart sliced lengthwise into 4 to 5 slices (see illustration below) (4 cups)
1　cup sugar
1　tablespoon powdered pectin for lower sugar recipes (such as Sure Jell)
　　Pinch salt
3　tablespoons cornstarch
　　Pinch ground cinnamon
2　tablespoons juice from one lemon
¼　teaspoon vanilla extract
1　prebaked 9-inch pie shell (see "The Secrets of Prebaking Pie Shells," September/October 1997)

1. Puree 1 pint (2 cups) halved berries in blender or food processor workbowl fitted with steel blade, scraping down sides as necessary, until smooth (you should have 1¼ cups; spoon off any extra). Bring puree, sugar, pectin, and a pinch salt to boil, stirring occasionally, in medium saucepan over medium heat. Increase heat to medium-high; boil hard until sugar and pectin are dissolved, about 1 minute. Off heat, skim foam from surface with large spoon.

2. Meanwhile, mix cornstarch and ¼ cup cold water in small bowl until absolutely smooth. Off heat, add cornstarch slurry to strawberry mixture, then return to boil, stirring constantly, over medium heat. Reduce heat to medium-low and,

continuing to stir constantly, simmer until mixture becomes thick and clear, about 3 minutes. Off heat, stir in cinnamon, lemon juice, and vanilla. Transfer glaze, reserving ¼ cup for topping, into large bowl; cool to room temperature, at least 15 minutes.

3. Using a rubber spatula, fold sliced strawberries into large bowl of glaze, turning several times to coat thoroughly. Turn glazed berries into pie shell; spread evenly and smooth surface with rubber spatula. Following instructions in photo caption, page 22, arrange remaining halved berries on pie. Stir 2 tablespoons water into reserved ¼ cup glaze to thin; brush over berry halves to finish pie. Refrigerate until cold, at least 2, and up to 6, hours. Serve.

DINER-STYLE FRESH STRAWBERRY PIE
SERVES 8

The process of thickening the glaze is easier and less involved with Instant Clearjel (see Resources, page 32), a commercially derived, modified food starch, than it is with the cornstarch and pectin in the recipe above. There is a hitch, though. You may have to mail order Instant Clearjel.

2　quarts fresh strawberries, washed, hulled, and halved (8 cups)
1　cup sugar
　　Pinch salt
　　Pinch ground cinnamon
2　tablespoons juice from one lemon
¼　teaspoon vanilla extract
3½　tablespoons Instant Clearjel
1　prebaked 9-inch pie shell (see "The Secrets of Prebaking Pie Shells," September/October 1997)

1. Bring 4 cups berries, ½ cup sugar, salt, and ¼ cup water to simmer in medium saucepan over medium heat; simmer, stirring constantly, until soft, about 8 minutes. Transfer mixture to sieve set over a large bowl; press on solids with back of wooden spoon to extract 1¼ cups juice into bowl (spoon off any extra) and discard solids. Add cinnamon, lemon juice, and vanilla to juice; set bowl over ice water and stir mixture occasionally until cold. (If juice is not cold, Instant Clearjel will not set up as smooth as it should.)

2. Mix Instant Clearjel with remaining ½ cup sugar in small bowl; whisk mixture into berry juice until thick and pudding-like, about 1 minute.

3. Fold remaining berries into glaze, turning several times with rubber spatula to coat thoroughly. Turn glazed berries into pie shell, using spatula to mound berries slightly at center. Refrigerate until cold, at least 2, and up to 6, hours. Serve.

Todd Butcher is a baker and food writer in Wilmington, North Carolina.

TECHNIQUE | BERRY SLICES

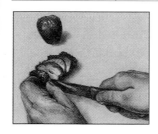

To preserve the shape of the strawberry, lay the berry on its side and slice it lengthwise into four or five pieces.

Testing Pie Thickeners

In search of the ideal thickener, we tried every option we could find with the following results:

GRAIN STARCHES
Cornstarch In the amounts normally recommended in most recipes, cornstarch set into a very stiff, opaque gel with a distinct cereal flavor.

Wheat flour Produced a thick, pasty gel with a strong cereal flavor and odor.

Wheat starch Produced a firm, cloudy gel with a distinct cereal flavor and odor.

Rice flour Produced a soft, white gel that smelled and tasted like rice.

ROOT STARCHES
Arrowroot With a thickening power equal to that of cornstarch, arrowroot produced a clearer gel. However, the texture had an unpleasant slimy consistency.

Potato starch Produced a stiff, flavorless gel.

Instant tapioca Lumps were too prominent to make it a suitable choice for a fresh pie glaze.

Tapioca starch This fine powder produced a thin, clear, flavorless gel that stuck in long strands to whatever it touched.

Kudzu This unusual starch (labeled "kuzu" at the Asian market) produced a soft, sticky, flavorless gel with a texture between tapioca starch and arrowroot.

VEGETABLE GUMS
Guar gum This health-food store offering had a strong malt-like odor and an unpleasant frothy consistency.

Xanthan gum Much like guar gum.

GELATINS
Nonflavored gelatin Produced a clear, flavorless gel that was much too firm.

Agar agar Performed about the same as unflavored gelatin, producing a clear, stiff, unflavored gel.

MODIFIED CORNSTARCHES
COLFLO 67 The best of the modified starches, it produced a silky-smooth, stable paste.

Clearjel Formed a soft, smooth paste, but had a tendency to become slightly rubbery when chilled.

Instant Clearjel Formed a soft, very clear, stable paste.

COMBINATIONS
Cornstarch + Jello strawberry gelatin mix Much too firm, with a phony flavor and color.

Cornstarch + Sure Jell for Lower Sugar Recipes Even texture of cornstarch combined with the water-binding power of pectin produced a good glaze using common ingredients.　—T.B.

Freshness, Not Fat, Makes Best Butter

High-fat designer butters make a difference when butter is the key ingredient; otherwise, go with your freshest grocery brand.

⋟ BY MARYELLEN DRISCOLL ⋞

When I buy butter I usually hesitate in front of my supermarket's dairy cooler, scan the prices, glance at the brands, and then scan the prices again before I toss the cheapest one into my cart.

I found out recently that I am not alone in selecting butter by the dime. Most Americans do not covet one brand over another, but purchase according to price: For every six people who buy the nationally available Land O'Lakes butter, there are ten who opt to save twenty-five to fifty cents a pound by selecting a generic supermarket brand. But I would bet that when selecting a butter most of them, like me, still wrestle with the question : Does the brand matter?

We at *Cook's* decided to find out.

Understanding Butter

Before we began, we wanted to learn more about butter and just what we should be looking for in our tasting.

Simply put, butter is overwhipped or churned cream. In cream, globules of fat protected by a phospholipid membrane float about in a suspension of water. When cream is agitated or churned, the fat globules collide with one another, causing the membranes to break. The freed fat globules then begin to clump together, trapping little pockets of water along with the broken membrane pieces and some intact fat crystals. After the cream is churned into a semisolid mass of butter, any remaining liquid is drawn off as buttermilk. So what begins as an oil-in-water emulsion known as cream is reversed to a water-in-oil emulsion known as butter. (*see* graphic, below).

All butter must consist of at least 80 percent milk fat, according to U.S. Department of Agriculture standards. Most commercial butters do not exceed this. European butters and Hotel Bar's Plugrá are exceptions, with anywhere from 82 to 88 percent milk fat. All butters contain about 2 percent milk solids and the remainder is water.

Despite tight government regulations for butter, batches of butter made by the same brand are prone to inconsistencies of color and texture. That is simply because butter is an agricultural product affected by factors like seasonal changes. During good-weather months, cows that graze in fields produce cream rich in carotene pigments from grass and other plants, which will make a butter more yellow. In the winter, cows eat feed and grains that will result in a whiter butter. The color of butter can also be affected by the cow's breed. Certain breeds, such as Jerseys, produce deeper yellow butters.

Winter milk also contains more hard fats, which remain solid at temperatures up to 100 degrees F. This makes for a stiffer butter that is slower to soften. In the summer, milk usually contains more of the softer polyunsaturated fats, which makes a more malleable butter that is quicker to melt, according to Manfred Kroger, a food science professor at Pennsylvania State University who was previously a buttermaker in Germany. The proportion of hard and soft fats in butter can vary, however, among brands and even among batches. So the time it takes for a stick of butter to soften at room temperature can be unpredictable.

Because American consumers demand consistency, many butter manufacturers have developed ways to minimize the fluctuations in color and texture. Some will simply mix summer and winter butters together, said Kroger. Tempering cream can alter the structure of the cream's hard fats to create a softer winter butter, while intensive mechanical working of summer butters can create a firmer butter. Many manufacturers also use natural pigments such as annatto seed extract to create a deeper yellow hue during the butter's paler-colored winter season.

In addition to standardizing butter composition, the USDA closely and frequently inspects butter manufacturing plants for sanitation, and grades batches of retail butter to assure that they are made with high-quality sweet cream.

A spokesperson for Challenge butter said their California dairy receives inspections from USDA and state agents weekly. At Land O'Lakes, USDA graders are there daily because of its mass production. All of the butters in our tasting were Grade AA, the highest mark for butter. The USDA letter grade surrounded by a shield is readily visible on butter cartons.

If a cream is not up to the potential of grade AA butter, a dairy will typically use it in cheese, ice cream, or other products that do not demand the clean, delicate flavor of the highest quality cream. Supermarkets can also sell Grade A butter, which is downgraded for having a slightly acidic flavor.

You can be sure that a Grade AA butter originated in premium form because of tight government standards on the quality of butter. But unfortunately, by the time you go to purchase it, you have no way of knowing how long or under what conditions it was sitting in frozen storage or in a market. And you cannot estimate its age by its expiration date, because there are no industry standards for such information. Each brand differs. So even if your butter is used before its expiration date or even immediately after purchase, you cannot be guaranteed the good taste of fresh butter.

We found this out with the first package of Breakstone's unsalted butter we tested. It had begun to spoil well before its expiration date. The second package, purchased from the same store a few weeks later, carried off flavors. Dr. Clair Hicks, a food science professor at the University of Kentucky, was not surprised. "You might get a Land O'Lakes that's extremely good in one store but not in another. It's typical of butter products," he said, explaining that Grade AA butter can easily deteriorate before purchase if

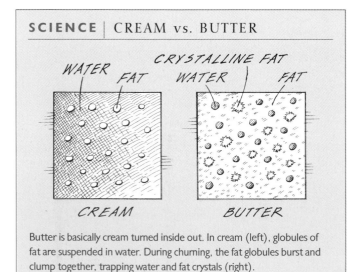

SCIENCE | CREAM vs. BUTTER

WATER FAT — CRYSTALLINE FAT WATER FAT

CREAM   BUTTER

Butter is basically cream turned inside out. In cream (left), globules of fat are suspended in water. During churning, the fat globules burst and clump together, trapping water and fat crystals (right).

TASTING UNSALTED BUTTERS

The following chart summarizes the results of our taste tests and cooking tests of butters. Members of *Cook's* editorial staff along with 15 chefs (*see* page 26) first tasted the butters plain (at room temperature and melted). They rated them for appearance, taste, and mouthfeel. *Cook's* editors then tasted each butter in a traditional pie crust, a basic yellow cake, and a plain buttercream. Other butter tests included melting in the microwave, melting two table-spoons in a saucepan at medium-low heat, clarifying, and sautéeing turkey cutlets with an oil and butter combination. Details on these last two tests and on the yellow cake test are omitted below because their results were judged insignificant. Butter prices fluctuate throughout the year and are based here on prices posted in December. Butters are listed in order of their overall performance based on combined scores from each quantified test.

Plugrá (KELLER'S CREAMERY, HARLEYSVILLE, PENNSYLVANIA)

➤ **$2.59 for one-half pound**

This butter is indulgence — but for twice the cost of regular butter. Made in America but in the European style of high-fat, cultured butters (with 82 percent milk fat), this butter placed first in the melted tasting and the buttercream tasting. It took third place in the pie crust test as well as when tasted plain, although tasters did note its rich, clean flavor in the latter. Sold in gourmet stores nationwide.

Celles Sur Belle (NORMANDY, FRANCE)

➤ **$2.49 for one-quarter pound**

From a region of France famous for its rich dairy products, this smooth butter had a "clean" flavor "reminiscent of homemade butter," according to one taster. Containing the highest milk fat content of all the brands (85 to 88 percent), it also sold for the highest price. In tests, this butter only faltered when its pie crust came out under-cooked (for further information, *see* page 26). Even then it ranked fourth because of the pastry's rich, buttery flavor. Sold in gourmet stores.

Challenge (DUBLIN, CALIFORNIA)

➤ **$2.53 for one pound**

This West Coast brand placed first in the pie crust test; tasters found its pastry the most flaky and flavorful. As a buttercream, it was in the tops for airiness. Tasted plain, it was described as "smooth" and "clean" but lacking in butter flavor.

Land O'Lakes (ARDEN HILLS, MINNESOTA)

➤ **$2.59 for one pound**

Tasters loved this national butter when tasted plain for its "clean and mild butter flavor." It also made one of the lightest buttercreams. But under the stress of heat it lost its stardom. In the pie crust test, it was the tasters' last choice, even behind its salted version. Tasters found the crust a bit "greasy."

Kellers/Hotel Bar (HARLEYSVILLE, PENNSYLVANIA)

➤ **$2.59 for one pound**

This butter's general performance was that of a "B" student. A bit on the soft side when tasted plain. One taster caught a "hint of onion," which could be because a cow happened to eat one—or because the butter, for some reason, was stored during distribution near an onion. The pie crust was one of the flakiest and had an okay flavor. The buttercream lagged because of mediocre texture and "off flavors." Sold in New England and the Philadelphia area under the label Kellers. Known as Hotel Bar in the New York City area.

Breakstone (GLENVIEW, ILLINOIS)

➤ **$2.26 for one pound**

Well, its pie crust was one of the flakiest. But in the first tasting the butter was rancid, and in a second tasting with a new butter, there was only slight improvement. Some of our editors were surprised, saying they have tasted better from this brand. Perhaps this was a case of mishandling during shipping or while in the market. Sold on the East Coast.

Crystal Farms (MINNEAPOLIS, MINNESOTA)

➤ **$2.01 for one pound**

For the first tasting we were inadvertently shipped this Midwest brand's salted version, which fooled and charmed few. As a buttercream, it was the airiest but was downgraded for mediocre flavor. In the pie crust, tasters observed it was "a bit heavy" and "a little hard."

Organic Valley (LAFARGE, WISCONSIN)

➤ **$3.79 for one pound**

This cultured butter stood out visually as a darker yellow than the other butters and took second in the pie crust tasting. Like European butters, natural cultures are added to Organic Valley's butter to enhance its flavor. This may have thrown some tasters off, however, because it was downgraded for tasting "tangy" and "weedy" when plain and "cheesy" and "oily" in the buttercream.

---

improperly shipped or stored at the market. Butter can also spoil in your refrigerator, turning rancid from the oxidation of fatty acids. Exposure to air or light are particular culprits, said Hicks, which explains why Land O'Lakes takes the precaution of wrapping its unsalted butter in foil.

The fats in butter are vulnerable not only to oxidation, but also to picking up odors. They are particularly susceptible at warmer temperatures, but can take on odors even when they are chilled or frozen. For this reason, we suggest not storing butter in a refrigerator's butter compartment, which tends to be warmer because it's inside the door. To find out how much of a difference this made, we stored one stick of butter in its original wrapper in the butter compartment and one in the center of the refrigerator. After one week, the butter in the compartment had begun to pick up off flavors, while the one stored in the center still tasted fresh.

Tasting Results

Now that we had learned a few essential things about butter, we were ready to begin testing the taste. We began by selecting five top-selling unsalted butters based on statistics provided by Information Resources, a Chicago company that tracks national sales trends. (We chose to test unsalted butters only because that is what is primarily recommended in *Cook's* recipes.) In addition to the top sellers, we included an organic butter, Organic Valley, as well as two higher-end, higher-fat butters, a French import called Celles Sur Belle, and an American-made European-style butter called Plugrá.

We served the eight butters, both at room temperature and melted, in a blind taste test. They were rated for appearance, taste, and mouthfeel by 15 chefs and pastry chefs from the Boston area, as well as by *Cook's* editors. Because butter is used for more than spreading on bread or melting to dip lobster into, we also decided to run the butters through a number of cooking tests that seemed particularly pertinent to a home cook. We used each butter to make a yellow cake, a pie pastry, a sautéed turkey cutlet, and a buttercream; we also melted each butter to observe any differences.

An ideal unsalted butter should, first and foremost, taste clean, free of any off flavors. Its flavor should be delicate and its texture waxy smooth. When our tasting panel used these criteria to rate the butters eaten plain, most of them scored reasonably high. The organic butter, Organic Valley,

was slightly downgraded for off flavors and a slow, uneven melting in the mouth, and Breakstone was disqualified because the butter had turned rancid, a problem most likely caused by poor handling during distribution or at the supermarket. Land O'Lakes was chosen as the best for its unadulterated flavor, with the two higher-fat butters following behind by only one- or two-tenths of a point.

The flavor of most of the butters was enhanced when we melted them. The two higher-fat butters solidly maintained their front standing, but we were surprised by a noticeable decline in the taste of Land O'Lakes; tasters complained of off flavors, which one described as "fishy." Kroger explained that flavor nuances in cool or room-temperature butter can sometimes be undetectable. At higher temperatures more chemicals are mobilized, which can reveal more nuances of the original cream's flavor — the good and the bad.

For the first cooking test, we made a basic yellow cake recipe with each of the eight butters. Nine of *Cook's* editorial staff tasted the cakes and rated them for texture, mouthfeel, and flavor. All the cakes received high ratings, and the scores were within close range of one another. Tasters confessed it was difficult to really taste the butter in the cakes.

We also tested the butters in a basic pie pastry recipe that used only butter for fat. While the higher-fat butters ranked among the top for flavor and flakiness, Challenge, a California butter, and Organic Valley, which had been downgraded in the first tasting, scored even better. Only Land O'Lakes was downgraded in this test, when several tasters found it "greasy." Tasters liked the rich, buttery flavor of the French-butter pastry but noted it was somewhat undercooked. That is simply because the higher the fat content, the longer the butter takes to fully melt, said one expert. So you might want to let a pie shell cook a little longer if it is made with a high-fat butter.

In another test, we tried a butter and oil sauté of turkey cutlets. (The addition of oil increases butter's tolerance of heat.) Here we were looking for the rate and uniformity of browning. All the cutlets browned evenly and at about the same speed, and all the butters burned slightly. The amount of burnt protein particles from each brand of butter was about the same.

We then melted each butter on medium-high heat in a saucepan and in the microwave to look for any noteworthy inconsistencies or difficulties. The first test proved interesting but not particularly significant (*see* "What Makes Butter Splatter?", left). For the microwave test, we melted the different brands at 50 percent power according to the instructions in "The Microwave Chronicles" (January/February 1998). Unlike melting butter at full power, which too often results in blowouts, there was no messy cleanup with any of the brands.

We conducted one last butter test, using each of the eight butters in a rich buttercream recipe. A number of pastry chefs predicted that this was the one test where the butter used would matter most. Using a standing mixer to beat slightly softened butter with confectioners' sugar and some milk, we made basic buttercreams with each butter. Most of these frostings were well liked (some more than others), but the one made with Plugrá was head and shoulders above the others for both a pleasant, delicate butter flavor and an airy texture. "Very creamy and buttery," one taster wrote with exclamations. The other high-fat butter, Celles Sur Belle, scored well but was not judged to have as light a texture.

Wrapping It Up

After all our tests were completed, not one brand stood out as a sure, consistent winner. Most of the butters eaten plain were well liked (except those that had picked up off flavors, and there are so many possible causes of this that one can't really blame the brand). The melted butters also finished close to one another, as did the butters used in the yellow cakes. The pie crust results suggested that when making a pastry, bakers should forget about the brand and find a butter that is as fresh as possible.

It was primarily with the buttercreams that we found that there was a certain luxury to the high-fat butters, with Plugrá, the more affordable of the pricey choices, clearly outperforming all others. So if you are making a recipe in which the delicate yet rich flavor of butter is particularly pronounced, then we suggest a little fatty indulgence.

Overall, however, we recommend that you pay more attention to the condition in which you buy the butter and the conditions under which you store it, than to the particular brand. Purchase your butter from a store you can depend on and that has a high turnover of products. The best way to store butter is sealed in an airtight plastic bag in your freezer, pulling out sticks as you need them. Frozen butter can easily be defrosted in a microwave (*see* "The Microwave Chronicles," January/February 1998). Butter will keep in the freezer for several months, and in the refrigerator for no more than two or three weeks.

The following pastry chefs from Boston and Cambridge, Massachusetts, participated in the tasting: David Broderick of Icarus Restaurant, Bobbi Corbin of the Four Seasons Hotel, Linda Gervich of Rosie's Bakery, Elaine Hayes and Judy Mattera of Grill 23, Evelyn Hermann of The Cake Lady, Suzi Parks of Wedding Angels, Amy Snyder of A Mano Catering, and freelance pastry chef Licia Gomes. Also attending were Boston-based food writer Sally Samson, and chefs Albert D'Addario, Scott Doughty, Albert Epstein, Helmut Kahlert, and Madonna Berry, all of Newbury College's culinary program.

What Makes Butter Splatter?

When we melted butter in a saucepan to compare their rates of melting and burning, we were most surprised at how explosively some of the butters splattered. We had expected the most volatile butters to be the ones with the highest moisture content, since splattering is common when water and fat are heated together. Yet observers had to jump back from the splatter of some, but not all, of the higher-fat butters.

Because there seemed to be no apparent trend to the splattering, we consulted Dr. Clair Hicks, a food science professor at the University of Kentucky. Hicks was not at all surprised by our results. He explained that splattering is inversely related to the phospholipid content in butter—that is, the more phospholipids, the less splatter and vice versa.

The reason for this is that phospholipids, which are structurally similar to fats, are hydrophobic, meaning they repel water. As a result, their presence in high proportion in a given butter helps prevent the formation of water pockets, which burst under high heat and result in splattering.

During the butter-making process, butter is rinsed repeatedly with cold water, a practice that washes away some of the phospholipids. Modern butter-making practices, however, do not rinse them away as thoroughly as the older churn methods. This means modern butter is less likely to splatter. The drawback is that these butters also tend to turn rancid more quickly, said Hicks. —M.D.

For Smokers, Go Electric

Electric smokers outperform charcoal models because they deliver steady, predictable heat.

⇒ BY JACK BISHOP ⇐

This magazine is dedicated to precision in the kitchen. We recognize that cooking can sometimes be an inexact science (different ranges and cookware can produce different results), but we try to provide enough detail in our stories and recipes so that different cooks working in different home kitchens can accurately reproduce our recipes.

Unfortunately, smoking does not submit to such standardization. In fact, testing smokers is a little like trying to quantify chaos. Very low cooking temperatures (often just above 200 degrees) and very long cooking times (up to 10 hours) translate into unpredictability. The cooking time for the same recipe made on the same smoker on two separate occasions can vary by an hour or two. That's because smokers are greatly affected not only by ambient conditions (wind and temperature) but also by minor variants in procedure, such as how often the smoker is opened to check on the food or to add wood.

But according to industry experts, smokers are the fastest-growing outdoor cooking tool in America, with annual sales now exceeding two million units. Given that fact, we wanted to make our best effort to determine which smoker made the most sense for the home cook. Many of the models look quite similar, but we figured there would be features that would make some units more user-friendly than others.

Since most people will use a smoker only occasionally, I set an upper price limit of $200, although it's possible to spend much more on specialized smoking equipment like that used in barbecue restaurants. I smoked briskets, ribs, and whole turkeys in each smoker, and repeated every test to make sure that my results were due to the smoker and not to ambient conditions or other factors out of my control.

It soon became evident that comparing ribs made in one smoker to ribs made in another was difficult if not impossible. One day, smoker A would produce tender, smoky ribs in four hours, while ribs cooked in smoker B were tough and not smoky enough and took five hours to cook. Based on this test, it would seem that smoker A was preferable. However, when I tried to duplicate those results, I couldn't. The next day, ribs on smoker A took five hours and did not really seem smoky enough. The ribs on smoker B were much smokier, but still a tad chewy and the cook-

ing time was now up to five and one half hours. After weeks of similar experiences, I was ready to throw in the towel.

But just as I was ready to give up, I began to observe some consistencies lurking behind the chaos. I found that I was having the same problems with some smokers each time I used them. As I continued to use the four models listed in the chart on page 28, it became clear that some smokers have features that increase the likelihood of great results, while others have design flaws that make success harder to achieve. The difference between the winner and the other models is the difference between a stripped-down car and one loaded with every feature imaginable. You can parallel park a car without power steering, but why would you want to?

In the end, then, I came to two general con-

clusions: First, since smoking itself is a very unpredictable cooking method, I would rather work with a smoker that's capable of maintaining a constant temperature, which means an electric smoker. On occasion, I had good results with the charcoal smoker I tested, but other times the fire died or was too low and the food took much longer to cook than I'd expected. (For more information, *see* "Smoking with Charcoal: Is It Worth the Bother?", page 28.)

Second, as I became more sophisticated and started experimenting with other foods in the smokers, I realized I wanted to be able not just to maintain a constant temperature, but to manipulate that temperature as well. True smoking, as practiced in barbecue pits in the South, often occurs at temperatures around 170 degrees. Given the worries about bacterial growth

EQUIPMENT | FEATURES OF ELECTRIC SMOKERS

All the electric smokers in our testing shared some common features: a coil, water pan, and lower and upper racks on which food is placed to be smoked. Additional features that we found useful include a heat regulator, temperature gauge, vents, and access doors. The manner in which the electrical plug attaches to the coil is also important.

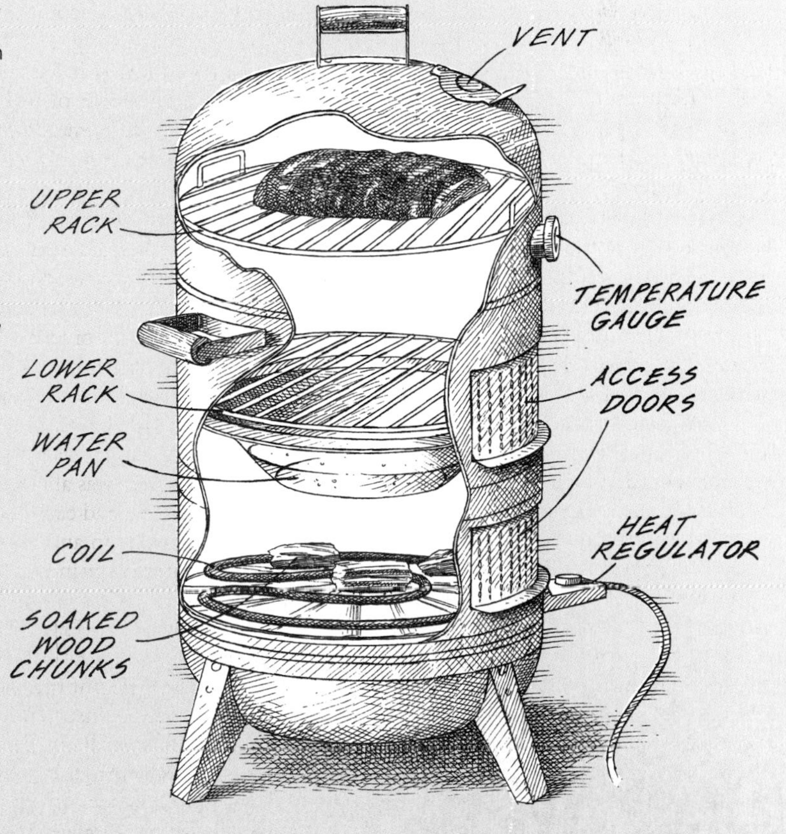

VENT

UPPER RACK

TEMPERATURE GAUGE

ACCESS DOORS

LOWER RACK

WATER PAN

HEAT REGULATOR

COIL

SOAKED WOOD CHUNKS

Meco Water Smoker
5030 XElectric Combo
Inexpensive model, has all the important features

Brinkmann Smoke 'n Grill
#810-5290-C
Nicely compact model, lacks heat regulator

Char-Broil Electric H20
Smoker #465-4512
Lacks vents and door, plug falls off easily

Weber Smokey Mountain
Cooker Smoker #2890
Requires experience to master, no temperature gauge

at such low temperatures, the manufacturers of smokers advise cooking at a higher temperature, around 225 degrees. Technically, food is being barbecued or low-roasted when cooked at 225 degrees.

Electric smokers are calibrated to run in this range when the dial is set to medium or high. But on several occasions, I played around with lower temperatures and liked the results. The food took longer to cook through but had more time to absorb smoke. Cooking a turkey at 170 degrees doesn't make much sense (because it would take

all day and part of the night and the risk of food illness is too high), but such slow cooking might not be a bad idea for a piece of cheese or a thin fish fillet.

While I recommend that you start by smoking at the suggested 225 degrees, I do think it's worthwhile getting a smoker that allows for easy manipulation of temperature. As you become more confident, these models will allow for experimentation. Just because you don't use cruise control every time you drive, doesn't mean you want to own a car without it.

Smoking with Charcoal: Is It Worth the Bother?

Without a doubt, an electric smoker is easier to use than a charcoal smoker and delivers more consistent results. After some practice, you can rest assured that a particular electric model will heat up to a certain temperature (given certain weather conditions). Charcoal, on the other hand, is fickle. I had fires die out, for example, because the charcoal did not get quite enough air through the vents.

More frustrating is the need to add charcoal every hour or so. While all you have to do is throw a dozen or so unlit briquettes onto the fire, if you forget to do this, the fire will die. (This happened to me once after waiting only an hour and a half to add charcoal.) You can light more charcoal in a chimney and then add the lit charcoal to the smoker, but at that point you've added at least an extra hour, if not two, to the cooking time.

Even when things go right, charcoal smokers do not hold onto heat as well as electric ones. If you build too big a fire, the smoker will start out too hot and food will brown prematurely and eventually burn. A decent but not roaring fire starts at 250 degrees but soon dips, and by the end of the first hour can be well below 200 degrees. This constant cycling up and down in temperature translates into an average cooking time that is 25 percent longer than in an electric smoker. That may not sound bad, but a twelve-pound turkey will take ten to 12½ hours (not the usual eight to ten hours) in a charcoal smoker. If you want to eat at six, that means starting the fire for the smoker at five in the morning.

Of course, there are people who must cook over a live fire and probably think electric smokers are for cheaters. For that reason, I included the Weber in the chart on page 29, although I left it out of the ratings. The apples-to-oranges metaphor really applies here.

One final note. I used the same amount of wood chunks in all my tests—three chunks added every three hours. I found that food cooked in the Weber was often a bit smokier than food cooked in electric models. I theorize that the longer cooking times, the use of charcoal as well as wood chunks, and the fact that a charcoal fire burns the wood chunks more thoroughly than electric coils all contribute to the stronger smoke flavor. But I found it easy enough to compensate for this in electric models by using an extra wood chunk or two, or adding wood more often.   -J.B.

Design Makes the Difference

The four water smokers in my test shared certain basic design features. All were shaped like torpedos (or giant coffee cans) and made of thin metal. An electric coil (or area for charcoal) rested on the bottom, and several inches above this was a water pan. Above the pan were two cooking racks—one on or just above the pan, the other close to the top of the smoker, which was covered with a domed lid.

Within this basic design, I found a few special features that I would highly recommend. First, an external temperature gauge was very helpful. While I often wished that the gauges were registering actual temperatures—instead of "warm," "ideal," and "hot"—I always found them helpful, especially as I got to know each smoker. By placing a separate grill thermometer (*see* Resources, page 32) on the cooking rack, I eventually learned that if the external temperature gauge read "ideal," the temperature inside the smoker was in a certain range. This became important because it allowed me to control the temperature without taking the lid off and letting the heat escape. The Meco and Char-Broil have temperature gauges.

Another special feature I found very useful was a heat regulator dial which, on both the Meco and the Char-Broil, plugged into the electric coil. Once I became accustomed to these models, I could lower or raise the heat level in the smoker by manipulating the dial and then watching the thermometer change. While I produced some good food without a regulator dial or thermometer in the small Brinkmann, the Meco has these features and costs less. Why buy a stripped-down model when the loaded car is cheaper?

Two other special features I found helpful were vents and doors. While I could always lift off the dome to let some heat escape, vents allowed me

TESTING WATER SMOKERS

I tested electric smokers from three leading manufacturers as well as a charcoal smoker from Weber. Electric models are listed in order of preference. The charcoal smoker is listed for comparison's sake at the end of the chart and has not been rated. For more information on the Weber smoker, *see* "Smoking with Charcoal: Is It Worth the Bother?", on page 28.

PRICE: Cost when ordering directly from manufacturer (*see* Resources, page 32). Smokers are often discounted, especially at large hardware or discount stores.

THERMOMETER: Some models come with a built-in thermometer that lets the cook know what the temperature is inside the cooking chamber without removing the lid.

Instead of numerical readings, dials register "warm," "ideal," or "hot." I have listed the dial-reading when the internal temperature measured 225 degrees on a separate thermometer on the cooking rack.

VENT/DOOR: Some models come with adjustable vents to regulate heat. Others have a door in the side for adding wood chunks.

TEMPERATURE RANGE: Some models have an adjustable dial that regulates heat. Range of possible temperatures (taken with dial set as low and as high it goes) is noted. Temperature was measured with thermometer placed on top cooking rack. In models with vents, they were completely closed.

Brand	Price	Temperature Gauge	Vent/Door	Temperature Range	Testers' Comments
BEST WATER SMOKER **Meco** Water Smoker 5030 XElectric Combo	$80	Dial runs cool, never getting out of warm range. At 225°, gauge is still in middle of warm range.	2 vents on dome; door on side for adding wood.	Adjustable. Registers 130° to 260°.	This inexpensive model has all the features I like—vents, a door for adding wood, a heat regulator dial, and an external temperature gauge.
Brinkmann Smoke 'n Grill #810-5290-C	$130	None	None	Not adjustable. Registers 250° to 270° all the time.	Compact and easy to work with, this smoker does not have a heat regulator and runs quite hot.
Char-Broil Electric H20 Smoker #465-4512	$80	Dial has separate scales for when ambient temperature is above or below 60°. At 225°, gauge is in middle of ideal range.	None	Adjustable. Registers 125° to 270°.	Similar to the Meco, with an external temperature gauge and heat regulator dial, but does not have vents or door. A serious design flaw causes the regulator dial and plug to detach easily from the electric coil.
Weber Smokey Mountain Cooker Smoker #2890	$180	None	3 vents on charcoal pan and 1 on dome; door on side for adding charcoal and wood.	Depending on intensity of fire, registers from 80° to 250°.	This charcoal smoker can be mastered, but is subject to the vagaries of cooking over a live fire. For the money, there should be an external temperature gauge to judge the fire intensity so cooks don't have to open the side door and let precious heat escape

to regulate the heat more precisely. Doors were another real convenience. On the Meco and Weber smokers, doors made it possible for me to add more soaked wood chunks or unlit charcoal simply and easily. Without doors, the Brinkmann and Char-Broil force the cook to lift off the body of the smoker that contains both the water pan and the food. Besides being a bother, this method allows much more heat to escape.

A final, very important design feature is the way the electric element is secured to the smoker. Most inconvenient was the plug on the Char-Broil smoker. It must be inserted into the electric element, but because it slides rather than snaps into place, it can easily fall out when you lift off the body to add more wood and jiggle the base. Twice I accidentally jarred loose the plug in this smoker and ended up cutting off the power supply for several hours. The first time it happened I was annoyed with my carelessness; the second time I realized that this smoker invites disaster, since even the gentlest bump can dislodge the plug and even the most careful cook might forget to check the connection each time the smoker is touched. The Meco plug must be inserted into the electric coil but stays firmly in place. The plug on the Brinkmann unit is fused into the coil so it can't come loose.

7 Tips for Better Smoking

In the course of testing for this article, I developed this list of simple tips that can make the difference between success and failure when smoking.

1. Line the water pan with heavy-duty aluminum foil. It will make cleanup much easier.

2. Fill the lined water pan with hot tap water. Cold water will increase the cooking time significantly. The only time I found it necessary to add water during the cooking process was when smoking a turkey. Otherwise, four quarts of water should last five or six hours, long enough to smoke most cuts of beef or pork.

3. Don't bother with flavorings in the water pan. I tried using beer instead of water or adding herbs and spices to the water and couldn't taste the difference. Apply a spice rub directly to the meat surface for maximum impact.

4. For a medium smoke flavor, add 3 tennis ball-sized wood chunks every 3 hours. To slow down the rate at which they burn, soak all chunks in cold water for at least 30 minutes, and preferably longer. For a smokier flavor or for foods that will smoke 3 hours or less, add 4 or 5 chunks every 2 hours.

5. Place a thermometer on the cooking rack so that you can see what the temperature is inside the smoker when you check on the meat. I found that a temperature of 200 to 250 degrees worked best. On electric smokers, the vents can be used to lower the temperature if it gets too hot. On charcoal smokers, opening the vents boosts the temperature at first because the fire is fed by more air, but over the long haul the temperature is lowered because the fire burns out faster.

6. On windy or cool days, plan on longer cooking times. The metal on most smokers is fairly thin and radiates heat. If the day is cool or there is a lot of wind to carry that heat away, expect the smoker to have trouble maintaining a particular heat level. Compensate by raising the temperature—set the dial as high as it will go or add more charcoal.

7. When smoking, it is necessary to cook all foods by internal temperature, not time. When you think something is done, insert an instant-read thermometer in the thickest part of the meat, away from the bone (or into the thigh in poultry). I cooked ribs to 160 degrees, brisket to 150 degrees, and turkey to 180 degrees.

Tasting Gewürztraminer

This distinctive white wine has always been difficult for West Coast winemakers—but our tasting shows that mastery may be imminent. BY MARK BITTMAN

Gewürztraminer is an unusual grape in many ways. It is probably indigenous to Alto Adige, the region of northeast Italy once called the Tyrol, yet the best wines made from this grape come from Alsace, in northeast France. It can be spicy and complex (the name means 'spicy' traminer, a reference to another grape), but is too often quite dull. And although ideally it is the deepest colored, most complex white wine of all, it is among the least well known. When fermented dry, Gewürztraminer can complement a variety of foods, but it can also be made sweet and used as a high-quality dessert wine. Either way, it is important that the spicy, flowery characteristics of the wine be subtle rather than overpowering. Unfortunately, because we don't often see Gewürztraminer at its best, many of us expect that this wine will be overly flowery, low in acid, and too sweet.

Given this, perhaps it makes sense that an assemblage of 16 bottles made for an unusual tasting. And although part of the results ran true to predictions, there were some very real surprises. Those of us with experience expected that in a tasting of theoretically dry, well-made Gewürztraminers, the top several finishers would be from Alsace and the wines that followed would be from the West Coast and would all be dreadful. But although the wines from Alsace were disproportionately represented in the top finishers, our first-ranked entry, a common-denominator wine that no tasters loved but all liked, was from the unlikely region of Columbia Valley (Washington), and had the added bonus of being an under-$10, widely available offering. Equally surprising, and delightful, was a third-place Californian (southern California, no less), priced at $10.

Perhaps even more of a shock was this: Although the wines from Alsace were characteristically bone-dry (tasters used adjectives like "hard" and "young" to describe them), the West Coast wines were not flowery and sweet, as the majority had been for many years.

We thus found a good, if not excellent, group of wines. While no entry made the kind of showing that would qualify it for a "Highly Recommended" rating, neither were any so dreadful that they fell into the "Not Recommended" category. In general, the wines ranged from quite dry to just slightly sweet, and almost all kept the grape's spicy,

flowery character in check, which made them delightful. Clearly, the West Coast winemakers represented here are now making Gewürztraminers that are not only tolerable with food but complement it well. In fact, most of the wines here complement the kind of food that can be difficult to pair with wine, most notably Asian food.

We included two ringers in this tasting, both of which led to interesting observations. The first was the 1995 Zind Humbrecht, an Alsatian wine that not only costs close to $40 but can be difficult to find. It really was in a class by itself—a class otherwise not represented here— and is worth looking for should you be so inclined. The other was a local wine from Sakonnet Vineyards in southern Rhode Island; in both price (about $14) and ranking, it would have fallen in the middle of the pack, and many readers who live on the East Coast should be able to find a bottle without much trouble.

THE JUDGES' RESULTS | GEWÜRZTRAMINER

The wines in our tasting—held at Mt. Carmel Wine and Spirits in Hamden, Connecticut—were judged by a panel made up of both wine professionals and amateur wine lovers. The wines were all purchased in the Northeast; prices will vary considerably throughout the country.

Within each category, wines are listed based on the number of points scored. In this tasting, the "Recommended" wines had a majority of positive comments. Those labeled "Recommended with Reservations" had mixed comments—some positive, some negative, with no clear majority.

RECOMMENDED

1996 Chateau Ste. Michelle, COLUMBIA VALLEY, WASHINGTON, **$9**
Strong finisher, largely on the strength of its "understated sweetness" and "knockout nose." Too sweet for some, but definitely worth a try, especially given its favorable price and ready availability.

1993 Trimbach, ALSACE, FRANCE, **$17**
"Real good nose" and "nice spice" in this "young" wine that will improve further despite its relative age. Dry as a bone, and representative of its region.

1996 Firestone, SANTA YNEZ VALLEY, CALIFORNIA, **$10**
Distinct "odors of coconut and chocolate" give this "elegant," "dry," and "crisp" wine an "interesting character." Like the Chateau Ste. Michelle, worth checking out.

1995 Leon Beyer, ALSACE, FRANCE, **$15**
"More earthy than others," the "strong flavor" of this wine makes it a "good food wine."

RECOMMENDED WITH RESERVATIONS

1993 Hugel, ALSACE, FRANCE, **$18**
An "anise-like," "young-tasting" wine.

1995 Becker Rimelsberg, ALSACE, FRANCE, **$13**
"Good nose" and "distinctive character" were offset, for some at least, by "barnyard" flavor.

1995 Bouchaine, RUSSIAN RIVER VALLEY, CALIFORNIA, **$14**
"Big nose unlike the others," but "too sweet to drink with most food."

1995 Joseph Phelps, CALIFORNIA, **$15**
"Subtle coconut flavor" of this wine might make it "great with Asian food." One taster found it "turned," another "too metallic."

1996 Beringer, CALIFORNIA, **$9**
"Good balance of fruit and acid," but some detected a "syrupy odor" or "bubble gum" flavor.

1996 Geyser Peak, CALIFORNIA, **$9**
"Big, flowery nose," "might make a nice aperitif but definitely not for dinner."

1996 Chateau St. Jean, SONOMA, CALIFORNIA, **$11**
"Nice wine," that was "kind of medicinal."

1997 Columbia Crest, COLUMBIA VALLEY, WASHINGTON, **$8**
Most found this "decent enough stuff."

1996 Napa Ridge, CENTRAL COAST, CALIFORNIA, **$8**
Too "sweet and insipid" for some, but many found it "fruity but well-balanced."

The New Making of a Cook

A useful tome by an accomplished culinary master falls short when it abandons rigor for idiosyncracy. BY CHRISTOPHER KIMBALL

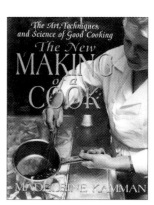

When the original *The Making of A Cook* appeared in 1971, there were few other serious, in-depth tomes on the subject of cooking. A seminal work, Madeline Kamman's first book became a mainstay reference, a kind of kitchen bible, for many of the staff of *Cook's Illustrated*, myself included.

The New Making of A Cook, however, comes at a different stage in our nation's culinary life cycle. There is an abundance of serious epicurean literature and French cooking is simply one choice among a vast world of cuisines; on the other hand, low-fat cooking has perverted good taste in the name of longevity, and the skill levels of home cooks have deteriorated. Faced with this changed landscape, Kamman had to make some hard choices about how to organize her new volume.

First, let it be said that this is an impressive work, if only for the sheer volume of material it contains and the well-researched and often useful commentary. The cheese, wine, egg, and sauce chapters are particularly lucid, and the book contains some real culinary gems, such as the illustration that details the conical interior section of a soufflé which should still be soft and loose when cooked. Simply put, there is an abundance of useful material here, enough to satisfy even the most avid cook.

But after even a cursory flip through the pages, the reader must begin to question how the author defined the parameters of this work. In fairness to Kamman, she did not set out to write a definitive cookbook of world cuisine—an impossible task even for someone as dedicated and determined an author as she—but even so, the curiously eclectic choice of recipes makes it difficult to find any unifying force at all. She casts her net far beyond French cuisine, gathering recipes from her extensive travels, from friends—even from her great-grandmother—but leaving out much that would be helpful to her readers. The section on roasting poultry, for example, begins with a discussion of roasting, including a useful list of baking times for different size birds. What follows, however, are four curiously limited recipes. There is no clearly presented master recipe for roasting poul-

try that takes into account attendant issues such as the use of a roasting rack, turning the bird in the oven, or basting. Instead we find Neil's Thanksgiving Turkey, The Treat of Capon, Tante Else's Gans, and Citrus Duck, a complex and exacting recipe which takes two days to make and 21 ingredients, including veal stock. If the book included more straightforward master recipes, the more personal, somewhat offbeat dishes such as these might be viewed as charming variations on a theme instead of offerings that pull the core of the book off center, where its message becomes diluted.

Delving further into the book also made it clear to me that, I suspect against her nature, Kamman is selectively waving the flag of low-fat cooking. In the salad dressing section, for instance, the basic recipe is low-fat, with classic dressings left to the introductory text. Yet the outstanding egg chapter offers five recipes for mayonnaise, four for flavored butters, and a lengthy discussion (space well-used in terms of her considerable expertise) of soufflés and omelets. How she reconciles her enthusiasm for both mayonnaise and low-fat dressings is problematic. A more consistent approach to low-fat cookery—raising the battle flag only when it really counts or as a variation on a standard high-fat recipe—might have been more helpful to her readers than her occasional and unpredictable willingness to do battle.

The basic structure of the book is also confusing. Many topics with nothing in common except a chapter heading are paired together: legumes and pasta, yeast breads and pie dough, mayonnaise and soufflés. I also wonder why 110 pages are devoted to sauces when only 150 pages are spent on baking, a vast, complex culinary topic that lends itself nicely to Kamman's experience and intelligence. She also organizes recipes within chapters by cooking technique, which makes some sense although it would have been nice to find all the carrot recipes in the vegetable chapter in one place. In addition, she frequently refers readers to other sections of the book which makes it hard to follow. The last of my gripes is that the author seems oddly out-of-date when it comes to

using modern appliances. The food processor is a wonderful machine for making pasta and pie dough in just seconds, yet these shortcuts are never offered.

The recipes themselves were generally of high quality. A high percentage passed our acid test—we liked them so well we would make them again. The ingredient lists are often quirky, though. One recipe calls for both medium and large eggs, while others require eggs from a vegetarian hen, quince, rose petals, or self-rising flour. Kamman cautions the reader that wild fennel seeds are to be gathered near river edges, not highways, "to prevent its contamination by the hydrocarbons of car exhaust." Probably true, but nonetheless an admonition that may be a bit rarified for home cooks. Some of the recipes are quick and easy, such as Ma and Pa Grilled Perch Fillets, but others start with the ominous instruction, "Day One." You never quite know what to expect. We also found a curiously low percentage of recipes we wanted to make based upon the ingredient lists and instructions.

For a book that is scientific in approach—and there is a lot of very worthwhile information here—it seems odd that some of the cooking techniques lack explanation. She suggests using three to four tablespoons of flour, for example, to thicken four cups of berries for a pie, yet recommends cornstarch or instant tapioca for other fruits. To understand her choices, it would help the reader to know what the differences are between thickeners in terms of texture and flavor.

In spite of its erratic organization and occasional inconsistencies, *The New Making of A Cook* is a serious book by a first-class cook and culinary mentor. There is a wealth of information in this hefty tome, and serious cooks will want to have it on their shelves as a reference despite its idiosyncrasies. Its fundamental flaw is one of organization and consistency. In many places it is thorough, the work of a master cook, but the choice of recipes is disappointingly whimsical and eclectic. It is ostensibly low-fat in approach, yet Kamman most warms to her subject when she cooks with butter, cream, and eggs. Many of the cooking techniques are tried and true, yet others seem to be matters of personal taste. When she is good, she is very, very good, but when she abandons rigor for idiosyncrasy, the book falls short of its considerable potential.

Most of the ingredients and materials necessary for the recipes in this issue are available at your local supermarket, gourmet store, or kitchen supply shop. The following are mail-order sources for particular items. Prices listed below were current at press time and do not include shipping or handling unless otherwise indicated. We suggest that you contact companies directly to confirm up-to-date prices and availability.

Smokers

Of the four electric smokers we tested for this issue, we liked the Meco Water Smoker 5030 Electric Combo for having all the right features to regulate heat so that food can be slowly infused with a smoky flavor without overcooking. It is also affordable, selling by mail for $90.43 (including shipping and handling) through its manufacturer, **Meco Corporation (1500 Industrial Road, Greenville, TN 37745; 800-346-3256)**. All the other smokers were obtained through the following mail-order sources: the Brinkmann Smoke 'n Grill for $130 from the **Brinkmann Corporation (4215 McEwen Road, Dallas, TX 75244; 800-468-5252)**; the Char-Broil Electric H2O Smoker for $80 through **Grill Lovers catalog (7100 Jamesson Road, Midland, GA 31820; 800-241-8981)**; and the Weber Smokey Mountain Cooker for $179.99 from **Armitage Hardware (925 West Armitage, Chicago, IL 60614; 888-469-3237; www.webergrills.com)**.

Grill Thermometer

Among our tips for better smoking (*see* page 27), we recommend placing a thermometer on the top cooking rack so that you can track the internal temperature of your smoker. Just stick the stem through the grate and the face will rest facing up. For our tests we used a replacement thermometer designed for Weber grills. The Weber thermometer measures a temperature range of 140 degrees to 550 degrees and can be bought by mail for $9.99 from **Armitage Hardware (925 West Armitage, Chicago, IL 60614; 888-469-3237; www.webergrills.com)**.

Instant Clearjel Powder

For our strawberry pie recipe on page 23 we were determined to find a thickening agent for the glaze that could be found at most any supermarket. During that search, however, we came across Instant Clearjel, a modified food starch primarily available to the food service industry. We could not resist how quick and simple it was to make the ideal strawberry pie glaze we were seeking with this product (*see* recipe for Diner-Style Fresh Strawberry Pie, page 23). An 8-ounce package of Instant Clearjel powder can be purchased for $2.95 by mail from **King Arthur Flour's The Baker's Catalogue (P.O. Box 876, Norwich, VT 05055-0876; 800-827-6836)**. This item is not listed in their current catalog but its order identification number is 1034.

Kitchen Shears

In many of our chicken recipes, such as Grilled Lemon Chicken on page 7 and our recent Master Recipe for Chicken and Rice (*see* March/April 1998), we recommend cutting up a whole chicken because often parts sold separately are from different sized chickens. That means one leg might be larger than the other and will not cook at the same rate. Though much of a chicken can be cut up with a chef's knife, a few bones need sharp, hefty shears, and poultry shears can be expensive. We found that a pair of sturdy kitchen shears work just fine. We tested a few makes and liked the Kitchen Partner shears. Their three-and-one-half-inch blades are longer than the others and allowed for better leverage. You could also comfortably wrap your fingers around them for a good grip. A serrated gap in the scissors' neck is designed to crack nuts. Sold by mail for $20 by **The Gooseberry (Route 7A, Manchester Center, VT 05255; 802-362-3263)**.

Grilling Basket

Manuevering 20 asparagus spears on the grill can be tedious. While developing the asparagus recipes on page 12, author Eva Katz discovered a solution—the Charcoal Companion grilling basket. With two or three shakes of the basket, the asparagus spears are easily turned all at once without any slipping into the fire. It has an open top, which makes it easy to get into with tongs to test for doneness. The Charcoal Companion basket measures nine-by-ten inches and three-and-one-half-inches deep. It is made of nonstick heavy steel wire grating that will not let small items, such as mushrooms and shrimp, slip through. There are handles on each side as well as a removable handle that hooks on the side. The grilling basket can be purchased for $18.95 from the **Sur La Table catalog (1765 6th Avenue South, Seattle, WA 98134-1608; 800-243-0852)**.

Corn Stick Pans

A trademark of Southern cornbread batter is the thin crisp crust that results from pouring the batter into a hot, greased cast-iron skillet (*see* page 19). You can get the same crisp crust for individual servings with a cast-iron corn stick pan that is shaped to give you seven five-inch-long ears of corn, including the details of the kernels. This pan sells for $7.95 through the **Sur La Table cata-** log **(1765 6th Avenue South, Seattle, WA 98134-1608; 800-243-0852)**. See page 9 of *Cook's* May/June 1997 issue for instructions on how to season cast iron.

Chipotle Peppers

If you cannot find chipotle peppers in your local markets or simply are a big fan of their smoky flavor, we recommend chipotles from **Tierra Vegetables (13684 Chalk Hill Road, Healdsburg, CA; 707-837-8366; www.tierravegetables.com)**. This family farm grows ten different varieties of chile peppers and then smokes them on site for five days at 140 degrees over prune, apple, and grapevine cuttings and, occasionally, fresh-cut basil. Each chile is hand-inspected for doneness. A 22-gram bag of chipotles sells for $4.95 (and a little goes a long way). While chipotles are most often made from jalapeños, Tierra Vegetables also makes them from scotch bonnet, serrano, fresno, Santa Fe, TAM jalapeño, New Mexico, Anaheim, and Hungarian Wax chiles. Habanero chipotles are sold in 16-gram packages.

EcoPump

We were recently introduced to the EcoPump, an environmentally safe alternative to the aerosol vegetable oil cans typically sold in supermarkets. The EcoPump has a specially designed cap that you simply pump up and down a few times before spraying to build pressure inside the clear plastic canister. The canister can be filled and refilled with your oil of choice or even water. **The Culinary Institute of America's** campus store and marketplace at Greystone sells the EcoPump for $5.95 by mail order **(2555 Main Street, St. Helena, CA 94574; 888-424-2433; www.digitalchef.com)**. The EcoPump holds up to three-quarters of a cup of oil.

Pastry Cutters

When testing steps for our puff pastry story on page 16, we found that the cookie cutters in our test kitchen were too flimsy for the quick, clean cut that this delicate pastry dough demands. So we tracked down replacements that were sturdy, easy to handle, but also affordable. Ateco pastry/biscuit cutters, carried by **A Cook's Wares (211 37th Street, Beaver Falls, PA 15010-2103; 800-915-9788)**, come as a set of nine tin steel circles neatly stacked inside one another in a storage can. The largest straight-edge circle cutter in the set measures about three inches in diameter; the innermost is just one inch. The set sells for $14. The scalloped-edge set sells for $15 with the cutters ranging in diameter from three-quarters of an inch to two-and-three-quarters inches.

RECIPE INDEX

Roast Potatoes with Garlic and Rosemary **PAGE 11**

Grilled Lemon Chicken, Asparagus with Anchovy Dressing and Country Bread **PAGES 7 AND 12**

Southern-Style Cornbread **PAGE 19**

Grilled Tuna with Watercress-Parsley Salad and Charmoula Vinaigrette **PAGE 9**

Perfect Lemon Bars **PAGE 21**

Fresh Strawberry Pie **PAGE 23**

PHOTOGRAPHY: CARL TREMBLAY   STYLING : RITCH HOLBEN

Green
oak leaf
lettuce

Green
romaine

Red Asian
mustard

Radicchio

Escarole

Arugula

Belgian
endive

Mâche

Beet leaf

Tatsoi

Mizuna

Frisée

SALAD GREENS

NUMBER THIRTY-THREE

JULY & AUGUST 1998

COOK'S
ILLUSTRATED

Fruit Crisps
We Put the Crunch Back

Juicy Grilled Chicken Kebabs
Acid-Free Marinades Preserve Flavor

First-Rate Lemonade
Mashing Lemons is the Key

Fork-Tender Barbecued Brisket
Use Heavy Foil and a Slow Oven

Testing Pie Plates
Light, Dark, or Pyrex?

Perfect Peach Ice Cream
Smooth, Not Icy

Tasting Canned Tuna

Great Pasta Salads

Best Turkey Burgers

How To Prep Vegetables

$4.00 U.S./$4.95 CANADA

CONTENTS

July & August 1998

COOK'S ILLUSTRATED

PUBLISHER AND EDITOR
Christopher Kimball

EXECUTIVE EDITOR
Pam Anderson

SENIOR EDITOR
John Willoughby

SENIOR WRITER
Jack Bishop

ASSOCIATE EDITORS
Adam Ried
Maryellen Driscoll

TEST KITCHEN DIRECTOR
Susan Logozzo

TEST COOKS
Anne Yamanaka
Dawn Yanagihara

CONTRIBUTING EDITORS
Mark Bittman
Stephanie Lyness

EDITORIAL INTERN
Garrett Peters

ART DIRECTOR
Amy Klee

CORPORATE MANAGING EDITOR
Barbara Bourassa

EDITORIAL PRODUCTION MANAGER
Sheila Datz

COPY EDITOR
Carol Parikh

MARKETING DIRECTOR
Adrienne Kimball

CIRCULATION DIRECTOR
David Mack

FULFILLMENT MANAGER
Larisa Greiner

CIRCULATION MANAGER
Darcy Beach

MARKETING ASSISTANT
Connie Forbes

PRODUCTS MANAGER
Steven Browall

VICE PRESIDENT PRODUCTION AND TECHNOLOGY
James McCormack

SYSTEMS ADMINISTRATOR
James Burke

DESKTOP PUBLISHING MANAGER
Kevin Moeller

PRODUCTION ARTIST
Robert Parsons

PRODUCTION ASSISTANT
Daniel Frey

CONTROLLER
Lisa A. Carullo

SENIOR ACCOUNTANT
Mandy Shito

OFFICE MANAGER
Bess Teuteberg

SPECIAL PROJECTS
Fern Berman

MELONS

MELONS, a fruit of the gourd family believed to have originated in Africa or India, come in an almost bewildering number of varieties. In the United States, the most familiar is the watermelon, available in standard or seedless varieties. Next in familiarity comes the muskmelon, which many Americans call cantaloupe, distinguished by its netted skin, and the smooth-skinned honeydew, which may have either green or yellow flesh. Sweet crenshaw, wrinkly-skinned casaba, and the aromatic Israeli hybrid called Galia are also becoming quite common. More unusual melons you might see in your supermarket include the bright yellow canary, the oval sharlyne, and the striped yellow Santa Claus with its pale green flesh.

COVER PAINTING: BRENT WATKINSON,   BACK COVER ILLUSTRATION: JOHN BURGOYNE

WORTH PRESERVING

Few of us are lucky enough to have a sense of history. I'm not talking about our country's heritage, but about something more personal—a finger pointed out the window to signal where old Crofut's car ran off the road, or the overgrown path up the mountain, the one we would take as kids to explore the lake by the monastery. And there are still a few of us who remember when dandelion, milkweed, and mustard greens were all picked on the farm, a familiar place where vegetables were also grown, where milk was churned into butter and converted into cheese. In those days meat came from wild game and domesticated hogs, and fresh berries never appeared in the winter. Beef tongue was pickled, fruits made into jam and fruit butters, corn turned into succotash, and root vegetables kept down in the cellar.

If you ask an old-timer about the past he is likely to shrug it off at first, saying something about hard work and long winters. But if you are patient and stay awhile, he'll remember sitting in a wagon with his girlfriend, bundled up against the cold, taking the team over to a square dance, or the time that he walked into the yellow farmhouse and Marie Briggs sat him down to tea, offering a big slab of warm country white spread with a thick yellow frosting of homemade butter. He may not admit it, but he knows the past is often replaced with something of lesser stature, men whose bones have no memory of the rhythm of a horse-drawn mower or the feel of a wet cornfield in April, the ground spongy and stubbled. He has but to close his eyes to see the warm froth floating in a pail of milk or sit quietly to hear a horse chomping on a bit, or take a deep breath to inhale the moist, sweet steam that rises from the evaporator during sugaring season. These memories are hard won and better for their poor beginnings.

For most of us, it is the small details of daily life that make the sweetest memories. Long after the wedding pictures are filed away forever, a glance, a taste, or a subtle fragrance are unexpectedly intimate, their essence recalled and savored forever. On a farm, the senses were offered a groaning board of such moments from the daily menu of milking, plowing, mowing, and baking. Even the cities, with their rowdy mix of ethnic neighborhoods offered a full menu of sensory experiences to the venturesome pedestrian who wandered by the bakeries, the food stalls, and the varied storefronts.

But these are not intimate times; personal experiences become more interchangeable each day. Eating out, shopping at malls, driving to work, and watching television are impersonal diversions, one experience and one day blending seamlessly into another. As my father, an experienced traveller, once put it, "After a while, all cities look like Cleveland." Although I disagreed with him at the time (Cleveland does have the best diner in America), his statement is increasingly apt. How often have we visited a new town only to find the same 30 stores that we have back home? Where are the neighborhoods, the dialects, and the ethnic foods?

We now find ourselves, in our lifelong race to have everything, in the pitiable state of experiencing almost nothing. I often wonder if it takes a hard life to build character and intimacy, as if modern times are simply too soft for such heavy lifting. I remember Fraiser Mears, the town dowser, who would cut a forked branch from an apple tree and hold it in front of him with his arms crossed. The

Christopher Kimball

branch would pull downwards when water was near. He spoke to his rod as if it were alive, saying, "Tell me, Mr. Stick, how far is it?" or "Tell me, Mr. Stick, is it deep?" Fraiser is long gone, his peculiar ways a reminder of days when towns had "characters," immune to the lure of convenience and efficiency.

As we have replaced letters with e-mails, visiting neighbors with television, and home-cooked dinners with takeout, I suspect that we are growing hungry for lives that are a bit more personal, more worthy of thought and reflection as we age. The great gift of the kitchen is to provide a full measure of taste memories; the full, ripe flavor of peach preserves in January recalls the March pruning, the spray of red buds on the trees in April, the long, slow maturing of the fruit, the still, hot days of July, the cooler nights in August, and then the final act of canning, wooden spoons streaked with sweet jam and children spreading hot spoonfuls on homemade bread.

Cooks are architects, building a present that is worth remembering, investing time and energy in simple tasks that grow in importance as time passes. For most of us, our crop of memories is hardly worth preserving—a small, scarred fruit without a gardener and a cook to see it through its simple beginnings to its ripe fruition. The wooded acres are cleared, the sod long ago broken into loose topsoil, abundance strewn carelessly about like weeds, stealing moisture from the young trees. I often think that in cooking one can find all things: experience, hope, nourishment, and a simple faith in providence. But most of all, cooking serves up home-grown fruit alive with the scent and taste of life's possibilities.

ABOUT COOK'S ILLUSTRATED

The Magazine Cook's Illustrated is published every other month (6 issues per year) and accepts no advertising. A one-year subscription is $24.95, two years is $45, and three years is $65. Add $6 postage per year for Canadian subscriptions and $12 per year for all other foreign countries. To order subscriptions, call 800-526-8442. Gift subscriptions are available for $24.95 each.

Magazine-Related Items Cook's Illustrated is available in an annual hardbound edition, which includes an index, for $24.95 plus shipping and handling. Discounts are available if more than one year is ordered at a time. Back issues are available for $5 each. The Cook's Illustrated 1998 calendar, featuring 12 of the magazine's covers reproduced in full color, is available for $12.95. Cook's also offers a 5-year index (1993-1997) of the magazine for $12.95. To order any of these products, call 800-611-0759.

Books Cook's Illustrated publishes a series of single-topic books, available for $14.95 each. Titles include: How To Make A Pie, How To Make An American Layer Cake, How To Stir Fry, How To Make Ice Cream, How To Make Pizza, How To Make Holiday Desserts, How To Make

Pasta Sauces, How To Grill, and How To Make Salad. The Cook's Bible, written by Christopher Kimball and published by Little, Brown, is available for $24.95. To order any of these books, call 800-611-0759.

Reader Submissions Cook's accepts reader submissions for both Quick Tips and Notes From Readers. We will provide a one-year complimentary subscription for each Quick Tip that we print. Send a description of your technique, along with your name, address, and daytime telephone number, to Quick Tips, Cook's Illustrated, P.O. Box 569, Brookline, MA 02147. Questions and suggestions should be sent to the same address.

Subscription Inquiries All queries about subscriptions or change of address notices should be addressed to Cook's Illustrated, P.O. Box 7446, Red Oak, IA 51591-0446.

Website Address Selected articles and recipes from Cook's Illustrated and subscription information are available on-line. You can access Cook's website at: www.cooksillustrated.com.

Testing Ice Cream Makers

Since *Cook's* evaluated ice cream makers in 1993, several new models, less fancy and expensive than your favorite $500 Simac, have come onto the market. I'd like to buy one, and I wonder if you have ever compared them or could make any recommendations?

DIONE SOBIN
SAN FRANCISCO, CA

➤ You could not have timed your inquiry better. While testing the peach ice cream recipe on page 23 in this issue, we experimented with two popular, inexpensive electric models, the Krups La Glaciere (model 358, $59.99) and the Cuisinart Automatic Frozen Yogurt–Ice Cream & Sorbet Maker (model ICE-20, $69.99).

Neither of these machines was difficult to assemble, though we preferred the layout of the Cuisinart. Both involve freezing a coolant-filled canister, preferably overnight. The primary difference is that after the ice cream mixture is placed in the canister of the Cuisinart, the paddle stays stationary and the canister revolves to churn the mixture, while the Krups has a top-mounted motor which rotates the paddle while the canister remains stationary. In addition, their capacities vary. The Cuisinart makes one quart of ice cream, whereas the Krups makes 1½ quarts.

Once assembled and going, though, the performance characteristics of these machines and the ice creams they produced were very similar. The Cuisinart took about 25 minutes to churn 3 cups of custard into 3½ cups of soft-serve-consistency ice cream. The Krups, even though it has a larger capacity, also took about 25 minutes, churning 4½ cups of custard into 5¼ cups of ice cream. (We should note, though, that to get a really firm texture, both ice creams had to be frozen after churning.)

Though several tasters thought the Krups-made ice cream was slightly lighter than the other, both were generally smooth, creamy, and dense. In operation, the Krups was a little quieter, but its canister is bulkier and more difficult to fit into a full freezer. Essentially, if larger capacity is important to you, the Krups is fine, but because the Cuisinart is easier and more intuitive to assemble, we give it the nod, if only by a hair.

Along the way, we developed a couple of hints to help ensure success with both machines. Freezing the canister thoroughly is important. We measured the temperature in several home freezers and found them to be consistently 3 to 6 degrees above the recommended 0 degrees. To counteract this drawback, allow plenty of time for the canister to freeze (overnight is best), place it at the back of the freezer, which is colder than the front, and do not overpack the freezer because that will limit air circulation. Second, chill the custard to 40 degrees before churning it. This is best accomplished at the back of an uncrowded refrigerator shelf. Third, to help limit the iciness that occurs when the custard comes into contact with the frozen canister wall, set up the machine and switch it on before adding the custard mixture through the hole in the cover. And finally, do not fill the canister to the very rim. Allow plenty of space for the ice cream to increase in volume as it churns by leaving about half an inch of headroom at the top.

See Resources, page 32, for availability of both the Krups and the Cuisinart.

Tube Pan Quick Breads

I was pleased with your recipe for banana bread in the March/April 1998 issue of *Cook's*, except for one thing. I found that by the time the center of this loaf was cooked properly, the exterior was approaching overcooked. I have had similar problems with other quick breads cooked in loaf pans. My solution has been to bake quick breads in tube pans. Though the final loaves are ring-shaped, the slices are almost the same as those from traditional loaves, and I find the breads cook more evenly and quickly.

BILL DERING
ORANGE, NJ

➤ We baked side-by-side banana breads, one in a regular loaf pan and the other in a tube pan, and found what you say to be true. Because the open center of the tube pan allows exposure to heat at the center as well as the outside of the pan, the bread cooked in 43 minutes versus 60 minutes for the traditional loaf. Also, the slices were almost the same shape as those from the regular loaf, though slightly smaller. But we'd like to add a counterpoint. We observed that the crust of the regular loaf, having spent a few extra minutes in the oven, browned more thoroughly and deeply than the tube pan loaf, and we enjoyed the more intensely caramelized flavor of that darker brown crust. Also, none of our tasters felt that the exterior of the loaf was appreciably overcooked. Nonetheless, if you are in a hurry and need to shave off some baking time, the tube pan is certainly worth a try.

Masa Harina

Thank you for the excellent article on chili (March/April 1998). It validated most of the things I know about making my state's signature dish. My one suggestion is to use cornmeal as the thickening agent. It works as well as masa harina and may be easier to find in some regions.

PAT GRAPPE
LEVELLAND, TX

➤ Having not tried cornmeal as a thickener while developing the chili recipe, we gave your suggestion a whirl. While the cornmeal did thicken the sauce effectively, it did not add the same flavor as masa harina—a distinctive taste element that we all unanimously associated with the Southwest and that lends the chili a note of authenticity.

Masa harina is a corn product that the Aztecs of Mexico started making many centuries ago. To begin with, they boiled dried corn kernels in an alkaloid solution of wood ash to free the hulls and germ. This also freed nutrients and converted niacin, an amino acid essential to human health that cannot be absorbed by the body from unprocessed corn. This enabled the Aztecs to have a healthy corn-based diet. The resulting product, which was similar to hominy, was then rinsed, dried, ground, and sifted to make the flour called masa harina.

A customer representative at the Quaker Oats Company, a leading producer of masa harina, explained that masa harina is still produced using essentially the same process. Corn is heated in a slaked lime solution containing calcium hydroxide, then rinsed and dried, ground, and dried again. Dr. Joseph Maga of the Department of Food Science and Human Nutrition at Colorado State University explained that the slaked lime imparts to the masa harina that distinctive flavor of the Southwest that attracted all our tasters.

Chilling Mayo Ingredients

For the most part, I found the article about mayonnaise in your July/August 1997 issue to be right on the money, offering several key tricks for your readers. I have been working in the industrial segment of this business with McCormick & Company for the past 23 years, and there are many similarities between the industrial and the household methods of manufacture. However, you left out one element that manufacturers find critical to the production of good mayonnaise—always use cold ingredients. This will significantly increase the body of the mayonnaise while decreasing its likelihood of breaking. Be sure, though, that the oil is not allowed to become cold enough to crystallize, as crystals can cause an emulsion to break.

JAMES E. SACHSE
BALTIMORE, MD

➤ Though we have made dozens of batches of

mayonnaise from room-temperature ingredients without difficulty, we tried using cold ingredients and had very good luck with them. Several food scientists with whom we checked offered theories regarding the effect of chilling on emulsions. Dr. Bruce Watkins, Associate Professor of Food Science and Nutrition at Purdue University, mentioned that chilling changes the behavior of some of the components in the egg yolk. For instance, lipoproteins gel at lower temperatures, and triglycerides, which are crystalline in structure, grow larger and more stable. Both of these factors might well contribute stability and body to the emulsion. Dr. Watkins also mentioned that these substances become less hydrophobic as temperatures decrease, which means they are less resistant to water. Their increased willingness to accept water would also add to the stability of an emulsion.

Dr. Kenneth Hall, Professor in the Department of Nutritional Sciences at the University of Connecticut, added that chilling slows down molecular activity, which, in effect, makes ingredients thicker. The thicker the ingredients are to begin with, the thicker and more stable the resulting emulsion will be. We chilled three-quarters cup of corn oil overnight in the refrigerator and poured it side by side with the same amount at room temperature. Certainly the chilled oil seemed thicker and cloudier, and it poured a tiny bit more slowly than the room-temperature sample.

Incidentally, we discovered that the amount of salt in our original July/August 1997 recipe was misprinted as 1½ teaspoons. The correct quantity of salt is ½ teaspoon. The complete recipe follows:

HOMEMADE MAYONNAISE

Each time you add oil, make sure to whisk until it's thoroughly incorporated, but it is fine to stop for a rest or to measure the next addition of oil.

1	large egg yolk
½	teaspoon salt
¼	teaspoon Dijon-style mustard
1½	teaspoons juice from 1 small lemon
1	teaspoon white wine vinegar
¾	cup corn oil

Whisk egg yolk vigorously in medium bowl for 15 seconds. Add all remaining ingredients except oil and whisk until yolk thickens and color brightens, about 30 seconds. Adding ¼ cup oil in a slow, steady stream, continue to whisk vigorously until oil is incorporated completely and mixture thickens, about 1 minute. Add another ¼ cup oil in same manner, whisking until incorporated completely, about 30 seconds more. Add last ¼ cup oil all at once and whisk until incorporated completely, about 30 seconds more. Serve.

Fumes from Overheated Nonstick Harmful to Birds

This is a belated response to your September/October 1997 "Notes From Readers" letter regarding nonstick cookware abuse. You stated that fumes from overheated nonstick cookware are: "unpleasant and have, in rare instances, caused mild and temporary flu-like symptoms, but they are not notably toxic." You should have added the words "to humans" at the end of that sentence, since the fumes are quite toxic to birds. This note of caution extends to nonstick lined bakeware, range burner drip pans, and self-cleaning ovens.

JOHANNA PETERSON
WALPOLE, MA

➤ You are among many, many bird owners who wrote to alert us to this risk. Avian veterinarian Dr. Bill Sager of the Littleton Animal Hospital in Littleton, Massachusetts, as well as Dr. Susan Brewer, University of Illinois Associate Professor of Food Chemistry and enthusiastic owner of several pet birds, both confirmed the danger to birds from nonstick coating fumes. They agreed that the two primary reasons birds are so susceptible to the fumes are their small body size and the extraordinary efficiency of their respiratory systems. "Pound for pound," said Dr. Sager, "birds extract far more oxygen...and toxins from the air than mammals do." Both doctors pointed out that it was the legendary sensitivity of birds to environmental pollutants that led to the use of canaries to check the air in coal mines. If coal gas, which is not detectable to humans, began to leak, the canary would stop singing and die, thus warning the miners before the gas reached a level that was harmful to them.

Christa Kaiser, communications manager for DuPont's Teflon finishes, acknowledged that DuPont recognizes the danger of overheated, vaporized nonstick material to birds. Kaiser added that fumes from scorched or overheated butter, cooking oil, or plastic handles on cookware can also be dangerous to birds. Annually, DuPont distributes copies of its bird-safety brochure to pet shops and veterinarians' offices. To receive a free copy of the brochure, contact DuPont by calling 800-441-7515 or check their website at www.dupont.com/teflon.

Bar Keeper's Friend

Several pieces of my stainless steel cookware have brown stains cooked onto their interiors. The pans still work just fine, but they look terrible and neither hard scrubbing nor a single one of the many cleaners I've tried has cleaned them up. Do you have any suggestions?

ANN ROSWELL
CHEYENNE, WY

➤ Some editors here have had the same problem with stainless steel cookware. We called All-Clad about it and they recommended Bar Keeper's Friend cleanser and polish, available nationwide in large grocery, hardware, or discount stores. We bought a can and will attest to its efficacy. Discolored stainless steel pans that we thought were permanently marred came clean with just light scrubbing. If Bar Keeper's Friend is difficult to find in your area, try ordering directly from the manufacturer, Servass Laboratories (1200 Waterway Boulevard, Indianapolis, IN 46202; 800-433-5818). The smallest quantity sold is four 12-ounce cans, which cost $10.00; 12 cans cost only $15.00.

WHAT IS IT?

Not long ago, we moved into an old house purchased from the estate of an elderly woman. While putting some things into the attic, we came across this small, oddly shaped vessel packed in a box. Cleaning off the tarnish revealed a beautiful copper exterior, and the interior appeared to be tin. The shape is so unusual that we figure the pot was designed for a specific use—couscous, perhaps? Can you tell us what it's really for?

MARJORIE MILNER
POUGHKEEPSIE, NY

➤ This pot was indeed designed for a specific purpose—not for cooking couscous but for steaming potatoes. In France this pot is called a *pommes vapeur*, which derives from the French for potato, *pomme de terre* (which literally means "apple of the earth") and steam, which is *vapeur*. The bulbous base holds about three cups of water. Separating the base and the V-shaped body is a perforated grate, which allows steam to rise and cook up to two pounds of new potatoes, which the body accommodates. The theory is that the distinctive shape prevents the potatoes from getting soggy by routing the condensation from the steam down the angled walls. This way, the water droplets don't fall back onto the potatoes. At roughly nine to 10 inches tall, with a top diameter of about six inches, the whole setup is quite compact. Though we find a regular saucepan more than adequate for steaming potatoes, you can order a *pommes vapeur* (at the high cost usually associated with copper cookware) from either Sur La Table (catalog division, 1765 Sixth Avenue South, Seattle, WA 98134; 800-243-0852) for $199.95 or La Cuisine, The Cook's Resource (323 Cameron Street, Alexandria, VA 22314-3219; 800-521-1176) for $190.00.

Quick Tips

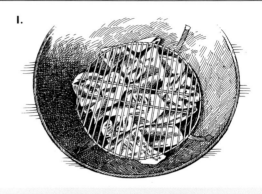

Starting a Grill Fire Without a Chimney Starter

Though his preferred method for starting a grill fire was to use a chimney, one year when his chimney had worn out and no replacement was available, Robert Barton of Richmond, Vermont, discovered that the same principle could be used without the chimney.

1. Place eight crumpled sheets of newspaper beneath the rack on which the charcoal sits.

2. With bottom air vent open, pile charcoal on rack and light paper.

Stabilizing Artichokes for Steaming

Without a steaming apparatus, it can be tricky to keep artichokes upright in the pan as they steam. If you simply sit an artichoke on its stem end, the air will not be able to circulate for even cooking, and the bottom of the artichoke can easily over-brown by the time the leaves are tender. Nancy Peterson of Clarkdale, Arizona, has discovered the perfect solution. Set each artichoke in the band of a canning jar lid, which will keep the artichoke stable and protect the stem end from the bottom of the pan.

Transporting Knives Safely

Shana Wagger of Washington, D.C., uses a cone-shaped paper coffee filter as a makeshift sheath for carrying a medium- or small-size knife on picnics.

1. Slip the knife into the filter, making sure the blade lies along the reinforced seam.

2. Roll the paper around the blade to form a sheath.

Slicing Scallions

Often scallions fail to separate fully when sliced (see top picture). Erica Foss, a cook at Aujourd'hui in Boston, Massachusetts, uses an unconventional knife technique to prevent this.

1. Rather than cutting the scallions with a rocking motion of the knife's heel, she draws the tip of the knife backward toward her across the scallions.

2. This method completely separates the scallion into rings without any jagged edges.

Keeping Flavor at Hand

To quickly add smooth, rich flavor to grilled or roast fish, chicken, chops, steaks, or even vegetables, Daniel van Ackere, of Boston, Massachusetts, makes up a batch of compound butter (softened butter flavored with citrus zest, chopped parsley, ginger, or like ingredients) and keeps it in the freezer. The butter will keep in this manner for 3 months.

1. Place the butter on top of waxed paper.

2. Roll it up into a long, narrow cylinder, and freeze it.

3. When you need it, just take butter out of freezer, cut off a slice, and place it to melt on top of freshly cooked food.

Damping a Grill Fire

Ben Utech, of Arlington, Virginia, uses this method to conserve charcoal when he has finished grilling. Close the bottom vents and place the top, with its vents shut also, on the grill. This starves the coals of oxygen, which will eventually extinguish them. Leave the unburned portion in the kettle to use the next time you grill. This also means that less fresh charcoal will be required.

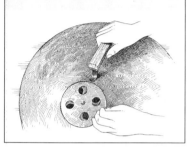

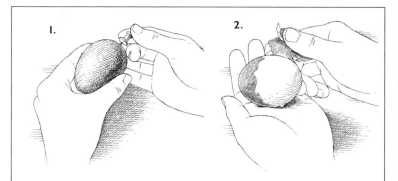

Peeling Hard-Cooked Eggs

Especially when making deviled eggs, you want the shell of a hard-cooked egg to slide off easily, leaving behind a pristine white with no shell chips or gouges. To ensure that the peels leave the whites intact, Janet van der Meulen of Newburyport, Massachusetts, uses a European method she learned from her Dutch husband.

1. Prick a tiny air hole in the large end of the egg using a common push pin or tack. Cook the eggs.

2. Remove the eggs from the hot water with a slotted spoon and plunge them into ice water. When the eggs are chilled thoroughly, their shells will peel right off.

Pitting Cherries Three Ways

Cherry pitters, though they work well, are oddball kitchen gadgets. Not every cook will have one on hand, which leaves many of us searching for alternative methods. Over the past several months, three readers have submitted their own personal cherry-pitting methods. With any of these methods, work over a bowl to catch the cherry juices.

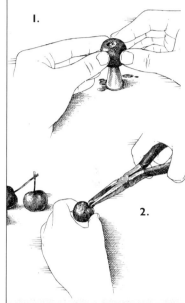

1. Barbara Connelly of Palm Harbor, Florida, pushes the cherries firmly down onto the pointed, jagged end of a pastry bag tip. Take care not to cut your fingers on the points as they pierce the fruit.

2. Carl Meuller of Pittsburgh, Pennsylvania, uses a pair of well-cleaned needle-nose pliers. All you do is pierce the skin at the stem, spread the pliers just enough to grasp the pit, and pull it straight out.

3. Patty Woodard of Eugene, Oregon, pushes a drinking straw through the bottom of the cherry, forcing the pit up and out the top.

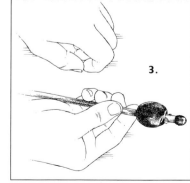

Lifting Canning Jars Easily

The handles on a jar caddy often fold down into the boiling water and get too hot to touch. Terry Nelson of Camas Valley, Oregon, uses her wooden spaghetti grabbers to solve this problem.

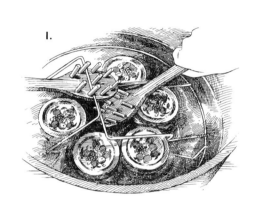

1. Grab one handle of the jar caddy with each of the upturned spaghetti grabbers so that the handles are nested securely among the pegs of the grabber.

2. Lifting with the grabbers, raise the caddy out of its water bath.

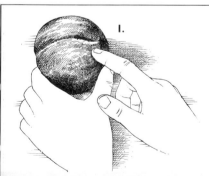

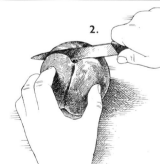

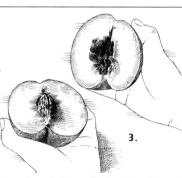

Halving Peaches and Nectarines

If you're tired of wrestling with peaches and nectarines to remove the pit, try this method from Carolyn Scheer of Irvine, California.

1. Locate the crease that marks the pointed edge of the pit.

2. Position the knife at 90° from the crease and cut the fruit in half, pole to pole.

3. Grasp both halves of the fruit and twist apart to expose the pit, which will not split open when cut this way and can be popped out easily.

Grilling Chicken Kebabs

The key to moist but well-grilled kebabs? Soak them in an acid-free marinade for about three hours before they hit the grill.

≥ BY LAUREN CHATTMAN ≤

Lemon juice in a marinade partially cooks the chicken, so if you want lemon flavors, we recommend that you simply squirt the kebabs with a lemon wedge after they come off the grill.

Grilled kebabs of chicken and fresh vegetables are delicious, simple, and practical. Just add a salad and a big bowl of fluffy white rice, or maybe some warm pita bread, and you've got a satisfying meal.

The kebabs of my dreams are succulent, well-seasoned, and really taste like they've been cooked over an open fire. They are complemented by fruits and vegetables that are equally satisfying—grill-marked but juicy, cooked all the way through but not incinerated or shrunken. When I started my testing for this article, I figured it would be simple. After all, skewered chicken is a standby of every street-corner grill cook from here to China.

But after some early attempts, I found that the difficulties in cooking and flavoring kebabs often result in skewers that look better than they taste. When I simply threaded the chicken and veggies on skewers, brushed them with a little oil, and sprinkled them with salt and pepper, I was always disappointed. Sometimes the components cooked at different rates, resulting in dry meat and undercooked vegetables. Even when they were nicely grilled, the quick-cooking kebabs didn't absorb much flavor from the fire and were bland. White meat seemed to lose moisture as it cooked, so that by the time it was safe to eat it was too dry to enjoy. With its extra fat, dark meat was invariably juicier than white meat, but still needed a considerable flavor boost before it could be called perfect.

I decided to attack the flavor problem first, reasoning that once I could produce well-seasoned, juicy chicken chunks, I could then work out the kinks of cooking fruits and vegetables at the same time. Having committed myself to dark meat, I started with the simplest solution, using a spice rub before cooking, but the results were disappointing. The chunks looked and tasted dry. If I rubbed the meat after cooking, the spices were a little powdery and raw-tasting.

Wanting to add a little moisture, I turned to "wet" preparations. I mixed a simple marinade of lemon juice, olive oil, garlic, and herbs and soaked the chicken in it for three hours, the time recommended for skin-on chicken parts in a previous *Cook's* article (*see* "Do Marinades Work?" July/August 1993). I liked the glossy, slightly moist grilled crust that the marinade produced and the way the garlic and herb flavors had penetrated the meat. But I found the flavor of the lemon juice, refreshing on larger pieces of chicken, overpowering on the smaller chunks. A more serious problem was the way the acid-based marinade tenderized the chicken. Even with shorter marinating times (I tried one hour and one-half hour), the chunks were mushy after cooking.

Was there a way to season the chicken all the way through and keep it moist on the grill without the acid? I ruled out brining because it would make the small skinless chicken chunks much too salty. But since I wanted the juiciness and flavor that brining imparts, I decided to try soaking the chicken in a lightly salted, acid-free marinade. I prepared two batches of acid-free olive oil marinade, one with salt and one without. I let the chunks sit in the marinade for three hours before grilling. The results were what I had hoped for. The salted marinade produced plump, well-seasoned kebabs. The chicken marinated without salt was drier and seemed to absorb less flavor from the garlic and herbs.

Fine-tuning the method, I settled on one teaspoon of salt (this quantity seasons the chicken without making it overly salty) for 1½ pounds of chicken and a marinating time of at least three hours. (During testing, chicken marinated for less time than this did not absorb enough of the marinade flavorings.) Because there is no acid in the marinade and thus no danger of breaking down the texture of the meat, the chicken can be soaked for up to 24 hours before cooking.

Since it was clear early on that cooking chicken and vegetables together enhances the flavor of

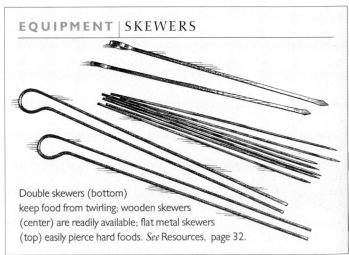

EQUIPMENT | SKEWERS

Double skewers (bottom) keep food from twirling; wooden skewers (center) are readily available; flat metal skewers (top) easily pierce hard foods. *See* Resources, page 32.

Double skewers are quite easy to thread. Use one hand to hold two skewers about ½-inch apart, then thread the chicken and vegetables on both skewers at once for easy turning on the grill.

both, I now needed to figure out how to prepare the vegetables so they would cook at the same rate as the chicken. I eliminated items like potatoes and yams, which need precooking. I also decided against marinating fruits and vegetables, partly because the chicken was already highly flavored from the marinade, and partly because I didn't like the way some of them lost their characteristic flavor after just a short dip. I found that simply tossing the fruits and vegetables with a little olive oil, salt, and pepper produced the best texture and flavor.

In general, resilient (but not rock-hard) vegetables such as zucchini, eggplant, and bell peppers cook thoroughly but stay moist and lend good flavor and crunch to chicken skewers. Cherry tomatoes, on the other hand, tend to disintegrate by the time the chicken is done. Firm-textured fruits like apples, pears, and pineapples grill beautifully, holding their shape while cooking all the way through. Fruits that tend toward softness when overripe, like peaches or nectarines, will work fine if still firm. Softer fruits like mangoes or grapes turn to mush over the fire, no matter what size you cut them.

Certain fruits and vegetables are obvious matches for certain marinades. With curry-marinated chicken, I liked pineapple cubes and slices of onion. With Middle-Eastern flavors, zucchini and eggplant are good choices.

As for the fire, medium-low is best (you should be able to keep your hand five inches above the fire for five seconds). A hotter fire chars the outside before the inside is done; a cooler fire won't give you those appetizing grill marks and may dry out the chicken. For the juiciest chicken with the strongest grilled flavor, cook skewers of white meat for eight minutes and dark meat skewers for about nine minutes, both uncovered.

After experimenting with various sizes and shapes, I chose 1- to 1½-inch chunks, small enough for easy eating but big enough to get some good grilled flavor. With smaller chunks or thin strips there's no margin for error; a few seconds too long on the grill and you'll wind up with a dry-as-dust dinner.

A final note on skewering itself. Chicken and vegetables simply skewered through the center may spin around when you try to turn them on the grill, inhibiting even cooking. I tried out some heavy-gauge twisted metal skewers designed to prevent this problem, but in the end found that threading the ingredients through two thinner skewers at once was more effective. I prefer thin but sturdy metal skewers that can fit two at a time through the kebabs but won't bend under the weight of the food.

MASTER RECIPE FOR GRILLED CHICKEN KEBABS

MAKES 8 KEBABS (4 SERVINGS)

Although white breast meat can be used, we prefer the juicier, more flavorful dark thigh meat for these kebabs. Whichever you choose, do not mix white and dark meat on the same skewer, since they cook at slightly different rates. During testing we discovered that wooden skewers do not need to be soaked in water before grilling.

Cut peeled eggplant and onions into half-inch cubes and zucchini into half-inch rounds; button mushrooms can be skewered whole, but portobello caps should be cut into half-inch chunks; seeded bell peppers work best as inch-wide squares, while peeled shallots can be skewered whole; apples and pears should be cored and cut into one-inch cubes, peaches pitted and cut into six sections, and pineapples peeled, cored, and cut into one-inch cubes.

- 1   recipe marinade of choice (*see* below)
- 1½   pounds skinless boneless chicken breasts or thighs, cut into 1- to 1½-inch chunks
- 3   cups vegetables and/or fruit, prepared according to above directions
- 2   tablespoons olive oil to coat vegetables and fruit
      Salt and ground black pepper for vegetables and fruit

1. Mix marinade and chicken in gallon-size zipper-lock plastic bag; seal bag and refrigerate, turning once or twice, until chicken has marinated fully, at least 3 and up to 24 hours.

2. Build a medium-low fire in grill (you can hold your hand 5 inches above grill surface for 5 seconds).

3. Meanwhile, lightly coat vegetables and/or fruit by tossing in medium bowl with oil and salt and pepper to taste.

4. Remove chicken chunks from bag; discard marinade. Following illustration above, thread a portion of chicken and vegetables and/or fruit onto 8 sets of double skewers. Grill, turning each kebab one quarter turn every 2 minutes, until chicken and vegetables and/or fruit are lightly browned and meat is fully cooked, about 8 minutes total for white meat and 9 minutes total for dark meat. Check for doneness by cutting into one piece when it looks opaque on all sides. Remove kebabs from grill when there is no pink at the center. Serve immediately.

MASTER RECIPE FOR GARLIC AND HERB MARINADE

MAKES SCANT ¾ CUP, ENOUGH TO COAT 1½ POUNDS CHICKEN CHUNKS

- ½   cup olive oil
- 6   small garlic cloves, minced (about 2 tablespoons)
- ¼   cup snipped chives, minced fresh basil, parsley, tarragon, oregano, cilantro, or mint leaves *or* 2 tablespoons minced fresh thyme or rosemary
- 1   teaspoon salt
      Ground black pepper to taste

Whisk all ingredients in small bowl.

CURRY MARINADE

Follow Master Recipe for Garlic and Herb Marinade, using ¼ cup minced fresh cilantro or mint leaves and adding 1 teaspoon curry powder.

CARIBBEAN MARINADE

Follow Master Recipe for Garlic and Herb Marinade, using ¼ cup minced fresh parsley leaves and adding 1 teaspoon cumin, 1 teaspoon chili powder, ½ teaspoon allspice, ½ teaspoon black pepper, and ¼ teaspoon ground cinnamon.

MIDDLE EASTERN MARINADE

Follow Master Recipe for Garlic and Herb Marinade, using ¼ cup minced fresh mint or parsley leaves, alone or in combination, and adding ½ teaspoon cinnamon, ½ teaspoon allspice, and ¼ teaspoon cayenne.

SOUTHWESTERN MARINADE

Follow Master Recipe for Garlic and Herb Marinade, using ¼ cup minced fresh cilantro leaves, decreasing salt to ½ teaspoon, and adding 1 teaspoon cumin, 1 teaspoon chili powder, 1 teaspoon turmeric, and 1 medium chile, such as jalapeño, seeded and minced.

ASIAN MARINADE

- 6   tablespoons vegetable oil
- 2   tablespoons Asian sesame oil
- ¼   cup soy sauce
- 6   small garlic cloves, minced (about 2 tablespoons)
- ¼   cup minced fresh cilantro leaves
- 1   piece (about 1-inch) fresh gingerroot, minced (about 1 tablespoon)
- 2   medium scallions, white and green parts, sliced thin

Whisk all ingredients in small bowl.

Lauren Chattman is the author of *Cool Kitchen* (William Morrow, 1998).

Solving the Barbecued Brisket Riddle

Extra-heavy-duty foil and a slow oven can turn any backyard into a barbecue pit.

⇛ BY CORT SINNES ⇚

Kansas City, where I live most of the time, is a town that takes its barbecue seriously. Nearly everyone in this town—from award-winning barbecue cooks to ordinary backyard barbecuers—has an opinion on how to cook a brisket. But this proved of little help in solving the riddle of why it's so hard to turn out a delicious barbecued brisket consistently.

Over the years, from one big barbecue blowout to another, I've had the benefit of a great cooking partner, my friend JP. We've racked up countless hours cooking together and, generally speaking, are fairly confident in our ability to pull some pretty good grub off the grill. That said, it took us years to figure out a method of barbecuing brisket that worked every time.

To understand the problem, it helps to know a little about this unique cut of meat, which most folks are only familiar with in its "corned" form as a St. Patrick's Day necessity.

The primary reason cooking a brisket is so difficult to get right is that it starts out as a very tough cut of meat. A full brisket, which can weigh upwards of 13 pounds, comes from the underside of a cow's chest. Most butchers separate the brisket into two cuts: the thicker pointed end known as the "point" cut, and the thinner squarish section called the "flat" cut (*see* illustration, page 10). A layer of fat runs along one side of a whole brisket, with a second layer sandwiched in the middle of the thick end. Depending on the butcher, these layers of fat may be either left thick or trimmed down to somewhere between one-fourth and three-eighths of an inch. Trimmed or untrimmed does not make much difference, as long as there's at least a quarter-inch layer to help keep the brisket moist and flavorful through a relatively long cooking period. (Once the brisket has been cooked, it's easy to remove any remaining fat in the carving process.) As far as which is the better end of the brisket—the point or the flat—it's a matter of personal opinion. If you like fattier meat, favor the point cut; if you like your meat

If you cook it for a long time over very low heat and slice it very thin against the grain, a tough brisket transforms itself into a tender, smoky-flavored treat.

leaner (and, therefore, a little tougher) and in long, uniform slices, the flat cut is for you.

Years of Experiments

As with any slightly esoteric pursuit, the deeper you get into the subject of barbecue, the more you realize you've entered a world unto itself, with its own language, traditions, rules, biases, folklore, and wisdom. In trying to figure out how to take a very large, very tough piece of beef and turn it into a mouth-watering, tender, and flavorful meal, I've listened to all manner of advice. Some of it was helpful, some interesting but of doubtful importance, and some downright silly. And none of it seemed to add up to the whole story of how to produce a good brisket consistently.

In the two-year period between 1990 and 1991, while I was writing *The Grilling Encyclopedia*, I can honestly say no single subject gave me more trouble than beef brisket. Everyone in the barbecue world was in agreement about one thing, however, that "low and slow" was the way to go. Translated, that means

that to produce a good barbecued brisket, you have to cook it over low heat over a long period of time. Beyond that, there was absolutely no agreement: Wrap the brisket in foil, don't wrap it in foil; use a pan of water in the bottom of the grill, don't use one; baste the brisket, don't baste the brisket. And when it came to dry rubs and sauces, the opinions and variations were as heated as they were limitless.

Ignoring some of the more questionable advice, such as basting the brisket with ginger ale, I tried everything I heard about. In addition to experimenting with cooking times, which I'll address later, the following techniques were all tried and eventually abandoned. Wrapping the brisket in foil when it was on the grill seemed like a good idea to keep the meat moist, but it kept the smoke flavor from permeating the brisket and the outside edges from taking on that dark brown crusty quality which many consider the best part of a barbecued brisket (known in barbecue circles as "burnt ends"). Placing a pan of water under an unwrapped brisket also seemed like a way to keep the meat succulent, but no one who tasted it could tell the difference between it and a brisket cooked without a pan of water under it.

Regularly basting the brisket also held some promise as a way of keeping the brisket moist, but again, no one could tell the difference between a basted brisket and one that hadn't been basted. Not only that, but repeatedly taking the lid off the grill wreaked havoc on the coals: Each time I opened the grill, the influx of air caused the briquettes to burn hotter and faster, two things I definitely didn't want. In publishing there are these things called deadlines, and eventually I had to settle on offering a set of instructions that worked for my book, but which I now consider impractical.

Long after the book came out, however, my friend JP and I continued to experiment with brisket. I'm happy to report that eventually we found that it is indeed possible to turn out a first-rate barbecued brisket without digging a pit in your backyard — but it involves barbecue heresy.

Oven to the Rescue

During our experimental period, we cooked briskets anywhere from 30 minutes per pound to 60 minutes per pound. Results aside, when you are dealing with a 10-pound piece of beef, you're talking about keeping the barbecue at a more or less even temperature of around 250 degrees for six to 12 hours! Unless you have nothing better to do, or make your living preparing barbecue, most people simply aren't willing or able to make that kind of time commitment to a piece of beef.

To get around this all-day-long-tending-the-barbecue problem, we found it necessary to commit barbecue heresy: We resorted to the partial use of an indoor oven. Suffice it to say that true barbecue loyalists wouldn't even consider such an option but, heresy or not, this two-stage cooking process solved all our problems and consistently turned out a great brisket. The time on the grill allowed the meat to absorb a nice smoky taste, didn't require adding additional coals, and produced that sought-after dark brown, crusty exterior. The time the brisket spent in the oven after it came off the grill and was wrapped in extra-heavy-duty foil allowed it to continue cooking at a constant temperature (with no attention required from the cook) and eventually produced a succulent, fork-tender piece of meat.

In fact, the foil was almost as important a discovery as the oven. It was crucial to our process, not only for the final cooking in the oven, but also for the smoking process. Conventional advice suggests soaking chips or chunks of smoking wood in water anywhere from 30 minutes to overnight before putting them directly on the hot coals. But wrapping dry chunks or chips of smoking wood in a double layer of foil not only eliminates the soaking step, it also releases the smoke over a longer period of time with no effect on the coals.

I am well aware that most (if not all) barbecue purists will take umbrage at finishing the brisket in the oven. But what this two-stage cooking process lacks in barbecue authenticity, it more than makes up for in results. Not only that, but there's a degree of satisfaction that comes from knowing that you'll be able to produce those results again when your guests tell you it's the best brisket they've ever tasted!

SPICY CHILI RUB
MAKES ABOUT 1 CUP

Adjust the ingredient amounts or add or subtract ingredients, as you wish. For instance, if you cannot abide spicy hot food, reduce or eliminate the cayenne.

- 4 tablespoons paprika
- 2 tablespoons chili powder
- 2 tablespoons ground cumin
- 2 tablespoons dark brown sugar
- 2 tablespoons salt
- 1 tablespoon ground oregano
- 1 tablespoon sugar
- 1 tablespoon ground black pepper
- 1 tablespoon ground white pepper
- 2 teaspoons cayenne pepper

Mix all ingredients in small bowl.

BARBECUED BEEF BRISKET
SERVES 18 TO 24

Barbecuing a whole brisket of roughly 10 pounds for almost six hours may seem like overkill. Although the process is time-consuming, it is easy, and the leftovers keep well in the refrigerator for up to four days. Don't worry if your brisket is a little larger or smaller; split-second cooking times are not critical since the meat is eaten very well-done. Small chunks or chips of hickory or mesquite wood give the meat its smoky, barbecued flavor, but don't be tempted to overdo a good thing: One packet of smoking wood is all you need. More than that, and you run the risk of

---

STEP-BY-STEP | THE BEST WAY TO BARBECUE BRISKET

1. Apply the dry rub generously to the brisket, pressing down to make sure the spices adhere. The meat should be completely obscured by the rub.

2. For controlled smoke release, wrap wood chips in foil and puncture the foil in several spots.

3. Place the brisket on the opposite side of the grill away from the coals and enclosed wood chips.

4. Wrap the grilled brisket in two 4-foot sections of heavy-duty foil that have been sealed together.

5. Seal foil sections together crosswise, then fold the sides of the foil packet tightly up against the sides of the meat.

6. When the brisket comes out of the oven, use potholders or oven mitts to lift the baking sheet and carefully pour the juices into a bowl. Reserve the juices.

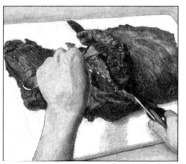

7. Since the grain on the two sections of the brisket goes in opposite directions, separate the two cuts before slicing.

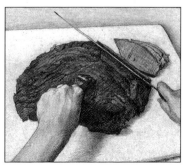

8. Carve the brisket into thin slices, going against the grain on the diagonal.

producing a bitter-tasting brisket. Moistening the sliced brisket with the meat juices adds flavor, and mixing the juices in equal proportion with good barbecue sauce improves it even further. Serve the brisket with traditional barbecue side dishes such as potato salad or french fries, soft white bread or cornbread, baked beans, coleslaw, dill pickle chips, or greens. Or for a real treat, do like we do in Kansas City and put a couple of slices of brisket on a single piece of regular white bread, add a little coleslaw, several dill pickle chips, and a squirt or two of your favorite barbecue sauce, and fold the whole thing into a neat triangle shape.

Barbecuing brisket for less than a crowd is easy to do. Simply ask your butcher for either the point or flat portion of the brisket, whichever cut you prefer. Then follow the master recipe, reducing the spice rub by half and grill-smoking for 1½ hours. Wrap the meat tightly in foil and reduce its time in the oven to 2 hours.

- whole beef brisket (point and flat cut together, *see* illustration at right), 9 to 11 pounds, trimmed
- recipe Spicy Chili Rub (*see* page 9)
- bottle (18 ounces) barbecue sauce

1. Following illustration 1, page 9, apply dry rub liberally to all sides of brisket; wrap tightly in plastic wrap. Refrigerate for at least 2 and up to 48 hours.

2. One hour prior to cooking, remove brisket from refrigerator and unwrap. Ignite about 2 quarts of hardwood charcoal or charcoal briquettes in pile on one side of grill; burn until

completely covered with thin coating of light gray ash, 20 to 30 minutes. Meanwhile, following illustration 2, assemble hickory chip pouch by wrapping 4 to 6 wood chunks (about 3 inches each) or 3 cups wood chips in double sheet of heavy-duty foil. Prick at least 6 holes in top of foil pouch with knife tip to allow smoke to escape; place on top of ash-covered coals.

3. Set grill rack in place and position brisket, fat side up, on side of rack opposite fire (illustration 3). Make sure that both top and bottom grill vents are open; position holes in lid directly over brisket and cover grill. Grill-smoke brisket without removing lid so that smoke flavor permeates meat, 2 hours.

4. Adjust oven rack to middle position and heat oven to 300 degrees. Attach two 48-inch long pieces heavy-duty foil by folding long edges together 2 or 3 times, crimping tightly to seal well, to form an approximately 48- x 36-inch rectangle. Position brisket lengthwise in center of foil. Bring short edges over brisket and fold down, crimping tightly to seal (illustration 4). Following illustration 5, repeat with long edges of foil to seal brisket completely. Place brisket on baking sheet; bake until fork-tender or instant-read thermometer inserted into thickest portion of meat registers 210 degrees, 3 to 3½ hours.

5. Remove brisket from oven, loosen foil at one end to release steam, and rest for 30 minutes.

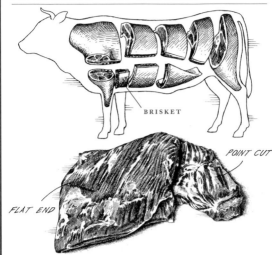

LOCATING THE BRISKET

BRISKET Butchers sometimes separate the whole brisket into two parts, the flat end (left portion) and the point cut (right portion).

Following illustration 6, drain juices into large bowl. De-fat juices (you should have 1½ to 2 cups) and mix in equal parts with barbecue sauce.

6. Unwrap brisket and place on cutting board. Following illustrations 7 and 8, separate into two sections. Slice each section, on the bias across the grain, into very thin slices. Moisten slices with some of the barbecue sauce mixture and serve, passing remaining sauce separately.

Cort Sinnes' latest grilling book is *The Gas Grill Gourmet* (Harvard Common Press, 1997).

How Does Brisket Become Tender?

Barbecuing a brisket is an ideal way to turn a tough cut of beef into a tender one. The test kitchen at *Cook's* conducted an experiment to better understand what happens to the brisket as it undergoes this transformation.

We took four 13.2-ounce pieces of brisket of equal shape, wrapped them tightly in foil, and cooked them in a 275-degree oven. Using an instant-read thermometer, we took the first one out when its internal temperature reached 160 degrees, the second one when it reached 180, the third at 200, and we took the last brisket out when it registered an internal temperature of 210 degrees. As we took each one out, we weighed both the meat and its exuded liquid, and checked it for tenderness and ease of chew. As we expected, as the internal temperature rose from 160 to 180, more liquid was lost and the meat became drier and therefore tougher. At 200 degrees, however, the meat began to be slightly less tough, although still quite dry. To our surprise, when the brisket reached 210 degrees it had the most appealing texture and the most pleasant chew, despite the fact that it had continued to lose moisture.

We found this surprising because many meats are most tender at a much lower internal temperature. Think of the silky-smooth texture of a steak cooked rare, for example, versus the much tougher texture of one cooked well-done. This is because as the internal temperature of the meat rises, the muscle proteins begin to uncoil and to bond together in tighter association, which drives out juice. This process begins at 147 degrees and intensifies as the internal temperature rises. The more juice lost, the tougher the meat becomes. By 210 degrees, most meats would be as tough as shoe leather.

But with meats like brisket, which start out tough, another process is going on at

the same time. According to Dr. Kathryn L. Kotula, Professor of Food Science at the University of Connecticut, brisket and other tough meats become tender when the connective tissue known as collagen, which is what makes these meats tough and chewy to begin with, dissolves and is transformed into gelatin. Three conditions are necessary for the gelatinization of collagen, said Dr. Kotula: high internal temperatures, moist heat, and time. Collagen begins to convert to gelatin at 150 degrees, just a few degrees higher than the point at which the muscle fibers begin to contract and force out juices. As the temperatures increase, so does the rate at which the collagen solubilizes.

So when cooking brisket, the effect of juice loss from the muscle groups pales in comparison to the importance of the gelatinization of collagen. When cooked to 210 degrees, a temperature at which collagen gelatinizes rapidly, the brisket was the most texturally pleasing and the easiest to chew; when cooked to only 160 degrees (a temperature at which collagen conversion was not significant) the brisket, while moist, was still tough and hard to chew.

It is important to point out that moist-heat methods of cooking are appropriate for cooking meats to such high internal temperatures because water is a more efficient conductor of heat than air. Meats cooked in moist environments heat up faster, and they can be held at high temperatures without burning or drying out. —Anne Yamanaka

Summer Tomato Salads

To create a nicely balanced acidic base for the dressings in these salads, salt the cut tomatoes and let them sit for 15 to 20 minutes to extract some juice.

≥ BY EVA KATZ ≤

A bonus of summer tomato salads is that the mildly acidic juices from the tomatoes themselves provide a delicious base for a dressing, so very little additional acid is needed in the dressing. To make this work, you need to extract a little of the juice from the tomatoes before you make the salads. This is easily done. Simply cutting the tomatoes into wedges and letting them sit for fifteen minutes provides enough time for the juices to exude. Salting the cut tomatoes helps this process and seasons the tomatoes and their juices at the same time.

Some cooks recommend peeling the tomatoes, but I find the skin on local vine-ripened tomatoes thin and unobtrusive. If homegrown tomatoes are unavailable, substitute halved cherry tomatoes.

TOMATO SALAD WITH CANNED TUNA, CAPERS, AND BLACK OLIVES
SERVES 6

- 4–5 large vine-ripened tomatoes (about 1 ½ pounds)
- ½ teaspoon salt
- 3 tablespoons extra-virgin olive oil
- 1 tablespoon juice from 1 lemon
- 3 tablespoons capers, chopped
- 12 large black olives, such as kalamata or other brine-cured variety, pitted and chopped
- ¼ small red onion, chopped fine (about ¼ cup)
- 2 tablespoons chopped fresh parsley leaves
  Ground black pepper
- 1 6-ounce can tuna, oil- or water-packed, drained

1. Core and halve tomatoes, then cut each half into 4 or 5 wedges. Toss wedges with salt in large bowl; let rest until small pool of liquid accumulates, 15 to 20 minutes.

2. Meanwhile, whisk oil, lemon juice, capers, olives, onion, parsley, and pepper to taste in small bowl. Pour mixture over tomatoes and accumulated liquid; toss to coat. Set aside to blend flavors, about 5 minutes.

3. Crumble tuna over tomatoes; toss to combine. Adjust seasonings and serve immediately.

TOMATO AND BREAD SALAD WITH GARLIC–ANCHOVY DRESSING
SERVES 6

- 4–5 large vine-ripened tomatoes (about 1 ½ pounds)
- ½ teaspoon salt
- 3 tablespoons extra-virgin olive oil
- 1½ tablespoons red wine vinegar
- 2 small garlic cloves, minced or put through garlic press
- ⅓ cup chopped fresh basil leaves
- 3 anchovy fillets, rinsed and mashed (about 1 tablespoon)
  Ground black pepper
- 4 large ¾-inch-thick slices chewy country-style bread, toasted or grilled until lightly browned, then cut into ¾-inch cubes

1. Follow step 1 in recipe for Tomato Salad with Canned Tuna, Capers, and Black Olives.

2. Meanwhile, whisk oil, vinegar, garlic, basil, anchovies, and pepper to taste in small bowl. Pour mixture over tomatoes and accumulated liquid; toss to coat. Set aside to blend flavors, about 5 minutes.

3. Add bread cubes; toss to combine. Adjust seasonings and serve immediately.

TOMATO SALAD WITH ARUGULA AND SHAVED PARMESAN
SERVES 6

- 4–5 large vine-ripened tomatoes (about 1 ½ pounds)
- ½ teaspoon salt
- 2 tablespoons extra-virgin olive oil
- 1 tablespoon balsamic vinegar
- 1 small garlic clove, minced or put through garlic press
  Ground black pepper
- 1 small bunch arugula, cleaned and chopped coarse (about 1 cup)
- 1 small chunk (about 2 ounces) Parmesan cheese, shaved into strips with vegetable peeler or paring knife

1. Follow step 1 in recipe for Tomato Salad with Canned Tuna, Capers, and Black Olives.

2. Meanwhile, whisk oil, vinegar, garlic, and pepper to taste in small bowl. Pour mixture over tomatoes and accumulated liquid; toss to coat. Set aside to blend flavors, about 5 minutes.

3. Add arugula and Parmesan; toss to combine. Adjust seasonings and serve immediately.

TOMATO SALAD WITH FETA AND CUMIN–YOGURT DRESSING
SERVES 6

- 4–5 large vine-ripened tomatoes (about 1 ½ pounds)
- ½ teaspoon salt
- ¼ cup plain yogurt, drained in fine sieve about 30 minutes (discard liquid)
- 1 tablespoon extra-virgin olive oil
- 1 tablespoon juice from 1 lemon
- 1 small garlic clove, minced or put through garlic press
- 1 teaspoon ground cumin
- 3 small scallions, white and green parts, sliced thin
- 1 tablespoon chopped fresh oregano leaves
  Ground black pepper
- 1 small chunk (about 3 ounces) feta cheese

1. Follow step 1 in recipe for Tomato Salad with Canned Tuna, Capers, and Black Olives.

2. Meanwhile, whisk drained yogurt, oil, lemon juice, garlic, cumin, scallions, oregano, and pepper to taste in small bowl. Pour mixture over tomatoes and accumulated liquid; toss to coat. Set aside to blend flavors, about 5 minutes.

3. Crumble feta over tomatoes; toss to combine. Adjust seasonings and serve immediately.

ISRAELI TOMATO AND CUCUMBER SALAD
SERVES 6

Thin-skinned English cucumbers, with or without the peel, work well in this salad.

- 4–5 large vine-ripened tomatoes (about 1 ½ pounds)
- ½ teaspoon salt
- 3 tablespoons extra-virgin olive oil
- 2 tablespoons juice from 1 lemon
- ¼ cup finely chopped red onion
- ¼ cup chopped fresh mint leaves
  Ground black pepper
- 2 medium cucumbers, peeled, quartered, seeded, cut into ¼-inch pieces, tossed with 2 teaspoons salt in strainer or colander set over bowl, and drained about 1 hour (discard liquid)

1. Follow step 1 in recipe for Tomato Salad with Canned Tuna, Capers, and Black Olives.

2. Meanwhile, whisk oil, lemon juice, red onion, mint, and pepper to taste in small bowl. Pour mixture over tomatoes and accumulated liquid and toss to coat. Rest to blend flavors, about 5 minutes.

3. Add drained cucumber pieces; toss to combine. Adjust seasonings and serve immediately.

Eva Katz, former Test Kitchen Director at *Cook's Illustrated*, now lives in Brisbane, Australia.

Beefing Up Turkey Burgers

For juicy and flavorful burgers, either grind your own turkey in the food processor or add ricotta cheese to lean, commercially ground turkey.

≥ BY PAM ANDERSON WITH MELISSA HAMILTON ≤

One summer vacation my 15-year-old daughter decided to become a vegetarian. After a week-long debate, we finally compromised on white meat. In other words, she was excused from lamb, beef, and pork as long as she would eat fish and fowl. Since hamburgers were one of her weaknesses, I thought she'd cave in pretty quickly. But what seemed like a teen fad has evolved into a way of life.

Since hamburgers are a regular summer supper for us, we needed to find a substitute sandwich for her. Ground turkey was the obvious first choice, but we found out pretty quickly that a lean, fully cooked turkey burger, seasoned simply with salt and pepper, was a weak stand-in for an all-beef burger. Simply put, it was dry, tasteless, and colorless. At the time, believing this was just a passing phase, I had very little energy for turkey burger exploration and simply switched to breaded chicken cutlets.

Now, three years later, finding my daughter's red-meat resolve still rock solid, I set out to develop a turkey burger that would rival her best beef burger memories. I wanted a turkey burger with beef burger qualities—dark and crusty on the outside and full-flavored and juicy with every bite.

The Meat Case

Finding the right meat was crucial to developing the best turkey burger. According to the National Turkey Federation, I had three options—white meat (with 1 to 2 percent fat), dark meat (over 15 percent fat), and a blend of the two (ranging from 7 to 15 percent fat).

At the grocery store, I found multiple variations on the white meat/dark meat theme, including preformed lean patties, higher-fat ground fresh turkey on Styrofoam trays or frozen in tubes like bulk sausage, lower-fat ground turkey breasts, and of course individual turkey parts I could grind up myself. I bought them all, took them home, and fired up a skillet.

We first tested the preformed lean patties—refrigerated and frozen—and found them mediocre. To varying degrees, the frozen ones had a week-old-roast-turkey taste. A few bites

A crusty exterior and a juicy interior define the best burger.

from one of the refrigerated varieties turned up significant turkey debris—tendon, ground up gristle, and bone-like chips. We moved on to bulk ground turkey.

The higher-fat (15 percent) ground turkey turned out to be flavorful and reasonably juicy with a decent, burger-like crust. Frankly, these burgers didn't need too much help. On the other hand, we didn't see much point in eating them either. Given that a great beef burger contains only 20 percent fat, a mere 5 percent fat savings didn't seem worth it.

At the other extreme with only 1 or 2 percent fat was ground turkey breast. As we were mixing and forming these patties, we knew we had about as much chance of making them look, taste, and feel like real burgers as we did of making vanilla wafers taste like chocolate chip cookies. They needed a binder to keep them from falling apart. They needed extra fat to keep them from parching and extra fat in the pan to keep them from sticking. And they needed flavor to save them from blandness.

With 7 percent fat, lean ground turkey was the most popular style at all the grocery stores I checked. Burgers made from this mix were dry, rubbery-textured, and mild-flavored. With a little help, however, these leaner patties were meaty enough to have real burger potential.

Most flavorful of all and only about 10 percent

fat were the boned and skinless turkey thighs we ground ourselves in the food processor. We first tried grinding the skin with the meat but found that it ground inconsistently and we had to pick it out. In the next batch we left it out and found the meat was equally flavorful and much lower in calories. As a matter of fact, my butcher declared our home-ground skinless turkey almost 90-percent lean when he tested it in his Univex Fat Analyzer.

For all the obvious reasons, I had sworn that even if I liked the outcome I wasn't going to make grind-your-own-turkey part of the recipe, but these burgers—meaty-flavored with a beef-like chew—were far superior to any we made with the commercially ground turkey. Of course, I had suspected as much, given my liking for grind-your-own-chuck beef burgers (see "A Better Burger," July/August 1995). If you are willing to take the time, food-processor-ground turkey thighs cook up into low-fat turkey burgers with great flavor and texture.

I Can't Believe It's Not Burger

For those with little time or energy for this process, we decided to see what we could do to improve the lean commercially ground turkey. To improve texture and juiciness, we started with the obvious—milk-soaked bread. For comparison we also made burgers with buttermilk- and yogurt-soaked bread. All these additions made the burgers feel too much like meat loaf and destroyed whatever meaty flavor there had been, since turkey is mild to start with. The bread and milk lightened the meat's color unpleasantly, while the sugar in both ingredients caused the burgers to burn easily and made it impossible to develop a good thick crust.

We tried other fillers to improve the texture, including cornmeal mush, mashed pinto beans, and minced tempeh, but they all tasted too distinct. Heat-and-serve mashed potatoes didn't mix well with the meat, making for a burger that not only fell apart easily but also had noticeable potato pockets.

Although most candidates were lackluster, two successful fillers emerged. Minced, rehydrated, dried mushrooms added a moist, chewy texture which the burgers desperately needed. They also offered an earthy, meaty flavor without tasting too distinct. Minced, sautéed fresh mushrooms also improved the texture, but we found their flavor too mild. The real winner—for flavor, texture, and easy availability—was ricotta cheese.

Moist and chewy, it gave the burger the texture boost it needed and required very little effort.

Finally, we decided to experiment a bit with added flavorings. We wanted only those that would enhance a burger's taste without drawing attention to themselves. We tried over 25 different flavorings—from fermented black beans to olive paste to teriyaki marinade—and found only four that we liked. Miso, a fermented soybean paste often used as a vegetarian soup base, offered a subtle savoriness, and fresh thyme flavored the burgers nicely. Worcestershire and Dijon mustard, which I actually prefer because they're more common pantry items, flavored the burgers equally well.

Well-Done But Juicy

Next we turned to the cooking method. Since turkey burgers must be well-done, cooking them can be a bit tricky—too high a heat and they burn before they're done; too low and they look pale and steamed. We tried several cooking methods, from broiling to roasting, but nothing compared in quality and ease to our stove-top method. Browning the burgers in a heavy-bottomed skillet over medium heat, then cooking them partially covered over low heat gave us a rich-crusted burger that was cooked all the way through.

Although our generous cooking times should ensure a fully cooked burger, as an extra precaution you may want to test for doneness by sticking an instant-read thermometer through the side and into the center of one of them. The burger is done at 160 degrees.

THE BEST TURKEY BURGERS
SERVES 4

We found that the extra step of grinding fresh turkey thighs ourselves made the most flavorful, best-textured burgers. If you want to save time, buy boneless turkey thighs. Panfrying develops a good, thick crust on the burgers, but grilling gives them a subtle smoky flavor that we love.

| | turkey thigh, about 2 pounds, skinned and boned (or 1 1/2 pounds skinless, boneless thighs) cut into 1-inch chunks and arranged in single layer on sheet pan and frozen until semifirm, about 30 minutes
1/2 | teaspoon salt
1/2 | teaspoon ground black pepper
2 | teaspoons Worcestershire sauce
2 | teaspoons Dijon mustard
1 | tablespoon vegetable or canola oil

1. Working in 3 batches, place semifrozen turkey chunks in workbowl of food processor fitted with steel blade; pulse until largest pieces are no bigger than 1/8-inch (see illustration 4), 12 to 14 one-second pulses.

2. Transfer ground meat to medium bowl. Stir in salt, pepper, Worcestershire sauce, and mustard until blended, and divide meat into 4 portions. Following illustration 5, lightly toss one portion from hand to hand to form a ball, then lightly flatten ball with fingertips into 1-inch-thick patty. Repeat with remaining portions.

3a. Heat a large, heavy skillet (preferably cast-iron or stainless steel with an aluminum core) over medium heat until very hot, 4 to 5 minutes. Swirl oil in pan to coat bottom, then add burgers. Cook over medium heat without moving burgers until bottom side of each is dark brown and crusted, about 5 minutes. Turn burgers over; continue to cook until bottom side is light brown but not yet crusted, 4 to 5 minutes longer. Reduce heat to low, position cover slightly ajar on pan to allow steam to escape, and continue to cook 5 to 6 minutes longer or until center is completely opaque yet still juicy, or an instant-read thermometer inserted from the side of the burger into the center registers 160 degrees. Remove from pan and serve immediately.

3b. Alternatively, grill burgers over medium-low fire (you can hold your hand about 5 inches above grill surface for 5 seconds) until dark spotty brown on bottom side, 7 to 9 minutes. Turn burgers over; continue grilling 7 to 9 minutes longer or until bottom side is dark spotty brown and center is completely cooked or instant-read thermometer registers 160 degrees. Remove from grill and serve immediately.

QUICKER TURKEY BURGERS
SERVES 4

This recipe will enrich store-bought ground lean turkey so that it makes excellent burgers. Ricotta cheese can burn easily, so keep a close watch on the burgers as they cook.

Follow recipe for The Best Turkey Burgers substituting 1 1/4 pounds 93 percent lean ground turkey for turkey thighs. Beginning with step 2, add 1/2 cup ricotta cheese to turkey mixture along with the salt, pepper, Worcestershire sauce, and mustard. If following step 3a, reduce cooking time to 3 to 4 minutes per side to prevent ricotta from burning yet still form deep brown crusts. Increase covered cooking time to 8 to 10 minutes, flipping burgers if necessary to promote deep browning, until center is completely cooked, or instant-read thermometer registers 160 degrees. Alternatively, follow grilling instructions in step 3b.

MISO TURKEY BURGERS

Japanese miso paste, made from soybeans, gives the turkey burgers a particularly savory, beefy flavor.

Follow recipe for either The Best or Quicker Turkey Burgers, omitting Worcestershire sauce and mustard. Thin 2 teaspoons pure soybean miso with 2 teaspoons water and add directly to turkey mixture for The Best Turkey Burgers or to ricotta for Quicker Turkey Burgers.

STEP-BY-STEP | MAKING HOME-GROUND TURKEY BURGERS

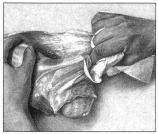
1. To remove the skin from the turkey thigh, grasp it with a paper towel for better traction and pull.

2. With a boning knife, cut along the top of the thigh bone, scrape the meat away on both sides and underneath, and discard bone.

3. After removing bone, cut the thigh meat into 1-inch strips and then cut each strip into 1-inch cubes. Freeze until semifrozen.

4. In three batches, pulse the semifrozen thigh meat in the food processor until it resembles coarsely ground burger meat.

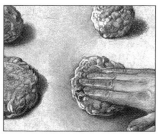
5. Divide the meat into four portions, form a ball, then flatten each into a 1-inch-thick patty.

6. To ensure burgers cook evenly, position the cover ajar on the pan so steam escapes.

Pasta Salad Made Right

This American invention can be delicious—as long as you stick with lemon juice in the vinaigrette and let the vegetables cool before dressing them.

> BY JACK BISHOP

I'll admit it. There is something appealing about the concept of pasta salad. Italians may gasp at the idea, but no one wants to eat a bowl of steaming hot pasta during the dog days of summer. A cooling pasta salad is another matter.

Since pasta salads make the most sense as a side dish for a summer meal, I've always found it odd that many recipes are heavy and creamy. A good pasta salad should be light and refreshing, with a fair amount of vegetables. (I find little bits of salami a greasy and distressing addition to deli pasta salads.) The dressing should help convey flavors and keep the pasta moist, not weigh it down. Vinaigrette (rather than mayonnaise) is the obvious choice.

Almost every deli in America sells a pasta salad dressed with vinaigrette. Often made with fusilli (tri-color fusilli in trendier markets), this salad invariably looks unappetizing. The pasta is so mushy you can see it falling apart through the glass deli case. And the vegetables are tired and sad. The broccoli has faded to drab olive green and the shredded carrots that most markets add (and that always strike me as a weird Americanization) have wilted. And as for the taste—these unattractive salads usually look better than they taste.

The problem with most of these pasta salads is that the acid causes the pasta to soften and dulls the color and flavor of many vegetables, especially green ones. But leave out the lemon juice or vinegar and the salad tastes flat. For this article, I wanted to develop a light, vinaigrette-dressed vegetable pasta salad that looked good and tasted even better.

I started my tests by making salads with four very simple vinaigrettes. Each contained a different acidic liquid, along with olive oil, salt, and pepper. Each was used to dress a simple pasta salad with blanched and cooled broccoli. The salads made with red wine vinegar and balsamic vinegar dyed the pasta and tasted too sharp. The salad made with white wine vinegar looked fine but tasted too acidic. The salad made with lemon juice was clearly the best. It had a nice bright flavor but was not puckery or sour. After half an hour, I noticed that the broccoli in the three salads with vinegar was turning olive green and starting to fall apart. But even after several hours, the broccoli in the salad with lemon juice was green and crunchy.

I was not quite ready to abandon vinegar, however. I was using a ratio of three parts oil to one

Although pasta salad is strictly American, Italian flavorings work very well in them. Here we use (clockwise from upper left) asparagus and red peppers; eggplant and tomatoes; and fennel, red onions, and sun-dried tomatoes.

part acid. Maybe this ratio was fine for lemon juice (with its acidity around 4 percent), but too high for the vinegars, which have a 6 to 7 percent acidity. I added more oil to a white wine vinegar dressing, but now the salad tasted greasy and the broccoli still lost its fresh color after half an hour. I concluded that the lemon juice simply tasted better and its lower acidity was helping to keep the vegetables green.

With lemon juice as my choice of acid, I focused on the sequence of assembling the pasta salad. Would hot vegetables absorb more dressing and taste better? Should I run the vegetables under cold water after cooking to set their color? Neither idea panned out. I found that green vegetables like broccoli lose their color most easily when they are hot. Letting them cool to room temperature helped stem any color loss, but unfortunately you can't speed up the process by running them under cold water. No matter how well I drained them,

the vegetables tasted waterlogged after being rinsed in cold water. The best method is to let them rest in the colander for at least 20 minutes, or until barely warm to the touch, before tossing them with the pasta and dressing.

At this point, I had a master recipe that I liked pretty well, but it needed some other flavors. An herb—I chose basil, but almost anything will work—perked things up. Olives (or sun-dried tomatoes) made everything more lively because they added some acidity and saltiness to a dish that otherwise was a bit bland.

When I turned my attention to other vegetables, I discovered that, as I suspected, other cooking methods added more flavor than blanching. A pasta salad made with roasted asparagus tasted better than one made with blanched asparagus, for example. Grilling also gave the vegetables a lot of flavor and made a better pasta salad. Four recipes follow, one with blanched broccoli, one with grilled fennel and red onions, one with grilled eggplant and diced tomatoes, and the last with roasted asparagus and bell peppers. If you want to create your own variation, *see* "Preparing Vegetables for Pasta Salad," at right.

PASTA SALAD WITH BROCCOLI AND OLIVES
SERVES 6 TO 8

If you prefer, increase the hot red pepper flakes or replace them with a few grindings of black pepper.

- 3 pounds broccoli (about 2 small bunches), florets cut into bite-size pieces (about 7 cups)
- 1/4 cup juice and 1/2 teaspoon grated zest from 2 lemons
  Salt
- 1 medium garlic clove, minced
- 1/2 teaspoon hot red pepper flakes
- 1/2 cup extra-virgin olive oil
- 1 pound short, bite-size pasta, such as fusilli, farfalle, or orecchiette
- 20 large black olives, such as Kalamata or other brine-cured variety, pitted and chopped
- 15 large fresh basil leaves, shredded

1. Bring 4 quarts water to boil in large pot over high heat. Cook broccoli according to chart directions; drain and cool to room temperature.

2. Meanwhile, whisk lemon juice and zest, 3/4 teaspoon salt, garlic, and red pepper flakes in large bowl; whisk in oil in slow, steady stream until smooth.

3. Add pasta and 1 tablespoon salt to boiling water. Cook until pasta is al dente and drain. Whisk dressing again to blend; add hot pasta, cooled broccoli, olives, and basil; toss to mix thoroughly. Cool to room temperature, adjust seasonings, and serve. (Can be covered with plastic wrap and refrigerated for 1 day; return to room temperature before serving.)

PASTA SALAD WITH FENNEL, RED ONIONS, AND SUN-DRIED TOMATOES

Grill or roast 2 large fennel bulbs and 2 large red onions according to chart directions; cool to room temperature. Follow recipe for Pasta Salad with Broccoli and Olives, substituting the cooked fennel and onions for the broccoli; ground black pepper to taste for hot red pepper flakes; and 1/2 cup oil-packed sun-dried tomatoes, sliced thin, for olives.

PASTA SALAD WITH EGGPLANT, TOMATOES, AND BASIL

Grill or broil 2 medium eggplants (about 1 pound, total) according to chart directions; cool to room temperature. Follow recipe for Pasta Salad with Broccoli and Olives, substituting the cooked eggplant and 2 large tomatoes, prepared according to chart directions, for the broccoli

and olives, and adding 1 medium garlic clove, minced, along with the basil.

PASTA SALAD WITH ASPARAGUS AND RED PEPPERS

Chives work particularly well with the asparagus and peppers, but you can substitute fresh mint, parsley, or basil.

Grill or roast 1 1/2 pounds asparagus and 3 large red peppers according to chart directions; cool to room temperature. Follow recipe for Pasta Salad with Broccoli and Olives, substituting the cooked asparagus and red peppers for the broccoli and olives; ground black pepper to taste for hot red pepper flakes; and 3 tablespoons snipped fresh chives for basil; and adding 1/3 cup grated Parmesan cheese.

Preparing Vegetables for Pasta Salad

The following list includes the vegetables I routinely add to salads. Grilling over a medium fire is my preferred cooking method, with the exceptions of broccoli and cauliflower, which are best blanched. Roasting is my second-choice cooking method for most of the vegetables, with the exception of eggplant, which is better broiled. When cool, cut vegetables into bite-size pieces if necessary. —J.B.

Vegetable	Preparation	Grilling Method	Stovetop or Oven Method
ASPARAGUS	Trim tough ends; toss with olive oil and salt and pepper to taste.	Grill until tender, and streaked with light grill marks, 5 to 7 minutes.	Roast in a 425-degree oven for 8 to 10 minutes, depending on thickness, shaking pan once halfway through the cooking time.
BROCCOLI/ CAULIFLOWER	Cut into bite-size florets.	Doesn't do well over live fire.	Blanch in boiling salted water until crisp-tender, about 2 minutes.
EGGPLANT	Cut into 1/2-inch-thick rounds; brush with olive oil to coat very lightly; toss with salt and pepper to taste.	Grill until marked with dark stripes on both sides, about 10 minutes.	Broil on baking sheet placed 4 inches from heating element, turning once, until tender and browned, about 7 minutes.
FENNEL	Cut off stalks and halve bulb through core; cut halves into 1/2-inch wedges; toss with olive oil and salt and pepper to taste.	Grill until tender and marked with dark stripes on both sides, about 15 minutes.	Roast in a 425-degree oven until tender and light brown on both sides, 15 to 17 minutes.
ONIONS	Peel and cut into 1/2-inch-thick rounds; toss with olive oil and salt and pepper to taste.	Grill until tender and marked with dark stripes on both sides, about 15 minutes.	Roast in a 425-degree oven until tender and light brown on both sides, about 15 minutes.
PEPPERS	Core, seed, and cut into 1 1/2-inch wedges; toss with olive oil and salt and pepper to taste.	Grill, using grill basket if you have one, until tender and lightly charred, about 8 minutes.	Roast in a 425-degree oven until tender and lightly browned, 15 to 17 minutes.
TOMATOES	Core, seed, and cut into 1/2-inch chunks.	Do not cook.	Do not cook.
ZUCCHINI	Cut lengthwise into 1/2-inch-thick strips; toss with olive oil and salt and pepper to taste.	Grill until tender and marked with dark stripes on both sides, about 10 minutes.	Roast in a 425-degree oven until tender and lightly browned on both sides, about 13 minutes.

Chefs' Vegetable Preparation Tips

When it comes to vegetables, there are some that can seem just too cumbersome, messy, or prone to pitfalls to prepare often. Even with the more straightforward vegetables it's common to wonder when carving with a knife: Is there an easier way? *Cook's* posed this question to chefs and cookbook authors across the country, who in turn shared some of their favorite tips for the quick and simple preparation of vegetables at home. By Maryellen Driscoll

SHARPENING PEELERS

Mary Sue Milliken and Susan Feniger have a quick method for restoring the edge of a dull vegetable peeler. Scrape the back side, between the blades, with the back tip of a paring knife to remove burrs. Then scrape the front side using the knife's back tip. Milliken and Feniger are chef-owners of the Los Angeles restaurant Border Grill and hosts of TVFN's "Too Hot Tamales."

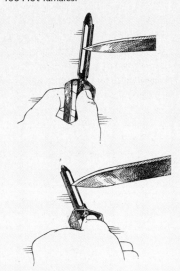

TAMING AND PEELING GARLIC

While attending John Ash's course on seasonal vegetarian cooking at the Culinary Institute of America in California's Napa Valley, one of our editors learned this tip for peeling garlic and slightly tempering its flavor. Toast the garlic cloves in a dry skillet on medium-high heat for about five minutes, shaking the skillet periodically to turn the cloves.

Remove the cloves from heat when the skins have begun to turn golden brown. After cooling, the once-sticky skins readily peel off. When testing this method, we also found that if you leave the cloves on the heat for about 15 minutes more, they soften to the creamy consistency of roasted garlic. Ash is the culinary director of Fetzer Vineyards and author of *From the Earth to the Table* (Dutton, 1995).

REMOVING BEET STAINS

To remove red beet stains from your cutting board or your hands, Julia Child recommends rubbing the stained area with salt, rinsing, then scrubbing with soap. She repeats the process until the stains are removed. Child is a world-renowned teacher, author, and cook.

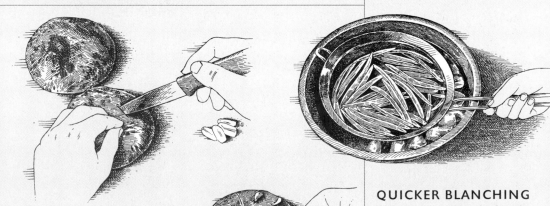

QUICKER BLANCHING

With green vegetables, shocking them in ice water after blanching is essential to preserving their color. To do so quickly, Norman Van Aken recommends laying a strainer, sieve, or perforated pan in the bowl of ice water so you don't have to fish for the vegetables when they are ready to be pulled out. Van Aken is the chef-owner of Norman's in Miami, Florida, and author of *Norman's New World Cuisine* (Random House, 1997).

FLAVORING PORTOBELLOS

Steve Raichlen has a simple technique for adding garlic and herb flavorings to portobello caps. Using the tip of a paring knife, he makes 10 to 12 narrow slits in the top of the cap and inserts a sliver of garlic and a strip of sage leaf into each slit. Raichlen is a Miami-based cooking instructor and author of many cookbooks, including *The Barbecue Bible* (Workman, 1998).

Illustration: John Burgoyne

CLEANING GREENS

To clean greens that tend to be sandy, such as kale, farm-stand spinach, whole heads of leafy lettuce, and arugula, the late Richard Sax recommended plunging them into a sink or dish pan of warm water. This relaxes the leaves, loosening the dirt for easier rinsing. The greens are then rinsed in a colander, crisped in several changes of cold water if limp, and dried in a salad spinner. Sax's most recent book is *Get In There & Cook* (Clarkson Potter, 1997), published posthumously.

SKINNING TOMATOES

During tomato harvest, when time to can batches of sauce is limited, David Hirsch freezes Roma and other medium-size tomatoes whole in a freezer bag. When it's time to retrieve a frozen tomato for a stew or sauce, he simply rubs off the skin by placing it under hot running tap water. Hirsch is a chef at the Moosewood Restaurant in Ithaca, New York, and author of *The Moosewood Restaurant Kitchen Garden* (Fireside, 1992).

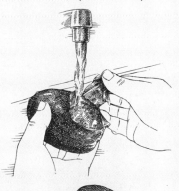

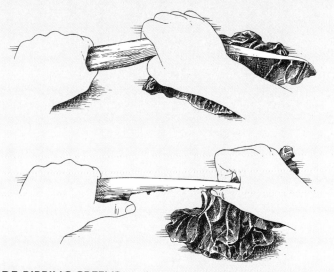

DE-RIBBING GREENS

To separate chard leaves, beet leaves, or large spinach leaves from their ribs, Steve Johnson loosely folds the leaf in half along the stem, grasps the folded leaf with one hand, and pulls it away from the rib. The leaf will separate cleanly and easily. Johnson is the chef and co-owner of The Blue Room in Cambridge, Massachusetts.

CUTTING SQUASH

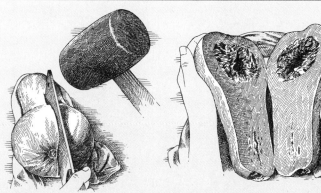

Deborah Madison uses a meat cleaver to cut through large, hard squashes. She places the cleaver lengthwise along the squash, then strikes the blunt edge of the cleaver with a mallet to drive it through and open the squash. (We recommend wrapping a damp cloth around the squash to hold it in place.) Madison is the founding chef at San Francisco's Green's restaurant and author of *Vegetarian Cooking for Everyone* (Broadway Books, 1997).

SEEDING ZUCCHINI

For easy removal of seeds when halving and stuffing zucchini or eggplant, Paula Wolfert rolls the vegetable with slight pressure under the palms of her hands to soften the insides and loosen the seeds. She then halves the vegetables lengthwise and scoops out the seeds with a spoon. Paula Wolfert is the author of many Mediterranean-based cookbooks, including *Mediterranean Grains & Greens* (HarperCollins, August 1998).

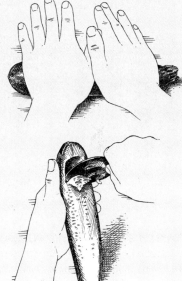

GARLIC PUREE IN SMALL AMOUNTS

We like Alice Water's solution for pureeing small amounts of raw garlic, as for a vinaigrette. Hold a fork with its tines resting face down on a cutting board. Rub a peeled clove of garlic rapidly back and forth against the tines close to their points. Mash any leftover large chunks with the fork turned over. Waters is the owner of Chez Panisse in Berkeley, California, and author of many cookbooks, including *Chez Panisse Vegetables* (Harper, 1996).

Quick Refrigerator Fruit Jams

For jam that jells easily and has real fruit flavor, make small batches
and use far less sugar than you think you need.

⇒ BY RUSS PARSONS ⇐

Jam is the original three-ingredient recipe: fruit, sugar, and lemon juice. Its cooking method is equally simple: one pan, high heat. But, as almost anyone who has tried to turn a lug of fruit into jam, jelly, or preserves can testify, this does not mean that making them is easy. I know, because I've been making jams and preserves for more than 15 years. I still remember my first batch of strawberry preserves. I was so proud when I had it bottled and sealed—and so disappointed when I opened the first jar and found nothing more than graying berries stuck in sweet water.

That was not an isolated instance. I can't give a good reason for my repeated failures, and the only way I can explain my persistence is by saying that it was like playing golf. The good jams were so good that the bad ones paled in comparison. And there were many good ones. To my taste, the perfect jam is lightly sweetened and tastes of fresh fruit. It doesn't need to be firmly set, the way commercial jams are. In fact it can even be spoonable as long as it isn't syrupy.

Despite my leniency about texture, I still found making jams a treacherous business. While there are some excellent recipe books that include preserving, very few set out the hows and whys of the process. If you want to deviate from the exact recipe, you are suddenly lost in unexplored territory.

Curious, I did a little homework. Jam-making, it turns out, hinges on a very delicate chemical balance of sugar, acid, and pectin that changes with each fruit. The trickiest part of the equation is balancing the pectin and the sugar. You can take a shortcut and use commercial pectin, but you need to follow the manufacturer's recipes to

These quick jams must be refrigerated and will last about two weeks.

the letter—recipes written by cooks with different palates than mine. I find the resulting jams both too sweet and too chewy.

Without artificial supplements, you need to consider the quality of the fruit very carefully. Some fruits are naturally high in pectin: Plums and apples (especially when underripe) come to mind. Some fruits are low, including strawberries and apricots. Fruits that are lower in pectin take more sugar to jell. Interestingly, this includes fruit that is very ripe—pectin content declines as the cell walls break during ripening—which helps to explain some of my early failures. Temperature is tricky, too. The jellying point is generally considered to be 220 degrees (or 8 degrees above boiling, depending on your altitude). But when I tried cooking to temperature, success was far from certain. I'd sit there—sometimes for as much as an hour—staring at my jelly thermometer, watching the mercury slowly inch upward. 216. 217. A little more, a little more. 218. I think you can, I think you can. 220! And sometimes, even then, the jelly wouldn't jell.

Then last summer I had a jam-

making epiphany. I'd like to claim that it came about as a result of rigorously controlled tests and continued experimentation. In reality, like so many revelations, it fell in my lap.

It came in two parts. The first occurred when I was working with a case of nectarines I'd picked up from a local farmer. I didn't have a recipe for nectarine preserves, so I looked, as I so often do, in Jeanne Lesem's *Preserving Today* (now reprinted in paperback by Owl Books under the title *Preserving in Today's Kitchen*). In the particular recipe I chose, two pounds of fruit were simmered in a big batch with the sugar, then left to stand overnight. (In the interest of saving time, this overnight rest was eliminated in the final recipe.)The next day I processed them in three- to four-cup lots.

This batch jelled effortlessly, almost eerily so. After the first boiling, I thought something was weird—the jam felt like it was already thickening. Sure enough, when I came back the next morning, it had cooled to a nice, light set. I quickly cooked it off. Within five minutes the jam was falling from my spoon in sheets, which is exactly the texture I was looking for. Disbelieving, I tried it again. The second time worked perfectly as well. And so did the third. Obviously something was different. I called my friend Sylvia Thompson, a wonderful cook and the author of *The Kitchen Garden Cookbook*. She said she'd had the same experience and that it had to do with cooking in smaller quantities.

A bulb lit up, though dimly, to be sure. The secret to Lesem's recipe had to be the quantity of jam in the batch. I'd always looked at canning as a semi-industrial hobby, the goal being to process as much fruit as possible. When my lemon tree was in full production, I'd make Meyer lemon marmalade in massive 8- to 10-cup quantities. Here I was dealing with less than half that amount.

I was hard pressed to explain why the size of the batch mattered. The ratios of pectin, sugar, and acid, after all, remained essentially the same. My best guess was that it comes down to temperature distribution. When you're pushing eight cups of jam past the boiling point, I reasoned, some of it

Preparing Fruit for Jam

The amounts of sugar in this chart are for one pound of fruit. Of course, since the jam will jell with various amounts of sugar, you may want to increase the amount slightly depending on the sweetness of the fruit.

Fruit (1 pound)	Preparation	Sugar (minimum amount)
STRAWBERRIES	Wash, hull, and slice thin	1 cup
APRICOTS	Peel, pit, halve, and slice very thin	1 cup
PLUMS	Wash, pit, halve, and slice very thin	1 cup plus 2 TB
PEACHES/NECTARINES	Peel, pit, halve, and slice very thin	1¼ cups

is bound to reach the desired temperature before the rest of it. This is not, after all, a uniform solution, being a combination of chunks of fruit and thickened liquid. So when some of the jam has reached 220 degrees, some of it is still lagging a degree or two or even more behind—enough to cause a problem. Conversely, by the time all of it has reached 220 degrees, some of it is much hotter; this is bad, too, since overcooking breaks down the support network of pectin fibers that we recognize as gel. The pectin turns to pectinic acid and then to pectic acid, which will not form a gel.

Dr. Elizabeth Andress, an author of the USDA's *Complete Guide to Home Canning* and a food-safety specialist at the University of Georgia, gave me an additional reason why the prolonged boiling necessary for larger batches of jam can cause problems. Heat converts table sugar (sucrose) into two different sugars (dextrose and levulose). The rate of this conversion is influenced by the heating time, the temperature, and the pH value of the solution. You need to achieve just the right balance between the sucrose and the two newly formed sugars. Too much heat will upset the balance and release water, which interferes with the gelling of pectin (*see* "Jammin' Science," above).

Less scientific but equally important is that when you're cooking with smaller amounts, the fine gradations of texture are more apparent. It is

much easier to see when three cups of jelly are thickening than when eight cups or more are. I tried to use a thermometer to see what temperatures the jams were reaching, but the jam was simply too shallow to be accurately measured.

I much prefer a different method for determining doneness, which I employ when the jam mixture begins to look syrupy. Chill a bowl in the freezer or suspend it over ice water. When you think the jam has jelled, spoon some of the liquid into the bowl and allow it to set for 30 seconds, then tip the bowl 45 degrees to one side. If it is done, the jam should be a soft gel that moves slightly, rather than a thin liquid that runs to the other side of the bowl.

Testing the Discovery

Emboldened by my discoveries, I embarked on a summer of rampant preserving. I made jam from strawberries, nectarines, raspberries, blackberries, peaches, and plums, and every one was a success. Then I began playing with the formula, reducing the sugar from the 60 to 65 percent recommended by most jam-making experts. Usually the jams still worked, though the set was noticeably soft—more spoonable than spreadable—which prompted me to wonder just how important the ratio of fruit to sugar really was. How much, I wondered, could I reduce the sugar and still end up with something that was recognizeable as jam.

I bought three pounds each of plums, peaches, apricots, and strawberries. I mixed a pound of each with varying quantities of sugar, starting with one cup and increasing the total amount to 1¾ cups in quarter-cup increments, then cooked them. For the strawberries and apricots, the best texture came from one cup of sugar. For the peaches, it was 1¼ cups. For the plums, one cup plus two tablespoons seemed the ideal amount. The odd thing was, though, that all the jams jelled—success was only a matter of degree.

Of course, texture isn't the only quality affected when you vary the amount of sugar. Taste changes, too. Interestingly, though my blind tasters consistently favored the jams made with the least sugar, they didn't say it was because they were less sweet. What they said instead was that the lower-sugar jams tasted more like fresh fruit. To be sure, even the sweetest of these wasn't as sweet as most com-

mercial mixtures, given that the ideal commercial ratio is 60 to 65 percent sugar and some of my recipes had as little as 33 percent sugar, not including the sugar in the fruit. With almost half as much sugar as most commercial jams, it is no wonder they had a brighter fruit taste.

A final advantage of this recipe is that using such small amounts of fruit allows you to make jam without having to worry about canning. This recipe makes about 2½ cups of jam—just enough to store in the refrigerator for the couple of weeks it lasts.

EASY FRESH FRUIT JAM
MAKES 2½ CUPS

The jam will continue to thicken as it cools, so err on the side of undercooking. Overcooked jam that is dark, thick, and smells of caramelized sugar cannot be saved. Note: Because of its reduced sugar amounts, this jam cannot be canned.

- 1　pound prepared fruit (*see* chart, page 18, for preparation), about 3 cups
    sugar (*see* chart, page 18, for amounts)
- 2　tablespoons juice from 1 lemon

1. Set small bowl over larger bowl of ice water; set aside.

2. In 10- or 12-inch skillet, bring fruit, sugar, and lemon juice to boil over medium-high heat, stirring occasionally. Reduce heat to medium and cook, stirring constantly and skimming foam as necessary, until mixture begins to look syrupy and thickens slightly, about 5 minutes for strawberries and apricots and 8 to 9 minutes for plums, peaches, and nectarines; remove from heat. Spoon ½ teaspoon fruit mixture into bowl over ice water; allow to set for 30 seconds. Tip bowl 45 degrees to one side; jam should be a soft gel that moves slightly. If mixture is liquid and runs to side of bowl, return skillet to heat and cook, stirring constantly, 1 to 2 minutes longer; then repeat test. Cool jam to room temperature before serving. (It will keep, covered and refrigerated, for up to two weeks.)

Russ Parsons is a food columnist for the *Los Angeles Times*.

TESTING | THE ACID TEST FOR JAM CONSISTENCY

After resting on a chilled bowl for 30 seconds, just-cooked jam should be a soft gel that moves slightly when tipped to one side (right), rather than a thin liquid that runs (left), or a thick gel that does not move (center).

The Problem with Fruit Crisps

After testing oats, corn flakes, cookie crumbs, Grape Nuts, graham crackers, and nuts, we found a simple way to put the crunch back in crisps.

≥ BY CHRISTOPHER KIMBALL WITH JEANNE MAGUIRE ≤

Simply stated, there is seldom anything crisp about a crisp. This simple baked dessert, made from sweetened fruit topped with a combination of sugar, butter, and flour, almost invariably comes out of the oven with a soggy top crust. A few recipes go so far as to refer to this classic dish as a crunch, a term that has no bearing on the flat, dull, overly sweetened crumble that serves as a streusel. The task, therefore, was quite simple. I wanted to put the crunch back in crisp.

As a first step, the *Cook's* test kitchen baked one crisp from a popular all-purpose cookbook and one from a well-regarded fruit cookbook. Although both used the classic, simple combination of sugar, flour, and butter for their topping, neither produced satisfactory results. The all-purpose recipe produced a very light, sandy-colored topping that was not at all crisp, and the fruit book's version was almost runny. Additional testing revealed that this simple combination of ingredients, regardless of proportions, could not produce a crispy topping.

My first thought was to test oats. When I wrote *The Cook's Bible* two years ago, I used an oat/flour topping for my fruit crisp recipe. After much testing, I had concluded that a 1:1 ratio of flour to oats was best. When I went back and made the recipe again recently, though, I found myself disappointed with the flour/oatmeal topping because it was chewy rather than crispy. In fact, I wondered if I wouldn't prefer baking the apples without any topping at all.

In search of a better, crunchier topping, I moved on to test a variety of other ingredients. My first set of tests included corn flakes, cookie crumbs made from vanilla wafers, graham cracker crumbs, and Grape Nuts. The corn flakes were crispy but made for an odd taste combination with the baked apple mixture; the cookie crumbs were also crispy but they were too sweet; the graham cracker crumbs were relatively crispy but their flavor was unwelcome on the fruit; and

Apples, pears, and stone fruits such as peaches all work perfectly with this topping.

Grape Nuts created the effect of chewing on tiny pebbles.

Obviously I had to look for other possibilities. I excluded cake crumbs because very few home cooks have extra slices of cake sitting around the house. I also left out bread crumbs since fruit baked with a bread-crumb topping is usually called a Betty or a crunch, not a crisp. Almost out of options, I once again reviewed my crisp recipe from *The Cook's Bible*. This time I noticed that I had included a variation that used nuts instead of oatmeal. When I tested it again, this version turned out to be the winner, just the topping I was searching for. The nuts not only produced a crispy streusel, they also added a pleasant complementary flavor to the underlying fruit. I preferred pecans and almonds to walnuts, since to me the latter had a slighty bitter aftertaste.

Mixing Butter, Choosing the Right Sugar

The next question was one of technique. It turned out that how you cut the butter into the flour is crucial to creating a good crisp topping.

When making a pie pastry, the flour-butter mixture should resemble a coarse meal. With a crisp, however, the topping should be thoroughly worked into the flour until the mixture has the consistency of crumbly wet sand. However, overprocessing will result in the mixture clumping together.

This is one task that is ideally suited to the food processor. I found it best to use three 4-second pulses to combine the flour and butter and then five to six 1-second pulses once the nuts are added. For this method, the butter must be very cold, taken straight from the refrigerator. If, however, you do not own a food processor, the mixture can be worked by hand. In this event, you want the butter to be cool but slightly softened. Unlike with pie pastry, if the flour is not thoroughly coated with butter, the streusel will be floury and not at all crisp. On the other hand, if the butter is melted (and we tried this method), the topping turns to mud.

The next issue was the sugar. Some recipes use only granulated sugar, some use only brown sugar, and others use a mixture of the two. We made crisps using each. The granulated-sugar version had little flavor, the dark-brown-sugar version was too strong, and the light-brown version seemed a bit soggy. We found that half granulated and half light brown was best. It was crisp but also had a nice flavor. The ratio of sugar to flour was also crucial. Too much sugar, and the topping was hard and overly sweet. Too little, and the topping was bland and floury-tasting, and did not hold together. The best ratio turned out to be ½ cup sugar to 6 tablespoons flour.

The best way to sweeten and thicken the fruit was also problematic. Many recipes use no sweetener and simply place a layer of very sweet streusel on top of the fruit and then bake it. The problem with this method is that fruit cooked without sugar often has a lackluster flavor; this is especially true of tart apples. It is much like boiling pasta in unsalted water and expecting the sauce to carry the flavor—you simply end up with dull, unsalted pasta. On the other hand, I found that it is best to keep the fruit mixture on the tart side to provide a nice contrast to the sweeter topping. So for eight cups of fruit, I deemed one-third cup of sugar optimal; with six cups, I liked one-fourth cup of sugar.

Although this recipe cries out for a juicy filling (since juices carry a great deal of flavor), I decided to try using a thickener. I chose Minute Tapioca because in a prior series of tests with baked fruit desserts I had found that it absorbs liquid nicely without leaving a gummy texture or a starchy aftertaste. But two tablespoons of tapioca proved too much, because there were almost no juices left in the pan after baking. One tablespoon was better, but no thickener at all was best. Letting the juices flow resulted in a dessert with a much brighter taste. Only plums, which tend to be very juicy, required a tablespoon of tapioca for thickening.

I also tested baking temperatures, starting at 325 degrees and running up to 425 degrees in 25-degree increments. At 325 degrees, the streusel never browned satisfactorily. At 350 degrees, the filling was overcooked by the time the topping browned and crisped properly. At the two higher temperatures, the fruit never cooked all the way through before the topping started to burn. The 375-degree oven was just right, delivering cooked fruit and a nicely browned topping. In a final refinement, I found that raising the oven temperature to 400 degrees for the last five minutes of baking produced a slightly crispier streusel.

FRUIT CRISP
SERVES 6

To make a larger crisp that serves 10, double all the ingredients, use a 13 x 9-inch baking pan, and bake for 55 minutes at 375 degrees, without increasing the oven temperature. If making an apple crisp, we recommend equal quantities of Granny Smith and McIntosh apples. Peel, core, and cut apples and pears into one-inch chunks. Peel, pit, and cut nectarines, peaches, and plums into half-inch wedges. If using plums, add one tablespoon quick-cooking tapioca to the fruit mixture. Half a teaspoon of grated fresh ginger makes a nice flavor addition to all the fruits.

Topping Mixture

- 6 tablespoons all-purpose flour
- 1/4 cup light brown sugar, packed
- 1/4 cup granulated sugar
- 1/4 teaspoon ground cinnamon
- 1/4 teaspoon ground nutmeg
- 1/4 teaspoon salt
- 5 tablespoons unsalted butter, cut into 1/2-inch pieces and chilled
- 3/4 cups pecans or whole almonds, chopped coarse (or chopped fine if mixing topping by hand) (about 3/4 cup)

- 2 1/2–3 pounds apples, nectarines, peaches, pears or plums (6 cups cut)
- 1/4 cup granulated sugar
- 1 1/2 tablespoons juice and 1/2 teaspoon grated zest from one lemon.

1. *For the topping:* Place flour, brown sugar, sugar, cinnamon, nutmeg, and salt in food processor workbowl fitted with steel blade. Add chilled butter and pulse until mixture moves from dry sand-like appearance with large lumps of butter to a coarse cornmeal texture, about three 4-second bursts. Add nuts and pulse until mixture resembles crumbly sand (*see* center photo, below), about five 1-second bursts. Do not overprocess or mixture will take on a smooth, cookie-dough-like texture. (To mix by hand, allow butter pieces to sit at room temperature for 5 minutes. Meanwhile, mix flour, brown sugar, granulated sugar, cinnamon, nutmeg, and salt in medium bowl. Add butter; toss to coat. Pinch butter chunks and dry mixture between fingertips until mixture looks like crumbly wet sand. Add nuts and toss to distribute evenly. Do not overmix.) Refrigerate mixture while preparing fruit, at least 15 minutes.
2. Toss cut fruit, sugar, lemon juice, and zest (along with 1 tablespoon quick-cooking tapioca if using plums as fruit) in medium bowl.
3. Adjust oven rack to lower-middle position and heat oven to 375 degrees.

TESTING | GETTING THE TOPPING RIGHT

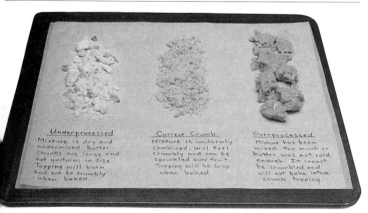

Underprocessed topping is dry and powdery with large, uneven chunks of butter (left). When properly processed, the topping will be crumbly and evenly mixed (center). Overprocessed topping is so smooth that it resembles cookie dough (right).

Crisps, Crunches, Crumbles, Betties, and Veiled Maidens

There are lots of old-fashioned desserts that consist of fruit baked with a topping of bread, cake crumbs, flour and butter, oats, crackers, and the like. In the days when home cooks were frugal, these easy desserts, based on older European recipes, used stale leftovers to vary the texture and flavor of baked fruit. One such old-world dish is called a veiled maiden or "Country Lass with A Veil" and is pretty much a Betty, or a crunch, made with fruit and browned bread crumbs. It often includes a bit of jam. The earliest version of this recipe I have found comes from Denmark.

Just how these topped fruit desserts differ from each other is not entirely clear. A crisp, for example, is fruit baked with a topping made from butter, sugar, and flour. However, many other variations qualify as crisps, including those with topping ingredients such as nuts, cake or cracker crumbs, or cornflakes. A crunch, often confused with a crisp by many authors, is, according to *The Joy of Cooking*, fruit sandwiched between two layers of buttered bread crumbs. A Betty, however, is fruit baked with buttered bread crumbs, not necessarily sandwiched between two layers, which makes it pretty close to a crunch. (However, I have seen recipes for Betties that do call for a top and bottom layer of bread crumbs.) A crumble, for which there seems to be some consensus, is a crisp that uses oats along with the flour.

All these definitions aside, common usage suggests that crisps have a top layer of streusel, crumbles are crisps that use oats, and crunches and Betties are layered with bread crumbs. —C.K.

Scrape fruit mixture with rubber spatula into 8-inch square (2 quart) baking pan or 9-inch round deep dish pie plate. Distribute chilled topping evenly over fruit; bake for 40 minutes. Increase oven temperature to 400 degrees; bake until fruit is bubbling and topping is deep golden brown, about 5 minutes longer. Serve warm or at room temperature.

APPLE–RASPBERRY CRISP

Follow recipe for Apple Crisp, reducing amount of cut apples to 5 cups (about 3 medium Granny Smith and 2 medium McIntosh) and adding 1 cup rinsed fresh raspberries to fruit mixture.

PEACH–BLUEBERRY CRISP

Follow recipe for Peach Crisp, reducing amount of cut peaches to 5 cups (about 5 medium peaches) and adding 1 cup rinsed fresh blueberries and 1 tablespoon quick-cooking tapioca to fruit mixture.

Texture Prevails Over Flavor in Tuna Tasting

Tasters turn up their noses at mushy chunk light despite its stronger tuna flavor.

=BY MARYELLEN DRISCOLL=

In most of our blind taste tests, taste has predictably reigned. That is, despite the many other characteristics that we assess—aroma, mouthfeel, appearance, texture—if it tastes good, it ranks well. No tough math.

Yet when it came to canned tuna, texture set the pace. Tasters were less concerned with flavor. But how it settled between the teeth—could you chew it, or just gum it?—determined their partiality. As one taster put it: "I can tolerate a bland tuna better than a mushy tuna. If I want a stronger flavor, I'll buy canned sardines or salmon."

As an inexpensive, readily available source of protein, canned tuna took off during World War I and really came into its own as a postwar lunchtime favorite. Today it is not only among the top-selling items in supermarkets, it is also the most frequently eaten seafood. The average American eats 8.5 cans of tuna a year, according to the U.S. Department of Commerce. And really, there is no mystery as to why. It's cheap; it's healthy; it's an easy sandwich filler; it keeps—for years and years; and it's almost always on sale.

We set out to determine which supermarket brands would make the best tuna salad, since that is its most popular use. We conducted our blind taste tests with two separate tasting panels. Our first was comprised of staff from *Cook's* and from the magazine's parent company, Boston Common Press. The second included staff from The East Coast Grill, in Cambridge, Massachusetts, where the day's catch can range from wahoo to scup.

Because there are a number of national brands of canned tuna, each of which makes several varieties, we decided to narrow the tasting down to the two top-selling varieties sold by the five major national brands—the chunk light and solid white varieties packed in water and made by Bumble Bee, Chicken of the Sea, Geisha, StarKist, and 3 Diamonds.

White vs. Light

Chunk light was the less expensive of the two varieties in our tasting, costing about 41 cents a can less than solid white. This may explain why it is also the top-selling type of canned tuna. Certainly our tasting results do not explain it, since tasters found only one of the five chunk light samples acceptable. (*See* "Tasting Canned Tunas," page 27.) In general, chunk light tuna is made of skipjack tuna or yellowfin tuna or both; skipjack contributes a stronger flavor than yellowfin. These two tuna species are found in warm waters all around the world.

While our tasters were not wild about the more pronounced flavor of chunk light (which often included an aftertaste of the tin can), what really upset the balance between the white and light tunas was the texture. White tuna you could eat, even pierce, with a fork; the light version was more appropriately scooped with a spoon. When blended with mayonnaise, the small flakes of chunk light tuna quickly broke down even further, taking on a texture that reminded many tasters of cat food. It is unusual to find a light tuna sold in solid form because it is lower in fat and more susceptible to breaking down into small pieces than white tuna when exposed to the duress of pressure cooking. Many tasters not only disliked the lack of chew this offered, but also found that the small shreds of fish held moisture too well, which created a sopping, mushy consistency.

Solid white, on the other hand, consists of large meaty chunks. In accordance with the U.S. Food and Drug Administration's standards, it is made up exclusively of albacore tuna. Because albacore do not swim in tight schools like yellowfin or skipjack, they have to be caught individually by lines dragging behind a slow-moving boat. This limits harvesting large quantities and, because of market forces, makes this a more expensive canned tuna—about $1.27 per six-ounce can.

Though known as "white" tuna, albacore can vary from nearly white to light pink or even beige. Its fat content can also vary, typically ranging from 1 to 5 percent. (The nutrition table on the can's label will indicate the percentage.) The amount of fat depends upon where the fish are caught—both the region and the depth. Despite these natural variances, tuna manufacturers are able to produce a relatively consistent product through quality control and special processing methods. Some of the white tuna products promote themselves as "Fancy Albacore" or "Premium Albacore." This is merely a marketing strategy. They do not differ.

With certain brands favored more than others, solid white was the tuna of choice among tasters for its mild flavor, milky-white appearance, and full flakes. (We broke down the large pieces with a fork before serving them to tasters so their consistency in the salad would be similar to chunky tuna.) However, it should be noted that 75 percent of our tasters were from New England, where white tuna sells more than in any other region, according to a representative of StarKist. She did not know why. One possibility is that New Englanders are more accustomed to mild-flavored, white, cold-water fish, such as haddock or scrod. Even so, when the scores of the non-New Englanders (mostly from the Midwest) were averaged separately, the results were consistent with the overall tasting.

Parenthetically, all the tunas in our tasting displayed a dolphin-safe logo, even though the danger of dolphins being caught in fishing nets and drowning applies only to light tuna—specifically, to yellowtail caught in the eastern Pacific Ocean, near Mexico and the United States. Only in this area is this species known to swim in schools beneath schools of dolphin.

Canned Tuna Breakdown

At a local supermarket we found that just one brand of tuna offered seven different varieties. With so many choices, it's easy to feel confused. Not only are there the options of white or light meat packed in oil or in water, but also there are various consistencies or "packs" to consider. Here's a quick rundown on the differences in how they are packed.

Solid tuna consists of one large piece of loin meat. If the segment is too small to fit perfectly into the can, a piece of another segment can be added. Free flakes broken from the loins can also be added but cannot exceed 18 percent of the total contents.

Chunk tuna consists of several pieces, more than half of which are required to be larger than 1/2 inch. The rest can consist of flakes, which sometimes makes the consistency mushy. Chunk is the main form in which light-meat tuna is sold, although there are some chunk white-meat tunas, too.

Flaked or grated tuna consists primarily of bits of meat smaller than 1/2 inch. It is less common than solid or chunk pack.

TASTING CANNED TUNAS

For our blind taste test we selected the best-selling canned tuna products sold in supermarkets nationwide. We drained five cans of each tuna and lightly blended them with mayonnaise. Large pieces from the solid white samples were broken down with a fork to a chunky consistency. No seasonings were added. Our first tasting was attended by 14 staff members from *Cook's* and its parent company, Boston Common Press. The second tasting was attended by 11 staffers from The East Coast Grill in Cambridge, Massachusetts.

RECOMMENDED

StarKist Solid White Tuna in Water NEWPORT, KENTUCKY

➤ $1.25 for six ounces

This tuna had it all. It showcased a "high quality (white) appearance" with a "big chunk consistency" that was flaky, chewy and yet firm — "doesn't compress into pastiness when being eaten." This tuna was unique among the typically bland white solids for carrying a subtle fishy flavor with a mild "tang." As one taster noted, "Most balanced flavor; true tuna taste." Many tasters preferred this tuna because it seemed to be of "high quality." A few, however, complained that it was slightly gritty.

3 Diamonds Solid White Tuna in Water LOS ANGELES, CALIFORNIA

➤ $1.19 for six ounces

This runner-up tuna was popular with tasters for visual and textural qualities reminiscent of the leading tuna: "large, solid (white) chunks." The flavor was clean though repeatedly described as "bland"—which many tasters did not consider much of a fault.

Chicken of the Sea Solid White Tuna in Water SAN DIEGO, CALIFORNIA

➤ $1.19 for six ounces

This tuna scored right on the tail of 3 Diamonds solid white. The flavor was described as "mild" to "bland" and somewhat salty. The texture held strong appeal—"firm," "meaty," "steak-like." And, as usual with the albacore tunas, tasters liked its appearance. "This had no terrible flaws," said one taster.

Bumble Bee Solid White Tuna in Water SAN DIEGO, CALIFORNIA

➤ $1.25 for six ounces

There was no clear consensus on this tuna except that it was salty. Some tasters liked the texture; some did not. Some liked the taste; some did not. Yet in the ranking for overall liking, it fared well. One taster amply put it, "Almost great." This tuna consisted of firm, chewy, "steak-y" chunks of fish, but they were on the sawdust side of dry.

Geisha Solid White Tuna in Water NEW YORK, NEW YORK

➤ $1.47 for six ounces

This tuna stayed above water with tasters primarily because it was a snowy white albacore tuna. But within this category, it was the least desirable. By those who were after a meek tuna fish, it was well liked, although a number of tasters complained that it had a canned flavor. It was downgraded for being dry, almost "chalky," but redeemed for consisting of big pieces of fish. "Tastes forgettable," one taster commented. Another concluded, "Not bad. Bland. I'd eat it."

Geisha Chunk Light Tuna in Water NEW YORK, NEW YORK

➤ 85 cents for six ounces

If light tuna is your preference (for reasons of flavor or affordability), this is the tuna to grab. Most agreed with the taster who wrote, "I don't usually like light tuna, but this is good tuna." Its saving grace was its texture: "You can chew this one instead of just gumming it." Tasters found it "mushy but not watery" and "tender and delicate, not dry or rubbery." Characteristic of light tunas, its flavor was assertively fishy, yet tasters did not seem to mind it here. Flavor comments included: "This is pretty tasty tuna," "assertive, you know what you're eating," and "strong-tasting but not unpleasant."

NOT RECOMMENDED

Chicken of the Sea Chunk Light Tuna in Water SAN DIEGO, CALIFORNIA

➤ 79 cents for six ounces

Think school lunches — on nonpizza days. "Cafeteria-style tuna that you could serve with an ice cream scoop" was one taster's response. This tuna scored better in terms of flavor than texture despite sour notes and metallic off flavors. That's because tasters found it not only "mushy" but "watery," "stringy," and "gritty."

Bumble Bee Chunk Light Tuna in Water SAN DIEGO, CALIFORNIA

➤ 99 cents for six ounces

Two tasters loved this tuna; the rest were anything but charmed. One remarked after the tasting that she suspected it was included in the tasting as a "punishment." This sopping wet, pinkish-gray tuna was beyond mush. "Water squirts out when you chew," observed one taster. And it did. Many noted a chemical-like off flavor. All in all, said one taster, "This has a strong, objectionable flavor coupled with low eye appeal and lots of wetness."

StarKist Chunk Light Tuna in Water NEWPORT, KENTUCKY

➤ 89 cents for six ounces

Sorry, Charlie. Another soggy flop among the "light" contenders. "Paté texture is a turn-off," said one taster. While true to the categorical tin-can aftertaste of chunk light tuna, its flavor was otherwise uncharacteristically drab. "If you blinded me I couldn't tell you what this is," wrote one taster. Some tasters noted unusual off flavors, like canned milk, anchovies, and mackerel.

3 Diamonds Chunk Light Tuna in Water LOS ANGELES, CALIFORNIA

➤ 79 cents for six ounces

Tasters found the texture of this tuna inconsistent. One bite was that of mush, the next of dry, thick chunks. The bitter taste evoked tin cans instead of fish. Tasters had a lot to bark about: "Thumbs down—way down." "Who would think tuna could taste so much like so nothing?" "The first bite was shocking — and so was the last."

Which Pie Plate Works Best?

Pyrex, that old American standard, proves its mettle when tested against everything from aluminum to ceramic.

⇒ BY ADAM RIED WITH SUSAN LOGOZZO AND ANNE YAMANAKA ⇐

While washing dishes a few weeks ago, wet soapy hands, a moment's distraction, and a hard-glazed kitchen sink cost me my glass pie plate. Later, as I stood in the store aisle reaching for another glass dish to replace it, I hesitated. To the left was an aluminum pie plate; to the right, a steel plate with holes in the bottom; and on the shelf below, a gorgeous ceramic model. There were more choices than I'd ever noticed before, which raised the question: "Might another plate prove superior to my old standby, Pyrex?" I turned to the test kitchen to sort out this issue.

From local cookware stores and supermarkets and well-known mail order catalogs, I culled 10 pie plates to test. All the plates were approximately nine inches from the inside edge of the rim to the opposite inside edge. Their depths were around 1½ inches and their sidewalls sloped. Materials from which they were made included clear ovenproof glass, glazed ceramic, heavy foil, aluminum, tinned steel, stainless steel, and nonstick coated steel. Several of the plates had unusual features, such as trough-like "juice saver" or fluted rims; on one, a ¾-inch extended rim at 9 and 3 o'clock formed integral handles, and on another, the bottom had ⅛-inch perforations that were supposed to allow more heat in to brown the bottom crust better. Prices ranged from a low end of $1.99 for three disposable foil plates to $29.00 for a heavy, glazed French ceramic dish.

A Tight Race

The tests were straightforward. First, we baked empty pie shells using the recipe from our September/October 1997 article "The Secrets of Prebaking Pie Shells." Ideally, we wanted crusts to be an even nut-brown color on both the sides and the bottoms.

With careful inspection, much comparison, and extensive discussion, the visual and tactile differences among the crusts became noticeable enough for us to assess and compare the plates. The Pyrex came closest to our ideal, browning the shell deeply and consistently, although it was not that far ahead of the other contenders since all the plates browned and crisped the crust. Some plates, however, including the Kaiser and the Ekco, did so very unevenly, and were downgraded for it. Nonetheless, the differences between those ranked good, fair, and acceptable were far from dramatic.

Ironically, in our second test, in which we filled raw pie shells with cherry pie filling and streusel topping, the differences between the crusts were even more difficult to detect than when we'd baked them empty. The sides of the crusts generally came out better than the bottoms, the worst of which—baked in E·Z Foil and the perforated and solid-bottomed Chicago Metallic Village Baker pans—showed very little hint of either browning or crisping. But even the best-baked bottom crusts—those baked in the Pyrex, Mirro, Ekco, and Progressive—were not great; in fact, they were limp and pale. From testing we did for the "All-Season Apple Pie" story in the November/December 1997 issue, we knew that partially prebaking the bottom crust, as well as trying to seal it with egg wash or bread crumbs, offered little promise of improvement. What we did try was moving the oven racks. We had baked our initial round of cherry pies on a rack positioned in the lower third of the oven. For the next round, we dropped the rack to the bottom position and found that all the bottom crusts improved, although not enough to change the ranking of the plates.

Minor Features Make the Difference

Because performance differences were so subtle, we turned to other characteristics of the pans to help us cement our impressions. First we considered the rim, which should be wide and sturdy enough to support a fluted edge; wider rims also make the plates easier to handle. The Pyrex and the Emile Henry ceramic, each with ½-inch rims, and the Progressive, with a ⅞-inch channeled rim, took top honors over the other plates, which had ⅜-inch rims. The Progressive's rim was ugly, but it successfully caught most of the fruit juices that would have dripped into the oven. The Ekco rim extended at either end to form ¾-inch tab handles,

The Pie Plates We Tested

BEST PIE PLATE
Corning Pyrex Originals
Performed well on all tests, has wide rim and advantage of being see-through.

Progressive Professional Quality Non-Stick
Extra-wide channeled rim is a definite plus; browned very evenly.

Mirro Comet
Browned and crisped well in blind baking test, but not when filled with fruit.

Chicago Metallic Bakers Heritage SilverStone No-Stick Perforated
Didn't brown as well as top pans.

Ekco Baker's Secret Non-Stick
Great for fruit-filled pie, poor for blind baking.

Emile Henry Le Potier
Pretty pan turned in a spotty performance.

Chicago Metallic Village Baker Commercial Weight Perforated
Left the bottom crust raw in baked filled pie.

Kaiser Backform
Overbrowned blind-baked crust, left center pale on filled pie.

Chicago Metallic Village Baker Commercial Weight
Browning action was at best uneven.

E·Z Foil Disposable Deep Pie Pan
Filled shell was disastrous due to flimsy aluminum and poor browning.

RATING PIE PLATES

We tested 10 pie plates according to the criteria listed below. Because performance differences were most apparent when baking unfilled pie shells, commonly called blind baking (for which we used the recipe from *Cook's* September/October 1997 article "The Secrets of Prebaking Pie Shells"), we placed greater emphasis on this test than on the filled pie shell test. For the latter test, shells were filled with 4½ cups canned cherry pie filling and 1½ cups streusel crumb topping and baked at 400 degrees for 50 minutes. The unfilled pie shells and the first round of fruit pies were baked in the same oven in our test kitchen, with the rack positioned in the lower third of the oven; a second round of fruit pies was baked with the oven rack in the very bottom position. Pie plates are listed in order of preference, and testers' comments augment the information on the chart with observations and working impressions of the pans.

PRICE: Retail price paid in local stores or mail-order catalogs.

MATERIAL/FINISH: Material from which the plate was made and the type of interior finish.

SIZE/RIM: Size of plate and width of rim.

BLIND-BAKED SHELL: Plates in which the bottoms and sides of the unfilled shells browned to a rich, even walnut shade and a crisp texture were rated good. Plates in which crusts turned a moderately darker or lighter brown or baked unevenly between bottoms and sides were rated fair. Plates that produced a burnt, very dark, or very light-colored crust and a wide discrepancy between bottoms and sides were rated poor.

FRUIT-FILLED SHELL: Rated good were the plates in which crust bottoms browned, especially at the center, and in which the sides browned evenly with some noticeable crispness. Soggy, pale bottom crusts, which were, unfortunately, the norm, were rated fair. Radically underbrowned edges and truly mushy bottom centers were rated poor.

TESTERS' COMMENTS: Observations and working impressions.

Brand	Price	Materials/Finish	Size:Rim	Blind-Baked Shell	Fruit-Filled Shell	Testers' Comments
BEST PIE PLATE **Corning** Pyrex Originals	$3.99	Ovenproof glass/Clear	9" : ½"	★★★	★★★	Good browning and crisping performance, low cost, and user-friendly features such as a see-through bottom and a rim wide enough to support a fluted edge made this the winner.
Progressive Professional Quality Non-Stick Pie Pan	$7.99	Steel/Nonstick coating	9⅜" : ⅞", channeled	★★	★★★	The extra-wide channeled rim makes this pan easy to handle. The bottom of the blind-baked shell was slightly dark by the time the edges were done, but the shell overall was well and evenly browned. The bottom and sides of the fruit pie were admirably crisp and brown.
Mirro Comet Pie Pan	$1.99	Aluminum/Brushed silver	9" : ⅜"	★★★	★★	Good browning and crisping performance in the blind baking, and middle-of-the-pack performance with the fruit-filled crust, which was cooked through and slightly colored, but not crisp.
Chicago Metallic Bakers Heritage SilverStone No-Stick Perforated Pie Pan	$3.99	Steel/Nonstick coating	9" : ⅜"	★★★	★★	Blind-baked shell was browned to a reasonably dark shade which was, for the most part, even. Sides of the fruit-filled shell achieved some browning, but the bottom, though it was cooked through, did not.
Ekco Baker's Secret Non-Stick Bakeware Pie Pan	$3.99	Tinned steel /Nonstick coating	9" : ⅜" with two ¾" tabs	★	★★★	Odd combination of performance strengths and weaknesses. Pan overbrowned the blind-baked shell, especially around the sides, but was among the best with the fruit-filled pie, producing crisp, well-browned sides and a bottom that was not raw.
Emile Henry Le Potier Pie Dish	$29.00	Ceramic/ Glazed	9" : ½" undulating rim	★★	★★	The most attractive (and expensive) of the dishes by a long shot, it turned in a spotty performance. Uneven browning from bottom to sides on both the empty and the filled shells. At 1¾-inches deep, it is about ¼-inch deeper than most of the other plates, giving it a deep-dish look.
Chicago Metallic Village Baker Commercial Weight Perforated Pie Pan	$4.99 for 2	Tinned steel/Shiny silver	9" : ⅜"	★★	★	Shell was sufficiently dark, but it was uneven from the bottom to the sides. Contrary to the label's claim that the holes in the pan prevent soggy crusts in fruit and cream pies, our bottom crusts were almost raw.
Kaiser Backform Pie Pan	$10.00	Tinned steel/Nonstick coating	9" : ⅜"	★	★★	Serious overbrowning of the blind-baked crust; the edges were practically burnt. Uneven browning. The sides of the fruit-filled crust had browned, but the center of the bottom crust was wet and pale.
Chicago Metallic Village Baker Commercial Weight Pie Pan	$2.95	Tinned steel/Shiny silver	9" : ⅜"	★★	★	The browning of the empty shell was uneven and concentrated at the edges. Browning of the filled shell was practically nonexistent.
E·Z Foil Disposable Deep Pie Pan	$1.99 for 3	Heavy aluminum foil/Shiny silver	9" : ⅜"	★★	★	Passable browning of the empty shell, but almost none of the filled shell. The flimsy aluminum buckled when we moved the pie. Also, we often cut right through the bottom of the pan when slicing the pie.

which proved to be a mixed blessing. Certainly the handles made the Ekco easy to pick up and move when filled with a hot pie, but they also made it difficult to use the inverted plate as a template to trim pastry.

We also considered the ease of cleaning the various plates. None of them, save the Emile Henry ceramic, were difficult to clean, but the nonsticks were easiest of all. The downside to the nonstick coating, though, is that it scratches easily when the pie is cut and served.

Another advantage of the Pyrex, along with its ½-inch rim, is that the glass is clear, making it especially easy to eyeball the color of the crust as it cooks to judge when it is done. Glass is also nonreactive, so storing a pie filled with acidic fruit for a couple of days is no problem. Neither is using the plate for a fruit cobbler or crisp. However, it's important to remember that glass is legendary for its good heat conductivity, which means that a pie crust in Pyrex pie plates tends to set up about two or three minutes faster than one in metal or ceramic. So keep a careful eye on the crust in a Pyrex plate, checking it well before the time specified in the recipe.

I know from experience that both Pyrex and ceramic plates break easily. Pyrex plates, however, are not costly to replace and offer a host of advantages. So the next time I need to replace a pie plate, I won't think twice while reaching for the Pyrex.

The Perfect Summer Wine?

At its best, dry rosé complements a wider range of hot-weather food than any other wine. But many of the wines we tried were too sweet to drink with anything. BY MARK BITTMAN

More than five years ago, I wrote in these pages that "dry rosés are increasing in popularity not only among open-minded wine drinkers but also among California winemakers." This was a trend that may have peaked at that very moment, because as I look back at the results of that tasting, I see that many of the wines we enjoyed then have become "too sweet" or "overly fruity" in the minds of today's tasters.

Perhaps the wines are indeed more sweet. Or perhaps the tasters' palates have changed, and individuals now prefer their wine to be even more dry. Whatever the reason, the optimism I felt based on that tasting has vanished. Once again you must look to Europe for consistency among dry rosés, at least if the results of our current tasting are to be trusted: Our top five wines were from France (our top seven from Europe), and our bottom three (and five of our bottom six) were from California. In '93, three of the top six wines were Californian.

Rosé wines can be made in such a wide variety of styles and from so many different kinds of grapes that perhaps it is no wonder that our tasters found little consistency even within particular labels. And because the term "rosé" isn't associated with any one style—you can find sickly sweet rosés, mostly made from the zinfandel grape, or nearly bone-dry specimens made from the grapes indigenous to Southern France—it's likely that winemakers feel free to change grapes and/or styles at will.

Rosé can be produced using any dark grape, and most winemaking regions—especially those with good red wines but poor white ones—have been making rosé from a portion of their grapes for as long as they've been making wine. The technique is simple—you allow red grapes to remain in contact with the juice just long enough to color it but not long enough to make the wine "red." The results vary in taste and color: A "rosé" (the word is French for "pink") may be pale amber, yellowish brown, pale rust, deep copper, hot pink, and even red. As far as our tasters could tell, color did not correlate with flavor in any way; any color wine might be sweet or dry, intensely flavored or watery.

One aspect of the tastings was strikingly consistent, however: the winner. In 1998, as in 1993, Chateau de Trinquevedel, a wine from Tavel (in the Southern Rhone valley of France), finished first by a mile. All our tasters enjoyed it, all ranked it, three had it as their top wine, and most had unmit-igated raves when writing about it. At $15, it is reasonably priced, and a no-brainer when you're looking for a wine to go with hot-weather food.

After that, however, the results were decidedly mixed; there was little agreement and there were no clear favorites. There were wines that drew positive comments that did not translate into high rankings, and those that scored well but which few people seemed to love. Although I had personal favorites among these wines (including one that finished in the bottom third), the winner and the value-priced second finisher are the only wines I can recommend with complete confidence.

Which is not to say that the other wines are all losers—many were enjoyed by many of our tasters, and some clearly vary greatly from one vintage to the next. The Bonny Doon Vin de Cigare, Vin de Mistral from Joseph Phelps, and Rene Barbier Rosé from Penedes were all solid finishers in our earlier tasting and remain competitively priced entries from—at least in the case of the first two—highly regarded houses. I wish I could write, as I did in 1993, that this was "a group of delightful, affordable wines." But there are some delightful and affordable wines in the group; you just have to be a little more picky than you did a few years ago.

THE JUDGES' RESULTS | DRY ROSÉS

The wines in our tasting—held at Mt. Carmel Wine and Spirits in Hamden, Conn.—were judged by a panel made up of both wine professionals and amateur wine lovers. The wines were all purchased in the Northeast; prices will vary throughout the country.

Within each category, wines are listed in order of preference. In this tasting, the "Highly Recommended" wines had almost all positive comments. Those labeled "Recommended" garnered mostly positive comments. The "Recommended with Reservations" group had decidedly mixed comments, and the "Not Recommended" category had almost all negative comments.

HIGHLY RECOMMENDED

BEST WINE: 1995 Chateau de Trinquevedel Tavel, $15. More-or-less universal praise for this classic rosé: "Deep full nose," "an enjoyable sipper," "smooth and mellow" with a "nice hint of raspberry." "Delicious." **BEST BUY: 1996 Domaine de la Gautiere en Provence, $8.** A "vigorous" organically grown wine that some found a bit "clumsy." Others, however, found it "dry and subtle," "quite fragrant, with hints of strawberries and cherries."

RECOMMENDED

1996 Domaines Ott La Déesse, $25. "Smooth and very drinkable," "clean," but "nondescript." "Nice fruit." **1995 Chateau St. Jean "Cuvée Natacha," Coteaux d'Aix en Provence, $8.50.** "Clean and acidic with plenty of fruit." Could be "watery in the finish." **1996 Chateau d'Aqueria Tavel, $15.** Perhaps "a little too sweet," but "distinctive" and "delightful." "Hints of raspberries" noted by many. **1996 Regaleali Tasca d'Almerita Rosata Sicilia, $9.** "Juicy and ripe" with "nice flavors" and "good finish." **1996 Domaine Tempier, Bandol, $22.** "Fragrant, strong, and slightly astringent." "Good fruit; complex."

1995 Heitz Cellar Napa Grignolino Rosé, $8. "Big wine for a rosé," "fruity and clean." "Nice and tart."

RECOMMENDED WITH RESERVATIONS

1996 Chateau Pradeaux, Bandol, $21. "Undefined but not unpleasant," "might as well be white." Let's call it "innocuous." **1994 Bonny Doon California Vin Gris de Cigare, $9.** "Strong but not unpleasant," "clean and well-balanced." **1996 Joseph Phelps California Vin de Mistral Grenache Rose, $12.** One admirer thought it had "good balance and good bite," but many found it "medicinal" and noticed other off flavors; some thought it "too sweet."

NOT RECOMMENDED

NV Rene Barbier Rosé, Penedes, $6. "Too sweet," with a "chemical nose and flavor." **1995 Mondavi California Rosato, $13.** "Has flavor but is one-dimensional." "Too sweet." **1996 Jed Steele Shooting Star Mendocino Zin Gris, $11.** "Too sweet," "way too sweet," "tutti fruity." **1996 Simi California Rosé of Cabernet, $12.** "Just drier than black cherry soda, not unlike it."

The Joy of Writing

A new form of culinary prose brings wit as well as research to bear on the subject of food. BY CHRISTOPHER KIMBALL

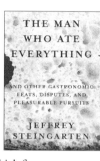

Food writing, which for too many years was primarily a forum for culinary cheerleading, has recently been upgraded by the likes of Jack Butler, Jeffrey Steingarten, and John Thorne. This new form of culinary prose is a cross between Hunter Thompson's gonzo journalism and the musings of a mad food scientist. You are entertained, you learn, and, on occasion, you cry with delight. Here are three new wave culinary books high on my list for summer reading. (Note that because these books are primarily about writing, not recipes, we have opted not to evaluate the recipes in our test kitchen.)

Jack's Skillet

➤ Jack Butler, Algonquin Books of Chapel Hill, $19.95

Butler is first and foremost a writer and poet. His vocation clearly shows in this charming, downhome, and eminently useful little book, which is based on the notion that most anybody can cook just about anything in his cast-iron skillet. And Jack is not talking about one of those flimsy aluminum jobs, either; he means a real, solid cast-iron skillet.

The premise is simple, and most of the recipes are, too. Since Butler believes that most things can be cooked in a cast-iron skillet by most anybody, even with the most meager collection of ingredients, there are plenty of recipes such as Refrigerator Soup, along with skillet-cooked pies, cobblers, hush puppies, chili, and quiche. There are also a number of recipes in the book that are not wedded to a skillet.

While Butler's love of cooking is infectious, his recipes are best described as "Southern bachelor." Boiled turnip greens and baked pork and bean sandwiches, for example, number among his favorites. I also have quibbles with his method for seasoning a skillet, and he could have been more helpful to those of us who might opt to purchase a new cast-iron skillet instead of seeking

one at a garage sale.

However, these are relatively minor points in the face of Butler's other charms. He writes with the same friendly banter one would expect to hear at a rural gas station in Arkansas, providing the reader with yet another good example of the literary benefits of a Southern childhood. For example, he describes the perfect skillet as having the texture of a "watermelon that has just been washed down with cold water from a garden hose." Describing his younger self, he says, "[I had] no more idea how to take care of myself than a baby frog on a rainy blacktop."

Most importantly, his comment that "most cooking is done in your mind, not in the oven" aptly describes his rabid appetite for the sport and sheer joy of cooking, an appetite that is refreshingly free of the ersatz enthusiasm and culinary worship that is the downfall of so many of today's food writers.

The Man Who Ate Everything

➤ Jeffrey Steingarten, Knopf, $38.50

If Hunter Thompson and Christopher Buckley were capable of jointly producing offspring, Steingarten would be their firstborn. Who else would ask himself, "Isn't ripening a chaotic, degenerative breakdown of the skin and flesh of a fruit as it plunges towards the death and decay that awaits us all?" Or sacrifice his body in the name of science to test firsthand the validity of La Method Montignac, a diet that promotes the consumption of chocolate and foie gras?

The magic of Steingarten lies not just in his wit and first-class writing talents but in his total, no-holds-barred commitment to any trend, news item, or cooking conundrum that catches his fancy. (My only reservation, albeit a minor one, is that about half of this volume is made up of older essays, mostly traditional food-travel pieces, nicely done but not up to the sheer insanity of his more recent work.) Few if any other modern writers would taste test 32 brands of bottled water and then, having designed the "perfect" recipe for water, go to a wholesale chemist supply company to fill his shopping list of ingestion-grade chemicals. They refused to sell him the compounds and so, in a last ditch effort to per-

suade them, he promised that he would first test the concoctions on his puppy. (He doesn't own one.) As he was about to quote from Horace ("Anger is a passing madness"), he was forcibly ejected from the premises.

Steingarten juxtaposes totally unrelated notions, such as the relative risk factors associated with skiing and eating raw shellfish, in a seemingly rational manner. (He concludes that oysters on the half shell are safer.) The unmatched genius of his work is not only his cleverness, which is more than sufficient to carry you through the 500-plus pages, but the fact that you read spellbound all the way through a 6,000-word essay about how to make french fries.

This minutely detailed scientific examination of the absurd reminds me of an English eccentric who's spent a very pleasant lifetime constructing an architectural folly. But Steingarten's "folly" will keep you glued to your armchair until every perfectly wacko premise has been investigated, carefully considered, and then brought to heel—as if you were watching a pince-nez-wearing trainer of mad dogs. And before you turn the last page, you might have begun to suspect that the trainer is as mad as his students.

Serious Pig

➤ John Thorne, North Point Press, $30

This book is a collection of essays, most of them a bit more weighty than those in the other two books reviewed here. Thorne is a Yankee (childhood summers in Maine having worked their magic) and his prose is a bit slower and more strait-laced than the ear-popping speed and wacked-out cadences of Butler and Steingarten. The word "serious" in the title was clearly deliberate, and when Thorne ruminates about cooking traditions and the methods for producing the perfect versions of such dishes as Bean Hole Beans, Crab Roll, or Summer Corn Chowder, we know that these issues really matter to him and are not just literary dalliance or exercises in culinary history. Thorne has done his homework, and I learned plenty about American cooking, including how and why one would want to make real salt pork, the secrets of oysters Rockefeller, and more about hoppin' John than my mother ever told me (and she grew up on it). Serious Pig is no casual read; rather, it's a perfect book for keeping by the fire to savor one essay at a time.

Most of the ingredients and materials necessary for the recipes in this issue are available at your local supermarket, gourmet store, or kitchen supply shop. The following are mail-order sources for particular items. Prices listed below were current at press time and do not include shipping or handling unless otherwise indicated. We suggest that you contact companies directly to confirm up-to-date prices and availability.

Pie Plates

The winner in our pie plate rating on page 28 was made by Pyrex, which has been manufacturing bakeware since 1915. The heat-tolerant glass of Pyrex products was originally developed in the early 1900s for the railroads. Corning scientists set out to solve the problem of glass lantern globes heating up and then shattering when exposed to sleet and snow. Pyrex pie plates are sold in clear, cobalt blue, and cranberry tints at supermarkets and hardware stores nationwide. If you cannot find this product in your local stores, you may order it for $4.25 by mail directly through **Corning Consumer Products Company (P.O. Box 1994, Waynesboro, VA 22980; 800-999-3436).** Call between 8 a.m. and 8 p.m. EST. The second place pie plate, the Progressive Professional Quality Non-Stick Pie Pan, can be purchased for $8.95 from **West 175 Enterprises (Department Prog., P.O. Box 84848, Seattle, WA 98124; 800-288-7834).**

Kebab Skewers

It would seem that spearing a series of ingredients for kebabs would make for very simple handling. Yet most of us have experienced the cherry tomato that tears off or the chunk of zucchini that dangles unmoved by the spin of the skewer. There is a two-pronged remedy for this. Skewers made with double prongs hold delicate meats and vegetables securely, make turning easy, and don't bend with the weight of ingredients. **Armitage Hardware (925 West Armitage, Chicago, IL 60614; 888-469-3237; www.webergrills.com)** sells a set of eight double-prong skewers for $9.99. Made of nickel-plated steel, the prongs are 13 inches long and dishwasher safe. They can get hot, though, so be sure to lift them off the grill with a mitt or potholder.

Brisket Slicer

With their sheer size and tender texture, barbecued briskets can give even experienced carvers fits. Not so if you outfit yourself with the Forschner/Victorinox meat slicer that features a kullenschiff edge. Unlike the saw-toothed edges of most meat slicer blades, a kullenschiff edge is straight with oval dimples along each side of the blade. The hollows create air pockets that minimize the surface contact between the meat and the side of the blade. They also trap juices, further reducing friction and thus the risk of the meat sticking to the blade and tearing. All this facilitates thin, clean, even slicing of meats. This kind of knife can also be used for roast beef, ham, and turkey breast. Do not use the knife when carving into bone or close to bone, though, because the hollows make for a thin blade which bone can nick or break. The Forschner/Victorinox meat slicer with a kullenschiff edge can be purchased by mail for $47.30 from **Professional Cutlery Direct (170 Boston Post Road, Suite 135, Madison, CT 06443; 800-346-3256; www.cutlery.com).** Made of high-carbon stainless steel with a textured black synthetic handle, the knife has a 12-inch long edge and a 1½-inch wide blade with a rounded tip.

Multipurpose Sieve

By coincidence, a number of recipes in this issue, including those for lemonade, peach ice cream, and tomato salads, require sieves. A sieve was also used to illustrate chef Norman Van Aken's tip for fuss-free shocking of blanched vegetables, a favorite among many of our editors. So we decided to look at the availability of sieves. We found that the extra-large fine-mesh sieve that is desirable for working with large batches and avoiding spillover is hard to come by. Most of the giants we found were made of tin-plated steel mesh, which is a sturdy metal fabric but discolors and rusts over time. We did, however, find a substantially large stainless steel sieve (9½ inches in diameter) sold through **Sur La Table's catalog division (1765 Sixth Avenue South, Seattle, WA 98134-1608; 800-243-0852).** This item is not listed in their current catalog but is available by mail order for $15.95.

Leverpull Savings

Thanks to reader James R. Talbot of Montpelier, Virginia, who tipped us off to a mail-order source that offers significant savings on the LeCreuset Leverpull LX, "the ultimate corkscrew" in our November/December 1997 equipment rating. Six months ago we saw prices for the Leverpull LX as high as $150 and no lower than $100 (on sale). Mr. Talbot has since informed us that **The Wine Club (953 Harrison St., San Francisco, CA 94107; 800-966-7835; sales@thewineclub.com)** sells the Leverpull by mail for $87.99. The Leverpull comes with a case, an extra uncorking worm, and a foil-cutter.

Ice Cream Makers

While testing the peach ice cream recipe on page 23 in this issue, we experimented with two popular, inexpensive electric models. We found both to be good for making smooth, creamy ice cream with just a hint of ice, but we preferred the construction of the Cuisinart for ease of use (for details *see* "Ice Cream Machines" in Notes From Readers, page 2). The Cuisinart Automatic Frozen Yogurt–Ice Cream & Sorbet Maker (model ICE-20) can be ordered for $69.99 from **Culinary Parts Unlimited (80 Berry Drive, Pacheco, CA 94553; 800-543-7549).** You can order the Krups La Glaciere (model 358) from **Kitchen Etc. catalog services (Department TM, 32 Industrial Drive, Exeter, NH 03833; 800-232-4070)** for $59.99. Both are white with plastic exteriors.

Sesame Oil

The recipe for Asian marinade on page 7 specifies the use of Asian sesame oil. This oil should not be confused with the mild, yellowish sesame oil you might find on your supermarket shelves and use in salads. Asian sesame oil is a dark-colored, thick oil with a rich, nutty flavor. Made from toasted or roasted pressed white sesame seeds, it is typically used to flavor stir-fried and sautéed foods but is not usually used for frying because of its low burning point. You can order a 10-ounce bottle of Asian sesame oil for $4.95 from **Adriana's Caravan (409 Vanderbilt Street, Brooklyn, NY 11218; 800-316-0820).** This catalog of international foods also sells a black sesame oil, which has a bitter, more assertive sesame flavor. A 12-ounce bottle of black sesame oil sells for $4.95.

Salad Spinner

Summer typically means abandoning the stove, lighting up the grill, and pulling out the salad spinner. While we applaud the invention of a gadget that uses centrifugal force to dry freshly washed leafy greens, many salad spinners have their failings. The drawstring propelled models are inclined to snap back and bring the spinning basket to an abrupt halt. The cord can also be prone to fraying. Those salad spinners with gear-operated handles tend to require a great deal of effort to spin them and to hold them down so they don't go skidding off the counter. A newly introduced salad spinner by Oxo Good Grips seems to avoid all these flaws. A large mushroom-shaped nonslip pump projects slightly from the center of the spinner's lid. Simply pump up and down repeatedly to spin the interior slatted basket. A non-slip ring on the base of the external bowl prevents it from spinning off the counter and a button on the lid's side acts as a quick brake. The Oxo Good Grips salad spinner has a 2½ quart capacity and comes in white. It is available by mail order for $25.99 from **A Cook's Wares (211 37th Street, Beaver Falls, PA 15010-2103; 800-915-9788).**

Garlic and Herb Grilled Chicken Kebabs **PAGE 7**

Turkey Burgers **PAGE 13** and Israeli Tomato and Cucumber Salad **PAGE 11**

Pasta Salad with (clockwise from upper left) Asparagus and Red Peppers; Eggplant, Tomatoes, and Basil; and Fennel, Red Onions, and Sun-Dried Tomatoes **PAGE 15**

Peach, Plum, and Strawberry Jams **PAGE 19**

Peach Crisp **PAGE 25**

Classic and Pink Lemonade **PAGE 21**

PHOTOGRAPHY: CARL TREMBLAY   STYLING : MYROSHA DZIUK

Casaba

Santa Claus

Sharlyne

Muskmelon

Seedless Watermelon

Canary

Watermelon

Crenshaw

Galia

Honeydew

MELONS

NUMBER THIRTY-FOUR

SEPTEMBER & OCTOBER 1998

COOK'S
ILLUSTRATED

Chicken Parmesan
Simplified
30 Minutes to Crisp Cutlets

Rating Chocolate
Chips
Soy-Laced Chips Win First Place

Foolproof Sponge
Cake
Moist, Tender Cake Every Time

Easy Hash Browns
Raw Grated Potatoes Taste Best

Testing Vegetable
Peelers
Which Model Is Truly All-Purpose?

Modern Minestrone
Deep Flavor Without Stock

Best Crème Caramel
How to Grill a Leg of Lamb
White Mushrooms Revisited
Cinnamon Swirl Bread

$4.00 U.S./$4.95 CANADA

CONTENTS

September & October 1998

COOK'S ILLUSTRATED

PUBLISHER AND EDITOR
Christopher Kimball

EXECUTIVE EDITOR
Pam Anderson

SENIOR EDITOR
John Willoughby

SENIOR WRITER
Jack Bishop

ASSOCIATE EDITORS
Adam Ried
Maryellen Driscoll

TEST KITCHEN DIRECTOR
Susan Logozzo

TEST COOKS
Anne Yamanaka
Dawn Yanagihara

CONTRIBUTING EDITOR
Stephanie Lyness

EDITORIAL INTERN
Garrett Peters

ART DIRECTOR
Amy Klee

CORPORATE MANAGING EDITOR
Barbara Bourassa

EDITORIAL PRODUCTION MANAGER
Sheila Datz

COPY EDITOR
Carol Parikh

MARKETING DIRECTOR
Adrienne Kimball

CIRCULATION DIRECTOR
David Mack

FULFILLMENT MANAGER
Larisa Greiner

CIRCULATION MANAGER
Darcy Beach

MARKETING ASSISTANT
Connie Forbes

PRODUCTS MANAGER
Steven Browall

VICE PRESIDENT
PRODUCTION AND TECHNOLOGY
James McCormack

SYSTEMS ADMINISTRATOR
James Burke

DESKTOP PUBLISHING MANAGER
Kevin Moeller

PRODUCTION ARTIST
Robert Parsons

PRODUCTION ASSISTANT
Daniel Frey

CONTROLLER
Lisa A. Carullo

SENIOR ACCOUNTANT
Mandy Shito

OFFICE MANAGER
Danielle Shuckra

SPECIAL PROJECTS
Fern Berman

MUSHROOMS An edible form of fungi, mushrooms have been highly prized since ancient times for their deep, rich, earthy flavors. The fact that they could be found only by foraging in the dark, cool, moist places where they grew wild made them particularly valuable. But in the 17th century, gardeners in Paris discovered how to cultivate the white, or button, mushroom. Today, several varieties of exotic mushrooms are cultivated, including the crimini and portobello, cousins of the common white mushroom, as well as the subtly flavored oyster, the smoky shiitake, and the odd, pin-shaped enoki. Chanterelles, morels, porcini, and the funnel-shaped horn of plenty are among those mushrooms that still grow only in the wild, and are therefore much more expensive.

COVER PAINTING: BRENT WATKINSON,   BACK COVER ILLUSTRATION: JOHN BURGOYNE

BUSY BEES

Two years ago, my wife Adrienne bought me an unusual birthday present: a beehive filled with 30,000 bees plus a subscription to *Bee Culture* magazine. Since then, I have added six additional hives, harvested two crops of honey, endured a few minor stings, and become an avid reader of this odd low-budget publication. Of most interest to me was a recent article containing a survey of American eating habits. It contained the following facts:

• The ideal food preparation time is 15 minutes. It is estimated that it will be five minutes by 2030.

• Only one-third of women over the age of 20 bake for fun, even once per year.

• Seventy-five percent of Americans do not know at 4 p.m. what they'll eat for dinner.

• Three-quarters of American children do not know how to cook.

• In 1995, restaurant sales were greater than supermarket sales.

• The sources of meals consumed at home are: fast food 41 percent; restaurant takeout 21 percent; and supermarket takeout 22 percent. This means that only 16 percent of the meals we consume at home are (presumably) home-cooked.

Another survey, this one reported by *The New York Times,* found that 75 percent of those polled did not know how to cook broccoli, 50 percent couldn't prepare gravy, and 45 percent didn't know the number of teaspoons in a tablespoon. The article went on to say that "in the last decade (the '80s), cooking has evolved into an optional activity, like skiing or playing chess." But this trend is not just a recent phenomenon. Back at the turn of the century, convenience foods were already being cleverly inserted into published recipes, often by magazine food writers who were heavily subsidized by the food industry, a practice that continues to this day.

The influence of advertising on food consumption became so enormous that one Iowa novelist quipped almost 100 years ago that "people in the United States do not eat for pleasure…eating is something done just in response to advertising." Another indication of things to come was that in the 1930s the average distance between growing fields and markets was already 1,500 miles.

Given where we find ourselves today (with fewer than 20 percent of the meals we eat at home being home-cooked) and despite relatively minor indications to the contrary (such as this magazine), we might begin to wonder at the meaning of the term "inconvenient." The dictionary states that it is the opposite of convenient, which itself is defined as "suited or favorable to a person's needs, comfort, or purpose." One then might reasonably ask, what is our purpose? I suspect that recent trends would indicate that our aim is to be comfortable, to have our physical needs fulfilled as easily and quickly as possible. Yet human history has always been driven by greater purposes than mere comfort, among them religion, spiritual awakening, freedom, and a lust for adventure. If convenience were truly the measure of life's activities, then Lewis and Clark would never have found a route to the West Coast, Jamestown would never have been settled, men would never have landed on the moon, and Martin Luther King would never have left his congregation. We would also be at great pains to explain the annual pilgrimage to Mecca and why anyone has ever voluntarily joined the armed forces. Boot camp is the epitome of inconvenience.

So why are Americans so lacking in spunk when it comes to the kitchen? After all, the rest of our

Christopher Kimball

life is consumed with "inconveniences"—like raising children and commuting to work. Perhaps we are lazy about our food because, for the first time in history, we don't have to cook to eat. Or perhaps we no longer find anything enlightening about the process of preparing food. Going to the moon is worth the effort; making chicken Parmesan is less noble.

Recently, as I was checking the hives, I took a moment to watch the bees build the honeycomb, the workers swarming over the beeswax foundation, engaged in an endless series of repetitive tasks. I began to wonder how bees see their short, hard lives. Maybe they dream about flying through a warm summer evening, laden with nectar, floating weightlessly down to the hive entrance, or perhaps they fall asleep thinking of fields of bright purple clover, orange and yellow Indian paintbrushes, and apple trees bursting with fragile white blossoms. The buzz and rich, moist air of the hive must act as a thick blanket, enveloping them as they sleep. And at the end of their life cycle, a mere six weeks at the height of the season, they must dream of the work itself, of building a honeycomb and filling it with thick goldenrod honey.

These are good thoughts—of hard work, of building a home, of working side by side with others. These are also the dreams of cooks, of those of us who have traded comfort for hard work and instant gratification for knowledge. In the kitchen, much like bees, we build foundations and fill them with sweet dreams that will be remembered by the next generation of cooks who will stand in our kitchens, preparing our recipes, long after our work is done.

ABOUT COOK'S ILLUSTRATED

The Magazine *Cook's Illustrated* is published every other month (6 issues per year) and accepts no advertising. A one-year subscription is $24.95, two years is $45, and three years is $65. Add $6 postage per year for Canadian subscriptions and $12 per year for all other foreign countries. To order subscriptions, call 800-526-8442. Gift subscriptions are available for $24.95 each.

Magazine-Related Items *Cook's Illustrated* is available in an annual hardbound edition, which includes an index, for $24.95 each plus shipping and handling. Discounts are available if more than one year is ordered at a time. Back issues are available for $5 each. The *Cook's Illustrated* 1998 calendar, featuring 12 of the magazine's covers reproduced in full color, is available for $12.95. *Cook's* also offers a 5-year index (1993-1997) of the magazine for $12.95. To order any of these products, call 800-611-0759.

Books *Cook's Illustrated* publishes a series of single-topic books, available for $14.95 each. Titles include: *How To Make A Pie, How To Make An American Layer Cake, How To Stir Fry, How*

To Make Ice Cream, How To Make Pizza, How To Make Holiday Desserts, How To Make Pasta Sauces, How To Grill, How To Make Salad, and *How To Make Simple Fruit Desserts.* The *Cook's Bible,* written by Christopher Kimball and published by Little, Brown, is available for $24.95. To order any of these books, call 800-611-0759.

Reader Submissions *Cook's* accepts reader submissions for both Quick Tips and Notes From Readers. We will provide a one-year complimentary subscription for each Quick Tip that we print. Send a description of your technique, along with your name, address, and daytime telephone number, to Quick Tips, *Cook's Illustrated,* P.O. Box 569, Brookline, MA 02147. Questions, suggestions, or other submissions for Notes From Readers should be sent to the same address.

Subscription Inquiries All queries about subscriptions or change of address notices should be mailed to *Cook's Illustrated,* P.O. Box 7446, Red Oak, IA 51591-0446.

Website Address Selected articles and recipes from *Cook's Illustrated* and subscription information are available online. You can access *Cook's* website at: www.cooksillustrated.com.

Lemon Bar Topping Problems

Please tell me how to prevent the confectioners' sugar from being totally absorbed into the delicious lemon bars (May/June 1998, page 20). I tried sprinkling them with extra sugar, but it adhered in some spots and melted into the lemon layer in others.

BELFIELD LESLIE
HUDSON, FL

➤ Several readers wrote to report similar difficulties with the confectioners' sugar topping on the lemon bars. In addition to having the same problem with the lemon bars, these readers all had one other thing in common: an address in the southeastern United States, including Florida, Georgia, and South Carolina. Late spring and summer weather in these states means plenty of humidity, which is the cause of the melting sugar problem. The sugar inevitably absorbs some of the moisture that's abundant in both the lemon filling and the air, and its melting destroys its decorative effect. Because we developed the lemon bar recipe in Boston during the winter months, we never encountered this problem. After receiving readers' letters, though, we made the bars on a hazy, humid 90 degree summer day and brought them outside, and sure enough, the sugar topping turned spotty.

You may find the same problem if you refrigerate leftover bars, because the environment inside a refrigerator is also humid. The confectioners' sugar is also likely to melt if the bars are even the slightest bit warm. They must truly be at room temperature or cooler before they're topped with the sugar.

That said, we can make a couple of suggestions. If you want to use the confectioners' sugar topping, sieve it onto the bars *just* before serving. Or, if you are willing to mail order, try Snow White Non-Melting Sugar from the King Arthur Flour Baker's Catalog (*see* Resources, page 32). Alternatively, you could try a topping that would be less susceptible to moisture and humidity. During the development of this recipe, we enjoyed the flavor of such toppings as very finely chopped almonds or pistachios and finely chopped or shredded dried coconut.

Do You Have to Skim Broth and Stock?

My grandmother, who was the resident cook at our house, always skimmed the foam from broth as she boiled the meat, bones, and vegetables. I have never understood the reason why. Is this necessary?

KAY DELL
CAMP HILL, PA

➤ New England Culinary Institute Chef/Instructor Andre Bournier explained why broths and stocks are usually skimmed. As meat, bones, and vegetables heat up in the water, Bournier said, they throw off a grayish foam referred to as "scum," which is composed of coagulated proteins from the blood, water soluble proteins called albumin, and melting fat. Common knowledge has it that this material might make the final broth or stock cloudy, or impart an off flavor if it is not removed. In addition, if the stock boils rather than simmers, even for a brief time, the agitation and heat of the boiling could cause any scum that has not been removed to emulsify with the liquid. This, too, could contribute to a cloudy appearance.

Though most traditionalists would probably disagree, we feel that constant skimming is a refinement, not a necessity. This is so, at least, with the beef and chicken broth recipes from previous issues of *Cook's* (January/February 1998 and March/April 1996, respectively), which begin by sautéing meat and bones, versus using raw meat and bones, as for a classic white stock.

To confirm our thinking, the test kitchen prepared two pots of *Cook's* beef broth and two of the chicken broth. We skimmed the scum off one pot of each type as it simmered, and left the other pots alone, scum and all. At the end of cooking, we strained all four broths and carefully skimmed away all the surface fat, steps which we do consider necessary. In neither the beef nor the chicken broth was taste impaired by the lack of repeated skimming; visually, the skimmed and not skimmed beef broths were practically indistinguishable. The chicken broth that had not been skimmed was, we admit, slightly cloudier than the skimmed broth. In the hearty, ingredient-rich soups for which these broths were destined, however, this small degree of cloudiness was of no concern.

Cleaning Doughy Bowls

I recently learned that cleaning a bowl in which you've made any kind of dough is much easier with cold water than with hot. I thought other bakers might appreciate this information, too.

ELLEN GREEN
NEW YORK, NY

➤ After using cold water to clean dozens of bowls covered with cookie, brioche, and bread dough, as well as cake and pancake batters, our test kitchen can enthusiastically endorse your trick. Shirley Corriher, our food science advisor and author of *CookWise* (Morrow, 1997), explained the advantages of cold water. Hot water, Corriher said, will swell the starches in the flour and begin to set, or harden, the proteins in the gluten, which can amount to a sticky mess on the sponge as well as in the bowl. Cold water, on the other hand, merely dilutes, and therefore weakens, the dough, rather than setting any of these cooking processes into motion.

The Neiman Marcus Cookie Recipe Legend

A woman and her daughter had lunch at the Neiman Marcus cafe in Dallas and decided to finish with a dessert of the "Neiman Marcus cookie." The cookie was delicious, so the woman asked the waitress for the recipe. The waitress would not give the recipe away, but agreed to sell it to the woman for "two fifty," which she added to the lunch tab.

A month later the woman's credit card statement arrived, and it listed "Cookie Recipe—$250." Upset, she called the credit office to return the recipe and have her account credited for it. The clerk denied her request, explaining that the bill would stand and that the recipe was expensive in order to discourage people from copying it. To get even, the woman thought, "Well, since they have my $250, I'll have $250 worth of fun," and she spread the recipe to as many cookie lovers as possible…for free.

NANCY LODGE
NEW HOPE, PA

➤ Many readers have passed this story about the expensive and misunderstood recipe purchase along to us. Even outside the office, several of our editors have gotten the letter, by both postal mail and e-mail, from friends and acquaintances. Invariably the letter ends: "This is a true story. Please pass the recipe on to everyone you know."

Since this story has become something of a culinary urban legend, even discussed by Marian Burros in *The New York Times* and published by Maida Heatter in *Maida Heatter's Brand New Book of Great Cookies* (Random House, 1995), we decided to investigate and called Neiman Marcus headquarters in Dallas. On two occasions, public relations representatives from the store said that the story, which they report has been in circulation for more than 20 years, was absolutely untrue. One representative said that she receives inquires about it almost weekly.

Regardless of the story's authenticity, the test kitchen tried the recipe, which works well and produces truly decadent cookies. The cookie dough is so loaded with ingredients—oats, two kinds of chocolate, nuts, and our addition of coconut—that it acts essentially as a sweet medium for the stir-ins. The oats give the cookies a cakey texture that helps hold all the stir-in ingredients in place, the coconut provides some chew, and the chopped chocolate gives them a mottled or speckled appearance. Here is the recipe, which has been slightly reproportioned by our test kitchen.

THE $250 COOKIE
(DELUXE CHOCOLATE CHIP COOKIES)
MAKES ABOUT 16 LARGE COOKIES

1	cup rolled oats, ground in food processor or blender until very fine
1	cup all-purpose flour
1/2	teaspoon baking powder
1/2	teaspoon baking soda
1/2	teaspoon salt
8	tablespoons (1 stick) unsalted butter, softened but still firm
1/2	cup packed light or dark brown sugar
1/2	cup granulated sugar
1	large egg
1/2	teaspoon vanilla extract
6	ounces semisweet chocolate chips
1/2	cup sweetened dried coconut
2	ounces semisweet or bittersweet chocolate, finely chopped
3/4	cup walnuts or pecans, chopped

1. Adjust oven racks to upper- and lower-middle positions and heat oven to 350 degrees. Line two large cookie sheets with parchment paper and set aside.

2. Whisk ground oats, flour, baking powder, baking soda, and salt in medium bowl.

3. Either by hand or electric mixer, beat butter, brown sugar and granulated sugar in large bowl until light and fluffy, about 3 minutes with mixer set at medium speed. Scrape sides of bowl with rubber spatula. Add egg and vanilla extract; continue beating until combined, about 40 seconds. Scrape sides of bowl. Add dry ingredients and beat at low speed until just combined, 30 to 45 seconds. Add chocolate chips, coconut, chopped chocolate, and nuts; stir to combine.

4. Working with 2 tablespoons of dough at a time, form dough into balls about 1¾ inches in diameter. Place balls on parchment-lined cookie sheets, leaving at least 2 inches between them. Bake, reversing position of cookie sheets halfway through baking, until edges of cookies begin to crisp but centers are still soft, 15 to 18 minutes. Cool cookies on sheets for 1 to 2 minutes before transferring to cooling racks with wide spatula.

Freezing Overripe Bananas
Mary Logozzo's March/April 1998 Quick Tip about freezing overripe bananas for use in banana bread, rather than throwing them out, is a good one. But have you ever peeled a frozen banana? If frozen, it is very difficult to remove the peel. Once thawed, the banana becomes a mushy mess. My solution is to peel the bananas before freezing them. Incidentally, freezing bananas is a great way to keep them on hand for making smoothies, as well as banana bread.

KARINA SCHUMACHER
ELBURN, IL

➤ We were surprised by the number of readers who wrote to voice the same addition to Mary Logozzo's tip. It is difficult to remove the peel from a fully frozen banana, and peeling them prior to freezing is an easy way to avoid the problem. This is especially true for bananas you plan to use in smoothies, since frozen fruit (thawed only, perhaps, for two to three minutes so it can be cut into smaller chunks) works beautifully for these drinks. In the case of banana bread, however, the bananas must be almost completely thawed so they can be mixed with the other ingredients.

If the banana is frozen with the peel intact, we found that the peel slips off easily once the banana has thawed for 15 to 20 minutes, which is well before it becomes truly liquidy, gooey, and unpleasant to touch.

Graham Flour and Crackers
While searching for a recipe for homemade graham crackers, I was told that they are made with graham flour. Is this true? If so, what is graham flour and where can I get it?

RAYMOND MULVEY
MIDDLESEX, NJ

➤ The four sources we consulted agree, and a representative from Nabisco, maker of Honey Maid Graham Crackers confirmed, that graham flour and graham crackers were both developed by a mid-19th century Presbyterian minister and diet reformer named Dr. Sylvester Graham. As we learned while working on the "Rediscovering Whole Wheat Bread" story and recipes in the January/February 1997 issue, graham flour is a whole wheat flour, containing all three elements of the wheat berry: the endosperm, which is the heart of the berry; the germ, which surrounds the endosperm; and the outer bran layer. It is graham flour's particularly coarse grind that distinguishes it from regular whole wheat flour, which is finely ground. (In older cookbooks, however, graham flour seems to have simply meant whole wheat flour; the distinction having to do with grinds came later.) When graham crackers were first introduced, they were billed as a health food because of the whole wheat flour, from which, according to the Nabisco representative, they are still made today.

The brand of graham flour we use is Hodgson Mill, which is available by mail order from the company for $3 per five-pound bag or $16 for a case of six five-pound bags. For more information or to order, contact Hodgson Mill (1203 Niccum Avenue, Effingham, IL 62401; 800-525-0177 or 217-347-0105).

Erratum
In the recipe for Perfect Lemon Bars on page 21 of the May/June 1998 issue, the two teaspoons of lemon zest called for in the list of lemon filling ingredients was unfortunately omitted from step three of the directions. The zest should be added along with the lemon juice, milk, and salt to the filling base. Our apologies for any confusion this may have caused for some readers.

WHAT IS IT?

This piece of kitchen equipment was donated to my kid's day-care center's big summer yard sale. You can see that it looks like an upside-down pot, only the bottom of the "pot" is actually the lid and the real bottom has holes. Regardless of the fact that we couldn't identify it, it did sell. So what was it?

SUZANNE GESARO
AUSTIN, TX

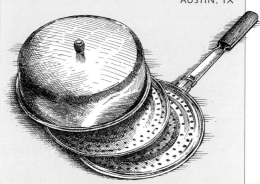

➤ Though it is designed for cooking, to label this device strictly "kitchen" equipment would be something of a misnomer. We know it primarily as a campsite cooking utensil called, appropriately enough, a camp oven. We also found sources that referred to it as an old-fashioned stove-top potato baker, warming oven, or Cape Cod baker. Commonly made of either tin, aluminum, or stainless steel, the camp oven does, as you note, look like an inverted pan. The body of the pan is actually a cover that fits tightly over a perforated base. The holes in the base let in the heat of a camp stove, campfire, grill, or even an indoor stove burner. The body accommodates three to four medium potatoes and can bake them, indoors or out, without the aid of an oven. In fact, the camp oven we found is also billed as "an economical alternative to large ovens for small baking needs...using less costly fuel and radiating less heat into your kitchen."

Though it is not pictured in their 1998 catalog, an American-made camp oven called the Bromwell Universal Efficiency Oven is available for $29.95 from Lehman's Non-Electric Catalog (P.O. Box 321, Kidron, OH 44636; 330-857-5757; GetLehmans@aol.com).

Quick Tips

Minimizing Standing Mixer Messes

Inspired by several tips we have published about avoiding spills while adding ingredients to a standing mixer, Leighton Bourgin of Savage, Maryland, wrote to share her method. When she is mixing dry ingredients that tend to puff out in a cloud or whipping wet ingredients that splatter, she drapes a clean, very damp dish towel over the front of the mixer and the bowl. Drawing the towel snug with one hand also helps.

Deciding When Bread Dough Has Enough Flour

Most bakers tend to add too much flour to their bread doughs, which can result in dry loaves. To tell if her doughs have enough flour before adding more, *Cook's* Test Kitchen Director Susan Logozzo squeezes the dough gently with her entire hand. Even with especially soft, sticky doughs, if her hand pulls away clean, she knows there is enough flour.

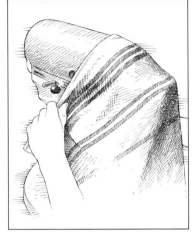

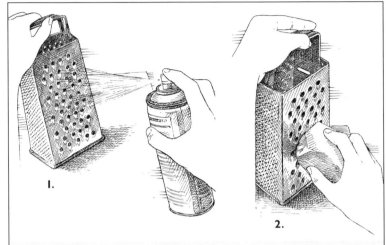

Shredding Cheese Cleanly

Try this tip from Gail McCormick of Chardon, Ohio, to prevent cheese from sticking to the grater.
1. Spray the grater with cooking spray before beginning.
2. The cheese will shred cleanly without sticking to the grater.

Keeping Plastic Wrap off Sticky Foods

The tried and true method for keeping plastic wrap from touching a gooey frosting or glaze is to stick the food with toothpicks and place the wrap over the toothpicks. Occasionally, though, as Barry Hand of Mt. Pleasant, South Carolina, found, the sharp point of the toothpicks puncture the wrap, which can then slide down and onto the food. To prevent this from happening, he developed this method.
1. Place a miniature marshmallow over the point of each toothpick.
2. Place the plastic wrap over the marshmallows. The plastic will be held away from the food and will not tear.

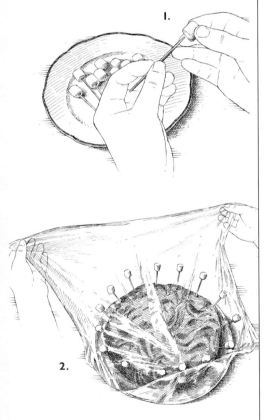

Cutting Parchment Paper to Line Pans

When lining cake pans for cakes like the sponge cake on page 23, it is important that you cut the right size piece of parchment paper. Here is an easy way to do this.
1. Trace the bottom of your cake pan roughly in the center of a sheet of parchment paper (use a double sheet if using two pans).
2. Fold the traced circle in half and then in half again, then cut just inside the outline of the quarter circle formed in this way. The resulting rounds of parchment will exactly fit your pan.

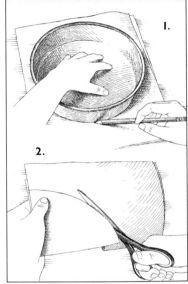

Lining a Loaf Pan With Plastic Wrap

When lining a loaf pan with plastic wrap to make a frozen mousse or semifreddo, Cathy Farr of Salem, Massachusetts, sprinkles the pan with water first. The water droplets cause the plastic wrap to cling smoothly to the metal without bunching or forming large air pockets.

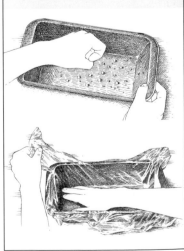

Send Us Your Tip We will provide a complimentary one-year subscription for each tip we print. See page 1 for information.

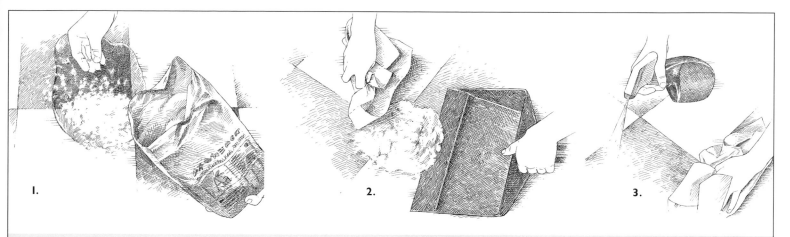

1.   2.   3.

Cleaning Up Spilled Oil

Anyone who has ever dropped a full glass bottle of oil on the floor and had it shatter knows how difficult it can be to clean up. Taking her cue from an old trick for cleaning oil stains out of garments, Elizabeth Johnston of Wakefield, Rhode Island, recommends using the following method to clean an oil-slicked floor.

1. Sprinkle a thick layer of flour over the spilled oil and wait a few minutes for the flour to absorb the oil.

2. With a paper towel, or a brush if there is any glass, move the flour around until it absorbs all the oil, and sweep it up with a dustpan and broom.

3. Spray the area with window cleaner and wipe away the last traces of oil and flour.

Boiling Water in a Hurry

Boiling four or five quarts of water for pasta can be slow and frustrating. Aaron Contorer of Kirkland, Washington, speeds up the process by boiling the water in two pots. When both pots are boiling, he carefully pours the water from the second pot into the stockpot, and he's ready to go.

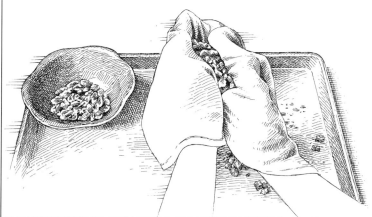

Testing Baking Powder

Olga Pitel of Wayland, Massachusetts, suggests that infrequent bakers check the potency of baking powder that may have been sitting in the cupboard for too long. To do so, mix 2 teaspoons of the baking powder into a cup of water. If there is an immediate reaction of foaming and fizzing (right), the baking powder is okay to use. If the reaction is at all delayed or weak (left), throw it away and buy a fresh can.

Cutting Pizza With Ease

When cutting pizza, a regular knife can catch and drag the melted cheese, and pizza wheels often dent the pan when you bear down to cut through the crust. Instead, Theresa Wilson of Salt Lake City, Utah, cuts pizza neatly and easily using her kitchen shears.

Flame Tamer

To make his own flame tamer when cooking foods that need to be maintained at a low simmer, Tim Allen of Chicago, Illinois, places the cooking pan inside a cast iron pan or skillet over low heat.

Skinning Toasted Walnuts

The skins from toasted walnuts can impart a bitter taste to dishes that include these nuts. To avoid this problem, Emma Dunn of Miami, Florida, removes the skins by rubbing the toasted nuts together inside a clean kitchen towel.

Impromptu Pie Weights

When blind baking pie pastry for a quiche recently, Sarah Jane Freymann of New York, New York, was not able to locate her metal pie weights. She went to her tool box and grabbed a handful of nails and screws, which proved to be an ideal substitute. To protect the pie from the sharp edges of the screws, she used a double layer of foil.

Minestrone Deconstructed

By adding a piece of cheese rind or pancetta to water, we created an excellent minestrone without the bother of homemade stock.

⇒ BY JACK BISHOP ⇐

Minestrone is not a light undertaking. Any way you cut it, there is a lot of dicing and chopping. Minestrone often has 10 vegetables and I've seen recipes with as many as 28. Given the amount of preparation, I thought it was important to discover which steps and ingredients were essential and which ones I could do without. Could I just add everything at once to the pot or would precooking some of the vegetables be necessary? Was stock essential or could I use water, as many traditional Italian recipes do? How many vegetables were enough? And which ones?

The word minestrone literally translates as "big soup," and this hearty soup is certainly loaded with vegetables. Some Italian cookbooks suggest mashing the vegetables into a thick porridge, but I did not want the consistency of my soup to resemble oatmeal. On the other hand, minestrone is not a brothy soup. Each spoonful should be mostly vegetables, with just enough liquid to keep it from becoming a stew.

While I wanted to pack the soup with vegetables, I was also determined to create a harmonious balance of flavors. I've had deli versions of this soup where one vegetable has dominated, but minestrone should be a group effort, with each element pulling equal weight. From the start, I knew I would jettison vegetables that were too bold as well as those that were too bland and added nothing to the soup.

Sketching Out a Recipe

Before tackling the issue of ingredients (I had more than 35 on my list to test), I figured I should devise a basic technique. My research turned up two possible paths. The majority of recipes dump the vegetables into a pot with liquid and simmer them until everything is tender. A smaller number of recipes call for sautéing some or most of the vegetables before adding the liquid along with any vegetables, such as spinach, that would not benefit from cooking in fat. This second method seemed appealing. If I wanted to use water as my base, I knew I would have to up the flavor of the vegetables.

Almost every minestrone recipe calls for leeks, onions, carrots, and celery—the standard aromatic vegetables used in most Italian soups. For my working recipe, I also added zucchini, potatoes, spinach, and tomatoes. I made two batches of soup

In addition to grated cheese as a topping, swirling pesto or a combination of rosemary and garlic into the finished soup builds flavor.

with these ingredients. For the first batch, I added all the ingredients plus water and simmered it for one hour. For the second batch, I sautéed the aromatics in a little extra-virgin olive oil until they began to brown around the edges (about 10 minutes), then added the water and remaining vegetables and simmered it for one hour.

The results were interesting but not as clear as I had hoped. Some tasters thought the soup with the sautéed vegetables had a slightly more intense flavor, but most tasters could not tell the difference. My conclusion was that sautéing the vegetables might help, but it was not enough. I prepared three more pots with the same vegetables but without sautéing any of them. I added homemade chicken stock to one pot, homemade vegetable stock to a second, and water and the rind from a wedge of Parmesan cheese to the third.

The results were unexpected. The soup made with vegetable stock tasted one-dimensional and overwhelmingly sweet; because the vegetables were already sweet, using vegetable stock, which is also fairly sweet, did not help to balance the flavors. I realized I wanted the liquid portion of the soup to add a layer of complexity that would play off the vegetables. The soup made with chicken stock fit

the bill. It was rich, complex, and delicious. However, several tasters (myself included) thought the chicken flavor overwhelmed the vegetables. Diluting the stock with water, on the other hand, created a rather bland soup. I, like most other tasters, preferred the soup made with water and the cheese rind. The cheese gave the broth a buttery, nutty flavor that contrasted nicely with the vegetables without overshadowing them.

My kitchen tests had also convinced me of several other points. Cooking times in the recipes I studied varied from 30 minutes to three hours. I wanted the vegetables to soften completely but not lose their shape, and an hour of gentle simmering accomplished this. Much longer and the vegetables began to break down. Any less time over the flame and the vegetables were too crunchy. I decided I liked the concentrating effect of simmering without the lid on. The house filled with the aroma of soup and the liquid was able to reduce as the vegetables cooked down and took up less space in the pot.

I also saw several recipes that added some fresh vegetables at the end of the cooking time. It sounded like a nice idea, but the fresh peas and green beans I added 10 minutes before the soup was done tasted uncooked and bland compared to the vegetables that had simmered in the flavorful broth for an hour. I tried other time-staggering regimens but always felt that the vegetables added in the later stages of cooking did not taste as good as those added at the start. For maximum flavor, all the vegetables, even ones that usually require brief cooking times, should be added at the outset.

Boosting Flavor

The cheese rind was an interesting find and my research also turned up two other flavor boosters that could be added upfront to the soup—rehydrated porcini mushrooms and their soaking liquid, and pancetta, unsmoked Italian bacon. I made a batch of soup with the porcini but felt that, like the chicken stock, the flavor of the addition was so strong it reduced the vegetables to bit roles.

Pancetta must be sautéed to render its fat and release its flavor. I cooked a little pancetta until crisp in some olive oil, then added the water and vegetables. Like the cheese rind, the pancetta contributed depth. While the soup made with the cheese rind was buttery and nutty, the soup with pancetta had a very subtle pork and spice flavor. I tried regular American bacon as well. It was a bit stronger, and lent the soup a smoky element. I prefer the subtler flavor the pancetta, but either pancetta or smoked bacon is a significant improvement over water alone.

Up until this point, I had focused on ingredients that went into the soup pot at the start. But many traditional Mediterranean recipes stir in fresh herbs or herb pastes just before the soup is served. Pesto is the most common choice. The first time I added pesto I was hooked. The heat of the soup releases the perfume of the basil and garlic and creates another delicious layer of flavor.

I tried several other ideas. Minced fresh herbs were fine, but could not compete with pesto. Gremolata, a mixture of parsley, rosemary, and lemon zest often sprinkled over osso buco just before serving, was good, but the lemon struck me as slightly out of place in this soup. However, a simple mixture of minced fresh rosemary, garlic, and extra-virgin olive oil was delicious. As with the pesto, the oil adds some fat to a soup that is otherwise very lean. The rosemary and garlic combo is very strong and must be used in smaller quantities than pesto.

MASTER RECIPE FOR CLASSIC MINESTRONE
SERVES 6 TO 8

The rind from a wedge of Parmesan cheese, preferably Parmigiano-Reggiano, adds complexity and depth to a soup made with water instead of stock. Remove the rind from a wedge of fresh Parmesan. (Rinds from which all the cheese has been grated can be stored in a zip-lock bag in the freezer to use as needed.) To use different vegetables or beans, *see* "Varying Minestrone," right.

- 2 small leeks (or 1 large), white and light green parts sliced thin crosswise (about ¾ cup) and washed thoroughly
- 2 medium carrots, peeled and cut into small dice (about ¾ cup)
- 2 small onions, peeled and cut into small dice (about ¾ cup)
- 2 medium celery stalks, trimmed and cut into small dice (about ¾ cup)
- 1 medium baking potato, peeled and cut into medium dice (about 1¼ cups)
- 1 medium zucchini, trimmed and cut into medium dice (about 1¼ cups)
- 3 cups stemmed spinach leaves, cut into thin strips
- 1 can (28-ounces) whole tomatoes packed in juice, drained, and chopped
- 8 cups water
- 1 Parmesan cheese rind, about 5 x 2 inches
  Salt
- 1 can (15-ounces) cannellini beans, drained and rinsed (about 1½ cups)
- ¼ cup basil pesto (or 1 tablespoon minced fresh rosemary mixed with 1 teaspoon minced garlic and 1 tablespoon extra-virgin olive oil)
  Pepper

1. Bring vegetables, tomatoes, water, cheese rind, and 1 teaspoon salt to boil in a soup kettle or pot. Reduce heat to medium-low; simmer, uncovered and stirring occasionally, until vegetables are tender but still hold their shape, about 1 hour. (Soup can be refrigerated in airtight container for 3 days or frozen for 1 month. Defrost if necessary and reheat before proceeding with recipe.)

2. Add beans and cook just until heated through, about 5 minutes. Remove pot from heat. Remove and discard cheese rind. Stir in pesto (or rosemary-garlic mixture). Adjust seasonings, adding pepper and more salt, if necessary. Ladle soup into bowls and serve immediately.

CLASSIC MINESTRONE WITH PANCETTA
SERVES 6 TO 8

Pancetta, unsmoked Italian bacon, can be used in place of a cheese rind to boost flavor in the soup. Because it has been smoked, American bacon can overwhelm the vegetables. Try cooking bacon strips in simmering water for one minute to wash away some of the smokiness.

Mince 2 ounces thinly sliced pancetta (or an equal amount of blanched bacon) and sauté in 1 tablespoon extra-virgin olive oil in soup kettle until crisp, 3 to 4 minutes. Proceed with Master Recipe, adding vegetables, tomatoes, and water but omitting cheese rind.

CLASSIC MINESTRONE WITH RICE OR PASTA
SERVES 6 TO 8

Adding pasta or rice makes this hearty soup appropriate as a dinner. If the soup seems too thick after adding the pasta or rice, stir in a little water. Pasta and rice do not hold up well when refrigerated or frozen, so serve this soup as soon as the pasta or rice is tender.

Follow Master Recipe or Classic Minestrone with Pancetta until vegetables are tender. Add ½ cup arborio rice or small pasta shape, such as elbows, ditalini, or orzo, and continue cooking until rice is tender but still a bit firm in the center of each grain, about 20 minutes, or until pasta is al dente, 8 to 12 minutes, depending on the shape. Add beans and continue with recipe.

Defining Hash Brown Potatoes

No need to precook the potatoes—freshly grated spuds cooked in a sizzling hot pan with melted butter are the taste test winner.

⇒ BY SUSAN LOGOZZO ⇐

The recollection of fragrant, crisply fried potato cakes being served in a diner by a short order cook provided the inspiration for me to perfect my own hash brown recipe.

After researching potato recipes, I decided I had to make a distinction between hash browns and their close relatives—home fries, potato pancakes, and roesti. To my mind, home fries, a close relative of hash browns, are made from potatoes that are always cooked first, then chopped or sliced, sautéed, tossed with onions in oil or bacon fat, and served in a mound. Potato pancakes are a more distant ethnic cousin, always made with egg and a starch binder, which give them a different appearance and a softer texture. Roesti, raw grated potatoes cooked in a large skillet, are the most similar to hash browns. However, they are much thicker and are usually cut into wedges and served as a potato accompaniment at dinner. I concluded that hash browns are best defined as thin, crisply sautéed potato cakes made with grated or chopped potatoes, raw or precooked.

The Potato

Even though I assumed a starchier potato would be best suited for this assignment, I began by testing every variety of potato in my local market. After thorough testing, the only type I completely eliminated were the waxy or low-starch varieties, such as red bliss, which did not stay together or brown well and were also lacking in flavor. The all-purpose potato sold in plastic bags in the supermarket, which has a medium starch content, worked well enough to be considered an adequate choice. I also liked the buttery color, as well as the taste, of Yukon golds, another medium-starch potato. But the russet or Idaho, a high-starch potato, yielded the best results overall. It adhered well, browned beautifully, and had the most pronounced potato flavor.

My next challenge was to decide between raw and precooked potatoes. My guess was that precooked potatoes would be my choice, but side by side taste tests convinced me I was wrong. Precooked potatoes tasted good, but when cut into chunks they did not stay together in a cohesive cake, and when grated they needed to be pressed very hard to form a cake. Unfortunately, this meant they ended up having the mouthfeel of fried mashed potato. Although this is an accept-

Although the potatoes will lose a bit of their original crispness, hash browns can be made ahead of time, placed directly on a baking sheet, covered with a paper towel or brown paper, and held in a warm oven at 250 degrees for 15 to 20 minutes.

able alternative if you have leftover cooked potatoes, I found that I preferred using raw, grated potatoes. Because they stayed together well while cooking, they could be made into individual rounds or formed into a single large round that could be cut into wedges or folded over, omelet style. I also liked the more textured interior, the pronounced potato taste, and the way the raw shreds of potatoes formed an attractive, deeply browned crust.

Choosing the best method for cutting the potatoes was easy. For the initial tests, I used raw potatoes and tried them coarsely chopped and diced as well as grated, since these three methods were mentioned in several recipes. The chopped potatoes never stayed together in the pan, regardless of how finely they were cut, nor did the diced version. They browned up nicely, but in my opinion, they were simply chopped, sautéed potatoes, not hash browns. I did the remainder of my testing with potatoes grated on the large-hole side of a box grater, which gave the hash browns the texture I was looking for. This could also be done

with the shredding attachment of a food processor, but I found doing it by hand easy and efficient.

To peel or not to peel the potato is a matter of personal preference, based on nutritional and aesthetic factors. The presence of the grated peel altered the taste a bit, but it did not negatively affect the overall cooking method and desired outcome.

Cooking the Hash Browns

After cooking countless batches of hash browns, I found that the pan itself was an important factor. A skillet with sloping sides made it considerably easier to press the potatoes into a flattened shape, invert them, and slide them from the pan. All these tasks were more difficult with a conventional straight-sided frying pan. As for browning, properly seasoned cast-iron pans and uncoated stainless steel pans produced the best exterior, with potatoes that were evenly colored and crusty; however, nonstick pans browned adequately and, obviously, were easy to use and clean.

I also found that lightly salted butter, brought just to the browning point over medium high heat before adding the potatoes, provided good color and a very rich, satisfying taste. (Unsalted butter was also fine, but I always ended up adding extra salt before serving.) Since I find the aroma and taste of fried bacon irresistible, though, I was still anxious to cook my hash browns in bacon fat. But while the rendered fat did add a bacon taste, the potatoes did not achieve the same golden brown color they did with just plain butter. I also found the overall flavor of the potatoes diminished by the lack of butter. Of course, if you're frying bacon for breakfast and have the fat sitting in your pan, add a little butter and use it to cook your hash browns. At this point in my testing, I could predict the outcome of using vegetable oil (canola or corn). The resulting crust was not as golden brown and the taste not as interesting. Mixing butter with the oil helped, but I would base the decision to use oil on dietary restrictions when making hash browns.

My last cooking-method test was to cover the potatoes during cooking. What I found was that the cover trapped steam in the pan, which reduced the crispness of the crust. This was usually not necessary anyway, because I began with a thin layer of potatoes in the pan, which cooked through adequately without covering.

While testing, I used only salt and freshly ground pepper for seasoning, planning to experiment with other ingredients at a later time, but I became so fond of the buttery salt and pepper taste that I decided to use only these seasonings for the master recipe. Of course, adding grated onion or chopped scallions and parsley (or other fresh herbs to suit your taste) is certainly an option. The onion or herbs can either be tossed with the grated potatoes before cooking or sprinkled over the potatoes in the pan before pressing them with the spatula.

I found that my hash browns could be made into one or more individual servings or one large portion (folded or not) that could be cut into wedges. I also liked using hash browns as the base for toppings or folding them over fillings like omelets.

Regardless of how you choose to present the hash browns, however, serve them steaming hot.

Stress-Free Spud Storage

Since potatoes seem almost indestructible compared with other vegetables, their storage is sometimes haphazard. But because various problems resulting from inadequate storage conditions turned up in my reading, I decided to find out how much difference storage really made. I stored all-purpose potatoes in five environments: in a cool (50-60 degrees), dark place; in the refrigerator; in a basket near a sunlit window; in a warm (70-80 degrees), dark place; and in a drawer with some onions at room temperature. I checked all the potatoes after four weeks.

As expected, the potatoes stored in the cool, dark place were firm, had not sprouted, and were crisp and moist when cut. There were no negative marks on the potatoes stored in the refrigerator, either; although some experts say that the sugar level dramatically increases in some potato varieties under these conditions, I could not see or taste any difference between these potatoes and the ones stored in the cool, dark but unrefrigerated environment.

My last three storage tests, however, produced unfavorable results. The potatoes stored in sunlight, in warm storage, and with onions ended up with a greenish tinge along the edges (top, right). According to Dr. Alfred Bushway of the University of Maine, when potatoes are stressed due to improper storage, the level of naturally occuring toxins increases, causing the greenish tinge known as solanine. This portion of the potato should be totally cut away, since solanine is not destroyed by cooking.

The skin of the potatoes stored in sunlight became gray and mottled, while the potatoes stored in a warm place and those stored with onions sprouted (bottom, right) and became soft and wrinkled. Sprouts also contain increased levels of solanine that should be cut away before cooking.

–S.L.

TECHNIQUE | MAKING HASH BROWNS

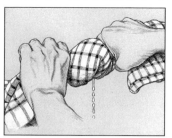

1. To release water from the grated potatoes, place them in a towel and, using two hands, twist towel tightly.

2. Before serving, fold the large flat of hash browns over, omelet style.

CLASSIC HASH BROWNS
SERVES 4

To prevent potatoes from turning brown, grate them just before cooking. For individual servings, simply divide the grated potatoes into four equal portions and reduce cooking time to 5 minutes per side. To vary flavor, add 2 tablespoons grated onion, 1 to 2 tablespoons herb of choice, or roasted garlic to taste, to the raw grated potatoes. You can also garnish the cooked hash browns with snipped chives or scallion tops just before serving.

- 1 pound high-starch potatoes such as russets or Idahos, peeled, washed, dried, grated coarse, and squeezed dry following illustration 1, above (1½ cups loosely packed grated potatoes)
- ¼ teaspoon salt
  Ground black pepper
- 1 tablespoon butter

1. Toss fully dried grated potatoes with salt and pepper in a medium bowl.

2. Meanwhile, heat half the butter in a 10-inch skillet over medium-high heat until it just starts to brown, then scatter potatoes evenly over entire pan bottom. Using a wide spatula, firmly press potatoes to flatten; reduce heat to medium and continue cooking until dark golden brown and crisp, 7 to 8 minutes.

3. Invert hash browns, browned side up, onto a large plate; add remaining butter to pan. Once butter has melted, slide hash browns back into pan. Continue to cook over medium heat until remaining side is dark golden brown and crisp, 5 to 6 minutes longer.

4. Fold the potato round in half; cook about 1 minute longer. Slide hash browns onto plate or cutting board, cut into wedges, and serve immediately.

HASH BROWN "OMELET" WITH CHEDDAR, TOMATO, AND BASIL
SERVES 4

The crisp potatoes offer a nice contrast to many filling ingredients. Fill with ¼ cup chopped ham, bacon, or sausage and/or ¼ cup cooked vegetables, such as mushrooms, peppers, or onions.

- 1 recipe Classic Hash Browns
- 1 medium tomato, cut into small dice
- 1 tablespoon chopped fresh basil leaves
- 1 ounce (¼ cup) grated cheddar cheese

Follow recipe for Classic Hash Browns, topping potatoes with tomato, basil, and cheddar as soon as they are inverted back into buttered skillet. Continue with recipe, folding potato cake and cooking until cheese melts. Serve immediately.

OPEN-FACED HASH BROWNS WITH HAM, TOMATO, AND SWISS CHEESE
SERVES 4

As with the Hash Brown "Omelet" (see above), these individual potato cakes can be topped with a host of ingredients. For an interesting variation, you can top the fully cooked hash browns with smoked salmon and sour cream after you remove them from the skillet.

- 1 recipe Classic Hash Browns
- 1 slice (about 1 ounce) deli-style baked ham, quartered
- 1 small tomato, sliced thin
- 1 ounce (¼ cup) grated Swiss cheese

Follow recipe directions for individual servings of Classic Hash Browns, turning them with a spatula rather than inverting them, and adding remaining butter as they are turned. Reduce cooking time to about 5 minutes per side. Once potatoes are fully browned, top each with a portion of ham, tomato, and cheese. Cover and continue to cook over medium heat until cheese melts, 1 to 2 minutes longer. Serve immediately.

Chicken Parmesan Simplified

Use boneless, skinless breasts without the tenderloins, keep the egg dip and bread-crumb dredge simple, then put the Parmesan on top and the herbs in the sauce.

⋑ BY PAM ANDERSON WITH MELISSA HAMILTON ⋘

Up until a couple of years ago, I hadn't made Parmesan anything except for the very occasional eggplant. I cook veal so infrequently that I could think of a hundred things I'd do with it before "parmesaning" it—breading and sautéing it, topping it with mozzarella cheese, then serving it with tomato sauce—and I had just never gotten around to trying it with chicken. But the first time I made chicken Parmesan, it became the instant family favorite—meaning, of course, the kids loved it. Why should I be surprised? Chicken Parmesan is little more than a plain cheese pizza, the boneless, skinless chicken breast standing in for the crust.

Chicken Parmesan is not a particularly hard dish to make, but there are a lot of piddly steps that can bog you down if you're in a hurry. First you must prepare and pound the chicken breasts. You must make an egg wash for dipping and a crumb mixture for dredging. And unless you buy them pre-grated, there's mozzarella and Parmesan cheese to grate as well. As simple as it is, you need to make a quick tomato sauce and boil water for pasta, since spaghetti is almost always served with this dish. And of course there's an impressive stack of pots, pans, pounders, and plates to wash and dry after dinner.

Since chicken Parmesan was such a family favorite, my goal was to ensure that this dish was the best it could be and doable for a weeknight supper—on the table in less than 30 minutes. I also wanted to avoid a common problem of this dish, a soggy cutlet.

How To Treat The Meat

Up to this point in my chicken Parmesan making, I had bought and pounded standard (6- to 8-ounce) boneless, skinless breasts. As you can imagine, these full-size breasts pounded into massive cutlets that demanded one of three choices: batch cooking, which was time-consuming; two skillets, which made an even bigger mess; or oven-frying, which didn't brown the cutlets as well. Semi-attached to these large breasts were the extra-tender tenderloin pieces that had a tendency to fall off during pounding or disintegrate when I removed the tendon.

These problems, however, were easily solved once I set my mind to it. Reducing portion size was a step in the right direction. A standard boneless, skinless breast half, when served with a side of spaghetti, a ladle of tomato sauce, and a topping of rich mozzarella cheese is too much for the average appetite. One breast half split horizontally with the tenderloin removed (*see* illustrations 1 and 2, below) was perfect for two people. In addition, I discovered that splitting the breast in this way drastically cut down on the need for pounding.

Specially trimmed chicken breasts—a relatively new product on the market—also worked well for chicken Parmesan. Fully trimmed with tenderloins removed, these boneless, skinless breast halves weigh 4 to 5 ounces each and require minimal pounding.

Pound Softly and Keep a Flat Surface

Whether you buy boneless, skinless breasts and split them or use the specially trimmed ones, you will need to do at least some pounding to make them thin enough to cook through before the coating begins to burn. I tried several different pounding gadgets—makeshift as well as purchased—and found that the best chicken breast pounders were relatively lightweight with large flat surfaces. The disk-style pounder with a handle in the center (*see* illustration, below) was one of my favorites. As long as I pounded lightly, its relatively large, round surface quickly and efficiently transformed breasts into cutlets. If you don't have this kind of pounder, I suggest pounding gently with a heavier version.

Pounding the chicken lightly with a flat surface was important, but I also discovered which side of the chicken breast I pounded. The pliable cut side of the breast easily flattened to perfection, while the skin side often split, resulting in an unsightly cutlet.

I also found that pounding the breast directly with no protection was messy and damaged the cutlet. I tried wax paper, but it disintegrated during pounding and bits of paper stuck to the breast. Flattening it between two sheets of plastic wrap ensured perfectly shaped cutlets.

Egg Dip, Bread Dredge

With pounded breasts in hand, I moved on to coating. Traditionally, chicken cutlets are dipped in an egg wash before being rolled in the crumb coating. Some recipes go even further, dredging the cutlet in flour before the egg dip. Was this

---

STEP-BY-STEP | PREPARING CHICKEN CUTLETS

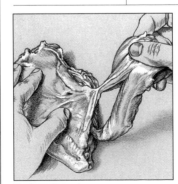

For large breasts:
1. Tenderloins tend to fall off or disintegrate during pounding, so they are best removed and reserved for another use.

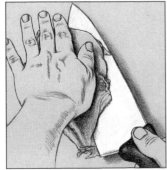

2. Halve breasts horizontally to form two cutlets. Cut this way, they need little or no pounding. If pounding, follow steps for small breasts.

For small breasts:
1. Place breasts, skinned side down, on a large sheet of plastic wrap. Cover with a second sheet and pound gently.

2. Breast pounded to 1/4-inch thickness (right) has considerably more surface area than unpounded breast (left).

extra flour step necessary? I thought not, and I was right. Although the coating of the flour-dipped cutlet was thicker, it tended to separate from the cutlet, peeling off in sheets. The simple egg and bread crumb coating seemed to form an almost inseparable skin.

I tried other dips—buttermilk, yogurt, even mayonnaise—but I didn't find anything better than just plain egg. Mayo-coated chicken sautéed into a greasy cutlet, while buttermilk and yogurt ones tasted too distinct to blend with the Parmesan flavors. A cutlet dipped in egg white was not an improvement over one dipped in whole egg—at least not enough to warrant the extra step of separating the egg. Since one egg perfectly coated four cutlets, I had no need to extend the egg with water or milk as some recipes did.

In my mind, dry bread crumbs were the coating to beat. A crushed potato chip coating was surprisingly good, but too distinctly flavored for chicken Parmesan. Cornflake crumbs were perfectly textured—fine and beautifully crisp—but, like the potato chips, they tasted too pronounced. Matzo meal cutlets were too bland, while those coated with crushed saltines were too soft. The cracker-meal-coated cutlets rivaled the dry bread crumb ones, but were not good enough to warrant a special purchase. Bread crumbs could not be beat, and panko (Japanese-style bread crumbs) turned out to be both my personal favorite and the favorite in a blind tasting (see "Finding the Best Bread Crumbs," right).

Of the three cooking options for the cutlets—oven-frying, broiling, and sautéing—I preferred sautéing. I found the oven method potentially unsafe, especially since lightweight roasting pans can warp at high temperatures (see "Rating Cookie Sheets," March/April 1998) and cause hot oil to spatter. Pulling a hot, oil-coated shallow pan in and out of the oven can also be dangerous. Broiling, the second method I tested, resulted in inconsistently and unimpressively browned cutlets. No other cooking method produced the beautiful, evenly golden brown color or the rich, satisfying flavor of sautéing. And using the smaller portions of chicken made it possible to cook four cutlets at the same time, eliminating the need for a second pan.

Which fat should be used for sautéing the cutlets? For a full-flavored dish like chicken Parmesan I might have guessed it didn't much matter. I was wrong. Cutlets sautéed in pure olive oil were markedly better than those sautéed in vegetable oil. Cutlets sautéed in a combination of pure olive oil and butter were acceptable but not superior to those sautéed in olive oil, and sautéing in pure butter produced too rich a taste.

Some recipes, especially older ones, instruct the reader to top cooked cutlets with mozzarella cheese and bake them on a bed of tomato sauce, covered, until the cheese melts. As far as I was concerned, this step not only added several minutes to the preparation time, it also destroyed my crisp, delicious coating and turned the cutlets into soggy mush. I simply sprinkled my cooked cutlets with mozzarella and Parmesan and broiled them until the cheeses melted and turned spotty brown. After that they were ready for tomato sauce and the accompanying pasta.

Buying trimmed chicken breasts saves time and preparation (although halving standard-size breasts is almost as easy). The egg dip and bread dredge couldn't be simpler. Buying shredded mozzarella and grated Parmesan cheese also shaves minutes off preparation time, and using crushed tomatoes renders sauce-making almost as simple as opening a can.

Chicken Parmesan in half an hour. Now all you need is someone to do the dishes!

CHICKEN PARMESAN, UPDATED
SERVES 4

Though not widely available, panko—Japanese bread crumbs—makes an excellent coating. It can often be found at Asian markets and can also be mail-ordered (see Resources, page 32).

Simple Tomato Sauce with Basil and Garlic
- 2   medium garlic cloves, minced
- ¼   cup extra-virgin olive oil
- 1   can (28 ounces) crushed tomatoes, preferably Red Pack, Progresso, or Muir Glen Ground Peeled
- ½   teaspoon dried basil
- ¼   teaspoon dried oregano
- ¼   teaspoon sugar
-   Salt and ground black pepper

Chicken Parmesan
- 1   large egg
-   Salt and ground black pepper
- ½–1   cup dry bread crumbs
- 2   large boneless, skinless chicken breasts (8 ounces each), or 4 trimmed chicken breasts (4 to 5 ounces each), prepared according to illustrations, page 10
- ¼   cup olive oil
- ¾   cup (3 ounces) grated part-skim mozzarella cheese
- ¼   cup (1 ounce) grated Parmesan cheese, plus extra for passing
- 8   ounces spaghetti or linguine

1. In a large saucepan or Dutch oven, heat garlic and oil together over medium-high heat until garlic starts to sizzle. Stir in tomatoes, basil, oregano, sugar, a pinch of salt, and a couple of grinds of pepper; bring to a simmer. Continue to simmer until sauce thickens a bit and flavors meld, 10 to 12 minutes. Taste sauce, adjusting salt if necessary. Cover and keep warm.

2. Bring 2 to 3 quarts of water to boil in a

large soup kettle. Beat egg and a heaping ¼ teaspoon salt in a small pie plate or other shallow dish until completely broken up. Mix bread crumbs, a heaping ¼ teaspoon salt, and a grind or two of pepper in another small pie plate or shallow baking dish.

3. Preheat broiler. Working with one at a time, dip both sides of each cutlet in the beaten egg, then in the bread crumb mixture. Set cutlets on large wire rack set over a jelly roll pan.

4. Add 2 teaspoons salt and the spaghetti to the boiling water. Boil while cutlets sauté (next step).

5. Heat oil over medium-high heat in a 12-inch skillet. When oil starts to shimmer, add cutlets and sauté until golden brown on each side, about 5 to 6 minutes total. Wash and dry wire rack and return to jelly roll pan. Transfer cutlets to wire rack and top each with equal portions of mozzarella and Parmesan cheeses. Place pan of cutlets 4 to 5 inches from heat source and broil until cheese melts and is spotty brown, about 3 minutes. Drain spaghetti.

6. Transfer a chicken cutlet and a portion of spaghetti to each of 4 plates. Spoon two or three tablespoons of sauce over part of each cutlet, then sauce the spaghetti as desired. Serve immediately with extra Parmesan passed separately.

White Mushrooms Revisited

High-heat roasting coaxes the inherent deep flavors out of these everyday mushrooms.

≥ BY JOHN WILLOUGHBY WITH ANNE YAMANAKA ≤

White mushrooms have a lousy reputation. Cooks who ooh and aah over porcini, portobellos, shiitake, and other exotic mushrooms often find the white mushroom, also called the button, to be beneath their consideration.

There is good reason for this. It has little to do, however, with the inherent character of the white mushroom. Instead, it results from the way these fungi were used in the '50s and '60s when, as the single commercially cultivated mushroom, they were the only choice available to most American cooks. Unfortunately, the versions that most of us got served were either overcooked or (even worse and even more often) jarred. These experiences left us feeling that white mushrooms were pallid, watery, tasteless, insipid, rubbery things, best left to the purveyors of third-rate commercial pizza.

A recent visit to my mother's house in our Iowa hometown caused me to reassess this conviction. Unlike markets in Boston or San Francisco or even Cleveland, the only mushrooms available in the single grocery store in Grundy Center, Iowa, were those familiar small, creamy white ones. But this time, instead of pitying the cooks of the town, I began to wonder if in fact this was so terrible. After all, I reasoned, these are mushrooms, and not cardboard. There must be ways of cooking them that would bring out the deep, rich, earthy flavors for which their tonier cousins are so highly prized. I decided to find out.

Searching for Flavor
I began my research not by consulting cookbooks, but by trying to figure out what exactly was the "mushroom flavor" that I wanted to elicit. This turned out to be a difficult task, since the taste of mushrooms is notoriously hard to pin down. But I was intrigued by the way "meaty" is so frequently used to describe mushrooms and decided to try treating my white mushrooms like steaks. In other words, I would cook them at high heat to brown the outside and bring out the flavor. At the same time, I knew that I would also have to address the most common issue in cooking mushrooms—how to deal with the moisture that makes up 80 percent of the fungi.

Parisians learned how to grow white mushrooms in the early 1700s, but managed to keep the process secret for several decades.

Now I turned to cookbooks, where I found that the most common method of cooking mushrooms is sautéing. Since that is also the initial step in cooking many meats, I decided to start there. The sautéing time seemed crucial, so I cut a handful of mushrooms into uniform ⅜-inch slices and sautéed them in a bit of oil over medium-high heat for times ranging from three minutes to eight minutes, removing one slice from the pan every minute. I preferred those cooked for six minutes, since at this point the mushrooms were moist all the way through—a condition I had learned to recognize as indicating doneness—and slightly browned but not burned on the exterior. Much of the moisture had been cooked out and evaporated, but some still remained in the pan. These mushrooms also tasted pretty good, with a fairly deep, somewhat complex, nutty flavor from the exterior browning. The texture, however, was not ideal; while tender, the mushrooms were also a bit rubbery.

I next tried sautéing the mushrooms until they were exuding no more liquid, as suggested by several cookbooks. This took about 12 minutes, though, and by that time the mushrooms had acquired a dark, almost burned taste, and again were slightly rubbery. Not terrible, but not great either. When I tried pan-frying the mushrooms longer at lower heat, the results were one notch further down the flavor/texture scale.

I decided to try some methods that mimicked even more closely the cooking of meat. I reasoned that an initial burst of high heat to brown the mushrooms, followed by a longer cooking period, might give me the texture as well as the flavor that I was looking for. So I tried both sautéing and high-heat roasting for the preliminary browning, followed by a longer roasting at a somewhat lower temperature. I also decided to throw in a slightly bizarre method suggested to me by a friend, who swore that it had been suggested to him by a celebrity chef: boiling the mushrooms for one minute before cooking them. This, he claimed, somehow extracted the liquid from the mushrooms and made them brown up quicker and better.

I divided a group of mushrooms of approximately equal size into three batches. The first I blanched in boiling water for one minute; the second I sautéed for four minutes over medium-high heat, reasoning that I should not fully cook them since they would finish in the oven; the third I tossed with a bit of oil and roasted for 10 minutes at 450 degrees, which was just long enough to get them nicely browned on the exterior. I then tossed each batch with a teaspoon of olive oil, put each of them in a separate small bowl, and roasted them all at 400 degrees for 20 minutes.

The differences were substantial. The pre-boiled mushrooms were an unappetizing tan color, and retained a vegetal taste that I did not particularly like. The pre-sautéed mushrooms had less than a teaspoon of liquid in the bowl and were moist throughout and relatively well browned. They also had a pleasant, rather rich flavor.

The pre-roasted mushrooms, however, were my clear favorite. Slight brown marks on the bottom of the bowl were all that remained of the evaporated liquid, and the mushrooms were not only moist all the way through but had a deep, rich, pronounced flavor that seemed at once meaty and nutty. This was the real mushroom flavor that I had been trying to coax from this everyday mushroom. After further testing of both higher and lower oven temperatures, I found that I could simply roast the mushrooms at a constant 450 degrees, as long as I turned them once near the end of the cooking time.

Stuffing the Caps
Although I liked simply tossing these roasted mushrooms with spice mixes or combinations of herbs and garlic, I started wondering if pre-roasting would improve that old cocktail party standby, stuffed mushroom caps. A final taste test showed that, as I'd

expected, pre-roasted caps had a fuller, deeper flavor than those I'd stuffed raw and roasted; the filling was also less soggy and more flavorful.

So whether you're going to simply toss them with other ingredients for a side dish or stuff them for an appetizer, the way to get the best flavor from white mushrooms is to stick them in the oven at high heat. Do that, and you will find yourself with new respect for these everyday fungi.

SIMPLE ROASTED MUSHROOMS
SERVES 4

    1   pound white mushrooms, washed and halved if small, quartered if medium, cut into sixths if large
    2   tablespoons olive oil
         Salt
         Ground black pepper

1. Adjust oven rack to lowest position and heat oven to 450 degrees.

2. Toss mushrooms with olive oil and salt and pepper to taste in medium bowl. Arrange in a single layer on a large low-sided roasting pan or jelly-roll pan. Roast until released juices have nearly evaporated and mushroom surfaces facing pan are browned, 12 to 15 minutes. Remove pan from oven and turn mushrooms with a metal spatula. Continue to roast until mushroom liquid has completely evaporated and mushrooms are brown all over, about 5 to 10 minutes longer. Serve.

ROASTED MUSHROOMS WITH GARLIC, OLIVES, AND THYME
SERVES 4

Follow recipe for Simple Roasted Mushrooms. While mushrooms roast, mix 1 minced small garlic clove, 1 tablespoon minced fresh thyme leaves, and 12 pitted, coarsely chopped brine-cured black olives in a medium bowl. Add roasted mushrooms to bowl along with 1 tablespoon balsamic vinegar; toss to coat. Serve warm or at room temperature.

ROASTED MUSHROOMS WITH WARM SPICES
SERVES 4

Follow recipe for Simple Roasted Mushrooms. While mushrooms roast, mix 1 teaspoon paprika, 1/4 teaspoon cinnamon, 1/4 teaspoon nutmeg, 1/4 teaspoon minced garlic, 1/4 teaspoon ground cumin, 3/4 teaspoon salt, and 1/2 teaspoon black pepper in a medium bowl. After the first 15 minutes of roasting, remove mushrooms from oven, add to spice mixture, and toss to coat. Return mushrooms to roasting pan in a single layer. Continue to roast on bottom rack 5 minutes longer. Return mushrooms to bowl; add 1 1/2 tablespoons lemon juice and toss to coat. Serve warm or at room temperature.

ROASTED MUSHROOM CAPS
SERVES 4

    24   large mushrooms, stems and caps separated and washed
    2   tablespoons olive oil
         Salt
         Ground black pepper

1. Adjust oven rack to lowest position and heat oven to 450 degrees.

2. Toss mushroom caps and stems, olive oil, and salt and pepper to taste in medium bowl. Arrange caps, gill side down, in a single layer on a large low-sided roasting pan or jelly-roll pan with stems placed alongside. Roast until mushrooms have released some juice and are brown around edges facing the pan, 12 to 15 minutes. Remove pan from oven and turn caps over with a metal spatula. Continue to roast until mushroom liquid has completely evaporated and mushroom caps and stems are brown all over, about 5 to 10 minutes longer. Use for the filling below or any other filling of your choice.

MUSHROOMS STUFFED WITH BACON, SPINACH, AND BLUE CHEESE
MAKES 24 STUFFED MUSHROOMS

    1   recipe Roasted Mushrooms Caps (*see* above)
    6   ounces (about 6 slices) bacon, cut crosswise into 1/4 inch strips
    1/2 medium red onion, minced
    1   large garlic clove, minced
    6   ounces spinach, stems removed, washed thoroughly and chopped coarse
    1/4 cup plain dried bread crumbs
    3   tablespoons ricotta cheese
    2   ounces blue cheese, crumbled
         Salt and ground black pepper

1. Follow recipe for Roasted Mushroom Caps, adjusting oven rack to center position and leaving oven temperature at 450 degrees. With cooked mushroom caps still on roasting pan, remove cooked stems and set aside.

2. Meanwhile, fry bacon in a large skillet over medium heat until crisp, 5 to 7 minutes. Remove and drain on paper towels; discard all but 1 tablespoon of drippings. Add onion; cook until soft, 6 to 8 minutes. Add garlic; cook about 1 minute longer. Add spinach; cook until wilted, about 2 minutes. Transfer spinach mixture to large bowl; let cool for 10 minutes.

3. Transfer spinach mixture to food processor, along with bread crumbs, ricotta, one ounce blue cheese, and roasted mushroom stems; process to a chunky puree, scraping down the sides of the processor at least once to ensure an even texture. Return spinach mixture to large mixing bowl; stir in bacon bits. Fill each mushroom cap with a heaping teaspoon of filling; top each with a portion of remaining blue cheese.

4. Roast stuffed mushrooms until cheese is melted and filling is hot throughout, about 8 minutes. Serve warm.

FUNGI COUSINS

Although they have very different reputations, white, crimini, and portobello are all varieties of the *Agaricus* mushroom. White mushrooms are usually sold with their gills closed but those with slightly open gills have a deep, rich flavor, more like that of crimini (left) or portobellos (right).

Grilled Leg of Lamb

Butterfly the leg, then grill it over a high heat, but an indirect fire. And don't worry about how to slice it.

⇒ BY STEPHANIE LYNESS ⇐

I was having a mob of serious meat-eaters to dinner. Summer was on the wane but it would be at least another month or two before I would be ready to retire the charcoal grill for the season. I didn't want to spend a fortune on steak or lamb chops, but I didn't want to be flipping burgers either. Leg of lamb seemed just the ticket.

I went to my local butcher and asked him to prepare a leg of lamb for grilling. He boned and then butterflied it (a technique in which several cuts are made in the boned flesh to open and flatten the leg so that its uneven topography is smoothed to an even thickness). The result was a large, unwieldy piece of meat, about ¾-inch thick and covered with a thin layer of fat. I used a 21-inch kettle grill and my preferred fuel—hardwood charcoal—to build a two-level fire. I seasoned the meat with salt and pepper and, wary of flaming, used no oil. I placed the meat fat-side-down over the coals, intending to brown it quickly over direct heat and then finish it over indirect.

The results dismayed me. The leg flamed and blackened. It was difficult to maneuver on the grill because of its size. The connective tissue in the shank retracted and curled so badly that eventually I had to cut it off and cook it overtime. The rest of the leg cooked unevenly and tasted oily as well as scorched from the flame. Because it was so thin, it was difficult to carve into attractive slices.

I made up my mind to start from scratch and find out the best way to grill a leg of lamb. I had several questions: First, is butterflying really necessary and if so, what's the best way to do it? Is there a way to grill the shank attached to the leg or must I always cut it off? Direct heat chars the leg more than I like, but how else can I grill it? Do I need to cover the grill to control the flaming? And is it necessary to carve a leg of lamb against the grain for the sake of tenderness?

My goal was to come up with a butchering technique that would yield an easy-to-manage piece of meat, thick enough to carve into attractive slices. And as always when grilling, I wanted a crust that was caramelized but not blackened and a moist, tender interior.

I decided to get an expert on the butchering: I called Patrick Boisjot, the chef at the Institute of Gastronomy and Culinary Arts at the University of New Haven. Boisjot approaches butchering from a restaurant's perspective, and his description of his procedure fascinated me. He began by boning a leg (*see* steps 1 through 12, pages 16 and 17) and showing me the six muscles—the meaty, dome-shaped top and smaller bottom rounds; the small cylindrical eye of round; the flat trapezoidal hip; the round knuckle; and the oblong shank. He explained that he prefers to separate the muscles from one another (they pull apart very easily) and then cook and carve each separately because that allows each muscle to be cooked perfectly and carved against the grain into large slices for optimal tenderness. (After the meat is butterflied, the grain runs every which way and it's impossible to carve against the grain.)

Cooking the muscles separately doesn't make sense for a home cook, particularly since people tend to turn to this cut when planning for a crowd. But I tried to adapt Boisjot's technique by boning the leg and cooking it as was—all the muscles intact and unbutterflied—planning to cut the muscles apart after cooking and carve each one separately.

This time, to solve the flaming problem, I cooked the lamb entirely over indirect heat. It browned beautifully and didn't flame, but after 40 minutes it was clear that there wasn't enough heat to cook through the larger muscles (the top round and knuckle).

I knew from previous experience that using the grill cover for anything other than very long cooking would impart an unwanted "off" flavor, so I decided to see if I could solve the problem in the butchering stage.

I was familiar with two methods of butterflying. One calls for cutting straight down into the meat and then spreading the meat open on either side of the cut. The second technique is to cut into the meat horizontally and then open it out like a book. I eventually found that a slightly different method worked best (*see* page 17). The butterflied leg was very large, however, so I cut it in half along a natural separation between the muscles. That not only made it easier to fit the meat on the limited grill space, it also enabled me to turn it with a single pair of tongs rather than struggling with a pair of tongs in each hand. It was also more practical to buy, since I could freeze half if I was cooking for only four.

Grilling with Indirect Heat

Satisfied with my butchering technique, I returned to the cooking. Working again over indirect heat, I grilled my butterflied leg, cut side up, for five minutes. Then I turned it 180 degrees and cooked it five more minutes to ensure that it cooked evenly all round. After 10 minutes the leg was well-browned on the skin side, so I turned it over and repeated the procedure, cooking it another 10 minutes until it registered 130 degrees on a meat thermometer. I let the meat rest 10 minutes and then sliced into it. The outside crust was perfect but inside I still had problems. While the meat in the center was a beautiful medium-rare, the perimeter of the leg was still pale because it had needed more time to rest. And the shank was still undercooked.

The problem with the shank was easy enough to solve; I decided to cut it off and save it for another use. (Some supermarkets also sell the leg without the shank.) Then I tested resting times, letting the meat rest 15, 20, and 25 minutes, and found that 20 minutes was ample time

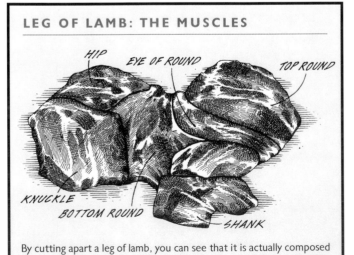

LEG OF LAMB: THE MUSCLES

HIP · EYE OF ROUND · TOP ROUND
KNUCKLE · BOTTOM ROUND · SHANK

By cutting apart a leg of lamb, you can see that it is actually composed of six separate muscles. The orientation of the muscles will differ depending on which of the animal's legs you happen to purchase.

for the juices to be redistributed through the leg. Finally, I experimented with carving to test for tenderness: I carved the meat into thin slices on an angle (to produce slices as large as possible) and disregarded the grain. As it turned out, this was a good decision: Although the different muscles varied in taste and texture, they were all plenty tender.

One final series of tests awaited me. I realized that having run all my tests with hardwood charcoal, I couldn't be sure that my cooking method would hold true for charcoal briquets. It's been my experience that briquets don't burn as hot as hardwood, so I was concerned that the indirect heat method wouldn't produce enough heat to brown and cook the lamb through. After several tests, I determined that I could use the same method with charcoal briquets if I made a pile that generously covered half the grill and was almost as high as the grate.

GRILLED BUTTERFLIED LEG OF LAMB
SERVES 12

Because it burns hotter than regular briquets, I prefer hardwood charcoal. However, since it might not be readily available, I also developed a grilling method for briquets. On those occasions when I want to cook only half a leg of lamb, I prefer the sirloin end.

1	7-pound leg of lamb, boned, butterflied, and halved between the eye and the bottom round (*see* illustrations page 16 and 17)
1½	tablespoons olive oil
	Salt and ground black pepper

1. Open all grill vents. Build a fire large enough to cover half a large (21-inch) charcoal grill and come within 1½ inches of the grill rack, about 5 pounds of hardwood charcoal. (If using briquets, build a fire large enough to cover half the grill and come all the way up to the grill rack, about 7.5 pounds.) Allow charcoal to burn down until the flames have died and all the charcoal is covered with a layer of fine gray ash, about 20 minutes. Return grill rack to position, open lid vents, cover grill with lid, and let rack heat for 5 minutes.

2. Rub olive oil onto all sides of both pieces of lamb and sprinkle with salt and pepper. Place lamb pieces, fat side down, on the side of the rack that is not directly over the coals. Lamb should sizzle when it hits the grill.

3. Grill lamb, uncovered, for 5 minutes. Fat side still down, rotate meat so that outside edges are now closest to the fire; grill, uncovered, until fat side of lamb is a rich dark brown, 3 to 5 minutes longer. With tongs or a large meat fork, turn both pieces over; repeat grilling procedure described above, rotating lamb to ensure even cooking, until an instant-read thermometer inserted into the thickest part of each piece registers 130 degrees for medium rare, about 10 minutes longer. Transfer meat to a large platter or cutting board, tent with foil, and let rest 20 minutes. Slice on an angle and serve.

Marinades and Flavorings
Omit the 1½ tablespoons of olive oil from the Grilled Butterflied Leg of Lamb recipe if you are going to use a marinade. To marinate, place the lamb in a large shallow pan or baking dish. Using hands, rub marinade over all sides. Cover with plastic wrap and refrigerate overnight (or at least 8 hours). Except for the Soy Marinade with Honey and Thyme, which is salty enough, season the marinated lamb with salt and pepper just before grilling.

TANDOORI MARINADE
ENOUGH FOR 1 BUTTERFLIED LEG OF LAMB

In a small bowl, mix ⅓ cup yogurt, 5 to 6 minced garlic cloves (4 teaspoons), grated ginger from a 1-inch piece (1 tablespoon), 2 tablespoons juice from 1 small lemon, 2 teaspoons each ground cumin and coriander, 1 teaspoon each turmeric and cayenne, and ½ teaspoon ground cinnamon.

LEMON MARINADE WITH GREEK FLAVORINGS
ENOUGH FOR 1 BUTTERFLIED LEG OF LAMB

In a small bowl, mix ¼ cup olive oil, 2 tablespoons juice from 1 small lemon, 3 to 4 minced garlic cloves (1 tablespoon), 1 tablespoon each dried oregano and thyme, and pinch of paprika.

GARLIC AND ROSEMARY OIL
ENOUGH FOR 1 BUTTERFLIED LEG OF LAMB

A leg of lamb need marinate only 3 hours in this flavored oil.

In a small bowl, mix 6 to 8 minced garlic cloves (2 tablespoons), 1½ tablespoons of minced fresh rosemary, and ¼ cup olive oil.

SOY MARINADE WITH HONEY AND THYME
(Adapted from a recipe by Jacques Pépin)
ENOUGH FOR 1 BUTTERFLIED LEG OF LAMB

In a small bowl, mix ⅓ cup each honey and soy sauce, 2 to 3 minced garlic cloves (2 teaspoons), grated ginger from a 1-inch piece (1 tablespoon), 1 teaspoon minced fresh thyme leaves, and a pinch of cayenne pepper.

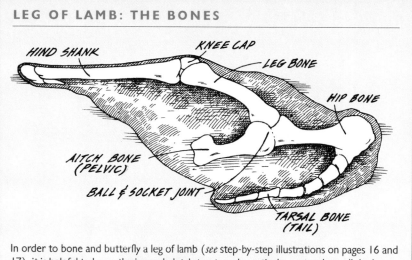

LEG OF LAMB: THE BONES

In order to bone and butterfly a leg of lamb (*see* step-by-step illustrations on pages 16 and 17), it is helpful to know the inner skeletal structure. In particular, note where all the bones come together in the center of the leg at the large ball and socket joint.

GROCERY STORE CUTS

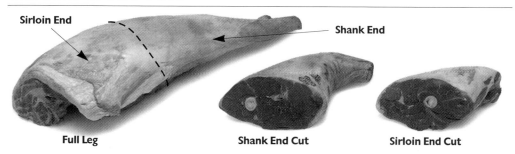

When you go to the grocery store, you will probably be able to buy either a full leg of lamb or a half leg. When buying a half, you can get either the sirloin (upper half) or shank (lower half). Of the two, we preferred the sirloin end because it was slightly more tender.

Boning and Butterflying a Leg of Lamb

The easiest way to get a boned and butterflied leg of lamb is to have your butcher do it for you. But if you don't have a cooperative butcher or you would prefer to do it yourself, it is easily done by following these illustrated steps. We found that we could do a neater job than the butcher—and besides, we had the bones left over for stock.
By Susan Logozzo

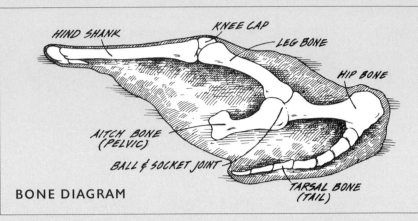

BONE DIAGRAM

HIND SHANK   KNEE CAP   LEG BONE   HIP BONE   AITCH BONE (PELVIC)   BALL & SOCKET JOINT   TARSAL BONE (TAIL)

BONING THE LEG

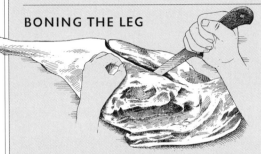

1. Using the tip of a boning knife, make the first cut at the top of the shank, cutting around the knee cap, and continuing down one side of the leg bone.

2. Cut straight down to the leg bone with the tip of the knife, and using the bone as a guide, cut until you reach the hip bone and must stop. Repeat on other side.

3. Cut under and around the knee cap and along the side of the leg bone, loosening the meat from the bone as you go.

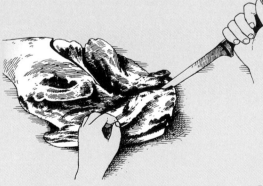

4. Cut around the hip bone to loosen the meat from the bone.

5. Using the tip of the knife, cut the meat away from the aitch or pelvic bone. Use the tip of the knife to scrape the meat away from the bone.

6. At this point, the meat should be free from the leg bone (center), the aitch or pelvic bone (lower left center), and the hip bone (lower right). Ball and socket joint is in center.

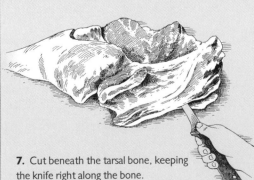

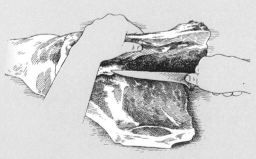

7. Cut beneath the tarsal bone, keeping the knife right along the bone.

Illustration: John Burgoyne

8. Lift the tarsal bone and continue scraping the meat away from the bone until you reach the ball and socket joint.

9. With the tip of the knife, scrape along and beneath the ball and socket joint to loosen it from the meat and cut between ball and socket to loosen.

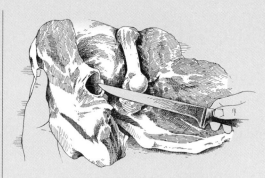

10. Snap the ball and socket apart and pull the tail, hip, and the aitch (pelvic) bones away from the leg bone (save this piece for stock or discard).

11. Continue to cut beneath the leg bone, lifting to release it from the meat as you cut.

12. Lift the leg bone and cartilage around the knee cap to totally separate the leg and shank portion (if your leg came with shank attached) and remove (save for stock or discard).

BUTTERFLYING THE BONED LEG

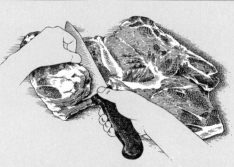

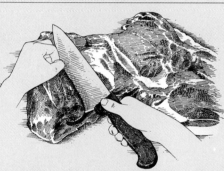

13. To butterfly, lay a large chef's knife flat on the center of the meat at the thinnest part parallel to the top round.

14. Keeping the knife blade parallel to the board, begin slicing through the muscle. Cut horizontally about 1 inch.

15. Begin to unroll the meat (like unrolling a carpet) with your other hand as you continue to cut into the muscle, always keeping the knife blade parallel to the board, cutting about 1 inch at a time, and unrolling as you cut.

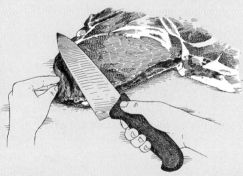

16. Stopping about 1 inch from the end, unfold the edge of the meat and flatten it.

17. The butterflied muscle should be even in thickness.

18. Turn the board around and cut the knuckle muscle on the other side using the same method as in steps 13 to 16.

19. Near the center of the bottom round locate a hard, thick section of fat. Using the tip of the boning knife, cut into the fat to locate the lymph node (a 1/2-inch round, grayish flat nodule). Remove and discard.

20. Divide the butterflied meat in half by cutting between the eye and the bottom round.

21. Turn the pieces of meat over and use a boning knife to cut away the thick pieces of fat, leaving about a 1/8-inch thickness for self-basting during grilling.

Cinnamon Swirl Bread

For the best texture and to avoid air pockets, be frugal with the flour, use a light hand when rolling, and keep a close eye on the proofing time.

⇒ BY SUSAN LOGOZZO ⇐

When I taught yeast bread classes at a culinary school, the cinnamon swirl bread sessions were invariably the most popular. The smells coming from the kitchen were heavenly, and the sometimes less-than-perfect loaves were still irresistible fresh from the oven.

Despite its forgiving nature, though, this bread did pose some problems. Often after baking there were gaps between the swirls of cinnamon filling and the bread, and the filling was prone to leaking out and burning in the pan. I wanted the baked texture to be moist and light, but also firm enough to be sliced fresh the first day and toasted for a few days after. To achieve the best texture and crust, I knew I

Through trial and error, we managed to eliminate the large air holes that often develop between the filling and the bread dough in this style of bread.

needed to perfect the baking time and temperature as well as fine-tune the ingredients. While I was at it, I decided to use this recipe to develop a technique for the ever-popular cinnamon rolls.

Getting the Dough Right

To get my bearings, I tried a range of yeast bread recipes, from rich brioche-type formulas with a high proportion of eggs, butter, and sugar to lean white-sandwich types. When these initial breads were tasted, everyone was drawn to the richer versions, as expected. However, for a more versatile bread that could be cut into thin or thick slices and toasted, I decided on a formula that was a compromise between the two.

I began my tests by focusing on milk, eggs, and sugar—the ingredients that most affect richness and texture. I tested loaves using all milk, all water, and a combination. All milk yielded a denser texture than I wanted; water had the opposite effect, producing a loaf that was too lean. An equal combination of milk and water was the answer. To lighten the texture a little bit more, I increased the 1½ eggs in my original recipe to two. Eggs contribute to the evenness of the crumb as well as to the color and flavor, but

using more than two produced a crumb that was too light and airy for this type of bread.

My final measurements of sugar and butter resulted in a crumb that was tender and soft the first day and retained some moisture for two to three days. The amount of sugar I had started with—one-third cup per loaf—was just enough to provide flavor for the bread without competing with the filling. Of course, since butter also contributes color and richness, I knew that to some extent the amount was a personal preference. For the everyday loaf I was after, I tested from two to eight tablespoons per loaf and settled on four tablespoons, since using more than that resulted in a loaf that was fattier than I wanted.

I tried adding yeast by the direct method (dissolving yeast in warm liquid and adding the remaining ingredients) and also by the rapid-mix method (mixing yeast with dry ingredients and then adding warm liquids), and found very little difference in the quality of the loaf. The rapid-mix method is quicker and works especially well with rapid-rise yeast. The direct method involves an extra step, but the doughs using this method took 20 minutes less for their first rise. Regardless of the method you use, just remember that you'll

kill the yeast if you use any liquid above 125 degrees. When mixing yeast with water initially, the recommended temperature is 110 degrees.

The Main Ingredient

I tested a range of flours, from bleached all-purpose to bread, and found surprisingly little difference. I detected a slight mushiness in bread made with bleached flour, and bread flour produced a slightly coarser texture, which was not objectionable. Overall, the breads made with unbleached all-purpose flours consistently tasted the best, with a fine, even crumb and a pleasant chew.

Almost more important than the particular type of flour you use is the total amount. Depending on a number of factors, including the humidity, the exact size of the eggs, and how precisely the liquids are measured, the dough will take anywhere between 3¼ and 3¾ cups of flour. Any of the doughs I made could have taken the full amount or more, if I forced it in, but when I did, the resulting loaves were dry. I had the best results when I held out the last half-cup of flour, adding it only as necessary, little by little, at the end while kneading, either by hand or machine. To test the dough to determine if the flour level is correct, squeeze it using your entire hand (completely clean with no dough clinging to it) and release it. When the dough does not stick to your hand, the kneading is complete. Even if the dough still feels soft, resist the temptation to add more flour.

Filling, Rolling, and Shaping

Now that I had perfected the dough, I was ready to tackle filling, rolling, and shaping the loaf. For the filling, I tried both brown and white sugar mixed with cinnamon. Although I like the taste of brown sugar, I finally had to rule it out because it melted more readily and leaked through the dough in places during baking.

The amount of filling was determined by one factor besides taste. I discovered that using too much more than one-quarter cup of the cinnamon-sugar mixture resulted in small separations between the filling and the bread because the excess sugar prevented the dough from staying together. I eventually discovered that one-quarter cup of sugar mixed with five teaspoons of cinnamon resulted in a tasty bread with no gaps.

Rolling and shaping the dough into a loaf are crucial steps. In order to create swirls in the finished bread and end up with a loaf that would fit into a 9-inch loaf pan, I rolled the dough out evenly into a rectangle 8 inches wide and 18 inches long. When I rolled the dough out longer than this, it was so thin that the filling popped through the edges in some places. Rolling the dough up evenly and closely was also important. When I rolled the dough too tightly, the filling popped through; rolling too loosely produced an uneven loaf and gaps between the swirls and the bread. Finally, I found that I could prevent the filling from leaking and burning in the pan while baking if I pinched the edges of the bottom seam and the ends of the roll together very tightly.

Proofing and Baking

Getting the dough mixed, risen, and shaped still doesn't guarantee great bread. Proofing time is also crucial. In fact, finding the proper proofing time entirely solved the gap puzzle. When I underproofed the shaped loaf by allowing it to rise just to the top of the pan, the baked bread was dense and did not have a fully risen, attractive shape. But, when I allowed the unbaked loaf to proof too much, 1½ inches or more above the pan, I ended up with those unwanted gaps between dough and filling. My overproofed loaves also collapsed in the oven. (Like a balloon, a loaf can only stretch so far before breaking.) I learned to control this by leaving room for the "ovenspring" or final burst of carbon dioxide before the yeast dies in the heat of the oven. Allowing the dough to rise just 1 inch above the top of a 9-inch loaf pan before baking resulted in a perfectly shaped loaf with no gaps.

To determine the best baking temperature, I first tested the bread in a slow oven (300 to 325 degrees). Because this allowed the unbaked loaf too long a time to continue to rise before the yeast died (at an internal temperature of 140 degrees), the bread rose too much and lost its

1. After rolling out dough, brush liberally with milk.

2. Sprinkle filling evenly over dough, leaving ½-inch border on far end.

3. Roll up dough, pinching gently with fingertips.

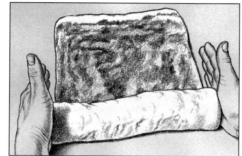

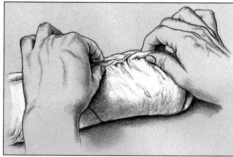

4. To keep loaf from stretching beyond 9 inches, use hands to occasionally push ends in as dough is rolled.

5. Use fingertips to pinch the dough ends together very tightly to form a secure seam.

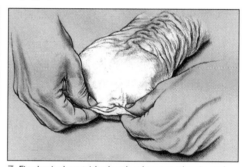

6. With seam side facing up, push in center of ends.

7. Firmly pinch outside dough edges together to seal.

shape. A hotter oven (375 to 425 degrees) resulted in a loaf that was too brown on the outside before it was cooked through. Since my bread formula contained milk, eggs, and sugar, all browning agents, I found that a moderate oven (350 degrees) baked the most evenly.

Inserting an instant-read thermometer into the top side edge of the bread proved to be an excellent method of testing doneness. The two other methods for testing doneness, by color and by tapping the bottom for a hollow sound, were unreliable. This bread colors pretty deeply before it is totally cooked internally, and because it is a soft bread, even when it is totally baked it does not sound hollow when tapped. I tested final internal temperatures between 180 and 210 degrees and found 185 to 188 to be the ideal range. Technically, bread is not totally finished

STEP-BY-STEP PROOFING AND BAKING THE LOAF

1. After shaping the dough into a loaf, place in prepared pan. It will fill the pan almost halfway.

2. After proofing, the shaped loaf will have risen about 1 inch above the top of the pan.

3. Finished loaf will have risen ⅓ more in the oven before the yeast succumbs—this is called "ovenspring."

baking until all the steam has evaporated and it has cooled completely on a rack, so resist the temptation to cut the bread while it's hot! The pressure of the knife will compress the loaf and you'll end up with a doughy slice.

My bread was nearly perfect, but because its natural look was rather dull, I decided to glaze it. Brushing it with milk resulted in a flat finish, and using egg yolk produced a very heavy coating. For a light, shiny finish, the answer was a whole egg thinned with two teaspoons of milk and brushed on just before baking. This was the finishing touch for a great loaf of cinnamon swirl bread.

CINNAMON SWIRL BREAD
MAKES 1 LOAF

If you like, the dough can be made one day, refrigerated overnight, then shaped, proofed, and baked the next day. This recipe also doubles easily.

Enriched Bread Dough
1/2	cup milk
4	tablespoons (1/2 stick) unsalted butter, cut into 1/2 inch pieces
1	package (2 1/4 teaspoons) dry active yeast
1/2	cup warm water (110 degrees)
1/3	cup sugar
2	large eggs
1 1/2	teaspoons salt
3 1/4–3 3/4	cups unbleached all-purpose flour

Filling and Glaze
1/4	cup sugar
5	teaspoons cinnamon
	Milk for brushing
1	large egg
2	teaspoons milk

1. *For the dough:* Heat milk and butter in small saucepan over medium heat until butter melts. Cool to lukewarm (about 110 degrees).

2. Meanwhile, sprinkle yeast over warm water in bowl of stand mixer fitted with paddle. Beat in sugar and eggs and mix at low speed to blend. Add salt, lukewarm milk mixture, 2 cups of flour; mix at medium speed until thoroughly blended, about 1 minute. Switch to dough hook attachment. Add 1 1/4 cups flour, and knead at medium-low speed, adding additional flour sparingly if dough sticks to sides of bowl, until dough is smooth and comes away from sides of bowl, about 10 minutes.

3. Turn dough onto work surface. Squeeze dough with a clean dry hand. If dough is sticky, knead in up to 1/2 additional cup flour to form a smooth, soft, elastic dough. Transfer dough to a very lightly oiled large plastic container or bowl. Cover top of container with plastic wrap and let rise until double in size, 2 to 2 1/2 hours. (Ideal rising temperature is 75 degrees.) After rise, punch down center of dough once (can be refrigerated, covered, up to 18 hours). Making sure not to fold or misshape dough, turn it onto unfloured work surface; let dough rest, to relax, about 10 minutes.

4. Grease sides and bottom of a 9-by-5-inch loaf pan. Mix sugar and cinnamon in small bowl.

5. Press dough neatly into an evenly shaped 6-by-8-inch rectangle. With short side of dough facing you, roll dough with rolling pin into evenly shaped 8-by-18-inch rectangle (flour counter lightly if dough sticks). Following illustrations 1 through 7, page 19, fill, roll, and seal.

6. Place loaf, seam side down, into prepared pan; press lightly to flatten. Cover top of pan loosely with plastic wrap and set aside to proof. Let rise until dough is 1 inch above top of pan, about 1 1/2 hours, or about 1 hour longer if dough has been refrigerated. As dough nears top of pan, adjust oven rack to center position and heat oven to 350 degrees.

7. Meanwhile, in small bowl, whisk together egg and milk. Gently brush loaf top with egg mixture; bake until loaf is golden brown and instant-read thermometer pushed through top side into center of loaf registers 185 to 188 degrees, 30 to 35 minutes. Remove bread from pan and cool on its side on wire rack until room

temperature, at least 45 minutes. (Can be double-wrapped in plastic wrap and stored at room temperature for four days or frozen up to three months.)

For mixing by hand: Beginning with step 2, sprinkle yeast over water in large bowl. Follow instructions in step 2, using hand mixer or wooden spoon, thoroughly blending ingredients with 2 cups flour. Using wooden spoon, mix in 1 1/4 cups flour. Knead by hand until dough is smooth and elastic, 12 to 15 minutes, adding additional flour if necessary. Transfer dough to lightly oiled container and follow rising instructions.

CINNAMON SWIRL ROLLS
MAKES 1 DOZEN

1	Recipe Enriched Bread Dough
1/3	cup sugar
2	tablespoons cinnamon
1	tablespoon milk
1/2	cup raisins, golden or dark (optional)
1/2	cup chopped nuts of choice (optional)

Cinnamon Roll Icing
1 1/4	cups confectioner's sugar, sifted
2	tablespoons milk
1/2	teaspoon vanilla extract

1. Follow steps 1 through 3 in Cinnamon Swirl Bread (*see* above).

2. Grease a 13-by-9-inch baking pan. Mix sugar and cinnamon in small bowl.

3. Roll dough with rolling pin into an evenly shaped 12-by-16-inch rectangle. Brush dough liberally with milk and sprinkle an even layer of cinnamon-sugar mixture, leaving a 1/2-inch border along one of the long sides. Sprinkle 1/2 cup raisins and/or 1/2 cup chopped nuts over cinnamon mixture. Roll, beginning with the long side of the rectangle. Use both hands to pinch dough with fingertips as you go, sealing edges firmly to form a seam. (Do not seal ends.)

3. Following illustrations 1 and 2 at left, cut into 12 even pieces using dental floss (or serrated knife with cutting board) and arrange in prepared pan.

4. Cover loosely with plastic and allow to rise until double in size (rolls will touch), about one hour. When rolls are almost fully risen, adjust oven rack to center position and heat oven to 350 degrees.

5. Bake until golden brown and thermometer inserted in center roll registers 185 to 188 degrees, 25 to 30 minutes. Invert rolls onto wire rack. Cool to room temperature, 20 to 30 minutes.

6. *For the icing:* Whisk sugar, milk, and vanilla in small bowl until smooth. Reinvert rolls and place rack over piece of parchment or wax paper. Following illustration 3 at left, drizzle icing over rolls with spoon. Cut or pull apart to separate, and serve.

STEP-BY-STEP | FORMING CINNAMON ROLLS

1. Cut formed roll in half, cut each half in half again, and then cut each piece into 3 rolls for a total of 12 rolls.

2. Space rolls evenly in a greased 9-x-13-inch baking pan.

3. When rolls have cooled to room temperature, use a spoon to drizzle icing over them.

ILLUSTRATION: ALAN WITSCHONKE

Foolproof Sponge Cake

This all-purpose recipe depends on a reliable combination of beaten yolks, whipped whites, and baking powder for lift.

≥ BY CHRISTOPHER KIMBALL WITH JEANNE MAGUIRE ≤

The coming of springtime in Vermont has all the usual keynotes: the firming up of muddy roads, an ocean of red buds sprayed across the mountainsides, the roar of the brook through the culvert, the early white blossoms of the plum and pear trees, and, for our family, the making of a Boston Cream Pie. This occurs in late April when we have a small birthday party for a neighbor who is partial to this cake. Over the years, I have made it with a standard yellow cake, a chiffon cake, a sponge cake, and even a génoise. Never quite satisfied, I decided last spring that what I really wanted was a lighter cake, one with a springy but delicate texture that stands up nicely to a rich custard filling and a sweet chocolate glaze. It should not be dry or tough, the curse of many classic sponge cakes, nor should it be difficult to make. I was seeking a basic building block cake recipe, just as dependable and useful as a classic American layer cake, a common choice for Boston Cream Pie.

The first step was to understand the different types of cakes used with Boston Cream Pie and how each is made. As I did research, I soon realized that, aside from the classic layer cake, the most likely cakes for this use—angel food, génoise, sponge, and chiffon—are all "foam" cakes. That is, they depend on eggs (whole or separated) beaten to a foam to provide lift and structure. But although they all use egg foam for structure, they differ in two ways: whether fat (butter, milk, or oil) is added and whether the foam is made from whole eggs, egg whites, or a combination. The leanest of the foam cakes is the angel food, which is made only with egg whites, using no yolks or added fat. A génoise is made by whipping whole eggs and calls for a small amount of melted butter, while a sponge cake calls for beating whole eggs and yolks together and then folding in whipped egg whites. (Traditionally no other fat was added.) A chiffon cake, the sturdiest of the lot, is a sponge cake with a good deal of added fat, usually a half cup or so of oil or butter.

The problem with these definitions is that cookbook authors ignore them, often using the terms "foam" and "sponge" interchangeably, or simply referring to the whole category of foam cakes as "sponge-style" cakes.

Despite these inconsistencies on the part of experts, I concluded that to fit the definition of a classic sponge cake, a recipe must call for beating at least some of the whites separately and then folding them into the whole egg foam. Otherwise the cake is nothing more than a classic génoise. (To make this category of cakes even more confusing, there are variations on classic sponge cakes that add fat in the form of milk and/or butter. Although, technically speaking, this addition would make a sponge cake into a chiffon cake, it seems that the defining factor for many experts is the amount of fat. The addition of just a few tablespoons of milk or butter does not disqualify a cake for the sponge designation, while adding a half cup or so of fat transforms it into a chiffon cake.)

To get things started, I asked *Cook's* test kitchen to try a variety of Boston Cream Pie recipes using different foam cakes as well as a traditional layer cake. The winner was a variation on a génoise. It was delicate but springy, light but firm. But, as I soon discovered, a génoise is anything but simple. This aerated mixture is dependent on the temperature of the ingredients, the ratio of eggs to flour, and even the speed with which the cake is put into the oven. During testing, we discovered that if the milk was added at room temperature, not hot as is suggested by most recipes, or if the eggs were a bit over- or under-beaten, the cake would not rise properly. This makes for a professional baker's cake, not the simple everyday cake recipe I was looking for.

My next thought was to turn to a sponge cake, which differs from a génoise only in that little or no fat is added and some or all of the egg whites are beaten separately, which delivers a more stable batter and thus a more foolproof recipe. I started by making a classic American sponge cake, which adds no fat in the form of butter or milk. I used my own recipe, which calls for eight beaten egg whites folded into four beaten egg yolks. The cake certainly was light, but it lacked flavor and the texture was dry and a bit chewy. To solve these

The texture of this sponge cake is rather delicate but can still stand up to a variety of fillings and frostings.

problems our test kitchen director, Susan Logozzo, suggested a recipe for a hot-milk sponge cake, in which a small amount of melted butter and hot milk are added to the whole egg foam. This cake turned out much better on all counts. The added fat provided not only flavor but also tenderized the crumb. This particular recipe also used fewer eggs than my original sponge cake recipe.

We were now working with a master recipe that used three-quarters cup cake flour, one teaspoon baking powder, three-quarters cup sugar, and five eggs. We started by separating out all five whites and found that the cake was too light, its insufficient structure resulting in a slightly sunken center. We then separated out and beat just three of the whites, and the resulting cake was excellent. When all-purpose flour was substituted for cake flour, the cake had more body and was a bit tougher than the version with cake flour. We then tried different proportions of the two flours, finally settling on a 2-to-1 ratio of cake flour to all-purpose. We also tested to find the proper ratio of eggs to flour and found that five eggs to three-quarters cup flour (we tested one-

Is Boston Cream Pie Really From Boston and Is It a Pie?

Well, yes and no. The foundation for Boston Cream Pie was a cake referred to by James Beard in *American Cookery* as the One-Egg Cake. It is made with cake flour, sugar, butter, milk, one or two eggs, vanilla, baking powder, and salt. Using this simple recipe, many different variations were created. According to Beard, they include Washington Pie, filled with jam and topped with powdered sugar; Boston Cream Pie, filled with a pastry cream and topped with powdered sugar; Martha Washington Pie, which is either the same as Washington Pie or split into three layers, one filled with jam and the other with pastry cream; and Parker House Chocolate Cream Pie, which is Boston Cream Pie topped with a thin layer of chocolate butter icing. The latter was invented either by a French chef, Sanzian, who was hired by Harvey Parker at his Boston hotel's opening in October

1855 at the extraordinary annual salary of $5,000 (a good chef in Boston could be hired at that time for $8 a week) or by a German baker named Ward who, shortly after the hotel opened, was also credited with inventing Parker House rolls. However, it is not clear whether, as Beard suggests, the term Boston Cream Pie already existed before the Parker House version. My guess is that Beard is right, since Fannie Farmer also lists a recipe for Boston Favorite Cake, which suggests that Boston Cream Pie is merely a variation.

As for why it is called a pie, Jim Dodge, author of *Baking with Jim Dodge*, suggests that the cake was originally baked in a pie pan by early New England cooks. My best guess is that since pies predated cakes in the American kitchen, pie pans were simply more common kitchen equipment than cake pans. No matter the origins, the editors of *Cook's* found, in a blind tasting of five different cakes, that our sponge cake recipe was ideal for Boston Cream Pie.   —C.K.

---

half cup and a full cup) was best. Five eggs also turned out to be appropriate: Six eggs produced an "eggy" cake, while four eggs resulted in a lower rise and a cake with a bit less flavor.

I had thought that the baking powder might be optional, but it turned out to be essential to a properly risen cake. Although angel food and classic sponge cakes, which use no added fat, do not require chemical leavening, in this sponge cake the addition of milk and melted butter combined with the relatively small amount of beaten egg whites in proportion to the flour make baking powder necessary.

Two tablespoons of melted butter was just the right amount; three made the cake a bit oily and the butter flavor was too prominent. As for the milk, three tablespoons was best; larger quantities resulted in a wet, mushy texture.

With our basic recipe in hand, we played with

the order of the steps. Beating the whole egg foam first, and then the whites, allowed the relatively fragile foam to deteriorate, producing less rise. We found that beating the whites first was vastly better. After much experimentation, we also found it best to fold together, all at the same time, the beaten whole eggs, the beaten whites, and the flour, and then, once the mixture was about half-mixed, to add the warm butter and milk. This eliminated the possibility that the liquid would damage the egg foam, and also made the temperature of the butter/milk mixture less important than it was with a génoise.

Determining when a sponge cake is properly cooked is a little more difficult than with a regular American layer cake. A sponge cake should provide some resistance and not feel as if one just touched the top of a soufflé. Another good test is color. The top of the cake should be a nice light

brown, not pale golden or a dark, rich brown.

We also tested the best way to handle the cakes once they are out of the oven. When left to cool in the baking pans, they shrink away from the sides and the edges become uneven. Quickly removing them onto a cooling rack works well, but it's tricky because the cake pans are very hot. We discovered that the best method is to place a plate over the hot cake, cover it with a towel, and invert the cake. Finally, reinvert the cake and slip it back onto a cooling rack.

FOOLPROOF SPONGE CAKE
MAKES TWO 8- OR 9-INCH CAKES

The egg whites should be beaten to soft, glossy, billowy peaks. If beaten until too stiff, they will be very difficult to fold into the whole-egg mixture.

- ½ cup cake flour
- ¼ cup all-purpose flour
- 1 teaspoon baking powder
- ¼ teaspoon salt
- 3 tablespoons milk
- 2 tablespoons unsalted butter
- ½ teaspoon vanilla extract
- 5 eggs, room temperature
- ¾ cup sugar

1. Adjust oven rack to lower middle position and heat oven to 350 degrees. Grease two 8- or 9-inch cake pans and cover pan bottoms with a round of parchment paper. Whisk flours, baking powder, and salt in a medium bowl (or sift onto waxed paper). Heat milk and butter in a small saucepan over low heat until butter melts. Remove from heat and add vanilla; cover and keep warm.

2. Separate three of the eggs, placing whites in bowl of standing mixer fitted with whisk attachment (or large mixing bowl if using hand mixer or whisk), reserving the 3 yolks plus remaining 2 whole eggs in another mixing bowl. Beat the 3 whites on high speed (or whisk) until whites are foamy. Gradually add 6 tablespoons of the sugar; continue to beat whites to soft, moist peaks. (Do not overbeat.) If using a standing mixer, transfer egg whites to a large bowl and add yolk/whole egg mixture to mixing bowl.

3. Beat yolk/whole egg mixture with remaining 6 tablespoons sugar. Beat on medium-high speed (setting 8 on a KitchenAid) until eggs are very thick and a pale yellow color, about 5 minutes (or 12 minutes by hand). Add beaten eggs to whites.

4. Sprinkle flour mixture over beaten eggs and whites; fold very gently 12 times with a large rubber spatula. Make a well in one side of batter and pour milk mixture into bowl. Continue folding until batter shows no trace of flour, and whites and whole eggs are evenly mixed, about 8 additional strokes.

5. Immediately pour batter into prepared baking pans; bake until cake tops are light brown and

---

STEP-BY-STEP | FOLDING WITHOUT DEFLATING

  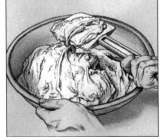

1. With spatula perpendicular to the batter, cut through the center down to the bottom of the bowl.

2. Holding the spatula blade flat against the bowl, scoop along bottom, then slide up the side of the bowl.

3. Fold over, lifting the spatula high so that the scooped batter falls without the spatula pressing down the batter.

feel firm and spring back when touched, about 16 minutes for 9-inch cake pans and 20 minutes for 8-inch cake pans.

6. Immediately run a knife around pan perimeter to loosen cake. Cover pan with large plate. Using a towel, invert pan and remove pan from cake. Peel off parchment. Re-invert cake from plate onto rack. (*See* illustrations 1 and 2, below.) Repeat with remaining cake and continue with one of the recipes that follow.

BOSTON CREAM PIE
SERVES 8

- 1 completed Foolproof Sponge Cake (*see* recipe, previous page)

Pastry Cream
- 2 cups milk
- 6 large egg yolks
- ¹/₂ cup sugar
- ¹/₄ teaspoon salt
- ¹/₄ cup cornstarch, sifted
- 1 teaspoon vanilla extract
- 1 tablespoon rum
- 2 tablespoons unsalted butter, optional

Rich Chocolate Glaze
- 1 cup heavy cream
- ¹/₄ cup light corn syrup
- 8 ounces semisweet chocolate, chopped into small pieces
- ¹/₂ teaspoon vanilla

1. *For the pastry cream*: Heat milk in a small saucepan until hot but not simmering. Whisk yolks, sugar, and salt in a large saucepan until mixture is thick and lemon-colored, 3 to 4 minutes. Add cornstarch; whisk to combine. Slowly whisk in hot milk. Cook milk mixture over medium-low heat, whisking constantly and scraping pan bottom and sides as you stir, until mixture thickens to a thick pudding consistency and loses all traces of raw starch flavor, about 10 minutes. Off heat, stir in vanilla, rum, and butter (if using) and transfer to another container to cool to room temperature, placing a piece of plastic wrap directly on surface of mixture to prevent skin from forming. Refrigerate pastry cream until firm. (Can be refrigerated overnight.) To ensure that pastry cream does not thin out, do not whisk once it has set.

2. *For the glaze*: Bring cream and corn syrup to a full simmer over medium heat in a medium saucepan. Off heat, add chocolate; cover and let stand for 8 minutes. (If chocolate has not completely melted, return saucepan to low heat; stir constantly until melted.) Add vanilla; stir very gently until mixture is smooth. Cool until tepid so that a spoonful drizzled back into pan mounds slightly. (Glaze can be refrigerated to speed up cooling process, stirring every few minutes to ensure even cooling.)

3. While glaze is cooling, place one cake layer on a cardboard round on cooling rack set over waxed paper. Carefully spoon pastry cream over cake and spread evenly up to cake edge. Place the second layer on top, making sure layers line up properly.

4. Pour glaze over middle of top layer and let flow down cake sides. Use a metal spatula, if necessary, to completely coat cake. Use a small needle to puncture air bubbles. Let sit until glaze fully sets, about 1 hour. Serve.

BLACKBERRY JAM CAKE

- 1 completed Foolproof Sponge Cake (*see* recipe, previous page)

- 1 jar (8 ounces) blackberry jam Confectioners' sugar for dusting

Place one cake layer on a cardboard round on a sheet of waxed paper. Evenly spread jam over cake. Place second layer over jam, making sure layers line up properly. Sieve confectioners' sugar over cake and serve.

SPONGE CAKE WITH RICH LEMON FILLING

- 1 completed Foolproof Sponge Cake (*see* recipe, previous page)

Rich Lemon Filling
- ³/₄ cup sugar
- ¹/₄ cup cornstarch
- ¹/₈ teaspoon salt
- 1 cup cold water
- 4 large egg yolks
- 2 teaspoons finely grated zest and ¹/₃ cup juice from 2 lemons
- 2 tablespoons unsalted butter

Confectioners' sugar for dusting

1. *For the filling*: Bring sugar, cornstarch, salt, and water to simmer in a large nonreactive saucepan over medium heat, whisking occasionally at beginning of process and more frequently as mixture begins to thicken. When mixture starts to simmer and turn translucent, whisk in egg yolks, two at a time. Whisk in zest, then lemon juice, and finally butter. Bring mixture to a steady simmer, whisking constantly. Remove from heat, and transfer to another container to cool to room temperature, placing a piece of plastic wrap directly on the surface of the filling to pre-vent a skin from forming. Let stand to room temperature. (Can be refrigerated overnight.) To ensure that lemon filling does not thin out, do not whisk or vigorously stir once it has set.

2. Place one cake layer on a cardboard round on a sheet of waxed paper. Carefully spoon filling over layer and spread evenly up to cake edge. Place the second layer on top making sure layers line up properly. Sieve confectioners' sugar over cake and serve.

The Science of Foams

Our recipe for sponge cake, which is a "foam" cake, depends on the proper aeration of both whole eggs and egg whites. When egg whites are beaten into a foam, their proteins partially unwind around air bubbles, lining the bubbles with protein strands that are loosely connected to one another. When the batter is heated, the bubbles increase in size, and the loose, elastic strands of protein allow this expansion without breaking their bonds. (If egg whites are overbeaten, on the other hand, the protein strands become inelastic and the mixture cannot expand.) This aeration is a good thing for leavening but it creates a less stable overall structure since the protein has been partially denatured through beating.

A whole egg foam is even more sensitive and unstable than an egg white foam because it is based on the process of emulsification and not, like egg whites, on a film of protein that traps air. During emulsification, tiny bubbles of air become suspended in the liquid of the egg through the medium of the lecithin in the eggs. This produces a very fragile and complex structure since water and air are not naturally inclined to bond.

Folding an egg white foam into a whole egg foam increases the protein content of the batter, which makes it more stable because of the air-protein construction. The beaten egg whites also set at a lower temperature than the whole egg foam, which means that the cake firms up quicker during baking. We also decided to add flour, a stabilizing influence, to this mixture before adding melted butter and milk, additional fats which often destabilize egg foams. —C.K.

STEP-BY-STEP | COOL CAKE, NO LINES

1. Position plate over cake. Place towel across plate, covering pan sides. Invert.

2. Remove the pan from the cake, reinvert the cake, and remove plate.

Classic Crème Caramel

With just the right proportion of whole eggs to yolks, you get a creamy, tender custard that stands up nicely on the plate. And the caramel? It's a snap.

≥ BY MARIE PIRAINO AND JAMIE MORRIS ≤

Crème caramel is a deceptively simple classic French dessert. Made with just a few ingredients that are readily available (sugar, eggs, and milk or cream), it is similar in construction and flavor to other baked custards. Slightly lighter and a little less sweet than a standard baked custard, what really makes it special is the caramel sauce.

For us, though, what made a perfect crème caramel was texture. We wanted a custard that was creamy and tender enough to melt in our mouths, yet firm enough to unmold without collapsing on the serving plate. We were also looking for a mellow flavor that was neither too rich nor too eggy.

As for the caramel, we learned one lesson early on: It's not for wimps. If we got nervous and took it off the heat too early, we had a pale, insipid, overly sweet caramel; if we braved it out for too long, we ended up with a bitter, dark, inedible sauce. But the caramel we were looking for was somewhere between the two: a rich, honey-colored sauce with just the right amount of sweetness and complexity.

Testing Ingredients

The first thing we discovered in our research was that the most important part of the recipe is the proportion of egg whites to egg yolks. Too many whites produced a custard that was almost solid and rubbery; too few egg whites, on the other hand, and our custard collapsed. After much tinkering, we came up with what we consider the ideal ratio: three whole eggs for two yolks—in other words, three whites to five yolks. The resulting custard was tender yet not overly rich, and firm enough to unmold easily.

Next, we examined the question of what liquid to use. Since we were making a classic crème caramel, our choices were limited to milk, heavy cream, light cream, and half-and-half. We made our initial custard using milk alone, but it tasted far too thin. Our custard with heavy cream and milk, on the other hand, was creamy but too rich. The high fat content of the cream caused the custard to coat our mouths as we ate, and the custard tasted less of eggs than of rich cream. Half-and-half was better, yet left us wanting something slightly richer. Light cream solved our problem. A mixture of equal parts of milk and light cream gave us just that extra edge of richness, creamy enough to satisfy both ourselves and our tasters.

Every bite combines sweet caramel and tender custard.

Our experiments with sugar were less extensive, since we had decided at the beginning that a crème caramel custard should be less sweet than a custard meant to be eaten unadorned. To us, that made the dessert more interesting and sophisticated. We initially used six tablespoons of sugar for the three cups of liquid in the recipe and were quite satisfied, but some tasters felt that this custard was bland. We then tried using one-half cup of sugar for the same amount of liquid. Opinions were divided on this custard. Some palates still wanted an even sweeter custard, so we tried two-thirds of a cup. This slightly sweeter custard became the new favorite for the majority, but if you prefer a less sweet custard, simply cut the sugar down to one-half cup.

Caramel Conundrums

There are basically two methods of making caramel. In the dry method, you use only sugar, cooking it slowly until it melts and caramelizes. The wet method uses a combination of water and sugar. The sugar begins to dissolve in the water, then the mixture is simmered until the water evaporates and the sugar caramelizes. Since neither one of us has ever successfully produced a smooth caramel with the dry method, we opted for the wet as a way of increasing the margin of success.

We had good success with the wet method, but it was a bit tricky and left us wondering if there was a foolproof method. At this point we remembered an interesting recipe in Shirley Corriher's *Cookwise* (Morrow, 1997). To her basic water and sugar mixture, Corriher added corn syrup and lemon juice. The corn syrup added another type of sugar (glucose) to the table sugar (sucrose) and the lemon juice (an acid) broke down the table sugar, making the dreaded crystallization difficult. This yielded great results every time. Even when crystallization occurred along the edges of the pan during the cooking process, as often happens to many home cooks, the caramel in the pan was still clear and perfect with no crystallization at all, time after time. We now had the foolproof caramel we had wanted.

Once our caramel was done, we poured it directly into our molds. While some cookbooks advised buttering the molds, we found that not only was this unnecessary, it solidified when cold and left the custard greasy. We then followed the common advice to pour the caramel into the molds, coat the bottom evenly, and then tilt the molds to coat the sides. An accident with hot caramel burning our fingers while the molds were tilted caused us to question this particular bit of advice. (A bowl of ice water nearby saved the day for the burned finger—a useful thing to have when you are making caramel or any type of candy.) We started to coat only the bottoms of the mold, reasoning that the caramel sinks to the bottom of the mold while baking anyway. When we unmolded the custards, the caramel still poured evenly over the tops of the custards. It was an easier and safer method.

Baking

How you bake crème caramel and how long you bake it can make the difference between a great one and a mediocre, or even disappointing, one. After considerable experimentation, we determined that baking the custards at 350 degrees in a bain marie, or water bath, in order to maintain an even, gentle heating environment, produced custards that were creamy and smooth.

As a final experiment, we decided to try lining the baking pan with a towel before adding the molds or the water. We found this in a couple of recipes and initially dismissed it as an extra step not worth the bother. However, our own testing at this point had given us custards that were wonderful, yet still had bubbles from overcooking near the bottom. We reasoned that the towel might absorb some of the heat from the bottom, preventing the custards from overcooking in this area. Custards baked with the towel contained significantly fewer bubbles, so we judged them worth the effort.

CLASSIC CRÈME CARAMEL
SERVES 8

Though you can make one large crème caramel, we find that custards baked in individual ramekins cook faster, are more evenly textured, and unmold more easily. You can vary the amount of sugar in the custard to suit your taste. Most tasters preferred the full two-thirds cup, but you can reduce that amount to as little as one-half cup to create a greater contrast between the custard and the sweetness of the caramel. Cook the caramel in a pan with a light-colored interior, since a dark surface makes it difficult to judge the color of the syrup. Caramel can leave a real mess in a pan, but it is easy to clean. Simply boil lots of water in the pan for 5 to 10 minutes to loosen the hardened caramel.

Caramel
1   cup sugar
1/3 cup water
2   tablespoons corn syrup
1/4 teaspoon juice from one lemon

Custard
1 1/2 cups whole milk
1 1/2 cups light cream
3   large eggs
2   large egg yolks
2/3 cup sugar
1 1/2 teaspoons vanilla extract
    pinch salt

1. *For the caramel:* In a medium nonreactive saucepan and without stirring, bring sugar, water, corn syrup, and lemon juice to simmer over medium-high heat, wiping sides of pan with wet cloth to remove any sugar crystals that might cause syrup to turn grainy. Continue to cook until syrup turns from clear to golden, swirling pan gently to ensure even browning, about 8 minutes. Continue to cook, swirling pan gently and constantly, until large, slow bubbles on mixture's surface turn honey-caramel in color, 4 to 5 minutes longer. Remove pan immediately from heat and, working quickly but carefully (the caramel is over

300 degrees and will burn you if it touches your skin), pour a portion of the caramel into each of 8 ungreased 6-ounce ovenproof ramekins. Allow caramel to cool and harden, about 15 minutes. (Can be covered with plastic wrap and refrigerated for up to 2 days; return to room temperature before adding custard.)

2. *For the custard:* Adjust oven rack to center position and heat oven to 350 degrees. Heat milk and cream, stirring occasionally, in medium saucepan over medium heat until steam appears and/or an instant-read thermometer held in the liquid registers 160 degrees, 6 to 8 minutes; remove from heat. Meanwhile, gently whisk eggs, yolks, and sugar in large bowl until just combined. Off heat, gently whisk warm milk mixture, salt, and vanilla into eggs until just combined but not at all foamy. Strain mixture through fine mesh sieve into large measuring cup or container with pouring spout; set aside.

3. Bring 2 quarts water to boil in kettle. Meanwhile, fold dish towel to fit bottom of large baking dish or roasting pan and position in pan. Divide reserved custard mixture among ramekins; place filled ramekins on towel in pan (making sure they do not touch) and set pan on oven rack. Fill pan with boiling water to reach halfway up ramekins; cover entire pan loosely with aluminum foil so steam can escape. Bake until a paring knife inserted halfway between center and edge of the custards comes out clean, 35 to 40 minutes. Transfer custards to wire rack; cool to room temperature (Can be covered with plastic wrap and refrigerated up to 2 days.)

4. To unmold, slide a paring knife around entire mold perimeter, pressing knife against side of the dish. Hold serving plate over top of ramekin and invert; set plate on work surface and shake ramekin gently to release custard. Serve immediately.

For one large crème caramel: Follow recipe for Classic Crème Caramel, pouring caramel and custard into 1 1/2-quart straight-sided soufflé dish rather than individual ramekins. Fill roasting pan with boiling water to reach halfway up sides of soufflé dish; increase baking time to 70 to 75 min-

PROCEDURES
POURING THE CARAMEL

When using a small mold, simply pour the caramel into the mold; there is no need to swirl to coat the sides.

utes or until an instant-read thermometer inserted in custard (*see* illustration) registers 175 degrees.

ESPRESSO CRÈME CARAMEL

Espresso beans ground in a coffee grinder will be too fine and impart too strong a coffee flavor to the custard. Instead, crush the beans lightly with the bottom of a heavy saucepan.

Follow recipe for Classic Crème Caramel, heating 1/2 cup lightly crushed espresso coffee beans with milk and cream mixture until steam appears and/or an instant-read thermometer held in the liquid registers 160 degrees, 6 to 8 minutes. Off heat, cover and steep until coffee flavor has infused milk and cream, about 15 minutes. Strain out beans and continue with recipe, reducing vanilla extract to 1 teaspoon.

Marie Piraino is a Boston-based food stylist and recipe developer and her sister, **Jamie Morris**, is a New York-based teacher.

PROCEDURES
TESTING FOR DONENESS

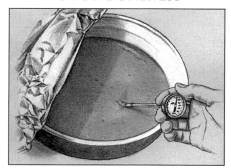

If making a single large crème caramel, test for doneness with a thermometer. Be sure to place it between the center and the perimeter of the mold.

Unorthodox Chocolate Chips Top Tasting

The winning chocolate chip contains tofu, while the second place finisher looks nothing like the pert little morsels we grew up with.

≥ BY MARYELLEN DRISCOLL ≤

At a young age I determined I'd been born with a "dessert box." Set smack above my stomach, it simply meant that no matter how big the dinner there was always room for dessert. Nowadays a certain level of health consciousness seems to have banished the box—except when there are chocolate chip cookies within reach. Yet during a recent chocolate chip cookie fit I was surprised to find myself picking out half the chips. A self-proclaimed "chocoholic" friend admitted she did the same.

I consulted a number of pastry chefs about this who were quick with a diagnosis. Chocolate chips, they said, are often too sweet, gritty, lacking in chocolaty flavor, and abundant in artificial flavors. And they were right, because these were the very qualities that proved the demise of nearly half the chocolate chips in our blind tasting. Those chips that excelled were noted for a balance of bitterness, sweetness, and smoothness—and turned out to hold a few curious secrets.

To prepare for the tasting, we at *Cook's* first had to identify the brands and the kind of chips we were to test. These days supermarkets will carry up to five chocolate chip brands which feature as many as five different varieties: semisweet, bittersweet, white, mint, and milk chocolate, not to mention the mini-chips and baby kisses. We decided to limit our taste test to the most popular variety, semisweet chocolate, and to include mostly brands found in supermarkets nationwide. Nestlé, which sold about 69 million bags of chips (or 4 billion cookies worth) in 1997, was an obvious pick. The other brands were Baker's, Hershey's, Guittard, and Ghirardelli. We also included Tropical Source, a brand found nationally in natural food stores, and Merckens, a gourmet brand available by mail order. All chips were tasted plain and in a traditional Toll House cookie recipe. They were rated for flavor (degree of chocolatiness, sweetness, off flavors, and overall flavor), mouthfeel (gritty or smooth), and overall liking. Our tasting panel consisted of 14 members of the *Cook's Illustrated* staff and eight professional pastry chefs.

The Nitty Gritty

Along the spectrum of chocolates, chips are generally considered the least refined. The most refined would be a coating chocolate, also known as couverture, an extremely glossy chocolate usually found only in specialty candy-making shops and primarily used by pastry chefs in confections. Chocolate chips lack the fluidity necessary for the technical and detailed work of a pastry chef, such as molds and truffles, or even for the thin, glossy effect of a simple chocolate-dipped strawberry. For example, a bowl of melted couverture will pour out smoothly, like cream, but a bowl of melted chips will slide sluggishly like glue. This high viscosity and low fluidity are what make the chip shape possible. When squeezed through a nozzle onto a moving belt in the factory, the chocolate quickly sets up into a pert morsel rather than collapsing into a small blob, explained Tricia Bowles of Nestlé Chocolate & Confections.

The chip that rated second in our tasting, however, defied the unspoken shape standard. Thalia Hohenthal, senior research and development scientist for Guittard, explained that her company wanted a high grade chocolate chip. To achieve this quality, Guittard grinds and blends its chip chocolate like it does its couverture. This helps to develop the flavor, says Hohenthal. The tradeoff, however, is that the chip is too fluid to hold the tightly pointed shape of a typical chip. Even so, some of our tasters liked the larger size and unorthodox disc shape of the chip.

The winning chip, Tropical Source, did showcase the typical pointed shape of a chip, but like the Guittard chip, it had an unusually high cocoa butter content. The average chip has 27 percent cocoa butter, but both Guittard and Tropical Source chips contain 30 percent. Cocoa butter is renowned for providing the melt-in-your-mouth lusciousness of chocolate. Because it is costly, though, most chocolate chip manufacturers limit the cocoa butter content. Tasters typically had to agitate chips between their tongues and the roofs of their mouths or even bite into some in order to break them down. Guittard and Tropical Source stood out because they melted notably more smoothly than the rest.

Tropical Source had some other peculiarities which helped explain its top finish. First, it was the only brand with tofu powder (roasted soy flour) listed as an ingredient, which the company's president said is used to lend a creaminess to the chip. (This is not to be confused with lecithin, another soy-based product used to evenly distribute cocoa solids in cocoa butter.) Another unusual ingredient was unrefined cane juice crystals used as a sweetener rather than standard sugar. Both sweeteners contain nearly the same amount of sucrose, according to the Sugar Association in Washington, D.C., yet tasters indicated that the Tropical Source chip seemed pleasantly less sweet than other chips. This could be the result of a differing ratio of sugar to other ingredients in the chips. Or it might well be a difference in perception of sweetness, because unrefined cane juice sugar can carry the characteristic

---

Do Chips Make the Mousse?

Many chocolate recipes, such as chocolate mousse, call for the chocolate to be chopped, a messy, tiring task. The reason for this chopping is to help the chocolate melt quickly to a smooth liquid without scorching. It would be much easier, we figured, if chocolate chips could be used in these recipes and the same results achieved.

To test the viability of substituting chips for chopped bittersweet chocolate, we used the top four chip finishers, along with two bar chocolates, to make the chocolate mousse recipe from the July/August 1996 issue of *Cook's Illustrated*. Nine staff members appraised the mousses on texture, airiness, chocolate flavor, and overall appeal.

The results were very positive; in fact, all the chocolates made great mousses. According to Steve Klc, a pastry chef and consultant in Washington, D.C., chocolate chips work well in a mousse because their high viscosity lends stability, texture, and structure to an otherwise delicate and unstable dessert. Ghirardelli and Tropical Source chips were judged particularly outstanding. On the basis of this test, we would say that using chocolate chips instead of chopping chocolate saves time and mess. —Garrett Peters

TASTING CHOCOLATE CHIPS

For our blind taste test we selected seven brands of semisweet chocolate chips that are available nationwide in stores or by mail order. The chips were tasted plain and in a traditional Toll House cookie (cooled to room temperature). Tasters rated the chips for flavor (degree of chocolatiness, sweetness, off flavors, and overall flavor), mouthfeel (gritty or smooth), and over-

all liking. The panel of 22 tasters consisted of professional pastry chefs (listed below) and *Cook's Illustrated* staff members. The chips are listed in order of preference based on each brand's combined scores from the two tastings. Prices were for purchases made from supermarkets in the Boston area.

RECOMMENDED

Tropical Source Semi-Sweet Chocolate Chips HOBOKEN, NEW JERSEY

> 10-ounce bag for $2.99

This natural food store brand ranked well above all the chips for its "velvety" smooth mouthfeel and its complex, slightly bitter chocolate flavor. Some tasters described it as "smoky." "Best mouthfeel yet, combined with deep, complex flavor makes for a good chip," one taster commented. A slight percentage of tofu is used in this chip to lend creaminess, according to the manufacturer. And the use of unrefined cane juice crystals (instead of refined white sugar) seems to have contributed an agreeably mellow sweetness. Available in natural food stores and by mail order from Natural Resources catalog (6680 Harvard Drive, Sebastopol, CA 95472; 800-747-0390).

Guittard Semi-Sweet Chocolate Super Cookie Chips BURLINGAME, CALIFORNIA

> 10-ounce bag for $1.85

This chip shared some of the winning chip's strengths. Tasters described Guittard chips as creamy with noticeable coffee subtleties, a "good bitter quality in front," "slightly fruity" notes, and an overall assertive chocolate flavor. A technician at Guittard attributed these qualities to a refined manufacturing process that is similar to that of a coating chocolate. The consequence of this, however, is that the chocolate is too fluid to stand upright in the shape of most commercial chips. Instead, these chips look more like a deflated chip about the size of a nickel. Super Chips are sold in supermarkets nationwide, though they can be hard to find. Call 800-468-2462 for further information on availability.

Ghirardelli Semi-Sweet Chocolate Chips SAN LEANDRO, CALIFORNIA

> 12-ounce bag for $2.89

This semisweet chip was more reminiscent of a bittersweet chip. "Strong chocolate flavor without killer sweetness." Tasters found the chips to be grainy when plain, yet they melted more rapidly in the mouth than many of the chips. The gritty, chalky character also smoothed out significantly when the chips were baked in a cookie. Some tasters noted a fruity essence. Sold in most supermarkets.

Nestlé Toll House Semi-Sweet Chocolate Morsels GLENDALE, CALIFORNIA

> 12-ounce bag for $2.75

The nation's first and best-selling chocolate chip carried a straightforward, "decent" chocolate flavor along with a relatively smooth mouthfeel. Some tasters did find it more sweet than they preferred. "Got milk?" commented one taster. Many tasters described the chip's flavor as "perfumey" or fruity. A reassuring solid finish for the brand of chocolate chips most likely to be found in cupboards across the country. Available at supermarkets nationwide.

NOT RECOMMENDED

Merckens Semi-Sweet Chocolate Chips MANSFIELD, MASSACHUSETTS

> 16-ounce bag for $3.25

There was little consensus as to this chip's flavor. Many found it full-flavored and pleasant, while others found the flavor lacking. The primary demise of this chip, however, was a strong aftertaste that one taster described as "celery-like." The plain chip was also grainy, "like melting sandpaper" in the mouth. In the cookie it melted smoothly, almost to the point of losing its shape. Available in gourmet stores.

Hershey's Semi-Sweet Chocolate Chips HERSHEY, PENNSYLVANIA

> 12-ounce bag for $2.19

This famous candy bar brand was "ok but..." it tasted artificial, "acidic," "sacchariney," "a little like sweet cough syrup," "flat," and "of cardboard box." Even more to its disadvantage was a "waxy" and "chalky" mouthfeel. It held up possibly too well under heat. Many tasters expressed the wish for more melting in the cookie. Available in supermarkets nationwide.

Baker's Semi-Sweet Real Chocolate Chips WHITE PLAINS, NEW YORK

> 12-ounce bag for $1.99

The bottom of the bags. "Hideously sweet" and "extremely waxy" were the major complaints. "It was like a sugar cube, with a chalky shortening quality to it," wrote one taster. Another likened it to the taste of cola. Like Hershey's, it proved too firm and waxy in a cookie. Available at supermarkets nationwide.

---

flavors of cane juice, including molasses, while refined sugar never does.

In our tasting it turned out that the best chocolate chip eaten plain also makes for the best tasting chip in a cookie. With this in mind we decided to find out if we could chop up a top bar chocolate and successfully use that in a cookie instead of a chip. We tested this with a Ghirardelli bittersweet bar and with a chunk of Callebaut bittersweet chocolate (both recommended in the 1994 *Cook's* tasting of bittersweet chocolates). The chunks created a more rugged-looking

cookie, a look that a few of our editors said they prefer. They did not melt excessively or leak out of the cookie, but we had trouble chopping them up. While the thin Ghirardelli bar broke up without too much trouble under the pointed pressure of fork tines, the Callebaut bar was too thick (about an inch) for a fork to penetrate. So we used a chef's knife, which was awkward and meant a loss of chocolate to shavings and shards. We were not the first to discover this. Such chopping difficulties are actually what inspired the evolution of the morsel shape. Forming chips

through a nozzle was more efficient than chopping, said Bowles of Nestlé, the first commercial manufacturer of chips.

The following Boston area professional pastry chefs participated in the tasting: David Broderick of Icarus Restaurant; Barbara Darnell of The Passionate Chocolatier; Clare Garland and Amy Rothenberg Snyder of A Mano Catering, Inc.; Judy Mattera of Grill 23; Lisa Beaudin, Roger Bencivenga, and Licia Gomes of the Professional Pastry Guild of New England.

Finding the Best All-Purpose Peeler

A model with an oversized grip wins hands-down for almost all peeling jobs.

≥ BY ADAM RIED ≤

In a cookware world where $500 ice cream makers and $3,000 gas grills no longer surprise us, the lowly vegetable peeler, averaging about 5 bucks, offers little cause for excitement. When we decided to test them for *Cook*'s, however, I learned that there's as much variation among these simple tools as among pots and pans. Some just plain work better than others, and having tested 10 different models here, I'll tell you which they are.

A shopping trip to some of our favorite kitchenware retailers around Boston and New York turned up an astonishing 25 different peelers from 15 separate makers. The major differences were the fixture of the blade, either stationary or swiveling; the material of the blade, either carbon steel, stainless steel, or ceramic; and the orientation of the blade to the handle, either straight in line with the body or perpendicular to it. This last arrangement, with the blade perpendicular to the handle, is referred to either as a "harp" peeler, because the frame is a loop that looks a little like the body of a harp, or, in Oxo's parlance, as a "Y" peeler, in that it also resembles the shape of the letter Y. Many of the kitchenware sources I consulted said that this type of peeler, which works with a pulling motion instead of a shucking motion, is of European origin and is more prevalent there than in the United States.

Preliminary testing on several huge sacks of potatoes and dozens of lemons helped us narrow the field down to a more manageable 10 models, which represented most of the manufacturers and most of the variables in blade type, fixture, and orientation. Those that made the cut to the full testing included relatively expensive stationary and swivel-blade peelers from the renowned German knife-maker Henckels; the Oxo Good Grips Swivel Peeler with its huge, soft plastic handle and nearly unanimous recommendation from store clerks; harp or Y-type models from Kuhn Rikon and Kyocera (the latter had a ceramic blade); familiar straight-handled swivel action peelers from Ekco with both carbon and stainless steel blades; and a Revereware and two Farberware models with large molded grips similar to the Oxo's.

We understand that peeler performance can vary to some degree based on the size and strength of particular user's hands. So in an effort to get a reliable overall impression, we recruited five testers to work with each peeler—two men with average size hands and three women, one with large, strong hands and one with exceptionally small hands.

Common Peeling Tasks

Asking co-workers and friends which vegetables they peel most often confirmed my suspicion—carrots and potatoes topped the list. Frankly, though, carrots posed little challenge to any of our peelers, all of which breezed through that testing without incident. As it did in all the tests, the ceramic-bladed Kyocera P-1 moved a little less smoothly down the vegetable than most others. So did the Farberware Euro Peeler.

Peeling potatoes was more effective at illuminating the peelers' pros and cons. We were looking for the peelers to allow quick, smooth action that required a minimum of downward pressure. We also focused on removing as little of the flesh along with the peel as possible. Peeling many, many pounds of spuds demonstrated just how comfortable the soft grip of the Oxo was for a variety of hands. With its sharp blade and effective potato bud remover (an indentation at the point of the frame meant for carving out potato eyes—all but the Kyocera had some form of this), this peeler created much less hand strain over the long haul than any of the others. Both Farberware models and the Revereware also had large molded grips, but neither proved as comfortable as the Oxo. The handle of the Henckels Swivel Peeler was also deemed comfortable by testers and the sharp blade did a good job peeling potatoes and zesting lemons.

The Oxo's ability to hug the curves of the pota-

The Peelers We Tested

BEST PEELER
Oxo Good Grips Peeler
Sharp blade, comfortable grip, great on curves, but bulky in small hands.

Kuhn Rikon Peeler
Efficient to use because it takes off wide strips of peel.

Kyocera P-1 Ceramic Yoke Peeler
Great for rough, craggy surfaces but takes off too much flesh with apple, potato, and lemon skins.

Ekco Deluxe Peeler
Familiar, cheap, and adequate for easy peeling, especially carrots and potatoes, but almost useless on tough jobs like squash.

Ekco Peeler
Carbon steel blade not appreciably sharper than the stainless steel Ekco, and it rusts.

Henckels Swivel Peeler
An expensive peeler that hugs the curves but glides right over the skin on the broad, flat surface of squash and the rough skin of celery root.

Farberware Stainless Soft Grip Euro Peeler
Blade does not feel sharp and it slides right over curved surfaces.

Henckels Vegetable Peeler
Exceptionally sturdy, but it feels like you're using a paring knife. Not for thin or delicate skins.

Farberware Euro Peeler
To get decent leverage with the blade, you must really choke up on the handle, which strains the hand.

Revereware Comfort Grip
The grip is simply too big; It feels bulky even in large hands. Blade does not feel sharp.

RATING VEGETABLE PEELERS

We peeled six different fruits and vegetables with each of 10 peelers. We wanted thin strips of peel with little flesh from apples, carrots, potatoes, and lemons, which we considered a single category. In a second category were tough-skinned butternut squash and celery root, from which we wanted thicker, fleshier strips of peel. In a third category,

maneuverability, we assessed each peeler's performance on items with curves, crevices, and rough skin. Other issues we evaluated, such as handle-grip comfort, hand strain, sharpness of the blade and its ease of travel, and the downward pressure required to peel, can depend on the hands of a particular user. Peelers are listed in order of preference.

Brand	Price	Blade Position	Blade Type	Thin Skin	Thick Skin	Maneuverability	Testers' Comments
BEST PEELER **Oxo** Good Grips Peeler	$6.00	STRAIGHT	Stainless Steel; Swivel	★★★	★★★	★★★	The top-rated peeler for almost all purposes. Easy to control for all but the smallest hands.
Kuhn Rikon Peeler	$3.25	Y	Carbon Steel; Swivel	★★	★★★	★★★	Takes off very wide, thick strips of peel, so it's especially good on a squash's broad surfaces and the rough skin of celery root. So good, in fact, we'd keep one around just for those tasks. For the same reasons, however, not well suited to lemons.
Kyocera P-1 Ceramic Yoke Peeler	$14.95	Y	Ceramic; Swivel	★★	★★★	★★★	Some of the same strengths as the Kuhn Rikon on thick-skinned vegetables, but the blade travel is less smooth and the price is much higher.
Ekco Deluxe Peeler	$2.49	STRAIGHT	Stainless Steel; Swivel	★★★	★	★	Quick to use and comfortable enough for apples, potatoes and carrots, but a bear on rougher customers. Hard to grip, slippery, bad on curves, and requires considerable effort.
Ekco Peeler	$1.29	STRAIGHT	Carbon Steel; Swivel	★★★	★	★	Performance is similar to the stainless steel Ekco model, i.e., not outstanding, and the blade rusts to boot. Zesting a lemon required an awkward sawing motion.
Henckels Swivel Peeler	$11.00	STRAIGHT	Stainless Steel; Swivel	★★★	★	★★	Some users found the unusual design very comfortable, while others disliked it. The blade was noticeably sharp and the potato eyer was great. Outstanding on lemons; equally dismal on squash.
Farberware Stainless Soft Grip Euro Peeler	$5.99	STRAIGHT	Stainless Steel; Swivel	★★	★★	★	Comfort totally depends on hand size; felt cumbersome and bulky in all but large hands. Blade travel is rough and the potato eyer is mediocre.
Henckels Vegetable Peeler	$8.00	STRAIGHT	Stainless Steel; Stationary	★	★★★	★	The blade angle feels awkward.
Farberware Euro Peeler	$3.99	STRAIGHT	Stainless Steel; Swivel	★	★	★	Blade is not particularly sharp, moves roughly, and takes off thick strips of peel. The handle felt awkward in all the testers' hands.
Revereware Comfort Grip Permasharp Peeler	$4.99	STRAIGHT	Stainless Steel with Grooves; Swivel	★	★	★	Blade is recessed so far into the frame that the frame often prevents the blade from hitting the food. Very poor job on the curves.

toes was also impressive, as were the thin strips of peel that left the flesh where it belongs—on the potato. The thickness of the peel was the downfall of both the sturdy-feeling Henckels Vegetable Peeler and the Y models, the Kuhn Rikon and Kyocera. Despite using very light pressure, all three removed the white pith from lemons as well as more flesh than we wanted to from potatoes, apples, and carrots. The Ekco models, which are the archetypal peelers to all but the youngest American cooks, did a fine job of peeling the potatoes, but after a few pounds, some hands began to ache. They simply were not as comfortable as those with the larger grips.

Oddly, though I had read that carbon steel blades are easier to sharpen and therefore sport sharper edges than their stainless steel counterparts, all our testers preferred the Ekco with the stainless steel blade, remarking that it felt both sharper and smoother in action. In addition, the stainless steel

blade does not rust, as did the carbon steel blade when we forgot to dry it after one washing.

Tougher Tasks
Peeling hard, tough-skinned butternut squash and celery root really separated the wheat from the chaff among the peelers. The curve where the neck and the base of the squash meet was an excellent test of maneuverability. The Oxo and the Kuhn Rikon did a nice job. The Kyocera also did well, but took off thick slices of the skin. (To be fair, I should mention that the care instructions for the Kyocera advised against peeling such thick skins.) All the others slipped off the peel at the curve. Digging into the squash at these points to get a good bite on the peel and resume the process—especially with the Ekcos, the Henckels Swivel, both Farberwares, and the Revereware—required an uncomfortable degree of strength and pressure for some testers.

Again, a sharp blade and great grip gave the Oxo both ease of movement and good control on the broad, flat surfaces and curves alike. In these cases, though, this peeler took off too little flesh with the peel, leaving behind a layer of slightly tough, green-veined flesh that we had to go over a second time to remove. For the majority of testers, both Y peelers really shone with the squash and celery root, taking off wide, thick strips of peel quickly, easily, and efficiently. Be warned, though, that our tester with the smallest hands felt somewhat out of control with these models.

So our conclusions are: If you want just a single peeler in your kitchen drawer choose the Oxo, which led the pack for its sharpness, comfort, and control. You can even hang onto it with wet hands. My kitchen drawer, however, has room for two peelers, so I'll put out the $3.25 for a Kuhn Rikon Y Peeler for peeling squash, which, until now, I have always found to be a real nuisance.

Tasting "Chillable" Reds

Beaujolais is the paradigm of picnic wines, and rightly so. But there are some fine alternatives that are equally inexpensive. BY MARK BITTMAN

Most red wines taste best at "cellar temperature," somewhat cooler than the "room temperature" at which they're usually served. But there are reds that are better when they're even cooler than that—chilled for an hour or longer in the refrigerator, or dunked in an ice bucket for a few minutes, until they have a decidedly cold edge to them. These are light, bright red wines, symbolized in the minds of many people by Beaujolais, the ultimate red quaffing wine for summer and the best red for a picnic. They're fruity wines that don't ask to be taken seriously and complement a wide variety of foods.

We have wanted to organize a Beaujolais tasting for years, but two aspects of the current state of the business mitigated against it. One is that the craze for Beaujolais Nouveau—immature wine rushed to the market each fall just a couple of months after the harvest—has greatly reduced the amount of grapes available to make "real" Beaujolais. The other is that Georges Duboeuf has cornered so much of the Beaujolais market that few other brands are available nationally—there are literally not enough wines in circulation to meet the standards of our tastings.

So we did the next best thing—we organized a tasting of light, chillable reds, including Beaujolais and others of its ilk. These include the fruity wines of the Côtes du Rhône; Chianti, the lightest of the well-known Italian reds; California wines made in the style of Beaujolais and the Côtes du Rhône; and a couple of other like wines. Because these are not intended to be "great" wines, they're mostly quite inexpensive, with the majority coming in at $10 or less.

Perhaps not surprisingly (although I was surprised), the Beaujolais wines showed best, a Duboeuf finishing first and three others finishing in the next five places. Beaujolais, a region south of Burgundy, makes a number of types of wines, all exclusively (or virtually so) from the Gamay grape, which is incapable of producing serious wines, but adept at making light, uncomplicated, and sometimes delightful ones.

There is "Beaujolais," presumably the simplest and most straightforward, and almost always the least expensive; it comes from the region's flatlands and may, in some cases, be labeled "Beaujolais Supérieur." And there is "Beaujolais-Villages" from the hillier northern area, whose favorable climate, soil, and viticultural techniques often produce a slightly more complex wine.

Then there is cru Beaujolais (cru usually refers to a vineyard of high quality) from 10 individual towns: Moulin à Vent, Fleurie, Morgon, St.-Amour, Chénas, Juliénas, Chiroubles, Régnié, Brouilly, and Côte de Brouilly. Some of the cru Beaujolais are almost never seen in the States, and few are nationally distributed; Château de la Chaize Brouilly, a standard in many wine shops and our second-place finisher, is an exception. Even fewer cru Beaujolais mention the word "Beaujolais" on their labels—presumably because their wines seem more special without the term—so to find them you must memorize (or at least carry a list of) their names. Although as a rule they are more expensive than either Beaujolais or Beaujolais-Villages, they are worth seeking out.

As for the other wines in our tasting, few generalizations can be made. Four of the Rhône-style wines, all of which rely on the Grenache grape—which can produce a somewhat richer wine than the Gamay—did nicely; their intrinsically light style makes them good candidates for chilling. While our Chianti entries did not fare so well, a reliable Chianti-style wine, Antinori Santa Cristina, fit in nicely with the group, as did the widely sold Bolla Bardolino, a light red from the Veneto region, in Italy's north.

THE JUDGES' RESULTS | CHILLABLE REDS

The wines in our tasting—held at Mt. Carmel Wine and Spirits in Hamden, Connecticut —were judged by a panel made up of both wine professionals and amateur wine lovers. The wines were all purchased in the Northeast; prices will vary throughout the country.

Within each category, wines are listed based on the number of points scored. In this tasting, the "Highly Recommended" wines had almost all positive comments. Those labeled "Recommended" garnered mostly positive comments; and the "Recommended with Reservations" group had decidedly mixed comments.

HIGHLY RECOMMENDED

1996 Duboeuf Beaujolais-Villages, $7.
"Has complexity," even "interest," and yet "remarkably easy drinking." A great quaffer.

1996 Château de la Chaize Brouilly, $12.
"Classy" wine, "smooth but tart," with "lush, lovely fruit." "Delicious."

1995 Guigal Côtes du Rhône, $10.
"Spicy," "tasty," "so much fun to drink." The lightest wine of a serious producer.

RECOMMENDED

1996 Jadot Beaujolais-Villages, $10.
"Pleasant," "mild," and "a bit tangy." "Good drinking."

1995 Domaine de la Gautière Vin de Pays, $8.
"Peppery" and "gorgeous." "Like Beaujolais, but deeper."

1996 Jadot Moulin à Vent, "Château de Jacques," $18.
Note price, not atypical of cru Beaujolais. "Big and well-balanced," "perhaps a bit young."

1995 Antinori Santa Cristina Sangiovese, $10.
"No nose," but "good fruit" and "nice drinking." "Light, fruity, and fun."

1995 Bolla Bardolino, $8.
"Very easy drinking," "most enjoyable."

1995 J. Vidal-Fleury Côtes du Rhône, $8.
"Strong pepper flavor," "surprisingly spicy."

1996 Poliziano Colli Senesi Chianti, $9.
"Easy drinking with a kick"; "nice tannin, good fruit."

RECOMMENDED WITH RESERVATIONS

1996 Clos de Gilroy California Grenache, $10.
"Lovely cherry-berry flavor," but "strange" aftertaste.

1995 Beringer California Gamay, $6.50.
"Fresh fruit," but "quite thin" and "clumsy."

1996 Paul Jaboulet Parallel 45 Côtes du Rhône, $9.
"Might open given time," but "very light—too light."

1996 Alaura Chianti, $8.
"Light" but "lacks character."

Easy as Pie?

Can a cookbook teach home cooks how to make foolproof pies and tarts?
Carole Walter's *Great Pies & Tarts* goes a very long way toward making this a reality.

BY CHRISTOPHER KIMBALL

An old friend of mine, a Vermont farmer, knows more about how to harness up a team of horses than most people. Yet as he once again shows me how to place the ancient wooden hames around the collars and then sort out and hitch up the tugs and traces, pole straps and lazy straps, whipple trees and eveners, britchens and back pads, I am once again lost in a sea of unfamiliar terms, confused by the tangled spaghetti of straps and buckles. He is an expert, not a teacher. In this he resembles my first cooking mentors, who would readily turn out perfect pie crusts, but whose explanations and advice about "pea-size" pieces of butter or warnings about not using too much liquid did not improve my efforts, which were very often disappointing, the crusts too tough, too dry, or too sticky. Carole Walter is, from all reports, an excellent and knowledgeable teacher, but when I first picked up her new book, *Great Pies & Tarts* (Clarkson Potter, $35), I couldn't help but wonder if she'd be as good an author as she is a teacher—if she'd be able to guide me safely through the perils of pastry making.

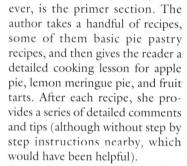

Simply put, making pies and tarts might be the most difficult culinary tasks faced by the home cook and *Great Pies & Tarts* goes a long way toward making them dependable and relatively foolproof. Carole Walter is a professional with rich baking experience that clearly shows in the depth of the commentary. The first half of the book is particularly helpful, offering, among other things, a detailed and useful section on ingredients. Walter also discusses techniques, pointing out some real gems: Whipping cream at lower speeds makes it more stable; egg whites can be whipped to four different stages rather than only three (frothy, soft peaks, firm peaks, and stiff peaks—this adds a good deal of precision to the process); and milk and white chocolates are too soft for chopping in a food processor. To sift flour, she admonishes those who use the "dip-and-sweep" method and instead recommends first sifting it onto waxed paper and then spooning it into a measuring cup. (She is correct when she claims that her method results in two table-

spoons less flour per cup, yet I wonder if sifting is really necessary for pie pastry.) The equipment section was good if a bit sketchy, Walter occasionally commenting on which brands to purchase but opting, for example, not to specify which food processors or thermometers are best.

The best feature of *Great Pies & Tarts,* however, is the primer section. The author takes a handful of recipes, some of them basic pie pastry recipes, and then gives the reader a detailed cooking lesson for apple pie, lemon meringue pie, and fruit tarts. After each recipe, she provides a series of detailed comments and tips (although without step by step instructions nearby, which would have been helpful).

But all this information only whetted my need to know what was really important. I wanted Walter to help me sort out her long lists of techniques and suggestions—she never, for example, really explains the essence of a good pie pastry recipe. Most cooks would agree that the key issue is the proportion of shortening to flour, but although her recipes get it just right, she never explicitly makes the point. Nor does she fully explore the issue of tough pastry, perhaps the home cook's most common problem. More information about things like gluten development, hydration, and overworked dough would have been useful, especially if appended to the basic pastry recipes. She also offers a choice between a hand and food processor method for making pie pastry without making it sufficiently clear that the latter is by far the easiest method. (I also noted that she does not offer a single-crust version of either of these two recipes, which is confusing, since she often refers back to them for recipes like Lemon Meringue Pie that require only a single prebaked crust.)

By the same token, she provides only a cursory discussion of prebaking pie shells, perhaps the single most difficult kitchen task. And the recipe is also not ideal. Much of the crucial information, such as chilling the dough, is not included in the numbered recipe instructions, and instructions to preheat the oven are given at the last second, when the pie shell is ready to bake. More information would have been help-

ful, especially about things such as chilling the shells and whether pricking the dough or buttering the foil is really necessary. (I find that refrigerating a pie shell for only 30 minutes is fine for an expert baker but not long enough for a home cook, who needs a greater margin of safety.) I was also curious about why she chose one thickener over another, using cornstarch with apples and instant tapioca with cherries.

The only other significant quibble I have with *Great Pies & Tarts* is its organization. The appealing but too often eclectic recipe titles and their organization into chapters such as "From Orchards, Vines and Bushes" and "Decadent and Delicious" make it difficult to see and appreciate the organizing principles of baking pies and tarts. It would have been helpful to go beyond the useful chapter introductions by starting with some simpler recipes and then showing how to build on them; kind of like seeing the old MS-DOS operating system that lurks just beneath the surface of Microsoft Windows. There is no recipe for a simple custard pie, for blueberry pie, for chiffon, or for simple fruit pie. As a result, the recipes don't quite match up to the excellent instructional information. This is no fatal error since the book is rife with solid cooking tips and techniques, but it would have sharpened its usefulness as a one-of-a-kind kitchen reference.

But what about the recipes themselves? We made eight recipes, five of which were winners, a more than respectable batting average. The flaky pie pastry was fine although the directions were sometimes confusing; a mistake-proof puff pastry delivered almost as promised since the resulting pastry was a bit doughy; a pumpkin pie had great flavor paired with a pecan crust; and a frozen honey yogurt tart and a chocolate ricotta tart were both unusual, a bit too sweet, but well received by dinner guests. Overall, some of us in the test kitchen would have preferred a simpler, less gussied-up collection of recipes, but that is simply a matter of personal taste.

Great Pies & Tarts is by no means perfect, but Walter does teach her readers how to get the horses harnessed and out of the barn, no mean feat given the difficulty of making pies and tarts. Although something is lost in the translation from pastry board to printed page, *Great Pies & Tarts* is an important contribution to its field.

RESOURCES

Most of the ingredients and materials necessary for the recipes in this issue are available at your local supermarket, gourmet store, or kitchen supply shop. The following are mail-order sources for particular items. Prices listed below were current at press time and do not include shipping or handling unless otherwise indicated. We suggest that you contact companies directly to confirm up-to-date prices and availability.

Vegetable Peelers

Oxo Good Grips Swivel Peeler, the number one peeler in our rating on page 28, can be found in cookware stores and department stores nationwide. If you cannot find it, **A Cook's Wares catalog (211 37th Street, Beaver Falls, PA 15010-2103; 800-915-9788)** sells the Oxo Good Grips peeler for $5.90 by mail order. While the Oxo peeler was the choice for everyday peeling tasks—apples, carrots, potatoes—the Kuhn Rikon was the preferred peeler for more challenging jobs, such as peeling off the thick skin of a butternut squash or the dry, coarse skin of a celery root. This "Y-peeler" can be purchased by mail for $3.50 through the **Sur La Table catalog division (1765 Sixth Avenue South, Seattle, WA 98134-1608; 800-243-0852)**. Its item identification number is 14663. While the Kyocera P-1 Ceramic Yoke Peeler (C I 89) was not the top pick among the peelers, it had its strengths, including a zirconium oxide blade that is supposed to never lose its edge. This is said to be so because, unlike steel, it does not oxidize, which contributes to dulling. If you quickly wear out peelers or your interest is piqued by the anomaly of the ceramic blade, the Kyocera P-1 peeler is available for $12.95 through **Professional Cutlery Direct (170 Boston Post Road, Suite 135, Madison, CT 06443; 800-859-6994)**.

Meat Pounder

While developing a recipe for chicken Parmesan, executive editor Pam Anderson found that the best tool for pounding out a chicken breast is a disc-shaped solid stainless steel meat pounder with an upright handle stemming from the center top(see illustration, page 10). It weighs a hefty 1.7 pounds, which means gravity does most of the work for you. This kitchen tool can be purchased for $24.95 from **Kitchen Arts (161 Newbury Street, Boston, MA 02116; 617-266-8701)**.

Japanese Bread Crumbs

Using a Japanese ingredient in chicken Parmesan might sound curious, but as we found out in a side-by-side blind tasting (see sidebar, page 11), neither Italian bread crumbs, plain American bread crumbs, nor matzo meal were able to surpass the light, crispy texture and toasty wheat flavor of Japanese-style bread crumbs, known as panko. Unlike American or Italian bread crumbs, which are finely ground, toasted, and dense, panko consists of large, untoasted, light flakes of wheat flour, shortening, yeast, sugar, and salt. The panko brand we tested, Wel-Pac, is not available by mail order. We were able to purchase it, however, in the international section of a large urban supermarket. **The Spice Merchant (P.O. Box 524, Jackson, WY 83001; 800-551-5999; stirfry@compuserve.com)** sells 5½ ounce bags of panko through the mail for $1.55, which we tested and found a suitable replacement for the Wel-Pac.

Commercial-Size Spatulas

The foolproof sponge cake recipe on page 22 requires gentle folding of the flour mixture into soft, moist beaten eggs. Our test kitchen recommends using a commercial-size rubber spatula because it is more efficient and less likely to disrupt the delicate egg foam. The one used in our test kitchen, manufactured by Rubbermaid, has a white 9½-inch plastic handle, with a 4½ x 2¾-inch rubber scraper. It can be purchased by mail order for $1.49 through the **Everything Rubbermaid store (115 South Market Street, Wooster, OH 44691; 330-264-7592)**. Its item identification number is 190. This store also sells a large rubber heat-resistant spatula (item #1963) for $6.99. It has a 13½-inch brick-red handle and a 4 x 2½-inch white scraper. This spatula is stain-resistant and can tolerate temperatures up to 500 degrees, so it can be used for stir-frying and will not scratch nonstick cookware. It is also dishwasher-safe and notched on one side for ease of scraping bowl edges. Because of their low price and general utility, we recommend stocking your kitchen with one of each.

Pyrophenalia

For the leg of lamb recipe on page 15, author Stephanie Lyness found that she preferred to set her chimney starter aside and instead tuck two paraffin fire-starter blocks into a pile of coals right in the grill. **Peoples Smoke'n Grill Shop (75 Mill Street, Cumberland, RI 02864; 800-729-5800)** carries wood paraffin fire-starter blocks that are nontoxic and odorless, comply with California air quality standards, and contain 10 percent recycled wood and paper products. One pound (36 blocks) sells for $2.50. The blocks can be used in a chimney starter instead of newspaper. People's also sells hardwood charcoal by mail—17.6 pound lots for $8.90 each or $7.90 each for two or more lots.

Ginger Grater

If you often cook with fresh ginger, it might be worthwhile to invest in a ginger grater and avoid gnashing your knuckles on a box grater. **Sur La Table catalog division, (1765 Sixth Avenue South, Seattle, WA 98134-1608; 800-243-0852)** sells a white porcelain ginger grater in the shape of a 5-inch wide shallow bowl for $10.95. In the center is a 3-inch raised circle with molded porcelain teeth to quickly shred the ginger fibers. We particularly like the fact that a moat surrounds the grater in order to catch not only the fibers but also the ginger juices. If you are looking for a grater you can safely stash in a utensil drawer, **King Arthur Flour's Baker's Catalogue (P.O. Box 876, Norwich, VT 05055-0876; 800-827-6836)** carries a stainless steel ginger grater that resembles a short, stubby metal spatula. Tiny teeth on the stainless steel base readily grate ginger into a thick paste. Slanted sides on the base prevent most of the juices from spilling off. This grater sells for $5.95.

Nonmelting Sugar

For some of our readers in the South who tried the lemon bar recipe in our May/June 1998 issue, humidity appeared to be the culprit of the disappearing confectioners' sugar topping. A few solutions to this were offered in this issue (see Notes from Readers, page 2), including the use of nonmelting sugar. Nonmelting sugar has the same fine texture and bright whiteness as confectioners' sugar. Yet place just a dab on your tongue and you will discover the difference—it doesn't dissolve instantaneously like other sugars, including confectioners' sugar. That is because each grain is encapsulated in a microscopic fatty layer of lecithin, which protects the sugar from breaking down under moist or warm conditions. Just to be sure, we sprinkled the nonmelting sugar on a batch of lemon bars while they were still warm from baking. No dissolving was apparent. While this sugar is not as sweet as confectioners' sugar, even the latter cannot compete with the flavor strength of the lemon filling in this dessert. You can mail order nonmelting sugar, called Snow White Sugar, for $3.75 per pound from the **Baker's Catalogue by King Arthur Flour (P.O. Box 876, Norwich, VT 05055-0876; 800-827-6836)**.

Erratum

The Forschner Victorinox Kullenschliff edge meat slicer for slicing brisket, recommended on our July/August 1998 Resources page, can be purchased by mail for $47.30 from **Professional Cutlery Direct (170 Boston Post Road, Suite 135, Madison, CT 06443; 800-859-6994)**.

RECIPE INDEX

Chicken Parmesan, Updated **PAGE 11**

Classic Crème Caramel **PAGE 25**

Classic Minestrone **PAGE 7**

Boston Cream Pie **PAGE 23**

Grilled Butterflied Leg of Lamb **PAGE 15**

Cinnamon Swirl Rolls **PAGE 20**

PHOTOGRAPHY: CARL TREMBLAY   PROP STYLING: MYROSHA DZIUK   FOOD STYLING: SUSAN LOGOZZO

Porcini

Oyster

Crimini

Enoki

White

Horn of Plenty

Chanterelle

Shiitake

Portobello

Morel

MUSHROOMS

NUMBER THIRTY-FIVE

NOVEMBER & DECEMBER 1998

COOK'S
ILLUSTRATED

Perfect Beef Tenderloin
High Heat Roasting Works Best

Fallen Chocolate Cake
Rich, Moist, and Foolproof

Testing Automatic Drip Coffee Makers
Do Any Make Decent Coffee?

Roast Duck Without Fat
Steam First, Then Roast

Rating Cinnamons
Is the Real Thing Best?

Yeast Coffee Cakes Perfected
Step-by-Step Guide to
3 Classic Shapes

Tetrazzini Updated

Nut Crescent Cookies

Oyster Taste Test

Oven-Baked Stuffings

$4.00 U.S./$4.95 CANADA

62805

12>

0 232816 4

CONTENTS
November & December 1998

COOK'S ILLUSTRATED

PUBLISHER AND EDITOR
Christopher Kimball

EXECUTIVE EDITOR
Pam Anderson

SENIOR EDITOR
John Willoughby

SENIOR WRITER
Jack Bishop

ASSOCIATE EDITORS
Adam Ried
Maryellen Driscoll

TEST KITCHEN DIRECTOR
Susan Logozzo

TEST COOKS
Anne Yamanaka
Dawn Yanagihara

CONTRIBUTING EDITOR
Stephanie Lyness

ART DIRECTOR
Amy Klee

CORPORATE MANAGING EDITOR
Barbara Bourassa

EDITORIAL PRODUCTION MANAGER
Sheila Datz

COPY EDITOR
Carol Parikh

MARKETING DIRECTOR
Adrienne Kimball

CIRCULATION DIRECTOR
David Mack

FULFILLMENT MANAGER
Larisa Greiner

CIRCULATION MANAGER
Darcy Beach

MARKETING ASSISTANT
Connie Forbes

PRODUCTS MANAGER
Steven Browall

VICE PRESIDENT
PRODUCTION AND TECHNOLOGY
James McCormack

SYSTEMS ADMINISTRATOR
James Burke

DESKTOP PUBLISHING MANAGER
Kevin Moeller

PRODUCTION ARTIST
Daniel Frey

SENIOR ACCOUNTANT
Mandy Shito

OFFICE MANAGER
Danielle Shuckra

SPECIAL PROJECTS
Fern Berman

Cook's Illustrated (ISSN 1068-2821) is published bimonthly by Boston Common Press Limited Partnership, 17 Station Street, Brookline, MA 02445. Copyright ©1998 Boston Common Press Limited Partnership. Periodical postage paid at Boston, MA and additional mailing offices. USPS #012487. For list rental information, contact List Services Corporation, 6 Trowbridge Drive, P.O. Box 516, Bethel, CT 06801; (203) 743-2600; fax (203) 743-0589. Editorial office: 17 Station Street, Brookline, MA 02147; (617) 232-1000; fax (617) 232-1572. Editorial contributions should be sent to: Editor, *Cook's Illustrated*. We cannot assume responsibility for manuscripts submitted to us. Submissions will be returned only if accompanied by a large self-addressed stamped envelope. Postmaster: Send all new orders, subscription inquiries, and change of address notices to: *Cook's Illustrated*, P.O. Box 7446, Red Oak, IA 51591-0446. PRINTED IN THE USA.

SHELLFISH One of the two main divisions of shellfish (along with crustaceans), mollusks are sea-dwelling invertebrates with soft bodies that are covered by one- or two-piece shells. Most of the edible mollusks are bivalves, which simply means they have a two-part shell. Edible bivalves include scallops, which may be either tiny bay scallops found only on the East Coast or the more widely available sea scallops; clams, which may be hard-shell such as cherrystones or soft-shell such as steamers; mussels, which include the common blue mussel and the lovely, green-lipped variety from New Zealand; and oysters, which come in many varieties (*see* page 10). Abalone and periwinkle snails are among the more popular of the edible gastropod mollusks, which have a one-piece shell.

COVER PAINTING: BRENT WATKINSON. BACK COVER ILLUSTRATION: JOHN BURGOYNE

A GUIDE FOR THE HOLIDAY SEASON

I recently met a fishing guide up on the Matapedia River in Canada. Richard, who was born in 1910, is a bowman for the Cold Spring Camp. This means that he springs into action as soon as one of the sports hooks a salmon, the biggest of which run up to more than 40 pounds. The fish must be allowed to run, the drag on the reel has to be set properly, and the large three-man canoe must be poled into the proper position to land the fish. Over half the big ones are lost before they can be reeled in due to improperly tied flies, smart fish that bang their heads against a rock to dislodge the hook, and lines that become tangled around a rock or the canoe itself. For a man of 88 years, Richard moves quickly, like a big cat that dozes most of the day but has large stores of coiled energy waiting to be released.

One afternoon I stopped down to his double-wide trailer for a visit. He told me that when he was growing up everyone had a large family, and his was no exception. There were eight children, four of whom are still alive. His mother kept a garden, growing turnips, potatoes, carrots, cabbage, beets, and beans, and stored much of it in a root cellar over the winter. Cream was stored in metal cans in the brook throughout the summer or hung by broom handles in barrels of cool water, and ice was cut in the winter and kept in the ice house with sawdust or hay as insulation.

His mother used to make brown sugar fudge, molasses cookies, sugar cookies, raisin pie, marble cake, dried apple pie, cucumber and mustard pickles, pumpkin jam, and doughnuts. Most every family he knew raised a few pigs and some beef. For Thanksgiving, the family would have a roast chicken and a glass of wine. For Christmas, a stocking filled with a few apples, an orange, and some hard candy was tied to the foot of his bed.

He left school at age 14, running off to the logging camps where he spent most of his life. The first of October they would start cutting, either up from the river or off one of the tributaries, using two-man saws. By Christmas, the cutting would stop and the logs would be hauled by horse down to the rivers where they were floated downstream. Log jams were common; a crew of 80 men used to do about five miles a day on the river, the logs getting stuck in a wing jam or on a rock. The camp cooks served baking powder biscuits, beans, and plenty of black tea for breakfast. There were no chickens or eggs; the only chicken Richard ever saw on those drives was the one in the picture on the wall.

Sporting long bushy white sideburns and dressed in thick woolen pants, Richard sits on the narrow porch attached to the trailer, legs outstretched, and remembers with relish the plate of beans and biscuits for breakfast, the long workdays hauling logs with the teams down to the river, the sweet smoke from hot campfires, and the winter days spent rabbit hunting; he used to sell rabbits for 25 cents apiece to the hotel down in Sillarsville.

I often think that happiness is in inverse proportion to the number of things one owns. The clothes on one's back, a warm, dry place for the winter, a good job, a few friends, and a bit of

Christopher Kimball

loose change can make a happy man. Happiness is being needed, not needing things.

So during this fall season, our family tries to take pleasure in simple chores, making coffee cake for church or greasing and storing equipment for the winter. We read up on beekeeping and pruning and the best methods for ridding ourselves of next year's crop of potato beetles. We spend time watching the view from our farmhouse, the light thinner now and the air so clear that I can look out across our valley and make out individual leaves, the five-pointed sugar maples, the jagged shagbark hickory, and the long, slender white ash. The timothy in the lower field no longer pushes up strongly from the earth but sits listlessly, pale green, mottled with browns, waiting for winter. The stand of corn is brown and withered; the heads of the giant sunflowers have turned dark, their necks broken.

And as I sit on my front porch, I wonder about the upcoming holidays. Perhaps this is the year we will make do with a roast chicken, a glass of wine, a raisin pie, and a stocking filled with tangerines and hard candy for the kids. In this day and age, it is a wistful thought, an idea to be hoped for, a fantasy just on the fragile edge of possibility.

But in a season that was born of simplicity and faith, we could all learn from Richard and find contentment in a plate of beans, a biscuit, and a cup of strong tea. I like to think that happiness would follow us the rest of our days.

ABOUT COOK'S ILLUSTRATED

The Magazine *Cook's Illustrated* is published every other month (6 issues per year) and accepts no advertising. A one-year subscription is $24.95, two years is $45, and three years is $65. Add $6 postage per year for Canadian subscriptions and $12 per year for all other foreign countries. To order subscriptions, call 800-526-8442. Gift subscriptions are available for $24.95 each.

Magazine-Related Items *Cook's Illustrated* is available in an annual hardbound edition, which includes an index, for $24.95 each plus shipping and handling. Discounts are available if more than one year is ordered at a time. Back issues are available for $5 each. The *Cook's Illustrated* 1998 calendar, featuring 12 of the magazine's covers reproduced in full color, is available for $12.95. *Cook's* also offers a five-year index (1993-1997) of the magazine for $12.95. To order any of these products, call 800-611-0759.

Books *Cook's Illustrated* publishes a series of single-topic books, available for $14.95 each. Titles include: *How To Make A Pie, How To Make An American Layer Cake, How To Stir Fry, How*

To Make Ice Cream, How To Make Pizza, How To Make Holiday Desserts, How To Make Pasta Sauces, and *How To Grill.* The *Cook's Bible,* written by Christopher Kimball and published by Little, Brown, is available for $24.95. To order any of these books, call 800-611-0759.

Reader Submissions *Cook's Illustrated* accepts reader submissions for both Quick Tips and Notes From Readers. We will provide a one-year complimentary subscription for each Quick Tip that we print. Send a description of your technique, along with your name, address, and daytime telephone number, to Quick Tips, *Cook's Illustrated,* P.O. Box 569, Brookline, MA 02147. Questions, suggestions, or other submissions for Notes From Readers should be sent to the same address.

Subscription Inquiries All queries about subscriptions or change of address notices should be addressed to *Cook's Illustrated,* P.O. Box 7446, Red Oak, IA 51591-0446.

Website Address Selected articles and recipes from *Cook's Illustrated* and subscription information are available online. You can access the *Cook's* website at: www.cooksillustrated.com.

Defining Custard Desserts

Custards confuse me. In *Cook's* alone, I've seen recipes, all slightly different, for rich baked custard, crème brûlée, and now, in the September/October 1998 issue, crème caramel. Also, I've eaten flans and pôts de crème. Clearly they are all in the same family, but can you clarify the characteristics that set them apart?

JOSEPH JOHNSON
CAMBRIDGE, MA

➤ While researching and testing for "Classic Crème Caramel," this same question occurred to authors Marie Piraino and Jamie Morris. Though recipes for these preparations vary widely, depending on the source, Piraino and Morris came up with the following general descriptions to help categorize these custard desserts, all of which are made with eggs, sugar, and a liquid dairy product, and served chilled. Flavorings such as vanilla, chocolate, coffee, or citrus are sometimes incorporated into the custards.

Simple Baked Custard: Because it uses milk as the dairy liquid and has a lower ratio of eggs to liquid than its richer custard cousins, simple baked custard is the lightest of these desserts. The lower egg-to-liquid ratio is sufficient because this custard is not unmolded before serving.

Crème Caramel: Also known in France as Crème Renversée, this fairly light custard, often made with milk as all or part of the dairy and with added yolks for some degree of richness, is baked in a mold lined with caramelized sugar. It is unmolded before serving, and the caramel becomes a sauce. A standard in French bistros and cafés, this dessert is now almost as American as it is French.

Flan: The preeminent dessert of Spain and much of Latin America, flan is similar to crème caramel (it often gets the same definition in cookbooks) in that it is also baked in a caramel-lined mold and turned out before serving. Flan, however, is usually richer and denser than crème caramel because the custard is made with more eggs and yolks, as well as some cream or evaporated or condensed milk.

Crème Brûlée: Many say that the origin of "burnt cream" can be traced not to France, as you might presume, but instead to Trinity College in 17th century England. Compared to crème caramel or flan, crème brûlée is very rich because the custard usually contains heavy cream and numerous egg yolks. Topped with a thin layer of sugar, which is caramelized under a broiler or salamander or with a torch just before serving, crème brûlée can be prepared either on the stove top, then poured into molds and chilled

to set, or baked. In neither case is it unmolded. The distinctive taste and texture of the crisp, warm sugar crust contrasts with the cold, creamy custard.

Pôt de Crème: This French cup custard literally means "pot of cream." Prepared either on the stove top or baked, it is served in very small portions in traditional lidded porcelain cups. This custard, like crème brûlée, is very rich because it uses a very high proportion of egg yolks to whole eggs (if any whole eggs are used at all).

Cocoa Dusting for Cake Pans

When I'm baking a dark-colored cake, I dust the greased cake pan with cocoa powder instead of flour. This eliminates the possibility of a hazy, whitish film of flour on the cake once it has been turned out of the pan.

KRIS ACKERMAN
DALLAS, TX

➤ Based on repeated tests with the individual and large fallen chocolate cakes on page 24 in this issue, we can say that your tip works very well. Cakes turned out of the cocoa-dusted baking cups and pans were extra dark and uniform in color, like good bittersweet chocolate, which added to their rich appearance. In comparison, cakes from the flour-dusted baking cups and pans had a slightly lighter crust, about the color of milk chocolate.

Apple Pie Airspace

My brother's apple pies taste great, but he is having trouble with the top crust forming a high dome over the apples once they are baked. He always heaps the apples, which do cook down as the pie bakes, but not all that much. He has tried cutting bigger slits in the top crust, but it didn't prevent the gap.

LINDA RUNEBERG
ELKO, MN

➤ Our solution to your problem is to increase the amount of fat, particularly butter, in your pie crust recipe. This was suggested by both P. J. Hamel, Senior Editor of the *King Arthur Flour Baker's Catalogue*, and Dr. Ronald Zelch, Director of Cake and Sweet Good Production at the American Institute of Baking. It was also born out in our test kitchen. In our November/December 1998 article "All-Season Apple Pie," the recipe for pie crust calls for two parts flour to one part fat (measured by volume) and the top crust sinks down snugly over the apples. When we tried a crust with three parts flour to one part fat, which is the typical ratio in many recipes, the pie baked up

with about 1½-inches of space between the apples and the top crust.

The reason for this is simple. The presence of additional fat in the dough makes it more pliable and prolongs the point at which the top crust will set into shape as it bakes in the oven. If the crust does not set until later, it will stick closer to the apples. However, if the crust sets into shape too quickly, it will not sink down with the cooking apples, which results in the unwanted gap between filling and crust. Zelch also explained that fat interferes with gluten formation in the pastry, and therefore weakens the overall structure, causing the crust to collapse onto the fruit. Zelch and King Arthur's Hamel both mentioned that butter has a lower melting point than shortening, so more butter will cause the crust to collapse sooner than shortening will.

Hamel and our test kitchen staff agreed on a few more pointers that should help. First, do your best to further limit gluten development in your dough by not overworking it. Moisture combined with any kind of movement, such as mixing or kneading, turns the proteins in flour into gluten, which makes a stronger, less collapsible (and less tender) crust. Second, lay the crust over the apples without stretching it, which will also increase gluten. Third, pat the apples down gently in the pie plate to compress them slightly before laying the top crust on them. This way, the fruit will sink a little less as it cooks, again helping to reduce the gap. Last, our editor Chris Kimball adds that you should let the dough hydrate as much as possible before rolling it out, preferably overnight. The hydration makes the dough more pliable and less likely to shrink when baked.

Tempered Glass Bakeware

In the article about apple pie in your December 1997 issue, there was a sidebar called "Do-Ahead Fresh-Baked Apple Pie" in which you recommend placing a frozen pie directly into a preheated oven (425 degrees, I assume, as in the master recipe). I use Pyrex pie plates. Can I really put a frozen Pyrex dish right into a hot oven without breaking it?

HORTENSE KABEL
MIDDLETOWN, CT

➤ The short answer is yes, it should be fine to transfer a filled Pyrex pie plate from the freezer into a preheated 425-degree oven. To double-check this point, we contacted Jim Kamandulis, Senior Quality Analyst at Corning Consumer Products Company, maker of Pyrex. Kamandulis emphasized preheating the oven, explaining that the pie plate would likely break if it came into contact with any direct heat source and also that some ovens may use the broiler as well as the bottom heating element to quickly heat up to the desired temperature, resulting in a heat intense enough to be regarded by Corning as the equivalent of direct heat.

The transfer from freezer to preheated oven is okay because the glass from which Pyrex products are made is tempered. Tempering, Kamandulis pointed out, is a mechanical strengthening process that increases the thermal shock resistance of the glass. The glass is heated to a uniform temperature and then quickly quenched with air, a process which amounts to rapid chilling. This creates compressive layers on the surface of the glass, which increase its impact- and thermal-resistance.

We did note that the use and care instructions printed on the back of the label on our pie plate caution against severe temperature changes. Though this warning is written in general terms, Kamandulis said that it applies especially to taking the glass from very high to very low temperatures, which is called "downshock." Downshock would result from adding cold liquid to a hot Pyrex dish, or placing the hot dish directly on a cold or wet surface.

Failed Limeade
The July/August 1998 recipe for lemonade was really good, so being a big limeade fan as well, I adapted the mashing method for limes. I was surprised that it didn't work out well, even though I didn't do anything different. The limeade was okay when it was first made, but after sitting for just 40 minutes, it had turned too strong to drink. What is going on with the limes here?

ART KOWITCH
PORTLAND, OR

➤ We had exactly the same experience, so we dropped the limeade variation we had originally wanted to include with the lemonade recipes. That said, there are a couple of factors that may be responsible for the excessive strength of the limeade. First, limes are more acidic and naturally have a stronger flavor than lemons. Jacquelyn Gibson, an extension agent with the Miami/Dade Cooperative Extension Service, said that limes contain about one-third more citric acid than lemons and that the oil content of lime zest is heavier than that of lemon zest. Even if limes did work well in this recipe, you could not substitute them one-for-one for the lemons.

As for the change over time, Dr. Robert Braddock of the University of Florida Citrus Research and Education Center in Lake Alfred, Florida, explained that limonin, one of the compounds that give both lemons and limes their bitterness, becomes even stronger when it reacts with the acid in the juice and with heat. Since there are greater concentrations of limonin in immature fruit, and limes are generally shipped and sold when they are less ripe than lemons (fully ripe limes take on a yellow tinge, like lemons), the extra limonin reacting with the juice may contribute to the undesirable change.

Expanding Ice Crystals
I like to make and freeze my own stock. Every time I open a container of frozen stock, though, I notice that the liquid has frozen with a visible peak in the middle. This seems to occur regardless of the container's size or shape. I am certain that it does not negatively affect the stock, but I'd love to know the cause.

DAVID BROMLEY
SAN FRANCISCO, CA

➤ The answer is expansion. Rob Brannan, Coordinator of the Food and Nutrition Extension at Kansas State University, explained, and the third edition of *Food Chemistry*, edited by Dr. Owen R. Fennema (Marcel Dekker, 1996) confirmed, that when liquids freeze, they expand to form ice crystals, which occupy roughly 9 percent more space than the same matter in liquid form. Because the liquid around the edges of the container is the most exposed to the cold air of the freezer, it freezes before the center portion. The walls of the container won't budge to accommodate the expanding volume, so the freezing liquid pushes toward the middle, forcing the liquid level there to rise just slightly (it has nowhere else to go) and form that familiar peak, which then freezes into position.

Warming Dinner Plates in the Microwave
I use a microwave technique that you did not write about in the January/February 1998 article "The Microwave Chronicles." Rather than heating the oven to warm my dinner plate, I put a little water onto the plate and microwave it for two minutes. This results in a plate warm enough to keep my food piping hot.

JEANNE FRANCAVILLA
NEW ROCHELLE, NY

➤ Warm dinner plates are a simple, enjoyable luxury, but since this is not strictly a cooking technique, it was not part of our original testing for the microwave piece. We did test your trick, though, on individual stoneware plates and on a stack of four. We suspect that our microwave may be more powerful than yours because we found the plates almost too hot to handle, at about 132 degrees on the surface of the plate, after two minutes, and quite hot enough after a minute and a half. The method also worked on the stack of four plates, though they reached a slightly cooler 125 degrees on the top plate and 112 degrees on the middle plates. Keep in mind, though, that we'd expect timing and temperature to vary according to your microwave oven's power and capacity. Regardless of your oven's specifics, make sure the plates you use are microwave-safe and free of metal trim or metallic glazes.

Virtually all the microwave books and manuals we consulted noted that you should never heat empty, dry dishes in the microwave oven. This is because of the way the microwaves work. Joy Daniel, a Senior Product Development Manager at Sharp Electronics Corporation, explained that a component called the magnetron tube generates short length electromagnetic waves and sends them through a covered wave guide into the cavity of the oven. Within the cavity, the waves are attracted to moisture, so there must be food, or in this case water, on the plate to absorb the energy. If not, the waves would reflect throughout the oven and back onto the porous wave guide cover. If there are any tiny food particles stuck to the cover, as there likely will be, the energy could burn holes in the wave guide cover over time.

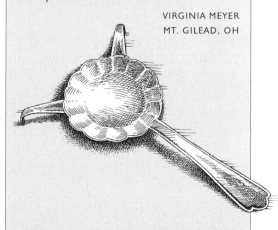

Quick Tips

Making Even-Sized Balls of Cookie Dough

Working on the nut cookie article in this issue, Test Cook Dawn Yanagihara found it difficult to accurately measure the diameter of balls of cookie dough with the ruler set right on the work surface. Moving the ruler to the top of a bowl solved her problem because the cookie could be easily measured across its equator.

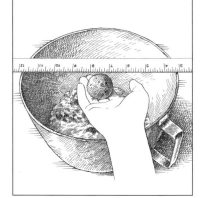

Indenting Cookies for Filling

The best thumbprint cookies have a deep, round indentation to hold the dollop of jam or chocolate securely. In her November/December 1997 tip, Anne Blumenfeld of San Diego, California, found a wooden honey dipper well-suited to the task. Laura Schafer of Romeoville, Illinois, who has no honey dipper, found that using the back side of an ordinary small melon baller makes a deeper, rounder indentation than either a spoon or her thumb.

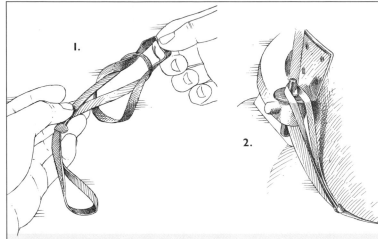

Stabilizing the KitchenAid Mixer Bowl

The KitchenAid KSM5 is an especially popular standing mixer model, but some readers, as well as our test kitchen staff, have experienced a problem with the bowl popping off the stand when the mixer is working on a batch of particularly stiff dough. When this problem occurred for Mark Loudon of Palmdale, California, he devised the following solution.

1. Loop together several sturdy rubber bands.

2. Hook one end of the long band around one of the prongs that hold the mixing bowl in place. Run the band underneath the mixing bowl and hook the other end around the opposite prong. The pressure the elastic exerts on the bowl keeps it steady even when the stiffest dough is being mixed.

Quick-Cooling for Pastry Creams and Puddings

Pastry creams and puddings come off the stove hot, but must be cooled to room temperature, or even chilled, before they can be used. Test Kitchen Director Susan Logozzo has found a way to speed the process by maximizing the surface area from which steam can escape.

1. Spread the pastry cream or pudding out across a rimmed, plastic wrap-covered baking pan, then cover it with another piece of plastic wrap to prevent a skin from forming.

2. Snip a number of holes in the plastic wrap to allow steam to escape.

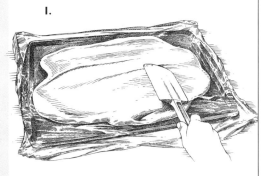

Safely Stacking Fine China

Many families have delicate china dishes handed down through the generations. As the dishes become worn and brittle with time, they crack and chip easily, sometimes even as they're being stacked in the cabinet. To provide an extra layer of cushioning and protection, Dulcie Camp of Greeley, Colorado, places paper plates between the china plates when she stacks them.

Improvisational Mortar and Pestle

Most cooks don't need a mortar and pestle very often. Instead of buying one for infrequent use, Melody Lewin of Glendora, California, uses a sturdy, shallow diner-style stoneware coffee cup and a heavy glass spice bottle.

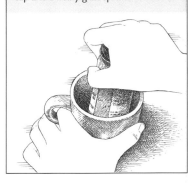

Gingerbread People Ornaments

Kim Fosbre of Jamaica Plain, Massachussetts, likes to decorate trees, wreaths, and tables with homemade gingerbread people. To ensure a sturdy hanging hole after baking, she pokes through the raw dough with a plastic drinking straw.

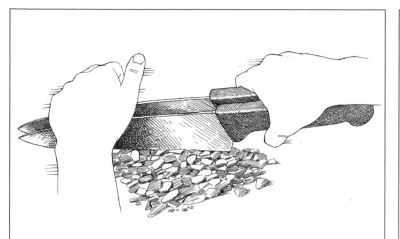

Chopping Nuts

When chopping nuts for the scores of test batches of nut crescent cookies, Test Cook Dawn Yanagihara found that using two chef's knives, held parallel, made the task go much faster.

Another Use for Frozen Citrus

Rather than throwing out the spent shells from juiced lemons and limes, Rachel Gregory of Lebanon, Tennessee, freezes them in a zipper-lock freezer bag, then pulls out a couple every time she needs acidulated water to hold peeled apples, potatoes, artichokes, and the like.

Makeshift Proofing Box

Cooking in a large, fairly drafty kitchen forced Steve and Diana Elder of Fort Collins, Colorado, to get creative about finding a "warm, draft-free" spot where bread or pizza dough could rise. Their solution was to place the dough in a lightly oiled food storage container, preferably shallow and with a flat bottom, and then to float the container in a large, covered stockpot almost full of warm (90 to 100 degrees) water.

Homemade Colored Sugar

Colored sugar is great for decorating holiday cookies, but often you don't use all that you buy, so some goes to waste. To solve this problem, Kathleen Collins of New York City uses this technique to make her own small batches of colored sugar.

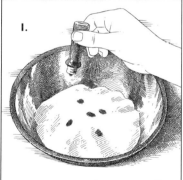

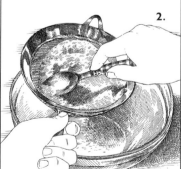

1. Sprinkle about ½ cup of granulated sugar evenly over the bottom of a pie plate or metal bowl, add about 5 drops of food coloring, and mix thoroughly.
2. To be sure the color is evenly distributed, push the sugar through a fine sieve. Spread the sugar on a pie plate or baking sheet and let dry.

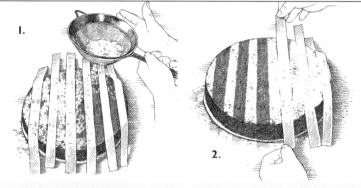

Decorating a Flourless Chocolate Cake

Karen Guillemin of Palo Alto, California, has found a neat way to give the top of her flourless chocolate cake an attractive striped look.
1. Lay strips of paper about ¾-inch wide across the top of the cake and then sieve confectioners' sugar over the top.
2. Carefully peel away the paper strips.

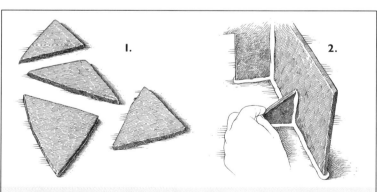

Gingerbread House Construction Tip

Elizabeth Flores of Golf, Illinois, went one up on our November/December 1997 gingerbread cottage construction instructions with her own method for supporting the walls.
1. When cutting out the wall and ceiling panels, cut four extra-small right triangles to bake along with the other pieces.
2. When it's time to assemble the house, pipe frosting on both perpendicular sides of the triangles and prop one up behind each wall to provide extra support.

Foaming Milk for Cappuccino, Redux

The tip in our January/February 1998 issue about foaming milk with a whisk inspired several other readers to offer their techniques for the same task. Kristen Rengren of Chicago, Illinois, found a method that frothed milk better than her espresso machine. Place a pot of heated milk on a pot holder or other protective surface and beat with a hand-held electric mixer. The resulting foam is not only velvety but also holds soft peaks after serving.

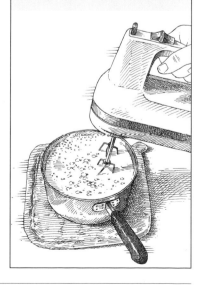

Making Beef Tenderloin Worth the Price

When you spend this much for a piece of meat, you want to be sure it comes out right.
Here's how to add a flavorful crust and end up with an evenly cooked roast.

⇒ BY PAM ANDERSON WITH MELISSA HAMILTON ⇐

For large holiday parties, few cuts top beef tenderloin. This elegant roast cooks quickly, serves a crowd, and its rich, buttery slices are fork-tender.

Despite its many virtues, however, beef tenderloin is not without its liabilities. Price, of course, is the biggest. Even at my local warehouse-style supermarket, the going rate for a whole beef tenderloin is $7.99 a pound—an average sticker price of about $50. But there are special occasions—Christmas and New Year's Eve among them—when what I really want is the traditional beef roast, and I'm willing to pay the price.

There is good reason for the tenderloin's hefty price. Because it sits up just under the spine of the cow, it gets no exercise at all and is therefore the most tender piece of meat (*see* "Locating the Tenderloin," page 7). It is one of the two muscles in the ultra-premium steak known as the porterhouse, so when it is removed from the cow as a whole muscle, it is going to go for ultra-premium prices.

But there are also other problems with this deluxe roast. The tenderloin's sleek, boneless form makes for quick roasting, but its torpedo-like shape—thick and chunky at one end, gradually tapering at the other end—naturally roasts unevenly (*see* "Parts of a Tenderloin," right). In addition, the flavor of this tender roast, while rich, is very mild, sometimes barely recognizable as beef. So with these challenges in mind, we headed to the supermarket and the local butcher and bought $550 worth of beef tenderloin. Despite the sound of it, we came home with just 11 roasts.

Let's Take It Off

A whole beef tenderloin can be purchased "unpeeled," with an incredibly thick layer of exterior fat left attached, but it's usually sold "peeled," or stripped of its fat. Because of our many bad experiences with today's overly lean pork and beef, we purchased six of the 11 roasts unpeeled, determined to leave on as much fat as possible. However, after a quick examination of the unpeeled roasts, we realized that the excessively thick layer of surface fat had to go. Not only would

The dark, flavorful crust created by a high roasting temperature is essential for tenderloin, but the additional crust of peppercorns is optional.

such a large quantity of rendering fat smoke up the kitchen, it would also prohibit a delicious crust from forming on the meat. We dutifully peeled the thick layer of fat from the six tenderloins, but even after removing the sheaths of fat, there were still large fat pockets and significant surface fat.

So does it make sense to buy an unpeeled roast and trim it yourself? We think not. We paid $6.99 a pound at the butcher for our unpeeled tenderloins, each weighing about eight pounds. After cleaning them up, the peeled tenderloins weighed about five pounds, a whopping three pounds of waste. We purchased peeled tenderloins of similar quality from another source for only $7.99 per pound. Clearly the unpeeled tenderloins were more expensive with no benefits.

Although we don't like tenderloins that have been picked clean, right down to the meat, we recommend buying peeled roasts, with their patches of scattered fat, and letting them be.

Fold It Under, Tie It Up, and Cook It High

Roasting a whole tenderloin is a little like cooking a whole fish. Both are thick at one end and tapered at the other, which makes for uneven cooking. For those looking for a range of doneness, this is not a problem, but for cooks who want a more

evenly cooked roast, something must be done.

Folding the tip end of the roast under and tying it bulks up the tenderloin center to almost the same thickness as the more substantial butt tender. This ensures that the tenderloin cooks more evenly. (Even so, the tip end is always a little more well-done than the butt end.) Tying the roast at approximately 1½-inch intervals further guarantees a more uniformly shaped roast, and more even slices of beef. Snipping the silver skin at several points (*see* illustration 1, page 7) also prevents the meat from bowing during cooking, when the silver skin shrinks more than the meat to which it is attached.

After cooking many roasts—beef, pork, and poultry—we've come to like slow-roasting for large roasts. The lower the heat, we've found, the more evenly the roast cooks. To develop a rich brown crust or skin on these low-roasted larger cuts, we either pan sear them up front or increase the oven temperature the last few minutes of roasting.

But a beef tenderloin is a different proposition. Though relatively large, its long, thin shape would seem to dictate a relatively quick cooking time. To determine the ideal roasting temperature, we started at the two extremes, roasting one tenderloin at 200 degrees, the other at 500. As expected, the roast cooked at 500 degrees not only created a very smoky kitchen from the rendering fat, it was also overcooked at each end and around the outside perimeter. However, the high oven heat had formed a thick, flavorful crust, crucial to this mild-flavored roast. Despite the even, rosy pink interior of the beef cooked at 200 degrees, this roast lacked the all-important meat crust. Neither oven temperature was ideal, so we kept roasting.

Since the higher roasting temperature offered the rich flavor this roast desperately needed, we

PARTS OF A TENDERLOIN

BUTT TENDER

SHORT TENDERLOIN   **TIP END**

A whole beef tenderloin comprises three sections. The thicker end of the roast is called the "butt tender"; the middle portion—virtually an even thickness—is called the "short tenderloin"; the tip end is sold as part of the whole tenderloin or removed and sold as "tenderloin tips."

LOCATING THE TENDERLOIN

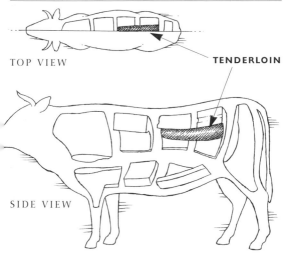

TOP VIEW

TENDERLOIN

SIDE VIEW

The tenderloin muscle is extremely tender because it is never used to move any part of the cow.

decided to roast it at as high a temperature as possible. A 450-degree oven still gave us smoke and uneven cooking, so we moved down to 425 degrees. For comparison, we roasted another tenderloin at 200 degrees, this time increasing the oven temperature to 425 degrees at the end to develop a crust. Both roasts emerged from the oven looking beautiful, and their meat looked and tasted almost identical. Since the tenderloin roasted at 425 degrees was done in just 45 minutes (compared with the slow-roasted tenderloin which took about 1½ hours), we chose the high-heat method.

Although all roasts should rest 15 to 20 minutes, we found that beef tenderloin improves dramatically if left uncarved even longer. If cut too soon, its slices are soft and flabby. A slightly longer rest, however, allows the meat to firm up into a texture we found much more appealing. Before carving, we preferred removing the big pockets of excess fat, which become more obvious at warm and room temperatures.

Some Like It Aged
To further improve flavor and texture, we tried aging the tenderloin in the refrigerator. To do so, we blotted dry a Kry-O-Vac-packed tenderloin, then simply refrigerated it on a wire rack set over a roasting pan. In addition, we salted another tenderloin, racking and refrigerating it like the other roast. For four days, we tasted the aging roasts, comparing them daily to tenderloin straight from the Kry-O-Vac .

Similar to our experience with prime rib (*see* "Perfect Prime Rib," November/December 1995), the salted roast tasted more like corned beef than tenderloin; if we wanted that flavor, we could have got it for half the money.

Our comparison of dry-aged to non-aged tenderloin revealed it was a matter of taste. We thought that aging for four days gave the tenderloin the increased flavor this mild cut needed. Interestingly, though, about half the tasting panel at *Cook's Illustrated* preferred the milder, fresher flavor and moister texture of the tenderloin roasted straight out of the Kry-O-Vac. Because it depends entirely on your taste, the choice is yours.

SIMPLE ROAST BEEF TENDERLOIN
SERVES 12 TO 16

To age the tenderloin, set it on a rack over a roasting pan and refrigerate it 3 to 4 days. If you do age the meat, you can reduce the post-roasting resting time to 15 to 20 minutes. To give the tenderloin a more pronounced pepper crust, increase the amount of pepper to 6 tablespoons and use a mixture of strong black and white and mild pink and green peppercorns. Be sure to crush the peppercorns with a mortar and pestle or with a heavy-bottomed saucepan or skillet. Do not use a coffee or spice grinder, which will grind the softer green and pink peppercorns to a powder before the harder black and white peppercorns begin to break up.

1 whole beef tenderloin peeled, (5 to 6 pounds), thoroughly patted dry

2 tablespoons olive oil
1 tablespoon kosher salt
2 tablespoons coarse-ground black pepper

1. Remove tenderloin from refrigerator 2 to 3 hours before roasting. Following illustration 1 below, use a sharp knife to carefully cut the silver skin on the side opposite the tail with shallow slashes at 1½-inch intervals. Tuck tail end under (illustration 2) and, following illustration 3, tie roast crosswise, knotting at 1½-inch intervals.

2. Adjust oven rack to upper middle position and heat oven to 425 degrees. Set meat on a sheet of plastic wrap and rub all over with oil. Sprinkle with salt and pepper; then, following illustration 4, lift plastic wrap up and around meat to press on excess.

3. Transfer prepared tenderloin from wrap to wire rack set on shallow roasting pan. Roast until instant-read thermometer inserted into the thickest part of the roast registers about 125 degrees (meat will range from medium-rare to medium in different areas of the roast), about 45 minutes. Let stand for about 30 minutes before carving. (Can be wrapped in plastic, refrigerated up to 2 days, sliced, and served chilled.)

4. Cut meat into ½-inch thick slices. Arrange on a serving platter and serve with the following sauce or another sauce of your choice.

PARSLEY SAUCE WITH CORNICHONS AND CAPERS
MAKES ABOUT 1¼ CUPS

¾ cup minced fresh parsley leaves
12 cornichons, minced (6 tablespoons), plus 1 teaspoon cornichon juice
¼ cup capers, chopped coarse
2 medium scallions, white and light green parts, minced
Pinch salt
¼ teaspoon ground black pepper
½ cup extra-virgin olive oil

Mix all ingredients in medium bowl; serve at room temperature.

STEP-BY-STEP | PREPARING THE TENDERLOIN FOR ROASTING

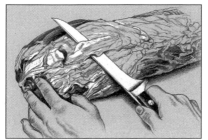

1. To keep the meat from bowing during roasting, slide a knife under the silver skin and flick the blade upwards to cut through the silver skin at 5 or 6 spots along the length of the roast.

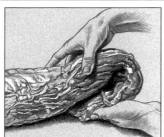

2. To ensure that the tenderloin roasts more evenly, fold the thin tip end of the roast under about 6 inches.

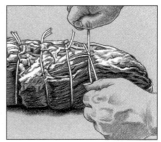

3. For more even cooking and evenly sized slices, tie the roast every 1½ inches.

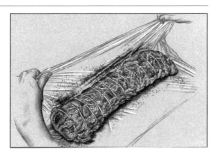

4. Set the meat on a sheet of plastic wrap and rub it all over with oil. Sprinkle with salt and pepper, then lift the plastic wrap up and around the meat to press on excess.

Roast Duck Without the Fat

The secret to delicious roast duck without a thick layer of fat is a two-step process.
Steam it first, then cut it into parts and roast it.

⇒ BY JACK BISHOP ⇐

Good ducks are delicious, but too often our pleasure in them is ruined because they are just too greasy. It wasn't always this way. Wild ducks are so lean they need to be covered with bacon to keep them from drying out in the oven. But only hunters encounter this problem. Supermarket shoppers must rely on domesticated Pekin (also called Long Island) ducks. And, boy, are these birds fatty. Although the sticker weight may say 4½ pounds, the final weight after roasting can be less than two pounds. No wonder a single duck yields two or maybe three servings.

My goals for this piece were simple—a knockout duck with crisp skin and moist, flavorful meat. To achieve this goal, I would have to rid the bird of a lot of fat.

At the outset, I decided I wanted an old-fashioned roast duck, cooked through without a trace of pink. Restaurants rely on different duck breeds with large breasts, in particular the muscovy, that can be cooked rare. But consumers must order such ducks by mail, and I wanted to stick with the duck you find in the supermarket. Since the breast on a Pekin duck is no thicker than half an inch, it can't be cooked rare or medium, especially if you are trying to get the legs to soften up.

Start Trimming

My initial tests demonstrated the need to start getting rid of the fat from the outset. I found that unless the skin rests directly on meat or bone it will never crisp properly. So before cooking even starts, the large clumps of white fat that line the body and neck cavity must be pulled out by hand and discarded. Any loose skin must also be trimmed away, including most of the flap that covers the neck cavity.

My next tests centered on roasting methods. Every source I consulted agreed that a roasting rack is necessary to keep the duck elevated above the rendered fat. After that, there was little agreement.

Many recipes suggest pricking the skin to help fat escape. I used a fork as well as the tip of a paring knife and both worked moderately well.

One chef told me he always starts duck in a 500-degree oven to render the fat quickly and then turns down the heat to 350 degrees to cook the duck through. My instincts told me this approach was problematic, and the billows of smoke that filled my kitchen (and worried my neighbors)

We like the contrasting flavors of glazes with duck, but the meat is so flavorful it can also be seasoned with just salt and pepper.

proved that this method only works in a kitchen equipped with an extremely powerful exhaust.

Next I tried the method advocated by most older sources—cooking in a moderate oven (350 degrees) for two hours, followed by a short burst at a higher temperature (425 degrees) to crisp the skin. The results were decent. The skin was good and the breast was fine. However, the legs were too fatty and the wings were flabby and totally unappetizing. My tasters devoured the breasts, but they ate around the fat in the legs and no one would touch the wings.

Many recent sources tout slow-roasting followed by a period of moderate roasting to crisp the skin. Of all the traditional methods that I tried, slow roasting and constant turning (so that the fat drips down from all sides) did the best job of getting rid of fat. However, even after four hours in the oven, the legs were still too fatty to eat with gusto. The internal fat, especially the fat that divides the thigh from the leg, was not melting away. And I noticed that the breast meat (which is hard to overcook because of the fatty skin on top) was actually starting to dry out after so many

hours in the oven. I had created a problem that duck wasn't supposed to have. Clearly, it was time to switch gears.

Asian Inspiration

Many Asian recipes for duck start with steaming or boiling. The theory is that moist heat melts some of the fat, and in fact it's true. Because moisture transfers heat more efficiently than dry air, moist cooking methods such as steaming cause more fluid loss than dry cooking methods such as roasting. After steaming or boiling, the duck can be roasted to render the rest of the fat and crisp up the skin. I decided to try a two-step cooking process, with moist heat followed by dry heat.

I bought three ducks and steamed one for an hour (a time suggested by several sources), blanched another for one minute (the method we'd found best for goose in previous tests), and boiled a third for 15 minutes. The steamed and boiled ducks were already cooked, so I roasted them in a 400-degree oven to crisp the skin. The blanched duck was roasted at a constant 350 degrees for two hours, followed by 425 degrees until the skin was brown and crisp.

The scale told the story here. When I roasted a duck without any treatment with water, I was able to reduce its initial weight by an average of 45 percent. Boiling or blanching pushed this number up to 48 percent and 46 percent, respectively. In contrast, the duck that was steamed lost an astonishing 58% of its weight. This duck also tasted less greasy, especially in the breast, and the skin was the thinnest and the crispest.

One problem remained. I still thought the legs were a bit too fatty. I wanted them to be dense, dark, and meaty, like the best confit. Steaming was melting all the fat right underneath the skin, but domesticated birds have a lot of intermuscular fat in the leg and thigh, which is shielded from the steam and the oven heat by skin, meat, and bone. I tried various steaming times and roasting regimens, but I just couldn't get the legs degreased.

At this point, I decided to cut the bird into six parts—two wings, two leg/thighs, and two breasts. I figured the fat in the leg/thighs would no longer be protected and would render quickly in the oven. And was I ever right. The difference was dramatic.

When I roasted a whole steamed duck for an hour, only two to three tablespoons of fat were rendered. However, when I roasted the parts from a steamed duck for less time and with far less body weight (I was saving the carcass and back for stock), I was able to coax a full one-third cup of fat out of the six parts. The skin was especially crisp and delicious because I was able to cook the parts skin side down directly on the pan, not on a rack. (I found it helpful to spoon off the fat when turning the parts.) The breast was moist, the wings were beautifully browned and very crisp, and I finally had a roast duck with legs that everyone at the table was fighting over.

There is a downside here—you can't bring a whole roasted duck to the table. But the duck tastes better, and I think it's easier to carve it before roasting than to do it with everyone gathered at the table. Also, because the duck is split into parts, you can roast two ducks at once in a regular large roasting pan.

As for the steaming step, I would never roast duck again without doing this first. It doesn't really add any time to the process because the duck roasts for such a short time. It can also be steamed a day in advance. Two-step duck may not be the easiest, but it produces the best results and minimizes last-minute kitchen work. You can roast duck for a small holiday gathering, knowing that every piece of the duck will be delicious—and mercifully free of grease.

CRISP ROAST DUCK WITH PORT WINE GLAZE
SERVES 2 TO 3

Pekin ducks, also called Long Island ducks, are the only choice in most supermarkets. Almost always sold frozen, the duck must defrost in the refrigerator for at least one day before cooking. To feed six people, steam one duck after the other and then roast all the pieces together in an oversized roasting pan or a large jelly roll pan.

Port Wine Glaze
1¼ cups port wine
2 medium garlic cloves, peeled and cut into thin slivers
4 fresh thyme sprigs

Crisp Roast Duck
1 whole Pekin duck (about 4½ pounds), neck and giblets discarded, prepared according to illustrations 1 and 2, and rinsed
Salt and ground black pepper

1. *For the glaze:* Bring all ingredients to boil in small saucepan. Reduce heat to medium-low and simmer until slightly thickened and reduced to scant ¼ cup, 25 to 30 minutes. Remove and discard garlic and thyme; set glaze aside until ready to use.

2. *For the duck:* Meanwhile, set V-rack in large, high-sided roasting pan and position duck, breast side up, on rack. Add water to just below bottom of duck. Bring water to boil over high heat, cover pan tightly with aluminum foil (or pan cover, if available), adjust heat to medium (to maintain a slow, steady boil), and steam, adding more hot water to maintain water level if necessary, until skin has pulled away from at least one leg. For duck with very moist, tender meat and slightly crisp skin once roasted, steam about 40 minutes. Steam 10 minutes longer for somewhat denser meat and very crisp skin after roasting. Transfer duck to carving board and, when cool enough to handle, follow illustrations 3 through 6 to cut into six pieces. (Cooled duck, either whole or cut into pieces, can be wrapped in foil and refrigerated overnight, reserving back and carcass for another use.)

3. Adjust oven rack to bottom position and heat oven to 425 degrees. Season pieces on both sides with salt and pepper to taste and position skin side down in lightly oiled roasting pan. Roast, carefully pouring off fat if more than two tablespoons accumulate in pan, until skin on breast pieces is rich brown color and crisp, about 25 minutes. Transfer breast pieces to platter and cover with foil to keep warm. Again, pour off excess fat from pan, turn leg/thigh and wing pieces skin side up, and continue roasting until skin on these pieces is deep brown and crisp, 15 to 20 minutes longer. Again, pour off excess fat from pan. Return breast pieces to pan and brush both sides of every piece with glaze. Roast until glaze is hot and richly colored on duck pieces, 3 to 4 minutes. Serve immediately.

ORANGE GLAZE

The lime juice keeps this thick, syrupy glaze from being too sweet.

Follow recipe for Port Wine Glaze, substituting 1 cup fresh squeezed orange juice, 2 tablespoons fresh lime juice, and 2 tablespoons honey for port and omitting garlic and thyme.

TECHNIQUE | CUTTING THE DUCK INTO PIECES

1. Any fat that is not directly above meat or bone should be trimmed away with a sharp knife.

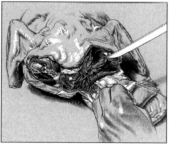

2. Pull back remaining skin in neck cavity and cut away pieces of fat on the underside of the skin to expose the back of the wing joints.

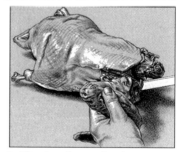

3. After steaming, cut the wings away at the shoulder joint.

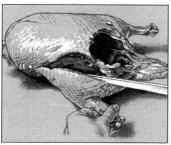

4. Cut around the leg, making sure to free the meaty oyster from the back of the duck.

5. Probe into the thigh joint with a knife to pop out the leg. The joint is much closer to the back than on a chicken. Cut down through the thigh joint to remove the leg and thigh in one piece.

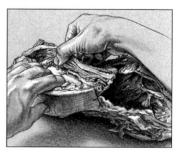

6. Using a paring knife and your fingers, peel the breast meat off the carcass in two separate pieces. Since the duck has been cooked, the meat should come off with minimal effort, and boneless breast pieces make easy eating.

How to Buy (and Open) Oysters

All oysters are not created equal. In a taste test, we found a wide range of flavors and textures from briny and firm to soft with a hint of melon.

⇒ BY MARK BITTMAN ⇐

It's easy to become overwhelmed by oysters. As if they weren't challenging enough in the first place—at least in their raw state, which is unquestionably their best state—there appear to be so many kinds that it's hard to get a handle. Walk into a good oyster bar, and you might be offered Gliddens from Maine; Wellfleet and Cuttyhunk from Massachusetts; Bras Dors from the Maritimes; Bluepoint from Long Island Sound; Chincoteague and Apalachicola from the South; Kumamoto, Hama-hama, and an assortment of flats from the West Coast. The question for most people is—what's the difference?

The first thing to know is that there are only five species of oysters seen in the United States. The three most important are the familiar Atlantic, grown all along the East and Gulf coasts; the European, grown in the Northwest and in a few spots in the far Northeast; and the Pacific, grown along the West Coast. In addition, there are the Olympia, the half dollar–size oyster indigenous to the Northwest and rarely seen elsewhere; and the now-trendy Kumamoto, once considered a variety of Pacific but recently declared a distinct species.

The problem is that within each of the three most popular species there are myriad nicknames and place names: The Atlantic is not only called the Eastern, but is casually referred to by many place names; the European is known as the "flat," and also—generically, but incorrectly—as the belon, a name that belongs to a small region in France; and the Pacific, which is also grown in Europe, not only has place names attached to it, but is sometimes called a Portuguese ("Portugaise"), from a now-extinct species that once made up the majority of oysters grown in Europe.

Can people tell the difference? Incredibly, they can—even those who have never tasted oysters before. An oyster from the mainland-facing side of Martha's Vineyard and one from the Atlantic side, for example, taste as different as, say, two good but distinct bottles of Napa Valley Merlot. In fact, oysters are quite a bit like wine: You have

Serve oysters on a bed of cracked ice with just a sprinkling of pepper and a squirt of lemon juice or a simple sauce such as a mignonette.

the species, which corresponds to the grape variety, and then you have the specific oysters from each location, which correspond to individual wines. Climate, water quality, and the age and condition of growing beds are among the factors that affect the taste of an individual oyster.

Nevertheless, just as all Merlot have some things in common, so do all oysters of a particular species.

Atlantic oysters are crisp and briny; you taste one and you get an intense hit of fresh, cold sea salt, lightly fishy. They're the easiest oysters to like, and the ones with the least complex flavor. They range from quite small, just two inches long, to the "tennis shoes" of the South that are nearly six inches long.

Pacific oysters are rarely as salty, but their flavors are more complex, often fruity—in tastings you see comparisons to cucumber and even watermelon. There's a certain sweetness there that can border on muddiness; when it does not, they're very enjoyable. But even the best Pacific oysters rarely have the crisp texture of the best Atlantic. They're usually midrange in size, three or four inches long.

Flats are said to be the most complex-tasting oysters, and they certainly have the most challenging flavor; many people find them repellent. A good one starts out crisp and briny, very much like an Atlantic, but it finishes with a strong metallic taste that either makes you cry for more or simply makes you cry. Flats might best be likened to very, very strong cheese—you either love it or you hate it. Flats are not only flat, they're almost round—not what you think of as oyster-shaped at all. Their shells can be as large as five inches across.

Tasting the Field

To see for myself whether people preferred one general type of oyster over another, I assembled 15 *Cook's Illustrated* staffers and guests at the East Coast Grill in Cambridge, Massachusetts, for a comparison tasting of 13 oysters from all over the country.

The results bore out my feeling that while it's pointless to see whether you like a Martha's Vineyard oyster more than a Nantucket oyster (because you're rarely going to find either when

FIVE OYSTER VARIETIES

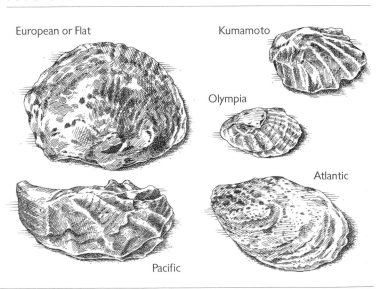

European or Flat

Kumamoto

Olympia

Atlantic

Pacific

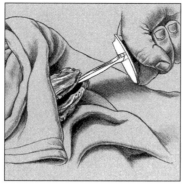

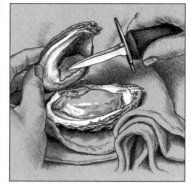

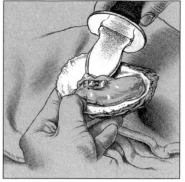

1. Holding oyster cupped side down, locate the hinge with the tip of the knife.

2. Push between the edges, wiggling back and forth to pry open the shell.

3. Detach the meat from the top half of the shell and discard the shell.

4. Sever the muscle that holds the meat of the oyster to the bottom shell.

it comes right down to it), you can certainly find Atlantic and Pacific oysters together, and maybe flats and Kumamotos, and you might generally enjoy one more than the others.

Few people liked the flats. Although their quality was unquestioned, their taste was too strong for most. ("What?" said one taster, incredulous. "You actually like that?") Tasters were more-or-less evenly divided in their appreciation of Atlantic and Pacific oysters. It's fair to say that most tasters liked both almost equally well, although they also appreciated the differences.

More people, including both veteran and novice tasters, had favorable reactions to Kumamoto oysters than to any other. The Kumamoto have some of the features of good Pacific oysters, but their flavor is less pronounced and a little sweeter. Almost all tasters also liked the northern Atlantic oysters more than the southern ones. They were crisper in texture and brinier in flavor.

Selecting an Oyster

In addition to the species and the obvious fact that oysters sold in the half shell must be alive and their shells undamaged, there are three things that are important in selecting oysters: freshness, season, and personal taste.

Oysters are a little bit like lobsters: Just because they're alive doesn't mean they're fresh. (The oysters we tasted were two days old; you can't get much better than that.) As long as they're kept cool and moist, oysters can live a long time after they're harvested. In fact, many 18th- and 19th-century New Englanders stored a barrel of oysters in their cellars all winter long, eating them at their leisure. But a separate test I conducted after our tasting, comparing oysters from the same beds harvested a week apart and tasted at the same time, clearly demonstrated what most oyster lovers routinely maintain: The best oyster is the freshest oyster. Older oysters are drier, flabbier, and less flavorful.

Unlike lobster, there is a way you can determine the freshness of an oyster, although it

requires assertiveness. Oysters, like other mollusks, are monitored by state agencies under the Federal Shellfish Sanitation Program. Every bag of oysters (and clams and mussels) that is harvested commercially must be tagged by the grower. And the retailer (or restaurateur) is required to keep the tag attached to the original container (usually a net bag) until that container is empty, then to keep the tag on file for 90 days thereafter. Any legitimate seller will show you the tag upon request and, if the date is within a couple of days of your purchase, you know you have a top-quality product—at least from the freshness standpoint. Of course, there are ways around this, just as there are ways around any laws governing the sale of anything, but it's the best you can do. As with any fish, finding a seller you can trust is your best line of defense.

Season is also key. The old saw about not eating oysters during months that don't contain the letter R is not as important as it used to be, when people spurned oysters in the summer because

they died quickly out of the water. But many oysters do spawn in the summer—when month names lack Rs—and that spawning makes their meat mushy and less appetizing.

A better generalization, born out not only by our tasting but by four similar tastings I've conducted over the last several years, is that regardless of the time of year the best oysters come from the coldest waters. While there are exceptions— especially on the West Coast, where coastal water temperatures are more even—it's generally true that with two oysters of the same species, the one from the colder bed will be crisper and more flavorful.

Of course, this does not take into account personal taste based on memory. One of our most experienced tasters, a southerner by birth, preferred a Gulf Coast Atlantic oyster to those from New England or Canada—he liked its size (oysters from warmer waters grow faster and are therefore usually larger) and its mild flavor. All the other tasters, however, preferred the northern oyster.

Will Any Oyster Knife Do?

If you want to open more than one oyster every 10 minutes and end up with the shell, your temper, and your hands intact, it's important to have the right oyster knife. We found this out when we gathered a sampling of oyster knives (as well as a can opener) and had both experienced shuckers and total newcomers open several oysters with each knife.

Our two favorites were the Oxo and the Dexter-Russell S121. Both these knives had blades with a slightly angled, pointed tip that made it surprisingly easy to make that first penetration into the hinge between the top and bottom shells. The handles of these knives were also contoured and textured for a secure, comfortable grip. A Wüsthof knife, which was the most expensive of those we tested, scored third because of its useful pointed tip and a guard at the base of the blade, but its shorter blade made detaching the oyster meat from the shell more cumbersome.

We also recommend the Mundial and the Dexter-Russell S1712, but with reservations, since their tips are not as pointed. Two knives by Capco with wooden handles were adequate, but not favored when compared with the others. When an oyster knife is nowhere to be found, the pointed end of a can opener will eventually open some oysters, but the task will be frustrating. —Susan Logozzo

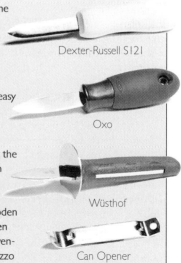

Dexter-Russell S121

Oxo

Wüsthof

Can Opener

The Return of Yeast Coffee Cakes

To give this rich, breadlike coffee cake a tender crumb and a melt-in-your-mouth texture, use plenty of butter, mix the dough very thoroughly, and make sure you let it rise twice.

⇒ BY SUSAN LOGOZZO ⇐

As a youngster, my favorite coffee cake was an Aunt Jemima all-in-one-box mix (which included a plastic bag for mixing and a foil pan for baking). In college I moved up to Entenmann's cheese streusel coffee cake, easily consuming an entire one, sliver by sliver, while cramming for exams. But when I began to study cooking formally and learned how to make yeast coffee cakes, they quickly took over as my favorite. Not only did I love the final product, I got great satisfaction from making the dough, watching it rise, shaping it however I wanted with fillings of my own choice, then seeing it balloon into its final shape in the oven as it turned a shiny golden brown and took on a heavenly aroma.

Unlike coffee cakes made with baking powder or soda (chemical leaveners), which are quick to put together and have a final texture that resembles a cake, yeast coffee cakes have a breadlike texture—in fact, they could easily be called "coffee breads." When I decided to create my own personal recipe, I knew what was most important to me: a flavorful, rich crumb that did not suffer from the dryness that is a common problem with this type of coffee cake. (I also wanted to avoid developing a hard, dark crust, which is very typical of rich coffee cakes because of the sugar and egg content.) I wanted to create a dough that could be shaped and filled in a variety of ways, and that was not overwhelming to make.

From previous experience, I knew that in order to create this paragon of a coffee cake, I would have to discover the ideal proportion of ingredients, the best mixing technique, and how to regulate rising times.

The Main Characters

I began by exploring the relative proportions of the primary ingredients—eggs, butter, sugar, flour, and yeast. Since the coffee cake I envisioned was very light yet rich, with a golden finish and a brioche-type texture, I knew that it would require a high proportion of eggs. Keeping the other ingredients constant, I tried the recipe with from one to six eggs. Six eggs added so much liquid that I had to increase the amount of flour, which resulted in a texture that I found a bit heavy and dry. One egg also threw off the proportions, requiring so much less flour that the baked dough was greasy and rather

To prevent the bottom crust of this rich dough from browning too much on the bottom, slip an extra baking sheet beneath the coffee cake before placing it in the oven on the middle rack.

coarse. Two or three eggs produced a decent crumb, but I still wanted a bit more lightness, so I settled on four eggs.

Next I tested amounts of butter, ranging from one-quarter cup to 1½ cups. One-half cup or less produced breads that were not rich enough for my vision of coffee cake; amounts over 1¼ cups produced doughs that had a slightly heavy quality. One cup of butter resulted in a soft texture that yielded a good buttery taste and aroma, a rich crumb, and a melt-in-your-mouth quality.

Sugar is an interesting ingredient because it is a flavor enhancer as well as a sweetener. Without a certain level of sugar, my baked doughs tasted flat; not bad, just not as flavorful as I wanted. Most of my testing was done with one-third cup of sugar (an average amount for this type of recipe), but when I made a few batches with one-half cup, they tasted better.

When it came to flour, I understood that the

amount, and not the type, would be the crucial factor. For the soft, moist texture that I wanted, 4¼ cups of all-purpose flour turned out to be the correct amount. When I added more than this, the coffee cake was slightly dry.

With yeast, as with flour, I was more concerned with the amount than with the type. Working with active dry yeast, I tried amounts ranging from one teaspoon to six teaspoons per recipe. Since rich doughs like this one take longer to rise than lean doughs, less than three teaspoons of yeast prolonged the rising time and did not produce good ovenspring (the last burst of yeast growth in the heat of the oven). Two packages of yeast, about 4½ teaspoons, produced the best results.

The Big Rise

In the process of working out the ingredient proportions, I realized that the mixing and rising times were also crucial to developing the desired texture. This rich dough requires a lot of beating; the eggs must be well incorporated, the butter has to be evenly combined into the mixture, and a great deal of gluten is needed for structure and strength. What worked superbly was a standing mixer equipped with, first, the paddle, to thoroughly combine ingredients, and then the dough hook, for kneading. I perfected the times and speeds for adding the eggs, most of the flour, then the butter. Doughs that were not beaten for a certain length of time did not rise well and the baked structure was heavy and gummy.

I tried mixing and working the dough with my hands, but because it was so soft I had to add flour to prevent it from sticking to my fingers and to the work surface. For this reason, I strongly recommend using a standing mixer or, if you do not have one, halving the recipe and mixing it in a food processor.

Using a straight-sided plastic container for rising proved to be a fine idea. Dough needs to be contained while it ferments, not spread out in a big bowl. A container two to three times the size of the dough is perfect. You can also mark the outside of the container to indicate the original volume of the dough, which makes it easy to gauge when the dough has doubled. In side-by-side tests, I found it unnecessary to grease the container.

The two rising or resting times, the first at room temperature and the second in the refrigerator, turned out to be important for both texture and flavor. When I tried working with dough that had no initial rising, the baked texture was coarse and the taste not very interesting. During the second rising in the refrigerator, which is actually more of a resting period, the dough develops further and, most importantly, it becomes firm, with a very smooth, luxurious texture that makes it easy to shape and fill.

During my testing I developed a few shortcuts to speed up the rising. For instance, setting the rising container in warm water (*see* Quick Tips, page 4) cut the total rising time in half. The second resting time, which takes place in the refrigerator, is usually overnight. But when I spread the risen dough out on a baking sheet and covered it with plastic and refrigerated it for two hours, the results were fine.

After shaping, the coffee cake must be proofed to achieve a light texture and attractive, full look. After proofing, the dough is ready for baking, or it can be refrigerated overnight and placed directly in a preheated oven to bake the next morning. Brushing with an egg wash (egg mixed with a little milk or cream) added a beautiful luster to the baked cake. (When I omitted the glaze, the baked crust was dull and very unattractive.)

One final technique that I had read about but not tried before these tests was freezing the dough raw. However, I had no success with frozen doughs (frozen one week) because very rich doughs will not rise again after defrosting. If you have extra dough it is best to shape and bake it before freezing.

RICH COFFEE CAKE DOUGH
ENOUGH FOR 2 SMALL CAKES

The finished cakes made from this dough freeze beautifully, so we like to make the full amount of dough, bake two smaller cakes (as the smaller pieces of dough are easier to work with), and freeze one for later. You can use the full quantity of dough to make one large cake if you prefer (increase the baking time to 35 to 40 minutes if you go this route), or the recipe can be halved, as it must be if you opt to mix the dough in a food processor rather than a standing mixer. Between rising, shaping, and proofing, preparing these cakes is time-consuming, though not at all labor-intensive. An early morning start will let you make, rise, shape, proof, and bake the dough all in one day. Alternatively, you can refrigerate the shaped, proofed loaf overnight and bake it the next morning for breakfast. The cake is best when eaten fresh from the oven and warm. Wrap any leftovers tightly in foil and warm in a preheated 300-degree oven for 20 to 25 minutes before serving.

2	packages (4 1/2 scant teaspoons) active dry yeast
1/4	cup warm water (110 to 115 degrees)
1/2	cup sugar
4	large eggs
2	tablespoons milk
1	teaspoon vanilla extract
4 1/4	cups all-purpose flour
2 1/4	teaspoons salt
1/2	pound (2 sticks) unsalted butter, cut into 1-inch pieces and slightly softened

1. Sprinkle yeast over warm water in bowl of standing mixer fitted with paddle; stir to dissolve. With mixer set on lowest possible speed, mix in sugar, eggs, milk, and vanilla until well combined. Add 3 1/4 cups flour and salt, mixing at low speed until flour is incorporated, about 1 minute. Increase mixer speed to medium-low and add butter pieces one at a time, beating until incorporated, about 20 seconds after each addition (total mixing time should be about 5 minutes). Replace paddle with dough hook and add remaining 1 cup flour; beat at medium-low speed until soft and smooth, about 5 minutes longer. Increase speed to medium and beat until dough tightens up slightly, about 2 minutes longer.

2. Scrape dough (which will be too soft to pick up with hands) into straight-sided plastic container or bowl using plastic dough scraper. Cover container tightly with plastic wrap and let dough rise at warm room temperature until doubled in size, 3 to 4 hours. Punch dough down, replace plastic, and refrigerate until thoroughly chilled, at least 4 or up to 24 hours. Alternatively, for a quick chill, spread dough about 1-inch thick on baking sheet, cover with plastic, and refrigerate until thoroughly chilled, about 2 hours.

RICH COFFEE CAKE DOUGH, FOOD PROCESSOR VERSION

1. Halve all ingredient quantities in recipe for Rich Coffee Cake Dough. In bowl of food processor fitted with stainless steel blade, sprinkle yeast over warm water; add sugar, eggs, milk, and vanilla and pulse to mix, about four 1-second bursts. Add 1 1/2 cups flour and salt and process until smooth, about 20 seconds; scrape down sides of bowl. Distribute butter pieces over dough, sprinkle 1/2 cup flour over butter, and pulse until butter is incorporated, about twelve 1-second bursts. Scrape down sides of bowl and beneath blade if any dough has stuck there; remove half the dough from bowl and reserve. Process dough that remains in bowl until soft and satiny, about 1 minute. Remove processed dough and repeat processing with reserved portion. Combine both dough portions on lightly floured work surface, sprinkle with remaining 2 tablespoons flour, and form dough into ball.

COFFEE CAKE SHAPES

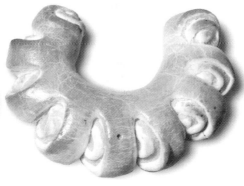

Coffee cakes from left: lattice top, horseshoe, and twisted coil. These shapes are illustrated in detail on pages 16 and 17.

2. Follow step 2 in recipe for Rich Coffee Cake Dough.

EGG WASH
ENOUGH TO BRUSH 2 SMALL CAKES

1 large egg
1 teaspoon heavy cream (preferably) or whole milk

Beat egg and cream or milk in small bowl until combined. Cover with plastic wrap and refrigerate until ready to use.

STREUSEL TOPPING
MAKES ABOUT 1 CUP, ENOUGH FOR 2 SMALL CAKES

1/3 cup light or dark brown sugar, packed
1 tablespoon granulated sugar
1/2 cup all-purpose flour
1/2 teaspoon cinnamon
1/4 teaspoon salt
5 tablespoons cold butter, cut into 8 pieces

Mix brown and granulated sugars, flour, cinnamon, and salt in small bowl. Add butter; toss to coat. Pinch butter chunks and dry mixture between fingertips until mixture is crumbly. Chill thoroughly before using. (Can be refrigerated in an airtight container up to 2 weeks).

COFFEE CAKE ICING
MAKES 1/3 CUP, ENOUGH FOR 2 SMALL CAKES

3/4 cup confectioners' sugar, sifted
3 1/2 teaspoons milk
1/2 teaspoon vanilla extract

Whisk all ingredients in medium bowl until smooth. (Can be refrigerated in an airtight container up to 1 week. Thin with a few drops of milk before using, if necessary.)

RICH COFFEE CAKE WITH SWEET CHEESE FILLING
MAKES 2 SMALL CAKES, EACH SERVING 8 TO 10

Use the Lattice Top or Twisted Coil shapes (*see* pages 16 and 17) when making this sweet cheese-filled coffee cake. For variety and color, equal proportions of cheese and fruit fillings can be used together in a single cake. Regardless of which fillings you choose, the cakes should have just under 1 cup of filling.

Sweet Cheese Filling
8 ounces cream cheese
1/4 cup sugar
2 1/2 tablespoons all-purpose flour
Pinch salt
2 teaspoons finely grated zest from 1 lemon
1 large egg
1/2 teaspoon vanilla extract

Cake
1 recipe Rich Coffee Cake Dough
1 recipe Egg Wash
1 recipe Streusel Topping (optional)
1 recipe Coffee Cake Icing (optional)

1. *For the filling:* Beat cream cheese, sugar, flour, and salt with hand-held electric mixer or in workbowl of standing mixer fitted with paddle at high speed until smooth, 2 to 4 minutes. Add lemon zest, egg, and vanilla; reduce beater speed to medium and continue beating, scraping down sides of bowl at least once, until incorporated, about 1 minute. Scrape mixture into small bowl and chill thoroughly before using. (Can be refrigerated in an airtight container up to 3 days).

2. *For the cakes:* Turn chilled dough, scraping container sides with rubber spatula if necessary, onto lightly floured work surface. Roll, shape, and top or fill following illustrations for Lattice Top or Twisted Coil cakes, pages 16 and 17.

3. Cover loosely with plastic wrap on parchment-covered baking sheet and let cakes rise until slightly puffed (will not increase in volume as dramatically as a leaner bread dough), about 1 1/2 to 2 hours. (After this final rise, unbaked cakes can be refrigerated overnight and baked the next morning.)

4. Adjust oven rack to middle position and heat oven to 350 degrees. Working with and baking one coffee cake at a time, brush Egg Wash evenly on exposed dough. Sprinkle evenly with streusel topping, if using. Slide baking sheet onto a second baking sheet to prevent bottom crust from overbrowning and bake until deep golden brown and/or an instant-read thermometer inserted in center of cake registers 190 degrees, 25 to 30 minutes. Slide parchment with coffee cake onto rack and cool at least 20 minutes. Following illustration 6 for Twisted Coil, drizzle icing over cake, if using, and serve.

RICH COFFEE CAKE WITH APRICOT–ORANGE FILLING
MAKES 2 SMALL CAKES, EACH SERVING 8 TO 10

Because of the stiff consistency of the Apricot-Orange filling, the Horseshoe shape is particularly nice for this cake. (Omit streusel topping if making Horseshoe shape.) The cake can be made in the Lattice Top and Twisted Coil shapes as well.

Apricot-Orange Filling
12 ounces dried apricots (about 2 cups)
3 tablespoons sugar
1 tablespoon finely grated zest and 3 tablespoons juice from 1 medium orange
2 tablespoons rum (optional)

Cake
1 recipe Rich Coffee Cake Dough
1 recipe Egg Wash
1 recipe Streusel Topping (optional)
1 recipe Coffee Cake Icing (optional)

1. *For the filling:* Bring apricots, sugar, and 1 cup water to boil in medium saucepan over medium-high heat. Reduce heat to medium and, stirring occasionally, boil gently until apricots are soft and water has nearly evaporated, 16 to 18 minutes. Off heat, add orange zest and juice (and rum, if using); transfer mixture to food processor workbowl fitted with steel blade and process until smooth, about 1 minute, stopping to scrape sides of bowl at least once. Scrape mixture into small bowl and cool to room temperature before using. (Can be refrigerated in an airtight container up to 3 days.)

2. *For the cake:* Turn chilled dough, scraping container sides with rubber spatula if necessary, onto lightly floured work surface; divide in half for two cakes. Roll, shape, and top or fill following illustrations for Horseshoe, Lattice Top, or Twisted Coil cakes, pages 16 and 17.

3. Complete cakes following steps 3 and 4 of Rich Coffee Cake with Sweet Cheese Filling.

RICH COFFEE CAKE WITH BERRY FILLING
MAKES 2 SMALL CAKES, EACH SERVING 8 TO 10

The Lattice Top or Twisted Coil shapes are best for this juicy, berry-filled cake.

Berry Filling
12 ounces fresh or frozen raspberries or blueberries (about 2 1/2 cups)
3 tablespoons sugar
2 tablespoons juice from 1 lemon
Pinch salt
Pinch cinnamon
1 1/2 tablespoons cornstarch dissolved in 2 tablespoons water

Cake
1 recipe Rich Coffee Cake Dough
1 recipe Egg Wash
1 recipe Streusel Topping (optional)
1 recipe Coffee Cake Icing (optional)

1. *For the filling:* Bring berries, sugar, lemon juice, salt, cinnamon, and cornstarch mixture to boil, stirring occasionally, in medium saucepan over medium heat. Continue boiling, stirring constantly, until mixture is thick and shiny, 1 1/2 to 2 minutes. Scrape mixture into small bowl, cover, and chill thoroughly before using. (Can be refrigerated in an airtight container up to 3 days.)

2. *For the cake:* Turn chilled dough, scraping container sides with rubber spatula if necessary, onto lightly floured work surface; divide in half for two cakes. Roll, shape, and top or fill following illustrations for Lattice Top or Twisted Coil cakes, page 16 and 17.

3. Complete cakes following steps 3 and 4 of Rich Coffee Cake with Sweet Cheese Filling.

Not-Too-Sweet Potato Casserole

For a great side dish that doesn't taste like a dessert, parboil the potatoes before baking, cut down on the butter, and sweeten with a combination of molasses and honey.

≥ BY SARAH FRITSCHNER AND LINDSAY ROBERTS ≤

Sweet potato casserole is a time-honored holiday tradition not only in the South, but wherever Thanksgiving dinner is served. But time has done peculiar things to this side dish—it has added sweeteners, fats, canned fruits, and even miniature marshmallows to what was once a seasonally appropriate and healthful side dish. Hoping to undo some of these evolutionary changes, we set out to find a recipe that was sweet without being cloying, rich enough without gratuitous fat, and didn't require the better part of the holiday weekend to prepare.

Our first step was to try baking the casserole without precooking the potatoes, a step that was called for in every recipe we had seen. We soon found out why: When we made a casserole with raw, sliced sweet potatoes, the sugar did not develop in the potatoes, and the potatoes were an odd color with a dryness that approached a crust. So which cooking method, we wondered, was the best for precooking?

We tested boiling, baking, microwaving, steaming, and parboiling, and liked parboiling best. The potatoes cook evenly and quickly, and are less cumbersome to handle because they're peeled before they're cooked—we didn't like having to cook potatoes and then set them aside to peel after they cooled. Parboiling the potatoes exposes them to hot water for a long enough time to lock in their bright orange color; it brings them to the point of releasing their sugars, but does not allow them to overcook.

The next step was to try different kinds and amounts of fats and sweeteners. Recipes from cookbooks run to the extreme—one we saw called for one cup of butter, one cup of sugar, and marshmallow topping for two pounds of canned sweet potatoes. From our research, the more recent the recipe, the more sugar it has.

But sweet potatoes are naturally very sweet; we thought that using less of a more interesting sweetener might complement the sweet potatoes without turning them into a dessert. Brown sugar, and even dark brown sugar, registered a somewhat bland sweetness, but molasses, honey, sorghum, and maple syrup offered other possibilities. Honey turned out to be too sweet and molasses too strong. Maple syrup was good, but sorghum was our favorite. Unfortunately, outside the deep South it's difficult to come by. So we combined dark molasses with gentler honey

and found it a perfect combination.

Butter and margarine are the favored fats for sweet potato casserole, and butter gives a better flavor. Knowing we didn't want to serve any vegetable side dish with a cup of butter in it (there is gravy on the table, after all), we gradually reduced the amount; six tablespoons added the rounded flavor of butter.

As for seasoning and flavorings, sweet potato casserole allows the creative cook a blank canvas. In our research we found recipes calling for dozens of different seasonings. Which you use is a matter of personal preference, but if you don't try fresh ginger at some point in your cooking venture, you're missing a great dish. Fresh ginger, peeled and grated, is by far the best, most natural seasoning that we've found for sweet potatoes.

We baked the sweet potatoes in wide, shallow dishes and narrower, deeper dishes and the former gave better results. Finally, stirring the potatoes during cooking allows them to cook more evenly.

SWEET POTATO CASSEROLE
SERVES 8 TO 12

If you can find sorghum, a sweetener popular in the deep South, substitute five tablespoons of it for the combined honey and molasses.

3	pounds (about 6 medium) sweet potatoes, peeled, halved lengthwise, and halves cut crosswise into 1/4-inch slices
6	tablespoons unsalted butter, melted
2	tablespoons honey
3	tablespoons molasses
1	tablespoon grated fresh ginger or 1 teaspoon powdered
3/4	teaspoon salt
1/4	teaspoon cayenne pepper
1 1/2	tablespoons cornstarch

1. Adjust oven rack to middle position and heat oven to 375 degrees. In large pot or Dutch oven of boiling water, parboil sweet potato slices over high heat until they are bright orange and the point of a paring knife easily pierces but does not break apart a few slices, 4 to 5 minutes. Drain potatoes well and turn into buttered 13-x 9-inch baking dish

2. Whisk melted butter, honey, molasses, ginger, salt, and cayenne in small bowl; set aside.

Mix cornstarch with 2 tablespoons cold water in small bowl until totally smooth, then whisk into butter mixture; pour over sweet potatoes and toss to coat well.

3. Cover dish tightly with foil and bake until liquid is bubbly, about 50 minutes. Remove foil, stir potatoes gently, and bake until liquid thickens to glaze potatoes, about 20 minutes longer. Cool slightly and serve hot or at room temperature.

MAPLE SWEET POTATO CASSEROLE

Follow recipe for Sweet Potato Casserole, substituting maple syrup for the honey and molasses.

ORANGE SWEET POTATO CASSEROLE

Follow recipe for Sweet Potato Casserole, adding 4 teaspoons finely grated orange zest to butter mixture.

LEMON–BOURBON SWEET POTATO CASSEROLE

Follow recipe for Sweet Potato Casserole, adding 3 tablespoons fresh lemon juice to butter mixture and substituting 1/4 cup bourbon for water in cornstarch mixture.

PECAN-TOPPED SWEET POTATO CASSEROLE

This variation is well suited to those with a sweet tooth.

Whisk 6 tablespoons light brown sugar and 1/4 cup all-purpose flour in small bowl. Add 4 tablespoons very cold butter, cut into 1/4-inch pieces, and toss to coat; pinch between fingertips until mixture is crumbly and resembles coarse cornmeal. Stir 1/2 cup chopped pecans into mixture; cover and refrigerate until ready to use. Follow recipe for Sweet Potato Casserole, sprinkling cold topping mixture over potatoes after removing foil. Continue with recipe, baking until topping is crisp and dark golden brown, about 20 minutes longer.

Sarah Fritschner is author of *Vegetarian Express Lane Cookbook* (Chapters, 1996). Lindsay Roberts is chef at Lynn's Paradise Cafe in Louisville, Kentucky.

Shaping Yeasted Coffee Cakes

The dough on page 13 can be formed into a variety of shapes after filling. By following the step-by-step directions below, you will be able to make three of our favorite shapes—the Horseshoe, the Twisted Coil, and the Lattice Top. Note that this dough is rather sturdy, so you can roll it in any direction, and lift and turn it if necessary. Use the cake recipes on page 14 to match the fillings to the shapes. When the coffee cakes are shaped and proofed, bake according to the instructions on page 14. You will need a separate sheet for each cake. By Susan Logozzo

HORSESHOE

1. Working with a half recipe of cold dough at a time, use your fingertips to shape the dough evenly into a 5-by-6-inch rectangle.

2. Roll the dough evenly into a 15-by-9-inch rectangle (dough should be about ¼-inch thick). During rolling, straighten the dough occasionally with a pastry scraper, as shown.

3. Spread the apricot-orange filling (*see* page 14) evenly over the dough, leaving a ½-inch border on one long side. Straighten the sides again with a pastry scraper to keep the rectangle even.

4. Using both hands, roll the dough up evenly lengthwise.

5. Pinch the dough securely to seal the seam. Do not seal the ends of the roll.

6. Place the roll in a semicircle on a prepared baking sheet. Using scissors, cut ⅔ of the way into the dough at 2-inch intervals.

7. Gently lift and separate the cut sections and flatten them slightly. Cover with plastic wrap and proof until slightly puffed, 1½ to 2 hours. Brush uncut surfaces with egg wash and bake as directed.

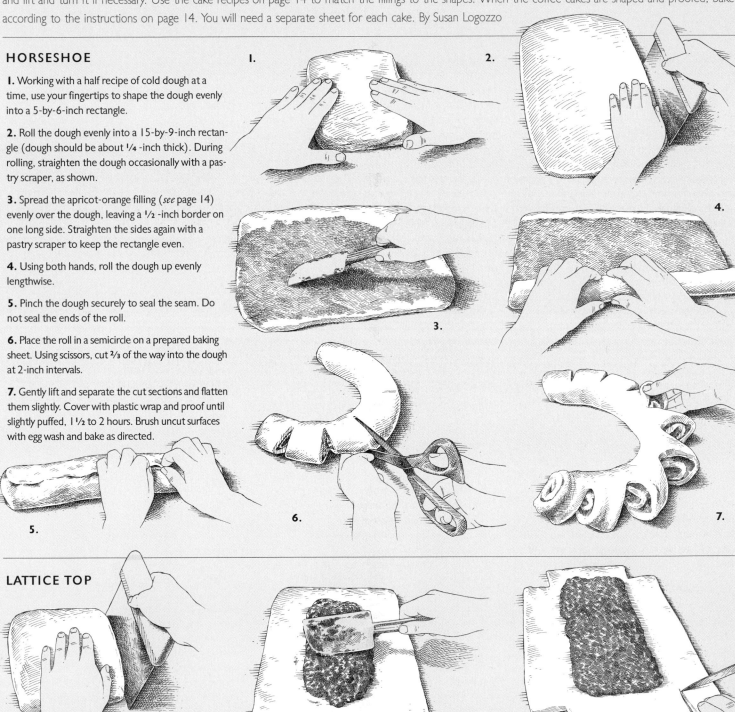

LATTICE TOP

1. Working with a half recipe of cold dough at a time, shape dough into a 5-by-6-inch rectangle, then roll into an 8-by-12-inch rectangle (dough should be about ⅓-inch thick). Straighten with a pastry scraper to keep the sides even.

2. Place on a prepared pan. Spread a 3-inch-wide strip of filling down the center of the dough, leaving a 1½-inch border at each short end.

3. Using a knife, cut a 1½-inch square out of each corner of the dough.

Illustration: John Burgoyne

LATTICE TOP (continued)

4. Using scissors, cut a triangle with 1½-inch sides in the center of one long side of the dough. Cut two more triangles (leaving a 1-inch strip of dough between each triangle) to the right and two to the left of the center triangle. Set aside dough scraps. Repeat with second long side.

5. Fold the ends over the filling, pinching the corner edges together to seal.

6. Bring the sections of dough from the long sides together in the center, overlapping the ends and pinching tightly to secure.

7. Cover lightly with plastic and proof until slightly puffed, 1½ to 2 hours. Brush with egg wash and sprinkle streusel topping down the center, leaving a 1-inch border down each side. Bake as directed.

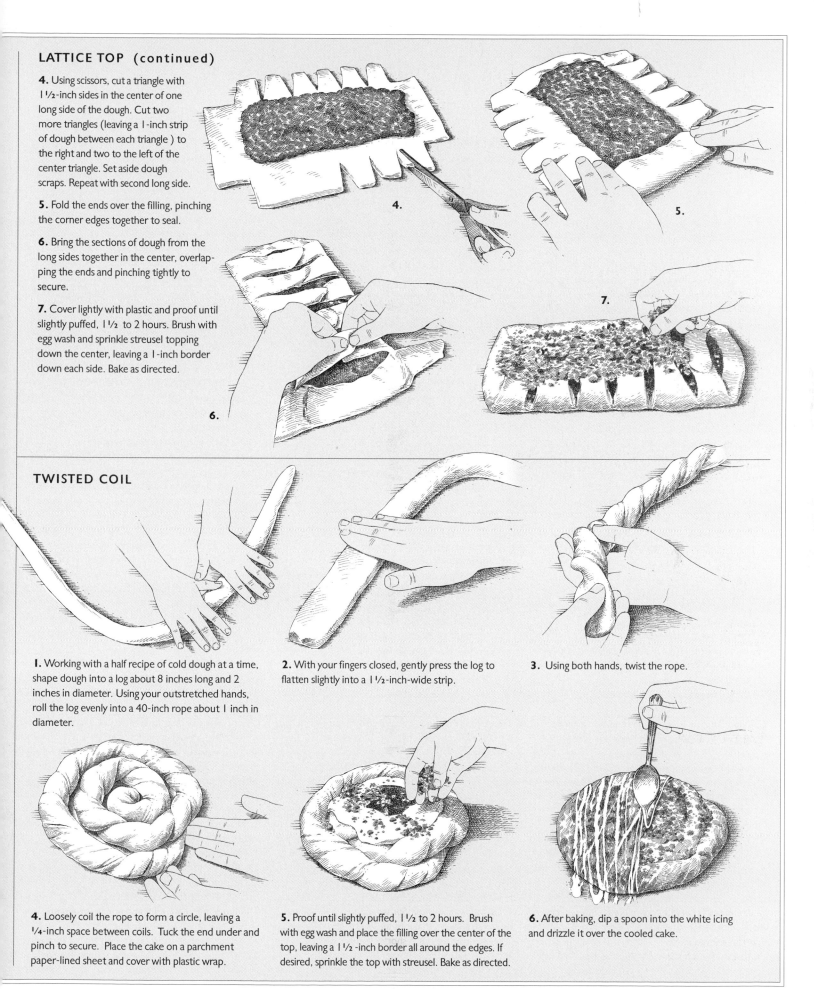

TWISTED COIL

1. Working with a half recipe of cold dough at a time, shape dough into a log about 8 inches long and 2 inches in diameter. Using your outstretched hands, roll the log evenly into a 40-inch rope about 1 inch in diameter.

2. With your fingers closed, gently press the log to flatten slightly into a 1½-inch-wide strip.

3. Using both hands, twist the rope.

4. Loosely coil the rope to form a circle, leaving a ¼-inch space between coils. Tuck the end under and pinch to secure. Place the cake on a parchment paper-lined sheet and cover with plastic wrap.

5. Proof until slightly puffed, 1½ to 2 hours. Brush with egg wash and place the filling over the center of the top, leaving a 1½-inch border all around the edges. If desired, sprinkle the top with streusel. Bake as directed.

6. After baking, dip a spoon into the white icing and drizzle it over the cooled cake.

Warm Winter Salads

Hardy-textured greens with strong flavors create salads that can stand up to a warm dressing or a single hot ingredient.

⇒ BY EVA KATZ ⇐

Tossing cool, crisp greens with a warm dressing or a single hot ingredient can create a great winter starter. Often, however, these salads can be bland or soggy or both. To avoid these problems, use greens that have hardy textures and assertive flavors.

The crisp texture of greens such as escarole, radicchio, arugula, and watercress can withstand a dousing with warm dressing or the addition of a hot ingredient without becoming so wilted they are no longer pleasurable, and their assertive flavors become pleasantly subdued, yet not overpowered.

The combinations of greens in the recipes below are interchangeable and can be mixed and matched to suit taste and availability. The total quantity of greens in each salad should be about nine cups, measured loosely packed after stemming.

ARUGULA AND ESCAROLE SALAD WITH BLUE CHEESE, FIGS, AND WARM PORT DRESSING
SERVES 6

- 1/3 cup port
- 1/2 teaspoon sugar
- 4 ounces dried figs (6 large or 12 small), stems removed
- 2 tablespoons balsamic vinegar
- 2 medium shallots or 1/4 small red onion, minced (about 3 tablespoons)
- 1/4 teaspoon salt
- 1/4 teaspoon ground black pepper
- 1/4 cup extra-virgin olive oil
- 2 large bunches arugula, washed, dried, stems trimmed, and leaves torn into bite-size pieces (about 3 cups, loosely packed)
- 1 medium head escarole, washed, dried, and torn into bite-size pieces (about 6 cups, loosely packed)
- 1/4 pound blue cheese (preferably Roquefort or Stilton), crumbled

1. Bring port, sugar, and figs to boil in medium saucepan over high heat. Cover pan, reduce heat to low, and simmer until figs are very soft but not mushy, about 15 minutes. Reserving liquid in pan, remove figs with slotted spoon and, when cool enough to handle, quarter and set them aside.

2. Whisk vinegar, shallots, salt, and pepper into port; gradually whisk in oil. Return figs to dressing and reheat over medium heat, stirring occasionally, until warm but not steaming.

3. Toss greens and warm dressing to coat in large mixing bowl. Divide dressed greens among 6 serving plates, sprinkle with a portion of blue cheese, and serve immediately.

ARUGULA AND RADICCHIO SALAD WITH WARM GOAT CHEESE AND OLIVE DRESSING
SERVES 6

Goat cheese can be difficult to slice neatly. If you have trouble, try wiping the knife blade with a cold, damp kitchen towel before each slice.

- 3 tablespoons fine, unflavored dried bread crumbs
- 2 teaspoons minced fresh thyme leaves
- 2 teaspoons minced fresh rosemary
- 1 small log (4 ounces) goat cheese, cut into 6 equal rounds
- 1 tablespoon extra-virgin olive oil, plus 1/3 cup
- 1 medium garlic clove, minced
- 3 tablespoons red wine vinegar
- 1/2 cup oil-cured black olives, pitted and chopped fine
- 1/4 teaspoon salt
- 1/8 teaspoon ground black pepper
- 4 large bunches arugula, washed, dried, stems trimmed and leaves torn into bite-size pieces (about 6 1/2 cups, loosely packed)
- 1 medium head radicchio, washed, dried, and leaves torn into bite-size pieces (about 2 1/2 cups, loosely packed)

1. Adjust oven rack to center position and heat oven to 375 degrees. Stir bread crumbs and 1 teaspoon each of the thyme and rosemary to combine in a shallow pie pan. Brush goat cheese rounds lightly with 1 tablespoon olive oil and gently press both sides and edges in bread crumb mixture to coat thoroughly with bread crumb mixture (can be done up to 1 hour before serving time and refrigerated on baking sheet until ready to bake).

2. Whisk garlic, vinegar, olives, remaining thyme and rosemary, salt, and pepper in small bowl; gradually whisk in remaining 1/3 cup olive oil; set aside.

3. Just before serving, bake breaded goat cheese rounds until warm throughout but not at all browned, 5 to 7 minutes. Meanwhile, whisk dressing to re-blend and toss greens and dressing to coat in large mixing bowl. Divide dressed greens among 6 serving plates. Remove cheese rounds from oven; top each salad with one round and serve immediately.

RADICCHIO AND WATERCRESS SALAD WITH WARM FENNEL AND WALNUT DRESSING
SERVES 6

- 1 large garlic clove, minced (about 1 1/2 teaspoons)
- 1 tablespoon juice from 1 small lemon
- 2 tablespoons sherry or white wine vinegar
- 1/4 teaspoon salt
- 1/8 teaspoon ground black pepper
- 1 tablespoon extra-virgin olive oil, plus 1/3 cup
- 1 cup walnuts, chopped coarse
- 1 medium fennel bulb (about 10 ounces), stems, fronds, and base trimmed; bulb halved, cored, and sliced thin (about 2 cups)
- 2–3 anchovy fillets, minced (about 1 tablespoon)
- 3 large bunches watercress, washed, dried, and stemmed (about 6 1/2 cups, loosely packed)
- 1 medium head radicchio, washed, dried, and torn into bite-size pieces (about 2 1/2 cups, loosely packed)
- 1 small chunk (about 1 1/2 ounces) Parmesan cheese, shaved into thin strips with a vegetable peeler

1. Whisk garlic, lemon juice, vinegar, salt and pepper in small bowl; gradually whisk in 1/3 cup olive oil until dressing is smooth and emulsified; set aside.

2. Heat walnuts in remaining 1 tablespoon oil in medium skillet (preferably nonstick) over medium heat, stirring occasionally, until lightly toasted and fragrant, about 3 minutes. Add fennel and cook until it just begins to soften and turns a very light golden, about 3 minutes longer. Stir anchovy fillets into fennel mixture and cook until fragrant, about 30 seconds longer. Whisk dressing to re-blend and, off heat, stir into fennel mixture to distribute evenly.

3. Toss greens and warm dressing mixture to coat in large mixing bowl. Divide dressed greens among 6 serving plates, sprinkle with a portion of shaved Parmesan, and serve immediately.

Eva Katz, the former Test Kitchen Director of *Cook*'s, now lives in Brisbane, Australia.

Tetrazzini Revisited

Cafeteria food or the real thing? If properly made, this noodle casserole bakes in just 15 minutes and is truly worth eating.

≥ BY CHRISTOPHER KIMBALL ≤

I am no fool for noodle casseroles. I prefer the fresh taste of just-picked vegetables, the caramelized juices of a good roast fowl, and the delicate interplay of pasta and sauce. When you throw them all together, the result is often a culinary train wreck in which the whole is less than the sum of its parts.

But when a country neighbor served up a simple meal of turkey Tetrazzini, my interest in casseroles was revived. It was very good food, an interesting blend of toasted breadcrumbs, silky sauce, and a modicum of turkey meat, all bound together by one of my favorite foods, spaghetti.

But it wasn't perfect. The downside of most casseroles, that individual tastes and textures are fused and thereby diminished, was true here as well. I then wondered if a basic noodle casserole could be re-engineered so that this eminently practical American dish could be made worthy of a well-laid table.

A bit of culinary sleuthing solved the most pressing problem, the fact that the ingredients are double-cooked. (Most casserole recipes are two-step affairs: Cook the ingredients, mix them together, and then bake them in a casserole.) In *American Cookery*, James Beard suggests using a shallow baking dish rather than a deep casserole. Paired with a very hot (450-degree) oven, this reduces the baking time to a mere 15 minutes, a fraction of the time suggested by most cookbooks. Tasted against longer baking times and slower ovens, this quick method won hands down; with its fresher-tasting vegetables, it easily avoided the wretched, overcooked dullness of cafeteria cuisine.

Next I adjusted the sauce. The traditional choice is bechamel, a sauce in which milk is added to a roux. I decided to use a velouté, a sauce based on chicken stock instead. This brightened up both the texture and the flavor, since dairy tends to dampen other flavors. I also played around a bit with the amount of sauce, trying larger and smaller quantities, and found that more sauce overran the taste of the other ingredients. In this case, less was more. It still needed a burst of flavor, however, so I spruced it up with a shot of sherry and a little lemon juice and nutmeg; a bit

A whopping three cups of mushrooms plus plenty of salt and pepper boost the flavor of this dish.

of Parmesan cheese provided tang and bite; and a full two teaspoons of fresh thyme also helped freshen the overall impression.

Most recipes do not toast the breadcrumbs before baking. This step does complicate the dish by adding an extra step (in a pinch, you can skip the toasting) but it is well worth it. Tossing the toasted breadcrumbs with a bit of grated Parmesan also helps to boost the flavor.

TURKEY TETRAZZINI
SERVES 8

Tetrazzini is also great with leftover chicken. Using a shallow baking dish without a cover and a very hot oven benefits both texture and flavor. Don't skimp on the salt and pepper; this dish needs aggressive seasoning.

Topping
- ½ cup fresh breadcrumbs
  Pinch salt
- 1½ tablespoons unsalted butter, melted
- 1 ounce Parmesan cheese, grated (about ¼ cup)

Filling
- 6 tablespoons (¾ stick) unsalted butter, plus extra for baking dish

- 8 ounces white mushrooms, cleaned and sliced thin (3 cups)
- 2 medium onions, chopped fine (1½ cups)
  Salt and ground black pepper
- ¾ pound spaghetti or other long-strand pasta, strands snapped in half
- ¼ cup flour
- 2 cups chicken stock or canned low-sodium chicken broth
- 3 tablespoons dry sherry
- 3 ounces Parmesan cheese, grated (about ¾ cup)
- ¼ teaspoon grated nutmeg
- 2 teaspoons juice from 1 small lemon
- 2 teaspoons minced fresh thyme leaves
- 2 cups frozen peas
- 4 cups leftover cooked boneless turkey or chicken meat, cut into ¼-inch pieces

1. *For the topping:* Adjust oven rack to middle position and heat oven to 350 degrees. Mix breadcrumbs, salt, and butter in small baking dish; bake until golden brown and crisp, 15 to 20 minutes. Cool to room temperature and mix with ¼ cup grated Parmesan in small bowl. Set aside.

2. *For the filling:* Increase oven temperature to 450 degrees. Heat 2 tablespoons butter in large skillet over medium heat until foaming subsides; add mushrooms and onions and sauté, stirring frequently, until onions soften and mushroom liquid evaporates, 12 to 15 minutes. Season with salt and ground black pepper to taste; transfer to medium bowl and set aside. Meanwhile, cook pasta in large pot of boiling, salted water until al dente. Reserve ¼ cup cooking water, drain spaghetti, and return to pot with reserved liquid.

3. *For the sauce:* Melt remaining 4 tablespoons butter in cleaned skillet over medium heat. When foam subsides, whisk in flour and cook, whisking constantly, until flour turns golden, 1 to 2 minutes. Whisking constantly, gradually add chicken stock. Adjust heat to medium-high and simmer until mixture thickens, 3 to 4 minutes. Off heat, whisk in sherry, Parmesan, nutmeg, ½ teaspoon salt, lemon juice, and thyme. Add sauce, sautéed vegetables, peas, and meat to spaghetti and mix well; adjust seasonings to taste. Turn mixture into a buttered 13- x 9-inch baking dish (or other shallow, ovenproof dish of similar size), sprinkle evenly with reserved breadcrumbs, and bake until breadcrumbs brown and mixture is bubbly, 13 to 15 minutes. Serve immediately.

Oven-Baked Holiday Stuffing

By using the right bread, getting the ratio of wet and dry ingredients just right, and baking it covered, you can make a rich, flavorful stuffing without the bird.

≥ BY ANNE YAMANAKA ≤

A year ago, unable to spend the holidays at home with my family, I was invited to have Thanksgiving dinner at a friend's house. My friend and her husband are both chefs and, as expected, every dish was fabulous, especially the stuffing. Richly flavored with butter, sausage, onions, celery, and herbs, and studded with just the right amount of nuts and fruit, this stuffing was nothing like the wet, mushy stuff that I had eaten in the past. Since it was cooked separately from the bird, it had developed a rich golden crust that contrasted nicely with the moist, fragrant contents within.

When I began testing bread stuffing for this article, I knew exactly what I was looking for. I wanted to create a recipe that did not rely on turkey drippings for richness and flavor, one that could be eaten as a side dish with a variety of holiday roasts. I also knew that I wanted a stuffing with the same great texture, richness, and balance of flavors that I had found so satisfying last Thanksgiving. Key to this would be the proper ratio of bread to liquid ingredients and the delicate blending of accompanying flavors—the essential herbs and aromatic vegetables and the optional meat, nuts, and fruit.

Laying the Foundation

Since bread would be the main vehicle for the other flavors in the stuffing, I decided to test it first. I wanted the bread to lend a subtle flavor and to hold up texturally to the liquid in the stuffing. To compare breads, I made the same basic stuffing recipe using eight different types. French bread turned out to be the answer; it held up well to the added moisture, maintaining some structure and chew, unlike many of the other breads, which became limp and wet. Unlike more assertive breads such as sourdough, it also served as a neutral base for accompanying flavors. Challah and potato bread were also attractive possibilities, adding a hint of sweetness and richness to the finished product.

Now that I had chosen the bread, I was ready to test other factors. Toasting the bread or cutting off the crusts made no real difference in the final product, and neither seemed to warrant the extra time and effort. After trying various sizes of cubed bread, I concluded that half-inch pieces were the optimal size—the stuffing was pleasantly chunky and all the ingredients were distributed evenly. Trying to cut pieces smaller than half an inch was tedious and time-consuming, and larger pieces made the stuffing too doughy.

Adding Moisture

I knew that the amount of liquid I used would determine the texture of my stuffing. I wanted to create a moist stuffing that still offered a bit of resistance and a hint of chew. Too much liquid and it would come out a sopping mess; too little and I'd end up with dry bread chunks.

To determine exactly what my liquid ingredients should be, I tested several stuffings moistened with chicken stock that I combined variously with wine, port, brandy, and cream. I was turned off by the stuffings made with alcohol because of their distracting boozy flavor. Tasters liked the stuffing that contained both chicken stock and cream, but after adding butter and eggs to the stuffing's list of ingredients, the final product was too rich. In the end, I chose plain, simple chicken stock, since it delivered a clean taste that wouldn't get drowned in the sea of flavors that would eventually be added to the final stuffing.

Next I tested different proportions of bread to stock. Other recipes offered little help, since most were designed for stuffing inside the bird. I began testing with as little as one cup and as much as three cups of stock for 12 cups of bread, and found that the bread absorbed the liquid quite unevenly. With both one and two cups, the bread was moist on the outside, but dry and hard on the inside. Increasing the liquid to three cups made the bread soggy, and the resulting stuffings were wet at the center.

Thus far I had been baking the stuffing uncovered, figuring that I would tackle the cooking technique after I had determined the proper proportion of bread and stock. Then I realized that covering the stuffing for at least a portion of time in the oven would trap moisture, directly affecting the amount of liquid necessary and perhaps solving the problem of uneven moisture distribution. Because this method meant steaming, it would also mimic cooking inside a bird. I retested the stuffing and sure enough, the stuffing made with two cups of stock and baked in a covered container emerged from the oven moist throughout, but not pasty or wet. I uncovered the stuffing for the last 15 minutes of cooking to develop a nice crust and a toasty flavor.

Adding Richness and Flavor

Stuffing cooked outside a bird requires not only a different proportion of liquid to bread, but also some way of adding the richness and flavor that the drippings would have provided. I found that eggs kept my stuffing from tasting flat and one-dimensional. Three eggs provided just the right amount of moisture and structure for 12 cups of bread; they made my stuffing rich and meaty, with a deep golden color and a superior flavor.

I chose to further enrich the stuffing by adding butter. In my preliminary testing of half a dozen recipes that called for different amounts of butter, my colleagues and I preferred those that were fairly rich. The butter added another level of flavor, which helped to compensate for the missing drippings. In the final recipe, I found six tablespoons to be just right, flavorful but not heavy or greasy. I drizzled an additional two tablespoons of butter on top to facilitate an even richer crust.

Pleased with the texture and body of my stuffing, I was now ready to refine the flavor. To be perfect, it needed the perfect amount of aromatic vegetables. I chose to stick to the classics—onion and celery—and after tinkering with various amounts, I found that 1½ cups of each with 12 cups of bread gave me a flavor base that was wonderfully fragrant without tasting vegetal.

My next test compared stuffings made with dried and fresh herbs. I was both surprised and relieved to find that although the stuffing made with fresh herbs was subtly brighter, it was not substantially better than the one with dried herbs.

I now had a stuffing that was rich and flavorful without any drippings from accompanying roasts. Including other ingredients in the stuffing is a matter of personal preference. Salt-cured meats add a nice hit of saltiness as well as body and richness, while nuts provide textural variety. The sweetness of fruit adds a bright counterpart to the rich and salty ingredients. These optional ingredients may be replaced by your own favorite flavors.

MASTER RECIPE FOR BREAD STUFFING WITH SAGE AND THYME
SERVES 10 TO 12 AS A SIDE DISH

Dry whichever bread you choose by cutting ½-inch slices, laying them in a single layer on baking sheets or cooling racks, and leaving them out overnight. The next day, cut the slices into ½-inch cubes and allow them to dry for another night. If you are in a hurry, rush the process by drying the slices in a 225-degree oven until brittle but not brown, 30 to 40 minutes. Then cut them into cubes and proceed.

Any of the stuffings can be cooked inside the holiday bird if you prefer; just reduce stock to 1 cup. Stuff a 12- to 15-pound turkey with 6 cups of stuffing. Then add an additional ½ cup of chicken stock to the remaining stuffing and bake it separately in an 8-inch pan.

- 8 tablespoons (1 stick) unsalted butter, plus extra for baking dish
- 1 large onion, chopped medium (about 1½ cups)
- 4 medium celery stalks, diced medium (about 1½ cups)
- ½ teaspoon each dried sage, thyme, and marjoram or 1½ teaspoons each minced fresh leaves
- ½ cup minced fresh parsley leaves
- ½ teaspoon ground black pepper
- 12 cups dried ½-inch cubes from one 1-pound loaf French, potato, or challah bread
- 2 cups chicken stock or low-sodium canned chicken broth
- 3 large eggs, beaten lightly
- 1 generous teaspoon salt

Adjust oven rack to center position and heat oven to 400 degrees (350 degrees if using challah). Heat butter in large skillet over medium-high heat until fully melted; pour off 2

tablespoons butter and reserve. Return skillet to heat; add onion and celery and sauté, stirring occasionally, until translucent, about 8 minutes. Stir in sage, thyme, marjoram, parsley, and black pepper and cook until just fragrant, about 1 minute longer. Turn onion mixture into large mixing bowl. Add bread cubes, stock, eggs, and salt and toss gently to distribute dry and wet ingredients evenly. Turn mixture into buttered 13-x 9-inch baking dish, drizzle with reserved melted butter, cover tightly with foil, and bake until fragrant, about 25 minutes (30 minutes for challah). Remove foil and bake until golden brown crust forms on top, 15 to 20 minutes longer. Serve warm.

BREAD STUFFING WITH SAUSAGE, PECANS, AND APRICOTS

Fry 1 pound crumbled sweet Italian sausage in large skillet over medium heat until browned and cooked through, about 10 minutes; remove with slotted spoon and place in large bowl. If necessary, add enough butter to rendered sausage fat to equal 6 tablespoons. Follow recipe for Baked Bread Stuffing with Sage and Thyme, adding reserved sausage, 2 cups toasted, chopped pecans, and 1 cup thinly sliced dried apricots along with bread cubes.

BREAD STUFFING WITH HAM, PINE NUTS, AND FENNEL

Follow Master Recipe for Bread Stuffing with

Sage and Thyme, substituting 1 large cored and thinly sliced fennel bulb for celery; 2 teaspoons dried (or 2 tablespoons minced fresh) basil for sage, thyme, and marjoram; adding 1 cup toasted pine nuts, ½ pound smoked ham cut into thin strips, and ½ cup finely grated Parmesan along with bread cubes; and reducing salt to ½ teaspoon.

BREAD STUFFING WITH BACON AND APPLES

During the course of testing, we found that caramelized onions add tremendous flavor to this stuffing. If you opt to caramelize them, increase the number of onions to 6, slice them thin instead of chopping, and caramelize them in a large pan over medium heat until deep, golden brown, about 45 minutes.

Fry 1 pound sliced bacon, cut into ¼-inch pieces, in large skillet over medium heat until crisp and brown, about 12 minutes. Transfer bacon with slotted spoon to paper towel–lined plate; pour off all but 6 tablespoons fat from pan. Follow recipe for Bread Stuffing with Sage and Thyme, adding 2 peeled, cored Granny Smith apples cut into ½-inch cubes (about 2 cups) to pan with onions and celery, increasing sage to 1½ teaspoons dried or 4½ teaspoons chopped fresh leaves, and adding reserved bacon along with bread cubes. Continue with master recipe, drizzling 2 tablespoons melted butter over stuffing before baking.

Rating Commercial Stuffings

After chopping, mincing, dicing, drying, and cubing our way through several batches of stuffing, we wondered if there was an easier, less time-consuming way to make this dish. To answer this question, the *Cook's* test kitchen decided to hold a blind taste test of seven different commercial stuffings prepared according to package directions. The stuffings included in the tasting were Bell's Family Style Stuffing, Kellogg's Croutettes Stuffing Mix, Arnold Sage and Onion Stuffing, Arnold Premium Herb Stuffing, Pepperidge Farm Herb

Seasoned Stuffing, Pepperidge Farm Cubed Herb Seasoned Stuffing, and Pepperidge Farm Cubed Country Style Stuffing.

Not surprisingly, all these commercial stuffings had disappointing scores, ranging from 10 to 17 out of a possible 25 points. Best of the lot was Bell's Family Style Stuffing, due to it's "herby" and "sweet" flavor. The remaining stuffings scored lower than 14 points with general complaints of saltiness, greasiness (one of the stuffings, a 6-ounce package, called for 1½ sticks of

butter), and lack of flavor. After reading the ingredient lists, it's easy to understand why: Following wheat flour in every one of the stuffings were corn syrup, salt, and soybean oil.

Results of the tasting reveal that taking the time to make stuffing from scratch is well worth the extra effort. High amounts of sugar, salt, and fat in boxed stuffings cannot mask the absence of fresh ingredients—the onions, celery, eggs, and stock that make a truly flavorful stuffing.

—A.Y.

 **17.0**
Bell's Family Style

 **13.5**
Kellogg's Croutettes

 **11.5**
Arnold Premium Sage & Onion

 **11.5**
Pepperidge Farm Cubed Herb

 **10.5**
Pepperidge Farm Cubed Country Style

 **10.0**
Arnold Premium Herb

 **10.0**
Pepperidge Farm Herb

Fallen Chocolate Cake

This undercooked chocolate cake baked in a ramekin, now a popular restaurant dessert, is easily translated for the home kitchen.

⋧ BY CHRISTOPHER KIMBALL ⋦

Every restaurant dessert has its life cycle. At least it seems that way to those of us who have lived through the birth and formative years of the emerging American restaurant scene. We survived the terrible twos, when cheesecake was ubiquitous; we made it through the awkward adolescence, when crème brûlée, like a body-pierced teenager, was disfigured with ingredients such as ginger and raspberries; and now we have arrived at young adulthood, featuring "fallen chocolate cake," an undercooked-in-the-center mound of intense, buttery chocolate cake, which ranges from a dense, brownielike consistency to something altogether more ethereal. When cutting-edge international chef Jean-Georges Vongerichten serves several hundred of these desserts every night in his three New York restaurants, we know something is afoot.

Despite its elegant appearance, this cake contains few ingredients and is very easy to make.

Having tasted Jean-Georges' recipe on a number of occasions and having also tried this dessert at other trendy eateries such as Olives in Boston, I became intrigued with the notion of turning a restaurant show-stopper into a practical recipe for home cooks. I knew that the ingredient list was short and suspected that the techniques would be relatively simple but, since restaurant recipes rarely work at home, it was clear that there would be a great deal of culinary translation ahead.

The first step, since this recipe concept encompasses a wide range of styles from half-cooked batter to a chocolate sponge cake, was to organize a tasting in the *Cook*'s test kitchen to decide exactly what we were looking for. We made three variations: the Warm, Soft Chocolate Cake from Jean-Georges, Fallen Chocolate Cake from Olives, created by chef-owner Todd English, and then an old favorite of mine entitled Fallen Chocolate Soufflé Cake, which was published by Richard Sax, a well-known food writer.

Sax's recipe, which is baked in a tube pan rather than in a ramekin, was quite delicious and soufflé-like in texture. However, it lacked the intense

whack of chocolate and the rich, buttery texture of the other two desserts. The recipe from Olives was the heaviest of the lot, very good but quite similar to an undercooked brownie. Jean-Georges' cake was the tasting panel's favorite, with the most intense chocolate flavor, a relatively light texture, and a very runny center. I then wondered if we might be able to capture some of the ethereal lightness of Sax's cake with the rich taste and buttery mouthfeel of Jean-Georges' dessert.

First we had to decide on the basic preparation method. There were two choices: We could beat the egg yolks and whites separately and then fold them together, or we could beat whole eggs and sugar to create a thick foam. The latter method proved superior, as it delivered the rich, moist texture we were looking for as well as making the recipe simpler. That left us with a recipe that consisted of melting chocolate; beating whole eggs, sugar, and flavorings into a foam; and then folding the two together, perhaps with a little flour or ground nuts for extra body.

Sorting Out Ingredients

Our next step was to determine what amounts of each ingredient made the best cake. After consid-

erable testing, we decided that one-half cup of melted butter made the dessert considerably moister. Some recipes use no flour or very little (Jean-Georges, for instance, uses only four teaspoons) but we finally settled on two tablespoons. The amount of chocolate was key and highly variable, running from a mere four ounces to a high of 12 ounces in Todd English's recipe. Eight ounces provided a good jolt of chocolate without being overbearing.

The eggs, however, were perhaps the most crucial element. We tested six whole eggs (light and airy sponge-cake texture), four whole eggs plus four yolks (moist and dark), and then the winner, four whole eggs plus one yolk (rich but light, moist, intense, and dark).

When baking these desserts in ramekins at 450 degrees, as called for in the Jean-Georges recipe, we found that the tops were slightly burned and the center was a bit too runny. At 350 degrees, the dessert took on a more cakelike quality and was also drier. Four hundred degrees was best, yielding a light, cakelike perimeter around a moist well of intense chocolate. (When using a cake pan rather than ramekins, though, we found it best to set the oven at 375 degrees.)

Final Steps

At this point we had the recipe pretty well in order. To finish the translation from restaurant to home kitchen, however, we still had some work to do. The biggest obstacle was the amount of last-minute cooking. One doesn't want to run out to the kitchen during dinner, whip up an egg foam, and throw it into the oven. Having had some experience with preparing chocolate soufflés ahead of time, we tested pouring the batter into the ramekins, refrigerating them, and then baking them during dinner. This worked, the batter holding for up to eight hours. Although the filled ramekins can be taken directly from the refrigerator to the oven with reasonably good results, they rise better if allowed to sit at room temperature for 30 minutes before baking.

I also wondered if most folks have eight ramekins at home. I could find only four, the others lost to breakage and my children's craft projects. Therefore, we developed variations using both 8- and 9-inch springform pans or cake pans with removable bottoms. As an added benefit for the home cook we discovered that, in cake form, this dessert can be baked up to one hour before serving, remaining warm right in the pan. (In a pinch, this dessert can be held up to two hours in the pan, but it will become slightly more dense as it cools.)

INDIVIDUAL FALLEN CHOCOLATE CAKES

SERVES 8

You can substitute 5 ounces of unsweetened baking chocolate for the semisweet if need be, but you'll also have to increase the sugar by 6 tablespoons, for a total of ⅞ cup. To melt the chocolate and butter in a microwave oven, heat chocolate alone at 50% power for 2 minutes; stir chocolate, add butter, and continue heating at 50% for another 2 minutes, stopping to stir after 1 minute. If chocolate is not yet entirely melted, heat an additional 30 seconds at 50% power.

8	tablespoons (1 stick) unsalted butter, plus extra for ramekins
8	ounces semisweet chocolate, coarsely chopped
4	large eggs
1	large yolk
1	teaspoon vanilla extract
¼	teaspoon salt
½	cup sugar
2	tablespoons all-purpose flour, plus extra for ramekins
	Confectioners' sugar or unsweetened cocoa powder for decoration, optional
	Whipped cream for serving, optional

1. Although acceptable in a standard cake, this texture is too dry for this recipe.

2. Just a bit of uncooked batter should ooze out of the center when the cake is cut.

3. A puddle of uncooked batter flowing out of the cake's center is unappealing.

1. Adjust oven rack to center position and heat oven to 400 degrees. Generously butter and flour (or use cocoa powder; *see* Notes From Readers, page 2) eight 6-ounce ramekins or Pyrex custard/baking cups; tap out excess flour and position ramekins on shallow roasting pan, jelly roll pan, or baking sheet. Meanwhile, melt 8 tablespoons butter and chocolate in medium heatproof bowl set over a pan of almost simmering water, stirring once or twice, until smooth; remove from heat. (Or melt chocolate and butter in microwave oven. *See* instructions above.)

2. Beat eggs, yolk, vanilla, salt, and sugar at highest speed in bowl of a standing mixer fitted with whisk attachment until volume nearly triples, color is very light, and mixture drops from beaters in a smooth, thick stream, about 5 minutes. (Alternatively, beat for 10 minutes using a hand-held electric mixer and large mixing bowl.) Scrape egg mixture over melted chocolate and butter; sprinkle flour over egg mixture. Gently fold egg and flour into chocolate until mixture is uniformly colored. Ladle or pour batter into pre-pared ramekins. (Can be covered lightly with plastic wrap and refrigerated up to eight hours. Return to room temperature for 30 minutes before baking.)

3. Bake until cakes have puffed about ½ inch above rims of ramekins, have a thin crust on top, and jiggle slightly at center when ramekins are shaken very gently, 12 to 13 minutes. Run a paring knife around inside edges of ramekins to loosen cakes and invert onto serving plates; cool for 1 minute and lift off ramekins. Sieve light sprinkling of confectioners' sugar or cocoa powder over cakes to decorate, if desired, and serve immediately with optional whipped cream.

FALLEN CHOCOLATE CAKE

SERVES 8 TO 10

One large fallen chocolate cake can be prepared in either a springform pan or a cake pan with a removable bottom. Do not use a regular cake pan, as the cake will be impossible to remove once baked. Though the cake is best when served warm, within about 30 minutes of being unmolded, it can also be held in the pan for up to two hours before serving.

Follow recipe for Individual Fallen Chocolate Cakes, substituting an 8- or 9-inch springform or removable-bottom cake pan for ramekins. Decrease baking temperature to 375 degrees and bake until cake looks puffed, a thin top crust has formed, and center jiggles slightly when pan is shaken gently, 22 to 25 minutes for 9-inch pan or 27 to 30 minutes for 8-inch pan. Cool cake for 15 minutes, run a paring knife around inside edge of pan, and remove pan sides. Sieve light sprinkling of confectioners' sugar or unsweetened cocoa powder over cake to decorate, if desired, just before serving, and serve warm, with optional whipped cream.

ORANGE CHOCOLATE CAKES

Follow recipe for Individual Fallen Chocolate Cakes or Fallen Chocolate Cake, folding 1 tablespoon finely grated zest from 2 medium oranges and 2 tablespoons orange liqueur (such as Grand Marnier or Triple Sec) into beaten egg and melted chocolate mixture.

Why Does This Cake Taste So Good?

One of the more interesting ideas I heard for the fantastic taste of this undercooked cake was proposed to me by Jean-Georges Vongerichten, who stated that the less one cooks chocolate, the better it tastes. I decided to check this out with Tom Lehmann, Director of Bakery Assistance at the American Institute of Baking, who agreed with Jean-Georges.

Chocolate, Lehmann explained, is a very delicate substance, full of highly sensitive volatiles. During baking, some of these volatiles, which give chocolate much of its flavor, are carried away by the steam produced by the liquids in the baked product. Anyone who has been in a kitchen while a chocolate cake was baking remembers the strong smell of chocolate. That's the good news. The bad news is that these volatiles are no longer in the cake where you want them to be. This situation is made even more acute by the fact that unwanted volatiles have already been driven off during the roasting and subsequent conching that are done to improve the flavor of chocolate beans. Additional exposure to heat, therefore, has no benefits; it simply makes the chocolate more bitter and less complex.

Another aspect of the wonderful flavor of this undercooked dessert is texture. It is my experience with many foods, including apple pie and tomato sauces, that flavor is enhanced by the presence of liquids. A juicy apple pie tastes better than a dry one, for example. In the same way, a very moist, liquid-in-the-center chocolate cake tastes better than a fully cooked one. My conjecture, which is supported by some of the food scientists I spoke with, is that liquids transport flavor to the tongue better than solids.

So, are there any lessons to be learned for home cooks who bake with chocolate? First, underbaking is always better than overbaking. Dry chocolate cakes, cookies, and brownies will have much less flavor and tend to be bitter. Second, use as much fat as possible. Fat increases the retention of volatile compounds. That's why "low-fat" chocolate cookies usually don't taste much like chocolate (or they are only slightly lower in fat). Finally, as we discovered in a chocolate tasting performed in our test kitchen some months ago, expensive chocolates with subtle flavor characteristics tend to lose their flavor edge when baked, so less expensive chocolate is fine for brownies, cakes, and cookies.

—C.K.

Nut Crescent Cookies

Superfine sugar and a combination of finely chopped and ground nuts yield tender, delicate, nutty cookies.

⋙ BY DAWN YANAGIHARA ⋘

Baking cookies has become a holiday tradition—as has the disposal of those with so little appeal that they go uneaten, even during a season of unabashed overindulgence. In my house, after the fruitcake, the first cookies to bite the dust are the balls and crescents coated in a pasty layer of melting confectioners' sugar. I have come to expect these cookies to be no more than stale, dry, floury, flavorless little chokeballs. They always fall short of the buttery, nutty, slightly crisp, slightly crumbly, melt-in-your-mouth nuggets they should be.

But that is a shame. Nut crescents are very much an "adult" cookie, low on sweetness, simple in flavor, and the perfect accompaniment to a cup of coffee or tea. When they are well-made, they are delicious, and I wanted to devise a recipe that would yield cookies that are eagerly awaited every holiday season, much like my mother's sugar cookies.

I gathered recipe after recipe from large, authoritative books and small, pamphlet-sized publications. These cookies, round and crescent-shaped, go by different names: Viennese crescents, butterballs, and Mexican wedding cakes, as well as almond, pecan, or walnut crescents. All the recipes are surprisingly similar, differing mainly in the amount and type of sugar and nuts. The standard ratio of butter to flour is one cup to two cups, with the flour in a few instances going as low as 1¾ cup and as high as 2½ cups. Across the board, the ingredients are simple: flour, sugar, butter, and nuts. Some add vanilla extract and salt. I chose four recipes and, with the input of a few tasters, formed a composite recipe to serve as the springboard for my testing.

Flour and Sweetness

Flour was my starting point. I certainly didn't need to go very far. Cookies made with two cups of all-purpose flour to one cup of butter were right on. The dough was easy to shape and handle, and the baked cookies were tender, delicate, and shapely. Any less flour and the rich cookies spread and lost some form in the oven; any more and they were dry and floury. I tried cake flour and cornstarch in place of some flour, thinking that one or another would provide extra tenderness. Both were failures. The resulting cookies lacked body and structure and disintegrated unpleasantly in the mouth.

Next I zeroed in on sugar. I liked the sweetness

To preserve the pristine appearance of these cookies, roll them in powdered sugar a second time just before serving.

of the cookies I had been making, but needed to discover the effects of granulated, confectioners', and superfine sugar. Granulated sugar yielded a cookie that was tasty, but coarse in both texture and appearance. Cookies made with confectioners' sugar were very tender, light, and fine-textured. Superfine, however, proved superior, producing cookies that were delicate, lightly crisp, and superbly tender, with a true melt-in-your-mouth quality. In a side-by-side tasting, the cookies made with superfine sugar were nuttier and purer in flavor, while the cornstarch in the confectioners' sugar bogged down the flavor and left a faint pastiness in the mouth.

As I tinkered with the amount of sugar, I had to keep in mind that these cookies are coated in confectioners' sugar after they are baked. One-third of a cup gives them a mildly sweet edge when they're eaten plain, but it's the roll in confectioners' sugar that gives them their finished look and just the right amount of extra sweetness.

When to give the baked cookies their coat of confectioners' sugar is a matter of some debate. Some recipes said to dust or dip them when they're still hot or warm. The sugar melts a bit,

and then they're usually given a second coat to even out their appearance and form a thicker coating. But I didn't like the layer of melting moistened confectioners' sugar, concealed or not. It formed a thin skin that was pasty and gummy and didn't dissolve on the tongue with the same finesse as a fine, powdery coat. I found it better to wait until the cookies had cooled to room temperature before coating them with confectioners' sugar.

Sifting sugar over the cooled cookies was tedious, and I wasn't able to achieve a heavy enough coating on the tops—or any at all on the bottoms. What worked much better was simply rolling them in confectioners' sugar. One coat resulted in a rather thin layer that was a bit spotty, but a second roll covered any blemishes, giving them an attractive, thick, powdery white coating.

If not served immediately, the cookies may lose a little in looks due to handling and storage. This problem can be easily solved by reserving the second coat of confectioners' sugar until just before serving.

Nut Case

During the nut testing, I concluded that what affected the cookies most was not the taste of the nuts but whether they were oily or dry. I found that when they were ground, the two types of nuts affected the cookies in different ways.

The flavor of oily nuts like walnuts and pecans is strong and distinct. These nuts are easier to chop and grind and, when finely ground, become quite oily. This is a definite advantage when making nut crescents, because the dough becomes softer and the resulting cookies are incredibly tender and delicate. Dry nuts like almonds and hazelnuts are rather subdued by comparison. Toasting ekes out their maximum flavor and crunchiness. Although these nuts are somewhat difficult to chop, that is the best form to use them in. Ground dry nuts did very little, if anything at all, to the texture of the cookies. Don't get me wrong: The almond and hazelnut cookies are delicious—they just don't melt in your mouth with the same abandon as the pecan and walnut ones.

In a recipe using one cup of butter and two cups of flour, various bakers called for anywhere from one-half cup to a hefty two cups of nuts, either roughly chopped, finely chopped, or ground. I wanted to cram as much nut flavor as I could into these cookies, but I found that two cups of ground nuts made them a tad greasy, while 1½ cups didn't give as much flavor as I was hoping for, so 1¾ cups was a happy compromise.

Chopped nuts were too coarse for the fine texture of the crescents and were quickly dismissed. Ground nuts, on the other hand, warranted further investigation. Oily ground nuts were flavorful, and because grinding really brought out the oils, they actually tenderized the cookies. I thought, though, that using a combination of ground and finely chopped nuts might tenderize, be flavorful, and add a pleasant bite. Hands down, a combo of one cup of finely chopped and three-fourths cup of ground nuts was the tasters' choice.

I had, up to this point, baked over 30 batches of cookies. I pressed on, however, knowing that I was very close.

Taking Shape

Recipes suggested baking temperatures ranging from a ridiculously low 300 degrees to a hot 400. At 375 degrees, the cookies browned too quickly, while at 300, they never achieved a nice golden hue, even after nearly half an hour of baking. Clearly the answer lay somewhere in between. My cookie-baking experience told me that many delicate, rich doughs like to bake at lower temperatures, and these cookies were no exception. Cookies baked at 350 degrees were good, but those baked at 325 degrees had a smoother, finer appearance, and were more tender and evenly textured and colored.

Whether for giving or keeping, these are cookies for eating, and not for the trash. The fruitcake may be a little lonely from now on.

PECAN OR WALNUT CRESCENT COOKIES
MAKES ABOUT 4 DOZEN COOKIES

You can buy superfine sugar in most grocery stores. You can also process regular granulated sugar to superfine consistency in about 30 seconds in the workbowl of a food processor fitted with a steel blade.

- 2 cups whole pecans or walnuts, chopped fine
- 2 cups bleached all-purpose flour
- ¾ teaspoon salt
- ½ pound (2 sticks) unsalted butter, softened
- ⅓ cup superfine sugar

TECHNIQUE | SHAPING THE COOKIES

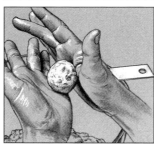

BALLS Roll the dough between your palms to form balls.

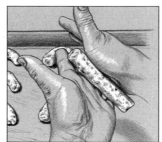

CRESCENTS I. To form crescent cookies, roll each ball into a 3½-inch rope of dough.

2. Shape each rope into a half circle and place about I inch apart on baking sheet.

RINGS For rings, shape each ball into a 4-inch rope, then push the ends together.

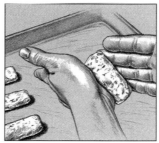

CIGARS To form cigar shapes, roll each ball into a 2½-inch log.

COATING SHAPES When cookies are cool, roll in confectioners' sugar. Repeat process just prior to serving.

- 1½ teaspoons vanilla extract
- 1½ cups confectioners' sugar for rolling cooled cookies

1. Adjust oven racks to upper- and lower-middle positions and heat oven to 325 degrees. Mix 1 cup chopped nuts, flour, and salt in medium bowl; set aside. In workbowl of a food processor fitted with a steel blade, process remaining chopped nuts until the texture of coarse cornmeal, 10 to 15 seconds (do not overprocess); stir into flour mixture and set aside. (To finely grind chopped nuts by hand, roll them between two large sheets plastic wrap with rolling pin, applying moderate pressure, until broken down to coarse cornmeal-like texture).

2. In bowl of an electric mixer at medium speed or by hand, beat butter and sugar until light and creamy, about 1½ minutes with an electric mixer or 4 minutes by hand; beat in vanilla. Scrape sides and bottom of bowl with rubber spatula; add flour mixture and beat at low speed until dough just begins to come together but still looks scrappy, about 15 seconds. Scrape sides and bottom of bowl again with rubber spatula; continue beating at low speed until dough is cohesive, 6 to 9 seconds longer. Do not overbeat.

3. Working with about one tablespoon dough at a time and following illustrations above, roll and shape cookies into balls, crescents, rings, or cigar shapes as desired. Bake until tops are pale golden and bottoms are just beginning to brown,

turning cookie sheets from front to back and switching from top to bottom racks halfway through baking, 17 to 19 minutes.

4. Cool cookies on sheets about 2 minutes; remove with metal spatula to wire rack and cool to room temperature, about 30 minutes. Working with three or four cookies at a time, roll cookies in confectioners' sugar to coat them thoroughly. Gently shake off excess. (They can be stored in an airtight container up to 5 days.) Before serving, roll cookies in confectioners' sugar a second time to ensure a thick coating, and tap off excess.

ALMOND OR HAZELNUT CRESCENT COOKIES
MAKES ABOUT 4 DOZEN COOKIES

Choosing almonds for your cookies automatically presents you with a choice: Whether to use them raw for traditional almond crescent cookies that are light in both color and flavor, or to toast them to enhance the almond flavor and darken the crescent. Toast hazelnuts and almonds in a preheated 350 degree oven until very lightly browned, stirring twice during baking, 12 to 14 minutes.

Follow recipe for pecan or walnut crescent cookies, substituting 2 cups toasted, skinned hazelnuts or a scant 1¾ cups whole blanched almonds (toasted or not) for pecans or walnuts. If using almonds, add ½ teaspoon almond extract along with vanilla extract.

Chinese "Cinnamon" Tops Tasting

Cinnamons vary widely in flavor, but our winner shares one important characteristic with all but one of the others—it's not really cinnamon.

⇛ BY MARYELLEN DRISCOLL ⇚

The warm, sweet, heady aroma of cinnamon is enough to weaken knees. Egyptians imported this spice from Asia as long ago as 4,000 years, and today, Americans love it, buying over 34 million pounds in 1995. And yet, more likely than not your last sticky bun or slice of cinnamon-raisin toast was not made with real cinnamon at all, but with a close cousin that has taken its place in the American pantry.

At *Cook's* we decided to hold a blind tasting of all the cinnamons, the true and the not-so-true, to see if we have been missing out on something. As it turns out we have, but not on what we expected. Let's backtrack.

In actuality true cinnamon, which is made from the dried bark of a tropical evergreen tree called *Cinnamomum zeylanicum*, has been all but unavailable in the United States for almost 100 years. Early in the 20th century, this spice became very popular for medicinal uses in Europe, and its cost skyrocketed. According to Pamela Penzey, of Penzeys Ltd., a mail-order spice house, a record from 1910 showed a cost of $100 per pound for Ceylon cinnamon.

This was far too expensive for culinary use, so American merchants imported cassia, which is the bark of a similar tropical evergreen, *Cinnamomum cassia*. Because of this, says Penzey, Americans have grown used to and prefer the stronger, fuller flavors of cassia.

While there is just one true cinnamon, there are a number of different cassias, typically identified by their place of origin. Some spice merchants will indicate this on their labels, but most supermarket brands do not, nor can you tell by appearance which one you are buying.

The Tasting

For our tasting, we included one sample of true cinnamon that we tracked down through a mail-order source, along with 10 samples from the three primary varieties of cassia currently available in the United States. They come from Indonesia, Vietnam, and China. Five of these cassia samples were from major supermarket brands, and five were purchased through major American spice houses. We tasted ground cinnamon instead of sticks, because it is more commonly used in cooking and carries the strongest flavor.

The tasting consisted of three tiers. In two separate tastings, held at Peter Kump's New York Cooking School and in *Cook's* test kitchen, a total of 20 different tasters assessed the appearance and aroma of each sample plain and also tasted a strong dose of each in apple sauce. In a third tasting, nine members of *Cook's* editorial staff also tasted the cinnamons in a cinnamon icebox cookie and in applesauce at a moderate dosage. The final results for both moderate and strong applesauce tests were consistent with one another, but the cinnamon-cookie ratings proved less predictable. Tasters said that the predominant flavors of butter, flour, and, in particular, sugar, made it difficult to concentrate on the taste of the cinnamon.

As predicted by our research, the one true cinnamon sample was unlike others in the tasting. While most tasters did not find anything offensive about it, it was, ironically, often downgraded for not tasting "cinnamon-y." While subdued, its flavor was complex with notes of citrus and clove, but many tasters found it medicinal or chalky.

As for the cassias, almost half the ones in our tasting were Indonesian cassia (also known as Korintje cassia), a variety that comprises the overwhelming majority of so-called cinnamon sold in the United States today. While some of these Indonesian cassias were notably spicy and bitter, the common denominator among those that tasters liked was a solid, familiar cinnamon flavor that was relatively strong and had no off flavors. The two mail-order varieties landed solidly in the recommended category. With one exception the supermarket brands also proved "acceptable," which is good news for those who are unlikely to buy spices through the mail.

The cassia that particularly grabbed the tasters came from China. Chinese cassia tends to have a stronger, sweeter flavor than Indonesian cassia. Both the samples in our tasting were also notably spicy, reminding many tasters of Red Hots candy. Penzeys Chinese cassia, which was anything but meek, secured the top ranking as excellent overall.

The second favorite sample was a Vietnamese cassia. Vietnamese cassias, which only recently became available in the United States with the relaxing of the U.S. trade embargo, tend to be expensive and hold a reputation for being the "world's finest." The two Vietnamese samples in our tasting, though, were quite different from each other. Penzeys Extra Fancy Vietnamese cassia finished second overall with big yet balanced flavors and a subtle complexity. The other Vietnamese cassia in our tasting, McCormick/Schilling Premium cinnamon, was also well received by tasters, but not for any kind of flavor intensity. Instead, they found it light and sweet with faint spice notes.

Whether cinnamon or cassia, their characteristic flavors and aromas come from their essential oils, which in turn are composed of hundreds of chemical compounds. One of the reasons that Ceylon or "true" cinnamon is so different from cassia is that the main components of its essential oils are different. The chemical compound cinnamaldehyde gives cassia its characteristic flavor. While Ceylon cinnamon contains cinnamaldehyde, it also contains a distinct amount of eugenol, the chemical compound that gives cloves their particular aroma and flavor. Cinnamon's essential oils are volatile, meaning they are quick to dissipate as gas. So it is important to seal cinnamon jars tightly and to store them somewhere dry and away from light and heat sources to prevent a loss of flavor. Smell and taste cinnamon a year after purchasing to determine if too much strength has been lost.

SPECIMEN | DIFFERENT BARKS, DIFFERENT USES

Bark from the large, old branches at the tree base is used to make ground cassia or cinnamon (above). The scrolled 3½-inch twigs sold commercially as cinnamon sticks (right) are cut from the cinnamon/cassia treetop.

TASTING THE CINNAMONS

For the *Cook's* cinnamon tasting, five products from major supermarket brands and six products available by mail order from major U.S. retail spice merchants were assembled. In the first blind taste test, ¼ teaspoon of each cinnamon sample was blended with ⅛ cup of applesauce and rated for strength and complexity of flavor, flavor appeal, and overall appeal. In a separate taste test, each cinnamon was served again in applesauce, but in the modest ratio of ¼ teaspoon for every 1¼ cups of applesauce. The cinnamons were also tasted in a basic cinnamon icebox cookie. Our first tasting was held at Peter Kump's New York Cooking School and attended by 11 New York City culinary professionals (see below). The remaining tests were conducted at the *Cook's* office and attended by nine editorial staff and test kitchen members. Each sample's three taste test scores for overall liking were totaled to determine ranking. Products are listed below in ranking order. Cinnamon products are subject to variations in quality, availability, and price, depending on market forces, the weather, and political/trade relations.

RECOMMENDED

Penzeys China Cassia Cinnamon
➤ 2.2-ounce glass jar sells for $2.99

It's no wonder this cassia cinnamon from Tunghing, China, is Penzeys' top-selling cinnamon. "I've never had such incredible cinnamon before in my life!" wrote one taster. "Perfection," wrote another. Spicy, sweet, and "pleasantly hot" characteristics seemed to be the love potion behind this cinnamon, which reminded many tasters of Red Hots candy with minty undertones. A few, however, were turned off by the pepper punch. Tasters felt that this spice also carried an "intense" flavor in the cookie. Available by mail order from Penzeys, Ltd (P.O. Box 933, Muskego, WI 53150; 414-679-7207).

Penzeys Extra Fancy Vietnamese Cassia Cinnamon
➤ 1.7-ounce glass jar sells for $4.29

Tasters found the aroma of this cinnamon from the remote north and west regions of Vietnam was "like a barnyard." Fortunately it did not deliver what it suggested. "Smooth, slightly spicy," with a "roundness to it" and "surprisingly sweet," it had a heat punch, a chalky aftertaste, and notes of clove, ginger, and allspice. Its big flavors with subtle complexity were significantly mellowed in the cookie. Available by mail order from Penzeys, Ltd.

Kalustyan's Korintje Cassia Cinnamon
➤ 2-ounce glass jar sells for $2.99

This cinnamon comes from the same island as many of the supermarket cinnamons in this tasting, yet it definitely stood out. Its flavor was described as "dark, deep, and brooding" with a confident spiciness. It was a little bitter, a little sharp, and a little sweet—"just the way I know and like my cinnamon," wrote one taster. The cookies particularly brought out its complexity. Available by mail order from Kalustyan's (123 Lexington Avenue, New York, NY 10016; 212-685-3451).

McCormick/Schilling Ground Cinnamon
➤ 2.37-ounce plastic jar sells for $2.79

This Korintje cassia spice shone in the cookie tasting as "bright" with a "strong cinnamon statement but not overkill." In the applesauce it was more "subtle" and "not so spicy." It had notably large flecks, which some found "gritty" in the applesauce. The McCormick label is sold in East Coast supermarkets. Schilling is sold on the West Coast.

Penzeys Indonesian Korintje Cassia Cinnamon
➤ 2.2-ounce glass jar sells for $2.99

This brand, lighter in color than most of the other Indonesian cassias, was extremely aromatic. Its flavor was "alive yet delicate," "earthy," sweet, and complex with a bitter finish. Available by mail order from Penzeys, Ltd.

Adriana's Chinese Cassia
➤ 2-ounce bag sells for $3.00

This agreeably spicy Chinese cassia had a lingering low heat and was sweeter than most other cassias, "full with some coarseness in the finish." Some tasters found a bitter aftertaste. A lot of this cinnamon's character seemed to get lost in the cookie. Available by mail order from Adriana's Caravan (409 Vanderbilt Street, Brooklyn, NY 11218; 800-316-0820).

McCormick/Schilling Premium Ground Cinnamon
➤ 1.87-ounce glass jar sells for $5.99

Available in the United States only in the past year, this coppery brown cinnamon from Saigon was "light"; "it doesn't slap you too hard." Like the other Vietnamese sample, it carried a noted sweetness but without much spiciness. The mouthfeel was described as dry. Available under the McCormick label in East Coast supermarkets and under the Schilling label in West Coast supermarkets.

ACCEPTABLE

Penzeys Ceylon Cinnamon
➤ 1.9-ounce glass jar sells for $5.69.

As the only true cinnamon in the tasting, this sample tripped up a number of tasters. As one of the misled wrote, "It's a wannabe." It looked completely different from the cassia cinnamons—pale, light, the color of putty. Its aroma was faint and its flavor less sweet than the cassias; it was notably aromatic, mild, yet complex, with notes of citrus, clove, and ginger. "Finishes round and spicy, lasts pleasantly in the mouth." This spice struck many tasters as out of place in applesauce or in a cookie. "It's unusual all around yet I like it that way," wrote one discriminating taster. Available by mail order from Penzeys, Ltd.

Durkee Ground Cinnamon
➤ 1.75-ounce plastic bottle sells for $2.89

This cassia cinnamon from Indonesia was delicate and somewhat mild in flavor with a spicy pungency "that sneaks up on you as an aftertaste." Available in supermarkets nationwide.

Tone's Ground Cinnamon
➤ 1.76-ounce bottle sells for $1.95

Red-hots thrill seekers found this fruity, delicate Midwest brand disappointing. The level of spiciness was faint. Also sold in a .7-ounce plastic bottle, which is ideal from someone who does not use a lot of cinnamon within a year's time. Available in supermarkets in the Midwest.

NOT RECOMMENDED

Spice Islands Ground Cinnamon
➤ 1.9-ounce glass jar sells for $4.37

This was the only product to combine Indonesian and Chinese cassias. Tasters consistently commented that it lacked "a cinnamon-y flavor." The cinnamon carried an unusual aftertaste, described as "green," "perfume-y," and "astringent." Available in supermarkets nationwide.

Tasting participants at Peter Kump's New York Cooking School were food writers Paul Grimes, Melissa Hamilton, and Dana Jacobi; freelance publicist Jeremy Meyers; pastry chefs Joanne Chang of Payard Patisserie, Maury Rubin of The City Bakery, and Dieter G. Schorner, instructor at the French Culinary Institute; culinary instructor Lynn Kutner of the New School; food consultant Kathleen Sanderson; Arlyn Blake of the James Beard Foundation; and Hope Flamm of Cooking by the Book Inc.

The Problem with Automatic Drip Coffee Makers

All models offer brew-in-your-sleep ease, but only one delivers the flavor to back it up—as long as you drink the coffee within a few minutes.

⇾ BY ADAM RIED ⇽

Almost every home kitchen I know has an automatic drip coffee maker. Yet when I began to ask around about them, I found that few people were actually satisfied with the coffee their machines produced. When we here at *Cook's* conducted a test of different coffee brewing methods (*see* "The Best Coffee-Brewing Method," January/February 1996), we agreed. The two automatic drip coffee makers included in that test, one with a glass carafe and burner plate and another with a thermal carafe, were disappointing. A second set of two machines in that test turned in somewhat better results, but still failed to dazzle us.

For a magazine dedicated to identifying the best kitchen equipment and appliances, though, automatic drip coffee makers were simply too important to write off. After all, most households own one, and top-of-the-line models like those tested here can cost an arm and a leg. At as much as $160 for the most expensive machine in our lineup, we'd expect not just bells and whistles, but decent, if not excellent, coffee.

Finding the Right Machines

Before choosing which models to test, we did some hard thinking about the types of features that were important to us. Generally, we broke features into two categories: those designed to enhance convenience, such as built-in clocks or grinders, programmability, automatic shut-off,

removable water reservoirs, and the like; and those aimed at improving the flavor of the coffee, such as water filtration systems, special coffee filters, and adjustable brew cycles or temperature controls. As a group, the editors felt strongly that convenience was not as important as flavor, so we focused on the second category of features.

Given the sheer number of different machines on the market—Mr. Coffee alone offers more than 40 models, for example — selecting specific models was difficult. For guidance, we turned to *Appliance Manufacturer* magazine, which provided a list of the top-selling coffee maker manufacturers for 1997. We then called representatives from the six top-selling brands and asked each to choose which model we should test, keeping in mind our focus on flavor.

Easy, but Flawed

The convenience of these machines goes undisputed. Provided you load ground coffee in the filter and water in the reservoir and set the clock with a pre-programmed brewing time, each one will literally brew coffee while you sleep. Despite brewing coffee easily, however, none brewed it perfectly.

Compared with our favorite coffee-making method, the manual drip, we found the quality of our test machines' freshly brewed coffee acceptable but not exceptional. We suspect that the shortcomings relate to several factors, including brewing time, filter-basket size, and water temperature.

To extract the desired degree of water-soluble flavor compounds (18 to 22 percent) from the coffee grounds, brewing time should be no more than six minutes. Longer brewing times can cause overextraction. None of our machines was able to brew a full pot of coffee in this time, a flaw that we thought was responsible for the harshness or bitterness we tasted in varying degrees in the coffee from every machine. To test this, we brewed the same amount of coffee in a cone-shaped manual drip coffee maker; it took 5 minutes and 45 seconds, and the coffee tasted much smoother and more balanced.

The small size of the filter baskets on most machines is another potential detriment to coffee quality. Coffee authorities, including Ted Lingle, executive director of the Specialty Coffee Association of America, agree that ground coffee should have ample headroom in the filter basket to be agitated and swollen by the water passing through it. When we filled the cramped filter baskets typical of our machines with enough grounds for a full pot, full flavor extraction was compromised because the grounds got compressed in some areas.

During the testing, temperature also arose as an issue that affected coffee quality. As we sipped our way through hundreds of cups of coffee, tasters commented consistently that the coffee from all the machines was not as hot as they would have liked. Ted Lingle explained that few automatic drip

The Coffee Makers We Tested

Krups ProAroma
Consistently brewed best-tasting cup of coffee.

Black & Decker Kitchentools
Carafe kept coffee hot with no burned taste.

Braun FlavorSelect
Easy to use, but brewed mediocre coffee.

Mr. Coffee Elite
Noisy machine yielded inconsistent coffee.

Betty Crocker Coffee Maker
Brewed watery, harsh coffee.

Hamilton Beach Aroma Express
Worst coffee of the lot.

RATING ELECTRIC DRIP COFFEE MAKERS

Machines from the brands with the top six 1997 market share percentages were tested. With each machine, we brewed three full pots according to the manufacturer's directions. The flavor of the freshly brewed coffee was our most important criterion. All the machines we tested included digital clocks programmable for delayed automatic brewing, as well as a feature that temporarily interrupts the flow of water to the pot when it is removed to pour a cup before the brew cycle is completed. Machines, which are listed in order of preference, were judged on the following criteria:

Price: Quoted by manufacturers. Actual retail prices may vary.

Full Pot Brewing Time: Averaged from three pots.

Full Pot Temperature, Fresh/30 Minutes: Each figure averaged from three pots.

Full Pot Flavor, Fresh/30 Minutes: Five tasters rated the flavor of three pots in each category based on perceptions of acidity, body, aroma, taste, and serving temperature.

Design/Testers' Comments: Testers' observations about particularly good or bad features.

BRAND	PRICE	BREW TIME	TEMP (Fresh)	TEMP (30 Minutes Later)	FLAVOR (Fresh)	FLAVOR (30 Minutes Later)	DESIGN/TESTERS' COMMENTS
BEST MAKER **Krups** ProAroma 12 Time with NaturActiv Filter Model 453	$140.00	12 minutes, 10 seconds	183°	172°	Good	Average	The most full-featured, electronically complicated, and second most- expensive coffee maker of the bunch brewed fine-tasting coffee, though not always hot enough for us. Some of the features, such as the carafe prewarming function, seem superfluous, but we appreciated others, including the well-designed water filter, adjustable burner-plate temperature, and automatic burner shut-off.
Black & Decker Kitchentools Model TCMKT800	$159.99	10 minutes, 45 seconds	186°	179°	Average	Average	This was the only model we tested that came with a thermal carafe. The flavor of the freshly brewed coffee was a notch below the first-place Krups. Hotter coffee and the thermal carafe, however, moved this machine to a solid second place. We did notice, though, that a small bit of coffee always collected in the pronounced spout of the carafe, and even after brewing multiple pots, tasters inevitably splashed the small bit of hot liquid on themselves.
Braun FlavorSelect Model KF 187	$99.99	11 minutes, 45 seconds	183°	172°	Average	Poor	Reasonably full-featured, yet easy and intuitive to use. The coffee, however, was nothing to write home about.
Mr. Coffee Elite Model PRX33	$49.99	13 minutes, 40 seconds	178°	175°	Average	Average	Turned in an uneven performance, with coffee ranging from average to awful according to no apparent pattern. Huffed, puffed, and sputtered far more than the other machines, but it was generally very easy to use.
Betty Crocker Coffee Maker Electronic 12-Cup Auto-Drip Model BC-1754	$34.99	15 minutes, 30 seconds	177°	175°	Average	Average	Fresh coffee from this machine tended to be watery, always with a slightly harsh, unpleasant flavor edge. Though easy to decipher and use, this machine felt light and shoddy, and not all the pieces fit flush against each other. Almost impossible to pour from this carafe without spilling.
Hamilton Beach Aroma Express Model 49271	$59.99	11 minutes, 55 seconds	178°	173°	Poor	Poor	Though this machine was very easy to figure out and use, it consistently brewed the worst-tasting coffee of the lot. Removing the water filter actually improved the flavor a little, though not enough to bump this machine out of last place.

machines are able to heat the water to the target brewing temperature of 195 to 205 degrees, largely because the power is divided among several different components, including burner plates and clocks and other electronic features, in addition to the heating element. To heat the water sufficiently, said Lingle, a machine should have a minimum of 1250 watts, a number rarely, if ever, encountered in home brewers. None of the ones that we tested came up to this wattage standard.

Don't Let it Age

All the machines except the thermal carafe model took a significant nose-dive when we tasted coffee that had sat in a glass carafe on the burner plate for 30 minutes. Across the board, the coffee lost a noticeable measure of quality, tasting flat and anywhere from slightly to very burnt after 30 minutes on the burner. This was especially bad news for Betty Crocker and Hamilton Beach, which produced coffees that tasted only marginally good when fresh.

Thirty-minute old coffee from the Black & Decker's thermal carafe was another story. There was much less flavor degradation after 30 minutes in the thermal carafe than on the burner plates of the other machines. The Black & Decker's 30-minute-old coffee received an average, rather than good, rating only because it started out as average, neither impressively hot nor full-flavored. In relation to the other machines, however, this 30-minute-old coffee was very good in that there was no burnt flavor. (Incidentally, Mr. Coffee, Krups, and a smaller company called Capresso, also make machines with thermal carafes.)

Though we are fans of the thermal carafe, another feature with a related purpose also struck us as worth mentioning. Adjustability of the burner plate temperature on the Krups, Braun, and Mr. Coffee helped mitigate, though not prevent, the coffee-burning problem. In particular, when the Krups burner plate was set to low, the coffee burned a little less than the other burner-plated models.

In addition to these attempts to deal with burning, many of the machines have other features intended to improve coffee flavor. These ranged from water filters to "small batch" brew settings to "brew ready" indicators. Sad to say, none of them worked very well in our tests.

Conclusions

As in our previous article on coffee-making methods, the electric drip machines, as a group, didn't wow us. The Krups offered a mix of some useful and some silly features, and it brewed the best-tasting coffee of the lot. In the end, after all the testing was complete, we reached for the Krups to brew our morning coffee in the test kitchen. Thus, the Krups is our pick, provided that your household drinks the pot of coffee while it is fresh. On the other hand, if your household is like many we questioned in an informal poll, pots of coffee are drunk over a period of time. In this case, try a thermal carafe model such as the Black & Decker Kitchentools.

Rich Red Wines

Maybe you can't have everything, but you can find rich, fruity reds at reasonable prices—they just come from unusual places. BY MARK BITTMAN

There are several qualities that make a great red wine—firm structure, richness, a certain soft silkiness, and complexity of flavor, to name a few. Finding them all in one wine is a real challenge. Fortunately, some reasonably priced wines excel at one or two of these features, and that's what we looked for in this tasting: rich, flavorful red wines from anywhere. Anywhere, that is, except Bordeaux, a region that produces plenty of these wines, but almost always at hefty prices. Instead, we concentrated on the wines of southern Europe, California, and the southern hemisphere. We did not include wines such as Rioja, which is soft and pleasant, or Chianti, which is light and fruity, because we were looking for something more distinguished. I settled on Cabernet Sauvignon as well as a few lesser-known grapes that have the potential to make big, full wines.

The tasting provided some pleasant surprises: A Spanish wine was at the top of the heap; an inexpensive selection from southern Italy took second place; and strong showings were made by a trio of Californians and a well-respected entry from Argentina. Generally speaking, the French wines that we did choose did not do well; they were light, or contained off-flavors or too little fruit. (Had our price limit been doubled—we put a ceiling of $25 on these wines—we would have had some beauties from France.)

It is not big news that you can buy rich reds from France, nor is it any longer surprising that good cabernet sauvignons can be made in California, but the three wine-growing regions that did best in this tasting are worth examining in a little more depth.

• Ribera del Duero is a Spanish region that concentrates on the same grape as neighboring Rioja—Tempranillo—although it calls it by a different name: Tinto del Pais. Whatever the name, this grape reaches its true potential here.

• Southern Italy is introducing some great wines this decade, and many are priced right. Salento is a region near the heel of Italy's boot—a peninsula in the middle of the sea—and Dr. Taurino is one of its most respected producers. His Salice Salentino (about $7) is a reliable inexpensive wine, but this Notarpanaro (a wine made from two indigenous grapes) was a real shocker.

• It's worth mentioning Argentina, too, a country whose wines get a fair amount of press

but so far have failed to make many inroads with consumers. The Trapiche Medalla cabernet blend was enthusiastically received, although it has plenty of stiff competition in the over-$20 price range.

Many of the world's wine-making regions produce reds that get occasional, or even frequent, good notice—Southern France, Australia, Chile, South Africa, and more—and we included some of the best of the lot, those with sound reputa-tions and widespread availability. It's odd, though: This was a strong tasting, with lots of sound wines that were enjoyed by all, but there were few true winners. This is probably because in the over-$20 price range wines have to be nearly unflawed to be worth buying, and that was hardly the case, as you'll see from the results below. My general recommendation is to try our big winners (and wines from their regions), or stick to sturdy Cabernets from California.

THE JUDGES' RESULTS | RICH REDS

The wines in our tasting—held at Mt. Carmel Wine and Spirits in Hamden, Connecticut —were judged by a panel made up of both wine professionals and amateur wine lovers. The wines were all purchased in the Northeast; prices will vary throughout the country.

Within each category, wines are listed based on the number of points scored. In this tasting, the "Highly Recommended" wines had almost all positive comments; those labeled "Recommended" garnered mostly positive comments; the "Recommended with Reservations" group had decidedly mixed comments; and the "Not Recommended" category had almost all negative comments.

HIGHLY RECOMMENDED

Best Wine: 1994 Arzuaga Ribera del Duero SPAIN, **$21.** All but two of our tasters ranked the wine first. "Big, rich, gutsy, round, and powerful"; "more elegant than anything else here."

Best Buy: 1990 Taurino Notarpanaro del Salento ITALY, **$11.** Note price. "Good, sturdy stuff"; "Bordeaux-like, with lavender perfume"; "quite delicious."

RECOMMENDED

1995 Trapiche Medalla ARGENTINA, **$22.** Garnered a slew of second-and third-place votes. "If this tasting is about rich, this wine is it."

1995 Ridge Geyserville Cabernet Sauvignon CALIFORNIA, **$25.** "Complex, fruity, deep, and rich," with "hints of apple and citrus."

1993 Burgess Vintage Selection Napa Cabernet Sauvignon CALIFORNIA, **$22.** "Perfect nose," "rich, almost sweet wine."

1995 Cline Contra Costa Carignane CALIFORNIA, **$11.** Cline wines almost always do well in our tasting, and this is no exception. Note the price for this "dark, big, rich" and "high-quality" entry, made from a strong Rhone Valley grape.

RECOMMENDED WITH RESERVATIONS

1995 Chateau de Saint Cosme, Gigondas FRANCE, **$23.** "Light but drinkable," which at this price is damning with faint praise.

1995 Chateauneuf du Pape Domaine de la Solitude FRANCE, **$20.** "Good fruit," but "more alcoholic than rich."

1995 Penfolds Koonunga Hill Shiraz-Cabernet AUSTRALIA, **$11.** "Decent wine," but "somewhat dull." At least the price is right.

1994 Rosenblum Sonoma Zinfandel CALIFORNIA, **$20.** "Complex" nose that some found "stinky." "Plenty of flavor."

1995 Kanakop Pinotage SOUTH AFRICA, **$23.** "Big" if "harsh" nose, with "plenty on the palate."

1990 Vallana Gattinara ITALY, **$20.** "Not as rich as some" (in fact, "a little thin") but "one of the better wines here."

1993 Quinta do Carmo PORTUGAL, **$20.** "Awkward" but "high-quality" wine.

NOT RECOMMENDED

1996 Casa Lapostolle Cabernet Sauvignon CHILE, **$20.**

1994 Jaboulet Crozes-Hermitages FRANCE, **$23.**

The Best Bread Ever?

Is the claim of the "best bread ever" mere hyperbole or has the author developed a precise scientific method that delivers superior results? BY CHRISTOPHER KIMBALL

Like physicists who specialize in quantum mechanics, arguing about the finer points of string theory and building vast underground pools hoping to catch the death of a single neutrino, bread bakers are a pretty mad lot. They get exercised about the carotene content of flour, claiming that this is the holy grail of authentic French bread. They spend weekends building replicas of commercial bakery ovens, devising ingenious methods of introducing steam, or, in the case of a friend of mine, renting a backhoe to dig a giant pit and move enough large rocks into it to build a Neapolitan pizza oven.

Many of these bread fanatics worship at the feet of Professor Calvel, the French éminence grise of bread baking, hanging onto every word, extracted over steak frites at a Paris bistro or perhaps at an industry lecture. The very thought of producing a baguette with a crackly thin crust and pillowy, pure white interior is just short of ecstasy, the equivalent of taking brush in hand and reproducing the ceiling of the Sistine Chapel right in one's own bedroom.

Charles Van Over is one of the smitten. He is an excellent bread baker and has garnered a deserved reputation for the bread served at his Restaurant du Village in Chester, Connecticut. He is also a true believer—even a short conversation will yield terms such as "base" temperature and "autolyse." So I expected his new book, *The Best Bread Ever,* to be the delightful rantings of a bread-baking maven, only modestly relevant to home cooking.

My first and most pleasant surprise upon opening his book was that Van Over is a devotee of the food-processor method of kneading bread dough. This technique is nothing new; many home bakers, myself included, use this method. Van Over, however, has taken it to the next step. He claims not only that this method is convenient (since the processing time is under one minute), but that it actually makes better bread. He believes that several factors are responsible for this. For one thing, he claims that standing mixers and commercial machines expose the dough to too much oxygen, which decreases the quality of the texture and flavor.

Another crucial factor, according to Van Over, is the pre-mixing temperature of the flour and water. For most food processors, the combined temperature of water and flour— what he calls the "base temperature"—should total 130 degrees.

In other words, if the flour measures 70 degrees, the water should be at 60 degrees, and vice versa. Van Over explains that this is crucial because when flour and water with a total temperature of 130 degrees are mixed in most food processors, they produce a dough that measures between 75 and 80 degrees, the ideal temperature for keeping the yeast alive but not so active that it causes the dough to rise too quickly.

Of course, the question that first came to my mind was, does it matter? Can't you use pretty much any temperature water, as long as it isn't ice cold or boiling hot?

To answer that question, our test kitchen made The Best Bread Ever, a recipe for baguettes, according to Van Over's precise instructions. Right off the bat, we found that his recipe was excellent, the best homemade baguettes we have ever had. However, when we made it again without bothering to measure the temperature of the flour or the water, the results were the same. I repeated this test at home but went to the extreme by making two batches, one in which the base temperature was 130 degrees (the flour was 74 degrees and the water 56 degrees) and one in which I used hot water (106 degrees) so that the base temperature reached 180 degrees. The dough from the second batch, rather than being in the 75 to 80 degree range, was a whopping 98 degrees. The results? Well, I actually liked the bread made with the "hot" dough more—it seemed to rise more fully and to be a bit lighter.

Despite the shaky science, though, further recipe testing revealed that many of Van Over's basic bread recipes were as top-notch as his baguettes. These included an outstanding New York bagel, very good pizza dough, and a great ciabatta. An anise-scented Moroccan bread was also outstanding, but we ran into trouble with some other recipes, including focaccia, garlic Parmesan breadsticks, Danish, and brioche. For many of these recipes, the baking times were very far off. But in general, if one adjusts the baking times, Van Over's recipes produce very high quality breads.

I have a few additional quibbles with *The Best Bread Ever.* It uses some uncommon ingredients that are hard for home cooks to find (in particular,

The Best Bread Ever
Charles Van Over
Broadway $27.50

instant yeast), and many of the recipes suffer from some imprecision. I also question the author's claim that all his breads are done when an instant-read thermometer reaches 205 to 210 degrees; this is true for European breads that use no sugar or fat, but the typical American bread is usually done at 190 degrees. I also wondered why the recipe for The Best Bread Ever is for a baguette. Why not structure it as a master recipe, offering the baguette as one of many variations? I also find it disappointing when cookbooks quickly scamper off into the land of specialty recipes, ignoring many of the really useful workhorse foods. I could not, for example, find a recipe for a whole wheat bread not made with sourdough or a rustic country loaf, yet the book was replete with things like Thai jasmine rice rolls, baba au rhum, and galette perougienne. Finally, Van Over never addresses the key reason I often do not use a food processor for kneading, which is volume. I like to make double recipes or large loaves when baking breads, which requires about six to seven cups of flour. This dictates that one must process the dough in two batches, which is more work than throwing everything into a standing mixer and walking away for eight minutes.

So where do we come out? Well, despite my doubts about the science behind it, I found that his method for kneading bread dough in a food processor works well— it is convenient (at least for smaller recipes), fast, and produces top-notch bread. And, for the most part, his recipes are quite good, especially the more basic ones. Generally, I would say the book is a must buy for any home bread baker. As for "the best bread ever," I find that claim a bit harder to swallow. The baguette recipe is, in fact, the "best ever," but some of the more complex breads, while fine, are not the best of their class. It may be that the food processor is a superior method for some breads but not all. (I began to suspect that this book started with the baguette recipe and then branched out from there. The farther we got from this white bread, the less satisfied we were with the results.) Yet Van Over should be given high marks for an original work, one that produces some outstanding breads, and recipes that, for the most part, are nicely adapted to home kitchens.

RESOURCES

Most of the ingredients and materials necessary for the recipes in this issue are available at your local supermarket, gourmet store, or kitchen supply shop. The following are mail-order sources for particular items. Prices listed below were current at press time and do not include shipping or handling unless otherwise indicated. We suggest that you contact companies directly to confirm up-to-date prices and availability.

Coffee Makers

Of the six automatic drip coffee makers tested, the best-tasting pot of coffee was brewed by Krups ProAroma 12 Time with NaturActiv Filter, Model 453. You can purchase the Krups by mail order for $90 from **A Cook's Wares (211 37th Street, Beaver Falls, PA 105010-2103; 800-915-9788)**. Available in both black and white, it has a 10-cup capacity and comes with a 1-year manufacturer's warranty.

If you are more likely to drink or serve coffee over an extended period of time, we recommend the Black & Decker Kitchentools Model TCMKT 800. This 8-cup coffee maker has a brushed stainless steel thermal carafe that can be brought to any part of the house. The Black & Decker comes with a reusable gold-toned filter and its reservoir detaches so you can fill it with water at the sink. It sells for $129.99 at **Kitchen Etc. catalogue services (Department TM, 32 Industrial Drive, Exeter, NH 03833; 800-232-4070)** and comes with a 5-year manufacturer's warranty. Like the Krups, it offers a programmable clock for delayed automatic brewing.

Fresh Oysters

If you do not have a market that sells cold-water oysters or are simply looking for guaranteed fresh oysters, we order from and recommend American Mussel Harvesters. This company supplies cold water shellfish to restaurants across the country and recently began a mail-order service for home cooks. American Mussel Harvesters obtains all its shellfish from certified waters and transplants them to closed salt-water holding tanks with state-of-the-art temperature controls, filters, and ultraviolet sterilizers. Their shellfish is harvested to order and shipped express in ice packs. American Mussel Harvesters carries more than a dozen varieties of Atlantic oysters and European flats. It also sells mussels and clams. For more information on products or to order, contact **American Mussel Harvesters (323 Great Island Road, Narragansett, RI 02882; 401-789-1678)**.

Oyster Knife

Novice and seasoned oyster shuckers at *Cook's* tested a variety of oyster knives for the story on page 10. Our favorites were from Oxo Good Grips and Dexter-Russell. Both had slightly angled, pointed tips, which made it easier to dig into the oyster's hinge and pry the shells apart. The Dexter oyster knife is made of a stain-free high carbon steel blade with a white "Grip-Tex" polypropylene handle. According to the manufacturer, bacteria, acid, moisture, fats, and grease cannot penetrate the handle. You can order the Dexter-Russell oyster knife model S121 for $9.95 from **Stoddard's (50 Temple Place, Boston, MA 02111; 617-426-4187)**. The Oxo oyster knife had a thick, comfortable grip handle made of Oxo's trademark black nonslip santoprene material. The handle's neck is ribbed so that your thumb holds steady, and a flared ring at the neck edge adds extra protection from slipping. You can order the Oxo oyster knife for $6.99 from **Kitchen Etc. catalogue services (Department TM, 32 Industrial Drive, Exeter, NH 03833; 800-232-4070)**.

Ramekins

The trouble with most ramekins is that they do not stack; as a result, they gobble up precious cabinet space or sit precariously on top of one another before they fall and chip. Since the recipe for individual servings of fallen chocolate cake on page 22 calls for eight 6-ounce ramekins, we decided it was time to find affordable ramekins that we could stack. **Kitchen & Company (100 Lake Drive, Newark, DE 19702; 800-747-7224; www.kitchenandcompany.com)** sells white 6-ounce ceramic ramekins for $1.99 each. With a 3½-inch diameter rim, the ramekin tapers slightly down to a 2¾-inch diameter base. This way one ramekin's base can fit into the bowl of another. It is not a perfectly snug fit, so we recommend placing a paper towel between each for protection and stacking no more than four. These ramekins are dishwasher safe and can go from the freezer to the oven.

Gravy Mate

When you are trying to get a full Thanksgiving meal on the table, there is not a whole lot of time to fuss over separating every globule of liquid fat from the gravy. We found a gadget that makes this task a cinch. Known as the Gravy Mate, this fat separator resembles equipment you might find in a chemistry lab. A clear plastic siphon fits into the lid of a clear plastic liquid measuring cup. As the prepared gravy (or stock or pan drippings) is poured into the siphon, the fat naturally floats atop the hot meat juices. A lever at the neck of the lid controls the flow of liquid into the measuring cup. Once nearly all the gravy has passed into the cup, just turn the lever and it cuts off the flow before the fat passes through. Barely any gravy is lost to the sep-

aration process. The Gravy Mate cup holds up to four cups of liquid. **A Cook's Wares (211 37th Street, Beaver Falls, PA 15010-2103; 800-915-9788)** sells the Gravy Mate for $24.95. The siphon fits into the cup for compact storage. It is dishwasher-safe if placed in the top rack.

Plastic Dough Scraper

In the recipe for coffee cake on page 12, the yeasted dough is too soft to be comfortably scooped by hand from the mixing bowl into a plastic container. To do the job, we recommend a plastic dough scraper. We stock two kinds in our test kitchen. The first is a flat, pliable scraper that looks like a large (5¾" by 3¾") white index card with an arch along one of the long edges. In addition to scraping or scooping dough out of bowls, we use this tool to cut dough and scrape it off counter tops. The second scraper we use is shaped like a teardrop. Though not as multipurpose as the first, its curved edges fit particularly well along the contours of a bowl. This scraper (item #510475) sells for $1.29, and the rectangular scraper (item #615642) mentioned first sells for 65 cents. They can be ordered from **Sweet Celebrations (P.O. Box 39426, Edina, MN 55439-0426; 800-328-6722)**.

Holiday Paper Baking Molds

The holiday season is a popular time for toting home-baked goods to neighbors' homes, holiday parties, or family gatherings. Neither foil nor cellophane provides enough structure to safely transport cakes or quick breads. We found an attractive solution to this, however. **Sur La Table (Catalog Division, 1765 Sixth Avenue South, Seattle, WA 98134-1608; 800-243-0852)** sells sturdy, festive paper molds that double as baking pans. The molds are made of a nonstick pure vegetable product, so there is no need for greasing. They can tolerate heat up to 450 degrees and are freezer- and microwave-safe, according to the manufacturer. The exterior is ribbed with a decorative gold ink design on a burgundy background.

The paper loaf-pan molds come in four sizes—large (9" x 2¾"), medium (8" x 2½"), small (6" x 2½"), and scalloped (11" x 4"). Each sells individually for less than $1. A set of 12 medium loaf molds sell for $9; 12 small molds for $6; and 12 scalloped loaf molds for $11.95. Paper baking molds for cakes come in 9½-inch and 8¼-inch diameters, each selling for 95 cents. A small panettone mold (2¾" diameter) sells for 25 cents or $6.50 for a set of 25. A medium panettone (5¼" diameter) sells for 50 cents, and a large (6⅝" diameter) sells for 75 cents.

RECIPE INDEX

Crisp Roast Duck and Sweet Potato Casserole **PAGE 9 AND PAGE 15**

Pecan Cresent Cookies **PAGE 25**

Individual Fallen Chocolate Cake **PAGE 23**

Rich Coffee Cake with Berry Filling **PAGE 14**

Simple Roast Beef Tenderloin with Parsley Sauce with Cornichons and Capers **PAGE 7**

Arugula and Escarole Salad with Blue Cheese, Figs, and Warm Port Dressing **PAGE 18**

PHOTOGRAPHY: CARL TREMBLAY PROP STYLING : MYROSHA DZIUK FOOD STYLING : SUSAN LOGOZZO